THE PRACTICAL GUIDE TO WRITING

WITH READINGS AND HANDBOOK | SECOND CANADIAN EDITION

SYLVAN BARNET
TUFTS UNIVERSITY

MARCIA STUBBS
WELLESLEY COLLEGE

PAT BELLANCA
HARVARD UNIVERSITY

PAMELA G. STIMPSON
UNIVERSITY OF ALBERTA

PEARSON
Longman

Toronto

Library and Archives Canada Cataloguing in Publication

The practical guide to writing : with readings and handbook / Sylvan Barnet ... [et al.] — 2nd Canadian ed.

Includes index.
ISBN 0-321-39930-7

1. English language—Rhetoric. 2. Report writing. 3. College readers. I. Barnet, Sylvan

PE1408.P733 2006   808'.042   C2006-901518-X

ISBN 0-321-39930-7

Vice-President, Editorial Director: Michael J. Young
Acquisitions Editor: Patty Riediger
Marketing Manager: Leigh-Anne Graham
Associate Editor: Jon Maxfield
Production Editor: Charlotte Morrison-Reed
Copy Editor: Anne Holloway
Proofreaders: Ann McInnis and Karen Alliston
Production Coordinator: Sharlene Ross
Composition: Jansom
Art Director: Mary Opper
Cover Design: Jennifer Stimson
Cover Image: David Muir/Masterfile

12 13 14 CP 16 15 14

Printed and bound in Canada.

PEARSON
Longman

Contents

CHAPTER 3: Shaping Paragraphs   44

CHAPTER 4: Revising Sentences for Conciseness   74

CHAPTER 5: Revising Sentences for Clarity   91

Preface

The Canadian edition of *The Practical Guide to Writing with Readings and Handbook* is designed for use in university and college courses in which essay writing is required. This guide enhances the learning process for both students and instructors by providing insight for students as they write, for instructors as they read, and for both as they discuss the writing together. The student who is looking for information about choosing a topic, writing an analysis, constructing a paragraph, or simply using a semicolon will find this guide indispensable. The instructor, by consulting the text and the accompanying manual, can suggest chapters or passages for the student to refer to before revising a draft or starting the next assignment. The explanations and suggestions offered in the text, the techniques used in the reprinted essays, and the exercises found throughout the book can all be used to initiate stimulating classroom discussions.

The Practical Guide includes over fifty short essays, as well as numerous excerpts from students, journalists, and academics. Approximately half of these pieces are written by Canadians and reflect Canada's geographic and cultural diversity. Aboriginal rights, bilingualism, and multiculturalism are some of the specifically Canadian topics covered, as well as more general subjects such as the environment, the Internet, and racism. These readings illustrate different forms, styles, and techniques of writing and, as such, provide students with useful models for critical thinking, reading, and composition.

The suggested writing topics that follow the readings often require students to write about something outside of themselves. Most of these topics present opportunities for introspection yet at the same time encourage students to look outward when writing, to other people, places, and especially ideas. We have tried, therefore, to balance advice such as "Trust your feelings" and "Ask yourself questions" with prescriptions such as "Keep your reader in mind" and "Avoid clichés." We have striven to make students aware that writing is both an exploration of self ("Choose a topic you can write about honestly") and a communication with others ("Revise for clarity").

This text emphasizes analysis, exposition, and argument, since these are chief activities in which we all engage, both in school and later in life. When students write papers, professors write articles, or social workers write case studies, their main purpose is to persuasively explain ideas and how they arrived at them. The guide also includes chapters on description, summary, and research, since these forms of writing are often incorporated into others.

Part I of *The Practical Guide* comprises the writing process from prewriting to revising for style. Sentence-level revisions are included in this section to reinforce how important revising is in arriving at a polished draft. Part II encompasses different analytic methods of development such as comparison, classification, and cause and effect. These methods are discussed both as strategies within other types of writing and as the main strategy for the essay as a whole. Part III includes some other forms of academic writing such as outlines, reviews, interviews, research, and exams, as well as a chapter dedicated to writing about literature. Part IV covers the final proofreading stage, focusing on punctuation and usage. And Part V provides a selection of further readings for both students and professors to consider as they approach the craft of writing.

Each chapter can stand by itself or be used in a variety of combinations to achieve the instructor's purpose and to act as a resource for the emerging writer. We trust you will find the information useful and hope that you appreciate our attempt to enliven this text with humour as you tackle the challenging tasks necessary to becoming a successful writer.

Acknowledgments

For this Canadian edition, I would like to acknowledge the support and suggestions of Mark Andrews, Geoff Stimpson, and Carolyn Guertin as well as those of my parents, Neil and Norma. I would like to thank my students, especially Paola Breda, Anita Coombes, Lydia Baker, Ally Alia, and Mark Facundo, whose writings you will find in this edition.

I would like to acknowledge the use of short excerpts or sentences from the following writers who are not recognized elsewhere in the textbook: R. Bennett, June Callwood, Bill Casselman, Monte Hummel, Michael Kerr, and Richard Lederer.

I am grateful to my editors at Pearson Education: Patty Riediger, Jon Maxfield, Charlotte Morrison-Reed, Anne Holloway, Ann McInnis, and Karen Alliston, as well as all the people who helped me to track down copyright permissions. I am also grateful to my reviewers, Georgia Milligan (Kwantlen University College), Carolyn Speakman (Lethbridge Community College), Marlene A. Sawatsky (Simon Fraser University), Bill Hay (College of New Caledonia), and Dr. Susan Birkwood (Carleton University).

My thanks to Sylvan Barnet, Marcia Stubbs, and Pat Bellanca for their dedication in producing such a high-quality text from which to work. Thanks also to their colleagues, students, editors, and others who contributed time, effort, and talent to the American edition of *The Practical Guide to Writing*.

Pam Stimpson
University of Alberta

PART ONE

An Overview of the Writing Process

The Balloon of the Mind

Hands, do what you're bid:
Bring the balloon of the mind
That bellies and drags in the wind
Into its narrow shed.

—*William Butler Yeats*

1

Discovering Ideas

All there is to writing is having ideas. To learn to write is to learn to have ideas.

—Robert Frost

To know what you want to draw, you have to begin drawing.

—Picasso

STARTING

How to Write: Writing as a Physical Act

"One takes a piece of paper," William Carlos Williams wrote, "anything, the flat of a shingle, slate, cardboard and with anything handy to the purpose begins to put down the words after the desired expression in mind." This is good advice from a writer who produced novels, plays, articles, book reviews, an autobiography, a voluminous correspondence, and more than twenty-five books of poetry, while raising a family, enjoying a wide circle of friends, and practising medicine in Rutherford, New Jersey. Not the last word on writing (we have approximately 85 000 of our own to add), but where we would like to begin: "One takes a piece of paper . . . and . . . begins to put down the words. . . ."

Writing is a physical act, like swimming, and like most physical acts, to perform it skilfully, to bring pleasure to both performer and audience, requires practice. Talent helps. Perhaps few of us are born to become great writers, just as few of us are born to become great swimmers. Nevertheless, we can learn to write, as we can learn to swim, for all practical purposes, including pleasure.

In this book we offer some suggestions, definitions, rules, and examples to help you learn not simply to write, but to write well. We hope they will help you to avoid some of the trials and errors—and the fear of drowning—that sometimes accompany uninstructed practice.

Why Write? Writing as Thinking

In life (as opposed to school), people are motivated by their jobs and other interests to put their ideas in writing. To secure contracts and research funding, scientists and engineers must put their proposals in writing, and then must report, again in writing, the results of their work to their sponsors and colleagues. Parents petition school boards and lawmakers; through prepared talks and newsletters, volunteers reach the communities they serve. In short, anyone who is engaged with ideas or who wants to influence the course of events finds it necessary to convert what Williams called "the desired expression in mind" into words on paper.

As a student, you may not always see a connection between the assignment you receive today and the need you will have several years from now to put your ideas in writing. The rewards of seeing your proposal accepted or of serving your community are probably a bit too distant to motivate you to write five hundred words on an assigned topic this week. There is, though, a closer reward. "To be learning something new," said Aristotle, "is ever the chief pleasure of humankind." We believe that. We also believe that writing is not simply a way to express ideas, but a way to discover them too.

We emphasize ideas because we are making some assumptions about you: that you are an adult, that you are acquiring an education, either in school or on your own, and that the writing skill you need most help with is not grammar or punctuation—though you may need help with them too—but the expression of ideas in clear and interesting expository essays. We begin, then, with some ideas about ideas.

Some Ideas about Ideas: Invention

Would-be writers have one of two complaints: either "I have the ideas but I don't know how to express them" or "I have nothing to say." When we are faced with a blank page, ideas and even words may elude us. We must actively seek them out. Since classical times the term "invention" has been used to describe the active search for ideas. ("Invention" comes from the Latin word *invenire,* "to come upon," or "to find.") Invention includes activities with which you may already be familiar, such as freewriting, brainstorming, listing, and clustering. A related activity is the practice of keeping a journal. In the following pages we will briefly describe several invention strategies and provide guidelines for keeping a journal. All of these activities have one step in common: starting to write by writing.

Starting to Write by Writing

Suppose your assignment is to choose and respond to a recent editorial. You have chosen one, read it several times, underlined a few key sentences, made a few notes. You have some ideas, but they do not seem connected; you do not know how to begin. Here are five suggestions for getting started.

1. Sit down and start writing. If you have the ideas but do not know how to express them, start writing anyway. Resist the temptation to check your email, to make a cup of coffee, or to call your mother. Now is *not* the time to do your laundry or to make your bed. Sit down and start putting one word after another.

2. Start with something easy. Start anywhere. Start with what comes to mind first. You might, for example, start by summarizing the editorial to which you are responding or by sketching one of your ideas about it. *Don't think you must start with an introductory paragraph;* you can write an introduction later, once your ideas have become better defined. It does not matter where you begin, only that you do begin. Start anywhere, and keep going.

3. Try freewriting. Put your hands on the keyboard or pick up a pen and *just start writing*. Forget the rules for a while. Forget about the five-paragraph essay; don't worry about grammar or spelling or punctuation. If you cannot think of the right word, write something close to it, or leave a blank space and move on. If you find yourself going in a direction you had not anticipated, keep writing anyway. Maybe there is something that will be worth thinking about down the road—you won't know until you get there. If, for example, you are writing about why you disagree with one argument in the editorial, a point may suddenly occur to you that supports the author's argument. Fine. Write it down now, while you are thinking of it. You can organize your points of agreement and disagreement later. But if you reach what appears to be a dead end, simply move on, or start again someplace else. You are writing to discover what you think, and it is a good idea to work as quickly as you can. (Take Satchel Paige's advice: Don't look back; something might be gaining on you.)

4. Plan to stop writing. Give yourself a time limit. If you tend to procrastinate (many writers do), try keeping your first sessions short. Promise yourself that you will stop working after twenty minutes—or thirty or fifteen—and *keep that promise*. If at the start you limit your writing sessions, you accomplish two things. You reduce anxiety: the thought of working at your desk for twenty minutes is not nearly as daunting as the thought of writing four or five pages. And after twenty minutes you will have *something* down on paper. You can gradually increase the length of the sessions—to an hour, or three, or whatever is reasonable, given the assignment and your schedule. Of course, you can follow this advice only if you have started to work on an assignment reasonably soon after receiving it. Setting a time limit for the initial stages of writing will help you to get an early start.

5. Revise later. After a few false starts (and probably more than one session), your ideas will begin to take form on the page. But don't, at this early stage, expect them to appear in final form; beautifully organized and in polished sentences. Ideas rarely exist that way in our minds. In fact, until we put them into words, ideas are usually only rough impressions or images rather than clear thoughts. (As E. M. Forster wrote, "How do I know what I think until I see what I say?") Once you do get some ideas down on paper, you can begin to see which ones should be developed or deleted, where connections need to be made, where details and examples need to be added. At this stage, you may be close to having a first draft. Whether or not you like what you've written (your response probably depends more on your temperament than on your actual accomplishment), take a rest from it. Do something else: make your bed or, if you like, just climb into it.

Listing

Listing is a way to discover ideas or to pin them down by writing. Like freewriting (which we discuss above) and like the other invention exercises we are about to discuss, listing may help those who believe they have nothing to say. The process is something like making a shopping list. You write down "soap" and are immediately reminded that you also must pick up dry cleaning. Similarly, if you plan to argue for a course of action, listing one reason for it may bring others to mind.

Listing is especially useful when you are making a comparison—of two figures in a photograph, for example, or two characters in a story or two positions on an issue. Start writing by listing the similarities and then the differences. Or, write both lists at once in parallel columns, making brief entries as they occur to you.

Listing can help you discover and develop ideas; it can also help you to find a topic to write about. Suppose, for example, you have been assigned to write an essay on a form of popular culture that interests you. You can begin simply by listing some of the forms of popular culture that initially occur to you as you think about the subject:

Popular Culture

movies, sci-fi, sci-fi movies?

TV movies, detective serials

soap operas (Why are they called operas? Why soap operas?)

cop shows–<u>Law and Order</u>, <u>Cold Squad</u>

male/female detectives

music videos

rock music

Having written "rock music" above, you begin to think of your favourite female singer, Alanis Morissette, and her songs:

"You Learn"	"Hand in My Pocket"
"All I Really Want"	"Ironic"
"So-called Chaos"	"Unprodigal Daughter"
"Offer"	

By the time you have written these titles, you have pretty much decided that you will write on Alanis Morissette. You are already familiar with her music, you like her songs, and you have some CDs at hand. An idea for an essay begins to form as the lyrics for one of her tunes pops into your head:

> An old man turned ninety-eight
> He won the lottery and died the next day
> It's a black fly in your Chardonnay
> It's a death row pardon two minutes too late
> Isn't it ironic . . . don't you think?

Why all this seeming cynicism and irony? (It is worth remembering that an unanswered question is an essay topic in disguise.) You begin to search your memory; perhaps you play some CDs, and maybe you take some notes. Her earlier songs are sharper, even unforgiving, you find. You also recall her popularity. You begin, once again, to make a list, to jot down words or phrases:

nominations and awards for Grammys, Juno host	playing God in the movies Dogma and Jay and Silent Bob Strike Back
Feast on Scraps and We're With the Band	her lyrics—"All I want is some patience / a way to calm the angry voice"
angry	unaffected
unapologetic	the passion of misspent youth
determined	

Your new list provides more than a topic; you are now several steps closer to a draft of an essay that you think you may be able to write on Alanis Morissette's appeal, the reasons for her popularity.

Clustering

Clustering (or mapping) is similar to listing, though it takes a different visual form. Sometimes ideas don't seem to line up vertically, one after another. Instead, they seem to form a cluster, with one idea or word related to a group of several others. It may be useful then to start by putting a key word or phrase (let's stay with Alanis Morissette) in a circle in the centre of a page, and then jotting down other words as they occur, circling them and connecting them appropriately. A map or cluster might look like the diagram shown here.

If you start writing by putting down words that occur to you in a schematic way—in a map or cluster—it may help you to visualize the relationship between

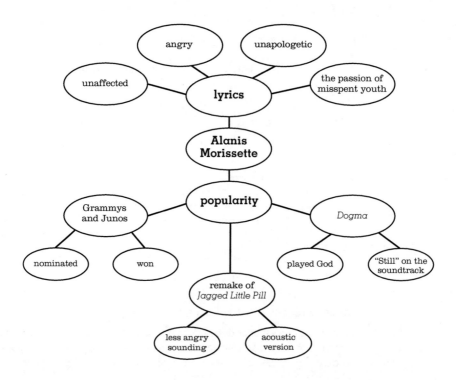

ideas. The visualization may also prompt still other ideas and the connections between them.

Asking Questions (and Answering Them)

Almost the first thing a journalist learns to do in getting a story is to ask six questions:

- who?
- when?
- why?
- what?
- where?
- how?

If you borrow this approach, asking yourself questions and answering them, you will often find that you can get a start on a writing project. The questions that journalists ask are appropriate to their task: to report what happened, who made it happen, how it happened, and so on. Learning to write academic essays is largely learning to ask—and to answer—questions appropriate to academic disciplines.

In analyzing a painting or a sculpture, for example, an art historian might answer certain basic questions:

- When, where, and by whom was the work made?
- Where would the work originally have been seen?
- What purpose did the work serve?
- In what condition has the work survived?

Depending on the work, more detailed questions may also be relevant. If, for example, the work is a landscape painting, the following questions may be appropriate:

- What is the relation between human beings and nature?
- What does the medium (oil paint or watercolour, for instance) contribute?
- What is the effect of light in the picture?
- What is the focus of the composition?
- How does the artist convey depth?

Similarly, a social scientist writing a review of research on a topic might ask about each study under review:

- What major question is posed in this study?
- What is its chief method of investigation?
- What mode of observation was employed?
- How is the sample of observations defined?

Students in all disciplines learn what questions matter by listening to lectures, participating in class discussions, and reading assigned books and articles. The questions differ from discipline to discipline, as the previous lists suggest, but the process—asking and answering questions that matter—is common to all.

An Exercise in Critical Reading: "The Myth of Canadian Diversity"

Writing assignments for English courses, like assignments in other disciplines, are designed to give students practice in critical reading, that is, practice in such skills as summarizing, analyzing, and evaluating written texts. We explain these skills in some detail in several places in this text. Here, by way of introduction, we take you through a brief exercise in discovering ideas about a text *by asking questions and answering them*—an exercise that combines invention and critical reading.

First read the following article from *The Globe and Mail*, June 13, 1994. (We have numbered the paragraphs to make it easier to refer to them.)

 ## Editorial (from *The Globe and Mail* of June 13, 1994)

The Myth of Canadian Diversity

1 Canadians cling to three myths about their country.

2 The first is that it is young. In fact, Canada is well advanced into middle age. At 127, it has existed as a unified state for longer than either Italy (unified in 1870) or Germany (1871). Less than a third of the 180-odd nations now belonging to the United Nations existed in 1945, when Canada was already a mature 78. We were 51 when Iraq and Austria—two countries many think of as old— came into being.

3 The second myth is that, in everything but geography, Canada is a small country—small in population, small in economic heft. In fact, our population of 27 million is a fair size by international standards, bigger than that of Austria, Hungary, Sweden, Norway, Finland, Romania, Greece, Algeria, Peru and Venezuela, to name only a few. Our economy, by traditional measures, is the seventh-largest in the world.

4 But the most important myth about Canada—the one that distorts our self-image, warps our politics and may one day tear us apart—is the myth of Canadian diversity. Almost any Canadian will tell you that his Canada is a remarkably varied place. "Canada, with its regional, linguistic and cultural diversity, has never been easy to govern," wrote *The Globe and Mail* when Jean Chrétien became Prime Minister last fall. Provincial politicians routinely parrot this myth to push for greater regional powers; federal politicians repeat it to let people know what a hard job they have.

5 In fact, Canada is one of the most homogeneous countries in the world. A foreign visitor can travel from Vancouver in the West to Kingston in the centre without finding any significant difference in accent, in dress, in cuisine or even, in a broad sense, in values. A high-school student in Winnipeg talks, looks and acts much like his counterpart in Prince George. Where they do exist, our regional differences are no match for those of most other countries.

6 Canada may have a few regional accents in its English-speaking parts—the salty dialect of Newfoundland, the rural tones of the Ottawa Valley—but these are nothing compared with the dozens in the United States or Britain. It may have two official languages, but that is unlikely to impress India, which has 14.

7 To be certain, we have our French-English divide, two "nations" living under one roof. That hardly makes us unique either. Spain has the Catalans and the Basques. Russia has the Tatars, Ukrainians, Belarussians, Chechens, Moldovians,

Udmurts, Kazakhs, Avars and Armenians. And, although few would dispute that francophone Quebec is indeed a distinct society, the differences between Quebec and the rest of Canada are diminishing over time. As Lucien Bouchard himself has noted, we share a host of common attitudes—an attachment to the Canadian social system, tolerance of minorities, a respect for government and law.[1]

8 Even our much-discussed ethnic differences are overstated. Although Canada is an immigrant nation and Canadians spring from a variety of backgrounds, a recent study from the C. D. Howe Institute says that the idea of a "Canadian mosaic"—as distinct from the American "melting pot"—is a fallacy. In *The Illusion of Difference*, University of Toronto sociologists Jeffrey Reitz and Raymond Breton show that immigrants to Canada assimilate as quickly into the mainstream society as immigrants to the United States do. In fact, Canadians are less likely than Americans to favour holding on to cultural differences based on ethnic background. If you don't believe Mr. Reitz and Mr. Breton, visit any big-city high school, where the speech and behaviour of immigrant students just a few years in Canada is indistinguishable from that of any fifth-generation classmate.

9 This is not to say that Canada is a nation of cookie-cutter people. The differences among our regions, and between our two main language groups, are real. But in recent years we have elevated those differences into a cult. For all our disputes about language and ethnicity and regional rights, our differences shrink beside our similarities; and the things that unite us dwarf those that divide us.

 Questions

Now answer the following questions.

1. a. What was the occasion for this article?
   b. What was the writer's response?
   c. How does the writer engage our interest in the first paragraph?
2. a. What are the three myths about Canada, according to the writer?
   b. How does the writer support his or her position about Canada's age? Why does he or she mention other countries?
3. a. Why does the writer dedicate more space to the third myth than to the first two?
   b. What are some examples that the writer gives to support his or her position that Canada lacks diversity?
4. How does the writer enlist our support for his or her point of view?
5. Optional: How successful is he or she?

If you were to write out your answers and then to review and revise them a bit, you would probably have a draft of an essay something like the student's essay that follows. (Numbers in parentheses refer to the questions.)

---

[1]A former leader of the Parti Québécois, Lucien Bouchard was premier of Quebec from 1996 to 2001. (Editors' note)

On "The Myth of Canadian Diversity"

This piece appeared in the newspaper during a provincial election campaign in Quebec (which was part of the sovereignty campaign leading up to the 1995 referendum), about five months after NAFTA took effect, and during ethnic violence in Rwanda and the former Yugoslavia. (1a) The writer in his or her article (The Globe and Mail, June 13, 1994) argues that our differences are not as great as we like to think and that we, as Canadians, have more in common than not. (1b) He or she supports this position by telling us about three ideas about Canada that Canadians hold dear, and then by discussing those ideas as "myths."

The writer challenges our "myths" that Canada is young, small, and diverse. (2a) At 127 years old, Canada is mature compared to many of the 180 countries in the United Nations that have come into existence since World War II. (2a and b) By international standards, Canada is relatively large in geography, population, and economic clout. In terms of diversity, Canada is a relatively homogeneous country with respect to regionalization, linguistics, culture, and ethnicity. (2a and b)

The writer singles out our ideas about Canadian diversity as the most important—and damaging—myth. (2a and 3a) He or she writes that from the west coast to the east coast there is very little difference in accent, dress, cuisine, and values. (3b) The regional differences that are noticeable, such as the Newfoundland dialect, are not different or significant enough to warrant heralding as "diversity" compared to differences within other countries. And, of course, nothing written about Canada and its views of itself is complete without mention of Quebec and of the country's two official languages. (3b) Even this "distinct" difference is minimized by the writer's example of India, with 14 official languages, and Russia, with nine nations living under one roof. (2b) Although the writer questions Canadians' views of their country and even their sacred cow, the Canadian mosaic, (1c) he or she acknowledges Canadians' differences while recognizing their commonalities such as respect for the social system and tolerance of minorities. By the last paragraph, the writer makes it clear why he or she criticizes the foundations of Canadians' sense of nation: the writer wants the reader to focus on what draws us together as Canadians rather than what divides us. (4)

To develop ideas about a text, then, you need to become a critical reader by asking questions and answering them. When you approach a text, and especially when you reread it, ask such questions as:

- Who wrote this?
- When was it written?
- Why and for what audience was it written?
- What main argument or points does the author make?
- How does the author make them?
- How successful (believable, interesting, persuasive) do I find it?

Keeping a Journal

Writing daily in a journal helps writers to remain fluent. As we said at the start, writing is a physical act, and to keep in trim, you should practise daily—or as close to daily as you can manage. Many writers also keep journals both to stimulate ideas and to record ideas for future use. We recommend that you keep a journal and that you use it to record your responses—however vague or fleeting—to the things you are reading and writing about in your courses. Rereading such journal entries can be a good way to get started on a new project.

Guidelines

1. Where to write: Your instructor may ask you to write in a loose-leaf notebook, so that you can turn in pages occasionally and your instructor won't have to stagger home with twenty or thirty notebooks. If you keep a journal strictly for your own use, write with whatever materials feel comfortable: pen, pencil, computer; loose sheets, bound notebook, or anything else that suits you.

2. When to write: Any time you can; ten to fifteen minutes a day is recommended. Some people find it helpful to establish a regular time for writing—just before they go to sleep, for example. Habits can be helpful, but not all of us can or should lead well-regulated lives. Writing for a minute or two several times a day may work best for you.

3. How long is an entry? An entry may be a few words, a line or two, or even a few pages. There is no required length, but do keep writing until you have put into words at least one thought or observation or question.

Dr. William Carlos Williams often wrote poems on prescription blanks.

4. Form: Write freely. Do not correct or revise. Do not worry about spelling, vocabulary, or punctuation. Use whatever language, idiom, or voice you wish. It is a good way to keep in touch with yourself and with the friends and family you have temporarily left. Date your entries.

5. Content: Write about anything that comes to mind. You can think of your journal as a record of your life now, which you might read with pleasure some years from now when many of the rich details of your daily experience would otherwise be forgotten. Write down your thoughts, feelings, impressions, responses, dreams, memories. May Sarton once said, "The senses are the keys to the past." If you have a strong sensory memory of something—the smell of salt-water mixed with sand and machinery oil, for example—try to describe it in words, and then to track it down. You may find a buried scene from your child-hood that you can rescue from your memory by a train of associations. If you keep tracking and writing, you may discover why that scene is important. Likewise, if you have a strong response—anger, perhaps, or confusion—to something you are reading, try to explain it, to get it down on paper. Doing so may help you begin to develop an idea for an essay (or may help you to study for an exam).

Examples: Journal Entries by Students

1. I guess I can see the writer's point about Canadian diversity, but
   believing in it is part of being Canadian. Of course, so is criticizing it.
   What an interesting paradox (right word?). Anyway, I can't take what
   he (she?) writes too seriously because I think we are more diverse than

he makes out. Besides, I like our difference from the United States, which has grown more diverse (!) since the editorial was written. With all the ethnic tensions in various parts of the world, we should be focusing on commonalities—as long as we understand that this is not mutually exclusive of accepting diversity.

2. It is difficult to believe that not understanding a physics problem isn't the worst problem in the world.

3. 9/20 Lab was a trip today. Right before my eyes, I observed an egg cell being invaded by an army of sperm cells. Think of it. That's how I began. I used to be a nothing, and now I'm something, an "I." (I was only looking at a sea urchin's egg, but that sure beats not looking at a sea urchin's egg.)

4. Intro to Women's Studies upset me today. We talked about the role of women in religion. We discussed how feminist theologians (thealogians?) believe that God is not necessarily a man but could be a woman. Their argument is that the Bible was translated and interpreted by men for their own purposes. They wanted to utilize the Bible to give women a subordinate role to men. I do believe that, or at least I think all this is worth questioning. But it's hard for me- -no, sad- -to think of God as a woman when I have grown to love him as a man, a father.

5. "Teruko-san! How come you don't understand what I am saying to you!! How come you are repeating these errors so many times!! One! Two! Three! Go!!" My arms, hands, fingers and even my brain are frozen. Tears are running down my cheeks. My both hands are sitting on the keyboard frighteningly. Silence. I hear my heart, beating thump thump thump. With a deep sigh, Mrs. Ikebuchi closes the page of a score which is blackened with fingering numbers, circles and crosses. Without saying any words, she leaves the room, and goes to the kitchen. The lesson is over. I sigh and wipe off my tears with the back of my hands, pick up the scores, go to the living room and sit on the tatami-floor stiffly. "By the way Teruko-san, did you see my gardenia? It is so beautiful! Come! come and see it!" She comes out from the kitchen with a big round black lacquer tray with tea and cookies on it. She puts the tray on the table and walks out to the garden to the gardenia bush. "Isn't this pretty?" "Yes." "Isn't this a nice smell?" "Yes." Mrs. Ikebuchi walks back to the living room and I follow her three steps behind and sit on the tatami-floor stiffly again. Mrs. Ikebuchi pours tea and asks me merrily, "How much sugar do you want? how much cream do you want? which cookie do you want? rabbit? elephant? or duck?" I answer politely, "two sugars, please? (it is cube sugar), that's enough, thank you (for cream). May I have a rabbit?" "Oh you like the rabbit! Good! By the way do you know the story about the rabbit? Ah—what was it? Ah, Peter Rabbit!" Her story is going on and on and on. Meanwhile I finish my tea and cookie. "Well, Teruko-san, see you next Monday." I stand up, my legs are numb from sitting on the tatami-floor, and start to walk slowly, my toes are tickling. I pick up my scores and bow and say "Thank you very much." Walk out the sliding door. Release! I skip home.

6. A belief I had when I was small: For some reason I thought every person was allowed only a certain number of words per lifetime. Of course, at that time in my life I was quiet, except when I was mad and all reason left me.

7. Anticipating something is like falling off a cliff and never reaching the bottom.

FOCUSING

What to Write About: Subject, Topic, Thesis

If you are taking a course in composition, you will probably receive assignments to write on something you are reading or on something out of your personal experience, which may include your experience of books. In other courses, it's usually up to you to choose a *subject* from those covered in the course, to focus on a *topic* within the subject, and to narrow the topic by formulating a *thesis.* Any assignment requires you to narrow the subject so that you can treat it thoroughly in the allotted space and time. Therefore, you write not on *Time* magazine, but on the political bias of *Time,* or on a comparison of *Time* and *Maclean's,* based on one or two issues of each, arguing for the superiority of one over the other; not on economic transfer payments to the provinces (a subject), but on a specific proposal to restructure them (a topic); not on penguins (a subject), but on the male penguin's role in hatching (a topic). A good general rule in finding a topic is to follow your inclinations: focus on something about the subject that interests you.

Suppose your assignment is to read the Book of Ruth in the Hebrew Bible and to write an essay of five hundred to one thousand words. If you start with a topic such as "The Book of Ruth: A Charming Tale," you are in trouble. The topic is much too vague. In writing about it you will find yourself hopping around from one place in the book to another, and in desperation saying things like "The Book of Ruth is probably one of the most charming tales in all literature," when you have not read all literature and could not define *charm* precisely if your life depended on it.

What should you do? Focus on something that interests you about the book. (If you read the book with pencil in hand, taking notes, underlining some passages, putting question marks at others, you will have good points to start with.) The book is named after Ruth, but perhaps you find Naomi the more interesting character. If so, you might jot that down: "Although the Book of Ruth is named after Ruth, I find the character of Naomi more interesting."

Stuck again? Ask yourself questions. *Why,* for example, do you find Naomi more interesting? To answer that question, reread the book, focusing your attention on all the passages in which Naomi acts or speaks or is spoken of by others. Ruth's actions, you may find, are always clearly motivated by her love for Naomi. But Naomi's actions are more complex, more puzzling. If you are puzzled, trust your feeling—*there is something puzzling there. What* motivated Naomi? Convert your question to "Naomi's Motivation" and you have a *topic.*

With this topic in mind, if you explore Naomi's actions one by one you may conclude that "although Naomi shows in many of her actions her concern for her daughter-in-law, her actions also reveal self-interest." Now you have a *working thesis,* that is, a brief statement of your main point. It's a bit awkwardly worded but you can work on a smoother, more natural expression later.

"Naomi's Motivation" is a topic in literary criticism, but if your special interest is, for example, economics, or sociology, or law, your topic might be one of these:

Economic Motivation in the Book of Ruth

Attitudes toward Intermarriage in the Book of Ruth

The Status of Women in the Book of Ruth

Any one of these topics can be managed in five hundred to a thousand words. But remember, you were assigned to write on the Book of Ruth. Formulate a thesis with evidence from that book. Suppress the impulse to put everything you know about economics or intermarriage or the status of women through the ages in between two thin slices, an opening sentence and a concluding sentence, on the Book of Ruth.

Let's take another example. Suppose that in a course on Modern Revolutionary Movements you are assigned a term paper on any subject covered by the readings or lectures. A term paper is usually about three thousand words and requires research. You are interested in Mexican history, and after a preliminary search you decide to focus on the Revolution of 1910 or some events leading up to it. Depending on what is available in your library, you might narrow your topic to one of these:

Mexican Bandits—The First Twentieth-Century Revolutionists

The Exploits of Joaquin Murieta and Tiburcio Vasquez—Romantic Legend and Fact

In short, it is not enough to have a subject (the Book of Ruth, revolutions); you must concentrate your vision on a topic, a significant part of the field, just as a landscape painter or photographer selects a portion of the landscape and then focuses on it. Your interests are your most trustworthy guides for choosing which portion of the landscape to study.

As you think about your topic and information relating to it, try to formulate a *tentative* or *working thesis.* Think of your tentative sentence—which may not appear in your final paper—as a working hypothesis, a proposition to be proved, disproved, or revised in light of information you discover.

Naomi's character is more interesting than Ruth's.

Murieta and Vasquez were in the vanguard of a revolution.

Your *working thesis* will help you to maintain your focus, to keep in mind the points that you must develop and support with evidence: quotations, facts, statistics, reasons, descriptions, and illustrative anecdotes. Be prepared to modify your working thesis, perhaps more than once, and perhaps substantially. Once you begin amassing evidence and arguments, you may find that they support a different thesis. Your best ideas on your topic may turn out to be radically different from the ideas with which you began. As we pointed out earlier, writing is not simply a way to express ideas you already have, but also a way to discover new ones.

Essays based on substantial research almost always include an explicit thesis sentence in the finished version, although short essays based on personal experience often do not. An essay recounting a writer's experience of racism, for example, or conveying the particular atmosphere of a neighbourhood, is likely to have a central idea or focus, a *thesis idea,* rather than a *thesis statement.* But whether stated or implied, the thesis idea must be developed (explained, supported, and proved) by evidence presented in the body of the essay. The kind of evidence will vary, of course, not only with your topic but also with your audience and purpose.

DEVELOPING IDEAS

Materials that writers use to develop ideas, to explain and support a thesis, are largely by-products of the reading, note taking, freewriting, questioning, and remembering that are part of the writing process from beginning to end. Materials for developing an essay on Naomi's motivation will be passages from the Book of Ruth, brief quotations that the writer introduces and explains. Similarly, materials for an essay on Alanis Morissette will be quotations from a thoughtful selection of lyrics. An essay on a memorable experience, one that led to an interesting idea, will rely on the writer's memory of that experience, examined with a reader in mind. In all of these instances, imagining a reader helps a writer develop ideas.

Thinking about Purpose and Audience

Purpose and audience, at their most basic level, are about the motivation for writing and the style of communication. Purpose and audience affect the what and the how of writing (the choice of materials, strategies, focus, style, and tone); they are interrelated and affect all aspects of the writing process. Thinking about purpose and audience can be helpful at both earlier and later stages of writing: when you are developing an idea and working up explanations and evidence to support it, and when you are evaluating the effectiveness of your own work.

Outside of class, you may find yourself writing by choice or by necessity for a general audience or for a knowledgeable audience. For example, you might write an essay or report for your colleagues in which you inform them about a new technology you think will help the business. Or, you might write an op-ed for the local newspaper in which you try to get your readers to see a subject from a different perspective. You will find your presentation of your subject affected by your writing aims and your perceived reader(s). For example, writing an annual self-evaluation letter to your boss is going to be quite different from writing a letter to a friend about the experience of trying to get the annual self-evaluation letter just right. As you read various essays in this textbook, you will notice that some are more academic while others are more informal and that some are more informative while others are more persuasive. The same differences will apply to your own writing in university and throughout life.

If you are writing about a particular assigned topic in a university course (this advice works for any writing you are likely to do), first ask yourself the following questions:

What is the purpose of the essay?
What is being asked of me?
What do I want to get out of the assignment?

Consider first what your professor's expectations are for the assignment. He likely wants both to ensure that you comprehend the course material and to evaluate your critical thinking and writing abilities. Read the assignment carefully; are you being asked to analyze, compare, define, inform, persuade, explain, and/or research? Take a moment to think about your own purpose in writing the essay. Obviously you want to get a good grade, but you also probably want to take on the challenge of learning something new and of communicating your ideas the best way you can. Whether you are given a topic or can choose your own, part of your purpose is to put your own stamp on the subject through the choices you make regarding your main argument and focus, strategies of writing, style and tone, and ideas about your reader(s).

If you are uncertain how to begin, or if you are overwhelmed by the materials you have unearthed and do not know how to sort them out, try asking yourself these questions:

- Who are my readers?
- What do they need to know?
- How can I best get them to be interested in my topic and to understand my argument?
- What do I want my readers to take away from their reading experience?

When you ask, "Who is my reader?" the obvious answer—the teacher who assigned the essay—is, paradoxically, the least helpful. Remember: *when you write, you are the teacher*, and your professor does not know your opinions, positions, interpretations on a subject. To learn to write well, you will likely find it easier to focus on a reader, real or imagined, who does not understand your material as well as you. It's probably easier to assume the role of the teacher if you imagine your reader to be someone in your class, that is, someone intelligent and reasonably well informed who shares some of your interests but who does not happen to be you and who therefore cannot know your thoughts unless you organize them and explain them clearly and thoroughly. For more on academic audiences, see "Academic Styles, Academic Audiences" in Chapter 7.

Thinking about your audience—about what you want your readers to understand about your topic or interpretation and to learn from their reading experience—is central to the revision process. You read over a draft you have written to see if it will be clear and interesting to someone else, to someone who is not you, does not know what you know, and does not necessarily share your beliefs. If you use a technical term, will the reader understand it? Should you define the term, or can you substitute a more familiar word? Do you have sufficient background information? Have you identified the source of a quotation? And is it clear why you are using the quotation at this point in your essay? Are the paragraphs arranged in a clear sequence? Have you provided effective transitions? And so on. Reading your draft (preferably aloud) while imagining an audience, you can often spot unclear patches and revise them. Reading your draft to an actual audience, a friend or classmate, is even better. And remember, whether your audience is real or imagined, specialized or general, sympathetic or resistant—and whether your essay is informal or academic—ultimately you are writing to communicate.

Writing from Experience: Two Essays by Students

Let's look at two essays, each written by a student during the first week of the semester in a composition course. Both students were asked to write from their own experience; the assignment was to describe or to explain something they knew well to others who were unfamiliar with it. Perhaps you are familiar with such an assignment. You try to think of something interesting you have done, but you have led a most unremarkable life. Your classmates, all strangers, seem to know more than you do about almost everything. They have all been to France or Mexico or Hong Kong—well, some of them. All you did last summer was file cards and run errands in an office full of boring people. Here is the first student's essay, on, as it happens, a boring job.

Example 1

A Lesson

As I look back at it, my first thought is that my job was a waste of time. It consisted of compiling information from the files of the Water and Assessor's Department in a form suitable for putting on the city's computer. Supposedly this would bring the water billing and property taxing to an efficient level. If the job sounds interesting, don't be deceived. After the first week of work, I seriously doubted that I would survive through the summer.

But I was able to salvage a lesson in the self-discipline of coping with people. Of course we all know how to succeed with friends, family, acquaintances, and employers. But try it in a situation where you have a distinct disadvantage, where you are the seller and they are the customers. And remember, the customer is always right.

By observing the situation, though I was not a participant, I learned that patience, kindness, and understanding can remove the difficulties you cross at the time.

Not a bad topic, really. We can learn something valuable from a boring, menial, frustrating job. Or if not, we can examine boredom (what exactly is it? is it the same as impatience? how does it come about? how does it feel?) and write about it without boring the reader. But this piece does not teach us anything about boredom. It does not allow us through concrete, specific details to feel with the writer that we too would have doubted we could survive the summer. Instead, it offers generalizations such as "compiling information from our files" and "a form suitable for putting on the city's computer," which give us no sense of the tedium of transferring numbers every day from five hundred manila index cards to five hundred grey index cards. In fact, the essay gives us almost no sense of the job. The second paragraph ends with the words "the customer is always right," but nothing in the essay suggests that the writer (whose work "consisted of compiling information from the files") had any contact with customers. We really do not know what she did. Nor does the essay present any evidence that the experience was redeemed by a lesson in "patience, kindness, and understanding."

As it turns out, there was no such lesson. In class discussion, the student admitted that the job was a waste of time. She had, out of habit, tried to come up with some pious thought to please the instructor. The habit had short-circuited the connection between the student's feelings and the words she was writing. The class discussion led to genuinely interesting questions. Why, for example, are we reluctant to admit that something we have done was a waste of time? "The job was a waste of time" would have been, for most of us, a more productive thesis than "I was able to salvage a lesson." What experiences lead to the conclusions "I must write what the instructor expects" and "The instructor expects a pious thought"? (We would like to hear from a student willing to explore that topic in five hundred to one thousand words.)

The class discussion revealed the student's real attitude toward her job. The questions that, as readers, the class asked also provided a focus for the writer, which helped her to formulate a more productive thesis. It is helpful to imagine such a discussion with real readers in the early stages of writing as you grope for what you have to say. For although it would be tidy if writers could simply, and in the following order, (1) choose a subject, (2) focus on a topic, (3) formulate a thesis, (4) support the thesis in the body of the essay, things do not often work out that way. More commonly, writers discover their topics, formulate their theses, and develop support for their theses in the act of writing and revising, in asking questions and in answering them, and in discarding the answers—or even the questions—and starting again.

Now look at the second essay, again on a common experience. Ask yourself as you read it, or reread it, what makes it uncommonly interesting.

Example 2

Dedication Doth Not a Good Teacher Make

The worst teacher I ever had was a brilliant and charming man. Fergy

(it was short for Mr. Ferguson) had written the textbook we used for

Chemistry. He had designed his house and built it himself, getting

professional help only for the electricity and plumbing. He could

remember the scores of all the football games he'd seen, and the names of

the players on each team. He never kept lists- -"Lists rot the memory," he

said- -so he memorized which type of lab implement he kept in which of fifty drawers, and he could tell you instantly, without pause. Sometimes we would ask him where a certain type of obscure bottle could be found just to test him, but he never failed. "Middle left-hand drawer in Lab Station Six," would say old Fergy, and in that middle left-hand drawer it would be. I never knew him to forget a name, a face, or a formula, either.

That, I think, was his failing as a teacher. Because he had no trouble grasping or recalling a concept, he had trouble in understanding how we could. The one thing his extraordinary mind seemed unable to comprehend was that it was extraordinary, that not everyone could think as completely and as easily as he. If the class had questions he would try to answer them, but he tended to complicate and expand on ideas, rather than to simplify them. He could not believe that we needed not expansion but explanation, with the result that we soon learned not to ask too many questions for fear of extra material to learn. And it did become a fear of learning, because, try as we would, we somehow never managed to pin down concepts like electron shells and the wave theory of gravitation, but we would still have to answer for them on tests- -and, ultimately, at home. (I never decided which was worse, knowing that once again I had made a complete fool of myself by taking a chem test, or having to listen to my parents sigh and claim that I could have done better if I'd tried.)

Fergy would have been horrified to know that he had this discouraging effect on us. He loved us and he loved teaching and he loved chemistry. He was always available for outside help, not only for chemistry, but for any problem, whether in English or your social life. He tried to make class interesting by telling little anecdotes and playing with the chemicals. Actually, he was funny, and interesting, and charming, and he kept us hoping that we'd understand chem so that he would approve of us and so we could relax and enjoy him. But although he is one of the best

people it has been my good fortune to have known, he never did manage to

teach me a lick of chemistry.

As you study this book, you'll frequently find questions following examples of writing. Critical reading and writing are closely intertwined. If you practise asking and answering questions as you read, as well as when you write, the skills you develop will reinforce each other. Try answering the following questions on "Dedication Doth Not a Good Teacher Make":

- What is the writer's thesis?
- How does she support the thesis?
- If you found the essay interesting, what makes it interesting?
- If you found it convincing, what makes it convincing?

The Groucho Marx Complex

Clearly—examining these essays should make it clear—there is no such thing as an uninteresting life, or moment in life. There are only uninteresting ways to talk about them. It is also clear that some people are more interested in introspection and in talking and writing about their personal experiences than others. The others may be suffering from the Groucho Marx Complex: as Groucho put it, "I don't want to belong to any club that would have me as a member." Students who freeze at the notion of writing about themselves or sharing their ideas often feel that everything they have done is so ordinary that no one else could possibly be interested in it; anything they know is so obvious that everyone else must already know it. Remember that no one else knows exactly what you know; no one else can know what it feels like to live inside your skin. If you work at summoning up from your memory concrete and specific details, you can turn the most ordinary experience into a first-rate essay.

Remember too that writing from your own experience does not necessarily mean writing about private experience. We all have areas of experience we would rather keep private, and we have a right to remain private about them. The important thing in writing about experience is, as Marianne Moore said, that "we must be as clear as our natural reticence allows us to be." Think, then, of experiences that you are willing to share and to be clear about. If, for example, you have just learned in a psychology course what "operant conditioning" means, define it for someone unfamiliar with the term. You might find yourself narrating an experience of your own to exemplify it; to be clear, you will have to provide an example. Or if an object in a local museum or craft exhibit or store interests you, ask yourself a question—why do I like it?—and you'll probably be able to turn an object into an experience. You will also be turning an experience into an object—an essay—that will interest your readers.

Writing academic papers usually requires examining and evaluating texts and other evidence beyond your personal experience or previous knowledge. Nevertheless, you still must trust your own ideas. Trusting your own ideas does not, of course, mean being satisfied with the first thought that pops into your head. Rather, it means respecting your ideas enough to examine them thoughtfully; it means testing, refining, and sometimes changing them. But it is always your reading of a text, your conduct of an experiment, your understanding of an issue that your essay attempts to communicate.

AN OVERVIEW: FROM SUBJECT TO ESSAY

We each must work out our own procedures and rituals (John C. Calhoun liked to plow his farm before writing), but the following suggestions may help. The rest of the book will give you more detailed advice.

1. If a topic is assigned, write on it; if a topic is not assigned, turn a subject into a topic. Get an early start, preferably the day you receive the assignment. Do this by employing any or all of the strategies—freewriting, listing, clustering, asking questions, keeping a journal—that we have discussed. When you look over your jottings, note what especially interests you, and decide what topic you can sensibly discuss in the assigned length. Unfortunately, few of us can write anything of interest on a large subject in only a few pages. We simply cannot say anything readable (that is, true and interesting to others) on subjects as broad as music, sports, ourselves, in five hundred words. Assigned such subjects, we have nothing to say, probably because we are desperately trying to remember what we have heard other people say. Trying to remember blocks our efforts to look hard and to think. To get going, we must narrow such subjects down to specific topics: from music to hip hop, from sports to commercialization of athletics, from ourselves to a term with a roommate.

2. Get a focus. Once you have turned a subject into a topic, you need to shape the topic by seeing it in a particular focus, by having a thesis, an attitude, *a point*:

Hip hop is popular because . . .

College athletes are exploited because . . .

Problems between roommates can be avoided if . . .

Probably you will not find your exact focus or thesis immediately, but you can begin to refine your thinking by *asking questions* about your topic. For example:

Why is hip hop popular?

What kind of people like it?

Why are some performers more successful than others?

If you ask yourself questions now, you may be able to answer them a day or two later. And you will probably find that reading what you have jotted down leads to something else—something that would not have occurred to you if you had not written down the first point. Few of us have good ideas about a topic at the start, but as we put our ideas into words, better ideas may begin to emerge.

Keeping your audience and your purpose in mind will help too. If, for example, you are writing about hip hop music to interest a reader who does not listen to it, you will begin to find things that you must say.

3. Turn your reveries into notes. Put aside, for a day or two, what you have written so far (assuming you have a couple of weeks to do the essay), but be prepared to add to it. Useful thoughts—not only ideas, but details—may come to you while you are at lunch, while you read a newspaper or magazine, or while your mind wanders in your other classes. Write down these thoughts in your journal, perhaps—don't assume that you will remember them when you come to draft your essay.

4. Sort things out. A few days before the essay is due, look over what you've written so far and see if you can discover a workable thesis. This might be a good moment to practise freewriting on your topic or to arrange your notes into what looks like a reasonable sequence. To help keep your thesis in focus, give your essay a provisional title. Do not be afraid to be obvious. If you look back at some of the titles of sections in this book, you will see such headings as

"Why Write?"

"Starting to Write by Writing," and

"Developing Ideas."

Simple as they are, these titles helped to keep us focused as we drafted and revised the chapter. And they tell you something about the topic at hand. Of course, sometimes wordplay produces an attractive but still informative title—for example, "If You Have *Time*, read *Maclean's*."

5. Write. Even if you are unsure that you have a thesis and a structure, start writing. Do not delay. You have already begun to capture and organize some of your ideas, and you have a mind that, however casually, has already been thinking. Don't worry about writing an effective opening paragraph (your opening paragraph will almost surely have to be revised later anyway); just try to state and develop your point, based on the phrases or sentences you have accumulated, adding all of the new details that flow to mind as you write. If you get stuck, *ask yourself questions*.

Have I supported my assertions with examples?

Will a comparison help to clarify the point?

Which quotation best illustrates this point?

Keep going until you have nothing left to say.

6. Save what you can. Immediately after writing the draft, or a few hours later, look it over to see how much you can salvage. Don't worry about getting the exact word here or there; just see whether or not you have a thesis, whether or not you keep the thesis in view, and whether or not the points flow logically. Delete irrelevant paragraphs, however interesting (you can save them in a separate file if you can't bear to throw them away); move paragraphs that are relevant but that should be somewhere else. Do not assume that tomorrow you will be able to remember that the paragraph near the bottom of page 3 will go into the middle of page 2. Move the block now so that when you next read the essay you will easily be able to tell whether in fact the paragraph does belong in the middle of page 2. Settle on a title, then put the draft aside until tomorrow.

7. Revise. Reread your draft, first with an eye toward large matters. Revise your opening paragraph or write one to provide the reader with a focus; make sure each paragraph grows out of the previous one, and make sure you keep the thesis in view. Remember, *when you write, you are the teacher*. As you revise, make certain that assertions are supported by evidence; try to imagine a reader (the person who sits next to you in class, perhaps), and let this imagined reader tell you where you get off the point, where you are illogical, where you need an example—in short, where you are in any way confusing.

Next, after making the necessary large revisions, read the draft with an eye toward smaller matters: make sure that each sentence is clear and readable. You can do this only by reading slowly—preferably aloud, unless you have developed the ability to hear each sentence, each word, in the mind's ear. Let's say that in telling a reader how to handle disks for a word processor, you have written, "When you write the label for the disk, use a felt pen." You notice, in revising, that the reader may wonder *why* a pencil or a ballpoint pen should not be used, and so you alter the sentence to "Because the pressure of a pencil or a ballpoint pen can damage the surface of the disk, label the disk with a felt pen."

Cross out extra words and recast unclear sentences. Keep pushing the paragraphs, the sentences, the words into shape until they say what you want them to say from the title onward. (This contest between writers and their words is part of what Muhammad Ali had in mind when he said, referring to his work on his autobiography, "Writing is fighting.") Correct anything that disturbs you—for instance, awkward repetitions that grate. Set the essay aside for a day or two, then come back to it with a fresh eye.

8. Edit. When your draft is as good as you can make it, take care of the mechanical matters: spell-check your document, double-checking in a dictionary if you have any doubts about a particular word; if you are unsure about a matter of punctuation, check it in this book. You will also find instructions about such things as title placement and margin size in Chapter 22, "Manuscript Form." And be sure to acknowledge the sources not only of quotations but also of any ideas that you borrowed, even though you summarized or paraphrased them in your own words. (See "Acknowledging Sources," pages 317-20.)

9. Prepare the final copy. If you are on schedule, you will be doing this a day or two before the essay is due. If you are pressed for time wait a few hours before you proofread it, because right now you are too close to your essay. If you put the essay aside for a while and then reread it, again aloud, you will be more likely to catch omitted words, transposed letters, inconsistent spelling of names, and so forth. Print out a final corrected copy if you have time. If not, you may make corrections—neatly and in black ink—right on the page. (See "Corrections in the Final Copy" in Chapter 22.)

10. Hand in the essay on time. In short, the whole business of moving from a subject to a finished essay on a focused topic adds up to Mrs. Beeton's famous recipe: "First catch your hare, then cook it."

Exercises

1. Quickly scan several editorials or op-ed pieces in *The Globe and Mail* (or another newspaper or newsmagazine) until you find one that you really want to read. Read it, and for each paragraph, or group of paragraphs, write one or two questions that call for a summary of the paragraph's content or an explanation of the paragraph's purpose. Overall, your questions should explore why the editorial is particularly interesting or effective.

2. Write journal entries on two or three assignments (of writing, reading, lab work, or problem sets) made in your courses in the first two weeks of classes.

3. Write a journal entry recalling, in as much detail as you can, your earliest memory.

4. Narrow the following subjects to a topic. For each, find a more specific focus for a five-hundred-word essay.

   ### Example:

   Parole system
   > Housing for parolees
   >> A controversial proposal to house parolees in a halfway house in my neighbourhood

   Homelessness
   Athletic scholarships
   The Internet
   The Olympics
   Gun control
   Animal rights
   AIDS
   The writing requirement

5. Formulate a thesis sentence for two topics chosen from Exercise 4.

Suggestions for Writing

1. Write a piece somewhat like the editorial on Canadian diversity (pages 8–9) in which you respond to a current proposal in your college community. (Suggested length: five hundred words.) Or, respond to the editorial. (Perhaps something the writer says reminds you of something you have read or experienced, or maybe you agree or disagree strongly with some point he or she makes.)

2. Explain clearly something—a process, a concept, a place, an experience—that you know well but that others in your class may not know about or may not understand as well as you. (Suggested length: 750 words.)

CHAPTER 2

Drafting and Revising

I have never thought of myself as a good writer. Anyone who wants reassurance of that should read one of my first drafts. But I'm one of the world's great revisers.

—James Michener

READING DRAFTS

In Chapter 1, we focused on how to have ideas and how to get them down on paper. We suggested that from the start of a project the writer is almost simultaneously inventing ideas and refining them. But we also advised that, particularly at the start, it is best to suspend critical judgment until you have begun to capture your thoughts, however roughly expressed, on paper. In this chapter, we will focus on ways to improve and refine rough drafts. First, we want to make what may seem like an obvious point: to improve the draft you have written, *you must first read it.* Moreover, you must try to read it objectively and critically.

Imagining Your Audience and Asking Questions

To read your draft objectively, to make sure that you have said what you intended to say, first put it aside for a couple of days, or at least for a couple of hours. Then read it through thoughtfully, as if you were not the writer, but someone reading it for the first time. As you read, try to imagine the questions such a reader might want or need to ask you to understand what you meant. Then, read your draft again, asking yourself the following questions:

1. Does the draft present an idea? Does it have a focus or make a unified point?
2. Is the idea or are the ideas clearly supported? Is there convincing evidence? Are there sufficient explanations and specific details?
3. Is the material effectively organized?

There are, of course, many other questions you might ask, and we will suggest some before we are done. But let's start with these.

1. Does the draft present an idea? Does it have a focus or make a unified point? If, on reading your draft objectively, you find that it does not have an idea or a point to develop, there is probably no reason to tinker with it (or to hand it in). It may be best to start again, using the invention techniques we discussed in Chapter 1. (Rereading the assignment is probably a good idea too.)

Let's suppose, however, that you do find some interesting material in your draft but that you are not yet sure what it adds up to. The chances are that extraneous material is getting in your way—false starts, needless repetition, or interesting but irrelevant information. Some pruning is probably in order.

Picasso said that in painting a picture he advanced by a series of destructions. A story about a sculptor makes a similar point. When asked how he had made such a lifelike image of an elephant from a block of wood, the sculptor answered, "Well, I just knocked off everything that didn't look like elephant." Often, revising a draft begins with similar "destruction." Having identified the main point that you want to pursue, do not be afraid to hack away competing material until you can see that point clearly in its bold outline. Of course you must first have a lot of writing on paper to begin with (at the start, nothing succeeds like excess). But often you must remove some of it before you can see that you have roughly formulated the main point you want to make and produced some evidence to support it.

2. Is the idea (or are the ideas) clearly supported? Is there convincing evidence? Are there sufficient explanations and specific details? Writers are always reluctant to delete. Students with an assignment to write five hundred or one thousand words by a deadline are, understandably, among the most reluctant. But, almost certainly, once you have settled on the focus of your essay, you will be adding material as well as deleting it. It is not enough simply to state a point; you must also explain, prove, and/or demonstrate it.

If you argue, for example, that smoking should be banned in all public places, including parks and outdoor cafés, you must offer reasons for your position and also meet possible objections with counter-arguments; perhaps you will cite statistics. If you are arguing that in Plato's *Apology* Socrates' definition of truth goes beyond mere correspondence to fact, you will need to summarize relevant passages of the *Apology* and introduce quotations illuminating Socrates' definition. Almost always, a draft needs the addition of specific details and examples to support and clarify its general points.

3. Is the material effectively organized? As you prune away the irrelevancies and add the specific details and examples that will clarify and strengthen your point, as your draft begins more and more to "look like [an] elephant," ask yourself if the parts of your draft are arranged in the best order. If you have given two examples, or stated three reasons, which one should be your starting point? Ask yourself if paragraphs are in a reasonable sequence. Will the relationship of one point to the next be clear to your reader? Does the evidence in each paragraph support the point of that paragraph? (The same evidence may be more appropriate to a different paragraph.) Does your opening paragraph provide the reader with a focus? Or, if it performs some other important function, such as getting the reader's attention, does the essay provide the reader with a focus soon enough?

When working on the organization of drafts, follow two general rules:

- Put together what belongs together.
- Put yourself in the position of your reader; make it as easy as possible for the reader to follow you.

Peer Review: The Benefits of Having a Real Audience

Occasionally a writing assignment will specify the reader you should address. For example: "Write a letter to the editor of your hometown newspaper arguing that . . ." More often, your reader must be imagined. We usually suggest imagining someone in your class who has not thought about your topic or considered the specific evidence you intend to examine.

In many writing classes, students routinely break up into small groups to read and to discuss each other's work. Peer review (as this practice is commonly called) is useful in several ways.

First, peer review gives the writer a real audience: readers who can point to what puzzles or pleases them, who ask questions and make suggestions, who often disagree (with the writer or with each other) and who frequently, though not willfully, misread. Though writers do not necessarily like everything they hear (they seldom hear "This is perfect. Don't change a word!"), reading and discussing their work with others almost always gives them a fresh perspective on their work, and a fresh perspective may stimulate thoughtful revision. (Having your intentions misread because your writing is not clear enough can be particularly stimulating.)

Moreover, when students write drafts that will be commented on, they are doing what professional writers do. Like journalists, scholars, engineers, lawyers—anyone whose work is ordinarily reviewed many times, by friends and spouses, by colleagues, and by editors, before the work is published—students who write drafts for peer review know they will have a chance to discuss their writing with their colleagues (other students) before submitting a final version for evaluation. Writers accustomed to writing for a real audience are able, to some extent, to internalize the demands of a real audience. Even as they work on early drafts, they are sensitive to what needs to be added or deleted or clarified. Students who discuss their work with other students derive similar benefits. They are likely to write and revise with more confidence and more energy.

The writer whose work is being reviewed is not the sole beneficiary. When students regularly serve as readers for each other, they become better readers of their own work and, consequently, better revisers. Learning to write is in large measure learning to read.

Peer review in the classroom takes many forms; we will look in a moment at an example as we trace a student's essay that is revised largely as a result of peer review. But even if peer review is not part of your writing class, you may want to work with a friend or another student in the class, reading each other's drafts.

When you work on your essay with your classmates or your friends, good manners *and* academic practice require that you thank them for their help, that you **document** their contributions. You can offer a sentence or two of general thanks at the end of the essay—something like this:

I'd like to thank the members of my peer revision group, Rebecca

Sharp and Isabella Thorpe, for helping me to clarify the main idea of my

essay and for suggesting ways to edit my sentences.

Or you can thank your peer reviewers for their specific contributions by inserting a footnote or endnote at the end of the sentence that contains an idea or words you wish to acknowledge, and then writing a sentence like this:

Kevin Doughten drew my attention to the narrator's play on words

here; I wish to thank him for helping me develop this point.

From Assignment to Essay: A Case History

On September 12, Suki Hudson was given the following assignment: Write an essay (roughly five hundred words) defining racism or narrating an experience in which you were either the victim or the perpetrator of a racist incident. Bring a first draft with two copies to class on September 16 for peer review. Revised essay due September 26.

Suki kept no record of her first thoughts and jottings on the topic, but what follows is an early attempt to get something down on paper. Because it was far from the finished essay she would write, not yet even a first draft, we label it a Zero Draft:

Zero Draft. Sept. 13

It was a warm sunny day in the playground. My three-year-old

brother and other children were playing gaily until one of the boys'

mothers interrupted. She called her son, whispered something, and when

he went back to the playground he excluded my brother from playing

together. I didn't know what to call the incident, but my heart ached as I

watched my little brother enviously looked at the other kids. I immediately

left the playground with him, and the playground has never been the same

since that day.

At that point, having reached the end of the anecdote, Suki stopped. What she had written was not yet an essay, and it was far short of the suggested five hundred words, but it was a start, which is all she had hoped to accomplish on this first try.

Later she read what she had written, and asked a friend to read it and see if he had any suggestions. It was a frustrating conversation. The friend didn't understand why Suki thought this was a "racist incident." Why did Suki leave the playground? Why hadn't she just asked the boy's mother for an explanation? The questions took her by surprise; she felt annoyed, then miserable. So she changed the subject.

But "the subject" did not go away. That evening, she wrote the following account of the conversation in her journal:

Sept. 13

I asked J to read my paper and he thought I was being paranoid. Why

didn't I just ask the boy's mother what was the matter? But I could not have

even thought of going up to the woman to question her motives. It was

beyond my control if she wanted to be ignorant and cruel to a different race.

(Or was it really my ignorance to walk away from a simple explanation?)

The following day, looking over what she had written, it occurred to her to try adding the journal entry to the anecdote. Maybe in a concluding paragraph she could explain why what happened in the playground was obviously a racist incident.

Here is the conclusion:

Sept. 14

Most people in modern society don't recognize the more subtle cases of

racism. People feel if they are not assaulting physically they are not

violating the law, and as long as they are living according to the law, racism

is not committed. However, the law or the constitution does not protect the

human heart from getting hurt, and without a doubt the most critical racist

action could be committed by close friends or their loved ones.

But having written that last line Suki was struck by something odd about it. The woman in the playground was not a loved one, nor was she a close friend. Still, it was true that racist acts can be committed by friends, and even if the acts are undramatic, they should be recognized as racist acts. At this point, she thought that she had a thesis for her essay, but she also realized that she had begun to recall a different experience. Starting again, she wrote the following account:

In Korea, I had a very close friend whose father was Chinese. Although

her mother was a Korean woman, they were treated as foreign people in

town, and they were singled out on many occasions. Her father died when

she was little but everyone in town knew she was a half Chinese. Her mother ran a Chinese restaurant, and they lived very quietly. My family knew her

mother well and I was close friends with the girl and for many years I was

the only friend she ever had. However, as I entered junior high school my

new group of friends didn't approve of her background, and I drifted away

from her. She was a very quiet, shy person and although I stopped calling or

visiting her, she always remembered me on holidays to send presents. After

graduating from junior high school she went to Taiwan to live with her

grandparents, whom she had never met. I gathered she could not stand the

isolation any longer at her age. Many years later I realized how cruel I have

been to her, and I tried to locate her without success.

The following day Suki combined the two drafts (hoping to come closer to the five hundred words), added a new concluding paragraph, and (rather disgusted with the whole assignment) typed up her first draft to hand in the next day. She photocopied it, as instructed, for peer review in class.

As we said earlier, peer review in the classroom takes many forms. Ordinarily, the instructor distributes some questions to be answered by both the writer and the readers. Typically, the writer is asked to speak first, explaining how far along he or she is in writing the essay and what help readers might give. The writer might also be asked, "What are you most pleased with in your writing so far?"

Readers are then asked to respond. Instructions may vary, depending on the particular assignment, but the questions distributed in Suki's class, shown on page 32, are fairly typical.

First Draft

What follows is the draft that Suki gave the two members of her group, and then a summary of the group's discussion. Before reading her draft aloud (the procedure the instructor recommended for this session), Suki explained how she had happened to narrate two experiences and asked which narrative she should keep or if she could keep both.

First Draft

S. Hudson

Sept. 16

It was a warm sunny day in the playground. My three-year-old

brother and other children were playing gaily until one of the boys'

mothers interrupted. She called her son to whisper something and when

Questions for Peer Review   Writing 125R
    Read each draft once, quickly. Then read it again, with the
following questions in mind:

1. What is the essay's topic? Is it one of the assigned topics or a
   variation from it? Does the draft show promise of fulfilling the
   assignment?
2. Looking at the essay as a whole, what thesis (main idea) is stated
   or implied? If stated, where is it stated? If implied, try to state it in
   your own words.
3. Looking at each paragraph separately:
   What is the basic point (the topic sentence or idea)? How does the
   paragraph relate to the essay's main idea or to the previous
   paragraph?
   Is each sentence clearly related to the previous sentence?
   Is the paragraph adequately developed? Are there sufficient
   specific details or examples?
   Is the transition from one paragraph to the next clear?
4. Look again at the introductory paragraph. Does it focus your
   attention on the main point of the essay? If not, does it effectively
   serve some other purpose? Does the opening sentence interest you
   in the essay? Do you want to keep reading?
5. Is the conclusion clear? Is the last sentence satisfying?
6. Does the essay have a title? Is it interesting? Informative?

he went back to the playground he excluded my brother from playing

together. I didn't know what to call the incident, but my heart ached as I

watched my little brother enviously looked at other kids. I immediately

left the playground with him, and the playground has never been the

same since that day.

A friend of mine said I was being paranoid. It would have been

appropriate to ask the boy's mother what was the matter, or if she had

anything to do with the kids excluding my brother from playing. But I could

not have even thought of going up to the woman to question her motives. It

was beyond my control if she wanted to be ignorant and cruel to a different

race, or perhaps my ignorance to walk away from a simple explanation.

Most people in modern society recognize only the dramatic instances of

racism, and on a daily basis people don't recognize the more subtle cases of racism. People feel if they are not assaulting physically they are not violating the law, and as long as they are living according to the law, the racism is not committed. However, the law or the constitution does not protect the human heart from getting hurt, and without a doubt the most critical racist action could be committed by close friends or their loved ones.

In Korea, I had a very close friend whose father was Chinese. Although her mother was a Korean woman they were treated as foreign people in town, and they were singled out on many occasions. Her father died when she was little, but everyone in town knew she was a half Chinese. Her mother ran a Chinese restaurant, and they lived very quietly. My family knew her mother well and I was close friends with the girl and for many years I was the only friend she ever had. However, as I entered junior high school my new group of friends didn't approve of her background and I drifted away from her. She was a very quiet, shy person, and although I stopped calling or visiting her, she always remembered me on holidays to send presents. After graduating from junior high school she went to Taiwan to live with her grandparents whom she had never met. I gathered she could not stand the isolation any longer at her age. Many years later, I realized how cruel I have been to her, and I tried to locate her without success.

She was a victim in a homogeneous society, and had to experience the pain she did not deserve. It is part of human nature to resent the unknown, and sometimes people become racist to cover their fears or ignorance.

Summary of Peer Group Discussion

1. The group immediately understood why the friend (in the second paragraph) had difficulty understanding that the first incident was racist. It might well have been racist, but, they pointed out, Suki had said nothing about the racial mix at the playground. It does become clear by the fourth paragraph that the writer and her brother are Korean, but we don't get this information early enough, and we know nothing of the race of the woman who whispers to her son. Suki had neglected to say—because it was so perfectly obvious to her—that she and her brother were Korean; the mother, the other child, in fact all others in the playground, were white.

2. Suki's readers confirmed her uneasiness about the third paragraph. They found it confusing. (a) Suki had written "people don't recognize the more subtle cases of racism." Did she mean that the mother didn't recognize her action as racist, or that Suki didn't? (b) In the first paragraph Suki had written "I didn't know what to call the incident." But then the second paragraph is contradictory. There she seems to accuse the mother of being "cruel to a different race." (c) And they agreed that the last sentence of the third paragraph, in which Suki writes of racist acts "committed by close friends," did not tie in well with the first part of the essay, although it did serve to introduce the second anecdote.

3. Her group was enthusiastic, though, about Suki's telling of the two stories and advised her to keep both. Both were accounts of more or less subtle acts of racism. One student thought that they should appear in chronological order: first the Korean story and then the more recent story, set in the playground. But both readers were sure that she could find some way to put them together.

4. They were less certain what the essay's thesis was, or whether it even had one. One student proposed:

> Subtle racist acts can be as destructive as dramatic instances (implied in paragraph 3).

The other student proposed unifying:

> It is part of human nature to resent the unknown

and

> . . . sometimes people become racist to cover their fears or ignorance (from the final paragraph).

All three members of Suki's group (Suki included) thought that the ideas in the essay were supported by the narrative. But the draft didn't yet hang together: Suki would have to work on the way the separate parts connected.

5. One member of the group pointed out that the second paragraph could be deleted. The friend mentioned in it (who called Suki "paranoid") had been important to Suki's thinking about her first draft, but served no useful purpose in the draft they were looking at, and other details in that paragraph were murky.

6. On the other hand, the first paragraph probably needed additional details about the setting, the people involved, what each did. How does a three-year-old know he's been excluded from a play group? What happened? What did the other children do? What did he do? And, as the group had seen at once, some details were needed to establish the racist nature of the incident. Her peers also reminded Suki that her essay needed a title.

7. Finally, some small details of grammar. Suki's English is excellent, although English is her second language (her third actually). But the other two in her group, being native speakers of English, were able to catch the slightly odd diction in

> she always remembered me on holidays to send presents

and the error in

> my heart ached as I watched my little brother enviously looked at other kids.

Suki asked if the past tense was right in

> I realized how cruel I have been to her

and the others supplied:

> I realized how cruel I had been to her

(though they could not explain the difference).

Several days later Suki consulted her notes and resumed work on her draft, and by September 25, the night before it was due, she was able to print the final version, which now included a title.

Suki Hudson

Ms. Cahill

Writing 125R

September 25, 1999

Two Sides of a Story

It was a warm sunny day in the playground. My three-year-old brother and two other small boys were playing together in the sandbox. My brother was very happy, digging in the sand with a shovel one of the other boys had brought, when one of the mothers sitting on a bench across from me called to her son. She bent over and whispered something to him, and he went right over to my brother and pulled the shovel out of his hand. He pushed my brother aside and moved to the other side of the sandbox. The other boy followed him, and they continued to play. My heart ached as I watched my little brother enviously looking at the other kids.

I didn't fully understand what had happened. I looked across at the mother, but she turned her head away. Then I picked up my brother and immediately left the playground with him.

I thought the woman was extremely rude and cruel, but I didn't think then that she was behaving in a racist way. We had only recently come here from Korea, and although I had been told that there was much racism in America, I thought that meant that it was hard for some people, like blacks, to find jobs or go to good schools. In some places there were street gangs and violence. But I didn't understand that there could be subtle acts of racism too. I was aware, though, in the playground that my brother and I were the only Koreans, the only nonwhites. When the woman turned her face away from me it felt like a sharp slap, but I was ignorant about her motives. I only guessed that she told her child not to play with my brother, and I knew that the playground was never the same since that day.

That incident was several months ago. When I started to think about it again recently, I thought also of another time when I was ignorant of racism.

In Korea, I had a very close friend whose father was Chinese. Although her mother was a Korean woman they were treated as foreign people in town, and they were singled out on many occasions. Her father died when she was little, but everyone in town knew she was half Chinese. Her mother ran a Chinese restaurant, and they lived very quietly. My family knew her mother well and I was close friends with the girl, and for many years I was the only friend she ever had. However, as I entered junior high school my new group of friends didn't approve of her background and I drifted away from her. She was a very quiet, shy person, and although I stopped calling or visiting her, she always remembered to send me presents on holidays. After graduating from junior high school, she went to Taiwan to live with her grandparents, whom she had never met. I gathered she could not stand the isolation any longer at her age. Many years later, I realized how cruel I had been to her, and I tried to locate her without success.

She was a victim in a homogeneous society, and had to experience pain she did not deserve. There was no law to protect her from that, just as there was no law to protect my little brother. Perhaps the woman in the playground did not realize how cruel she was being. She probably didn't think of herself as a racist, and maybe she acted the way I did in Korea, without thinking why. It isn't only the dramatic acts that are racist, and maybe it isn't only cruel people who commit racist acts. It is part of human nature to fear the unknown, and sometimes people become racist to cover their fears, or ignorance.

Acknowledgments

I would like to thank Ann Weston and Tory Chang for helping me to develop my main point, and to organize and edit my essay.

Notes, Drafts, Revisions: A Teacher Writes an Essay

As we face the empty computer screen, we imagine that other, better, more experienced writers are efficiently filling up their computer screens with brilliant ideas, organized paragraphs, lucid sentences. Not so—or at least, not usually so. Only in our most optimistic moments can we imagine essays popping out of our heads fully formed like the cartoon image of the head that opens as if upon a hinge to let out ideas in physical form. For most writers most of the time, ideas emerge through the writing process, which involves generating ideas, writing, and revising; focus, organization, and clarity result from rereading and rewriting.

By way of illustration (and, perhaps, inspiration), we reprint here "My Essays Are a Dog's Breakfast" in which Dennis York takes a different and humorous approach to advising students about the writing process. One of his students asked him for simple, detailed suggestions on how to get started and how to structure a basic essay. After going over the basics with the student, York decided to provide the information in a way that he thought might be more effective than making notes on a blackboard. As York explains,

> The other day, I had a student ask if there was an easy way to write essays. She just couldn't write them, she said, and she gave me plenty of reasons why she couldn't do so. I spent some time trying to help her and hopefully gave her a better understanding of how to write essays. Afterwards, I thought it would be interesting to use student explanations for why they find essay writing so difficult to show them one fairly easy way to write an essay. I would write an essay about not being able to write an essay—and this essay would illustrate how to overcome the very difficulties being discussed in the essay itself. While I was at it, I would teach them a little bit about irony.

This essay is what York describes as "Essays for Dummies," an allusion to the series of books such as *Calculus for Dummies, Canadian History for Dummies, Sex for Dummies,* and *Knitting for Dummies.* While the essay's narrator, "A. Student," grumbles about not being able to write essays, he inadvertently gives his readers the basics for getting the job done. The result is a well-structured essay on the writing process that students can use as a model. Following the piece, we reprint portions of York's brainstorming and drafting to show the process of writing and revising.

 **DENNIS YORK**

Dennis York is a freelance writer, editor, and consultant and an instructor at Algonquin College in Ottawa. He has published numerous essays in magazines and newspapers.

My Essays Are a Dog's Breakfast

by A. Student

1   I find it very hard to write essays. I know I'm supposed to have a good topic and thesis, but I don't seem to be able to get that right. And even when I do decide on a topic and thesis, I find it difficult to come up with things to say about them. Not that it matters much, because I have a terrible time putting my ideas in order and can't write decent introductions for my essays. Apparently, I also don't have proper flow and coherence between my sentences and paragraphs. So, having messed up everything else, it's not much of a surprise that I then end my essays with a confused whimper, rather than a focused and forceful conclusion.

2   I think the main reason that I can't get my topic and thesis straight is because I haven't really thought about how they affect my essay. I sometimes pick a topic I know very little about and that often leads to difficulties. Besides having to look everything up and not always finding what I need, I usually find that there's either too little or too much information. Apparently, what I need to do is write about something that I can discuss properly using the number of words I'm going to have in my essay—something that's not too big, or so small that I won't have enough to talk about.

3   They say one way to make sure I'm not taking on too much is to focus my topic by writing a good thesis statement. If I can just restrict my topic a bit by saying something about it, I will have an essay that is better focused and probably a lot more interesting. I mean, it's one thing to write an essay on schizophrenia and another thing to write an essay about how certain medications can control the symptoms of schizophrenia. Schizophrenia is such a big topic that I'd probably have to write a book to deal with that one. Focusing my topic by coming up with a thesis statement makes it much more manageable. At least, that's what they tell me.

4   Now if "they" could just help me to come up with some ideas, I'd be even happier. Usually, I just start writing. Or, actually, I don't start writing. Most of the time, I just sit there looking at the computer screen or blank sheet of paper and can't even begin. They tell me it wouldn't be so hard if I had some idea of

what I was going to say. As if I didn't know that! What I need is a way to come up with something good. Well, apparently one way is to try a bit of brainstorming before I do anything else. I should think about my purpose in writing my essay and about who's going to read it. Then I should write the topic and thesis down on a piece of paper and come up with every idea I can think of that might have something to do with that topic and thesis. I'm not supposed to worry about which ideas are good or bad at this stage. If I try too hard and get too fussy, I could miss out on some good ideas. I'm supposed to worry about which ideas are good ones and which are bad ones after I've written down everything that I can think of. Apparently, there'll be a lot more ideas than I expect—and some should be good ones that I can actually use.

5   If I do manage to come up with some useful ideas for my essay, they tell me I need to organize them and draw up an outline. This is supposed to give me a kind of map so that I know where I'm going when I write my essay. It will also give the big picture and help me decide what things I need to research. A lot of times the essay topic and thesis are supposed to make it pretty obvious how I should arrange my ideas. Like, if I'm trying to explain how to build something, I have to start at the beginning and go from there. If I'm describing a room, I'd probably want to do something like start from one place and work my way to another, say from front to back. Mind you, it's not always clear what order I should use for the ideas in my essay. When this happens, they say I'm supposed to think about how I would explain it if I were talking to the reader. There's often more than one way to arrange things in an essay, but I need to choose the best one for my topic and thesis, and for the reader who is going to be reading my essay.

6   This still doesn't sound easy, but apparently if I manage to come up with a good outline and do some research to get the information I need, writing the essay will just be changing that outline into sentences and paragraphs. And apparently, the outline could be especially useful for helping me write my first paragraph. That's because one simple way to write an introductory paragraph is to just state my topic and thesis in the first sentence and then use the next sentences to briefly mention the things that I will talk about in my essay when I discuss my topic and thesis. I could even list these things in the same order that I'm going to place them in my essay. If nothing else, an outline will at least give me a clearer idea of what I'm planning to write about and how my essay will be structured.

7   The problem is, even if I do come up with a good topic, thesis and outline I can't find the right words to get started, let alone find enough of those good words to write a decent essay. Even when I know what I want to say, I can't put it in writing. "So don't try to put it in writing, yet," one teacher told me. Start by just explaining it to a friend and use that to help you get started, but don't forget the type of person who will be reading your essay and make sure you're writing for that reader. If it helps, you could try beginning your first sentence by thinking, "I want to tell you that . . ." and then just start writing the words you would use after those first words. Apparently, a lot of us try too hard when we start writing and that makes things worse. What we need to do is just relax a bit and write more simply and clearly, almost as though we were talking to the reader. Reading our work out loud is supposed to help.

8   Yeah, right. They teach us about things like compound-complex sentences, tell us not to write short choppy sentences, and then turn around and tell us to keep it simple. They say these longer sentences are all right if they work, but long,

complicated sentences aren't better if they're full of mistakes or don't help the reader understand what we mean. Let's see how this might work: I want to tell you that . . . "You should keep your sentences simple enough to be understood."

9   Okay, but what about coherence and flow? I'm always getting criticized about that. So even if I do manage to get the rest of it right, I'm still going to lose marks because of these flow and coherence things. Again, they tell me I may be closer to getting this right when I'm speaking than when I'm writing. And just as with talking, we should have a clear purpose in mind and write for our reader the way we talk for our listener, only without the slang, clichés and sentence fragments.

10   Anyway, coherence is supposed to be something like "sticking." Things have to stick together in a logical way. You say one thing and then you say another thing, and those should go together and make sense.

11   Flow is having sentences and paragraphs move along smoothly and not sound choppy when read out loud. A lot of us speak reasonably clearly and smoothly, though we probably shouldn't overdo things like the "like" thing, the way we do when we're talking. Like, it's not used in essays much. Like, they're probably going to write comments on your paper, and, like, take marks off. And, like, they also don't like sentence fragments and slang in essays. Like, writing should be closer to the way we talk, but not always exactly how we speak, unless we're writing dialogue, of course. We can test our essays for smoothness, flow and appropriate language by reading them out loud after we think they're finished. That's more work, but it could get us better marks if we find things that need fixing and then fix them before we hand in our essays. Maybe I'll try that. So far, most of my essays move like students danced when they did the Jerk back in the sixties.

12   Anyway, there you have it: a real dog's breakfast. Not only do I usually manage to choose a poor topic and thesis, but I then continue on when I really should have stopped right there. That's right, I just continue on and throw in whatever I can think of, in whatever order it happens to come to mind. Given that it's so mixed up, it's not surprising that my essays don't read well and seem to just jump around, rather than flow nicely. And once I've gotten that down, it's also no surprise that I can't write a decent concluding paragraph. As I say, a real dog's breakfast. So maybe I should just buy a dog; my essays could certainly keep it fed.

York's motivation for writing the piece was to provide a basic essay model to the nervous writers under his tutelage and to reinforce the stages of the writing process—as overviewed and discussed in Part One of this textbook. York began with the subject of essay writing and the topic of how difficult some students find it is to write an essay. As a writing instructor, he already had the information that he wanted to provide to his readers, but he still needed to figure out the best way to present it. First, he made a list of the types of comments he had heard from his students about their writing frustrations:

Writing is hard.
I don't know how to get started.
I have nothing to say.
My topics are either too general or too narrow.
I often go off the topic.
My essays often don't read well; they sound awkward.
My ideas end up all over the place.
I can't end my essays well.

As York thought about how best to address these writing concerns with his students (his audience), he suddenly felt inspired to write the essay from a student's perspective (rather than as the instructor to the students). He then needed to refine his brainstorming list and chosen voice into a structure for his essay.

Topic and Thesis:

> I find essay writing to be extremely difficult.

Main points:

> I know that I should have a clear topic and a thesis that is not too broad or narrow for the length of the essay, but I just do not seem to be able to get that right.
>
> Having gotten off on the wrong track, I then have a hard time thinking of all the things I need to say to discuss what I have managed to choose for a topic and thesis.
>
> It gets worse, because I then take what few ideas I have managed to think of and have a terrible time trying to find a way to put those in an appropriate order.
>
> Having things out of order may also contribute to the difficulty I have in getting my writing to flow nicely.
>
> I just don't have any coherence between my sentences and between my paragraphs.
>
> It's not much of a surprise that I then end with a confused whimper, rather than a focused and forceful conclusion.
>
> My essay writing truly is a mess.

Now that York had a subject, topic, thesis, outline, audience, and point of view, he began writing his essay as though it was written by "A. Student." Here are the first two paragraphs of his rough draft:

> I find essay writing to be extremely difficult. I know that I should have a clear topic and a thesis that is not too broad or too narrow for the length of the essay, but I just do not seem to be able to get that right. Having gotten off on the wrong track, I then have a hard time thinking of all the things I need to say to discuss what I have managed to choose for a topic and thesis. It gets worse, because I then take what few ideas I have managed to think of and have a terrible time trying to find a way to put those in an appropriate order. Having things out of order may also contribute to the difficulty I have in getting my writing to flow nicely. I just do not have any coherence between my sentences and between my paragraphs. Having no clear thesis or organization, it is not much of a surprise that I then end with a confused whimper, rather than a focused and forceful conclusion. Yes, my essay writing truly is a mess.
>
> I think the main reason that I cannot get my topic and thesis straight is because I have not really thought about what those are and how they affect my essay. I often pick a topic I know very little about, and that pretty well always leads to difficulties. Besides having to look

everything up and not always finding what I need, I often find that there is either too little or too much information. What I need to do is pick a topic that is suitable for the size of the essay I am writing: one that isn't too broad or too narrow, and one that I can at least find information on. One way to make sure I am not taking on too much is to focus my topic by having a good thesis statement . . .

Because York is trying to keep his explanation straightforward, he has worked his first outline into his introduction, to show the structure of the essay. In this basic introductory paragraph, A. Student has chosen to state the main points he will discuss in the body of the essay. (We will discuss writing introductions and conclusions in Chapter 3.) Because the voice of his essay is meant to be that of a student, and he wants to make the essay humorous to keep his students' attention, he needs to engage in revision. If we compare these first two rough paragraphs with the final first two paragraphs, we can see how he reworks his writing to reinforce the desired effect. He edits the tone to make it less formal by adding contractions (e.g., "cannot" to "can't") and by fine-tuning the diction (e.g., "Having no clear thesis or organization" becomes "So, having messed up everything else" and "extremely difficult" becomes "very hard"), and he edits out some of the detail that is unnecessary in an introduction (e.g., "that is not too broad or too narrow for the length of the essay"). He also needs to think about the most effective way to structure his paragraphs logically and to make each paragraph flow into the next. Notice, for example, how the last sentence of his second paragraph in the rough draft becomes the topic sentence for his third paragraph in the final draft.

York has written a focused, well-structured, lucid essay. The essay includes explanations and examples to develop his main points. Each paragraph develops an aspect of the central idea of the piece and is carefully linked to the paragraphs that precede and follow it. Now, go back and carefully analyze the essay written by "A. Student."

 ## Topics for Critical Thinking and Writing

1. Dennis York began the process of writing the piece by asking himself a question: "What is the most effective way to allay students' concerns about writing and to explain writing to them?" What makes York's essay effective?

2. Reread "My Essays Are a Dog's Breakfast" and analyze the topic and the writing: What areas of the writing process does he cover in the essay? What strategies does he use to make one paragraph flow into the next? What methods of development does he use (e.g., narration, definition, examples, and so on) and how? Are his topic sentences clear? Why does he conclude the way he does? Why might he have chosen that particular title?

3. York explains that he wants students to learn "a little bit about irony." What is irony? What are some examples of irony in the essay? How does "A. Student" use irony to engage his audience?

Suggestions for Writing

1. Write an essay in response to the assignment Suki Hudson received: in five hundred words, narrate an experience in which you were either the victim or the perpetrator of a racist incident.

2. Think about how you usually respond to a writing assignment—or how you responded to a particular assignment. Try to trace, step by step, your thoughts, actions, and feelings from the moment you receive an assignment to the moment you turn in a finished essay.

3. Looking back, what experiences have you had as a writer, in class or out, that have led to your current writing practices and to your attitude toward writing? Do you find writing under some circumstances (writing letters, for example, or writing for a school newspaper) easier than others? Turn your reflections into an essay of about five hundred words.

Shaping Paragraphs

PARAGRAPH FORM AND SUBSTANCE

It is commonly said that a good paragraph has

- *unity* (it makes one point, or it indicates where one unit of a topic begins and ends);
- *organization* (the point or unit is developed according to some pattern); and
- *coherence* (the pattern of development, sentence by sentence, is clear to the reader).

We will say these things too. Moreover, we will attempt to demonstrate that, generally speaking, they are true and that, of course, a good paragraph needs substance. Along the way we also hope to show you how to shape your ideas into effective paragraphs. But first we feel obliged to issue this warning: you can learn to write a unified, organized, coherent paragraph that no one in his or her right mind would choose to read. Here is one such example, written by a student:

Charles Darwin's great accomplishments in the field of natural science resulted from many factors. While innate qualities and characteristics played a large part in leading him to his discoveries, various environmental circumstances and events were decisive factors as well. Darwin himself considered his voyage on the <u>Beagle</u> the most decisive event of his life, precisely because this was to him an educational experience similar to if not more valuable than that of college, in that it determined his whole career and taught him of the world as well.

Notice that the paragraph is unified, organized, and coherent. It has a **topic sentence** (the first sentence). It uses **transitional devices** ("while," "as well," "Darwin himself") and, as is often helpful, it **repeats key words**. But notice also that it is wordy, vague, and inflated ("in the field of," "many factors," "qualities and characteristics," "circumstances and events," "precisely because," "educational experience," "similar to if not more valuable than"). It is, in short, thin and boring. What does it teach and to whom?

Consider, by contrast, these paragraphs from another essay on Darwin, this time by Darwin scholar Philip Appleman:

> Charles Darwin's youth was unmarked by signs of genius. Born in 1809 into the well-to-do Darwin and Wedgwood clans (his mother was a Wedgwood, and Darwin himself was to marry another), he led a secure and carefree childhood, happy with his family, indifferent to books, responsive to nature. The son and grandson of impressively successful physicians, he eventually tried medical training himself, but found the studies dull, and surgery (before anesthesia) too ghastly even to watch. So, for want of anything better, he followed the advice of his awesome father (6' 2", 336 pounds, domineering in temperament) and studied for the ministry, taking his B.A. at Christ's College, Cambridge, in 1831.
>
> Then a remarkable turn of events saved Darwin from a country parsonage. His science teacher at Cambridge, John Stevens Henslow, arranged for Darwin the invitation to be naturalist on H.M.S. *Beagle* during a long voyage of exploration. Despite his father's initial reluctance, Darwin got the position, and at the end of 1831 left England for a five-year voyage around the globe that turned out to be not only a crucial experience for Darwin himself, but a passage of consequence for the whole world.

Notice how full of life these paragraphs are compared with the paragraph that begins by asserting that "Charles Darwin's great accomplishments in the field of natural science resulted from many factors." These far more interesting paragraphs are filled with specific details, facts, and names that combine to convey ideas. We finish reading them with a sense of having learned something worth knowing, from someone fully engaged not only with the topic, but also with conveying it to someone else.

The one indispensable quality of a good paragraph, the quality that the first paragraph on Darwin lacks, is **substance**. A paragraph may define a term, describe a person or a place, make a comparison, tell an anecdote, summarize an opinion, draw a conclusion; it may do almost anything provided that it holds the readers' attention by telling them something they want or need to know, or are reminded of with pleasure.

But even a substantial paragraph, as we shall soon see, does not guarantee that you will hold the attention of your readers, because readers (like writers) are often lazy and impatient. The important difference is that readers can afford to be. If they find that they must work too hard to understand you, if they are puzzled or confused by what you write, if the effort they must expend is greater than their reward, they can—and will—stop reading. The art of writing is in large part the art of keeping your readers' goodwill while you teach them what you want them to learn. Now, experienced writers can usually tell—not so much while they are writing as while they are revising—what does or does not make a satisfactory unit, and their paragraphs do not always exactly follow the principles we are going to suggest. But we think that by following these principles, more or less as you might practise finger exercises in learning how to play the piano, you will develop a sense of paragraphing. Or, to put it another way, you will improve your sense of how to develop an idea.

PARAGRAPH UNITY: TOPIC SENTENCES, TOPIC IDEAS

The idea developed in each paragraph often appears, briefly stated, as a **topic sentence**. This sentence states the topic and says something *about* that topic (i.e., it makes a point or sets up an argument). Topic sentences are most useful, and are therefore especially common, in paragraphs that offer arguments; they are much less common, because they are less useful, in narrative and descriptive paragraphs.

The topic sentence usually is the first sentence in the paragraph—or the second, following a transitional sentence—because writers usually want their readers to know from the start where the paragraph is going. Sometimes, though, you may not wish to forecast what is to come; you may prefer to put your topic sentence at the end of the paragraph, summarizing the points that earlier sentences have made or drawing a general statement based on the earlier details. Even if you do not include a topic sentence anywhere in the paragraph, the paragraph should have a topic idea—an idea that holds the sentences together.

Examples of Topic Sentences at Beginning and at End, and of Topic Ideas

1. The following paragraph begins with a topic sentence.

To fans of the horror genre, *The Kiss*'s climax may recall David Cronenberg's parasites in *Shivers*. However, the origin and function of the all-important monster differs significantly in this film. Whereas Cronenberg's monsters were products of science and repressed sexual energy, the creature in *The Kiss* belongs safely in the realm of magic and witchcraft. In terms of its meaning, this monster therefore lacks potential for the social criticism that the beasts in Cronenberg's earlier films have, arguably, suggested. In accordance with his decision to go with a more familiar formula, director Pen Densham has created a film that, despite its flirtation with strangeness, lands firmly on the side of the traditional nuclear family.

—Annie Ilkow

The first sentence announces the topic: the monster in Densham's *The Kiss* compared with the one in Cronenberg's *Shivers*. Everything that follows this topic sentence develops or amplifies it, first by setting up the more specific focus on the "origin and function" of the monster, then by speaking of the differences between the two monsters, and then by offering the implications of the contrast and a return to *The Kiss* with a statement about the film as a whole. The writer begins by stating or summarizing her idea, provides specific evidence to support it, then offers a closely related general statement. (In a sense, the paragraph delivers on the promise the writer makes in its first sentence.)

2. The next paragraph has its topic sentence at the end:

> If we try to recall Boris Karloff's face as the monster in the film of *Frankenstein* (1931), most of us probably think of the seams holding the pieces together, and if we cannot recall other details we assume that the face evokes horror. But when we actually look at a picture of the face rather than recall a memory of it, we are perhaps chiefly impressed by the high, steep forehead (a feature often associated with intelligence), by the darkness surrounding the eyes (often associated with physical or spiritual weariness), and by the gaunt cheeks and the thin lips slightly turned down at the corners (associated with deprivation or restraint). The monster's face is of course in some ways shocking, but probably our chief impression as we look at it is that this is not the face of one who causes suffering but of one who himself is heroically undergoing suffering.
>
> —LESLIE RODRIGUEZ

When the topic sentence is at the end, the paragraph usually develops from the particular to the general, the topic sentence serving to generalize or summarize the information that precedes it. Such a topic sentence can be especially effective in presenting an argument: the reader hears, considers, and accepts the evidence before the argument is explicitly stated, and if the evidence has been effectively presented the reader willingly accepts the argument.

3. The next paragraph has no topic sentence:

> A few years ago when you mentioned Walt Disney at a respectable party—or anyway this is how it was in California, where I was then—the standard response was a headshake and a groan. Intellectuals spoke of how he butchered the classics—from *Pinocchio* to *Winnie the Pooh*, how his wildlife pictures were sadistic and coy, how the World's Fair sculptures of hippopotamuses were a national if not international disgrace. A few crazies disagreed, and since crazies are always the people to watch, it began to be admitted that the early Pluto movies had a considerable measure of *je ne sais quoi*, that the background animation in *Snow White* was "quite extraordinary," that *Fantasia* did indeed have *one* great sequence (then it became two; now everyone says three, though there's fierce disagreement on exactly which three).
>
> —JOHN GARDNER

The topic here is, roughly, "Intellectuals used to scorn Disney, but recently they have been praising him." Such a sentence could easily begin the paragraph, but it is not necessary because even without it the reader has no difficulty following the discussion. The first two sentences talk about Disney's earlier reputation; then the sentence about the "crazies" introduces the contrary view and the rest of the paragraph illustrates the growing popularity of this contrary view. The paragraph develops its point so clearly and consistently (it is essentially a narrative, in chronological order) that the reader, unlike the reader of a complex analytic paragraph, does not need the help of a topic sentence either at the beginning, to prepare for what follows, or at the end, to pull the whole together.

UNIFYING IDEAS INTO PARAGRAPHS

Although we emphasize **unity** in paragraphs, do not assume that every development or refinement or alteration of your thought requires a new paragraph. Such an assumption would lead to an essay consisting entirely of one-sentence paragraphs. A good paragraph may, for instance,

- ask a question and answer it, or
- describe an effect and then explain the cause, or
- set forth details and then offer a general comment.

Indeed, if the question or the effect or the details can be set forth in a sentence or two, and the answer or the cause or the general overview can be set forth in a sentence or two, the two halves of the topic should be pulled together into a single paragraph. Only if the question (for example) is long and complex and the answer equally long or longer, will you (or, more precisely, your reader) need two or more paragraphs.

Let us consider three paragraphs from an essay titled "The Darker Implications of Comedy." The essay is about the wisdom of some writers to acknowledge the double mask of tragedy and comedy in the lives of their characters, and hence in the experiences of humanity. The author begins with personal experience and his initial ponderings about comedy in his readings. He then goes on to define his terms and provide specific examples with explanations. Note that in the paragraphs printed below, the first is on personal experience as a younger man reading comedy, the second blends the personal with the more formal and shifts to a different kind of comedy, a darker humour, and the third extends an example of the black comedy in an attempt to figure out why certain types of comedy make him nervous. In other words, each paragraph is about one thing—personal experience with reading comedy and different types of comedy—and each paragraph builds on what the reader has learned in the previous paragraphs. That the third paragraph is more focused on the text, *My Present Age*, than on the personal response does not mean that it lacks unity: it is a unified discussion leading up to an extended discussion of tragi-comedy.

When I was a grad student, my test of good comedy was whether it made me laugh out loud in the graduate library. When I read Evelyn Waugh's *Vile Bodies* I broke out into a silly giggle. When I read Rabelais, I broke out into a raucous belly laugh. I suspect my laughter for *A Midsummer Night's Dream* was light and merry. For Mark Twain it was a barbaric yawp. Immediately after reading Alexander Pope, I suspect that I went around with a witty smirk.

But whenever I read Harold Pinter or Samuel Beckett there was this nervous laughter that was anything but joyful. When I finished grad school, I had run the gamut from Shakespearean comedy to

Restoration and eighteenth-century satire to early French ribaldry to frontier humour to black humour and farce. So when I talk about the darker implications of comedy, I'm also trying to get at why my laughter in the presence of contemporary comedy was so uneasy.

This uneasy laughter of modern-day black comedy is to me the most interesting of all. Reading Guy Vanderhaeghe's *My Present Age* for the first time I laughed my way through nearly every chapter until the last few pages. At the end of the novel I beheld the protagonist Ed alone in his basement apartment, deluded into thinking that his former wife Victoria will be looking for him, unable to go outside and face the world, unable to go to sleep because he is terrified of what he will see when he closes his eyes. He really has reached bottom. He is in the throes of a severe nervous breakdown, and only in the last sixteen lines of the novel does he have a guarded hope of recovery. And his voyage to the bottom has been outrageously funny. I have to ask myself why, in *Modern Times*, Charlie Chaplin gets turned into a twitching, mechanized monster because he has been working at one machine in a factory for too long. Or, in *The Gold Rush*, he gets so hungry in his Klondike shack, he has to cook and eat his shoe. I habitually explode with laughter, and again, I am beginning to wonder why.

—DAVID CARPENTER

Now contrast the unity of any of the previous three paragraphs on comedy with the lack of focus in this paragraph from a book on athletic coaching.

Leadership qualities are a prerequisite for achievement in coaching. A leader is one who is respected for what he says and does, and who is admired by his team. The coach gains respect by giving respect, and by possessing knowledge and skills associated with the sport. There are many "successful" coaches who are domineering, forceful leaders, gaining power more through fear and even hate than through respect. These military-type men are primarily from the old school of thought, and many younger coaches are achieving their goals through more humanistic approaches.

Something is wrong here (beyond the gender-exclusive language). The first half of the paragraph tells us that "a leader is one who is respected for what he says and does," but the second half of the paragraph contradicts that assertion, telling us that "many" leaders hold their position "more through fear and even hate than through respect." The trouble is *not* that the writer is talking about two kinds of leaders; a moment ago we saw that a writer can in one paragraph talk about different kinds of comedy. The trouble here is that we need a unifying idea if these two points are to be given in one paragraph. The idea might be: there are two kinds of leaders, those who are respected and those who are feared. This idea might be developed along these lines:

Leadership qualities are a prerequisite for achievement in coaching, but these qualities can be of two radically different kinds. One kind of leader is respected and admired by his team for what he says and does. The coach gains respect by giving respect, and by possessing knowledge and skills associated with the sport. The other kind of coach is a domineering, forceful leader, gaining power more through fear than through respect. These military-type men are primarily from the old school of thought, whereas most of the younger coaches achieve their goals through the more humane approaches of the first type.

ORGANIZATION IN PARAGRAPHS

A paragraph needs more than a unified point; it needs a reasonable **organization** or sequence. After all, a box containing all of the materials for a model airplane has unity (all the parts of the plane are there), but not until the parts are joined in the proper relationship do we get a plane. In the following paragraph, a sentence is out of place.

> The Depression hit Canada at a time when the country was in a development policy vacuum, although this was little recognized at the time as international trade collapsed and with it investment. Government economic intervention came from the politics of necessity, not of design. Even Conservative Prime Minister Bennett's eleventh-hour conversion in 1935 to the necessity of social security programs was a victim of the deluded, politically motivated Judicial Committee of the British Privy Council. On the other hand, government intervention in the form of investment in commerce, communications, and transportation was more successful, as evidenced by the formation under the Conservatives of the Bank of Canada and the Canadian Wheat Board, both at first in essence public support for private capital. Other rescue policies, such as the aid given to the attempted cartelization of the pulp and paper industry, were less successful. Later in the decade, the Liberals formed the Canadian Broadcasting Corporation and Trans-Canada Airlines.
>
> —PAUL PHILLIPS AND STEPHEN WATSON

Which sentence is out of place in the paragraph you have just read? How might you work it into its proper place?

Exactly how the parts of a paragraph will fit together depends, of course, on what the paragraph is doing.

1. If it is *describing* a place, it may move from a general view to the significant details—or from immediately striking details to some less obvious but perhaps more important ones. It may move from near to far, or from far to near, or from the past to the present.

2. If it is *explaining,* it may move from cause to effect, or from effect to cause, or from past to present; or it may offer an example.

3. If it is *arguing,* it may move from evidence to conclusion, or from a conclusion to supporting evidence; or it may offer one piece of evidence, for instance an anecdote (a short narrative) that illustrates the argument.

4. If it is *narrating,* it will likely move chronologically; in the following paragraph about going home after the first day at school as a new immigrant to Canada, we move from the children getting practical help from a teacher, to getting lost and finally to recognizing the house, and then to the response of the children's mother and landlady to their arrival home, and finally to a glimpse of just how different the author finds life in the new land.

> When the school day is over the teacher hands us a file card on which she has written, "I'm a newcomer. I'm lost. I live at 1785 Granville Street. Will you kindly show me how to get there? Thank you." We wander the streets for several hours, zigzagging back and forth through seemingly identical suburban avenues, showing this deaf-mute sign to the few people we see, until we eventually recognize the Rosenbergs' house. We're greeted by our quietly hysterical mother and Mrs. Rosenberg, who, in a ritual she has probably learned from television, puts out two glasses of milk on her red Formica counter. The milk, homogenized, and too cold from the fridge, bears little resemblance to the liquid we used to drink called by the same name.
>
> —EVA HOFFMAN

5. If a paragraph is *classifying* (dividing a subject into its parts), it may begin by enumerating the parts and go on to study each, perhaps in climactic order. Here is an example:

> The chief reasons people wear masks are these: to have fun, to protect themselves, to disguise themselves, and to achieve a new identity. At Halloween, children wear masks for fun; they may, of course, also think they are disguising themselves, but chiefly their motive is to experience the joy of saying "boo" to someone. Soldiers wore masks for protection, in ancient times against swords and battle-axes, in more recent times against poison gas. Bank robbers wear masks to disguise themselves, and though of course this disguise is a sort of protection, a robber's reason for wearing a mask is fairly distinct from a soldier's. All of these reasons so far are easily understood, but we may have more trouble grasping the reason that primitive people use masks in religious rituals. Some ritual masks seem merely to be attempts to frighten away evil spirits, and some seem merely to be disguises so that the evil spirits will not know who the wearer is. But most religious masks are worn with the idea that the wearer achieves a new identity, a union with supernatural powers, and thus in effect the wearer becomes—really becomes, not merely pretends to be—a new person.

Notice that the first sentence offers four reasons for wearing masks. The rest of the paragraph amplifies these reasons, one by one, and in the order indicated in the first sentence. Because the writer regards the last reason as the most interesting and the most difficult to grasp, it is discussed at the greatest length, giving it about as much space as is given to the first three reasons altogether.

The way in which a paragraph is organized, then, will depend on what the writer is trying to do—what the writer's purpose is. Almost always one of the writer's purposes is to make something clear to a reader. Among the common methods of organizing a paragraph and keeping things clear are the following:

1. General to particular (topic sentence usually at the beginning)
2. Particular to general (topic sentence usually at the end)

3. Enumeration of parts or details or reasons (probably in climactic order)
4. Question and answer
5. Cause and effect
6. Comparison and contrast
7. Analogy
8. Chronology
9. Spatial order (e.g., near to far, or right to left)
10. Most to least important or interesting (or vice versa).

We might say that a paragraph is like an upside-down gem—let's say a diamond (below). You begin with a topic sentence (a precise statement about the paragraph), expand upon it in the body (explanation, detail, and examples), and then narrow down to a concluding sentence (a statement rounding out the paragraph). However, this sense of shape is perhaps too rigid for the complex process of writing a paragraph. After all, you might include a transition at the beginning or end of your paragraph. Or, you might write a paragraph with the topic sentence at the end. The paragraph is rather complex!

The only rule that can cover all paragraphs is this: readers must never feel that they are stumbling as they follow the writer to the end of the paragraph. They should not have to go back and read the paragraph again to figure out what the writer had in mind. A paragraph is not a maze like *Spaghetti* on page 53; it should be organized so that readers can glide through it in seconds, not minutes.

COHERENCE IN PARAGRAPHS

In addition to having a unified point and a reasonable organization, a good paragraph is **coherent**; that is, the connections between ideas in the paragraph are clear. Coherence can often be achieved by inserting the right transitional words or by taking care to repeat key words.

Transitions

Richard Wagner, commenting on his work as a composer of operas, once said, "The art of composition is the art of transition," for his art moved from note to note, measure to measure, scene to scene. **Transitions** establish connections between ideas; they alert readers to what will follow. Here are some of the most common transitional words and phrases.

1. **amplification or likeness:** similarly, likewise, and, also, again, second, third, in addition, furthermore, moreover, finally
2. **emphasis:** chiefly, equally, indeed, even more important
3. **contrast or concession:** but, on the contrary, on the other hand, by contrast, of course, however, still, doubtless, no doubt, nevertheless, granted that, conversely, although, admittedly
4. **example:** for example, for instance, as an example, specifically, consider as an illustration, that is, such as, like

Vladimir Koziakin. *Spaghetti.*

5. **consequence or cause and effect:** thus, so, then, it follows, as a result, therefore, hence
6. **restatement:** in short, that is, in effect, in other words
7. **place:** in the foreground, further back, in the distance
8. **time:** afterward, next, then, as soon as, later, until, when, finally, last, at last
9. **conclusion:** finally, therefore, thus, to sum up

Consider the following paragraph:

> Folklorists are just beginning to look at Africa. A great quantity of folklore materials has been gathered from African countries in the past century and published by missionaries, travelers, administrators, linguists, and anthropologists incidentally to their main pursuits. No fieldworker has devoted himself exclusively or even largely to the recording and analysis of folklore materials, according to a committee of the African Studies Association reporting in 1966 on the state of research in the African arts. Yet Africa is the continent supreme for traditional cultures that nurture folklore. Why this neglect?
>
> —RICHARD M. DORSON

The reader gets the point, but the second sentence seems to contradict the first: the first sentence tells us that folklorists are just beginning to look at Africa, but the next tells us that lots of folklore has been collected. An "although" between these sentences would clarify the author's point, especially if the third sentence were hooked on to the second, thus:

> Folklorists are just beginning to look at Africa. Although a great quantity of folklore materials has been gathered from African countries in the past century by missionaries, travellers, administrators, linguists, and anthropologists incidentally to their main pursuits, no fieldworker has devoted himself or herself . . .

But this revision gives us an uncomfortably long second sentence. Further revision would help. While it is smothered, the real point of the original passage is that although many people have incidentally collected folklore materials in Africa, professional folklorists have not been active there. The contrast ought to be sharpened:

> Folklorists are just beginning to look at Africa. True, missionaries, travellers, administrators, linguists, and anthropologists have collected a quantity of folklore materials incidentally to their main pursuits, but folklorists have lagged behind. No fieldworker . . .

In this revision the words that clarify are the small but important words "true" and "but." The original paragraph is like a jigsaw puzzle that is missing tiny but necessary pieces.

Repetition

Coherence is also achieved through the **repetition** of key words. When you repeat words or phrases, or when you provide clear substitutes (such as pronouns, demonstrative adjectives, and synonyms), you are helping the reader to keep step with your developing thoughts. Grammatical constructions too can be repeated, the repetitions or parallels linking the sentences or ideas.

In the following example from Allan Gould's *Canned Lit*, in which he satirizes Canadian writers, notice how the repetitions provide continuity (as well as the humour of the paragraph).

> Over the past half century, Northrop Frye has not only given the University of Toronto a reputation it had never before achieved, he has proceeded to create several masterpieces of world-class scholarship. In *Fearful Symmetry* (1957) he explained William Blake to everyone who hadn't understood the great British poet and artist before, which included every other Blake scholar before Frye. In *Anatomy of Criticism* (1957) he explained how myth and archetype worked in literature to everyone who hadn't understood it before, which included every other scholar of literature before Frye. In *The Bush Garden* (1971) he explained why Canadian literature is bush to everyone who is bright enough to listen (we won't discuss numbers here). In *The Great Code* (1982) he explained the patterns of the Old and New Testaments to all those willing to find them . . . And much, much more, including years of profound musings in the *University of Toronto Quarterly* (which he improved by halves in every issue) and his inspired Conclusion to the *Literary History of Canada* in 1965.

Notice not only the exact repetitions of words and phrases, and sentence structures ("explained," "everyone who hadn't understood," "before Frye," and "much, much") and the slight variations ("everyone who is bright enough to listen"), but also the exaggeration (the build from "every other Blake scholar" to "every other scholar of literature," "improved by halves in every issue," and the "Conclusion" to literary history in Canada).

LINKING PARAGRAPHS TOGETHER

Each paragraph in an essay generally develops a single idea, a single (new) aspect of the main point of the essay, as one paragraph follows another, and readers should feel they are getting somewhere—smoothly and without stumbling. As you move from one paragraph to the next—from one step in the development of your main idea to the next—you probably can keep your readers with you if you link the beginning of each new paragraph to the end of the paragraph that precedes it. Often a single transitional word (such as those listed on pages 52-53) will suffice; sometimes repeating key terms will help connect a sequence of paragraphs together and make your essay (as many writers put it) "flow."

Consider the movement of ideas in the following essay by Cheryl Lee written in response to an assignment for her writing class that asked students to analyze a family photograph.

The Story Behind the Gestures

1   At the close of my graduation ceremony, my entire family gathered together to immortalize the special moment on film. No one escaped the flash of my mother's camera because she was determined to document every minute of the occasion at every possible angle. My mother made sure that she took pictures of me with my hat on, with my hat off, holding the bouquet, sitting, standing, and in countless other positions. By the time this family picture was taken, my smile was intact, frozen on my face. This is not to say that my smile was anything less than genuine, for it truly was a smile of thankfulness and joy. It is just that after posing for so many pictures, what initially began as a spontaneous reaction became a frozen expression.

2   The viewer should, however, consider not so much the frozen expressions of those in the photograph, but rather the fact that the picture

is posed. A posed picture supposedly shows only what the people in the picture want the viewer to see- -in this case, their happiness. But ironically the photograph reveals much more about its subjects than the viewer first imagines. The photograph speaks of relationships and personalities. It speaks about the more intimate details that first seem invisible but that become undeniable through the study of gestures.

3   In the photograph, the most prominent and symbolic of gestures is the use and position of the arms. Both my father and mother place an arm around me and in turn around each other. Their encircling arms, however, do more than just show affection; they unify the three figures into a close huddle that leads the viewer's eye directly to them as opposed to the background or the periphery. The slightly bended arms that rest at their sides act as arrows that not only reinforce the three figures as the focal point but also exclude the fourth figure, my brother, from sharing the "spotlight." Unlike the other members of the family whose arms and hands are intertwined, Edwin stands with both hands down in front of him, latching onto no one. The lack of physical contact between the huddled

figures and Edwin is again emphasized as he positions himself away from the viewer's eye as he stands in the periphery.

4   Edwin's position in the photograph is indicative of him as a person, for he always seems to isolate himself from the spotlight, from being the centre of attention. Thus, it is his decision to escape public scrutiny, not the force of my parents' arms that drives him to the side. His quiet, humble nature directs him away from even being the focal point of a picture and leads him towards establishing his own individuality and independence in privacy. His long hair and his "hand-me-down" clothes are all an expression of his simply being himself. The reason behind his physical independence is the emotional independence that he already possesses at the age of sixteen. He stands alone because he can stand alone.

5   While Edwin stands apart from the other three figures, I stand enclosed and protected. The lock of arms as well as the bouquet restrain me; they dissuade me from breaking away in favour of independence. Although my mother wants me to achieve the same kind of independence that Edwin has achieved, she works to delay the time when I actually will move away to the periphery. Perhaps my being the only daughter, the only other female in the family, has something to do with my mother's desire to keep me close and dependent as long as possible. Her arm reaches out with bouquet in hand as if to shield me from the world's unpleasantness. Even though my father also holds onto me with an encircling arm, it is my mother's firm grip that alone persuades me to stay within the boundary of their protective arms.

6   Her grip, which proves more powerful than my father's hold, restrains not only me but also my father. In the picture, he falls victim to the same outstretched hand, the same touch of the bouquet. Yet this time, my mother's bouquet does more than just restrain; it seems to push my father

back "into line" or into his so-called place. The picture illustrates this exertion of influence well, for my mother in real life does indeed assume the role of the dominant figure. Although my father remains the head of the household in title, it is my mother around whom the household revolves; she oversees the insignificant details as well as the major ones. But my father doesn't mind at all. Like me, he also enjoys the protection her restraining arm offers. It is because of our mutual dependence on my mother that my father and I seem to draw closer. This dependence in turn strengthens both of our relationships with my mother.

7   At the time the picture was taken, I seriously doubt that my mother realized the significance of her position in the picture or the import of her gestures. All of us in fact seem too blinded by the festivity of the occasion to realize that this photograph would show more than just a happy family at a daughter's graduation. The family photograph would inevitably become a telling portrait of each member of the family. It would, in a sense, leave us vulnerable to the speculative eyes of the viewer, who in carefully examining the photograph would recognize the secrets hidden in each frozen expression.

A few observations on these paragraphs may be useful. First, notice that each paragraph in the sequence examines a different aspect of the photograph and introduces a new point into the discussion. The first paragraph gives background information (the photograph was taken at Lee's graduation); the second paragraph states the writer's point—that studying the gestures of her family members enables us to understand their "personalities and relationships." Each succeeding paragraph treats one of these gestures (paragraph 3, for example, considers the encircling arms) or one of the personalities or relationships. Paragraph 4 focuses on the writer's brother Edwin; paragraph 5 focuses on Lee's relationship to her mother; paragraph 6 focuses on her mother and father. We might think that symmetry requires that each family member get a single paragraph, but given the complexity of their relationships to each other, and given the mother's dominance in the family, it makes sense that things don't break down so neatly and that Lee devotes two paragraphs to her mother.

Second, notice how Lee makes the essay cohere. Although she uses some transitional words ("however" at the beginning of the second paragraph; "while" at the beginning of the fifth paragraph), she establishes coherence in this essay primarily by repeating the key terms of her discussion. The first sentence of each new paragraph picks up a word or phrase from the last sentence of the paragraph preceding it. The phrase "frozen expressions" links the beginning of the second paragraph to the end of the first; "gestures" links the second paragraph to the third; "position" links the third to the fourth; "stands" links the fourth to the fifth; and so on. These links are hardly noticeable on a first reading, but because Lee uses transitions and repetition effectively, the writing flows, and the reader never stumbles.

PARAGRAPH LENGTH

There are no hard-and-fast rules about paragraph length, but most good paragraphs are between one hundred and two hundred words, consisting of more than two or three but fewer than ten or eleven sentences. It is not a matter, however, of counting words or sentences; paragraphs are coherent blocks, substantial units of your essay, and the spaces between them are brief resting places allowing the reader to take in what you have said. One double-spaced, word-processed page of uninterrupted writing (approximately 250 words) is about as much as the reader can take before requiring a slight break. On the other hand, a single page with half a dozen paragraphs is probably faulty because the reader is too often interrupted with needless pauses and because the page has too few *developed* ideas: an assertion is made, and then another and another. These assertions are unconvincing because they are not supported with detail. To put it another way, a paragraph is a room in the house you are building. If your essay is some five hundred words long (about two double-spaced word-processed pages), you probably will not break it down into more than four or five rooms or paragraphs; if you break it down into a dozen paragraphs, readers will feel they are touring a rabbit warren rather than a house.

The Use and Abuse of Short Paragraphs

A short paragraph can be effective when it summarizes a highly detailed previous paragraph or group of paragraphs, or when it serves as a transition between two complicated paragraphs, but unless you are sure that the reader needs a break, avoid thin paragraphs. A paragraph that is nothing but a transition can usually be altered into a transitional phrase or clause or sentence that starts the next paragraph. But of course there are times when a short paragraph is exactly right. Notice the effect of the three-sentence paragraph between two longer paragraphs:

> Though never on display, the suit's exact whereabouts is never in doubt. Whenever weather changes, or soldiers are imagined, it is always his brother's suit that comes first to Uncle Henry's mind. It has to do with refusing to give up. The suit has been there since my father went to get an elevator, waited for the door to open, and stepped into an elevator shaft that turned out to be empty and fell to the bottom. He lay there unconscious for a day until he was discovered. His head was

smashed and his brain stem injured. My father, a Holocaust survivor, died in Toronto two days later at the age of thirty-three. Uncle Henry was visiting from New York at the time, looking into setting up a furniture business with my father. I was seventeen months then, my brother two months. Now, in my thirties myself, I think of the empty suit.

Perhaps I saw the awe-inspiring but silent suit on its hanger six or seven times. I can't remember my father wearing it, and I don't think I can remember my father. But I remember the suit.

Where there are no readily retrievable memories, substitutes must suffice. I knew him as one knows the numbness of the phantom limb which out of nowhere speaks out to say "I am here, but I am missing"; I had the indelible knowledge that a number was tattooed on his arm but didn't know the number; I know stories of him telling stories to survive and his life-giving gift of the gab; heard others hum the songs he was always singing; I remember standing as a child of four or five with my mother and brother, staring at his tombstone, and I know that the name of the stone was not his real name, Leon Greenspan, but the alias that he used to escape and that he became saddled with after the war. And yes, I knew his suit.

—NORMAN DOIDGE

If the content of the second paragraph were less momentous, it would hardly merit a paragraph. Here the brevity contributes to the enormous impact; those three sentences that emphasize the importance of the suit and that foreshadow the first sentence of the next paragraph, set off by themselves, seem equal in weight to the longer paragraphs that precede and follow. They are the hinge on which the door turns.

When used for emphasis, short paragraphs can be effective.

Often, though, short paragraphs (like the one directly above) leave readers feeling unsatisfied, even annoyed. Consider these two consecutive paragraphs from a draft of a student's essay on D. C. Scott's poem "The Forsaken."

The winter imagery in the first half of Scott's poem is cold and bitter.

The Chippewa woman is far away from the Fort during a storm.

In the second half of his poem, the scene shifts. The woman is now old.

Her son leaves her during winter on the same island where she struggled

to survive all those years ago.

Sometimes you can improve a sequence of short paragraphs merely by joining one paragraph to the next. But unsatisfactory short paragraphs usually cannot be repaired so simply. The reason is that the source of the problem is usually not that sentences have been needlessly separated from each other, but that general statements have not been supported by details, or that claims have not been supported by evidence. Here is the student's revised version, strengthening the two thin paragraphs of the draft.

In the first half of Scott's poem, the winter scene is depicted as very harsh, isolating, cold, and bitter, as the Chippewa woman with her baby son is far away from the Fort in the middle of a storm. The images evoke an anxious mood:

Of millions of iceflakes

Hurled by the wind

.   .   .   .

With the voice of the storm

In the deeps of the cedars

(Scott 25-31)

The woman, however, with her strong characterization as "valiant" and "unshaken" creates an opposing mood more resolute in nature.

In the second half of Scott's poem, the scene shifts dramatically. The woman is now described as old and withered. The son whom she had protected so many years before from the cruel realities of the winter storm now leaves her on the island near the place where she had so valiantly confronted nature years before. This time nature greets her in more reverent terms, accepting the now aged woman as the warrior she is. Still "valiant, unshaken," she courageously accepts her fate, as is indicated by her smoothing her locks of hair under her kerchief, straightening her shawl, and folding her aged hands on her breasts as she lies waiting for her time to expire (71-74). Winter delicately blankets her with millions of snowflakes from a "windless cloud," covering her with a "beautiful crystal shroud" (80-81). Nature treats her with respect this time. Even as she takes her dying breath, the wintry snow recedes to accept this final sign of her spirit.

This revision is not simply a padded version of the earlier paragraphs; it is a necessary clarification of them, for without the details the general comments mean almost nothing to a reader.

INTRODUCTORY PARAGRAPHS

As the poet Byron said, at the beginning of a long part of a long poem, "Nothing so difficult as a beginning." Woody Allen thinks so too. In an interview he said that the toughest part of writing is "to go from nothing to the first draft."

Almost all writers—professionals as well as amateurs—find that the first paragraphs in their drafts are false starts. As we suggest in Chapter 1, we think you shouldn't worry too much about the opening paragraph of your draft; you will almost surely want to revise your opening later anyway. (Surprisingly often your first paragraph may simply be deleted; your second, you may find, is where your essay truly begins.)

When writing a first draft you merely need something—almost anything may do—to break the ice. But in your finished paper the opening cannot be mere throat-clearing. The opening should be interesting. Among the commonest *un*interesting openings are:

1. A dictionary definition ("Webster says . . .")
2. A restatement of your title. The title is (let's assume) "Winter Imagery in D. C. Scott's 'The Forsaken,' " and the first sentence says, "This essay will discuss D. C. Scott's use of winter imagery in his poem 'The Forsaken.' " True, the sentence announces the topic of the essay, but it gives no information about the topic beyond what the title already offers, and it provides no information about you either—that is, no sense of your response to the topic, such as might be present in, say, "In D. C. Scott's 'The Forsaken,' the Native woman is associated with two winter scenes at different times in her life to evoke various emotions regarding life's experiences and journey toward death."
3. A broad generalization, such as "Ever since the beginning of time, human beings have been violent." Again, such a sentence may be fine if it helps you to start drafting, but it should not remain in your final version: it is dull—and it tells your readers almost nothing about the essay they are about to read. (Our example, after all, could begin anything from an analysis of *Pulp Fiction* to a term paper on World War II.) To put it another way, the ever-since-the-beginning-of-time opening lacks substance—and if your opening lacks substance, it will not matter what you say next. No one will bother to read more—or if someone does, a bad first impression has already been made.

What is left? What *is* a good way for a final version to begin? Your introductory paragraph will be at least moderately interesting if it gives information, and it will be pleasing if the information provides focus—that is, if it lets the reader know exactly what your topic is and where you will be going. Remember, when you write, *you* are the teacher; it will not do to begin,

George Orwell says he shot the elephant because . . .

We need some information identifying the text you are writing about.

George Orwell, in "Shooting an Elephant," says he shot the elephant because . . .

Even better is

In "Shooting an Elephant," George Orwell sets forth his reflections on his service as a police officer in Burma. He suggests that he once shot an elephant because . . . but his final paragraph suggests that we must look for additional reasons.

Compare, for example, the opening sentences from three essays written by students on Margaret Atwood's *The Journals of Susanna Moodie*. In this group of poems Atwood speaks through Moodie, an early Canadian pioneer and writer.

Canadian writers tend to write about the landscape and about survival.

This is what we call a **zonker** (see page 76), an all-purpose sentence that serves no specific purpose well. Notice also the unnecessary repetition of "writers" and "write," the weaselling of "tend," and the vagueness of lumping all Canadian writers into an oversimplified, narrow category.

I think Margaret Atwood chose Susanna Moodie to write about and through as she was the first female Canadian poet, and she wrote about many of the things that are still being written about in poetry today.

This example is more specific because it mentions the text being discussed and tells you something about it, but it is wishy-washy with "I think," includes an ambiguous pronoun (is "she" Atwood or Moodie?), and is vague with "many of the things."

Margaret Atwood's The Journals of Susanna Moodie follows Moodie's search for her identity as a Canadian pioneer while Atwood searches for hers as a Canadian poet.

Surely this is the best of the three openings. Informative and focused, it identifies the book's theme and method, and it offers an evaluation. The essayist has been considerate of her readers: if we are interested in the experiences of women pioneers and in Canadian poetry, we will read on. If we are not, we are grateful to her for letting us off the bus at the first stop.

Let us look now not simply at an opening sentence but at an entire first paragraph, the opening paragraph of an analytic essay. Notice how the student provides the reader with the necessary information about the book being discussed (the diary of a man whose son is brain-damaged) and also focuses the reader's attention on the essay's topic (the quality that distinguishes this diary from others).

Josh Greenfeld's diary, <u>A Place for Noah</u>, records the attempts of a smart, thoughtful man to reconcile himself to his son's autism, a severe mental and physical disorder. Most diaries function as havens for secret thoughts. And Greenfeld's diary does frequently supply a voice to Greenfeld's darkest fears about who will ultimately care for Noah. It provides, too, an intimate glimpse of a family striving to remain a coherent unit despite their tragedy. But beyond affording such urgent and personal revelations, <u>A Place for Noah</u>, in chronicling the isolation of the Greenfelds, reveals how inadequate and ineffectual our medical and educational systems are in responding to families victimized by catastrophic illness.

This example is engaging and fairly direct—but of course you can provide interest and focus by other, more indirect means, such as:

- A quotation
- An anecdote or other short narrative
- An interesting fact (a statistic, for instance, showing the reader that you know something about your topic)
- A definition of an important term—but not merely one derived from a desk dictionary
- An assertion (in an essay offering a proposal) that a problem exists
- A glance at a view different from your own
- A question—but an interesting one, such as "Why do we call some words obscene?"

Many excellent opening paragraphs do not use any of these devices, and you need not use any of them if they feel forced. But in your reading you may observe that these devices are used widely. Here is an example of the second device, **an anecdote** that makes an effective introduction to this student essay on the importance of economic independence for the realization of creative and intellectual potential.

When I consider the relationship between money and artistic/ intellectual potential, a scene from a film I saw years ago, one set in 1930s Paris, floats to the top of my mind. It looks like this: a writer, virtually penniless, hunched and hammering away at his typewriter (or did he write longhand?) at his makeshift desk, in his shabby, roach-infested—yet

against all odds, quaint—room. I then recall that he, the writer, had

rejected materialism, sexual prudery, and the literary conventions of the

time. He refused to waste himself on gainful employment, choosing instead

to hoard his creative energies and pour them into his unique vision. He ate

and drank heartily when provisions were offered but was able, apparently,

to be equally productive and brilliant on an empty stomach. For him,

dispossession and fecundity could co-exist.

The third strategy, **an interesting detail**, shows the reader that you know something about your topic and that you are worth reading. We have already seen (page 45) a rather quiet example of this device, in a paragraph about Charles Darwin that began "Charles Darwin's youth was unmarked by signs of genius." Here is a more obvious example, from an essay on protecting endangered spaces in Quebec.

> In addition to being the midpoint of the Endangered Spaces campaign, 1995 is a significant year for the Québec park system because Mont Tremblant, its oldest park, celebrates its centennial.

(Such information is to be had by spending about thirty seconds with a dictionary or encyclopedia or the Internet.)

The fourth strategy, **a definition**, is fairly common in analytic essays; the essayist first clears the ground by specifying the topic. (For more on definition, see Chapter 11, "Defining.") Here is the beginning of an essay on bilingual education in the United States.

> Let's begin by defining "bilingual education." As commonly used today, the term does *not* mean teaching students a language other than English (almost everyone would agree that foreign-language instruction should be available, and that it is desirable for Americans to be fluent not only in English but also in some other language); nor does "bilingual education" mean offering courses in English as a second language to students whose native language is, for example, Chinese, or Spanish or Navajo or Aleut. (Again, almost everyone would agree that such instruction should be offered where economically possible.) Rather, it means offering instruction in such courses as mathematics, history, and science *in the student's native language,* while also offering courses in English as a second language. Programs vary in details, but the idea is that the nonnative speaker should be spared the trauma of total immersion in English until he or she has completed several years of studying English as a second language. During this period, instruction in other subjects is given in the student's native language.
>
> —Tina Bakka

The fifth strategy, **the assertion that a problem exists**, is common in essays that make proposals. The following example is the first paragraph of a (successful) grant proposal written by engineers seeking government funding for their research project, a new method for treating liver cancer. Notice that the paragraph does not in fact offer the authors' proposal; it simply points out that there really is an unsolved problem, and the reader infers that the proposal will offer the solution.

> Liver cancer, especially metastatic colorectal cancer, is a significant and increasing health concern. In the United States, half of the 157,000 new cases of colorectal cancer will develop metastases in the liver. These metastases will lead to over 17,000 deaths annually. And while not as significant a health risk as colorectal metastasis, hepatocellular carcinoma is being diagnosed with increasing frequency. The current standard of practice for treating liver cancer is surgical resection, but only 10% of patients are eligible for this procedure. (Circumstances limiting eligibility include the tumor location, the number of lobes affected by the cancer, the patient's general poor health, and cirrhosis.) Further, less than 20% of those patients who undergo resection survive for three years without recurrence. Transplantation is an alternative to resection, but this technique is not appropriate for metastatic disease or for larger cancers, and the shortage of liver grafts limits the usefulness of this technique. Systemic chemotherapy has been shown to have a therapeutic effect on metastases, but it has also been shown to have no effect on long-term survival rates.
>
> —MICHAEL CURLEY AND PATRICK HAMILTON

The sixth strategy, **a glance at the opposition**, is especially effective if the opposing view is well established, but while you state it, you should manage to convey your distrust of it. Here is an example:

> One often hears, correctly, that there is a world food crisis, and one almost as often hears that not enough food is produced to feed the world's entire population. The wealthier countries, it is said, jeopardize their own chances for survival when they attempt to subsidize all of the poorer countries in which the masses are starving. Often the life-boat analogy is offered: There is room in the boat for only X people, and to take in $X + 1$ is to overload the boat and to invite the destruction of all. But is it true that the world cannot and does not produce enough food to save the whole population from starving?
>
> —V. NAGARAJAN

The seventh strategy, **a question**, is briefly illustrated by the opening paragraph of an essay about whether it is sometimes permissible for doctors to lie to their patients.

> Should doctors ever lie to benefit their patients—to speed recovery or to conceal the approach of death? In medicine as in law, government, and other lines of work, the requirements of honesty often seem dwarfed by greater needs: the need to shelter from brutal news or to

uphold a promise of secrecy; to expose corruption or to promote the public interest.

—Sissela Bok

Clearly, there is no one way to write an opening paragraph, but we want to add that you cannot go wrong in beginning your essay—especially if it is an analytic essay written for a course in the humanities—with a paragraph that includes **a statement of your thesis**. A common version of this kind of paragraph

- offers some background (if you are writing about a novel, for example, you will give the author and title as well as relevant information about the novel's plot, characters or literary techniques);
- suggests the problem or question the essay will address (in the paragraph below, the problem is implied: In *Frankenstein* similar characters meet very different fates; how can we account for the difference?); and
- ends with a sentence that states the main point, or thesis, and indicates the direction the essay will take.

In <u>Frankenstein</u>, Mary Shelley frames the novel with narratives of two similar characters who meet markedly different fates. Frankenstein, the medical researcher, and Walton, the explorer, are both passionately determined to push forward the boundaries of human knowledge. But while Walton's ambition to explore unknown regions of the earth is directed by reason and purpose, Frankenstein's ambition to create life is unfocused and misguided. This difference in the nature of their ambitions determines their fates. Walton's controlled ambition leads him to abandon his goal in order to save the lives of his crew members. When we last see him, he is heading toward home and safety. Frankenstein's unchecked ambition leads to his own death and the self-destruction of his creature.

CONCLUDING PARAGRAPHS

Concluding paragraphs, like opening paragraphs, are especially difficult if only because they are so conspicuous. Fortunately, you are not always obliged to write one. Descriptive essays, for example, may end merely with a final paragraph, not with a paragraph that draws a conclusion. In an expository essay explaining a process or mechanism you may simply stop when you have finished. Just check to see that the last sentence is a good one, clear and vigorous, and stop. In such essays there is usually no need for a crescendo signalling your farewell to the reader. Persuasive essays are more likely to need concluding paragraphs, not merely final paragraphs. But even persuasive essays, if they are short enough, may end without a formal conclusion; if the last paragraph sets forth the last step of the argument, that may be conclusion enough.

If you do have to write a concluding paragraph—and you almost certainly will in a humanities course—say something interesting. It is not of the slightest interest to say "Thus we see . . ." and then echo your title and first paragraph. There is some justification for a summary at the end of a long essay because the reader may have half-forgotten some of the ideas presented thirty pages earlier, but an essay that can easily be held in the mind needs something different, some-thing more. A good concluding paragraph rounds out the previous discussion. Such a paragraph may offer a few sentences that summarize (without the obvi-ousness of "We may now summarize"), but it will probably also draw an infer-ence that has not previously been expressed. To draw such an inference is not to introduce an entirely new idea—the end of an essay is hardly the place for that. Rather it is to see the previous material in a fresh perspective, to take the discus-sion perhaps one step further.

Because all writers have to find out what they think about any given topic and have to find the strategies appropriate for presenting these thoughts to a par-ticular audience, we hesitate to offer a do-it-yourself kit for final paragraphs, but the following simple devices often work:

- End with a new (but related) point, one that takes your discussion a step further.
- End with an allusion, say to a historical or mythological figure or event, putting your topic in a larger framework.
- End with a glance at the readers—not with a demand that they mount the barricades but with a suggestion that the next move is theirs.
- End with a quotation, especially a quotation that amplifies or varies a quotation used in the opening paragraph.
- End with some idea or detail from the beginning of the essay and thus bring it full circle.

If you adopt any of these devices, do so quietly; the aim is not to write a grand finale but to complete or round out a discussion.

Here are the beginning and the end of an essay on change in Emily Dickinson's poetry. (We reprint the beginning as well as the end of the essay to illustrate the last two suggestions above.) Note the way the writer begins the last paragraph with a quotation that amplifies the opening paragraphs' point about Dickinson's troubled response to change; note also that the word "palsy," found in an opening paragraph, appears again in the last paragraph.

Emily Dickinson's life knew little change of the conventional sort. As

her sister-in-law Susan wrote in an 1886 obituary, "Miss Emily Dickinson

of Amherst,"

The death of Miss Emily Dickinson, daughter of the late Edward

Dickinson, at Amherst on Saturday, makes another sad inroad on the small circle so long occupying the old family mansion. It was for a long generation overlooked by death, and one passing in and out of there thought of old-fashioned times, when parents and children grew up and passed maturity together, in lives of singular uneventfulness, unmarked by sad or joyous crises.

Dickinson lived in the same house all her years but the one she spent at seminary; she never married; she never worked. Yet in spite of this permanence- -or because of it- -change seemed to fascinate her and to inspire much of her poetry. She says as much in a June 1862 letter to her mentor T. W. Higginson, whom she tells that when "a sudden light on Orchards, or a new fashion in the wind trouble my attention," she feels a "palsy" that "the Verses just relieve" (Selected 174). Indeed Dickinson is probably best known for her many verses on the most troubling of all changes: "Because I could not stop for Death / He kindly stopped for me." Yet changes- -deaths, seasonal changes, shifts in the quality of light (as at sunset or sunrise)- -both trouble and charm Dickinson. A remark from a letter of April 1873 to her cousins Louise and Frances Norcross reveals the dichotomy in her attitude. . . .

Now for the final paragraph:

"Poetry is what Dickinson did to her doubts and incomprehension," writes critic David Porter (328), and she surely felt doubt about things she knew or feared would change. "Because I could not say it- -I fixed it in the Verse- -for you to read- -when your thought wavers," she wrote in an 1862 letter to Samuel Bowles (Selected 170). Dickinson wrote about change to give it the kind of order she understood, to control it and to fix it and so relieve her "palsy." To this extent, poetry for her must have had an immortal quality, like the wine of Indian Summer, and writing it must have been an ultimate act of faith.

Here are the beginning and end of David Suzuki's "The Road from Rio," in which he brings the essay full circle by reintroducing the metaphor of the car on the road that is set out in the introduction. He ends with a two-paragraph conclusion, in which the first paragraph briefly summarizes his main points and proposes a solution and the second calls the world to action.

The beginning:

The earth summit in Rio in June 1992 can best be described by a metaphor. Picture the participants at the Earth Summit as passengers in a packed car heading for a brick wall at 150 kilometres an hour. Most of them ignored the danger because they were too busy arguing about where they wanted to sit. Some occupants did notice the wall but were still debating about whether it was a mirage, how far away it was, or when the car would reach it. A few were confident the car was so well built that it would suffer only minor damage when it plowed into the wall. Besides, they warned, slowing down or swerving too sharply would upset everyone inside the car.

The end:

If we are to take a different road from Rio, the directions are clear. The rich nations of the world now hoard a disproportionate share of the world's wealth, consume far beyond a sustainable level, and are the major polluters and destroyers. It is our responsibility to cut back drastically while sharing efficient technologies and paying for family planning and debt reduction in the poor countries.

We can't afford to wait another twenty years for another opportunity to look in the mirror. If Rio did anything, it informed us that it's up to us, and we have to begin now.

All essayists will have to find their own ways of ending each essay; the five strategies we have suggested are common but they are not for you if you don't find them useful. And so, rather than ending this section with rules about how to end essays, we suggest how *not* to end them: do not merely summarize, do not say "in conclusion," do not introduce a totally new point, and do not apologize.

A Checklist for Revising Paragraphs

✔ Does the paragraph *say* anything? Does it have substance?
✔ Does the paragraph have a topic sentence? If so, is it in the best place? If the paragraph doesn't have a topic sentence, might one improve the paragraph? Or does it have a clear topic idea?
✔ If the paragraph is an opening paragraph, is it interesting enough to attract and to hold a reader's attention? If it is a later paragraph, does it easily evolve out of the previous paragraph, and lead into the next paragraph?
✔ Does the paragraph contain some principle of development, for instance from cause to effect, or from general to particular?

✔ Does each sentence clearly follow from the preceding sentence? Have you provided transitional words or cues to guide your reader? Would it be useful to repeat certain key words, for clarity?

✔ What is the purpose of the paragraph? Do you want to summarize, or tell a story, or give an illustration, or concede a point, or what? Is your purpose clear to you, and does the paragraph fulfill your purpose?

✔ Is the closing paragraph effective, and not an unnecessary restatement of the obvious?

Exercises

1. Reread the paragraph on page 46, in which a topic sentence (about comparing *The Kiss* to *Shivers*) begins the paragraph. Then write a paragraph with a similar construction, clarifying the topic sentence with details. You might, for example, begin thus: "When facing a right-handed batter, a left-handed pitcher has a distinct advantage over a right-handed pitcher." Another possible beginning: "All three major television networks offer similar kinds of entertainment during prime time."

2. Reread the paragraph on page 47 discussing the face of Frankenstein's monster and then write a paragraph on some other widely known face, ending your paragraph with a topic sentence. The cover of a recent issue of *Maclean's* or *Chatelaine* may provide you with the face you need.

3. The following paragraph is unified but incoherent. How could it be reorganized?

   Abortion, the expulsion of a fetus that could not develop and function alone successfully, is an issue that has caused much discussion in the past decade. There exist mainly two opposing groups concerning this subject, but many people's opinions lie somewhere in the middle. Some believe that abortions should be legalized unconditionally throughout Canada, while others believe that abortions should be illegal in all cases.

4. The following paragraph is both unified and fairly well organized, but it is still lacking in coherence. What would you do to improve it?

   The cyclist must also master prerace tactics. Not only what to wear and what food to bring are important, but how to strip the bike of unnecessary weight. Cycling shoes are specially designed for bike racing. They have a metal sole that puts the energy directly to the pedal, thus efficiently using one's power. The food that one brings is important in a long-distance race. It must not only be useful in refuelling the body, but it must be easily eaten while pedalling. Candy bars and fruit, such as bananas, satisfy both requirements. The bike must be stripped of all unnecessary weight, including saddlebags and reflectors. Some cyclists drill holes in parts of the frame, saddle post, and handlebars to lessen the weight of the bike.

5. On page 49 we printed a paragraph on athletic coaching, and we also printed a more unified revision of the paragraph. But the revision is still weak for it lacks supporting details. Revise the revision, giving it life.
6. Here is a newspaper report—chiefly in paragraphs of one sentence each—of an unfortunate happening. Imagine how it could be reorganized into one paragraph, into two paragraphs, and into three. Decide which organization would be most effective and revise the report accordingly.

 **REUTERS**

Fish Eat Brazilian Fisherman

1   MANAUS, BRAZIL—Man-eating piranha fish devoured fisherman Zeca Vicente when he tumbled into the water during a battle with 300 farmers for possession of an Amazon jungle lake.

2   Vicente, a leader of a group of 30 fishermen, was eaten alive in minutes by shoals of the ferocious fish lurking in Lake Januaca.

3   He died when the farmers—packed in an armada of small boats—attacked the fishermen with hunting rifles, knives, and bows and arrows after they refused to leave.

4   The farmers, who claimed the fishermen were depleting the lake's fish stocks, one of their main sources of food, boarded the fishing vessels and destroyed cold storage installations.

5   Last to give way was Vicente, who tried to cut down the farmers' leader with a knife. But farmers shot him and he fell wounded into the water, and into the jaws of the piranhas.

6   Fifteen persons have been charged with the attack which caused Vicente's death and the injury of several other fishermen.

7   Lake Januaca, about four hours from this Amazon River town by launch, is famous for its pirarucu and tucunare fish which are regarded as table delicacies.

7. Here is the opening paragraph of an essay (about 750 words) on the manufacture of paper in the fifteenth century, the days of the earliest printed

books. On the whole it is very good, but the unity and the organization can be improved. Revise the paragraph.

We take paper for granted, but old as it is it did not always exist. In fact, it was invented long after writing was invented, for the earliest writing is painted or scratched on cave walls, shells, rocks, and other natural objects. Paper was not even the first manufactured surface for writing; sheets made from papyrus, a reed-like plant, were produced about 2500 BCE, long before the invention of paper. Although the Chinese may have invented paper as early as the time of Christ, the oldest surviving paper is from early fifth-century China. The Arabs learned the secret of paper-making from the Chinese in the eighth century, but the knowledge travelled slowly to Europe. The oldest European paper, made by the Moors in Spain, is of the twelfth century. Early European paper is of poor quality and so not until the quality improved, around the fourteenth century, did paper become widely used. Most writing was done on parchment, which is the skin of a sheep or goat, and vellum, which is the finer skin of a lamb, kid, or calf. Whatever the animal, the skin was washed, limed, unhaired, scraped, washed again, stretched, and rubbed with pumice until a surface suitable for writing was achieved. Until it was displaced by paper in the fourteenth century, parchment was the chief writing surface in Europe.

8. Here is the concluding paragraph of a book review. What repetitions do you find? What is their effect?

Mr. Flexner's book is more than a political argument. He has written so vividly and involved us so deeply that there are moments when we yearn to lean over into the pages, pull Hamilton aside, and beg him to reconsider, to pity, to trust, to wait, or merely to shut up. Yet the book's effect is not melodramatic. It is tragic—a tragedy not of fate but of character, the spectacle of an immensely gifted man who tried to rule a nation and could not rule himself.

—NAOMI BLIVEN

Revising Sentences for Conciseness

Excess is the common substitute for energy.

—Marianne Moore

All writers who want to keep the attention and confidence of their audience revise for conciseness. The general rule is to say everything relevant in as few words as possible. The opening of Rick McConnell's article about beginning to write—"All Beginnings Are Hard"—says it all in four words.

The writers of the following sentences talk too much; they bore us because they do not make every word count.

There are two pine trees which grow behind this house.

On his left shoulder is a small figure standing. He is about the size of the doctor's head.

The judge is seated behind the bench, and he is wearing a judicial robe.

Compare those three sentences with these revisions:

Two pine trees grow behind this house.

On his left shoulder stands a small figure, about the size of the doctor's head.

The judge, wearing a robe, sits behind the bench.

We will soon discuss in some detail the chief patterns of wordiness, but here it is enough to say that if you prefer the revisions you already have a commendable taste for conciseness. What does your taste tell you to do with the following sentences?

A black streak covers the bottom half. It appears to have been painted

with a single stroke of a large brush.

The time to begin revising for conciseness is when you think you have an acceptable draft in hand—something that pretty much covers your topic and comes reasonably close to saying what you believe about it. As you go over it, study each sentence to see what can be deleted without loss of meaning or emphasis. Read each paragraph, preferably aloud, to see if each sentence supports the topic sentence or idea and clarifies the point you are making. Leave in the concrete and specific details and examples that support your ideas (you may in fact be adding more) but cut out all the deadwood that chokes them:

- extra words
- empty or pretentious phrases
- weak qualifiers
- redundancies
- negative constructions
- wordy uses of the verb *to be*
- other extra verbs and verb phrases.

We will discuss these problems in the next pages, but first we offer some examples of sentences that cannot be improved upon; they are so awful there is nothing to do but delete them and start over. Zonker, in Garry Trudeau's cartoon, is a master of what we call Instant Prose (stuff that sounds like the real thing, but is not).

DOONESBURY   **by Garry Trudeau**

INSTANT PROSE (ZONKERS)

Here are some examples of Instant Prose from students' essays:

> Frequently a chapter title in a book reveals to the reader the main point that the author desires to bring out during the course of the chapter.

We could try revising this, cutting the twenty-seven words down to seven:

> A chapter's title often reveals its thesis.

But why bother? Unless the title is an exception, is the point worth making?

> The two poems are basically similar in many ways, yet they have their significant differences.

True, all poems are both similar to and different from other poems. Start over, perhaps with something like "The two poems, superficially similar in rough paraphrase, are strikingly different in diction."

> Although the essay is simple in plot, the theme encompasses many vital concepts of emotional makeup.

> Following a transcendental vein, the nostalgia in the poem takes on a spiritual quality.

> Cassell only presents a particular situation concerning the issue, and with clear descriptions and a certain style sets up an interesting article.

Pure zonkers. Not even the writers of these sentences know what they mean.

Writing Instant Prose is an acquired habit, like smoking cigarettes or watching soap operas; fortunately it is easier to kick. It often begins in high school, sometimes earlier, when the victim is assigned a ten-page paper, or is told that a paragraph *must* contain at least three sentences, or that a thesis is stated in the introduction to an essay, elaborated in the body, and repeated in the conclusion. If the instructions appear arbitrary, and the student is bored or intimidated by them, the response is likely to be, like Zonker's, meaningless and mechanical.

Students like Zonker have forgotten—or have never learned—the true purpose of writing: the discovery and communication of ideas, attitudes, and judgments. They concentrate instead on the word count: stuffing sentences, padding paragraphs, stretching and repeating points, and adding flourishes. Rewarded by a satisfactory grade, they repeat the performance, and in time, through practice, develop some fluency in spilling out words without thought or commitment, and almost without effort. Such students enter, as Zonker would say, the college of their choice, feeling somehow inauthentic, perhaps even aware that they do not really mean what they write: symptoms of habitual use of, or addiction to, Instant Prose.

How to Avoid Instant Prose

1. Trust yourself. Writing Instant Prose is not only a habit; it is also a form of alienation. If you habitually write zonkers, you probably don't think of what you write as your own but as something you produce on demand for someone else. (Clearly Zonker is writing for that unreasonable authority, the teacher, whose mysterious whims and insatiable appetite for words he must somehow satisfy.) Breaking the habit begins with recognizing it and then acknowledging the possibility that you can take yourself and your work seriously. It means learning to respect your ideas and experiences (unlearning the passive habits that got you through childhood) and determining that when you write you will write what you mean—nothing more, nothing less. This involves taking risks, of course; habits offer security, or they would have no grip on us. Moreover, we all have moments when we doubt that our ideas are worth taking seriously. Keep writing honestly. The self-doubts will pass; accomplishing something—writing one clear sentence—can help make them pass.

2. Learn to recognize Instant Prose Additives. This advice applies to your own writing, as well as to what you read, and you *will* find Instant Prose Additives in what you read—in textbooks and in academic journals, notoriously.

Here is an example from a recent book on contemporary theatre:

> One of the principal and most persistent sources of error that tends to bedevil a considerable proportion of contemporary literary analysis is the assumption that the writer's creative process is a wholly conscious and purposive type of activity.

Notice all the extra stuff in the sentence: "principal and most persistent," "tends to bedevil," "considerable proportion," "type of activity." Cleared of deadwood, the sentence might read:

> The assumption that the writer's creative process is wholly conscious bedevils much contemporary criticism.

3. Acquire two things: the habit of revising for conciseness; and what Isaac Singer calls "the writer's best friend," a wastebasket.

EXTRA WORDS AND EMPTY WORDS

Extra words should, by definition, be eliminated; vague, empty, or pretentious words and phrases should be replaced by specific and direct language.

Wordy

However, it must be remembered that Ruth's marriage could have positive effects on Naomi's situation.

Concise

> Ruth's marriage, however, will also provide security for Naomi.

In the second version, the unnecessary "it must be remembered that" has been eliminated and specific words communicating a precise point have been substituted for the vague "positive effects" and "situation." The revision, though briefer, says more.

Wordy

> In high school, where I had the opportunity for three years of working with the student government, I realized how significantly a person's enthusiasm could be destroyed merely by the attitudes of his or her superiors.

Concise

> In high school, during three years on the student council, I saw students' enthusiasm destroyed by insecure teachers and cynical administrators.

Again, the revised sentence gives more information in fewer words. How?

Wordy

> The recurring image of nature versus culture appears frequently in the writings of Susanna Moodie as the pioneers toil in the hostile environment to break the soil and clear the fields, or perhaps it is the writer who is hostile to the environment as she struggles to form a new identity in her new land?

"Nature versus culture" is a trite statement of the situation; the discussion of what is hostile to whom is pretentious. Both are Instant Prose.

Concise

> Susanna Moodie's love-hate relationship with the land on which she toiled helped to form her identity.

Wordy

> It creates a better motivation of learning when students can design their own programs involving education. This way students' interests can be focused on.

Concise

> Motivation improves when students design their own programs focused on their own interests.

Now revise the following wordy sentences:

1. Perhaps they basically distrusted our capacity to judge correctly.
2. The use of setting is also a major factor in conveying a terrifying type atmosphere.

Notice how, in the examples provided, the following words crop up: *basically, significant, situation, factor, involving, effect, type*. These words have legitimate uses but are often no more than Instant Prose Additives. Cross them out whenever you can. Similar words to watch out for: *aspect, facet, fundamental, manner, nature, ultimate, utilization, viable, virtually, vital.* If they make your writing "sound good," don't hesitate—cross them out at once.

Weak Intensifiers and Qualifiers

Words like *very, quite, rather, completely, definitely,* and *so* can usually be struck from a sentence without loss. Paradoxically, sentences are often more emphatic without intensifiers. Try reading the following sentences both with and without the bracketed words:

> At that time I was [very] idealistic.
>
> We found the proposal [quite] feasible.
>
> The remark, though unkind, was [entirely] accurate.
>
> It was a [rather] fatuous statement.
>
> The scene was [extremely] typical.
>
> Both films deal with disasters [virtually] beyond our control.
>
> The death scene is [truly] grotesque.
>
> What she did next was [completely] inexcusable.
>
> The first line [definitely] establishes that the father had been drinking.

Always avoid using intensifiers with *unique.* Either something is unique—the only one of its kind—or it is not. It cannot be very, quite, so, pretty, or fairly unique.

Circumlocutions

Roundabout ways of saying things enervate your prose and tire your reader. Notice how each circumlocution in the first column is matched by a concise expression in the second.

I came to the realization that	I realized that
She is of the opinion that	She thinks that
The quotation is supportive of	The quotation supports
Concerning the matter of	About
During the course of	During
For the period of a week	For a week
In the event that	If
In the process of	During, while
Regardless of the fact that	Although
Due to the fact that	Because
For the simple reason that	Because
The fact that	That
Inasmuch as	Since
If the case was such that	If
It is often the case that	Often
In all cases	Always
I made contact with	I called, saw, phoned, wrote
At that point in time	Then
At this point in time	Now

Now revise this sentence:

> These movies have a large degree of popularity for the simple reason that they give the viewers insight in many cases.

Wordy Beginnings

Vague, empty words and phrases clog the beginnings of some sentences. They are like elaborate windups before the pitch.

Wordy

> By analyzing carefully the last lines in this stanza, you find the connections between the loose ends of the poem.

Concise

> The last lines of the stanza connect the loose ends of the poem.

Wordy

> What the cartoonist is illustrating and trying to get across is the greed of the oil producers.

Concise

> The cartoon illustrates the greed of the oil producers.

Wordy

> Dealing with the crucial issue of the year, the editorial is expressing ironical disbelief in any of the possible solutions to the Middle East crisis.

Concise

> The editorial ironically expresses disbelief in the proposed solutions to the Middle East crisis.

Wordy

> In the last stanza is the conclusion (as usual) and it tells of the termination of the dance.

Concise

> The last stanza concludes with the end of the dance.

Wordy

> In opposition to the situation of the younger son is that of the elder who remained in his father's house, working hard and handling his inheritance wisely.

Concise

> The elder son, by contrast, remained in his father's house, worked hard, and handled his inheritance wisely.

Notice that when the deadwood is cleared from the beginning of the sentence, the subject appears early, and the main verb appears close to it:

The last lines . . . connect . . .

The cartoon illustrates . . .

The editorial . . . expresses . . .

The last stanza concludes . . .

The elder son . . . remained . . .

Locating the right noun for the subject, and the right verb for the predicate, is the key to revising sentences with wordy beginnings. Try revising the wordy beginnings in the following sentences:

1. The way that Mabel reacts toward her brother is a fine representation of her nature.
2. In David Carpenter's case, he began thinking about the effects of comedy in graduate school.

Empty Conclusions

Often a sentence that begins well has an empty conclusion. The words go on but the sentence seems to stand still; if it's not revised, it requires another sentence to explain it.

Empty

    "Those Winter Sundays" is composed so that a reader can feel what the poet was saying.

(How is it composed? What is the writer saying?)

Concise

    "Those Winter Sundays" describes the speaker's anger as a child, and his remorse as an adult.

Empty

    In both Orwell's and Baldwin's essays the feeling of white supremacy is very important.

(Why is the feeling of white supremacy important?)

Concise

    Both Orwell and Baldwin trace the insidious consequences of white supremacy.

Empty

    Being the only white girl among about ten Native girls was quite a learning experience.

(What did she learn?)

Concise

> As the only white girl among about ten Native girls, I began to understand the experiences of isolation, helplessness, and rage regularly reported by minority students.

Wordy Uses of the Verbs *To Be, To Have,* and *To Make*

Notice that in the preceding unrevised sentences a form of the verb *to be* introduces the empty conclusions "*was* saying," "*is* very important," and "*was* quite a learning experience." In each revision, the right verb added substance and clarified the writer's meaning. In the following sentences, substitutions for the verb *to be* invigorate and shorten otherwise substantial sentences. (The wordy expressions are italicized, and so are the revisions.)

Wordy

> The scene *is taking place* at night, in front of Parliament Hill.

Concise

> The scene *takes place* at night, in front of Parliament Hill.

Wordy

> In this shoe shining and early rising *there are indications* of church attendance.

Concise

> The early rising and shoe shining *indicate* church attendance.

Wordy

> The words "flashing," "rushing," "plunging," and "tossing" *are suggestive of* excitement.

Concise

> The words "flashing," "rushing," "plunging," and "tossing" *suggest* excitement.

As a general rule, whenever possible you should replace a form of the verb *to be* with a stronger verb.

To Be	*Strong Verb*
and a participle ("is taking")	takes
and a noun ("are indications")	indicate
and an adjective ("are suggestive")	suggest

Revise the following sentence:

> The rising price of oil is reflective of the spiralling cost of all goods.

Sentences with the verbs *to have* and *to make* can similarly be reduced:

Wordy

> The Friar *has knowledge* that Juliet is alive.

Concise

> The Friar *knows* that Juliet is alive.

Wordy

> The stanzas *make a vivid contrast* between Heaven and Hell.

Concise

> The stanzas *vividly contrast* Heaven and Hell.

Like all rules, this one has exceptions. We do not list them here; you will discover them by listening to your sentences.

Redundancy

The word *redundancy*, derived from a Latin word meaning "overflowing, overlapping," refers to unnecessary repetition in the expression of ideas. "Future plans," after all, are only plans, and "to glide smoothly" or "to scurry rapidly" is only to glide or to scurry. Unlike repetition, which often provides emphasis or coherence (for example, "government of the people, by the people, for the people"), redundancy can always be eliminated.

Redundant

> Any student could randomly sit anywhere. (If the students could sit anywhere, the seating was random.)

Concise

> Students could sit anywhere.
> Students chose their seats at random.

Redundant

> I have no justification with which to excuse myself.

Concise

> I have no justification for my action.
> I can't justify my action.
> I have no excuse for my action.
> I can't excuse my action.

Redundant

> In the orthodox Cuban culture, the surface of the female role seemed degrading. (Perhaps this sentence means what it says. More probably "surface" and "seemed" are redundant.)

Concise

In the orthodox Cuban culture, the female role seemed degrading.
In the orthodox Cuban culture, the female role was superficially degrading.

Redundant

In "Araby" the boy feels alienated emotionally from his family.

Concise

In "Araby" the boy feels alienated from his family.

Try eliminating redundancy from the following sentences:

1. The reason why she hesitates is because she is afraid.
2. Marriage in some form has long existed since prehistoric times.

What words can be crossed out of the following phrases?

a. throughout the entire article
b. her attitude of indifference
c. a conservative type suit
d. all the different tasks besides teaching
e. his own personal opinion
f. elements common to both of them
g. emotions and feelings
h. shared together
i. falsely padded expense accounts
j. alleged suspect

Many phrases in common use are redundant. For example, there is no need to write "blare noisily," since the meaning of the adverb "noisily" is already in the verb "blare." Watch for phrases like these when you revise:

round in shape	resulting effect
purple in colour	close proximity
poetic in nature	connected together
tall in stature	prove conclusively
autobiography of her life	must necessarily
basic fundamentals	very unique
true fact	very universal
free gift	the reason why is because

Negative Constructions

Negative constructions are often wordy and sometimes pretentious.

Wordy

Housing for married students is *not unworthy of* consideration.

"See what I mean? You're never sure just where you stand with them."

Concise

Housing for married students is worth considering.

Better

The trustees should earmark funds for married students' housing. (This is probably what the author meant.)

Wordy

After reading the second paragraph *you aren't left with* an immediate reaction as to how the story will end.

Concise

The first two paragraphs create suspense.

The following example from a syndicated column is not untypical:

Although it is not reasonably to be expected that someone who fought his way up to the presidency is less than a largely political animal and sometimes a beast, it is better not to know—really—exactly what his private conversations were composed of.

The Golden Rule of writing is "Write for others as you would have them write for you," not "Write for others in a manner not unreasonably dissimilar to the manner in which you would have them write for you." (See the discussion of *not un-* in the Glossary, page 467, for effective use of the negative.)

EXTRA SENTENCES, EXTRA CLAUSES: SUBORDINATION

Sentences are sometimes wordy because ideas are given more elaborate grammatical constructions than they need. In revising, these constructions often can be reduced. Two sentences, for example, may be reduced to one, or a clause may be reduced to a phrase.

Wordy

> The Book of Ruth was probably written in the fifth century BCE. It was a time when women were considered the property of men.

Concise

> The Book of Ruth was probably written in the fifth century BCE, when women were considered the property of men.

Wordy

> The first group was the largest. This group was seated in the centre of the dining hall.

Concise

> The first group, the largest, was seated in the centre of the dining hall.

Wordy

> The colonists were upset over the tax on tea, and they took action against it.

Concise

> The colonists, upset over the tax on tea, took action.

Who, Which, That

Watch particularly for clauses beginning with *who, which,* and *that.* Often they can be shortened.

Wordy

> George Orwell is the pen name of Eric Blair, *who was* an English writer.

Concise

> George Orwell was the pen name of English writer Eric Blair.

Wordy

> They are seated at a table, *which* is covered with a patched and tattered cloth.

Concise

> The table they are seated at is covered with a patched and tattered cloth.

Wordy

> There is one feature *that is* grossly out of proportion.

Concise

> One feature is grossly out of proportion.

It Is, This Is, There Are

Also watch for sentences and clauses beginning with *it is, this is, there are* (again, wordy uses of the verb *to be*). These expressions often lead to a *which* or a *that*, but even when they do not they may lead to wordy sentences.

Wordy

> The trail brings us to the timberline. This is the point where the trees become stunted from lack of oxygen.

Concise

> The trail brings us to the timberline, the point where the trees become stunted from lack of oxygen.

Wordy

> This is a quotation from Black Elk's autobiography which discloses his prophetic powers.

Concise

> This quotation from Black Elk's autobiography discloses his prophetic powers.

Wordy

> It is frequently considered that *Hamlet* is Shakespeare's most puzzling play.

Concise

> *Hamlet* is frequently considered Shakespeare's most puzzling play.

Wordy

> In Phil Bergerson's grid photographs of single images reprinted many times, there is a transformation of the mundane into a tapestry of colour and texture.

Concise

> Phil Bergerson's grid photographs of single images reprinted many times transform the mundane into a tapestry of colour and texture.

Try revising the following sentences:

1. There are many writers who believe that writing can't be taught.
2. Always take more clothes than you think you will need. This is so that you will be prepared for the weather no matter what it is.
3. This is an indication that the child has a relationship with his teacher which is very respectful.

(For further discussion of subordination see pages 128–29. On *which* clauses, see also Chapter 21, "Usage," page 472.)

SOME CONCLUDING REMARKS ABOUT CONCISENESS

We spoke earlier about how students learn to write Instant Prose and acquire other wordy habits by trying to write what they think the teacher has asked for. We have not forgotten that instructors assign papers of a certain length in college too. But the length given is not an arbitrary limit that must be reached; the instructor who asks for a five-page or twenty-page paper is probably trying to tell you the degree of elaboration expected in the assignment. Such, apparently, was the intention of William Randolph Hearst, the newspaper publisher, who cabled to an astronomer, "Is there life on Mars? Cable reply 1000 words." The astronomer's reply was, "Nobody knows," repeated five hundred times.

What do you do when you have been asked to produce a ten-page paper and after diligent writing and revising you find you have said everything relevant to your topic in seven and a half pages? Our advice is to hand it in. We cannot remember ever counting the words or pages of a focused, substantial, interesting essay; we assume that our colleagues elsewhere are equally reasonable and equally overworked. If we are wrong, tell us about it—in writing, and in the fewest possible words.

Exercises

1. First identify the fault or faults that make the following sentences wordy, then revise them for conciseness.

   a. There were quite a number of contrasts that White made between the city school and the country school which was of a casual nature all throughout.
   b. The study of political topics involves a careful researching of the many components of the particular field.
   c. Virtually the most significant feature of any field involving science is the vital nature of the technical facilities, the fundamental factor of all research.
   d. Like a large majority of North American people, I, too, have seen the popular disaster films.
   e. Something which makes this type of film popular (disaster) is the kind of subconscious aspect of "Can man overcome this problem?" Horror

films, on the other hand, produce the aspects of whether or not man can make amends for his mistakes.

f. The average person becomes disappointed and downtrodden due to the fact that he can't help himself and is at the mercy of inflation and unemployment.

g. The last of the Doukhobor refugee ships left the Black Sea port of Batum in the summer of 1899 carrying twenty-three hundred people. These ships make up the largest single shipment of immigrants in Canadian history, on a journey that would end on the steep, eroded banks of the North Saskatchewan River on the prairies of Canada.

h. Reading has always been a fascinating and exciting pastime for me for as long as I can remember.

i. The province of Alberta once formed part of the great domain of the Hudson's Bay Company, known as the North-West Territories, and was made a province in 1905, and entered in to the Confederation.

j. Only once in the first two sentences does the author make reference to the first person.

k. The length of the sentences are similar in moderation and in structural clarity.

l. The magnitude of student satisfaction with the program ranged from total hatred to enthusiastic approval.

m. Taking a look at the facial expressions of the man and the woman in both pictures one can see a difference in mood.

n. One drawing is done in watercolour and the other is done in chalk which is a revision of the watercolour.

o. The dialogue places the role of the two gods on a believable basis.

p. Senseless crimes such as murder and muggings are committed on a daily basis.

q. One must admire the lowly toque because it is surviving being tasselled, plastered with logos of NHL hockey teams, and tarted up in fluorescent glow-in-the-dark colours.

r. The two major aspects behind the development of a performer are technique and musicianship.

s. I remember my first desire to smoke cigarettes as I watched my father smoke. My father often sat in his favourite easy chair idly smoking cigarettes.

t. Christopher Stone's article "Putting the Outside Inside the Fence of Law" is concerning the legal rights of the environment. He comments on the legal rights of other inanimate entities which seem to be acceptable. Just as these entities are represented, so should the environment be represented.

2. In the following paragraph, from a student essay on Charlotte Perkins Gilman's short story "The Yellow Wallpaper," circle all forms of the verbs *to be, to have,* and *to make.* Then, wherever possible, eliminate these verbs by reducing clauses or by substituting stronger, more exact, or active verbs.

Charlotte Perkins Gilman's story "The Yellow Wallpaper" is about a woman who has been diagnosed with a "temporary nervous depression" and who is moved by her husband to a house in the country so that she may have the opportunity to rest and recuperate from her illness. As the story progresses, however, her depression is combined with her isolated situation, and her mental state is made more fragile as a result. Gradually, her ability to make distinctions between reality and fantasy is lost, and she is overcome with madness. Her madness is reflected in her descriptions of the yellow wallpaper with which the walls of her bedroom is covered. At first the wallpaper is simply described as "ugly" and "repellent." By the end of the story, though, the narrator is seeing a figure of a woman who is trapped behind the wallpaper, a woman who shakes and pulls at the wallpaper and who seems to be making an effort to free herself from its confinement.

3. When you complete the draft of the essay you are currently writing, identify and circle all forms of the verbs *to be, to have,* and *to make.* Replace as many of them as possible with stronger verbs.

Revising Sentences for Clarity

Here's to plain speaking and clear understanding.

—Sidney Greenstreet, in *The Maltese Falcon*

CLARITY

We have seen new realities created by the advance of physics. But this chain of creation can be traced back far beyond the starting point of physics. One of the most primitive concepts is that of an object. The concepts of a tree, a horse, any material body, are creations gained on the basis of experience, though the impressions from which they arise are primitive in comparison with the world of physical phenomena. A cat teasing a mouse also creates, by thought, its own primitive reality. The fact that the cat reacts in a similar way toward any mouse it meets shows that it forms concepts and theories which are its guide through its own world of sense impressions.

—ALBERT EINSTEIN AND LEOPOLD INFELD

Skills constitute the manipulative techniques of human goal attainment and control in relation to the physical world, so far as artifacts or machines especially designed as tools do not yet supplement them. Truly human skills are guided by organized and codified *knowledge* of both the things to be manipulated and the human capacities that are used to manipulate them. Such knowledge is an aspect of cultural-level symbolic processes, and, like other aspects to be discussed presently, requires the capacities of the human central nervous system, particularly the brain. This organic system is clearly essential to all of the symbolic processes; as we well know, the human brain is far superior to the brain of any other species.

—TALCOTT PARSONS

Why is the first passage easier to understand than the second?

Both passages discuss the relationship between the brain and the physical world it attempts to understand. The first passage, by Einstein and Infeld, is, if anything, more complex both in what it asserts and in what it suggests than the second, by Parsons. Both passages explain that the brain organizes sense impressions. But Einstein and Infeld further explain that the history of physics can be understood as an extension of the simplest sort of organization, such as we all make in distinguishing a tree from a horse, or such as even a cat makes in teasing a mouse. Parsons only promises that "other aspects" will "be discussed presently." How many of us are eager for those next pages?

Good writing is clear, not because it presents simple ideas, but because it presents ideas in the simplest form the subject permits. A clear analysis does not falsely reduce a complex problem to a simple one; it breaks the problem down into simple, comprehensible parts and discusses them, one by one, in a logical order. A clear paragraph explains one of these parts coherently, thoroughly, and in language as simple and as particular as the reader's understanding requires and the context allows. Where Parsons writes of "organized and codified *knowledge* of . . . the things to be manipulated," Einstein and Infeld write simply of the concept of an object. And even "object," a simple but general word, is further clarified by the specific, familiar examples "tree" and "horse." Parsons writes of "the manipulative techniques of . . . goal attainment and control in relation to the physical world, so far as artifacts or machines especially designed as tools do not yet supplement them." Einstein and Infeld show us a cat teasing a mouse.

Notice also the clear organization of Einstein and Infeld's paragraph. The first sentence, clearly transitional, refers to the advance of physics traced in the preceding pages. The next sentence, introduced by "But," reverses our direction: we are now going to look not at an advance, but at primitive beginnings. And the following sentences, to the end of the paragraph, fulfill that promise. We move back to primitive human concepts, clarified by examples, and finally to the still more primitive example of the cat. Parson's paragraph is also organized, but the route is much more difficult to follow.

Why do people write obscurely? Surely some students learn to write obscurely by trying to imitate the style of their teachers or textbooks. The imitation may spring from genuine admiration for these authorities. Or students may feel that a string of technical-sounding words is what the teacher expects. If this thought has crossed your mind, we cannot say you are entirely wrong. Learning a new discipline often involves acquiring a specialized vocabulary. But we add the following cautions:

- Teachers expect your writing to show thought and make sense. They are likely to be puzzled by the question "Do you want me to use technical terms in this paper?"
- If you try to use technical terms appropriate to one field when you write about another, you are likely to write nonsense. Do not write "the machine was viable" if you mean only that it worked.
- When you do write for specialists in a particular field, use technical terms precisely. In an art history paper, don't write "This print of van Gogh's *Sunflowers*" if you mean "This reproduction of van Gogh's *Sunflowers*."

- No matter what you are writing, do not become so enamoured of technical words that you cannot write a sentence without peppering it with *input, interface, death-symbol, parameter, phallocentric, feedback,* and so on.

But to return to the question "Why do people write obscurely?" It is difficult to write clearly.[1] Authorities may be obscure not because they want to tax you with unnecessary difficulties, but because they do not know how to avoid such difficulties. If you have ever tried to assemble a mechanical toy or to install a computer upgrade by following the "easy instructions," you know that the simplest kind of expository writing, giving instructions, can foil the writers most eager for your goodwill (that is, those who want you to use their products). Few instructions, unfortunately, are as unambiguous as "Go to jail. Go directly to jail. Do not pass Go. Do not collect $200."

You can, though, learn to write clearly, by learning to recognize common sources of obscurity in writing and by consciously revising your own work. We offer, to begin with, three general rules:

1. Use the simplest, most exact, most specific language your subject allows.
2. Put together what belongs together, in the essay, in the paragraph, and in the sentence.
3. Keep your reader in mind, particularly when you revise.

Now for more specific advice and examples: the cats and mice of revising for clarity.

CLARITY AND EXACTNESS: USING THE RIGHT WORD

Denotation

Be sure the word you choose has the right *denotation* (explicit meaning). Did you mean *sarcastic* or *ironic*? *Fatalistic* or *pessimistic*? *Disinterested* or *uninterested*? *Biannual* or *semi-annual*? *Enforce* or *reinforce*? *Use* or *usage*? If you are not sure, check the dictionary. You will find some of the most commonly misused words discussed in Chapter 21, "Usage." Here are examples of a few others:

1. Daru faces a dilemma between his humane feelings and his concept of justice. (Strictly speaking, a dilemma requires a choice between two equally unattractive alternatives. "Conflict" would be a better word here.)
2. However, as time dragged on, exercising seemed to lose its charisma. (What is charisma? Why is it inexact here?)
3. Ms. Wu's research contains many symptoms of depression which became evident during the reading period. (Was Ms. Wu depressed by her research? We hope not. Probably she described or listed the symptoms.)
4. When I run I don't allow myself to stop until I have reached my destiny. (Which word is inexact?)

[1] Our first draft of this sentence read "Writing clearly is difficult." Can you see why we changed it?

"I'm not quite clear on this, Fulton. Are you moaning about your prerequisites, your requisites, or your perquisites?"

Connotation

Be sure the word you choose has the right *connotation* (association, implication). As Mark Twain said, the difference between the right word and the almost right word is the difference between lightning and the lightning bug.

1. Boston politics has always upheld the reputation of being especially crooked. ("Upheld" inappropriately suggests that Boston has proudly maintained its reputation. "Has always had" would be appropriate here, but pale. "Deserved" would, in this context, be ironic, implying—accurately—the writer's scorn.)
2. This book, unlike many other novels, lacks tedious descriptive passages. ("Lacks" implies a deficiency. How would you revise the sentence?)
3. Vancouver, notorious for its scenic setting and good food . . . (Is "notorious" the word here? "Famous"? "Renowned"?)
4. "It was easier to keep myself from becoming a success as an actor. Critics were careful not to outrage my modesty by their praise, and the public scrupulously refused to debauch me with applause." (In this passage by Robertson Davies, the ironic use of "outrage my modesty" and "scrupulously refused to debauch" strikingly makes his point in a way that "The lack of enthusiasm from the critics and audiences told me that my acting skills left something to be desired" would not.)

Because words have connotations, most writing—even when it pretends to be objective—conveys attitudes as well as facts. Consider, for example, this passage by Eric Robinson and Henry Bird Quinney, which provides a history as part of their views on Canada's constitutional discussions of the 1980s:

> When the Europeans first bumped into our Island on their way to the Far East, there were over 11 million people living in what is now Canada and the United States . . . Since that time we have been treated as prisoners in our own homeland. The invaders took over more and more of our lands until we were confined in concentration camps which they called Reserves.

Here, as almost always, the writers' purpose in large measure determines the choice of words. Probably the sentences accurately describe part of the history, but they also, of course, record the authors' contempt for the attitudes of the Europeans. Suppose, for example, the same historical overview were being written by someone from the federal government. Instead of "bumped into our Island," it would be "discovered the new land," and instead of "invaders," it would be "immigrants" or "pioneers," and the reference to reserves as "concentration camps" would be omitted. The authors' words would be the wrong words for a federal politician, but, given Robinson and Quinney's purpose, they are exactly the right ones because they convey the authors' perspective and anger with great clarity.

Notice, too, that many words have social, political, or sexist overtones. We might read for example of the *children* of the rich, but the *offspring* of the poor. What is implied by the distinction? Consider the differences in connotation in each of the following series:

1. friend, boyfriend, young man, lover (What age is the speaker?)
2. dine, eat (What was on the menu? Who set the table?)
3. spinster, bachelor (Which term is likely to be considered an insult?)
4. underdeveloped nations, developing nations, emerging nations
5. preference, bias, prejudice
6. upbringing, conditioning, brainwashing
7. message from our sponsor, commercial, advertisement, plug
8. intelligence gathering, espionage, spying
9. emigrate, defect, seek asylum
10. anti-abortion, pro-life; pro-abortion, pro-choice

Reprinted with permission of King Features Syndicate.

Quotation Marks as Apologies

When you have used words with the exact meanings (denotations) and appropriate associations (connotations) for your purpose, don't apologize for them by putting quotation marks around them. If the words *copped a plea, ripped off,* or *kids* suit your purpose better than *plea-bargained, stolen,* or *children,* use them. If they are inappropriate, don't put them in quotation marks: find the right words.

Being Specific

In writing descriptions, catch the richness, complexity, and uniqueness of things. Suppose, for example, you are describing a scene from your childhood, a setting you loved. There was, in particular, a certain tree . . . and you write: "Near the water there was a big tree that was rather impressive." Most of us would produce something like that sentence. Here is the sentence Ernesto Galarza wrote in *Barrio Boy:*

> On the edge of the pond, at the far side, there was an enormous walnut tree, standing like an open umbrella whose ribs extended halfway across the still water of the pool.

We probably could not have come up with the metaphor of the umbrella because we would not have seen the similarity. (As Aristotle observed, the gift for making metaphors distinguishes the poet from the rest of us.) But we can all train ourselves to be accurate observers and reporters. In our original sentence, instead of "the water" (general) we can specify "pond"; for "near" we can say how near, "on the edge of the pond," and add the specific location, "at the far side"; for "tree" we can give the species, "walnut tree"; and for "big" we can provide a picture, its branches "extended halfway across" the pond: it was, in fact, "enormous."

Galarza does not need to add limply, as we did, that the tree "was rather impressive." The tree he describes *is* impressive. That he accurately remembered it persuades us that he was impressed, without his having to tell us he was. For writing descriptions, a good general rule is: show, don't tell.

Be as specific as you can be in all forms of exposition too. Take the time, when you revise, to find the exact word to replace vague, woolly phrases or clichés. In the following examples we have to guess or invent what the writer means.

Vague

> The clown's part in *Othello* is very small.

Specific

> The clown appears in only two scenes in *Othello.*
>
> The clown in *Othello* speaks only thirty lines. (Notice the substitution of the verb "appears" or "speaks" for the frequently debilitating "is." And in place of the weak intensifier "very" we have specific details to tell us how small the role is.)

Vague

> He feels uncomfortable at the whole situation. (Many feelings are uncomfortable. Which one does he feel? What is the situation?)

Specific

He feels guilty for having distrusted his father.

Vague

The passage reveals a somewhat calculating aspect behind Antigone's noble motives. ("A somewhat calculating aspect" is vague—and wordy—for "calculation." Or did the writer mean "shrewdness"? What differences in connotation are there between "shrewd" and "calculating"?)

Vague

She uses simplicity in her style of writing. (Do we know, exactly, what simplicity in style means?)

Specific

She uses familiar words, normal word order, and conversational phrasing.

Vague cliché

Then she criticized students for living in an ivory tower. (Did she criticize them for being detached or for being secluded? For social irresponsibility or studiousness?)

Specific

Then she criticized students for being socially irresponsible.

Using Examples

In addition to exact words and specific details, illustrative examples make for clear writing. Einstein and Infeld, in the passage quoted on page 91, use as an example of a primitive concept a cat teasing not only its first mouse, but also "any mouse it meets." Here are two more paragraphs that clarify their topic sentences through examples; the first is from Pierre Berton's *The Great Depression.*

> In retrospect, we see it as a whole—a neat decade tucked in between the Roaring Twenties and the Second World War, perhaps the most significant ten years in our history, a watershed era that scarred and transformed the nation. But it hasn't been easy for later generations to comprehend its devastating impact. The Depression lies just over the hill of memory; after all, anyone who reached voting age in 1929 is over eighty today. There are not many left who can remember what it was like to live on water for an entire day, as the Templeton family did in the Parkdale district of Toronto in 1932, or how it felt to own a single dress—made of flour sacks—as Etha Munro did in the family farmhouse on the drought-ravaged Saskatchewan prairie in 1934.

In the next paragraph, Northrop Frye, writing about the perception of rhythm, illustrates his point:

> Ideally, our literary education should begin, not with prose, but with such things as "this little pig went to market"—with verse rhythm rein-

forced by physical assault. The infant who gets bounced on somebody's knee to the rhythm of "Ride a cock horse" does not need a footnote telling him that Banbury Cross is twenty miles northeast of Oxford. He does not need the information that "cross" and "horse" make (at least in the pronunciation he is most likely to hear) not a rhyme but an assonance. . . . All he needs is to get bounced.

Frye does not say our literary education should begin with "simple rhymes" or with "verse popular with children." He says "with such things as 'this little pig went to market,'" and then he goes on to add "Ride a cock horse." We know exactly what he means. Notice, too, that we do not need a third example. Be detailed, but know when to stop.

Your reader is likely to be brighter and more demanding than Lady Pliant, who in a seventeenth-century play says to a would-be seducer, "You are very alluring—and say so many fine Things, and nothing is so moving to me as a fine Thing." "[F]ine Things," of course, are what is wanted, but only exact words and apt illustrations will convince intelligent readers that they are hearing fine things.

Now look at a paragraph from the essay of a student whose thesis is that rage can be a useful mechanism for effecting change. Compare the left-hand paragraph with the same paragraph, revised, at the right. Note the specific ways, sentence by sentence, the student revised for clarity.

In my high school we had little say in the learning processes that were used. The subjects that we were required to take were irrelevant. One had to take them to earn enough points to graduate. Some of the teachers were sympathetic to our problem. They would tell us about when they were young, how they tried to oppose their school system. But when they were young it was a long time ago, for most of them. The principal would call assemblies to speak on the subject. They were entitled "The	In my high school we had little say about our curriculum. We were required, for example, to choose either American or European History to earn enough points for graduation. We wanted, but were at first refused, the option of Black History. Some of our teachers were sympathetic with us; one told me about her fight opposing the penmanship course required in her school. Nor was the principal totally indifferent- -he called assemblies. I remember one talk he gave called "The Value of an Education in

Value of an Education" or "Get a Good Education to Have a Bright Future." The titles were not inviting. They had nothing to do with our plight. Most students never came to any agreements with the principal because most of his thoughts and views seemed old and outdated.

Today's World," and another, "Get a Good Education to Have a Bright Future." I don't recall hearing about a Black History course in either talk. Once, he invited a group of us to meet with him in his office, but we didn't reach any agreement. He solemnly showed us an American History text (not the one we used) that had a whole chapter devoted to Black History.

Jargon and Technical Language

Most dictionaries give three meanings for *jargon:* technical language, meaningless language, and inflated or pretentious language.

The members of almost every profession or trade—indeed, almost all people who share any specialized interest—use technical language. Composition teachers talk of conjunctions, misplaced modifiers, and writer's block; baseball fans talk of southpaws, the hit-and-run, and the hat trick; Freudians talk of cathect, libido, and the oral phase; magicians talk of the French drop, double lifts, and second dealing.

Properly used, technical language communicates information concisely and clearly, and it can create a comfortable bond between speakers, or between the writer and the reader. But to the outsider it may seem meaningless, hence the second definition of the word, meaningless talk. In fact, *jargon* originally meant (some six hundred years ago) the twittering of birds—and this is what the language of specialists sounds like to the outsider's ear. The third meaning, pretentious language, comes from the outsider's impatience with other people's technical language. We wonder if all of that twittering—all of the mysterious vocabulary—really is necessary, and we suspect that perhaps the speaker is making a big deal out of what can be said much more simply, maybe in an effort to impress us.

Consider, for instance, a twenty-eight-page manual issued in Dallas, Texas, to parents of children in kindergarten through the third grade. The manual, intended to help parents decipher their children's report cards, is titled *Terminal Behavioral Objectives for Continuous Progression Modules in Early Childhood Education.* Terminal objectives, it seems, means goals. What does the rest mean? If you were one of the parents, would you expect much help from the manual? It was intended to be helpful, but it sounds like a parody, doesn't it?

And finally, here is an example from the Government of Canada website on The Office of Critical Infrastructure Protection and Emergency Preparedness (OCIPEP):

OCIPEP conducts threat, incident, and vulnerability analysis, and co-ordinates consequence management with respect to the cyber and physical risks to our critical infrastructure. This work includes identifying national critical infrastructure elements and assessing their vulnerabilities and dependencies.

In general, when you write for non-specialists, avoid technical terms; if you must use them, define them. If you use a technical term when writing for specialists, be sure you know its precise meaning. But whenever you can, even among specialists, use plain English.

Clichés

Clichés (literally, in French, moulds from which type is cast) are trite expressions, mechanically—that is, mindlessly—reproduced. Since they are available without thought, they are great Instant Prose Additives (see pages 76–88). Writers who use them are usually surprised to be criticized: they find the phrases attractive and may even think them exact. (Phrases become clichés precisely because they have wide appeal and therefore wide use.) But clichés, by their nature, cannot communicate the uniqueness of your thoughts. Furthermore, because they come instantly to mind, they tend to block the specific detail or exact expression that will let the reader know what precisely is in your mind. In revising, when you strike out a cliché, you force yourself to do the work of writing clearly. The following example is full of clichés:

> Finally, the long-awaited day arrived. Up bright and early. . . . [S]he peered at me with suspicion; then a faint smile crossed her face.

The following example from Ronnie Hawkins about his career plays with a cliché:

> "The bigtime for you is just around the corner." They told me that first in 1952—boy, it's been a long corner. If I don't hit the bigtime in the next 25 or 30 years, I'm gonna pack in the music business and become a full-time gigolo.

Other examples:

first and foremost	time-honoured
the acid test	bustled to and fro
fatal flaw	short but sweet
budding genius	few and far between
slowly but surely	D-Day arrived
little did I know	sigh of relief
the big moment	last but not least

In attempting to avoid clichés, however, do not go to the other extreme of wildly original, super-vivid writing: "'Well then, say something to her,' he roared, his whole countenance gnarled in rage." It is often better simply to say "he said." (Anyone who intends to write dialogue should memorize Ring Lardner's intentionally funny line, "'Shut up!' he explained.") Note also that such common expressions as "How are you?" "Please pass the salt," and "So long" are not clichés; they make no claim to be colourful.

Metaphors and Mixed Metaphors

Ordinary speech abounds with metaphors. We speak or write of the foot of a mountain, the germ (seed) of an idea, the root of a problem. Metaphors so deeply embedded in the language that they no longer evoke pictures in our minds are called *dead metaphors.* Ordinarily, they offer us, as writers, no problems: we need neither seek them nor avoid them; they are simply there. (Notice, for example, "embedded" two sentences back.) Such metaphors become problems, however, when we unwittingly call them back to life. Howard Nemerov observes: "That these metaphors may be not dead but only sleeping, or that they may arise from the grave and walk in our sentences, is something that has troubled everyone who has ever tried to write plain expository prose."

Dead metaphors are most likely to haunt us when they are embodied in clichés. Since we use clichés without attention to what they literally say or point to, we are unlikely to be aware of the dead metaphors buried in them. But when we attach one cliché to another, we may raise the metaphors from the grave. The result is likely to be a mixed metaphor; the effect is almost always absurd.

Water seeks its own level whichever way you want to slice it.

Traditional liberal education has run out of gas and educational soup kitchens are moving into the vacuum.

The low ebb has been reached and hopefully it has turned the corner.

Her energy, drained through a stream of red tape, led only to closed doors.

We no longer ask for whom the bell tolls but simply chalk it up as one less mouth to feed.

"You're right as rain. It's the dawn of history, and there are no clichés as yet. I'll drink to that."

As comedian Joe E. Lewis observed, "Show me a man who builds castles in the air and I'll show you a crazy architect."

Fresh metaphors, on the other hand, imaginatively combine accurate observations. They are not prefabricated ideas; they are a means of discovering or inventing new ideas. They enlarge thought and enliven prose. Here is an example from a student's journal:

I have some sort of sporadic restlessness in me, like the pen on a

polygraph machine. It moves along in curves, then suddenly shoots up,

blowing a bubble in my throat, making my chest taut, forcing me to move

around. It becomes almost unbearable and then suddenly it will plunge,

leaving something that feels like a smooth orange wave.

Bob Schieffer, a CBS news anchor, comments upon the government's slow response to the terrible damage in Louisiana and Mississippi caused by Hurricane Katrina:

> Yet as scenes of horror that seemed to be coming from some Third World country flashed before us, official Washington was like a dog watching television. It saw the lights and images, but did not seem to comprehend their meaning or see any link to reality.

And here is a passage from an essay in which a student analyzes the style of a story he found boring:

Every sentence yawns, stretches, shifts from side to side, and then

quietly dozes off.

Experiment with metaphors, let them surface in the early drafts of your essays and in your journals, and by all means, introduce original and accurate comparisons in your essays. But leave the mixed metaphors to politicians and comedians.

Euphemisms

Euphemisms are words substituted for other words thought to be offensive. In deodorant advertisements there are no armpits, only *underarms,* which may *perspire,* but not sweat, and even then they do not smell. Parents reading a report card may learn not that their child got an F in conduct, but that the child "experiences difficulty exercising self-control: (a) verbally (b) physically." And where do old people go? To Sun City, "a retirement community for senior citizens."

Euphemisms are used for two reasons: to avoid giving offence and, sometimes unconsciously, to disguise fear or animosity. We do not advise you to write or speak discourteously; we do advise you, though, to use euphemisms consciously and sparingly, when tact recommends them. It is customary in a condolence letter to avoid the word *death,* and, depending on both your own feelings and those of the bereaved, you may wish to follow that custom. But there is no reason on earth to write "Hamlet passes on" in an English essay. You should be aware, moreover, that some people find euphemisms themselves offensive. Margaret Kuhn, for instance, argues that the word *old* is preferable to *senior.* "Old," she says "is the right word. . . . I think we should wear our gray hair, wrinkles, and crumbling joints as badges of distinction. After all, we worked damn hard to get them." She has organized a militant group called the Gray Panthers to fight ageism.

In revising, replace needless euphemisms with plain words. Your writing will be sharper, and you might, in examining and confronting them, free yourself of a mindless habit, an unconscious prejudice, or an irrational fear.

A Digression on Public Lying

There is a kind of lying that, in the words of Walker Gibson, we may call *public lying.* Its rules are to avoid substance, direct answers, and plain words. Its tendency is to subvert the English language. It employs and invents euphemisms, but the public liar intends to protect not his listeners, but himself and his friends, and he misleads and deceives consciously. Public lying was not invented during the Vietnam War (in 1946 George Orwell had already written what some people call the definitive essay on it, "Politics and the English Language"). But this war produced classic examples, from which we select a few.

The war in Vietnam, of course, was not a war, but a "conflict" or an "era." "The Americans, our side" never attacked "the other side," but made "protective reaction raids"; Americans didn't invade, but "incursed." They didn't bomb villages, but "pacified" them; peasants were not herded into concentration camps, but "relocated." The Americans didn't spray the countryside with poisons, destroying forests, endangering or killing plant, animal, and human life, but "practised vegetation control." When American intelligence agents drowned a spy, they referred to their action as "termination with extreme prejudice." And the much-used term "friendly fire" referred to the deadly incidents in which one side inadvertently fired on its own troops.

Feiffer

There is a Gresham's law in rhetoric as there is in economics: bad language drives out good. Bad language is contagious. Learn to detect the symptoms: use of vague words for clear words; use of sentences or phrases where a word or two would suffice; evasive use of the passive voice; and outright lying.

Passive or Active Voice?

1. I baked the bread. (Active voice)
2. The bread was baked by me. (Passive voice)
3. The bread will be baked. (Passive voice)

Although it is the verb that is in the active or the passive voice, notice that the words *active* and *passive* describe the subjects of the sentences. That is, in the first sentence the verb "baked" is in the active voice; the subject "I" acts. In the second and third sentences the verbs "was baked" and "will be baked" are in the passive voice; the subject "bread" is acted on. Notice also the following points:

- The *voice* of the verb is distinct from its *tense.* Do not confuse the passive voice with the past tense. (Sentence 2 above happens to be in the past tense, but 3 is not; both 2 and 3 are in the passive voice.)
- The passive voice uses more words than the active voice. (Compare sentences 1 and 2.)
- A sentence with a verb in the passive voice may leave the doer of the action unidentified. (See sentence 3.)
- Finally, notice that in each of the three sentences the emphasis is different.

In revising, take a good look at each sentence in which you have used the passive voice. If the passive clarifies your meaning, retain it; if it obscures your meaning, change it. More often than not, the passive voice obscures meaning.

Passive voice

The revolver given Daru by the gendarme *is left* in the desk drawer. (Left by whom? The passive voice here obscures the point.)

Active voice

Daru leaves the gendarme's revolver in the desk drawer.

Passive voice

More than sixty NHL records were broken by Wayne Gretzky during his career.

Active voice

During his career, Wayne Gretzky broke more than sixty NHL records.

Avoid what has been called the Academic Passive: "In this essay it has been argued that . . ." This cumbersome form used to be common in academic writing (to convey scientific objectivity), but "I have argued" is usually preferable to such stuffiness.

When is the passive voice appropriate? The passive is appropriate when (1) the doer is obvious ("Campbell was elected premier in 2001"), or (2) the doer is unknown ("The picture was stolen between midnight and 1:00 A.M."), or (3) the doer is unimportant ("Unexposed film should be kept in a light-proof container").

The Writer's "I"

It is seldom necessary in writing an essay (even on a personal experience) to state "I think that" or "in my opinion." Your reader knows that what you write is your opinion. Nor is it necessary, if you have done your job well, to apologize. "After reading the story over several times I am not really sure what it is about, but . . ." Write about something you are reasonably sure of. Occasionally, though, when there is a real problem in the text—for example, the probable date of the Book of Ruth—it is not only permissible to disclose doubts and to reveal tentative conclusions, but it may be necessary to do so.

Note also that there is no reason to avoid the pronoun *I* when you are in fact writing about yourself. Attempts to avoid *I* ("this writer," "we," expressions in the passive voice such as "it has been said above" and "it was seen") are noticeably awkward and distracting. And sometimes you may want to focus on your subjective response to a topic in order to clarify a point. The following opening paragraph from "French Is a *Must* for Canadians" uses the "I" as an example of a typical English-speaking Canadian:

> The old proverb about people who live in glass houses applies perfectly to me when I write about bilingualism in Canada. I can't blame my fellow Canadians of the English language for being unable to speak French because I speak it brokenly myself, and my ears are painfully slow to catch it from others. I read French reasonably well, but that is not the same thing at all. In a country like ours, I should be able to speak it almost as well as English. My inability to do so is a constant shame to me, and I recognize it as the severest educational handicap in my entire life.
>
> —HUGH MACLENNAN

Students who have been taught not to begin sentences with *I* often produce sentences that are eerily passive even when the verbs are in the active voice. For example:

1. Two reasons are important to my active participation in dance.
2. The name of the program that I enrolled in is the Health Careers Summer Program.
3. An eager curiosity overcame my previous feeling of fear to make me feel better.

It makes more sense to say:

1. I dance for two reasons.
2. I enrolled in the Health Careers Summer Program.
3. My curiosity aroused, I was no longer afraid.

A good rule: **Make the agent of the action the subject of the sentence.**

CLARITY AND COHERENCE

Writing a coherent essay is hard work; it requires mastery of a subject and skill in presenting the subject; it always takes a lot of time. Writing a coherent paragraph often takes more fussing and patching than you expect, but once you have the hang of it, it is relatively easy and pleasant. Writing a coherent sentence requires only that you stay awake until you get to the end of it.

We all do nod sometimes, even over our own prose. But if you make it a practice to read your work over several times, at least once aloud, you give yourself a chance to spot the incoherent sentence before your reader does and to revise it. Once you see that a sentence is incoherent, it is usually easy to recast it.

Cats Are Dogs

Looking at a picture of a woman, a man once said to the painter Henri Matisse, "That woman's arm is too long." "That's not a woman," Matisse replied, "it's a painting."

In some sentences a form of the verb *to be* mistakenly asserts that one thing is in a class with another. Is a picture a woman? Are cats dogs? See the following examples of students' writing:

Incoherent

> X. J. Kennedy's poem "Nothing in Heaven Functions as It Ought" is a contrast between Heaven and Hell. (As soon as you ask yourself the question "Is a poem a contrast?" you have, by bringing the two words close together, isolated the problem. A poem may be a sonnet, an epic, an ode—but not a contrast. The writer was trying to say what the poem does, not what it is.)

Coherent

> X. J. Kennedy's poem "Nothing in Heaven Functions as It Ought" contrasts Heaven and Hell.

Incoherent

> Besides, he tells himself, a matchmaker is an old Jewish custom. (Is a matchmaker a custom?)

Coherent

> Besides, he tells himself, consulting a matchmaker is an old Jewish custom.

Try revising the following:

> The essay is also an insight into imperialism.

In a related problem, one part of the sentence doesn't know what the other is doing.

Incoherent

> Ruth's devotion to Naomi is rewarded by marrying Boaz. (Does devotion marry Boaz?)

Coherent

> Ruth's marriage to Boaz rewards her devotion to Naomi.

Incoherent

> Canadians are not those from whom unpleasant facts should be concealed: the people of this country were born optimists, but they were born realists as well. (Can a person be born both an optimist and a realist?)

Items in a Series

If you were given a shopping list that mentioned apples, fruit, and pears, you would be puzzled and possibly irritated by the inclusion of "fruit." Do not puzzle or irritate your reader with a **false series** of this sort. Analyze sentences containing items in a series to be sure that the items are of the same order of generality. For example:

False series

> His job exposed him to the "dirty work" of the British and to the evils of imperialism. ("The 'dirty work' of the British" is a *specific* example of the more *general* "evils of imperialism." The false series makes the sentence incoherent.)

Revised

> His job, by exposing him to the "dirty work" of the British, brought him to understand the evils of imperialism.

In the following sentence, which item in the series makes the sentence incoherent?

> Why should one man, no matter how important, be exempt from investigation, arrest, trial, and law-enforcing tactics?

Modifiers

A modifier should appear close to the word it modifies (that is, describes or qualifies). Three kinds of faulty modifiers are common: misplaced, squinting, and dangling.

Misplaced Modifiers

If the modifier seems to modify the wrong word, it is called *misplaced*. Misplaced modifiers are often unintentionally funny. The judo parlour that advertised "For $20 learn basic methods of protecting yourself from an experienced instructor" probably attracted more amused readers than paying customers.

Misplaced

> Orwell shot the elephant under pressure. (Orwell was under pressure, not the elephant. Put the modifier near what it modifies.)

Revised

Orwell, under pressure, shot the elephant.

Misplaced

Orwell lost his individual right to protect the elephant as part of the impe-rialistic system. (The elephant was not part of the system; Orwell was.)

Revised

As part of the imperialistic system, Orwell lost his right to protect the elephant.

Revise the following:

1. Last week Toronto police buried one of their own—a 22-year-old consta-ble shot with his own revolver in a solemn display of police solidarity rarely seen in Canada.
2. Sitting Bull and William Cody stand side by side, each supporting a rifle placed between them with one hand.
3. Complete with footnotes the author has provided her readers with some background information.

Sometimes other parts of sentences are misplaced:

Misplaced

We learn from the examples of our parents who we are. (The sentence appears to say we are our parents.)

Revised

We learn who we are from the examples of our parents.

Misplaced

It is up to the students to revise the scheme, not the administrators. (We all know you can not revise administrators. Revise the sentence.)

Squinting Modifiers

If the modifier is ambiguous, that is, if it can be applied equally to more than one term, it is sometimes called a *squinting modifier:* it seems to look both forward and backward.

Squinting

Being with Jennifer more and more enrages me. (Is the writer spending more time with Jennifer, or is she more enraged? Probably more enraged.)

Revised

Being with Jennifer enrages me more and more.

Squinting

Writing clearly is difficult. (Is this sentence about "writing" or about "writing clearly"?)

Revised

> It is clearly difficult to write.

Revised

> It is difficult to write clearly.

Squinting

> Students only may use this elevator. (Does "only" modify students? If so, no one else may use the elevator. Or does it modify elevator? If so, students may use no other elevator.)

Revised

> Only students may use this elevator.
>
> Students may use only this elevator.

Note: The word *only* often squints, seeming to look in two directions. In general, put *only* immediately before the word or phrase it modifies. Often it appears too early in the sentence. (On *only,* see the Glossary in Chapter 21.)

Dangling Modifiers

If the term being modified appears nowhere in the sentence, a modifier is called *dangling*.

Dangling

> The first Canadian postage stamp, issued on April 23, 1851, was designed by Sandford Fleming, which was the world's first pictorial stamp. (The name of the first pictorial stamp is missing from the sentence, and it is the stamp, not Fleming, that was the world's first.)

Revised

> The first Canadian postage stamp, the Three Penny Beaver, which was the world's first pictorial stamp, was designed by Sandford Fleming and was issued on April 23, 1851.

Dangling

> A meticulously organized person, his suitcase could be tucked under an airplane seat. (How would you revise the sentence?)

The general rule: **When you revise sentences, put together what belongs together.**

Reference of Pronouns

A pronoun is used in place of a noun. Because the noun usually precedes the pronoun, the noun to which the pronoun refers is called the *antecedent* (Latin: "going before"). For example:

> **antecedent**   **pronoun**
>
> When *Sheriff Johnson* was on a horse, *he* was a big man.

But the pronoun can also precede the noun:

    pronoun   **noun**

When *he* was on a horse, *Sheriff Johnson* was a big man.

The word *antecedent* can be used here too. In short, the antecedent is the word or group of words referred to by a pronoun.

    Whenever possible, make sure that a pronoun has a clear reference. Sometimes it is not possible: *it* is commonly used with an unspecified reference, as in "It's hot today," and "Hurry up please, it's time"; and there can be no reference for interrogative pronouns: "What's bothering you?" and "Who's on first?" But otherwise always be sure that you have made clear what noun the pronoun is standing for.

Vague Reference of Pronouns

Vague

Apparently, they fight physically and it can become rather brutal. ("It" doubtless refers to "fight," but "fight" in this sentence is the verb, not an antecedent noun.)

Clear

Their fights are apparently physical and sometimes brutal.

Vague

I was born in Colón, the second largest city in the Republic of Panama. Despite this, Colón is still an undeveloped town. ("This" has no specific antecedent. It appears to refer to the writer's having been born in Colón.)

Clear

Although Colón, where I was born, is the second largest city in Panama, it remains undeveloped. (On *this,* see the Glossary in Chapter 21.)

Revise the following sentence:

They are applying to medical school because it is a well-paid profession.

Shift in Pronouns

This common error is easily corrected.

1. In many instances the child was expected to follow the profession of your father. (Expected to follow the profession of whose father, "yours" or "his/hers"?)
2. Having a tutor, you can get constant personal encouragement and advice that will help me budget my time. (If "you" have a tutor, will that help "me"?)

Revise the following sentences:

1. Schools bring people of the same age together and teach you how to get along with each other.
2. If asked why you went to the dance, one might say they were simply curious.

Ambiguous Reference of Pronouns

A pronoun normally refers to the first appropriate noun or pronoun preceding it. Same-sex pronouns and nouns, like dogs, often get into scraps.

Ambiguous

Her mother died when she was eighteen. (Who was eighteen, the mother or the daughter?)

Clear

Her mother died when Mabel was eighteen.

Her mother died at the age of eighteen. (Note the absence of ambiguity in "His mother died when he was eighteen.")

Ambiguous

Joe Clark lost the Tory leadership to Brian Mulroney on June 11, 1983, and he later became one of the most hated Canadian politicians in this country's history. (Both Clark and Mulroney are male, and so it is not clear who became so hated.)

Clear

Brian Mulroney, who defeated Joe Clark for the Tory leadership on June 11, 1983, later became one of the most hated Canadian politicians in this country's history.

The general rule: **Put together what belongs together.**

Agreement

Noun and Pronoun

Everyone knows that a singular noun requires a singular pronoun, and a plural noun requires a plural pronoun, but writers sometimes slip.

Faulty

    singular   **plural**
A *dog* can easily tell if people are afraid of *them.*

Correct

    singular   **singular**
A *dog* can easily tell if people are afraid of *it.*

Faulty

                    singular   **plural**
Cutbacks have hit *Parks Canada* so badly that *they've* had to downgrade
plural
their official logo from a beaver to a muskrat.

Correct

singular   singular   singular

Cutbacks have hit *Parks Canada* so badly that *it* has had to downgrade *its* *its* official logo from a beaver to a muskrat.

Each, everybody, nobody, no one, and *none* are especially troublesome. See the entries on these words in the Glossary in Chapter 21.

Subject and Verb

A singular subject requires a singular verb, a plural subject a plural verb.

Faulty

plural   singular

Horror films bring to light a subconscious fear and *shows* a character who succeeds in coping with it.

Correct

plural   plural

Horror films bring to light a subconscious fear and *show* a character who succeeds in coping with it.

The student who wrote "shows" instead of "show" thought that the subject of the verb was "fear," but the subject really is "Horror films," a plural.

Faulty

The manager, as well as the pitcher and the catcher, were fined.

Correct

The manager, as well as the pitcher and the catcher, was fined.

If the sentence had begun "The manager and the pitcher," the subject would have been plural and the required verb would be *were:*

The manager and the pitcher were fined.

But in the sentence as it was given, "as well as" (like *in addition to, with,* and *together with*) does *not* add a subject to a subject and thereby make a plural subject. "As well as" merely indicates that what is said about the manager applies to the pitcher and the catcher.

Revise the following:

About mid-morning during French class the sound of sirens were heard.

Three Additional Points

1. A collective noun—that is, a noun that is singular in form but that denotes a collection of individuals, such as *mob, audience, jury*—**normally takes a *singular* verb:**

Correct

The mob is at the gate.

Correct

An audience of children *is* easily bored. (The subject is "an audience," *not* "children.")

Correct

The jury is seated.

But when the emphasis is on the individuals within the group—for instance when you are calling attention to a division within the group—you can use a plural verb:

The jury disagree.

Still, because this sounds a bit odd, it is probably better to recast the sentence:

The jurors disagree.

2. Sometimes a sentence that is grammatically correct may nevertheless sound awkward:

One of its most noticeable features is the lounges.

Because the subject is "one"—*not* "features"—the verb must be singular, "is," but "is" sounds odd when it precedes the plural "lounges." The solution: Revise the sentence.

Among the most noticeable features are the lounges.

3. When a singular and a plural subject are joined by *or, either . . . or,* or *neither . . . nor,* use a verb that agrees in number with the subject closest to the verb.

Correct

Either the teacher *or the students are* mistaken.

Correct

Either the students *or the teacher is* mistaken.

The first version uses "are" because the verb is nearer to "students" (plural) than to "teacher" (singular); the second uses "is" because the verb is nearer to "teacher" than to "students."

Repetition and Variation

1. Don't be afraid to repeat a word if it is the best word. The following paragraph from "Riot Rocks Toronto" repeats "African," "Canada," "native," "US," "American," and variations of the words "racism" and "slavery"; notice also "racism" and "prejudice" as well as the alliteration of "resisting racism" and "racist reality." Repetition, a device necessary for continuity, clarity, and emphasis, holds the paragraph together.

> It is not just those of African heritage who are resisting racism in Canada. Many other immigrants—South Asians (from Sri Lanka, India, and Pakistan), South East Asians (from Vietnam, Hong Kong, China), Latin Americans and those from the Middle East—are all discovering the racist reality in Canada. Nor is racism a new phenomenon here. The indigenous people in Toronto have also been struggling for their rights as urban natives, and against the prejudice and racism they face in the city, as part of their historical struggle for self-determination and survival. The African community in Canada, which goes back to the very beginning of non-Native settlement, began in the chains of slavery. There is pride that Canada was a haven for escaped slaves from the US before the American civil war. Little mention is made of the fact that most of these former American slaves chose to return to the US after emancipation, since their conditions here were no better than what they experienced on the other side of the border.
>
> —JIM CAMPBELL

2. Use pronouns, when their reference is clear, as substitutes for nouns. Notice Campbell's use of pronouns. Substitutions that neither confuse nor distract keep a sentence and a paragraph from sounding like a broken record.

3. Do not, however, confuse the substitutions we have just spoken of with the fault called Elegant Variation. A groundless fear of repetition sometimes leads students to write first, for example, of "Campbell," then of "the writer," then of "our author." Such variations may strike the reader as silly. They can, moreover, be confusing. Substitute "he" for "Campbell" if "he" is clear and sounds better. Otherwise, repeat "Campbell."

4. But don't repeat a word if it is being used in two different senses.

Confusing

> My theme focuses on the theme of the essay. (The first "theme" means "essay"; the second means "underlying idea" or "motif.")

Clear

> Campbell's essay focuses on the theme of racism in Canada.

Confusing

> Caesar's character is complex. The comic characters, however, are simple. (The first "character" means "personality"; the second means "persons" or "figures in the play.")

Clear

> Caesar is complex; the comic characters, however, are simple.

5. Finally, eliminate words repeated unnecessarily. Use of words such as *surely, in all probability, it is noteworthy* may become habitual. If they do not help your reader to follow your thoughts, they are Instant Prose Additives. Cross them out.

In general, when you revise, decide if a word should be repeated, varied, or eliminated by testing sentences and paragraphs for both sound and sense.

Euphony

The word is from the Greek for "sweet voice," and though you need not aim at sweetness, try to avoid cacophony, or "harsh voice." Avoid distracting repetitions of sounds, as in "The story is marked by a remarkable mystery," and "This is seen in the scene in which . . ." Such echoes call attention to themselves, getting in the way of the points you are making. When you revise, tune out irrelevant sound effects.

Not all sound effects are irrelevant; some contribute meaning. James Baldwin, in his essay "Stranger in the Village," argues that the American racial experience has permanently altered black and white relationships throughout the world. His concluding sentence is

This world is white no longer, and it will never be white again.

As the sentence opens, the repetition of sounds in "*w*orld is *w*hite" binds the two words together, but the idea that they are permanently bound is swiftly denied by the most emphatic repetition of sounds in *no, never, again,* as the sentence closes. Or take another example:

Canada, Love It or Leave It.

If it read, "Canada, Love It or Emigrate," would the bumper sticker still imply, as clearly and menacingly, that there are only two choices, and for the patriot, only one?

Transitions

Repetition holds a paragraph together by providing continuity and clarity. Transitions such as *next, on the other hand,* and *therefore* also provide continuity and clarity. Because we discuss transitions at length on pages 52–54 in our chapter on paragraphs, we only remind you here to make certain that the relation between one sentence and the next, and one paragraph and the next, is clear. Often it will be clear without an explicit transition: "She was desperately unhappy. She quit school."

But do not take too much for granted; relationships between sentences may not be as clear to your readers as they are to you. You know what you are talking about; they do not. After reading the passage readers may see, in retrospect, that you have just given an example, or a piece of contrary evidence, or an amplification, but readers like to know in advance where they are going; brief transitions such as *for example, but, finally* are enormously helpful.

CLARITY AND SENTENCE STRUCTURE: PARALLELISM

Make the structure of your sentence reflect the structure of your thought. This is not as formidable as it sounds. If you keep your reader in mind (and remember that you are explaining something to someone who understands it less well than you do), you will almost automatically not only say *what* you think but also show *how* you think.

In revising, read your work as if you were not the writer of it, but your intended reader. If you reach a bump or snag where the shape or direction of your thought isn't clear, revise your sentence structure. Three general rules help:

- Put main ideas in main (independent) clauses.
- Subordinate the less important elements in the sentence to the more important.
- Put parallel ideas and details in parallel constructions.

The time to consult these rules consciously is not while you write, but while you revise. (The first two rules are amplified in Chapter 6, "Revising Sentences for Emphasis." Clarity and emphasis are closely related, as the following discussion of parallel construction makes evident.)

Consider the next sentence and the revision:

Awkward

He liked eating and to sleep.

Parallel

He liked to eat and to sleep.

In the first version, "eating" and "to sleep" are not grammatically parallel; the difference in grammatical form blurs the writer's point that there is a similarity. Use parallel constructions to clarify relationships—for instance to emphasize similarities or to define differences.

I divorce myself from my feelings and immerse myself in my obligations.

—FROM A STUDENT JOURNAL

She drew a line between respect, which we were expected to show, and fear, which we were not.

—ERNESTO GALARZA

I will not accept if nominated and will not serve if elected.

—WILLIAM TECUMSEH SHERMAN

Fascist art glorifies surrender; it exalts mindlessness; it glamorizes death.

—SUSAN SONTAG

In the following examples, the parallel construction is printed in italic type.

Awkward

The dormitory rules needed revision, a smoking area was a necessity, and a generally more active role for the school in social affairs were all significant to her.

Parallel

> She recommended that the school *revise* its dormitory rules, *provide* a smoking area, and *organize* more social activities.

Awkward

> According to the 1996 census, 22.1 percent of the Canadian population is rural and 77.9 percent live in cities.

Parallel

> According to the 1996 census, 22.1 percent of the Canadian population *is rural* and 77.9 percent *is urban*.

Revise the following sentence:

> The Rogallo glider is recommended for beginners because it is easy to assemble, to maintain, and it is portable.

In parallel constructions, be sure to check the consistency of articles, prepositions, and conjunctions. For example, "He wrote papers on a play by Shakespeare, a novel by Dickens, and a story by Davies," *not* "He wrote papers on a play by Shakespeare, a novel of Dickens, and a story by Davies." The shift from "by" to "of" and back to "by" serves no purpose and is merely distracting.

Let's study this matter a little more, using a short poem as our text.

 **ROBERT BLY**

Love Poem

> When we are in love, we love the grass,
> And the barns, and the lightpoles,
> And the small mainstreets abandoned all night.

Suppose we change "Love Poem" by omitting a conjunction or an article here and there:

> When we are in love, we love the grass,
> Barns, and lightpoles,
> And the small mainstreets abandoned all night.

We've changed the rhythm, of course, but we still get the point: the lover loves all the world. In the original poem, however, the syntax of the sentence, the consistent repetition of "and the . . ." makes us feel, without our thinking about it, that when we are in love we love the world, everything in it, equally. The list could extend infinitely, and everything in it would give us identical pleasure. In our altered version, we sacrifice this unspoken assurance. We bump a little, and stumble. As readers, without consciously being aware of it, we wonder if there is some distinction being made, some qualification we have missed. We still get the point of the poem, but we don't feel it the same way.

To sum up:

A pupil once asked Arthur Schnabel (the noted pianist) whether it was better to play in time or to play as one feels; his characteristic mordant reply was another question: "Why not feel in time?"

—David Hamilton

Exercises

1. In the following sentences, underline phrases in which you find the passive voice. Recast the sentences, using the active voice:
   a. The phrases in which the passive voice is found should be underlined.
   b. The active voice should be used.
   c. In the letter from Ms. Mike advice was sought regarding her problem with her tenant.
   d. The egg is guarded, watched over, and even hatched by the male penguin.
   e. After the Industrial Revolution, the workers' daylight hours were spent in factories.
   f. Tyler found that sexual stereotyping was reinforced in kindergarten: the girls were encouraged to play with dolls and the boys with Mack trucks.
   g. Insufficient evidence was given in the report to prove her hypothesis that reading problems originate in peer relationships.
2. Revise the following sentences to eliminate faults in modifiers:
   a. At the age of ten years, my family moved to Kamsack, Saskatchewan.
   b. Without knowing the reason, my father's cheeks became red with embarrassment.
   c. Buffalo Bill became friends with Sitting Bull while performing together in the Wild West Show.
   d. During a drought, annual plants will succumb without help.
   e. Looking out from my window, the sky was inky black.
   f. Mr. Von Karajan conducted the orchestra three times during the weekend before returning to his home in the Alps to the delight of the audience.
3. In the following sentences, locate the errors in agreement and correct them.
   a. Locate the error and correct them.
   b. One must strive hard to reach their goal.
   c. I would recommend the book to anyone who wants to improve their writing.
   d. Her collection of antique toys fill the house.
4. Recast the following sentences, using parallel constructions to express parallel ideas:
   a. Jacoby's aim in writing is to disgrace the passively committed and opposition to feminism.
   b. The boys segregated themselves less, the girls showed broader career interests, and unromantic, cross-sex relationships were achieved.

   c. The study shows parents and educators that it is important to change and it can be done.

   d. I do believe that there should be equality between men and women: equal pay for equal work; everybody should have an equal chance to attain whatever goals they may have set for themselves; and everybody should share the same responsibilities toward society.

5. Identify the specific faults that make the following sentences unclear, then revise each sentence for clarity. (Note that you will often have to invent what the writer thought he or she had said.)

   a. Actually, she was aging, and quite average in other respects.

   b. If technology cannot sort out its pluses and minuses, and work to improve them, humans must.

   c. Brooks stresses the farm workers' strenuous way of life and the fact that they have the bare necessities of life.

   d. Instead of movable furniture, built-in ledges extend into the centre of the room to be used as tables or to sit on.

   e. The issue has been saved for my final argument because it is controversial.

   f. I am neither indifferent nor fond of children.

   g. When the students heard that their proposal was rejected a meeting was called.

   h. A viable library is the cornerstone of any college campus.

   i. Her main fault was that she was somewhat lacking in decision-making capabilities.

   j. After industrialization a swarm of immigrants came battering to our shores.

   k. Each group felt there was very personal rapport and thus very candid feedback resulted.

   l. He can tolerate crowding and pollution and seems disinterested or ignorant of these dangers.

   m. The wooden door occupies the majority of the stone wall.

   n. Yale students frequently write to Ann Landers telling her fictional stories of their so-called troubles as a childish prank.

   o. At my grandmother's house vegetables were only served because meat was forbidden.

   p. My firm stand seemed to melt a little.

   q. The conclusion leaves the conflict neatly tied in smooth knots.

   r. The paragraph reeks of blandness.

6. The following sentences, published in *AIDE,* a magazine put out by an insurance company, were written to the company by various policyholders. The trouble is that the writers mean one thing but their sentences say another. Make each sentence clearly say what the writer means.

   a. The other car collided with mine without giving warning of its intentions.

   b. I collided with a stationary truck coming the other way.

   c. The guy was all over the road; I had to swerve a number of times before I hit him.

   d. I pulled away from the side of the road, glanced at my mother-in-law, and headed over the embankment.

 e. In my attempt to kill a fly, I drove into a telephone pole.

 f. I had been driving for forty years when I fell asleep at the wheel and had the accident.

 g. To avoid hitting the bumper of the car in front, I struck the pedestrian.

 h. The pedestrian had no idea which direction to run, so I ran over him.

 i. The indirect cause of this accident was a little guy in a small car with a big mouth.

7. In 1983, while conflicting reports were being broadcast about an invasion of Grenada by U.S. troops, Admiral Wesley L. McDonald, in the Pentagon, answered a reporter's question thus: "We were not micromanaging Grenada intelligencewise until about that time frame." Bruce Felknor, director of yearbooks for the *Encyclopaedia Britannica,* says that he was "inspired" by that answer to translate "a small selection of earlier admirals' heroic prose for the edification, indeed enjoyment, of our young." Below we list Felknor's translations and, in parentheses, the names of the admirals, the battles, and the dates of their heroic prose. What were the original words?

 a. "Combatwise, the time frame is upcoming." (John Paul Jones, off the English coast, September 23, 1779)

 b. "Area accessed in combat mode; mission finished." (Oliver Hazard Perry, after the Battle of Lake Erie, September 10, 1813)

 c. "Disregard anticipated structural damage. Continue as programmed." (David Farragut, Mobile Bay, August 5, 1864)

 d. "Implementation of aggressive action approved; time frame to be selected by fire control officer." (George Dewey, Manila Bay, May 1, 1898)

8. Translate the following euphemisms into plain English:

 a. revenue enhancement

 b. atmospheric deposition of anthropogenically derived acidic substances

 c. resize our operations to the level of profitable opportunities (spoken by a business executive)

 d. reconcentrate (or redeploy) our forces

Revising Sentences
for Emphasis

In revising for conciseness and clarity, we begin to discover something we may have been largely unaware of in the early stages of writing: what in our topic most concerns us and precisely why it interests us. That moment or those several discrete moments of discovery yield more pleasure than any other in writing. From there on we work, sometimes as if inspired, to make our special angle of vision seem as inevitable to our readers as it is to us. Now as we tighten sentences or expand them, as we shift the position of a word, a sentence, or a paragraph, or as we subordinate a less important idea to a more important one, we are assigning relative value and weight to each of our statements. The expression of value and weight is what is meant by emphasis.

Inexperienced writers may *try* to achieve emphasis as Queen Victoria did, by a style consisting *almost entirely* of italics and—dashes—and—exclamation marks!!! Or they may spice their prose with clichés ("little did I realize," "believe it or not") or with a liberal sprinkling of intensifiers ("really beautiful," "definitely significant," and so on). But experienced writers abandon these unconvincing devices, preferring to exploit the possibilities of position, of brevity and length, of repetition, and of subordination.

EMPHASIS BY POSITION

First, let's see how a word or phrase may be emphasized. If it appears in an unusual position it gains emphasis, as in "This course he liked." Because in English the object of the verb usually comes after the verb as in "He liked this course," if the object appears first, it gains emphasis. But this device is tricky; words in an unusual position often seem ludicrous, the writer fatuous: "A moose toward the forest raced."

Let's now consider a less strained sort of emphasis by position. The beginning and the end of a sentence or a paragraph are emphatic positions, and the end is usually the more emphatic of the two. What comes last is what stays most in the mind. Compare these two sentences:

The essay is brief but informative.

The essay is informative but brief.

The first sentence leaves the reader with the impression that the essay, despite its brevity, is worth looking at. The second, however, ends more negatively, leaving the reader with the impression that the essay is so brief that its value is fairly slight. Because the emphasis in the two sentences is different, they say different things.

The rule: **It usually makes sense to put the important point near the end, lest the sentence become anticlimactic.** Here is a sentence that properly moves to an emphatic end:

Although I could not read its six hundred pages in one sitting, I never willingly put it down.

If the halves are reversed, the sentence trails off:

I never willingly put it down, although I could not read its six hundred pages in one sitting.

This second version straggles away from the real point—that the book was interesting.

Anticlimactic

Besides not owning themselves women also could not own property.

Emphatic

Women could not own property; in fact, they did not own themselves.

The most common anticlimaxes are caused by weak qualifiers (*in my opinion, it seems to me, in general,* etc.) tacked on to interesting statements. Weak qualifiers usually can be omitted. Even useful ones rarely deserve an emphatic position.

Anticlimactic

Poodles are smart but they are no smarter than pigs, I have read.

Emphatic

Poodles are smart, but I have read that they are no smarter than pigs.

The rule: **Try to bury dull but necessary qualifiers in the middle of the sentence.**

EMPHASIS BY BREVITY AND LENGTH: SHORT AND LONG SENTENCES

How long should a sentence be? What comes to mind is Lincoln's remark to a heckler who asked him how long a man's legs should be: "Long enough to reach the ground." No rules about length can be given, but be careful not to bore your reader with a succession of short sentences (say, under ten words) and be careful not to tax your reader with a monstrously long sentence. In *Les Misérables* Victor Hugo wrote a sentence containing 823 words and punctuated by ninety-three commas, fifty-one semicolons, and four dashes—not a good model for beginners. Conversely, consider this succession of short sentences:

> The purpose of the refrain is twofold. First, it divides the song into stanzas. Second, it reinforces the theme of the song.

These sentences are clear, but since the points are simple, readers may feel they are being addressed as if they were children. There is too much emphasis (too many heavy pauses) on too little. The reader can take all three sentences at once:

> The purpose of the refrain is twofold: it divides the song into stanzas, and it reinforces the theme.

The three simple sentences have been turned into one compound sentence, allowing the reader to keep going for a while.

Now compare another group of sentences with a revision.

> Hockey is one of the fastest-moving team sports in Canada. The skaters are constantly on the go. They move at high speeds. The action rarely stops.

These four sentences, instead of suggesting motion, needlessly stop us. Here is a revision:

> Hockey is one of the fastest-moving team sports in Canada. The skaters, constantly on the go, move at high speeds, and the action rarely stops.

By combining the second, third, and fourth sentences, the writer keeps the reader on the go, like the players.

Next, a longer example that would be thoroughly delightful if parts of it were less choppy.

Conceit

At my high school graduation we had two speakers. One was a member of our class, and the other was a faculty member. The student speaker's name was Alva Reed. The faculty speaker's name was Mr. Williams. The following conversation took place after the graduation ceremony. Parents, relatives, faculty, and friends were all outside the gymnasium congratulating the class of 1989. Alva was surrounded by her friends, her parents, and some faculty members who were congratulating her on her speech. Standing not far from her was Mr. Williams with somewhat the same crowd.

"Alva, dear, you were wonderful!"

"Thanks, Mom. I sure was scared though: I'm glad it's over."

At that moment, walking towards Alva were her grandparents. They both were wearing big smiles on their faces. Her grandfather said rather loudly, "That was a good speech dear. Nicely done, nicely done." Walking past them at that moment was Mr. Williams.

He stuck his head into their circle and replied, "Thank you," and walked away.

The first four sentences of this amusing anecdote seem to be written in spurts. They can easily be combined and improved thus:

> At my high school graduation we had two speakers. One was a member of our class, Alva Reed, and the other was a faculty member, Mr. Williams.

If we think that even this version, two sentences instead of four, is a little choppy, we can rewrite it into a single sentence:

> At my high school graduation we had two speakers, Alva Reed, a member of our class, and Mr. Williams, a faculty member.

or:

> The two speakers at my high school graduation were Alva Reed, a member of our class, and Mr. Williams, a faculty member.

The rest of the piece is less choppy, but reread it and see if you can discover some other sentences that should be combined.

Sometimes, however, the choppiness of a succession of short sentences is effective. Look at this description of the methods by which imprisoned Black Panther George Jackson resisted efforts to destroy his spirit:

> He trains himself to sleep only three hours a night. He studies Swahili, Chinese, Arabic and Spanish. He does pushups to control his sexual

urge and to train his body. Sometimes he does a thousand a day. He eats
only one meal a day. And, always, he is reading and thinking.

—JULIUS LESTER

These six sentences add up to only fifty-one words. The longest sentence—the
one about pushups—contains only thirteen words. That the author is at ease also
with longer and more complicated sentences is evident in the next paragraph,
which begins with a sentence of forty-two words.

Yet, when his contact with the outside world is extended beyond his
family to include Angela Davis, Joan, a woman who works with the
Soledad defense committee, and his attorney, he is able to find within
himself feelings of love and tenderness.

Can we account for the success of the passage describing Jackson's prison routine? First, the short sentences, with their repeated commonplace form (subject,
verb, object) in some degree imitate Jackson's experience: they are almost
monotonously disciplined, almost as regular as the pushups the confined
Jackson does.

He trains himself. . . .

He studies Swahili. . . .

He does pushups. . . .

Sometimes he does a thousand. . . .

He eats only one meal a day.

Later, when Jackson makes contact with activist and prison reformer
Angela Davis and others, the long sentence (forty-two words) helps to suggest
the expansion of his world. Second, the brevity of the sentences suggests
their enormous importance, certainly to Jackson and to Julius Lester and,
Lester hopes, to the reader.

Keep in mind this principle: **Any one sentence in your essay is
roughly equal to any other sentence**. If a sentence is short, it must be relatively weighty. A lot is packed into a little. Less is more. (The chief exceptions are transitional sentences such as, "Now for the second point.")
Consider the following passage:

It happened that in September of 1933 Lord Rutherford, at the British
Association meeting, made some remark about atomic energy never
becoming real. Leo Szilard was the kind of scientist, perhaps just the
kind of good-humored, cranky man who disliked any statement that
contained the word "never," particularly when made by a distinguished
colleague. So he set his mind to think about the problem.

—JACOB BRONOWSKI

The first two sentences are relatively long (twenty-three words and thirty-one
words); the third is relatively short (ten words), and its brevity—its weight or
density—emphasizes Szilard's no-nonsense attitude.

EMPHASIS BY REPETITION

Do not be afraid to repeat a word if it is important. The repetition will add emphasis. In these lucid sentences by Helen Gardner, notice the effective repetition of "end" and "beginning."

> *Othello* has this in common with the tragedy of fortune, that the end in no way blots out from the imagination the glory of the beginning. But the end here does not merely by its darkness throw up into relief the brightness that was. On the contrary, beginning and end chime against each other. In both the value of life and love is affirmed.

The substitution of "conclusion" or "last scene" for the second "end" would be worse than pointless; it would destroy Ms. Gardner's point that there is *identity* or correspondence between beginning and end.

EMPHASIS BY SUBORDINATION

Five Kinds of Sentences

Before we can discuss the use of subordination for emphasis, we need to talk about what a sentence is, and about five kinds of sentences.

If there is an adequate definition of a sentence, we have not found it. Perhaps the best definition is not the old one, "a complete thought," but "a word or group of words that the reader takes to be complete." This definition includes such utterances as "Who?" and "Help!" and "Never?" and "Maybe." Now, in speaking, "While he was walking down the street" may be taken as a complete thought if it answers the question "When did the car hit him?" In writing, however, it would be a sentence fragment that probably should be altered to, say, "While he was walking down the street, he was hit by a car." We will discuss intentional fragments on pages 127–28. But first we should take a closer look at complete sentences.

Usually a sentence names someone or something (this is the subject) and it tells us something about the subject (this is the predicate); that is, it "predicates" something about the subject. Let us look at five kinds of sentences: simple, compound, complex, compound-complex, and sentence fragments.

1. A **simple sentence** has one predicate, here italicized:

Shakespeare *died.*

Shakespeare and Jonson *were contemporaries.*

The subject can be elaborated ("Shakespeare and Jonson, England's chief Renaissance dramatists, were contemporaries"), or the predicate can be elaborated ("Shakespeare and Jonson were contemporaries in the Renaissance England of Queen Elizabeth"), but the sentence remains technically a simple sentence: it consists of only one main (independent) clause with no dependent (subordinate) clause.

2. A **compound sentence** has two or more main clauses, each containing a subject and a predicate. It is, then, two or more simple sentences connected by a comma plus a coordinating conjunction (*and, but, for, nor, or, so, yet*) or by *not only . . . but also,* or by a semicolon or colon.

Shakespeare died in 1616, and Jonson died in 1637.

Shakespeare not only wrote plays, but he also acted in them.

Shakespeare died in 1616; Jonson died twenty-one years later.

3. A **complex sentence** has one main (independent) clause and one or more subordinate (dependent) clauses. The main clause (here italicized) can stand as a sentence by itself.

Although Shakespeare died, *his plays survived.*

Jonson did not write a commemorative poem when Shakespeare died.

The parts not italicized are subordinate or dependent because they cannot stand as sentences by themselves.

4. A **compound-complex sentence** has two or more main clauses (here italicized) and one or more subordinate clauses.

In 1616 Shakespeare died and *his wife inherited the second-best bed* because he willed it to her.

Each of the two italicized passages could stand by itself as a sentence, but "because he willed it to her" could not (except as the answer to an oral question). Each italicized passage, then, is a main (independent) clause, and "because he willed it to her" is a subordinate (dependent) clause.

We will return to subordination, but let us first look at the fifth kind of sentence, the sentence fragment.

5. A **sentence fragment** does not fit the usual definition of a sentence, but when the fragment is intended the thought is often clear and complete enough. Intentional fragments are common in advertisements:

Made of imported walnut. For your pleasure. At finer stores.

More native than the Limbo. More exciting than the beat of a steel drum. Tia Maria. Jamaica's haunting liqueur.

And yet another example, this one not from an advertisement but from an essay on firewood:

Piles of it. Right off the sidewalk. Split from small logs of oak or ash or maple. Split. Split again.

—JOHN MCPHEE

All these examples strike us as pretentious in their obviously studied efforts at understatement. Words are hoarded, as though there is much in little, and as though to talk more fully would demean the speaker and would desecrate the subject. A few words, and then a profound silence. Here less is not more; it is too much. The trouble with these fragmentary sentences is not that they do not convey complete thoughts but that they attract too much attention to themselves; they turn our minds to their writers and conjure up images of unpleasantly self-satisfied oracles.

Here, however, is a passage from a student's essay where the fragmentary sentences seem satisfactory to us. The passage begins with a simple sentence and then gives three fragmentary sentences.

The film has been playing to sellout audiences. Even though the

acting is inept. Even though the sound is poorly synchronized. Even

though the plot is incoherent.

If this passage is successful, it is because the emphasis is controlled. The author is dissatisfied, and by means of parallel fragments (each beginning with the same words) she conveys a moderately engaging weariness and a gentle exasperation.

Then, too, we see that if the first three periods were changed to commas we would have an orthodox complex sentence. In short, because the fragments are effective we find them acceptable.

For ways to correct ineffective or unacceptable fragments, see pages 432–33 in Chapter 20.

Subordination

Having surveyed the kinds of sentences, we can now talk about using subordination to give appropriate emphasis.

Make sure that the less important element is subordinate to the more important. Consider this sentence about the painter Vincent van Gogh, who was supported by his brother, Theo.

Supported by Theo's money, van Gogh painted at Arles.

The writer puts van Gogh in the independent clause ("van Gogh painted at Arles"), subordinating the relatively unimportant Theo.

Had the writer wished to give Theo more prominence, the passage might have read:

Theo provided money, and van Gogh painted at Arles.

Here Theo (as well as van Gogh) stands in an independent clause, linked to the next clause by "and." The two clauses, and the two people, are now of approximately equal importance.

If the writer had wanted to emphasize Theo and to de-emphasize van Gogh, he might have written:

While van Gogh painted at Arles, Theo provided the money.

Here van Gogh is reduced to the subordinate clause, and Theo is given the position of the only independent clause.

In short, though simple sentences and compound sentences have their place, they make everything of approximately equal importance. Since everything is not of equal importance, you must often write complex and compound-complex sentences, subordinating some things to other things.

Exercises

1. Here is one way to test your grasp of the relationship of independent and subordinate elements in a sentence. This *haiku* (a Japanese poetic form) consists of one sentence that can be written as prose: "After weeks of watching the roof leak, I fixed it tonight by moving a single board."

   ### Hitch Haiku

   After weeks of watching the roof leak
   I fixed it tonight
   by moving a single board.
   —GARY SNYDER

   a. Identify the independent clause and the subordinate elements in the poem.
   b. The "I" in the poem's sentence does or has done three things. Write three simple sentences, each expressing one of the actions.
   c. Write one sentence in which all three of the poem's actions are expressed, but put in the independent clause one of the two actions that appear in a subordinate element in the poem.
   d. Compare your sentence with the poem's. Both sentences should be clear. How do they vary in emphasis?
   e. Optional: compare the original sentence written as poetry and written as prose.

2. First identify the fault or faults that make the following sentences unemphatic, and then revise them for emphasis.

   a. He lists some of the rights given to humans and to non-humans and both admits and accounts for the oddity of his proposal well by citing examples.
   b. Rights for women, African Americans, and the insane were granted though many couldn't see the value in it and so now our environment should be granted rights even though it takes some getting used to the idea.
   c. Thus Creon's pride forces Antigone's death which drives his son to suicide and then his wife.
   d. Stock breeding will give the same result as population evolution, defenders of positive eugenics claim.
   e. The family today lacks the close relationship it had before the industrial age, for example.
   f. The woman's face is distraught, her hair is unkempt, and her dress is rumpled.

g. There is probably no human being who would enjoy being eaten by a shark.

3. Analyze the ways Peter Newman achieves emphasis in these two paragraphs from "To Kill a People—Dash Their Dream," about the effect of the moratorium on people involved in the East Coast fishing industry.

To be a Newfie is to be a survivor. A survivor, not with any negative connotation of trying to outlive others, but in an exhilarating, nose-thumbing sense of tempting the fates that have never stopped trying to bring you down. That great spirit—that feeling of Darwinian pride that has allowed Newfoundlanders to claim with brassy validity that they are a race apart—is in jeopardy.

They are about to become an endangered species. Dash a people's dreams often enough, and you eventually kill their culture that depends for its sustenance on perpetuating the way of life that gave it birth.

The Writer's Voice

The friends that have it I do wrong
When ever I remake a song,
Should know what issue is at stake:
It is myself that I remake.

—William Butler Yeats

DEFINING STYLE

Style is not simply a flower here and some gilding there; it pervades the whole work. Van Gogh's style, or Walt Disney's, let us say, consists in part of features recurring throughout a single work and from one work to the next: angular or curved lines, hard or soft edges, strong or gentle contrasts, and so on. A picture of a seated woman by van Gogh is utterly different from a picture of the same subject by Disney, and if we have seen a few works by each, we can readily identify who did which one. Artists leave their fingerprints, so to speak, all over their work. Writers leave their voiceprints.

The word *style* comes from the Latin *stilus,* a Roman writing instrument. Even in Roman times *stilus* had acquired a figurative sense, referring not only to the instrument but also to the writer's choice of words and arrangement of words into sentences. But is it simply the choice and arrangement of words we comment on when we speak of a writer's style, or are we also commenting on the writer's mind? Don't we feel that a piece of writing, whether it is on constitutional debates or on genetics and intelligence, is also about the writer? The writing, after all, sets forth the writer's views of his or her topic. It sets forth perceptions and responses to something the writer has thought about. The writer has, from the choice of topic, revealed that he or she found it worth thinking about. The essay, in attempting to persuade us to think as the writer does, reveals not only how and what the writer thinks, but also what he or she values.

When we write about things "out there," our writing nevertheless reveals the shape of our minds, just as every work of art reveals its creator as well as its ostensible subject. A portrait painting, for example, is not only about the sitter, but is also about the artist's perceptions of the sitter; hence the saying that every portrait is a self-portrait. Even photographs are as much about the photographer as they are about the subject. Richard Avedon said of his portraits of famous people, "They are all pictures of me, of the way I feel about the people I photograph." A student's essay similarly, if it is truly written, is not exclusively about "Satan in a Sleigh: A Revelation into the Evils of Santa Claus"; it is also about his perceptions and responses to the commercialization of Christmas.

STYLE AND TONE

> *The style is the man.*
>
> —Buffon

> *The style is the man. Rather say the style is the way the man takes himself.*
>
> —Robert Frost

Suppose we take a page of handwriting, or even a signature. We need not believe that graphology is an exact science to believe that the shape of the ink lines on paper (apart from the meaning of the words) often tells us something about the writer. We look at a large, ornate signature, and we sense that the writer is confident; we look at a tiny signature written with the finest of pens, and we wonder why anyone is so self-effacing.

   More surely than handwriting, the writer's style reveals, among other things, his or her attitude toward the self (as Frost's addition to Buffon's epigram suggests), toward the reader, and toward the subject. The writer's attitudes are reflected in what is usually called *tone*. It is difficult to separate style from tone but we will try. Most discussions of style concentrate on what might be thought of as ornament: figurative language ("a sea of troubles"), inversion ("A leader he is not"), repetition and parallelism ("government of the people, by the people, for the people"), balance and antithesis ("It was the best of times, it was the worst of times"). Indeed, for centuries style has been called "the dress of thought," implying that the thought is something separate from the expression; the thought, in this view, is dressed up in stylistic devices. But in most of the writing that we read with interest and pleasure, the stylistic devices are not ornamental and occasional but integral and pervasive. When we talk about wit, sincerity, tentativeness, self-assurance, aggressiveness, objectivity, and so forth, we can say we are talking about style, but we should recognize that style now is not a matter of ornamental devices that dress up some idea, but part of the idea itself. And "the idea itself" includes the writer's unified yet appropriately varied tone.

   To take a brief example: the famous English translation of Caesar's report of a victory,

   I came, I saw, I conquered,

might be paraphrased thus:

   After getting to the scene of the battle, I studied the situation. Then I devised a strategy that won the battle.

But this paraphrase loses much of Caesar's message; the brevity and the parallelism of the famous version, as well as the alliteration (came, conquered), convey tight-lipped self-assurance—convey, that is, the tone that reveals Caesar to us. And this tone is a large part of Caesar's message. Caesar is really telling us not only about what he did, but also about what sort of person he is. He is perceptive, decisive, and effective. The three actions, Caesar in effect tells us, are (for a man like Caesar) one. (The Latin original is even more tight-lipped and more unified by alliteration: *veni, vidi, vici.*)

Let's look now at a longer sentence, the opening sentence of Lewis Thomas's essay "On Natural Death":

> There are so many new books about dying that there are now special shelves set aside for them in bookstores, along with the health, diet and home-repair paperbacks and the sex manuals.

This sentence could have ended where the comma is placed: the words after "bookstores" are, it might seem, not important. One can scarcely argue that by specifying some kinds of "special shelves" Thomas clarifies an otherwise difficult or obscure concept. What, then, do these additional words do? They tell us nothing about death and almost nothing about bookshops, but they tell us a great deal about Thomas's *attitude* toward the new books on death. He suggests that such books are faddish and perhaps (like "the sex manuals") vulgar. After all, if he had merely wanted to call up a fairly concrete image of a well-stocked bookstore, he could have said "along with books on politics and the environment," or some such thing. His next sentence reads:

> Some of them are so packed with detailed information and step-by-step instructions for performing the function you'd think this was a new sort of skill which all of us are now required to learn.

Why "you'd think" instead of, say, "one might believe"? Thomas uses a colloquial form, and a very simple verb, because he wants to convey to us his common-sense, homely, down-to-earth view that these books are a bit pretentious—a pretentiousness conveyed in his use of the words "performing the function," words that might come from the books themselves. In short, when we read Thomas's paragraph we are learning as much about Thomas as we are about books on dying. We are hearing a voice, perceiving an attitude, and we want to keep reading, not only because we are interested in death but also because Thomas has managed to make us interested in Thomas, a thoughtful but unpretentious fellow.

Now listen to the introduction from Basil H. Johnston's "One Generation from Extinction." Johnston is writing about the necessity of language for the preservation of culture and identity, and about the disappearance of many of the original Aboriginal languages in Canada.

> Within the past few years Gregor Keeshig, Henry Johnston, Resime Akiwenzie, Norman McLeod, and Belva Pitwaniquot died. They all spoke their tribal language, Anishinaubae (Ojibwa). When these elders passed away, so did a portion of the tribal language come to an end as a tree disintegrates by degrees and in stages until it is no more; and, though infants were born to replenish the loss of life, not any one of

them will learn the language of their grandfathers or grandmothers to keep it alive and to pass it on to their descendants. Thus language dies.

Try, in a word or two, to characterize the tone (the attitude, as we sense it in the inflection of the voice) of the first sentence. Next, the tone of the second, and then of the third. Suppose the passage had been written thus:

Older people who speak Anishinaubae (Ojibwa) are dying without the younger generations learning the language of their heritage. Although babies are being born to replace the loss of life, the loss of the language is a major problem. When language dies, in many ways so too does the culture.

How has the tone changed? What word(s) can you find to characterize the tone of the whole, as Johnston wrote it?

Now the next paragraph from Johnston's essay:

In some communities there are no more Gregor Keeshigs, Henry Johnstons, Resime Akiwenzies, Norman McLeods, and Belva Pitwaniquots; those remaining have no more affinity to their ancestral language than they do to Swahili or Sanskrit; in other communities the languages may not survive beyond a generation. Some tribal languages are at the edge of extinction, not expected to survive for more than a few years. There remain but three aboriginal languages out of the original fifty-three found in Canada that may survive several more generations.

Do you find traces of Johnston's voiceprint here?

Finally, a longer passage by the same writer. After you read it, try to articulate the resemblances between this and the other passages—qualities that allow us to speak of the writer's tone.

There is cause to lament, but it is the native peoples who have the most cause to lament the passing of their languages. They lose not only the ability to express the simplest of daily sentiments and needs, but they can no longer understand the ideas, concepts, insights, attitudes, rituals, ceremonies, institutions brought into being by their ancestors; and, having lost the power to understand, cannot sustain, enrich, or pass on their heritage. No longer will they think Indian or feel Indian. And though they may wear "Indian" jewellery and take part in pow-wows, they can never capture that kinship with and reverence for the sun and the moon, the sky and the water, or feel the life beat of Mother Earth or sense the change in her moods; no longer are the wolf, the bear, and the caribou elder brothers but beasts, resources to be killed and sold. They will have lost their identity which no amount of reading can ever restore. Only language and literature can restore the "Indianness."

ACQUIRING STYLE

In the preceding pages we said that your writing reveals not only where you stand (your topic) and how you think (the structure of your argument), but also who you are and how you take yourself (your tone). To follow our argument to its limit, we might say that everything in this book—including rules on the comma—is about style. We do. What more is there to say?

Clarity and Texture

First, a distinction Aristotle makes between two parts of style: that which gives clarity and that which gives texture. Exact words, concrete illustrations of abstractions, conventional punctuation, and so forth—matters we treat in some detail in the sections on revising and editing—make for clarity. On the whole, this part of style is inconspicuous when present; when absent, the effect ranges from mildly distracting to ruinous. Clarity is the foundation of style. It can be achieved by anyone willing to make the effort.

Among the things that give texture, or individuality, are effective repetition, variety in sentence structure, wordplay, and so forth. This second group of devices, on the whole more noticeable, makes the reader aware of the writer's particular voice. These devices can be learned too, but seldom by effort alone. In fact, playfulness helps here more than doggedness. Students who work at this part of style usually enjoy hanging around words. At the same time, they are likely to feel that when they put words on paper, even in a casual letter to a friend, they are putting themselves on the line. They will come to recognize the rules of play in John Holmes's advice to young poets: "You must believe that your feelings and your words for your feelings are important. . . . That they are unique is a fact; that you believe they are unique is necessary."

A Repertory of Styles

Second, a distinction between perspectives on style: the reader's and the writer's. The style as the reader perceives it is static: it's fixed in writing or print; we can point to it, discuss it, analyze it. But the writer's experience of his or her own style changes as the writer changes. In his essay "Why I Write" George Orwell says, "I find that by the time you have perfected any style of writing, you have always outgrown it." An exaggeration that posits a truth. The essay concludes, however, "Looking back through my work, I see that it is invariably where I lacked a political purpose that I wrote lifeless books and was betrayed into purple passages, sentences without meaning, decorative adjectives and humbug generally." A suggestion surely, that through trial and error, and with maturity, a writer comes to a sense of self, a true style, not static and not constantly changing, but achieved.

Undergraduates seldom know what purpose, in Orwell's sense, they will have. You may be inclined toward some subjects and away from others, and you may have decided on a career—many times. But if your education is worth anything like the money and time invested in it, your ideas and feelings will change more rapidly in the next few years than ever before in your memory, and perhaps more than they ever will again. Make use of the confusion you are in. Reach out for new experiences to assimilate; make whatever connections you can from your reading to your inner life, extending back into your past and forward into your future. And keep writing.

To keep pace with your changing ideas—and here is our main point—you will need to acquire not one style, but a repertory of styles, a store of writing habits on which you can draw as the need arises.

Originality and Imitation

Finally, a paradox: a person starts to acquire an individual style by studying and imitating the style of others. This paradox is not limited to writing. Stylists in all fields begin as apprentices. The young ballplayer imitates the movements of Raul Mondesi; the aspiring filmmaker studies the work of Denys Arcand; the chess player hangs around the park or club watching the old pros, then finds a book that probably recommends beginning with Ruy Lopez's opening. When Michelangelo was an apprentice he copied works by his predecessors; when Millet was young he copied works by Michelangelo; when van Gogh was young he copied works by Millet. Would-be writers may be lucky enough to have a teacher to imitate; more likely they will, in W. H. Auden's words, serve their "apprenticeship in the library."

Practice in Acquiring Style

Benjamin Franklin's Exercise

Benjamin Franklin says in his *Autobiography,* "Prose writing has been of great use to me in the course of my life, and was a principal means of my advancement," and he reveals how he acquired his ability in it. (He had just abandoned, at about the age of eleven, his ambition to be a great poet—after his father told him that "verse-makers" were "generally beggars.")

> About this time I met with an odd volume of the *Spectator.* It was the third. I had never before seen any of them. I bought it, read it over and over, and was much delighted with it. I thought the writing excellent, and wished, if possible, to imitate it. With that view I took some of the papers, and making short hints of the sentiment in each sentence, laid them by a few days, and then, without looking at the book, tried to complete the papers again by expressing each sentiment at length, and as fully as it had been expressed before, in any suitable words that should come to hand. Then I compared my *Spectator* with the original, discovered some of my faults, and corrected them.

A few pages later Franklin confides, with characteristic understatement (which he learned, he thought, by imitating Socrates), "I sometimes had the pleasure of fancying that in certain particulars of small import I had been lucky enough to improve the method or the language."

Exercises

1. Outline, in a list of brief notes, Franklin's exercise.
2. Choose a passage of current prose writing whose style you admire and follow Franklin's method. (Don't forget the last step: where you have improved on your model, congratulate yourself with becoming modesty.)

Paraphrasing

Do not confuse a paraphrase with a summary. A summary is always much shorter than the original; a paraphrase is sometimes a bit longer. Your sentence should say substantially what the original says, but in your own words, and in a fluent, natural style. Each word or phrase in the sentence you are paraphrasing should be replaced with one of your own. (Articles, pronouns, and conjunctions need not be replaced.) The structure of the sentence should be yours as well. Consider the following sentence by W. H. Auden and the paraphrase that follows it:

> Owing to its superior power as a mnemonic, verse is superior to prose as a medium for didactic instruction.
>
> —W. H. AUDEN

> Because it is more easily memorized and can be retained in the mind for a longer time, poetry is better than prose for teaching moral lessons.

Paraphrasing is useful for several reasons. First, paraphrasing helps you to increase your vocabulary. (Many students say that a limited vocabulary is their chief source of difficulty in writing.) You may know, for example, that "didactic" means "intended for instruction, or instructive." But why then does Auden say "didactic instruction"? Are the words redundant, or is Auden stipulating a kind of instruction? Your dictionary, which may list "tending to teach a moral lesson" as one of three or four meanings of "didactic," will help you understand Auden's sentence. But notice, first, that you will have to choose the appropriate definition and, second, that you will not be able to insert that definition as is into your sentence. To paraphrase "didactic instruction" you will have to put "didactic" in your own words. (If you look up "mnemonic" you will find an even more complex puzzle resolved in our paraphrase.) Paraphrasing, then, expands your vocabulary because to paraphrase accurately and gracefully you must actively understand the denotative and connotative meanings of an unfamiliar word, not simply memorize a synonym for it.

Paraphrasing also helps you to focus your attention on what you read. If you want, for example, to become a better reader of poetry, the best way is to *pay attention,* and the best way of paying attention is to try paraphrasing a line whose meaning escapes you. So too with understanding art history or economics or any specialized study. If you come across a difficult passage, don't just stare at it, paraphrase it. (If you have too little time to stop and puzzle through a sentence that is not entirely clear to you, you can always make time to jot the sentence down. As Stanislav Andreski says, "Paper is patient.")

Finally, in paraphrasing, you are observing closely and actively the way another mind works. You are, in effect, serving as an apprentice stylist. (Some masters, of course, are not worth serving or emulating. Be discriminating.)

Exercise

Try paraphrasing the following sentences:

> Generally speaking and to a varying extent, scientists follow their temperaments in their choice of problems.
>
> —CHARLES HERMITE

> The scholar's mind is a deep well in which are buried aborted feelings that rise to the surface as arguments.
>
> —NATALIE CLIFFORD BARNEY

The more extensive your acquaintance is with the works of those who have excelled, the more extensive will be your powers of invention, and what may appear still more like a paradox, the more original will be your composition.

—Sir Joshua Reynolds

Anyone who has ever struggled with poverty knows how extremely expensive it is to be poor.

—James Baldwin

What is expressed is impressed.

—Aristotle

A prairie sunset is often enigmatic: one moment it smiles with dazzling color and radiant light, and seconds later may reveal a more sinister countenance.

—Courtney Milne

When the shoe fits, the foot is forgotten.

—Chuang Tzu

Imitating the Cumulative Sentence

When you write, you make a point, not by subtracting as though you sharpened a pencil, but by adding. When you put one word after another, your statement should be more precise the more you add. If the result is otherwise, you have added the wrong thing, or you have added more than was needed.

—John Erskine

In *Notes Toward a New Rhetoric,* Francis Christensen cites "Erskine's principle" and argues that "the cumulative sentence" best fulfills it. The cumulative sentence makes a statement in the main clause; the rest of the sentence consists of modifiers *added* to make the meaning of the statement more precise. The cumulative sentence adds *texture* to writing because as the writer adds modifiers she is examining her impressions, summarized in the main clause. At the same time she reveals to the reader how those impressions impinged on her mind. Here are some of Christensen's examples:

He dipped his hands in the bichloride solution and shook them, a quick shake, fingers down, like the fingers of a pianist above the keys.

—Sinclair Lewis

The jockeys sat bowed and relaxed, moving a little at the waist with the movement of their horses.

—Katherine Anne Porter

The Texan turned to the nearest gatepost and climbed to the top of it, his alternate thighs thick and bulging in the tight trousers, the butt of the pistol catching and losing the sun in pearly gleams.

—WILLIAM FAULKNER

George was coming down in the telemark position, kneeling, one leg forward and bent, the other trailing, his sticks hanging like some insect's thin legs, kicking up puffs of snow, and finally the whole kneeling, trailing figure coming around in a beautiful right curve like points of light, all in a wild cloud of snow.

—ERNEST HEMINGWAY

Exercise

Try writing a cumulative sentence. First, reread Christensen's sample sentences out loud. Then, during a second reading, try to sense the similarities in structure. For the next few days, train yourself to observe people closely, the way they walk, move, gesture, smile, speak. Take notes when you can. Then, after reading the sentences again, try writing one. Either imitate one of the sentences closely, word by word (substituting your own words), or start with your subject, imitating the structure you have detected or have simply absorbed.

ACADEMIC STYLES, ACADEMIC AUDIENCES

When you write an essay for a course, you are to some degree learning how people working in that academic discipline express themselves. To communicate with other people in the discipline, you must adapt your voice to the conventions of the discipline and the audience's expectations about writing within that discipline. Some disciplines call for an abstract at the beginning of the paper, and some do not. Some call for an immediate statement of purpose, and some do not. Some disciplines (literature, for example) frown on passive verbs. But in lab reports in the sciences passive verbs are acceptable—even encouraged—in part because they help focus the reader's attention on the experiment rather than on the person who conducted it and thereby help to establish authority.

To make matters even more complicated, the conventions are changing, and they vary to some degree from class to class, and instructor to instructor. For example, one literature instructor might accept an essay containing the word "we" (as in "we see here the author's fascination with landscape"); another might object to its use, arguing that the "we" falsely implies that all readers—regardless of race, class, gender, and so on—read all texts in the same way.

These differences make some students frustrated, even cynical. To them, writing an essay becomes a game of figuring out What the Instructor Wants. (For what it's worth, such students can make instructors a bit frustrated too.) It may help both students and instructors to keep in mind that there is no one *right* style (although there are incorrect styles)—and that the differences among styles are not a matter of arbitrary and inscrutable personal taste, but rather a matter of disciplinary convention, and (to some degree) theoretical approach.

It would be impossible to list here all the different conventions you will encounter in university or college. You do not need to learn them all anyway. You simply need to be alert to the ways in which people talk to each other in the disciplines within which you are writing, and do your best to follow the conventions you observe. We illustrate a few of these differences below.

Here is the first paragraph of an article from a recent issue of the *Cambridge Journal of Economics*:

> In this paper I shall develop a framework which may be used to examine several alternative theories of the rate of interest. The four most widely accepted approaches are the Neoclassical Loanable Funds, Keynes's Liquidity Preference, Neoclassical Synthesis ISLM, and Basil Moore's Horizontalist (or endogenous money). I will use the framework developed here to present a fifth: an integration of liquidity preference theory with an endogenous money approach. I first briefly set forth the primary alternative approaches, then develop an analytical framework based on an asset or stock approach and use it to discuss several theories of the interest rate: those advanced by Keynes, by Moore, by neoclassical theory and the monetarists, by Kregel, and by Tobin. Finally, I shall use the framework to reconcile liquidity preference theory with an endogenous money approach.
>
> —L. Randall Wray

Note the use of the pronoun "I," the direct statement of what the writer will do ("In this paper I shall develop a framework . . ."), and the listing of the steps of his procedure ("I first briefly set forth," and so on). An English professor is likely to cringe at seeing "In this paper I shall . . ." A literary critic would be unlikely to present his or her ideas so methodically, as the next example suggests.

Here is the first paragraph of a chapter from a recent study of Bram Stoker's *Dracula,* in which a literary critic analyzes the novel in its social and political context:

> "In obedience to the law as it then stood, he was buried in the centre of a *quadrivium,* or conflux of four roads (in this case four streets), with a stake driven through his heart. And over him drives for ever the uproar of unresting London!" No, not *Dracula* (1897), but the closing lines of a much earlier nineteenth-century work, Thomas De Quincey's bleakly ironic essay "On Murder Considered as One of the Fine Arts" (1854). De Quincey is describing how in 1812 the London populace dealt with the body of one of his prize exhibits, a particularly grisly serial killer who had escaped the gallows by hanging himself in his cell in the dead of night. Yet it is difficult for us to read this gleefully chilling passage today without thinking of Bram Stoker's classic vampire novel. The quirky Christian symbolism, the mandatory staking down of the monster to keep it from roaming abroad, the sense of busily self-absorbed London unaware of its proximity to a murderous presence that haunts its most densely populated byways: together these features seem virtually to

define a basic iconography for the vampire Gothic as it achieved canonical status in *Dracula*.

—David Glover

Note the absence of the pronoun "I" and the presence of the pronoun "we." Note also the playfulness of the style (the reference to a "gleefully chilling passage" and the "staking down of the monster"), the specificity of the language, and the variety in punctuation and sentence structure.

Finally, here is the opening paragraph of a chemistry student's study of the enzyme calf alkaline phosphatase.

Enzymes, protein molecules that catalyze reactions, are crucial for many biochemical reactions. This research project studies the actions of the enzyme calf alkaline phosphatase on the substrate p-nitrophenyl phosphate. The focus of this research project is the relation of alkaline phosphatase denaturation to temperature. Heat denaturation has been well documented in major biology and chemistry texts, but few textbooks mention how extreme cold affects enzyme structure and function. This study will examine how alkaline phosphatase responds to both high and low temperatures.

—Hilary Suzawa

Note the absence of personal pronouns (the *research project* "studies"), the orderly and careful presentation of information (including the brief definition of the word "enzymes" in the first sentence), and the clear statement of purpose. (You might compare this writer's first sentence with Glover's—deliberately misleading—opening.)

THE WRITER'S VOICE: SIX EXAMPLES

1. The following passage is from the Introduction to *Fire and Ice: The United States, Canada and the Myth of Converging Values*.

For all the pressing of Canadian noses against the glass of American prosperity and achievement, we cherish our separateness—our unassuming civility, our gift for irony and understatement in a world of exaggerated claims and excess, the myriad "intangibles" we are certain set us apart—and wring our hands over what will become of our quirks and idiosyncrasies as the leviathan to the south continues to thrash its ever more powerful tail and the self-declared prophets of globalization augur the death of difference.

—Michael Adams

   a. How does Adams give this one-sentence paragraph clarity and texture? What would be lost if it were written as two or three sentences?
   b. Given Adams's title, tone, and diction, how should we as readers take his exaggeration of the stereotype of Canadians' views of ourselves? Is it playful? Insulting? How do you think Adams feels about Canadians and our nation's relationship with the United States?

2. The following paragraph, from an essay called "The View from the Cheap Seats," comes from a broadcast of *This Hour Has 22 Minutes* and was published in *Streeters: Rants and Raves from This Hour Has 22 Minutes*:

And then, out of the blue, one MP called another MP a liar. Well, the place went up. Because apparently the worst thing you can do in the House of Commons is call someone a liar. If you call someone a liar, and you do not apologize, you are kicked out of the House, which is ironic, seeing as that is how most of them get in there in the first place. But if you're an MP, you can lie all you want and nobody will call you a liar, because that would be the truth, and the truth is not allowed when it comes to lying, because in the House there are no liars. Just like in the big house, here are no guilty men.

—Rick Mercer

   a. How does Mercer present himself here? What is his tone and attitude toward his subject?
   b. Mercer writes that "in the House there are no liars." Does he mean what he says, or is he being ironic? How do you know?
   c. Why might he have ended the paragraph with the simile about prisons?

3. The following paragraph comes from a speech by the British mathematician and philosopher Alfred North Whitehead:

Style, in its finest sense, is the last acquirement of the educated mind; it is also the most useful. It pervades the whole being. The administrator with a sense for style hates waste; the engineer with a sense for style economizes his material; the artisan with a sense for style prefers good work. Style is the ultimate morality of mind. . . . With style the end is attained without side issues, without raising undesirable inflammations. With style you attain your end and nothing but your end. With style the effect of your activity is calculable, and foresight is the last gift of Gods to men. With style your power is increased, for your mind is not distracted with irrelevancies, and you are more likely to attain your object.

   a. Suppose that the first sentence of Whitehead's passage had begun thus: "I want to point out to you today that style may be regarded not only as the last acquirement of what I consider the mind that has been well educated, but it is also the most useful, I definitely believe." What would be lost?

4. Here is the opening paragraph of a chapter on "apparition belief" from a recent cultural history of eighteenth-century England:

Why do we no longer believe in ghosts? In his nostalgic celebration *The Book of Dreams and Ghosts* (1897), Andrew Lang blamed the skeptical eighteenth century: "the cock-sure common-sense of the years from 1650 to 1850, or so, regarded everyone who had an experience of a hallucination as a dupe, a lunatic, or a liar." Enlightenment thinking—to put it bluntly—made spirits obsolete. Keith Thomas takes up a similar theme in *Religion and the Decline of Magic* (1971), but develops it rather more ingeniously. Men and women of the eighteenth century "stopped seeing ghosts," he asserts, not so much because ghosts came to seem "intellectually impossible" (though this was certainly the case) but because ghosts gradually lost their "social relevance." In traditional English society, he suggests, the belief in apparitions performed a powerful community function. The idea that spirits of the dead might come back to haunt murderers, locate stolen objects, enforce the terms of legacies, expose adulterers, and so on, functioned as a kind of implicit social control—a restraint on aggression and a "useful sanction for social norms." With the emergence after 1706 of new and bureaucratic forms of surveillance—with the rise of an organized police force, grand juries, insurance companies, and other information-gathering bodies— the need for a spectral monitoring agency, composed of ethereal headless ladies, morose figures in shrouds, and other supernatural busybodies, gradually began to fade.

—Terry Castle

    a. How would you characterize Castle's attitude toward her topic? Her audience? How would you describe her attitude toward the scholars she cites?

    b. Recall the distinction Aristotle makes between the two parts of style: that which gives clarity (exact words, concrete illustrations of abstractions, conventional punctuation), and that which gives texture (effective repetition, variety in sentence structure, wordplay). Analyze the paragraph in terms of these two "parts": where, for example, does Castle supply "concrete illustrations of abstractions"? Which words and phrases could be described as giving "texture" to the paragraph?

5. Here is the opening paragraph of an essay on Jane Austen's *Pride and Prejudice*:

In a famous and lovely chapter of *Pride and Prejudice*, Elizabeth Bennet first sees Pemberley, the splendid estate of the splendid Mr. Darcy, whose rather insulting offer of marriage she has rather insultingly refused. Jane Austen reports that Elizabeth felt "an embarrassment impossible to be overcome" when the place's owner, whom she had supposed absent, suddenly appears and finds her, accompanied by relatives whom she thinks *he* thinks beneath his notice, admiring his property like any common tourist. "Embarrassment" seems the right word— she feels confused, ill at ease, disconcerted, flustered, to be discovered rubbernecking at the home of someone she knows as an approximate social equal. But after this first encounter the terms change: Elizabeth now feels "overpowered by shame and vexation" to suppose that she has given Darcy reason to think she has "thrown herself in his way," though his gracious, cordial behavior soon suggests even to her that he thinks no such thing.

—Thomas R. Edwards

    a. Read this passage out loud. What is the most noticeable feature of Edwards's style? What effect does it create?

    b. How would you describe the writer's tone? How does it differ from Castle's tone in the earlier paragraph on ghosts?

6. Following is a passage from *The Alchemy of Race and Rights* (1991) by Patricia J. Williams, a lawyer and professor of law at Columbia University.

Walking down Fifth Avenue in New York not long ago, I came up behind a couple and their young son. The child, about four or five years old, had evidently been complaining about big dogs. The mother was saying, "But why are you afraid of big dogs?" "Because they're big," he responded with eminent good sense. "But what's the difference between a big dog and a little dog?" the father persisted. "They're *big*," said the child. "But there's really no difference," said the mother, pointing to a large slathering wolfhound with narrow eyes and the calculated amble of a gangster, and then to a beribboned Pekingese the size of a roller skate, who was flouncing along just ahead of us all, in that little fox-trotty step that keeps Pekingese from ever being taken seriously. "See," said the father. "If you look really closely you'll see there's no difference at all. They're all just dogs."

    And I thought: Talk about your iron-clad canon. Talk about a static, unyielding, totally uncompromising point of reference. These people must be lawyers. Where else do people learn so well the idiocies of High Objectivity? How else do people learn to capitulate so uncritically to a norm that refuses to allow for difference? How else do grown-ups sink so deeply into the authoritarianism of their own world view that they can universalize their relative bigness so completely that they obliterate the subject positioning of their child's relative smallness? (To say nothing of the position of the slathering wolfhound, from whose own narrow perspective I dare say the little boy must have looked exactly like a lamb chop.)

    a. At what point in the first paragraph do you begin to get Williams's attitude toward the little boy? How does the cumulative sentence in the middle of the paragraph convey her attitude toward the boy's parents? (What would be lost if Williams simply said that the mother pointed to a wolfhound and a Pekingese?)

    b. Describe Williams's voice at the beginning of the second paragraph. How does her style express her attitude here?

    c. Paraphrase the second-paragraph sentence that begins "How else do grown-ups sink so deeply."

PART TWO

The Writer's Materials and Strategies

A Note on Using the Writer's Materials and Strategies

In Part Two, we discuss various methods of development or what we sometimes call rhetorical modes:

classification	*narration*
cause and effect	*definition*
description	*persuasion*
comparison	

Although we discuss these strategies individually, keep in mind that what works well in one place may not work well in another. In any piece of writing you do, you may blend various methods of development (and forms of academic writing: see Part Three), or you may employ only one or two in an essay, depending upon your subject, purpose, audience, and voice.

8

Analytic Thinking and Writing

Look at this drawing by Pieter Brueghel the Elder, *The Painter and the Connoisseur* (circa 1565), and jot down your responses to the questions that follow.

ANALYZING A DRAWING

1. One figure is given considerably more space than the other. What might this fact imply?
2. What is the painter doing (besides painting)?
3. What is the connoisseur doing?
4. What does the face of each figure tell you about the character of each of the men? The figures are physically close; are they mentally close? How do you know?

Now consider this brief discussion of the picture.

> The painter, standing in front of the connoisseur and given more than two-thirds of the space, dominates this picture. His hand holds the brush with which he creates, while the connoisseur's hand awkwardly fumbles for money in his purse. The connoisseur apparently is pleased with the picture he is looking at, for he is buying it, but his parted lips give him a stupid expression and his eyeglasses imply defective vision. In contrast, the painter looks away from the picture and fixes his eyes on the model (reality) or, more likely, on empty space, his determined expression suggesting that he possesses an imaginative vision beyond his painting and perhaps even beyond earthly reality.

The author of this paragraph uses analysis to interpret the drawing, to discover its meaning. The paragraph does not simply tell us that the picture shows two people close together; it separates the parts of the picture, pointing out that the two figures form a contrast. It explains why one figure gets much more space than the other, and it explains what the contrasting gestures and facial expressions imply. The writer of the comment has "read" or interpreted the drawing by examining how the parts function, that is, how they relate to the whole.

ANALYZING TEXTS

Most of what you read and write in most of your courses is analytical: you read of the various causes of a revolution, of the effects of inflation, or of the relative importance of heredity and environment; you write about the meaning of a short story or painting, the causes and effects of poverty, the strengths and weaknesses of some proposed legislative action. And much (though not all) of this reading and writing is based on the analysis of *texts*. The word *text* derives from the Latin for "woven" (as in textile), and it has come to refer not only to words stitched together into sentences (whether novels or letters or advertisements), but also to all kinds of objects of interpretation: films, paintings, music videos, even food on a plate.

For that reason, much—but not all—of our discussion in this chapter focuses on textual analysis. Of course writing an analysis of a drawing differs from writing an interpretation of a poem (or, for that matter, a legislative proposal or an argument about the causes of inflation). Nevertheless, we believe that there are important similarities between these processes. In all cases, the reader must be able to envision the object under scrutiny, so the writer must summarize it or describe it precisely. In all cases, the writer must be able to explain what the text *means,* so the writer must pay close attention to its details, to its parts—to how they work, to what they imply or suggest, to their relationship to each other and to the whole.

CLASSIFYING AND THINKING

Analysis (literally a separating into parts) is not only the source of much writing that seeks to explain; it is also a way of thinking, a way of arriving at conclusions (general statements), a way of discovering meaning. One form of analytic thinking, classifying, is, at its simplest, an adult version of sorting out cards with pictures of baseball players on them. Now, if you have identical items—for instance, one hundred bricks to unload from a truck—you can't sort them; you can only divide them for easier handling into groups of, say, ten, or into armloads. But if the items vary in some way you can sort them. You can, for example, put socks into one drawer, underwear into another, trousers or dresses in a closet—all in an effort to make life a little more manageable.

Thinking, if broadly defined, includes intuitions and even idle reveries, but much of what we normally mean by analysis requires classifying things into categories and seeing how the categories relate to each other. When you think about choosing courses, for example, you classify the courses by subject matter, or by degree of difficulty ("Since I'm taking two hard courses, I ought to look for an easy one"), or by the times at which they are offered, or by the degree to which they interest you, or by their merit as determined through the grapevine. When you classify, you establish categories by breaking down the curriculum into parts, and by then putting into each category courses that significantly resemble each other but that are not identical. We need categories: we simply cannot get through life treating every object as unique.

In classifying, the categories must be established on a single basis of division: you cannot classify dogs into purebreds and small dogs, for example, for some dogs belong in both categories. You must classify them into consistent, coordinate categories. Let's pause to look more thoroughly at the world of canine classification. In the early days of kennel clubs and dog shows, says a spokesperson for the Canadian Kennel Club, it became necessary to gather the many and varied breeds of purebred dogs into some sort of order for the purpose of comparison and record keeping. The most logical method of doing so was grouping based on tasks for which they were best suited. Today's kennel club lists seven groups that reflect the "original purpose" common to each dog in that group:

- Group 1, sporting dogs—pointing breeds, game flushers, setters, and retrievers
- Group 2, hounds—hunters with a keen sense of smell and sight
- Group 3, working—guard dogs and draft workers
- Group 4, terriers—hunters of vermin and bred to go into burrows
- Group 5, toys—pets and lap dogs for companionship
- Group 6, non-sporting—dogs that perform a variety of tasks
- Group 7, herding—livestock herder (primarily cattle and sheep)

Non-sporting! What a category. Why not non-working or non-hound? And things start getting complex when you consider size. Off the top of your head, would you feel more comfortable grouping a standard poodle with the non-sporting Dalmatian or over in lap-dog country with its toy poodle relatives?[2] Still, the classifications are by now established. Every purebred must fit into one and only one, and thus every purebred can be measured against all of the dogs that in significant ways are thought to resemble it.

Examples of Classifying

If you think about examinations—especially if you think about them with the aid of pencil and paper—you may find that they can serve several purposes. Examinations may test knowledge, intelligence, or skill in taking examinations; or they may stimulate learning. Therefore, if you wish to discuss what constitutes a good examination, you must decide what purpose an examination *should* serve. Possibly you will decide that in a particular course an examination should chiefly stimulate learning, but that it should also test the ability to reason. To arrive at a reasonable conclusion, a conclusion worth sharing and, if need be, defending, you must first recognize and sort out the several possibilities.

Often the keenest analytic thinking considers not only what parts are in the whole, but also what is *not* there—what is missing in relation to a larger context that we can imagine. For example, if we analyze the women in the best-known fairy tales, we find that most are either sleeping beauties or wicked stepmothers. These categories are general: "sleeping beauties" includes all passive women valued only for their appearance, and "wicked stepmothers" includes Cinderella's cruel older sisters. (Fairy godmothers form another category, but they are not human beings.) Analysis helps us to discover the almost total absence of resourceful, productive women. ("Almost total," rather than "total," because there are a few resourceful women in fairy tales, such as Gretel.) You might begin a thoughtful essay with a general statement to this effect and then support the statement with an analysis of "Cinderella," "Little Red Riding Hood," and "Snow White."

 **AMY WILLARD CROSS**

Amy Willard Cross was born in the United States and currently lives in Canada. She has written for several Canadian magazines, including Chatelaine.

Life in the Stopwatch Lane

1   If time is money, the rates have skyrocketed and you probably can't afford it. North Americans are suffering a dramatic time shortage since demand greatly exceeds supply. In fact, a recent survey revealed that people lost about 10 hours of leisure per week between 1973 and 1987. Maybe you were too busy to notice.

---

[1]The kennel club categories, though, are perhaps a bit more precise than those given in an old Chinese encyclopedia, whose fourteen classifications of dogs (according to Jorge Luis Borges) include "those belonging to the Emperor," "stuffed dogs," "free-running dogs," "those getting madly excited," "those that look like flies from the distance," and "others."

2   Losing that leisure leaves a piddling 16.6 hours to do whatever you want, free of work, dish-washing or car-pooling. In television time, that equals a season of 13 *thirtysomething* episodes, plus $3^{1}/_{2}$ reruns. Hardly enough time to write an autobiography or carry on an affair.

3   How has replacing free time with more billable hours affected society? It has created a new demographic group: the Busy Class—who usurped the Leisure Class. Easy to recognize, members of the Busy Class constantly cry to anyone listening, "I'm soooooo busy." So busy they can't call their mother or find change for a panhandler. Masters of doing two things at once, they eke the most out of time. They dictate while driving, talk while calculating, entertain guests while nursing, watch the news while pumping iron. Even business melts into socializing—people earn their daily bread while they break it.

4   In fact, the Busies must make lots of bread to maintain themselves in the standard of busy-ness to which they've become accustomed. To do that, they need special, expensive stuff. Stuff like call waiting, which lets them talk to two people at once. Stuff like two-faced watches, so they can do business in two time zones at once. Neither frenzied executives nor hurried housewives dare leave the house without their "book"—leather-bound appointment calendars thick as bestsellers. Forget hi-fi's or racing cars, the new talismans of overachievers also work: coffee-makers that brew by alarm; remote-controlled ignitions; or car faxes. Yet, despite all these time-efficient devices, few people have time to spare.

5   That scarcity has changed how we measure time. Now it's being scientifically dissected into smaller and smaller pieces. Thanks to digital clocks, we know when it's 5:30 (and calculate we'll be home in three hours, eight minutes). These days lawyers can reason in 1/10th of an hour increments; they bill every six minutes. This to-the-minute precision proves time's escalating value.

6   Time was, before the advent of car phones and digital clocks, we scheduled two kinds of time: time off and work hours. Not any more. Just as the Inuit label the infinite varieties of snow, the Busy Class has identified myriad subtleties of free time and named them. Here are some textbook examples of the new faces of time:

7   *Quality time.* For those working against the clock, the quality of time spent with loved ones supposedly compensates for quantity. This handy concept absolves guilt as quickly as rosary counting. So careerist couples dine à deux once a fortnight. Parents bond by reading kids a story after nanny fed and bathed them. When pressed for time, nobody wastes it by fighting about bad breath or unmade beds. People who spend quality time with each other view their relationships through rose-coloured glasses. And knowing they've created perfect personal lives lets the Busy Class work even harder—guilt-free.

8   *Travel time.* With an allowance of 16.6 hours of fun, the Busy Class watches time expenditures carefully. Just like businesses do while making bids, normal people calculate travel time for leisure activities. If two tram rides away, a friendly squash game loses out. One time-efficient woman even formulated a mathematical theorem: fun per mile quotient. Before accepting any social invitation, she adds up travel costs, figures out the time spent laughing, drinking and eating. If the latter exceeds the former, she accepts. It doesn't matter who asks.

9   *Downtime.* Borrowed from the world of heavy equipment and sleek computers, downtime is a professional-sounding word meaning the damn thing broke, wait around until it's fixed. Translated into real life, downtime counts as neither work nor play, but a maddening no-man's land where nothing happens!

Like lining up for the ski-lift, or commuting without a car phone, or waiting a while for the mechanic's diagnosis. Beware: people who keep track of their downtime probably indulge in less than 16 hours of leisure.

10   *Family time.* In addition to 60-hour weeks, aerobics and dinner parties, some people make time for their children. When asked to brunch, a young couple will reply, "We're sorry but that's our family time." A variant of quality time, it's Sunday afternoon between lunch and the Disney Hour when nannies frequent Filipino restaurants. In an effort to entertain their children without exposure to sex and violence, the family attends craft fairs, animated matinees or tree-tapping demonstrations. There, they converge with masses of family units spending time alone with the kids. After a noisy, sticky afternoon, parents gladly punch the clock come Monday.

11   *Quiet time.* Overwhelmed by their schedules, some people try to recapture the magic of childhood when they watched clouds for hours on end. Sophisticated grown-ups have rediscovered the quiet time of kindergarten days. They unplug the phone (not the answering machine), clutch a book and try not to think about work. But without teachers to enforce it, quiet doesn't last. The clock ticks too loudly. As a computer fanatic said, after being entertained at 16 megahertz, sitting still to watch a sunset pales by comparison.

12   As it continues to increase in value, time will surely divide into even smaller units. And people will share only the tiniest amounts with each other. Hey, brother, can you spare a minute? Got a second? A nanosecond?

Amy Willard Cross examines the trend of dividing time into smaller and smaller units, which results in dividing and classifying time into various categories of non-work time. Using structure to reinforce content, this author includes subheadings for the classifications: there is "quality time," "travel time," "downtime," "family time," and "quiet time," which she implies are only some examples of a larger categorization. She also divides and classifies groups of people. Cross's sardonic tone reflects her point that "spare time" has diminished because the technological innovations that should add, not detract from, "leisure time" have actually added too much efficiency to people's lives.

CAUSE AND EFFECT

Analytical reasoning from cause to effect is also often expected in academic discussions, which are much given to questions such as the following:

What effect did the Riel Rebellion have on settlement on the Prairies?

What is the effect of labelling on mental patients?

What is the function of Mrs. Linde in Ibsen's *A Doll's House*?

How does the death penalty affect jury verdicts?

Why do people enjoy horror movies?

What are the effects of atrocity myths?

Let's look at the following short essay by Michael Ignatieff, which addresses the last question on the above list with an argument that uses cause and effect primarily but also comparison and example.

 **MICHAEL IGNATIEFF**

Michael Ignatieff writes fiction and non-fiction, for which he has won the Governor General's Literary Award and the Gelber Prize, and has been nominated for the Booker Prize. Born and raised in Canada, he has taught at Harvard, Cambridge, and Oxford universities, the University of London, and the London School of Economics; been awarded seven honorary doctorates; and been a commentator and host for the BBC and the CBC. He is currently a Liberal member of parliament.

Myth and Malevolence

1   In the summer of 1992, when Serbian militias were viciously "cleansing" the Muslim villages of southeastern Bosnia, journalists asked the Serbs of Foca and Goradze why people they had lived with for centuries deserved such treatment. The Serbs seemed surprised by the question. Didn't everybody know that Muslims killed Serbian children and floated their crucified bodies down the river Drina? Several old women, doing their washing by the riverbank, swore they had seen them with their own eyes.

2   No one could persuade these old women otherwise. They were in the grip of one of the oldest atrocity myths in Western culture. The Romans accused the early Christians of just this sort of child sacrifice. When the Christians got a state church of their own, they turned the same myth against the Jews. The earliest recorded accusation occurred in the English town of Norwich in 1144, when the Jewish community was accused of killing a Christian child and draining his blood for use in satanic rituals. In all its apparitions, the tortured or crucified child surfaces, like an image in a nightmare, whenever an ethnic or religious majority has to read into its subconscious to justify the persecution of a minority. As the millennium ends, Muslim Europeans find themselves the target of a myth that, when the millennium began, was a blood libel against the Jews.

3   Myths endure because they offer repertoires of moral justification. Myths turn crime into fate and murder into necessity; they both justify atrocity and perpetuate it. The Balkan wars have been among the most inhuman in an inhuman century. Intrastate wars, the war of village against village, neighbor against neighbor, will usually engender more atrocities than the impersonal wars between states. Small wonder that the three urban communities most thoroughly destroyed by the Balkan conflict—Vukovar, Mostar, and Sarajevo—had the highest rates of ethnic intermarriage.

4   It is as if the very intermingling of the combatants forced these communities into displays of terror and destruction to demarcate the territories and values they were defending. What Serbs once shared with their neighbors had to be defiled, so that sharing would never be possible again. Atrocities draw the innocent bystander into collusion with the guilty perpetrator and engrave the myth of inhuman otherness in the subconscious of both sides.

5   This myth of inhuman otherness does such violence to the acts that it can gain a foothold only if ordinary people on every side can be made to forget that in reality their differences are small. It is nonsense to call the Balkan communi-

ties ethnic groups at all. Intermarriage down the centuries has blurred ethnic differences to the vanishing point; religious differences have collapsed in the general secularization of Balkan culture; modernization has converged material aspirations toward the same Mercedes cars and Swiss-style chalets. Nationalism in the Balkans is what Freud called the narcissism of minor difference. Lies, demagoguery, and propaganda have turned permeable identities into bunkered mentalities. Serbs and Croats who once shared the same language are being told that Serbian and Croatian are as distinct as the Cyrillic and Latin scripts in which they are written. Nationalistic narcissism is a hothouse for atrocity myths that blossom forth in order to portray each community as the blameless victim of the motiveless malevolence of the other.

6   In the Balkans these myths collapse time. The past can never safely become the past. It remains immobilized in a neurotic, hysterical present. The very name each group gives the other locks both sides into a past that is a nightmare. Serbs call all Croatian fighters Ustase, the fascist minority of World War II Croatia. Croatians call the Serbs Chetniks, the fascist minority on the other side. The naming process is intended to visit the sins of the fathers upon the sons forever.

7   Renaming enemies rewrites the past so that their very identity can be expunged from history. The Bosnian Serbs assert that the Muslims don't really exist, since they are renegade Serbs who converted to Islam in order to gain land and privileges from their Ottoman overlords. Thorvald Stoltenberg, the former U.N. mediator, has been heard to repeat this preposterous fable. In other ways too the outside world ignorantly colludes in Balkan mythmaking. The Western fantasy that all Muslims are fanatics and all Islam is fundamentalist underwrites the Serbs' myth that they, like the Christian host turning back the Turks at the gates of Vienna in 1683, are holding the Islamic tide from Europe's southern flank.

8   There is no easy awakening from the nightmare of their history. But outsiders can do something to break the demonic hold of myth. War-crimes tribunals and human-rights commissions are not the irrelevance they seem. Their function is to plunge the burning coals of myth into the icy bath of evidence; to hold the remaining ember of truth aloft for all to see; to show that history never justifies crime; and to teach people that they need truth as much as they need peace, and can't hope to get one without the other.

Now let's analyze this short essay. In the first paragraph Ignatieff introduces his topic through an example, and he indicates in the first sentence what his essay is about by drawing attention to the use of the euphemistic word *cleansing*, which means genocide, by placing it in quotation marks. At the beginning of the third paragraph, Ignatieff clearly states his argument: "Myths endure because they offer repertoires of moral justification. Myths turn crime into fate and murder into necessity; they both justify atrocity and perpetuate it." He has prepared us for this argument through the title of his essay, through the example in the first paragraph, and through placing these myths in a historical context in the second paragraph. He implies that the horror and the enduring nature of this kind of destructive stereotyping is what makes this kind of myth-making worth writing about.

The cause-and-effect essay or the method of cause and effect within an essay may be structured as listing the causes and then discussing the effects or blending the two together. Ignatieff has chosen the latter method in the body of his essay. Focusing primarily on a modern example of an ongoing atrocity myth, he explains both the causes and effects together, such as in paragraph 4 where he states that one of the causes of this atrocity myth is to renew the hatred between the groups so that intermingling will not be possible again and so that everyone gets drawn into the violence and destruction. What other cause-and-effect relationships does Ignatieff raise? In the larger context of the whole piece, Ignatieff has stated the cause of the atrocity myth and its need to be ingrained "in the subconscious of both sides," and the possible effect of outside intervention in the form of war-crimes tribunals and human-rights commissions.

Your writing course may offer you some practice in writing cause-and-effect analyses; other academic courses, especially in the sciences and social sciences, almost certainly will. You can also practise by noticing patterns as you read assigned academic texts as well as newspapers and magazines. Make it a habit to underline or highlight such phrases as *The three causes everyone agrees on were . . .*, or *Among the most notable effects . . .*, and then number the causes and effects in the margins of the text. When you are studying for a quiz or an exam, make lists of causes and effects; make lists too when your writing calls for an analysis of cause and effect. In the essays at the end of this chapter, see where you can spot this pattern of thinking and writing.

ANALYSIS AND DESCRIPTION

In Chapter 10 we discuss in more detail some strategies for writing effective descriptions. But it is worth noting here that passages of description are commonly used in essays to support analysis. In the preceding cause-and-effect essay, for example, Ignatieff opens his piece with a description of journalists questioning the Serbs of Foca and Goradze. And, in the classification essay before that, Cross describes "the Busy Class." Both of these essays are primarily analytical; reading them, we share the writers' thoughts, but these thoughts are not the random and fleeting notions of reverie. They have been organized for us, and the description is employed to draw in the reader and to support and exemplify the writers' points.

Description, however, is not analysis, and if you are asked to analyze a painting for your art history class or an advertisement for your media studies class, it will not be enough simply to describe the thing in detail. It may be useful, then, to make some distinctions between the two processes, *description* and *analysis*. Cross *describes* "the Busy Class" when she writes that they "dictate while driving, talk while calculating, entertain guests while nursing, watch the news while pumping iron" and that "lawyers can reason in 1/10th of an hour increments; they bill every six minutes." These statements do not offer inferences; they do not offer evaluations (although of course Cross's diction and tone and the context of the essay do influence our responses to these descriptions). Cross goes on, though, to say, "In fact, the Busies must make lots of bread to maintain themselves in the standard of busy-ness to which they've become accustomed. To do that, they need special, expensive stuff," and "This to-the-minute precision proves time's escalating value." In both of these excerpts she is making an inference: she is telling her readers what the descriptions *imply* or *suggest*, and as such she is *analyzing*.

Topics for Critical Thinking and Writing

1. Look closely at Wally Houn's photograph of the older man sitting under a photograph of himself as a younger man. What would you say about Houn's photograph if you were to describe it for a person who had not seen it?
2. What does Houn's photograph mean? What does it imply or suggest about its subject? You might begin to answer this question by considering how you respond to the man it represents and by comparing the "two" men.

This photograph by Wally Houn was part of the Ontario Art Gallery exhibition *Exposure: Canadian Contemporary Photographers* in November 1975. (Reproduced by permission of Wally Houn.)

3. *How* does the photograph mean? How does it make its point? Consider the angles of the heads, the attire, and the facial expressions of the older man and the younger one as well as the beam of light separating them and the use of light and shadow.
4. In an essay of two to three pages, describe and analyze Houn's photograph.

A NOTE ON THE USE OF SUMMARY IN THE ANALYTIC ESSAY

When a writer analyzes an image, the first task is to describe it, make it present to the reader. When a writer analyzes a written text, she must do something similar, and that is provide enough information about the text at hand to enable a reader to follow the discussion. This information often appears in the form of a brief *summary* at or near the beginning of an essay. The word *summary* is related to *sum*, the total something adds up to. (We say "adds *up* to" because the Greeks and Romans added upward, and wrote the total at the top.)

A summary is a condensation or abridgement; it briefly gives the reader the gist of a longer work. Or, to use an analogy, it boils down the longer work, resembling the longer work as a bouillon cube resembles a bowl of soup. For example, the student who wrote about "The Myth of Canadian Diversity," reprinted in Chapter 1 of this book, is *summarizing* when she writes that the editorial "argues that our differences are not as great as we like to think and that we, as Canadians, have more in common than not." She is *summarizing* because she is briefly reporting what the author of the piece said, and of course her readers need to know what the author of "The Myth of Canadian Diversity" said before they can make sense of what she'll say about it. On the other hand, she is *analyzing* when she writes, "By the last paragraph, the writer makes it clear why he or she criticizes the foundations of Canadians' sense of nation: the writer wants the reader to focus on what draws us together as Canadians rather than what divides us." In this sentence, the student writer is not reporting *what* the editorial writer wrote but is explaining *the implications* of the editorial piece.

Your writing about other writing will be for the most part analytic, but for the benefit of the reader, it will probably include an occasional sentence or even a paragraph summarizing some of your reading. (And part of your preparation for writing your essay may involve writing summaries as you take notes on the reading you are going to analyze.) Needless to say, if the assignment calls for an analysis, it will not be enough simply to write a summary. (You will find a detailed explanation of how to write a summary on pages 284–86.)

COMPARING

We began this chapter with a brief analysis of a Brueghel drawing. We *compared* Brueghel's handling of the two figures: the amount of space each figure occupied, their activities, their facial expressions, the directions of their gaze; we thereby arrived at an interpretation of the *meaning* of Brueghel's drawing. We might say that the drawing invites the comparison, and in so doing communicates Brueghel's understanding of the artist's vision or of the value of art.

Writers, too, often use comparisons to explain a concept or idea or to arrive at a judgment or conclusion. As in drawing or painting, the point of a comparison in writing is not simply to list similarities or differences but to explain something, to illuminate what the similarities and differences add up to. What the comparison—or analysis—adds up to is sometimes referred to as a *synthesis*, which is a combination of separate elements that form a coherent whole.

The following paragraph is from an essay titled "England, Your England," written during World War II by George Orwell. Notice how Orwell clarifies our understanding of one kind of military march, the Nazi goose-step, by calling attention to how it differs from the march used by English soldiers. Notice, too, the point of his comparison, which he makes clear in his second sentence and which resonates throughout the comparison.

One rapid but fairly sure guide to the social atmosphere of a country is the parade-step of its army. A military parade is really a kind of ritual dance, something like a ballet, expressing a certain philosophy of life. The goose-step, for instance, is one of the most horrible sights in the world, far more terrifying than a dive-bomber. It is simply an affirmation of naked power; contained in it, quite consciously and intentionally, is the vision of a boot crashing down on a face. Its ugliness is part of its essence, for what it is saying is "Yes, I *am* ugly, and you daren't laugh at me," like the bully who makes faces at his victim. Why is the goose-step not used in England? There are, heaven knows, plenty of army officers who would be only too glad to introduce some such thing. It is not used because the people in the street would laugh. Beyond a certain point, military display is only possible in countries where the common people dare not laugh at the army. The Italians adopted the goose-step at about the time when Italy passed definitely under German control, and, as one would expect, they do it less well than the Germans. The Vichy government, if it survives, is bound to introduce a stiffer parade-ground discipline into what is left of the French army. In the British army the drill is rigid and complicated, full of memories of the eighteenth century, but without definite swagger; the march is merely a formalised walk. It belongs to a society which is ruled by the sword, no doubt, but a sword which must never be taken out of the scabbard.

—GEORGE ORWELL

Organizing Short Comparisons

An essay may be devoted entirely to a comparison, say of two kinds of business organizations. An essay may include only a paragraph or two of comparison as one method of development—for example, explaining something unfamiliar by comparing it to something familiar. Let's spend a moment discussing how to organize a paragraph that makes a comparison—though the same principles can be applied to entire essays.

The first part may announce the topic, the next part may discuss one of the two items being compared, and the last part may discuss the other. We call this method *blocking* (sometimes known as *lumping*), because it presents one item in a block, and then the other in another block. Thus Orwell says all that he wishes to say about the goose-step in one block, and then says what he wishes to say about the British parade-step in another block. But in making a comparison a writer may use a different method, which we call *alternating* (sometimes known as *splitting*). The discussion of the two items may run throughout the paragraph, the writer perhaps devoting alternate sentences to each. Because almost all writing is designed to help the reader see what the writer has in mind, it may be especially useful here to illustrate this second structure, alternating, with a discussion of visible distinctions. The following comparison of a Japanese statue of a Buddha with a Chinese statue of a bodhisattva (a slightly lower spiritual being, dedicated to saving humankind) shows how a comparison can run throughout a paragraph.

The Buddha sits erect and austere, in the lotus position (legs crossed, each foot with the sole upward on the opposing thigh), in full control of his body. In contrast, the bodhisattva sits in a languid, sensuous posture known as "royal ease," the head pensively tilted downward, one knee elevated, one leg hanging down. The carved folds of the Buddha's garments, in keeping with his erect posture, are severe, forming a highly disciplined pattern, whereas the bodhisattva's garments hang naturalistically. Both figures are spiritual but the Buddha is remote, constrained, and austere; the bodhisattva is accessible, relaxed, and compassionate.

In effect the structure of the paragraph is this:

the Buddha (posture)
the bodhisattva (posture)
the Buddha (garments)
the bodhisattva (garments)
the Buddha and the bodhisattva (synthesis)

Sakyamuni Buddha.
Wood, 85 cm; Japanese,
late tenth century.

Notice, again, that although this paragraph on two images is chiefly devoted to offering an analysis, it also offers a *synthesis*. That is, the analytic discussion of the Buddha calls attention to the posture and garments, but it also brings these elements together, seeing the figure as "remote, constrained, austere." Similarly, the discussion of the bodhisattva calls attention to the posture and garments, and synthesizes these, or brings them together, by characterizing the image as "accessible, relaxed, compassionate." And notice, finally, that the paragraph brings the two images together, characterizing both as "spiritual."

Whether in any given piece of writing you should compare by blocking or by alternating will depend largely on your purpose and on the complexity of the material. We cannot even offer the rule that alternating is good for brief, relatively obvious comparisons, blocking for longer, more complex ones, though such a rule usually works. We can, however, give some advice:

Bodhisattva Kuan Yin. Wood, 144 cm; Chinese, twelfth century.

1. If you alternate, in rereading your draft

   - *imagine your reader,* and ask yourself if it is likely that this reader can keep up with the back-and-forth movement. Make sure (by the topic sentence and perhaps a summary sentence at the end) that the larger picture is not obscured by the zigzagging;
   - *do not leave any loose ends.* Make sure that if you call attention to points 1, 2, and 3 in *X,* you mention all of them (not just 1 and 2) in *Y.*

2. If you block, do not simply comment first on *X* and then on *Y.*

   - *Let your reader know where you are going,* probably by means of an introductory sentence or two;
   - *Don't be afraid in the second half to remind your reader of the first half.* It is legitimate, and even desirable, to relate the second half of the comparison to the first half. A comparison organized by blocking will not break into two separate halves if the second half develops by reminding the reader how it differs from the first half.

Longer Comparisons

Now let's think about a comparison that extends through two or three paragraphs. If you are comparing the indoor play (for instance, board games or play with toys) and the sports of girls with those of boys, you can, for example, devote one paragraph to the indoor play of girls, a second paragraph to the sports of girls, a third to the indoor play of boys, and a fourth to the sports of boys. If you are thinking in terms of comparing girls and boys, such an organization uses blocks, girls first and then boys (with a transition such as "Boys on the other hand . . ."). Or, you might alternate, writing four paragraphs along these lines:

> indoor play of girls
> indoor play of boys
> sports of girls
> sports of boys

Or you might organize the material into two paragraphs:

> play and sports of girls
> play and sports of boys

There is no rule, except that the organization and the point of the comparison be clear.

Consider these paragraphs from the essay "Eat Your Hearts Out Cinephiles, The Tube Is Where It's At" by John Haslett Cuff, comparing movies and television shows. The writer's thesis in the essay is that television is superior to movies in quality, information, and relevance. After beginning the essay with a narrative of his own experiences growing up with television and movies and outlining his shift in preference from the latter to the former, he provides an overview of his subjective impressions and then he moves into more qualitative reasoning (the overview and reasoning are reprinted here). Notice that whether a paragraph is chiefly about television or chiefly about movies (and chiefly about the author's own preferences or chiefly about reasoned arguments), he keeps us in mind of the overall point: the reasons why television is better than movies.

1   The obvious advantage television has over movies is its accessibility and the familial intimacy it has established with its audience after decades in the home of virtually every class of person. Even without TV's unquestioned rule as the primary provider of news and information, the culture of television drama and comedy is clearly superior to most of the $30-million-plus (the budget of an average studio movie) offerings available in cinemas.

2   Any five episodes of *Seinfeld, Frasier,* or *Roseanne* are arguably funnier and more meticulously crafted than a Jim Carrey, Robin Williams, or Eddie Murphy blockbuster, not to mention more sophisticated and relevant. The same comparison can be made of a top-flight TV drama such as *NYPD Blue* or *ER*. On an ongoing basis, these fine shows deliver more emotional punch and subtlety, as well as character and plot development, than almost any $100-million-grossing action flick.

3   While this is true even of some of the most commercial network shows, the quality gap is even more marked when imported and specialty television is brought into the mix. There is simply no equivalent in contemporary, mainstream moviemaking to the oeuvre of a Dennis Potter or Alan Bleasdale, British TV writers who make most movies look like puerile drivel.

4   But these are highly subjective, qualitative comparisons and television is also superior in other significant and quantifiable ways. Most obviously, network television produces more entertainment for much less money than the Hollywood studios. Carrey's payday for a 90-minute movie would almost finance a whole season (22 hours) of prime-time TV drama.

5   Culturally, television is richer in ideas and issues and in its representation of society. Just look at the number and range of roles for women in television, and compare them with the paucity of good parts for women of any age in the movies. There are no film-actress superstars who can open a film and command the money that such muscle-bound hacks as Sly Stallone or Arnold Schwarzenegger routinely earn.

6   Yet television abounds with women stars, young and middle-aged, fat and anorexic. Many of the most enduringly popular sitcoms, such as *Roseanne, Murphy Brown, Grace Under Fire, Ellen,* and *Caroline in the City,* dominate the ratings, and TV shows employ award-winning movie actresses such as Christine Lahti, Madeline Kahn, and Mercedes Ruehl in increasing numbers.

7   Television engenders loyalty and empathy with its characters in a way that movies don't, because over the course of a season viewers develop relationships with TV characters, sharing in their development in a way that is impossible in one-off movie fare. Such characters as Dr. Frasier Crane have been visiting us in our homes for years, and we have watched them age through story lines that reflect changes in fashion, society, and even politics.

8   While television has produced a rich mix of exceptional dramas over the past decade, movies have all but abandoned them, preferring high-octane, live-action cartoons instead. Perhaps the most important difference is that TV writers are forced to be more creative with language, plot, and even sex than the creators of movies. Since TV writers are not allowed to use profanity, nudity, or violence with the graphic abandon of their movie peers, the resulting drama is often more powerful, suggestive, and complex.

The first paragraph reproduced here directly states the author's main thesis about the superiority of television over movies and focuses on the point that television is more accessible and intimate (a point he returns to six paragraphs later).

The second paragraph discusses the craft involved in producing television shows and provides examples (a point he returns to six paragraphs later), but he also refers to movie stars and blockbuster movies to reinforce the comparison. The rest of the paragraphs in this excerpt go on to discuss quality, cost, and representation. In each paragraph Haslett Cuff mentions both television and movies, but even with this sort of see-saw alternating structure, we never lose sight of his thesis.

Ways of Organizing an Essay Devoted to a Comparison

Let's now talk about organizing a comparison or contrast that runs through an entire essay, say a comparison between two political campaigns or between the characters in two novels. Remember, first of all, that one writes such a comparison not as an exercise, but in order to make a point, let's say to demonstrate and explain the superiority of *X* over *Y*.

Probably your first thoughts, after making some jottings, will be to block rather than to alternate, that is, to discuss one half of the comparison and then to go on to the second half. We will discuss this useful method of organization in a moment, but here we want to point out that many instructors and textbooks disapprove of such an organization, arguing that the essay too often breaks into two parts and that the second part involves a good deal of repetition of categories set up in the first part. They prefer alternating. Let's say you are comparing the narrator of *Huckleberry Finn* with the narrator of *The Catcher in the Rye* in order to show that despite superficial similarities, they are very different and that the difference is partly the difference between the nineteenth century and the twentieth. An organization often recommended is something like this:

1. first similarity (the narrator and his quest)
    a. Huck
    b. Holden
2. second similarity (the corrupt world surrounding the narrator)
    a. society in *Huckleberry Finn*
    b. society in *The Catcher in the Rye*
3. first difference (degree to which the narrator fulfills his quest and escapes from society)
    a. Huck's plan to "light out" to the frontier
    b. Holden's breakdown

And so on, for as many additional differences as seem relevant. Here is another way of alternating and organizing a comparison:

1. first point: the narrator and his quest
    a. similarities between Huck and Holden
    b. differences between Huck and Holden
2. second point: the corrupt world
    a. similarities between the worlds in *Huck* and *The Catcher*
    b. differences between the worlds in *Huck* and *The Catcher*
3. third point: degree of success
    a. similarities between Huck and Holden
    b. differences between Huck and Holden

But a comparison need not employ either of these methods of alternating. There is even the danger that an essay employing either of them may not come into focus until the essayist stands back from the seven-layer cake and announces, in the concluding paragraph, that the odd layers taste better. In your preparatory thinking you may want to make comparisons in pairs, but you must come to some conclusions about what these add up to before writing the final version. The final version should not duplicate the thought processes; rather, it should be organized so as to make the point clearly and effectively. *The point of the essay is not to list pairs of similarities or differences, but to illuminate a topic by making thoughtful comparisons.* Although in a long essay you cannot postpone a discussion of the second half of the comparison until page 30, in an essay of, say, fewer than ten pages, you can set forth half of the comparison and then, in the light of what you have already said, discuss the second half. True, an essay that uses blocking will break into two unrelated parts if the second half makes no use of the first or fails to modify it, but the essay will hang together if the second half looks back to the first half and calls attention to differences that the new material reveals.

The danger of organizing the essay into two unrelated blocks can be avoided if in formulating your thesis you remember that the point of a comparison is to call attention to the unique features of something by holding it up against something similar but significantly different. If the differences are great and apparent, a comparison is a waste of effort. ("Blueberries are different from elephants. Blueberries do not have trunks. And elephants do not grow on bushes.") Indeed, a comparison between essentially and evidently unlike things can only obscure, for by making the comparison the writer implies there are significant similarities, and readers can only wonder why they do not see them. The essays that do break into two halves are essays that make *un*instructive comparisons: the first half tells the reader five things about baseball, the second half tells the reader five unrelated things about football.

 ## A Checklist for Revising Comparisons

- ✔ Is the point of the comparison—your reason for making it—clear?
- ✔ Do you cover all significant similarities and differences?
- ✔ Is the comparison readable, that is, is it clear and yet not tediously mechanical?
- ✔ Is blocking or is alternating (see page 157) the best way to make this comparison?
- ✔ If you are offering a value judgment, is it fair? Have you overlooked weaknesses in your preferred subject and strengths in your less preferred subject?

ANALYZING A PROCESS

Popular writing offers many examples of the form of writing known as process analysis. Newspaper articles explain how to acquire a home aquarium or how to "detail" your car to improve its resale value; magazine articles explain how to begin a program of weight training or how to make a safe exit in an airplane

emergency. The requirements for writing such an article, sometimes called a
directive process analysis, can be simply stated. The writer must:

Know the material thoroughly.

Keep his or her audience in mind.

Set forth the steps clearly, usually in chronological order.

Define unfamiliar terms.

In addition, in the introductory paragraph or in the conclusion, writers often
express their pleasure in the process or their sense of the utility or value of the
process. But such comments must be brief, must not interrupt the explanation
of the process, and must not gush. Surely everyone has one such article to write,
and you may be asked to write one.

Explaining a process is common in academic writing too, though usually the
explanation is of how something happens or has happened, and it is thus sometimes called an *informative process analysis.* The writer's purpose is for the
reader to understand the process, not to perform it. You may find yourself reading
or writing about a successful election strategy or a botched military campaign.

In an exam you may explain your plan to solve a mathematical problem, or
you may explain how the imagery works in a Shakespearean sonnet. You might
write an essay on the camera techniques Hitchcock used in a sequence, or a
term paper based on your research in marine biology. Once again, you will need
to keep your reader in mind, to organize your explanation clearly and logically,
and, of course, to write with expert knowledge of your subject.

We reprint below two process analysis essays. The first, "Tennis Tips to a
Beginning Player," is a *directive process analysis* written by a student for a college writing class. The second, "It's the Portly Penguin That Gets the Girl, French
Biologist Claims" (pages 166–67), reports on a lecture that was, from the evidence, an entertaining example of an *informative process analysis.*

Two Essays Analyzing a Process

 SUSAN POPE

Tennis Tips to a Beginning Player

1   The beginning player needs tennis tips on the two basic skills of tennis: foot-

work, the way in which you move to prepare to hit the ball, and form, the way

in which you hit the ball. The most important coaching command relevant to

both skills is "Concentrate and keep your eye on the ball." As soon as you see the

opposing player hit the ball, determine where it will land and move quickly to

that spot, never taking your eyes from the ball.

2   Moving requires footwork, the most subtle and often overlooked aspect of tennis. In order to hit the ball well, you must first reach it in plenty of time. When receiving a serve you should stand behind the point where you expect to receive the ball; you may then run smoothly forward to receive it rather than tripping backwards. Stand, facing the net, with your feet shoulder width apart, knees flexed, and holding the neck of your racket lightly in your free hand. This is called the ready position. Bounce up and down on the balls of your feet and prepare to move. The instant the server makes contact with the ball, jump; this enables you to move quickly in any direction. Move laterally by jumping and sliding with your feet parallel; never cross your feet. After completing your swing, return immediately to the center of the backcourt line, assume the ready position, bounce on the balls of your feet, and prepare to move again. If you can predict where your opponent will return the ball, move to this area instead and assume your ready stance. The objective of footwork is to reach the ball quickly so you can prepare to hit it with good form.

3   Form involves the position and use of the parts of your body as you hit the ball. By the time you have reached the place where you intend to hit the ball, you should have completed your backswing, cocking your racket back until it points behind you. A short backswing resulting from not bringing your racket back soon enough will almost always result in a mistake. On the other hand, by having your racket back, you still may be able to successfully return a ball hit beyond the physical range you can usually reach.

4   As you wait for the ball with your racket held back, plant your feet firmly, shoulder width apart. If you are using forehand, your left shoulder should be pointing approximately in the direction you wish to hit the ball. Concentrate on firmly gripping the racket handle because a loose grip can result in a wobbly shot. As the ball comes toward you, bend your knees and step with your lead foot

toward the ball, the left foot when using forehand. The ball often goes in the net if you hit it standing stiffly. Keep your wrist and elbow rigid as you swing at the ball; using either of these joints for the force of your swing will cause inconsistency in your groundstrokes and promote tennis elbow. Use your arm and shoulder as a unit and twist your torso, throwing the weight of your body onto your lead foot and into your swing. Make your swing quick, snappy, and parallel to the ground. If your stroke is not level, the ball will either be scooped up into the air by a rising swing or be hit directly into the net by a swing directed toward the ground. Stroke through the ball as if it were not there and then follow through with your swing bringing the racket up over your shoulder close to your ear. You will have good control over the ball if you hit it in the middle of your racket, the sweet spot, when it is slightly in front of you. Deviations from these basic coaching instructions may cause problems with your form and weaken your groundstrokes. Try to concentrate on them while you practice until you develop an unconscious, smooth, consistent swing.

5   It requires conscious effort to pinpoint the flaws in your tennis game but often your repeated errors will indicate what you are doing incorrectly. Footwork and form, the basics of the game of tennis, may be constantly improved with attention to a few coaching tips. Most important, however, remember to "keep your eye on the ball."

 Topics for Critical Thinking and Writing

1. The essay addresses itself to a beginning player. How successful, for a beginner, would you expect these tips to be?
2. An earlier draft of the essay began with the following paragraph:

   Playing tennis requires determined practice and hard work. There are many well-known coaching suggestions which can help improve the consistency of your groundstrokes and thereby increase your confidence in your game. With practice, you can integrate these coaching prompts until you execute them automatically. Your concentration may then be focused on game strategy, such as how to capitalize on your opponent's weaknesses, and on more difficult strokes, such as the top spin.

Do you agree with the writer's decision to drop the paragraph from her revised essay? Why, or why not?

 ## ANNE HEBALD MANDELBAUM

It's the Portly Penguin That Gets the Girl, French Biologist Claims

1   The penguin is a feathered and flippered bird who looks as if he's on his way to a formal banquet. With his stiff, kneeless strut and natural dinner jacket, he moves like Charlie Chaplin in his heyday dressed like Cary Grant in his.

2   But beneath the surface of his tuxedo is a gallant bird indeed. Not only does he fast for 65 days at a time, sleep standing up, and forsake all others in a lifetime of monogamy, but the male penguin also guards, watches over, and even hatches the egg.

3   We owe much of our current knowledge of the life and loves of the king and emperor penguins to—*bien sûr*—a Frenchman. Twenty-eight-year-old Yvon Le Maho is a biophysiologist from Lyons who visited the University last week to discuss his discoveries and to praise the penguin. He had just returned from 14 months in Antarctica, where he went to measure, to photograph, to weigh, to take blood and urine samples of, to perform autopsies on—in short, to study the penguin.

4   Although his original intent had been to investigate the penguin's long fasts, Monsieur Le Maho was soon fascinated by the amatory aspect of the penguin. Copulating in April, the female produces the egg in May and then heads out to sea, leaving her mate behind to incubate the egg. The males huddle together, standing upright and protecting the 500-gram (or 1.1-pound) egg with their feet for 65 days. During this time, they neither eat nor stray: each steadfastly stands guard over his egg, protecting it from the temperatures which dip as low as –40 degrees and from the winds which whip the Antarctic wilds with gusts of 200 miles an hour.

5   For 65 days and 65 nights, the males patiently huddle over the eggs, never lying down, never letting up. Then, every year on July 14th—Bastille Day, the national holiday of France—the eggs hatch and thousands of penguin chicks are born, M. Le Maho told his amused and enthusiastic audience at the Biological Laboratories.

6   The very day the chicks are born—or, at the latest, the following day—the female penguins return to land from their two-and-a-half month fishing expedition. They clamber out of the water and toboggan along the snow-covered beaches toward the rookery and their mates. At this moment, the males begin to emit the penguin equivalent of wild, welcoming cheers—*"comme le cri de trompette,"* M. Le Maho later told the *Gazette* in an interview—"like the clarion call of the trumpet."

7   And, amid the clamorous thundering of 12,000 penguins, the female recognizes the individual cry of her mate. When she does, she begins to cry to him. The male then recognizes *her* song, lifts the newborn chick into his feathered arms, and makes a beeline for the female. Each singing, each crying, the males and females rush toward each other, slipping and sliding on the ice as they go, guided all the while by the single voice each instinctively knows.

8   The excitement soon wears thin for the male, however, who hasn't had a bite to eat in more than two months. He has done his duty and done it unflaggingly, but even penguins cannot live by duty alone. He must have food, and quickly.

9   Having presented his mate with their newborn, the male abruptly departs, heading out to sea in search of fish. The female, who has just returned from her sea-going sabbatical, has swallowed vast quantities of fish for herself and her chick. Much of what she has eaten she has not digested. Instead, this undigested food becomes penguin baby food. She regurgitates it, all soft and paplike, from her storage throat right into her chick's mouth. The chicks feed in this manner until December, when they first learn to find food on their own.

10   The penguins' reproductive life begins at age five, and the birds live about 25 years. Their fasting interests M. Le Maho because of its close similarities with fasting in human beings. And although many migratory birds also fast, their small size and indeed their flight make it almost impossible to study them closely. With the less-mobile and non-flying penguin, however, the scientist has a relatively accessible population to study. With no damage to the health of the penguin, M. Le Maho told the *Gazette,* a physiobiologist can extract blood from the flipper and sample the urine.

11   "All fasting problems are the same between man and the penguin," M. Le Maho said. "The penguin uses glucose in the brain, experiences ketosis as does man, and accomplishes gluconeogenesis, too." Ketosis is the build-up of partially burned fatty acids in the blood, usually as a result of starvation; gluconeogenesis is the making of sugar from non-sugar chemicals, such as amino acids. "The penguin can tell us a great deal about how our own bodies react to fasting conditions," M. Le Maho said.

12   He will return to Antarctica, M. Le Maho said, with the French government-sponsored *Expéditions Polaires Françaises* next December. There he will study the growth of the penguin chick, both inside the egg and after birth; will continue to study their mating, and to examine the penguin's blood sugar during fasting.

13   During the question-and-answer period following his talk, M. Le Maho was asked what the female penguin looks for in a mate. Responding, M. Le Maho drew himself up to his full five-foot-nine and said, *"La grandeur."*

 Topics for Critical Thinking and Writing

1. In three or four sentences explain the male penguin's role in hatching chicks.
2. Pick out three or four sentences that strike you as especially interesting or provoking, and explain what makes them so.
3. Addressing an audience pretty much like yourself—say, your class-mates—in three hundred to five hundred words explain a process with which you are familiar but which is likely to be new to them. Examples: how to perform a card trick, make Chinese dumplings, housebreak a puppy, refinish a table, prepare for a marathon, develop a photograph. If you choose a topic you are strongly interested in, you will probably find that an interesting voice emerges and that the process will engage the reader.

EXPLAINING AN ANALYSIS

As we have suggested, the writer of an analytic essay arrives at a thesis by asking questions and answering them, by separating the topic into parts and by see-ing—often through the use of lists and scratch outlines—how those parts relate. Or, we might say, analytic writing presupposes detective work: the writer looks over the evidence, finds some clues, pursues the trail from one place to the next, and makes the arrest. Elementary? Perhaps. Let's observe a famous detective at work by reading the following report by Dr. Watson.

 ## ARTHUR CONAN DOYLE

Arthur Conan Doyle (1859–1930), after studying medicine in Edinburgh, Scotland, became a novelist of historical fiction, science fiction, and detective fiction. This excerpt is from A Study in Scarlet, *Doyle's first Sherlock Holmes story.*

The Science of Deduction

1   "I wonder what that fellow is looking for?" I asked, pointing to a stalwart, plainly dressed individual who was walking slowly down the other side of the street, looking anxiously at the numbers. He had a large blue envelope in his hand, and was evidently the bearer of a message.

2   "You mean the retired sergeant of Marines," said Sherlock Holmes.

3   "Brag and bounce!" thought I to myself. "He knows that I cannot verify his guess."

4   The thought had hardly passed through my mind when the man whom we were watching caught sight of the number on our door, and ran rapidly across the roadway. We heard a loud knock, a deep voice below, and heavy steps ascending the stair.

5   "For Mr. Sherlock Holmes," he said, stepping into the room and handing my friend the letter.

6   Here was an opportunity of taking the conceit out of him. He little thought of this when he made that random shot. "May I ask, my lad," I said, in the bland-est voice, "what your trade may be?"

7   "Commissionaire, sir," he said, gruffly. "Uniform away for repairs."

8   "And you were?" I asked; with a slightly malicious glance at my companion.

9   "A sergeant, sir, Royal Marine Light Infantry, sir. No answer? Right, sir."

10   He clicked his heels together, raised his hand in salute, and was gone.

11   I confess that I was considerably startled by this fresh proof of the practical nature of my companion's theories. My respect for his powers of analysis increased wondrously. There still remained some lurking suspicion in my mind, however, that the whole thing was a prearranged episode, intended to dazzle me, though what earthly object he could have in taking me in was past my compre-hension. When I looked at him, he had finished reading the note, and his eyes had assumed the vacant, lack-lustre expression which showed mental abstraction.

12   "How in the world did you deduce that?" I asked.

13   "Deduce what?" said he, petulantly.

14   "Why, that he was a retired sergeant of Marines."

15   "I have no time for trifles," he answered, brusquely; then with a smile, "Excuse my rudeness. You broke the thread of my thoughts; but perhaps it is as well. So you actually were not able to see that that man was a sergeant of Marines?"

16   "No, indeed."

17   "It was easier to know it than to explain why I know it. If you were asked to prove that two and two made four, you might find some difficulty, and yet you are quite sure of the fact. Even across the street I could see a great blue anchor tattooed on the back of the fellow's hand. That smacked of the sea. He had a military carriage, however, and regulation side-whiskers. There we have the marine. He was a man with some amount of self-importance and a certain air of command. You must have observed the way in which he held his head and swung his cane. A steady, respectable, middle-aged man, too, on the face of him—all facts which led me to believe that he had been a sergeant."

18   "Wonderful!" I ejaculated.

19   "Commonplace," said Holmes, though I thought from his expression that he was pleased at my evident surprise and admiration.

Even when, as a writer, after preliminary thinking you have solved a problem—that is, focused on a topic and formulated a thesis—you are, as we have said before, not yet done. It is, alas, not enough simply to present the results of your analytic thinking to a reader who, like Dr. Watson, will surely want to know "How in the world did you deduce that?" And like Holmes, writers are often impatient; we long to say with him, "I have no time for trifles." But the real reason for our impatience is, as Holmes is quick to acknowledge, that it "was easier to know it than to explain why I know it." However, explaining to readers why or how, presenting both the reasoning that led to a thesis and the evidence that supports the reasoning, is the writer's job.

In your preliminary detective work (that is, in reading, taking notes, musing, jotting down thoughts, and writing rough drafts) some insights (perhaps including your thesis) may come swiftly, apparently spontaneously, and in random order. You may be unaware that you have been thinking analytically at all. In preparing your essay for your reader, however, you become aware, in part because *you must become aware.* You must persuade *your* Dr. Watson that what you say is not "brag and bounce." To replace your reader's natural suspicion with respect for your analysis (and for yourself), you must, we repeat, explain your reasoning in an orderly and interesting fashion, and you must present your evidence.

In the hypothetical example on pages 5–6, we showed a writer of an essay musing over the popularity of Alanis Morissette. Perhaps, we imagined, those musings were triggered by a few lines he happened to remember or to hear. The writer then began to ask himself questions, to listen to some CDs, to jot down some notes. His thesis (which turned out to be that she is popular because her songs are cynical, angry, and unapologetic with a focus on the passions of misspent youth) might have been formulated only in a late draft. But it might easily have occurred to the writer much earlier. Perhaps the thesis came almost simultaneously with the writer's first musings. But no matter when or how he arrived at a conclusion interesting enough to offer as the thesis of an essay, he still had the job of explaining to his reader (and perhaps to himself) how he had arrived at it. He probably had to examine his own thought processes carefully—replaying them in slow motion to see each part separately. He would certainly have had to marshal some evidence from available books and CDs. And he would have had to arrange the parts of his analysis and the supporting evidence clearly and interestingly to demonstrate the accuracy of his conclusion to a reader who knew less about Morissette's lyrics than he did.

To turn to another example, notice how Jeff Greenfield, on pages 177-79, solves and presents his case, one involving another famous detective. We will never know in what order the thoughts leading to his thesis came to him. But we can observe how Greenfield organized and supported his analysis. How can we do this? Elementary. By asking questions and answering them.

 ## Topics for Critical Thinking and Writing

1. It is often said that television has had a bad effect on sports. If you believe this, write an essay of five hundred to a thousand words setting forth these effects. If you don't believe this, write an essay refuting these effects.
2. An aunt has offered to buy you a subscription to *National Geographic* or *Canadian Geographic*. Compare in about 750 words the contents of the current issues, the length and depth with which they are treated, and other special features (photographs, essays, layout). Explain which magazine you prefer. (If neither magazine is of interest, try comparing *Sport* and *Sports Illustrated* or *Chatelaine* and *Canadian Living*.)

Canadian soldier Patrick Cloutier and Saskatchewan Native Brad Laroque (aka Freddie Krueger) come face to face during the standoff at the Kahnesatake reserve in Oka, Quebec, in 1990. (Canadian Press Photograph/Shaney Komulainen)

3. Write a paragraph comparing a contemporary magazine advertisement with a counterpart of the 1950s. (You can easily find ads for cars and cigarettes in old copies of magazines or microfiche newspapers in your library.) How are the appeals similar and how are they different? Include copies of the advertisements with your paper.

4. In a paragraph or two, describe and analyze a magazine advertisement that promotes gender stereotypes or one that is aimed at gay men.

5. In a paragraph or two explain why you like your favourite television show so much and why it is effective viewing pleasure.

6. Think about Haslett Cuff's point about the superiority of television over movies and, in an essay of two or three pages, describe and compare a television drama with a Hollywood blockbuster. Or, compare a Canadian film with an American mainstream movie. Or, compare television and video games.

7. The photograph shown on the previous page was taken at the Kahnesatake reserve in Oka, Quebec, during the Oka crisis of 1990. Reread the discussion of Brueghel's drawing on page 147, and then write two or three paragraphs describing and analyzing the photograph of the Canadian soldier and the Native who called himself Freddy Krueger, paying special attention to the body positions and attire of the two figures in this tense stand-off. Reading some historical information about the confrontation will help you to understand the photograph. Append a list of Works Cited to your paper and document where appropriate. (See Chapter 17, "Documenting the Research Essay.")

Francisco de Goya y Lucientes. Spanish, 1746–1828. *Woman Holding up Her Dying Lover.* Brush and grey wash, touched with brown wash. (234 x 145 mm). Gift of Frederick J. Kennedy Memorial Foundation. 1973. Courtesy, Museum of Fine Arts, Boston.

Francisco de Goya y Lucientes, *El amor y la muerte* (Love and Death), 197 x 141 mm. Courtesy, Museo del Prado, Madrid.

8. Reread the discussion of Brueghel's drawing on page 147, and of the comparison on page 157, and then study the two drawings on page 172 by Francisco Goya (1746–1828). They show a woman holding a dying lover who has fought a duel for her. The first version is a watercolour; the revision is in chalk. Write a brief essay of three to four paragraphs comparing them.

Analysis at Work

 **PAOLA BREDA**

First-year university student Paola Breda wrote this essay in response to an assignment that called for students to compare the extent to which the female protagonists are victimized by their environments in the two Canadian short stories.

Caged: Ross's "A Field of Wheat" and Munro's "Thanks for the Ride"

1   In their respective short stories "A Field of Wheat" and "Thanks for the Ride," Sinclair Ross and Alice Munro write about victimization as the horrible caging of people within their environments. The victimization of the female protagonists within these stories occurs not only because of their physical surroundings but also because of their social environments. In one sense, they are at the mercy of their physical environments, and in another sense, they are victims of the social framework in which they live. In Martha's case, women are virtually countless during the depression era Prairies, especially in terms of decision-making. For Lois, on the other hand, dead-end life in this small town is a complete and persistent form of caging. Martha, at least, has some form of hope as she realizes some value in her marital life after the hailstorm. But for Lois, there is no value; there is no hope. For both women, there is an overall sense of hopelessness and various levels of victimization from the obstacles of the physical and social environs in which they live.

2   Hostile physical environments are easily victimizing. In "A Field of Wheat," the natural setting somewhere on the Canadian Prairies is a case in point. The characters in this story, like the many wheat farmers of the Great Depression, are at the mercy of their farm, their fields, and the respective success of their crops. In the simplest of terms, working the fields is physically draining: "Martha . . . stood a moment with her shoulders strained back to ease the muscles that were sore from bending" (Ross 161). She is not even allowed to walk freely, "placing her feet edgeways between the rows of wheat to avoid trampling and crushing the stalks" (161). Martha is then faced with the completely destructive forces of a hailstorm. There is no way for her to win against the unbearable heat, the "ominous darkness" (166), and the inevitable hailstorm. These strong, almost unbeatable elements of nature lead to yet another failure of the field.

3   In "Thanks for the Ride" the physical environment is not natural, as in a field or crop, instead it is man-made. The town's socio-physical limits are in evidence everywhere, most notably in the "bare yards" (Munro 83) and the lack of life and growth: "only the hardy things like red and yellow nasturtiums, or a lilac bush with brown curled leaves, grew out of that cracked earth" (83). The few trees in the yards that were actually growing had "fine leaves greyed with dust" (83), a testament to the dusty grey ambiance. The town's main street completely lacked life: "There were no trees along the main street, but spaces of tall grass and dandelions" (83). The tackiness of Lois's house symbolizes the limits of this home and therefore the social level of the people who live within it. Even the smell of the home is notable to a visitor: "I noticed the smell in the house, the smell of stale small rooms, bedclothes, frying, washing and medicated ointments" (87). The old

woman, Lois's grandmother, also plays a role in creating the doomed and stale feeling of this town: "Some of the smell in the house seemed to come from her. It was a smell of hidden decay" (87).

4   Both writers use symbols within the physical environments of their stories to convey the theme of victimization. Ross's wheat field initially symbolizes life and vitality; the lone strands of wheat remaining after the hailstorm symbolize renewed hope; these strands are "headless" but standing defiantly (Ross 70). The poppy in the garden symbolizes youth, which can be easily taken away. Munro's grey town, decaying houses, and life-lacking main road symbolize the stagnation and hopelessness of the town's residents. These two hostile and hopeless environments and the physical symbols within them exemplify the debilitating nature and victimizing environments of these two women.

5   Not only is the physical environment a debilitating factor for these female protagonists, but it is also the social environment which is victimizing. Martha in "A Field of Wheat" is victimized by her husband and the beliefs of the society in which she lives, and in her subservient female state. She hopelessly remembers that she had wanted insurance on the crop. Even though it would have been prudent, it was not her place to suggest this; the social degradation of women during this era is blatant. Lois in "Thanks for the Ride" is not overtly and specifically denigrated by a husband, but she is victimized by the "summer boyfriends" who come up from the city for the summer, just to ride through the town, without the intention of committing to life there: "He just went around with me for the summer. That's what those guys from up the beach always do. They come down here to the dances and get a girl to go around with for the summer" (Munro 91). She hopelessly, aimlessly, and knowingly allows them to use her for the season.

6   These women have both been caged to degrees by the society in which they live. Martha accepts her state as a subservient woman, probably due to the social designations of the depression era historical period. Although she has valuable input and obviously intelligent ideas, she must live in subservience to her husband who makes all the decisions. Lois also accepts her state as a woman with an apathetic future in small-town Ontario by acquiescing to the pre-written road of high school dropout leading to a future of a dead-end job. She follows the permanent destiny of this apathetic, dehumanizing subsistence.

7   Even in the areas of love and romance, these women both lose. Martha no longer knows her husband as he was; he is no longer the man she knew. She has lost him: "for these sixteen years [she] had stood close, watching while he died—slowly, tantalizingly, as the parched wheat died" (Ross 163). There is no love, no romance. In short, there is no life with him; because of this, there is no life for her. Lois also allows herself to be shortchanged in the area of love and romance. She sets herself up for a sexual encounter, which she intuitively knows will lead nowhere. She has no illusions about the intent of these young men; she is resigned to allow it. The only scrap of happiness she has is the perfect date fantasy, which she knows must end with inevitable rejection. The permanently empty love life of Martha and Lois is depressing, demoralizing, and permanently victimizing.

8   Martha and Lois are destined to believe in their own inescapable and permanent desolation. The continued hopelessness and the listless atmosphere in both the Prairie countryside and small-town Ontario doom the lives of these women to failure. Yet, in Martha's life, there is a ray of hope, so her ultimate victimization is by degrees lower and not as harsh as that of Lois. Martha learns that there is

some value in her marital relationship when they are both vulnerable after the storm. There is a short interlude where she and he touch (170), but for "the sake of the children" they must separate once again. For that short while, they are united in struggle, pain, and marriage: "It was more of him than she had had for years" (170). So, not all is lost in love and fulfilment. Martha's renewed sense of hope is also symbolized by the remaining strands of wheat not abolished by the natural forces of the hailstorm. They stand alone, albeit headlessly! These remaining strands of wheat also symbolize the renewed strand of hope that comes with overcoming life's tragedies, even in some small way, or with some small new beginning. For Martha, there is escape. There is life. The victimization is only partial. These strands of hope reaching into the sunshine do not compare with anything offered to Lois. Instead, that story starts and ends with desolation. Nothing remains standing defiantly after life deals its harsh cards to resigned and apathetic Lois; she just continues to subsist. There is no grain of wheat symbolizing strength and continued commitment or hope for the future. There is no meaningful touch from a man. In fact, there is nothing for her; she is left by a line of young men; first the summer boyfriend, then Dick, and then inevitably, those of the future. The empty future promise of a fur jacket provides no real hope for a meaningful life. In short, there is no grain of hope for Lois. For her, the victimization is complete, consistent, and permanent.

Works Cited

Munro, Alice. "Thanks for the Ride." <u>The Story Makers</u>. Ed. Rudy Wiebe. Toronto: Macmillan, 1987. 80-95.

Ross, Sinclair. "A Field of Wheat." <u>The Story Makers</u>. Ed. Rudy Wiebe. Toronto: Macmillan, 1987. 161-73.

Topics for Critical Thinking and Writing

1. In this essay, Breda combines the alternating and the block methods by discussing the physical environment for Martha and for Lois and then the social environment for Martha and for Lois. Do you think the structure of this essay is successful?
2. What is the function of Breda's opening paragraph? Does it effectively introduce the topic of the essay? Does she have a clear thesis?
3. Evaluate the final paragraph as a concluding paragraph. (See pages 67–70 for a discussion of final paragraphs.)
4. Following Breda's example, analytically compare two short stories, two poems, or two essays. See, in Part Five, Bharati Mukherjee's "An Invisible Woman" for another example of a comparison essay.

 ## JEFF GREENFIELD

Jeff Greenfield wrote speeches for Robert F. Kennedy and has exchanged sharp words with William F. Buckley on television. He has published essays on sports and on other popular entertainments, has appeared regularly on Nightline, *and is currently a senior analyst on CNN, a contributor to* Inside Politics, *and a columnist at* Time. *The following essay, which seeks to account for the long-running popularity of the television series* Columbo, *originally appeared in* The New York Times *more than a quarter of a century ago. Reruns of* Columbo *can still be seen regularly on television.*

Columbo Knows the Butler Didn't Do It

1   The popularity of *Columbo* is as intense as it is puzzling. Dinner parties are adjourned, trips to movies postponed, and telephone calls hastily concluded ("It's starting now, I gotta go." "Migod, it's 8:40, what did I miss?"), all for a detective show that tells us whodunit, howhedunit, and whyhedunit all before the first commercial.

2   Why? Peter Falk's characterization is part of the answer of course; he plays Lieutenant Columbo with sleepy-eyed, slow-footed, crazy-like-a-fox charm. But shtick—even first-class shtick—goes only so far. Nor is it especially fascinating to watch Columbo piece together clues that are often telegraphed far in advance. No, there is something else which gives *Columbo* a special appeal—something almost never seen on commercial television. That something is a strong, healthy dose of class antagonism. The one constant in *Columbo* is that, with every episode, a working-class hero brings to justice a member of America's social and economic elite.

3   The homicide files in Columbo's office must contain the highest per-capita income group of any criminals outside of antitrust law. We never see a robber shooting a grocery store owner out of panic or savagery; there are no barroom quarrels settled with a Saturday Night Special; no murderous shoot-outs between drug dealers or numbers runners. The killers in Columbo's world are art collectors, surgeons, high-priced lawyers, sports executives, a symphony conductor of Bernsteinian charisma—even a world chess champion. They are rich and white

(if Columbo ever does track down a black killer, it will surely be a famous writer or singer or athlete or politician).

4   *Columbo's* villains are not simply rich; they are privileged. They live the lives that are for most of us hopeless daydreams: houses on top of mountains, with pools, servants, and sliding doors; parties with women in slinky dresses, and endless food and drink; plush, enclosed box seats at professional sports events; the envy and admiration of the Crowd. While we choose between Johnny Carson and *Invasion of the Body-Snatchers,* they are at screenings of movies the rest of us wait in line for on Third Avenue three months later.

5   Into the lives of these privileged rich stumbles Lieutenant Columbo—a dweller in another world. His suspects are Los Angeles paradigms: sleek, shiny, impeccably dressed, tanned by the omnipresent sun. Columbo, on the other hand, appears to have been plucked from Queens Boulevard by helicopter, and set down an instant later in Topanga Canyon. His hair is tousled, not styled and sprayed. His chin is pale and stubbled. He has even forgotten to take off his raincoat, a garment thoroughly out of place in Los Angeles eight months of the year. Columbo is also unabashedly stunned by and envious of the life style of his quarry.

6   "Geez, that is some car," he tells the symphony conductor. "Ya know, I'll bet that car costs more than I make in a year."

7   "Say, can I ask you something personal?" he says to a suspect wearing $50 shoes. "Ya know where I can buy a pair of shoes like that for $8.95?"

8   "Boy, I bet this house musta cost—I dunno, hundred, what, hundred fifty thousand?"

9   His aristocratic adversaries tolerate Columbo at first because they misjudge him. They are amused by him, scornful of his manners, certain that while he possesses the legal authority to demand their cooperation, he has neither the grace nor wit to discover their misdeeds. Only at the end, in a last look of consternation before the final fadeout, do they comprehend that intelligence may indeed find a home in the Robert Hall set. All of them are done in, in some measure, by their contempt for Columbo's background, breeding, and income. Anyone who has worked the wrong side of the counter at Bergdorf's, or who has waited on tables in high-priced restaurants, must feel a wave of satisfaction. ("Yeah, baby, *that's* how dumb we working stiffs are!")

10   Further, Columbo knows about these people what the rest of us suspect: that they are on top not because they are smarter or work harder than we do, but because they are more amoral and devious. Time after time, the motive for murder in *Columbo* stems from the shakiness of the villain's own status in high society. The chess champion knows his challenger is his better; murder is his only chance to stay king. The surgeon fears that a cooperative research project will endanger his status; he must do in his chief to retain sole credit. The conductor owes his position to the status of his mother-in-law; he must silence his mistress lest she spill the beans and strip him of his wealth and position.

11   This is, perhaps, the most thorough-going satisfaction *Columbo* offers us: the assurance that those who dwell in marble and satin, those whose clothes, food, cars, and mates are the very best, *do not deserve it.* They are, instead, driven by fear and compulsion to murder. And they are done in by a man of street wit, who is afraid to fly, who can't stand the sight of blood, and who never uses force to take his prey. They are done in by Mosholu Parkway and P. S. 106, by Fordham U. and a balcony seat at Madison Square Garden, by a man who pulls down $11,800 a year and never ate an anchovy in his life.

12   It is delicious. I wait only for the ultimate episode: Columbo knocks on the door of 1600 Pennsylvania Avenue one day. "Gee, Mr. President, I really hate to bother you again, but there's *just one thing. . . .*"

 Topics for Critical Thinking and Writing

1. What is Greenfield's thesis? Where does he state it?
2. Describe what Greenfield is doing in his first paragraph; in his second paragraph.
3. Beginning with the third paragraph, Greenfield looks first at the characterization of the hero and villains, then at the underlying conflict, and finally at the implicit meaning of the conflict. Why does he present the parts of his analysis in this order?
4. In an essay of about 750 words, analyze the appeal of a popular television show—e.g., *E.R.*, *Law & Order*, or *This Hour Has 22 Minutes.*

 WARREN CARAGATA

Warren Caragata is a Canadian journalist and has been a senior staff writer at Maclean's *and* Asiaweek; *he specializes in technology and business coverage. He has also worked overseas as a foreign correspondent from Jakarta, Indonesia, and he is the author of a book on trade unions and labour history titled* Alberta Labour: A Heritage Untold.

Crime in Cybercity

1   It is quite a neighborhood. *Penthouse* magazine is there, along with amateur pornography purveyors offering graphic portrayals of seemingly every form of sexual activity, from kiddie porn to bestiality. There is Ernst Zundel's proclamation that the Holocaust never happened. And the forbidden secrets of the Karla Homolka case are revealed for those who cannot wait for the evidence to be presented in the Paul Bernardo murder trial. The neighborhood is the Internet, and the criminals have moved in. Some of the crimes, like obscenity, are familiar, but others have taken new forms, from information theft to the sabotage of computer systems with data-destroying viruses.

2   Although the neighborhood has much to recommend it, the dark side of the Net has people worried. There have been calls for laws to regulate and censor what moves across the wires. New laws, says Liberal MP Rey Pagtakhan, who is pushing for tighter control, will demonstrate that "we will not tolerate these types of activity." The problem is figuring out how to impose those laws on a computer network originally designed to withstand a nuclear war. "The Internet regards censorship as a hardware failure and just works around it," says Michael Martineau, vice-president of NSTN Inc., a Halifax company that provides Internet connections.

3   Canada has so far not experienced the kind of cybercrime wave seen in the United States, where most of the reported cases have occurred. In one of the most celebrated U.S. cases, computer hacker Kevin Mitnick was arrested last

February in North Carolina and charged with stealing more than $1 million worth of data and thousands of credit-card numbers. In another, Jake Baker, a University of Michigan student, was arrested on threat charges against a fellow student after he wrote a fictitious article about a woman—named after one of his classmates—who was raped and tortured. In Canada, only a last-minute check prevented the online version of February's federal budget from spreading an unwanted computer virus. Then, last March, officials at the University of British Columbia in Vancouver found that hackers had broken into the university's computer system and stolen about 3,000 passwords. And in April, Calgary police charged Alan Norton, 52, with multiple counts of possession of child pornography, alleging that he was part of a porn ring linked by international computer networks.

4   The Internet has stretched the concept of what the law means, where it applies, and to whom it applies. Copyright law, privacy law, broadcasting law, the law against spreading hate, rules governing fair trials: all are running up against the technology of the Internet. "It presents challenges to the law because of the fact that it is presented in a substantially different form," explains David Johnston, a law professor at Montreal's McGill University who chairs the federal government's advisory council on the information highway. "That form, therefore, requires some adjustment and, some would say, very substantial stretching."

5   Last week in Ottawa, MPs approved Pagtakhan's motion urging the government to get tough with hate on the Internet, with members from all parties voicing their support. "Cyberspace is a free-for-all," says Reform MP Keith Martin. Pagtakhan, a soft-spoken Winnipeg pediatrician, told *Maclean's* that the hate messages he has seen have been "very scary" and would have a hurtful effect on young children. While he acknowledges enforcement would not be easy, he says that is not the point: "To any degree we can, we have to confront this." The government, Pagtakhan believes, will move quickly to set up new rules. The reason for his optimism lies in remarks by Justice Minister Allan Rock—made over the Internet—suggesting that Ottawa was on the verge of action. "We are now considering new laws to establish limits on the use of the Internet and other forms of communication," Rock said. But one justice department official, on condition of anonymity, said that no decision has been taken on how to toughen up enforcement.

6   In fact, the government is still trying to come to grips with the nature of the beast, conscious of the reality that this electronic neighborhood of bits and bytes can be a force of good. Sgt. Craig Hannaford, an RCMP Internet expert in Ottawa, says: "The vast majority of the use of the Internet is totally and completely legitimate." But, he adds, "Like any community, you have a small percentage of people who are criminals."

7   Michael Binder, assistant deputy minister at the industry department, asks another key question: "How would you regulate it?" Computer and legal experts all agree that enforcement is difficult. Still, a committee of the Canadian Association of Chiefs of Police has made several recommendations. One would make it illegal to possess computer hacking programs, those used to break into computer systems. Another would make the use of computer networks and telephone lines used in the commission of a crime a crime in itself. The committee also recommends agreements with the United States that would allow police officials in both countries to search computer data banks. But for the time being, Binder says, the government is in no rush to rewrite the statute books. "We don't know how it will evolve," he said. "We don't want to stifle communication. We don't want to shut down the Net."

8   It is pornography that stirs the most controversy. But while there is no doubt that pornography is popular, it amounts to a trickle compared with everything else available on the Net. And as any walk past a magazine stand will demonstrate, dirty pictures are not automatically obscene under the Criminal Code. David Jones, president of Electronic Frontier Canada and a computer science professor at McMaster University in Hamilton, says the Internet should be governed in the same way as other media. "Pornography is not illegal in Canada," Jones said. "Visit Yonge Street in Toronto or watch cable TV if you have any doubt."

9   Much of the debate about the Internet arises because it is so new. "We're just sort of waking up to it," says Ian Kyer, president of Computer Law Association Inc. and a lawyer with the Toronto firm of Fasken Campbell Godfrey. "Now that it's an everyday thing, it's coming to the attention of the legislators and police forces, and I think they're not going to like what they see." But the debate is actually age-old and boils down to the limits that society sets on free expression. In an e-mail message, Troy Angrignon, a University of Victoria computer science graduate, told *Maclean's*: "This is NOT a computing issue—it is a civil liberties issue."

10   Freedom of expression is enshrined in the Charter of Rights, and the courts have generally protected it from government encroachment. Although the Supreme Court has not yet ruled on any Internet cases, a speech late last year by Justice John Sopinka gave some hint of how it might respond. While Sopinka observed that rights are not absolute, he made it clear that the court would not easily endorse wide-ranging restrictions. The court had struck down a municipal by-law prohibiting posters on public property, he said, and then tellingly added: "It may be said that the electronic media such as the Internet are the posters of the late 20th century."

11   Almost like posters on telephone poles, the Internet appears to defy regulation, an irony given its roots as a research network for the U.S. defence department, which is no fan of anarchy. No one owns the Net, so no one controls it. Messages are passed from computer system to computer system in milliseconds, and the network literally resembles a web of computers and connecting telephone lines. It crosses borders in less time than it takes to cross most streets, and connections to Australia or Asia are as commonplace as dialling Ottawa or Washington. It is the Net's very lack of frontiers that makes law enforcement so difficult. "One of the real problems with the law of the Internet is deciding, where does the offence occur?" says Kyer.

12   The elusive nature of the Net is illustrated by a recent case in which a postal inspector in Tennessee downloaded pornography from a computer bulletin board in California. The board operator in California was charged and convicted in Tennessee, based on that state's community standards. That decision, says Richard Pitt, CEO of Wimsey Information Services, a Vancouver-based Internet provider, strikes terror into the hearts of computer network operators. They may discover, says Kyer, that the Net may fall subject to regulation in every jurisdiction it touches. "It's a frightening prospect to think that we are all then bound by the laws of the most strict and puritanical jurisdictions in the world."

13   The problems of enforcing one nation's laws on the Net are illustrated by the gambling craze. A company called Sports International has established a betting operation on the World Wide Web. For two years, the bookmaker, based on the island of Antigua, has been taking bets on Canadian and American sports events, with bets paid by bank transfers. Next fall, it will become a virtual casino, offering roulette and blackjack to clients—including Canadians—sitting thou-

sands of miles away at their computer screens. Is it illegal? "The question," says Hannaford, "is where is it taking place." On balance, he says, "Probably there's not a whole lot that can be done."

14   Zundel, a Toronto publisher with international neo-Nazi credentials, has an outpost on the World Wide Web, an Internet service that combines text and graphics with the seamless ability to move from one database to another using a technology known as hyper-text links. Information about Zundel's cause is posted on an Orange County, Calif., computer by Greg Raven, associated with the Institute for Historical Review. Raven says he set up the Web site to disseminate Zundel's views after a previous site, also in the United States, was shut down by the Internet provider. In addition, the on-line magazine of the white supremacist Heritage Front is found on a Web server in Florida.

15   The saying on the Net is that bits have no boundaries, and that is equally true of smut. Pornography might be sent from a computer in Manitoba to a computer in the United States and then to a computer in Europe, where it may reside, perfectly within the laws of that country. Canadian police forces can ask for help from foreign investigators—but may not get it. A case may not be a priority, especially if the alleged crime is not illegal in that country. "International investigations don't move that quick," Hannaford notes. And Kyer points out that just as some small countries have sometimes set themselves up as money-laundering havens, others could find it profitable to become data havens. The problems are pushing governments to talk about international treaties governing data flows, but so far little has been done.

16   Confronted with the difficulty of trying to grab on to something as amorphous as the Net, some critics and government officials are hoping that Internet service providers—companies like NSTN or Wimsey that, for a fee, will hook up companies and individuals—can police the Net themselves. The information highway council is expected later this month to approve a recommendation that would encourage the providers to develop a code of ethics, in the same way that broadcasters have been "encouraged" to regulate themselves in the transmission of violent television programs. The Net providers say they cannot hope to control what floods over their networks and trust that they will eventually be considered common carriers, as the telephone companies are, freed from liability for what people say and do over the phone. There have been no clear Canadian court tests. But a U.S. decision suggests that as long as on-line services do not provide content, they may not be liable for the information they carry; in other words, they would be treated as a library or bookstore, not a publisher.

17   At Wimsey, Pitt says postings in newsgroups—the equivalents of computer-based bulletin boards—add up to more than 100 megabytes a day, the equivalent of maybe 20 million words. On the advice of his lawyers, Wimsey does not provide its subscribers with access to the newsgroups dealing with pedophilia or bestiality. But there is nothing stopping someone from posting an obscene picture to any newsgroup, no matter what the subject.

18   Wimsey was overwhelmed in trying to control the newsgroup discussions about the Bernardo-Homolka case, which quickly became a place to exchange information covered by a court-ordered publication ban. It was, says Pitt, like sticking a finger in a leaking dike. "It showed up in so many places on our machines that there was no possibility" that they could control it, he says. As the Supreme Court noted late last year in a decision setting new rules for publication bans: "In this global electronic age, meaningfully restricting the flow of information is becoming increasingly difficult."

19   As Canadians try to come to grips with the Internet, one legal expert says the government should tread cautiously to avoid strangling a powerful resource. Jon Festinger, a professor of media law at the University of British Columbia and legal counsel for WIC, Western International Communications Ltd., says the Internet and the debate over it could help Canadians redefine the limits of control. "We should err on the side of tolerance," he says, "and we should err on the side of freedom of expression."

 ## Topics for Critical Thinking and Writing

1. What does the expression "bits have no boundaries" mean? Is it an accurate statement about the Internet?
2. According to Caragata, what recommendations have been made to the Canadian government to regulate the Internet? What challenges would be involved in enforcing these regulations?
3. Do you agree with Jon Festinger (quoted in the concluding paragraph) that we "should err on the side of tolerance . . . and we should err on the side of freedom of expression"? What are the implications of following this advice?
4. What methods of development does Caragata use in his essay?
5. Do you think the Internet should be regulated by the government? Can it be regulated? Are there any regulations currently in place?

 ## DAVID SMITH

David Smith, former chair of the Department of Culture and Values in Education at McGill University in Montreal, is currently an emeritus professor.

De-militarizing Language

1   Linguistic research over the last quarter century has exposed the influence of language on our thinking patterns and processes. We are seldom aware that the kind of language we use affects our behaviour in significant ways. One example of these revelations is the militarization of English over a long period of time. The result is that our conceptual and higher-level thinking is shaped in ways that we might not consciously wish it to be, and that the language we use in some cases may actually prevent us from attaining our goals.

The History of Military Metaphors

2   Military metaphors have become part of our language over hundreds of years. This has been a normal process, since people tend naturally to draw upon experiences in one area of life in order to give fresh insight and understanding to experiences in another. Think of the language that sailors have brought from the sea to the land (Know the ropes), that urban dwellers have adapted from farms (Put the cart before the horse), or that people have brought home from their places of work (Strike while the iron is hot).

3   Soldiers have had vivid, sometimes traumatic, experiences during military duty that they have then applied to non-military situations. Today, we may ask

someone to "spearhead the discussion" or to "get off your high horse." From marching, someone may "get off on the wrong foot" or "mark time"; from strategy, we might "close ranks" or "beat a hasty retreat"; from weapons, we can "cross swords" with an adversary or "look daggers." From the military hierarchy, we refer to "the top brass" or "the rank and file." There are literally hundreds of military metaphors used in everyday speech and writing.

4   One might well argue that at the relatively shallow level of vocabulary, or even of metaphorical expression, the use of militaristic language is harmless and serves to make our communication more colorful, more precise and perhaps, as Aristotle claimed, to convey fresh meaning or perspective. Indeed, there are words in use that we do not link at all to their origins with the military establishment (such as "harbinger," someone who went before an army to find accommodation, especially for officers). If no violence or military meaning is associated with the word, surely its use is innocuous. But is the use of military language in our society cause for concern at a deeper level?

Metacognitive Thinking

5   What has concerned some linguists and philosophers is not the use of military language per se, but patterns of metaphorical thinking at the metacognitive level. In their book, *Metaphors We Live By*, George Lakoff and Mark Johnson give clear examples of such metaphorical thinking. They assert that in English-speaking society, we conceive of "argument as war" as shown by the following set of conceptual metaphors:

- Your claims are *indefensible*.
- He *attacked* every point in my argument.
- I have lots of *ammunition* in my *arsenal*.
- His criticisms were right on *target*.
- I *demolished* his argument.
- If you use that *strategy*, she'll *wipe* you out.
- You disagree? Okay, *shoot*.
- He *shot down* all my arguments.

6   While there are many alternative metaphors, we may often think of "love as war":

- She *fought* for him, but his mistress *won out*.
- He is slowly *gaining ground* with her.
- He *won* her hand in marriage.
- She is *besieged* by suitors.
- She has to *fend* them *off*.
- He made an *ally* out of her mother.
- He is known for his many *conquests*.

7   Both of the overriding ideas that "argument is war" and "love is war" consist of coherent and consistent sets of metaphorical expressions. Such related clusters are referred to as structural metaphors, and it is these metaphors that may become part of our generally unarticulated belief system.

8   In order to explore these ideas further over the past year, I have been reading and analyzing a variety of newspaper and magazine articles mainly in the areas of politics, economics, environment, and health. My analysis has involved the identification of structural metaphors and their supporting evidence.

Perhaps I can give one example from the recent federal election campaign, as reported in the *Gazette* of February 24. Under the headline "Charest *broadsides* Liberals," we find the following (italics are mine):

- Charest made a *blistering attack* on the Liberal record.
- He's not *targeting* the Bloc.
- He has a *shot* at becoming prime minister.
- Federalist *forces* could easily *rally* against separatists.
- He has been an *underdog, fighting* to keep the politicians in Ottawa honest.
- They played the song, *Another One Bites the Dust.*
- He devoted his entire speech to *attacking* the Liberals.

9   In all, there were 13 military metaphors that supported the structural metaphor, "electoral campaigning as war." In the same article, there were three conceptual metaphors supporting the structural metaphor "election campaigning is a race." The dominant metaphor was clearly that of war.

10   Analysis of articles such as these yields an interesting variety of structural metaphors. However, the dominant theme of war emerges repeatedly: Politics is war, Electoral reform is war, Improvement of the economy is a battle, Marketing is war, Environmental protection is a battle, Medical progress is a battle, and so on.

11   In their book, *Language and Peace*, Christina Schaffner and Anita Wenden assert that structural metaphors like these do not exist in our belief systems as separate ideas but are related to one another and are systematically organized into metaphors at an even higher, ideological level. The metaphor Life is a (an uphill) battle would be one such ideological metaphor. In presenting the research of linguists and philosophers over the past ten years, the authors arrive at a number of sobering conclusions.

12   They conclude that the language of journalists and diplomats frequently represents ideological stances that accept and promote war as a legitimate way of regulating international relations and settling intergroup conflict (legitimization); that language unquestioningly promotes values, sustains attitudes, and encourages actions that create conditions that can lead to war (propagation); and that language itself creates the kind of enemy image essential to provoking and maintaining hostility that can help justify war (justification).

Critical Language Education

13   Recognition of the kind of metaphor contained in the language we use should become part of the education of every person. Schaffner and Wenden write about the need for critical language education in *Language and Peace*. The elements of such education might include the following:

1. *Develop an awareness of metaphorical language*. The study of metaphor could be introduced at the elementary level, beginning with simple examples (such as White Tiger Kung Fu, Blockbuster Video, Arrow Taxi, Check-Mate Investigations) and proceeding to more sophisticated ones at the secondary and tertiary levels. We already study metaphor in poetry and novels; to study its use in political and other discourse would create an understanding of the way in which language reflects ideologies and can influence the exercise of power.

2. *Develop skills in decoding metaphorical language*. One model of formal analysis is to identify conceptual and structural metaphors and map

the latter by showing the intended parallels between the structural metaphor and the issues under discussion. This can then provide the basis for a critical summary of the mode of metaphorical reasoning.

3. *Recognize the limitations of metaphors.* Sure, metaphors are helpful in enlarging our understanding of something we may already be familiar with, yet the system that allows us to comprehend one aspect of a concept in terms of another (for example, argument in terms of war) will necessarily hide some aspects of the concept. There may well be aspects of argument that are inconsistent with war. We may lose sight of the opportunities for cooperation in an argument, of sharing viewpoints that do not support our own position, or of learning from the points raised by the other person.

4. *Become more self-critical to enhance communication skills.* Many kinds of discourse use metaphorical language that is inconsistent with the purpose of the speakers or writers. An example is the one-page article on influenza that includes 13 conceptual metaphors to support the structural metaphor, "preventing flu is war." The mental set of the person who accepts the article is to fight the flu. However, the article concludes with the contrary advice, "Finally, remember to be a nice person; studies have shown that feelings of hostility reduce immune system levels, while being at peace with your world will actually increase your body's ability to resist infection." We need to ensure that the language we use is consistent with the message we wish to convey.

5. *Encourage creativity through the use of alternative metaphors.* Suppose instead of thinking about argument in terms of war, we were to think of argument as a pleasing, graceful dance. How would such a metaphor cause us to conceptualize argument in a different way? It is initially difficult for us to accept such a creative challenge because the present cultural metaphor gets in the way of conceiving argument in terms other than war. We may even conclude that thinking of argument in terms of dance produces a concept that is not argument at all. That is precisely the power of metaphors to control and limit our thinking; yet it is also their power to create a breakthrough (military metaphor intended) to renew and reconstruct.

Topics for Critical Thinking and Writing

1. What are "conceptual metaphors" and "structural metaphors," according to Smith?
2. In a couple of sentences summarize Smith's discussion of metaphors in language.
3. Do you think, as Schaffner and Wenden conclude, that the use of the war metaphor affects our belief systems because metaphors set up relationships and comparisons and that "language unquestioningly promotes values [and] sustains attitudes"?
4. How many war metaphors can you list beyond what Smith provides?
5. How many metaphors can you list under the structural metaphor of argument as dance? What other metaphor might you use?
6. Think about your day-to-day language. What kinds of conceptual metaphors do you use on a regular basis? In a 500-word essay, decode the metaphorical language that you use most.

Narrating

THE USES OF NARRATIVE

Usually we think of **narrative** writing as the art of the novelist or short story writer, but narratives are not always fictional. History books, travel books, biographies, and autobiographies are also largely narrative—although they are likely to contain substantial portions of **analysis** and **description** as well. A history of the Second World War might provide an analysis of the causes of the war and descriptions of devastated battlefields, as well as a narrative account of the major battles. An essay that is mostly **persuasive** or analytic might begin with a narrative designed to capture a reader's attention or to illustrate a point. (The narrative introduction reprinted below does both, we believe.) And even essays that are mostly narrative can make implicit arguments. Later in this chapter you will find an autobiographical narrative by Myrna Dey. As you read it, ask yourself what point or idea the author communicates by telling the story. (You might ask yourself the same question if you read George Orwell's celebrated narrative essay, "Shooting an Elephant," in Part Five, "Readings.")

Narrative Introductions

Narrative paragraphs frequently appear in analytic essays, to introduce or illuminate an idea. Here is the way Fan Shen introduces an article in a journal whose audience is primarily teachers of college composition courses. She begins with an incident from her life in China:

> One day in June 1975, when I walked into the aircraft factory where I was working as an electrician, I saw many large-letter posters on the walls and many people parading around the workshops shouting slogans like: "Down with the word 'I'!" and "Trust in masses and the Party!" I then remembered that a new political campaign called "Against Individualism" was scheduled to begin that day. Ten years later, I got back my first English composition paper at the University of Nebraska–Lincoln. The professor's first comments were: "Why did you

always use 'we' instead of 'I'?" and "Your paper would be stronger if you eliminated some sentences in the passive voice." The clashes between my Chinese background and the requirements of English composition had begun. At the center of this mental struggle, which has lasted several years and is still not completely over, is the prolonged, uphill battle to recapture "myself."

The two brief narratives, the first introduced by "One day in June 1975" and the next by "Ten years later," placed one after the other in the opening paragraph, dramatize Fan Shen's struggle. At the end of the paragraph the word "myself" is in quotation marks; the two incidents described here have prepared us to understand why.

Here is another *narrative introduction* to an essay. Flannery O'Connor begins "The King of the Birds" (an essay on her passion for collecting and raising peacocks) with the following story:

When I was five, I had an experience that marked me for life. Pathé News sent a photographer from New York to Savannah to take a picture of a chicken of mine. This chicken, a buff Cochin Bantam, had the distinction of being able to walk either forward or backward. Her fame had spread through the press, and by the time she reached the attention of Pathé News, I suppose there was nowhere left for her to go—forward or backward. Shortly after that she died, as now seems fitting.

What makes this anecdote arresting? First of all, we can hardly read that an experience marked a person for life without wanting to know what the experience was. We expect to learn something sensational; perhaps, human nature being what it is, we hope to learn something horrifying. But O'Connor cannily does not gratify our wish. Instead she treats us to something like a joke. The chicken, whose fame had "spread through the press," has her picture taken by Pathé News (one of the companies that made the newsreels shown regularly in cinemas before television became popular) and then dies. If the joke is partly on us, O'Connor takes the sting out of it by turning it around on herself. In her second paragraph she explains:

If I put this information in the beginning of an article on peacocks, it is because I am always being asked why I raise them, and I have no short or reasonable answer.

But of course her answer, contained in the first paragraph, *is* short, and about as reasonable an explanation as any of us can offer about our passion for collecting anything. If these opening paragraphs persuade us to keep reading, it is not because they deliver the melodrama they at first hinted at, but because O'Connor's irony persuades us that she is entertaining, and that she is honest about her experience. We want to learn more about her, and we may thereby be seduced into learning what she wants to teach us about peacocks. Moreover, O'Connor's explanation that she tells the story because "I have no short or reasonable answer" reveals a profound truth about the impulse to tell stories. When a writer, even the writer of an essay, tells a story, it is because that story happens to be the best way to make the particular point he or she wants to make.

Narratives in Other Positions in an Essay

Although writers often use narratives in opening paragraphs of essays (just as speakers often begin their speeches with anecdotes), narration can be introduced effectively in almost any position in an essay. If you look back at essays that appear in earlier chapters of this book, you will see that one student, Suki Hudson, introduces her essay "Two Sides of a Story" (page 35), naturally enough, with a story, but she tells another story (which illuminates the first) in the second half of her essay. In contrast, the brief essay "A Lesson" (page 18), an account of what a student learned from a boring job, would have been invigorated had the writer included a narrative—an account of what happened during one day or one hour on the job. Not only would we have better understood what the "lesson" was, very likely she would have understood it better herself. Recounting an event or experience, *reliving* it, so that someone else can understand it, deepens our own understanding of it as well.

DISCOVERING STORIES

Some people are more apt to tell stories than others, but we all have stories to tell. We have stories about our childhood, or work, or travel; the beginning of a relationship, the death of a friend. Sometimes a memory is contained in an image, a sense impression, an emotion, even a dream, and we must examine the traces of memory to remember the event and its meaning. Once on the track of a story, you can capture and develop it by writing about it. Try *freewriting* or *asking yourself questions*. The journalist's questions are specifically designed to elicit stories. They are, you may remember:

- *What* happened?
- *Who* was involved?
- *When* did it happen?
- *Where* did it happen?
- *Why* did it happen?
- *How* did it happen?

NARRATIVE PACE: SCENE AND SUMMARY

In telling a story, you have some decisions to make: will you present it as a scene or will you summarize it? A **scene** brings the characters and actions before the eyes and often, with dialogue, before the ears of your readers. A **summary** briefly comments on an action, giving your readers a synopsis. Brent Staples, in his essay "Just Walk On By: A Black Man Ponders His Power to Alter Public Space" (page 565), begins with a scene, his encounter with a white woman on a deserted street in Hyde Park. The scene dramatizes his first experience of "being perceived as dangerous." Later in the essay he summarizes "the standard unpleasantries with police, doormen, bouncers, cab drivers, and others whose business it is to screen out troublesome individuals *before* there is any nastiness." When you are writing an essay, as opposed to a novel, you can't present everything as a scene. When you read Staples's essay, ask yourself why he summarizes the "unpleasantries" instead of presenting them as scenes.

The general rule is to keep the point of the story in mind and to cut any details or incidents that clog the action or blur the point. Flannery O'Connor describes her chicken only enough to convince us of its reality—it was a "buff Cochin Bantam." The point of the anecdote lies not in the unremarkable chicken (which achieves fame and dies in three sentences) but in the effect on the writer of a brief moment of celebrity. On a deeper level, the point of the anecdote is the writer's wish to secure our attention and goodwill.

ORGANIZING A NARRATIVE

The usual way to organize a narrative is chronologically. As the King tells the White Rabbit in *Alice's Adventures in Wonderland:* "Begin at the beginning, and go on till you come to the end: then stop." Sometimes, though, it's effective to start with the end of the action, or somewhere in the middle, and then tell the story through a *flashback.* If you have seen the classic film *Sunset Boulevard,* you will remember the opening scene: as we look down at a man's corpse in a swimming pool, his voice begins the story of how he got there! Narratives, however they are organized, are almost always told in the past tense; and good storytellers help us to follow the succession of events, the passage of time, by using such transitional words as *first, then, next, at last,* and *finally.*

Finally, we reprint a letter to the editor in which a college student, an assault victim, tells her experience. You may observe that the organization is for the most part chronological, made clear by transitions, and framed by the writer's analysis of her experience and her reasons for revealing it. As readers, we may or may not notice these points; gripped by the story being told, we are largely unaware of the techniques of successful writers. As students of writing, however, we study these techniques.

 ## A Letter to the Editor

1   I write this letter out of concern for women of the college community. I am one of the two students who were assaulted during the winter recess. I do not feel any shame or embarrassment over what happened. Instead, I want to share some of my experience because in doing so I may help other women to think about rape and rape prevention.

2   First I think it is important for the community to understand what happened to me. At my request, during the vacation a well-intentioned employee let me into my residence hall to collect some things from my room. It was after dark. I was alone in my room when a man appeared at the door with a stocking over his head and a knife in his hand. He said he was going to rape me. I had no intention of submitting, and I struggled with him for about five minutes. One of the reasons why I chose not to submit but to resist was that as a virgin I did not want my first sexual experience to be the horror of rape. While struggling I tried to get him to talk to me, saying such things as "Why do you want to rape me? Don't you

understand I want no part of this? I am a woman, not an object. In God's name, please don't rape me." He finally overpowered me and attempted to rape me, but stopped when he realized I had a Tampax in. Then at knifepoint he asked me a number of questions. He ended by threatening that if I reported and identified him he would kill me. As he was leaving he made me lie on my bed and count to five hundred, which I started to do. Then as I reached one hundred he returned and told me to start over. Thus it was good I did not get up right after he left.

3   It is impossible to say what should be done in all instances of assault. Each incident is different and requires a different response. I think what helped me most was my ability to remain calm, assess the situation, and then act firmly. I did struggle, I did talk, but I also did act in such a way as to ensure my own safety at knifepoint.

4   I believe there are some reasons why I was able to cope with the situation. One is that I had talked with other women about rape and self-defense. As a result I was more aware of the possibility of rape and had thought some about what I might do if confronted with an attacker. Also my active involvement in the women's movement has helped me develop confidence in myself, especially in my strength, both emotional and physical. I believe such confidence helped me not to panic. Another reason why I was able to cope was that I prayed.

5   I think it is important also to share with you the aftermath of the attack. The first thing I did after leaving my room was to report the incident to security and to the campus police. I did not hesitate to report the attack since I realized that reporting it was vital to protect the safety of the college community. The police were efficient and helpful in taking the report and starting search procedures. (The police also told me they did not think I was in further danger, despite the threats on my life. There seemed to be little reason for him to come back.) Also, two female members of the student services staff stayed with me most of the evening. Their presence and support were very helpful to me, especially while I talked to the police. Since the incident, I have also found support from professional staff and from friends. The residence office, the medical and psychiatric staff, the dean's office, and the chaplaincy staff have all been helpful. All have protected my confidentiality.

6   At first I did not realize that I would want or need to seek out people's help, but now I am glad I did. The rape experience goes beyond the assault itself. I have come to understand the importance of dealing with the complex emotions that follow. Also I now know that there is no reason for women to feel ashamed, embarrassed, or scared about seeking help.

7   I hope you now have a greater concern for your own safety after reading about what happened to me. I think this is the most important point of my writing. It never occurred to me that entering an unoccupied residence hall was dangerous. We all have been too accustomed to doing things on and off this campus without considering our own safety or vulnerability to attacks. But we ourselves are our own best security, so please protect yourselves and each other.

8   I am aware I will be working through this experience for a long time to come. I am thankful that there are people in this community to help me do that. I in turn want to be helpful in any way I can. So I invite women who are genuinely concerned about rape and assault to join me in sharing experiences and thoughts next Tuesday, February 18 at 7 p.m. in the Women's Center.

—NAME WITHHELD UPON REQUEST.

Topics for Critical Thinking and Writing

1. In one or two paragraphs tell a story that illustrates an abstraction, such as anger, courage, endurance, a misunderstanding, a put-down, pride, the generation gap, embarrassment, racism, loneliness. For an example, see "Conceit" (page 123) and the brief discussion following it.
2. In 750 to 1000 words, survey your development as a writer and explain your current attitude toward writing. Include a narrative or two contrasting narratives to exemplify what you have learned and how you learned it.
3. For an essay on any topic you choose, write an opening paragraph that includes an anecdote. Don't write the essay, but indicate from the anecdote and, if you wish, an additional sentence or two, the topic of your essay.
4. In five hundred to a thousand words narrate an experience in such a way that you communicate not only the experience but also the significance of it. For example, you might tell of an interview for a job that gave you some awareness of the attitude of people with jobs toward those without jobs. Or you might narrate an experience at school that seems to you to illuminate the virtues or defects or assumptions of the school. A variation: John Keats in a letter says, "Nothing ever becomes real till it is experienced—Even a proverb is no proverb to you till your life has illustrated it." Recount an experience that has made you feel the truth of a proverb.

Narration at Work

 MYRNA DEY

Myrna Dey is a long-time writer whose work has appeared in sources such as Canadian Living, Reader's Digest, *and the* National Post. *She lives in Kamsack, Saskatchewan.*

A Present from the Past

1   *Phoebe, age five, tries so hard to read. "Where does it say 'wizard'?" she demands when I read to her. For two years she has been pleading with me to let her inside her storybooks. When Pinocchio turns into a donkey, she points with agitation: "Can you get me onto the page so I can help that boy run away?"*

2   *Annelisa, still cuddly at three, lifts her father's weights like a strongman. Last week she asked, out of the blue, "How do you know God is a 'him'?"*

3   *Gillian, at seven, is less physical than Phoebe and Annelisa. She's more of a director, organizing musicals in the backyard or playing school and house, while they wrestle like bear cubs on the floor until she calls them to participate. Annelisa is always willing to take whatever role Gillian assigns; Phoebe takes off somewhere else as soon as the production starts.*

4   These passages are written in a once-forgotten scribbler from the '70s. For a year I had filled it with notes about my three young daughters. Its discovery was a

delightful surprise to me—and an even bigger one to my grown-up girls, all living in different cities. After receiving the transcribed pages, they were immediately on the phone with one another and with me.

5   *Last night Gillian came down wailing that, instead of getting ready for bed, Phoebe was writing on her (Gillian's) doll. When I investigated, Phoebe had printed neatly all over the doll "I love you, Gillian."*

6   *Lamenting her own doll's broken arm, Phoebe thought how terrible it would be to have only one arm. With great seriousness, she asked, "What if you wanted to shake hands with two people at the same time?" Then, as a secondary hardship, she added, "Or hug someone?"*

7   The notebook also reminded me of her scary dreams: *Last night Phoebe woke up from a nightmare in which a witch had turned her chin into a fish's chin. Not long ago she dreamed that people without noses were trying to steal them from those who had them. She had managed to talk them out of stealing hers.*

8   An innocent exchange from another entry could have come from a self-help manual: *Annelisa asked me in private yesterday who was my favourite in our family. I said I loved everybody the same. She said that, no, I had to pick just one, so I obliged: "Okay, you." Then I asked who her favourite was, and she replied, "Me. You can't forget yourself, you know."*

9   This early self-assurance served Annelisa and her sisters well growing up as racially mixed children in a small town:

10   *Annelisa: "Is our skin black?"*

11   *Me: "What do you think?"*

12   *Annelisa: "It's brown."*

13   *Gillian: "No, we're golden."*

14   *Annelisa: "Alex and Nick told me today that we had black skin."*

15   *Phoebe (with understated disgust): "Well, I'd say Alex and Nick don't know their colours very well."*

16   The notes go on and on. *Gillian is growing like a flower whose soil is love. Give her love and encouragement, she guarantees it in return.* There's more on Gillian's ballet exam and adenoidectomy; on Phoebe's need to explore on her own; on Annelisa being chosen to present flowers to the teacher on stage at the end of a dance recital, then sitting back down with them, thinking they were for her—the confidence that just wouldn't quit.

17   While my daughters found their childhoods in the notebook, I found clues to the women they have become. It chronicles their most spontaneous words and behaviours—the parts of their personalities that were uncoached by their father or me, the parts that define them.

18   Now that her sisters have outgrown her tutelage, Gillian is an elementary school teacher, sharing her imagination and responsive soul with other children. Phoebe, a journalist, finally does get right into people's stories on the page. And, in covering all her beats, she must surely shake hands sometimes with two people at once. Fearless Annelisa (did I mention that she could ride a bicycle without training wheels before she was three?) surprised us the most; after formative years filled with dancing, figure skating, band, sports and theatre, she joined the RCMP and fights crime with Canada's largest detachment. Indeed, my daughters are the golden girls they said they were. The code was there to be deciphered.

19   I wish I had continued writing in that scribbler. I have a cupboard filled with photo albums and scrapbooks that offer some consolation, but pictures can't preserve the words and thoughts of childhood.

20   From now on, I've decided, my gift to new parents will be a journal—a remembrance of things future.

Topics for Critical Thinking and Writing

1. In blending a narration from the past with a narration from the present, what is Dey illuminating and what is her main point?
2. Is the essay with its past and present interwoven together and demarcated by italics and standard font effective? What would be the effect on the piece if Dey had chosen to write chronologically?
3. What do you make of the discussion about skin colour and the way that Dey works it in later in her narration?

RICHARD MURPHY

Richard Murphy has taught writing and English at Radford University; his books include The Calculus of Intimacy: A Teaching Life *and* Symbiosis: Writing and an Academic Culture. *The following essay was originally published in the journal* College English.

Anorexia: The Cheating Disorder

1   I wanted to pray. A part of me would not let myself ask Him for help. I did it to myself. God understood my confusion. I tried to figure out why it was happening to me, and how. It only happens to weak girls, girls who have no self-control, girls who are caught up with society's standards—not me. But was I one of them? It was happening to me, just like the cases I read about in magazines.

2   This is the first paragraph of an essay I received from a young woman purporting to describe her own experience with anorexia nervosa. Before I had finished reading one page, I suspected it was plagiarized. I cannot easily explain my hunch. Something canned about the writing, its confessional sentiment exactly like the cases in the magazines. I ran a quick search through the *Magazine Index* in the library and then through recent issues of *Teen, McCall's, Glamour,* and *Mademoiselle.* In a half-hour, I had six articles: "Anorexia Nearly Killed Me," "Starving Oneself to Death," "Starving for Attention," "Two Teens," "My Sister and I," and "One Teen's Diet Nightmare." I did not accuse the student of plagiarism on the evidence of this search, but I decided to talk with her before I would comment on or evaluate her paper. I guessed that in our talk she would reveal that she had copied her essay or in some other way falsified it. She did.

3   I am not inquiring here into the causes of plagiarism among students nor describing how teachers ought to respond to it. I am simply telling two stories in order to convey something of its perversity.

4   Several years before I received the anorexia paper, a student submitted a brief analysis of James Joyce's "The Dead." As I was reading it, the paper tripped some wire in my mind. It seemed both accomplished and incompetent, full of discontinuities like those in the following two sentences:

> The physical movement of the main character, Gabriel Conroy, from a house in the western part of the city eastward to a hotel at the very center expresses in spatial terms his commitment to the ways and the doom of his fellow Dubliners. His spiritual movement westward, in our imaginative vision, symbolizes his supremeness of that doom through recognition of its meaning and acceptance of this truth of his inward nature.

Much of the first sentence here is sensible; the character's physical movement expresses his commitment. It is also syntactically sophisticated. The grammatical subject, "movement," is sustained through five prepositional phrases before its meaning is completed by the verb "expresses." The verb itself is modified by a prepositional phrase ("in spatial terms") that parallels and reiterates the adjective "physical." The second sentence, however, is nonsense. The grammatical kernel (movement symbolizes supremeness) is unintelligible. The pronoun sequence creates nothing but blur (his-our-his-that-its-this-his). One sentence, then, is substantial and coherent. The next is gummed with vagueness. So stark is the contrast between the two that it was difficult for me to imagine the same person writing both.

5   When I had assigned the paper, I explicitly restricted the use of secondary sources. I asked students to select a short reading from the literature we had been studying and to write an essay defining and explaining what they considered its central aesthetic purpose. I asked them to write about the work only as it presented itself to them in their reading. They were not to read or refer to any critical or historical background discussions of it.

6   In spite of the assignment's restriction, however, parts of this student paper about Gabriel Conroy seemed to me surely to have been copied. I scanned several library collections of critical essays on Joyce, browsed in longer works that made reference to *Dubliners,* and then, without having found anything but still persuaded the paper was plagiarized, asked the student to come to my office to talk with me.

7   "Before I give you credit for this paper," I said, "I need to ask a couple of questions: Did you use any outside materials when you wrote this? Did you read any books or articles about Joyce or about this story?"

8   To both of these questions he answered, "No," simply and firmly. But the look on his face was perplexed, and I realized once again how difficult it is to confront plagiarism without proof, how important it is not to accuse a student of cheating without sufficient cause. I hurried to soften the impression that I thought he had cheated by saying that my reason for asking was the strange inconsistency in the paper between specific recounting of the story line and abstract discussion of thematic issues. I was trying to understand the combination, I said, and I thought that perhaps he had looked at some outside sources which had influenced what he wrote. He still looked puzzled, but said, "No," again, and our brief conference ended.

9   Plagiarism irritates, like a thin wood splinter in the edge of one's thumb. With any sort of reasonable perspective, I realize that one student's possibly copying part of one paper on James Joyce is a small matter. In a typical semester, I teach 120 students and read perhaps 600 student papers. In a typical day, I have two classes to prepare and teach, committee meetings to attend, confer-

ences with individual students, the utility bill to pay, a child to pick up from a Cub Scout meeting. But everything I touch rubs the sliver in my thumb and sets its irritation pulsing. As much as I try, I cannot ignore it.

10   So when I happened to be sitting in a colleague's office, waiting for her to finish a phone call, my eye seized upon the book of Joyce criticism on her shelf. I had to look. It took only a moment. The phrases of the student's jumbled sentences were everywhere. I borrowed the book, took it back to my office, double-checked its lines with the lines of the paper, and then went again to the library.

11   I wanted to verify that our library collection contained the book and thus that it had actually been available to the writer. It was checked out. "To whom?" I asked. The circulation clerk said that library policy prohibited his divulging that information, but if I wished I could have the book recalled. I did, and reconciled myself to waiting several days for it to arrive.

12   In order to make the story complete, I have to explain some of the mixture of my feeling during this episode. Though I should not have had time to play detective, I made room among all the duties of my life to pursue this student. I was thrilled by the chase. When I happened on those sentences in my colleague's office, I was exhilarated. They promised the solution to a puzzle that had eluded me. They reinforced my sense of judgment and my sense of self-satisfaction at the thought that, in a small way, I was preserving the integrity of the university.

13   I was also dismayed, however, and angry at what I came to feel as the obligation to play out this scene, at my exhilaration, at the student's distortion of our whole working relationship. When I thought about his voice, about his poise in denying that he had used any outside sources, I thought too about the other 119 students and wondered what his cheating meant about them. When I went into class in the following days and watched their faces, I realized that I had lost some of my faith in them. For no more reason than my experience with him, I found myself wondering what the rest of them had copied.

14   The recall notice came shortly afterward. I hurried to the library to pick up the book. When I could not find the sentences I was looking for, I first imagined that I had inadvertently recalled the wrong book. Then I thought that perhaps this was a different edition. I walked away from the circulation desk flipping the pages and wondering—through the electronic gate at the library door, out through the foyer past the philodendrons in their huge pots, onto the columned porch—and then I saw it. The gap in the pagination, page 98 followed immediately by page 113, and, in the fold of the binding so neatly done as to be almost invisible, the seven razor-bladed stumps.

15   He still denied it, first in my office, then in the Dean of Students' office, sitting with his legs crossed in an upholstered armchair next to a whirring tape-recorder. He began by denying that he had even used the book, then that he had damaged it in any way: he went so far as to say that he had noticed the missing pages and reported them to the library himself. He hadn't wanted to be blamed, he said. What kind of person did we think he was, he asked, how did we suppose he had been brought up? He was offended at the very thought of it. But when I finally left the hearing room, he admitted to the Dean both that he had copied and that he had cut out the pages he had used. Within the week he was suspended from the university.

16   Nearly every year I encounter students who cheat in their writing. Their stories are all different, and all the same: they were worried about their school work, rushed, unclear about the assignment, afraid. My stories are all different, and all the same: an intuition, some feeling on the surface of the page, something

about the dye of the ink that whispers this is counterfeit currency; the excitement of judicial self-satisfaction, the slanderous suspicion that all students are cheating. Though particularly vivid, my experience with the *Dubliners* paper is like all the others, obsessive and bilious. Like all the others, it has nothing whatever to do with what the job of teaching should be.

17   "Did this really happen?" I asked my student when we met to talk about her essay on anorexia. She was already nodding yes when I thought that I shouldn't seem rude in my disbelief. "I mean," I said, trying to make the edge of my question sharp, "I mean, did this happen the way you tell it here?"

18   "Yes," she nodded again. "Why do you ask?"

19   "Well, I don't know exactly." I looked up from the paper at her face, then back down to the typed page. "It's sort of vague in places, as if . . . I don't know . . . as if you didn't remember what happened in your own story."

20   Now she was shaking her head. "I don't know what you mean."

21   She played the correct gambit—my move, force me to commit myself. But I didn't want to move yet. I was after proof, and I needed to go after it slowly. This was a parody of a writing conference. I was asking her about the details of her story, trying to appear helpful, as if I were attempting to help her revise, when in fact I was trying to tease out the insincerity of her paper.

22   "I mean, I'm sort of confused by your essay," I said. "In the part here on page three where you say you ran to the bathroom to vomit—'I would run to the toilet to vomit, screaming the entire way' and 'The vomiting ceased after awhile'— when did that happen? Did that happen before you went to the hospital or after?"

23   "After."

24   "And here where you say, on page two, that your father stroked your hair and rubbed behind your ears, and then on the next page you say that your father was a monster who yelled at you and forced food down your throat constantly. Are you talking about what caused your anorexia or what happened afterward?"

25   She didn't answer this question at all, just sat there looking at me: so I tried a different tack.

26   What struck me as I read and reread her paper were the seams, the joints, where the parts were pushed together with no bonding. She is lying in a hospital bed staring at the ceiling tiles. She is trying to listen to the doctor talk to her. She is using and abusing a whole series of diet plans. She is flipping through a magazine looking at the pictures of models. She is taking a laxative every night before she goes to bed. She is listening to her father tell her that she is going home.

27   The effect on me was two-fold. I thought that the details she included were completely credible: only a person who had lain in a hospital bed would think to mark off the ceiling tiles: only a girl whose father actually rubbed behind her ears would think to mention that specific caress. At the same time, the vague and abrupt transitions between these highly individual details seemed to me understandable only if I assumed that she had copied them in fragments from a magazine memoir. My guess was that she had taken them from an article that was too long to copy in its entirety and so had included just selected parts in her essay.

28   "Did you write this?" I finally asked unexpectedly. I did not plan to say it like that, but I couldn't seem to approach the real point of my questions by just skirting the issue.

29   Her face looked so blank that I immediately switched to a different question. "Is this story really about you?"

30   She paused for a moment and then asked quietly, "What would happen if it weren't?"

31   I told her that I could not accept such a paper since the assignment was to write about a personal experience of her own. I told her, too, that it would help explain the vagueness I had been trying to point out to her: if she wrote the paper about someone else's experience, then she would be likely to leave gaps in the story that she couldn't fill.

32   "What grade would I get on it if it were about someone else?" she asked. To pin me down.

33   "I wouldn't grade it at all. I wouldn't give you any credit for doing it. It's not the assignment."

34   "OK," she said. "It's not about me. It's about a friend of mine."

35   My reaction to this admission was complicated. I had been expecting it, in fact working toward it, trying to get her to tell me where the paper had come from. I was glad finally to have its pretense uncovered but disappointed because I knew immediately that I would have to accept this substitute explanation though I didn't believe it either. I was sorry I had not been able to find the magazine story that provided the actual source of her paper and so would have to settle for this second lie about its roots. And I was angry at the whole situation: at the wasted time in the library, at the wasted conference with her, at my own inability to define the fakery of the piece, and at her apparent inability to see the purpose of our work together. I wanted her to write truthfully about her own experience and to use my responses, along with others', to help her convey the meaning of that experience more surely and vividly. As it was, her paper seemed just a hoax.

36   The deep flux of such feeling is just one of the dimensions for me of the problem of plagiarism. Another is the comic peculiarity of my claiming to be committed to helping students learn but sometimes spending large chunks of everyone's time trying to corner them in a fraud. Then there is the distance, the surprising separation I discover in such situations between myself and students. Because I assume their good will and candor and my own, both their cheating and my response to it shock me. I take for granted that we are working together and thus am amazed each time at the unimagined distance between us.

37   But even if I had expected the fakery of the anorexia paper, I would not have been prepared for what happened. Even if I had remembered the pages sliced out of the book of Joyce criticism and the self-righteous posturing of that frightened student writer trying to elude me, I would not have anticipated the journal of the woman who had told me that her essay on anorexia was not really about herself but about her friend.

38   I gave her a zero on the paper. She completed the rest of the semester's assignments, and at the end of the term, as required, she turned in a binder containing all her work for the course. As I was rereading her finished essays and the background notes and drafts she had made while working on them, I came upon the following entries in her journal:

> Feb. 7. My roommates and I did watch the Miss America pageant. I believe pageants are my favorite programs to watch. They are so inspiring. But sometimes that can make you sick.

> Feb. 21. The title of Miss America is such a distinguished title. Whoever is chosen for this honor represents the dreams of millions of young girls.

Feb. 22. My next paper I am writing about when I had anorexia. The thought of going all through that again scares me but I think it would be a good experience to write about.

Feb. 22. Skinny. Healthy. Slim. Muscle. Diets. Firmness. Roundness. All thoughts of women in today's society. Is this such a healthy attitude to have? Women can be obsessed with these listed thoughts to the point of worshipping, slimness, firmness, healthiness etc.—

Feb. 22.

. . . It really hurt.

"You're fat" my brother said to me.

I looked in the mirror.

You're fat I said to myself.

March 1. Blindness is a scary experience or at least it was for me. I haven't experienced blindness but something close to it. The world diminishes. Your only hope is through touch.

March 2. Scared and alone. I laid in my hospital bed. I wanted to pray. I thought prayer would make me feel closer to the only friend I had left. My situation had done this to me. I thought it only happened to weak girls, girls who have no self-control, girls concerned w'society.

39   These journal entries astonished and appalled me. Their sincerity was unmistakable. These were not descriptions of a friend's experience. These were not fragments copied from the pages of a popular magazine. They were threads of memory—a brother's teasing, a father's touch. As closely as I can reconstruct it, she and I met in conference to discuss her essay on anorexia nervosa March 12, eighteen days after she began writing it, thirty-three days after she had begun to remember in her journal about her feelings that led both to her sickness and to her writing.

40   What must she have been thinking as I began to ask her those strange questions in our conference? At what point did she catch a glimmer of what I was really doing there? And when she saw it—if she saw it—what must she then have thought about it all—the course, me, the whole project of learning in school? What calculation, what weariness with it all, must have led her to deny her own paper? "Is this paper about you?" I asked her.

41   "No," she said.

42   I did not mean for it to come to this.

 ## Topics for Critical Thinking and Writing

1. In paragraph 2, Murphy says, "I am not inquiring here into the causes of plagiarism among students nor describing how teachers ought to respond to it. I am simply telling two stories in order to convey something of its perversity." Why does he tell *two* stories? Who, exactly, is perverse in these stories?

2. Why does Murphy tell first about the essay on *Dubliners,* and then about the essay on anorexia?

3. At the beginning of this chapter we say that a writer may make a point by means of a story. What is Murphy's point? If he had decided to offer an explicit thesis, what might have been his thesis statement?

4. Murphy ends his narrative with a one-sentence paragraph: "I did not mean for it to come to this." To what does "this" refer?

5. Murphy does not discuss at length the causes of plagiarism, but in paragraph 18 he does mention some of the reasons students cheat: they are "worried about their school work, rushed, unclear about the assignment, afraid." What other reasons might there be?

6. Using Murphy's essay as a model, write a narrative about a similar experience, an experience of being wrong—but for complicated reasons.

 # WU-TSU FA-YEN

Wu-tsu Fa-yen (1025–1104) was a Chinese Zen Buddhist priest. More exactly, he was a Ch'an priest; Zen is Japanese for the Chinese Ch'an.

The practitioner of Zen (to use the more common name) seeks satori, "enlightenment" or "awakening." The awakening is from a world of blind strivings (including those of reason and of morality). The awakened being, free from a sense of the self in opposition to all other things, perceives the unity of all things. Wu-tsu belonged to the branch of Zen that uses "shock therapy, the purpose of which is to jolt the student out of his analytical and conceptual way of thinking and lead him back to his natural and spontaneous faculty" (Kenneth Ch'en, Buddhism in China *[1964, rptd. 1972], p. 359).*

Zen and the Art of Burglary[1]

1   If people ask me what Zen is like, I will say that it is like learning the art of burglary. The son of a burglar saw his father growing older and thought, "If he is unable to carry on his profession, who will be the breadwinner of the family, except myself? I must learn the trade." He intimated the idea to his father, who approved of it.

2   One night the father took the son to a big house, broke through the fence, entered the house, and, opening one of the large chests, told the son to go in and pick out the clothing. As soon as the son got into it, the father dropped the lid and securely applied the lock. The father now came out to the courtyard and loudly knocked at the door, waking up the whole family; then he quietly slipped away by the hole in the fence. The residents got excited and lighted candles, but they found that the burglar had already gone.

3   The son, who remained all the time securely confined in the chest, thought of his cruel father. He was greatly mortified, then a fine idea flashed upon him. He made a noise like the gnawing of a rat. The family told the maid to take a candle and examine the chest. When the lid was unlocked, out came the prisoner,

---

[1]The title of this story, from *The Sayings of Goso Hōyen,* is the editors'.

who blew out the light, pushed away the maid, and fled. The people ran after him. Noticing a well by the road, he picked up a large stone and threw it into the water. The pursuers all gathered around the well trying to find the burglar drowning himself in the dark hole.

4   In the meantime he went safely back to his father's house. He blamed his father deeply for his narrow escape. Said the father, "Be not offended, my son. Just tell me how you got out of it." When the son told him about his adventures, the father remarked, "There you are, you have learned the art."

 Topics for Critical Thinking and Writing

1. What assumptions about knowledge did the father make? Can you think of any of your own experiences that substantiate these assumptions?
2. Is there anything you have studied or are studying to which Zen pedagogical methods would be applicable? If so, explain by setting forth a sample lesson.

Describing

Looking is not as simple as it looks.

—Ad Reinhardt

OBSERVING DETAILS

Description represents in words our sensory impressions caught in a moment of time. In much descriptive writing visual imagery dominates. Look at the following example, part of a letter Vincent van Gogh wrote to his brother, Theo.

> Twilight is falling, and the view of the yard from my window is simply wonderful, with that little avenue of poplars—their slender forms and thin branches stand out so delicately against the gray evening sky; and then the old arsenal building in the water—quiet as the "waters of the old pool" in the book of Isaiah—down by the waterside the walls of that arsenal are quite green and weatherbeaten. Farther down is the little garden and the fence around it with the rosebushes, and everywhere in the yard the black figures of the workmen, and also the little dog. Just now Uncle Jan with his long black hair is probably making his rounds. In the distance the masts of the ships in the dock can be seen, in front the Atjeh, quite black, and the gray and red monitors—and just now here and there the lamps are being lit. At this moment the bell is ringing and the whole stream of workmen is pouring towards the gate; at the same time the lamplighter is coming to light the lamp in the yard behind the house.

First, notice that van Gogh does not attempt to describe the view from the window at all times of day, but only now, when "twilight is falling." Thus, the figures of the workmen, the little dog, the masts in the distance, appear black; the evening sky is grey, and "just now here and there the lamps are being lit."

Second, notice that Vincent tells Theo that he sees not "a row of trees" but a "little avenue of poplars—their slender forms and thin branches stand out so delicately against the gray evening sky." These details, the result of close observation, help the reader to see what van Gogh saw, and to feel as he felt.

Third, notice that while van Gogh describes primarily what he *sees* (not surprising in a painter) he also notices and tells Theo what he *hears:* "At this moment the bell is ringing." And through every detail he communicates what he feels about the scene he describes: "the view of the yard from my window is simply wonderful."

We note in Chapter 8 that description is an important strategy in **analytic writing**. An urban planner writing an analysis of billboards must describe them before she can explore their meaning; a student analyzing Buddhist sculptures must describe them before he can compare them. But description is often also a kind of **persuasion**. Writers wish to persuade us to share their judgment that what they describe is beautiful or ugly, noble or ignoble, valuable or worthless.

If we are persuaded, it is not so much because the writer tells us what to feel (often the judgment is not stated, but implied) as it is because the writer skilfully represents to us what he or she sees, or experiences through other senses.

ORGANIZING A DESCRIPTION

Patient observation of details and willingness to search for exactly the right words with which to communicate our impressions are both part of the secret of good descriptive writing. Still another part is organization, the translation of our disorderly, even chaotic, impressions into orderly structures. Limiting the description to what is sensed at a particular moment in time in itself imposes some order. But in addition, our descriptions must have some discernible pattern, such as from left to right, from bottom to top, from general to particular, or, as in van Gogh's description, from near to far.

Notice this structure, from near to far, as Walt Whitman uses it in his poem "A Farm Picture."

> Through the ample open door of the peaceful country barn,
> A sunlit pasture field with cattle and horses feeding,
> And haze and vista, and the far horizon fading away.

Although the poem is only three lines long, the view is leisurely, beginning where the observer stands, inside the "ample open door," and then stretching slowly out to the "sunlit pasture field," still distinct, because still close up, then to the slightly more general "cattle and horses," and last to the indistinct "far horizon fading away." The leisurely pace persuades us that the scene is indeed "peaceful"; the orderly structure of the poem allows us to feel that it is.

Now look, by contrast, at a description not of a place, but of a phenomenon, a phenomenon not seen but felt, not peaceful, but "uneasy."

> There is something uneasy in the Los Angeles air this afternoon, some unnatural stillness, some tension. What it means is that tonight a Santa Ana will begin to blow, a hot wind from the northeast whining down through the Cajon and San Gorgonio Passes, blowing up sandstorms out along Route 66, drying the hills and the nerves to the flash point. For a few days now we will see smoke back in the canyons, and hear sirens in the night. I have neither heard nor read that a Santa Ana is due, but I know it, and

almost everyone I have seen today knows it too. We know it because we feel it. The baby frets. The maid sulks. I rekindle a waning argument with the telephone company, then cut my losses and lie down, given over to whatever it is in the air. To live with the Santa Ana is to accept, consciously or unconsciously, a deeply mechanistic view of human behavior.

—JOAN DIDION

Here the governing pattern of the description is more complex—from the general to the specific, and back to the general. Didion begins with the relatively general statement "There is something uneasy in the Los Angeles air this afternoon." She then moves to the specific details that support the general statement: the visible effects of the unseen wind first on the landscape and then on people (the baby, the maid, Didion herself). In the final sentence, again a relatively general one, she summarizes a further effect of what it is "to live with the Santa Ana." The organization is complex, but the passage is not disorderly. Or, we might say, it is just disorderly enough to make us feel, with the writer, "something uneasy in the Los Angeles air."

Specific details and concrete language help us to imagine what the writer has observed; a suitable organization further assists us in following the writer's representation of impressions and feelings.

Establishing the Observer's Position

In addition to observing closely, finding the right word, and organizing the material, there is yet another technique that helps persuade the reader to accept the writer's observations as true, and his or her judgment as sound. This technique can be discovered by comparing two descriptions of a building on fire. The first is by a student.

The thick, heavy smoke, that could be seen for miles, filled the blue July sky. Firemen frantically battled the blaze that engulfed Hempstead High School, while a crowd of people sadly looked on. Eyes slowly filled up with tears as the reality of having no school to go to started to sink in. Students that had once downed everything that the high school stood for and did, began to realize how much they cared for their school. But it was too late, it was going up in smoke.

This is surely a competent description, and it is well organized. But compare it to the second description by a professional writer, a practised hand.

We were on the porch only a short time when I heard a lot of hollering coming from toward the field. The hollering and crying got louder and louder. I could hear Mama's voice over all the rest. It seemed like all the people in the field were running to our house. I ran to the edge of the porch to watch them top the hill. Daddy was leading the running crowd and Mama was right behind him.

"Lord have mercy, my children is in that house!" Mama was scream-ing. "Hurry, Diddly!" she cried to Daddy. I turned around and saw big clouds of smoke booming out of the front door and shooting out of cracks everywhere. "There, Essie Mae is on the porch," Mama said. "Hurry, Diddly! Get Adline outta that house!" I looked back at Adline. I couldn't hardly see her for the smoke.

George Lee was standing in the yard like he didn't know what to do. As Mama got closer, he ran into the house. My first thought was that he would be burned up. I'd often hoped he would get killed, but I guess I didn't really want him to die after all. I ran inside after him but he came running out again, knocking me down as he passed and leav-ing me lying face down in the burning room. I jumped up quickly and scrambled out after him. He had the water bucket in his hands. I thought he was going to try to put out the fire. Instead he placed the bucket on the edge of the porch and picked up Adline in his arms.

Moments later Daddy was on the porch. He ran straight into the burning house with three other men right behind him. They opened the large wooden windows to let some of the smoke out and began rip-ping the paper from the walls before the wood caught on fire. Mama and two other women raked it into the fireplace with sticks, broom handles, and anything else available. Everyone was coughing because of all the smoke.

—ANNE MOODY

What can we learn from the professional writer? First notice her patience with detail, the concreteness of the passage. In the first passage we read: "Firemen fran-tically battled the blaze that engulfed Hempstead High School." Moody, by con-trast, shows us individuals and exactly what each does. The first passage general-izes the reaction of the observers—"Eyes slowly filled up with tears" and "Students . . . began to realize how much they cared for their school"—while in Moody's passage Mama screams, "Lord have mercy, my children is in that house!"

But equally important, the professional writer captures the reader's atten-tion and secures the reader's identification with the observer or narrator by establishing the observer's physical position. At the beginning she is on the porch, looking toward the field. It is only when she hears her mother scream that she turns around and sees the smoke. And notice that she *does have to turn,* and the writer has the patience to tell us "I turned around and saw . . ." We could, if we wished to, place the position of the observer, exactly, throughout the action, as if we were blocking a scene in a play. By contrast, notice that there is no real observer in the student's description. If there were, she would first have to be miles away from the scene and looking up into the sky to see the smoke. Then, in the second sentence she would be across the street, watching the firefighters. By the third sentence she'd be closer still—not close to the fire, but close to the other observers. In fact, she'd have to be inside their heads to know what they were thinking. As readers we sense this lack of focus; we have no one to identify with. Though we may find the passage interesting, it will not engage us and we will soon forget it.

Establishing the Observer's Point of View

In addition to the observer's physical location, a good description provides a consistent psychological position, or *point of view,* with which we can identify ourselves. In the following passage from *Black Elk Speaks,* Black Elk, an Oglala Sioux holy man, is describing the Battle of Little Bighorn (1876).

> The valley went darker with dust and smoke, and there were only shadows and a big noise of many cries and hoofs and guns. On the left side of where I was I could hear the shod hoofs of the soldiers' horses going back into the brush and there was shooting everywhere. Then the hoofs came out of the brush, and I came out and was in among men and horses weaving in and out and going upstream, and everybody was yelling, "Hurry! Hurry!" The soldiers were running upstream and we were all mixed there in the twilight and the great noise. I did not see much; but once I saw a Lakota charge at a soldier who stayed behind and fought and was a very brave man. The Lakota took the soldier's horse by the bridle, but the soldier killed him with a six-shooter. I was small and could not crowd in to where the soldiers were, so I did not kill anybody. There were so many ahead of me, and it was all dark and mixed up.

Black Elk was an old man when he told this story. How old would you guess he was at the time it happened? How do you know?

DESCRIBING AN ACTION

At the beginning of this chapter we defined description as a representation, in words, of sensory impressions caught in a moment of time. Strictly speaking, description is static. The passage from van Gogh's letter and Whitman's poem most nearly conform to this definition: they each describe a scene caught in a single moment, like a snapshot. Didion's paragraph about the Santa Ana is less static; it implies the passage of time. That time passes is, however, somewhat masked because Didion represents almost everything as happening simultaneously: "The baby frets. The maid sulks. I rekindle a waning argument with the telephone company." By contrast, in Moody's description of a house on fire, we not only hear (with Essie Mae) "a lot of hollering," and see "big clouds of smoke booming out of the front door and shooting out of cracks everywhere," we also know that moments have passed between the first sensory impression and the second, and that several more have passed before the passage ends with the women raking the burning wallpaper into the fireplace. The description is thoroughly interwoven with narration. Black Elk's account of the Battle of Little Bighorn is similarly a blend of description and narration.

Long passages of pure description are rare. The reason is simple. A description of a place will be much more interesting if the writer shows us something happening there. Similarly, descriptions of people are seldom (except briefly) static. In real life we seldom observe people at dead rest; we see them in action; we form our impressions of them from how they move, what they do. Good descriptions, then, frequently show us a person performing some action, a particularly revealing action, or a characteristic one. If, for example, you want to suggest a person's height and weight, it's much more interesting to show him manoeuvring through a subway turnstile, perhaps laden with packages, than to say, "He was only five feet four but weighed 185 pounds" or "He was short and stocky." Here is the opening description of Elly

May from Bill Richardson's *Scorned and Beloved: Dead of Winter Meetings with Canadian Eccentrics.*

1   Elly May's eyelashes are beautifully groomed and expertly attached. Longer than long. Fracturers of time and space. Exquisite, extravagant receptors. At any minute they might register a distant seismic trembling, or crackle with radio waves beamed over light-years from a remote and intelligent corner of the universe. If you were to see one out of context—flaccid and strewn across the bar, say—you might mistake it for one of those cunning brushes waiters use, postprandially, for clearing crumbs from tables. When Elly May bats her lids, which is often, they generate a breeze that sets the candle flames to shimmying. These, as the inquisitor said to the heretic, are holy lashes. Everything about their architecture—their anti-gravitational sweep, their unlikely heft, their evidence of the divinely inspired human inventiveness we call Art—funnels attention heavenward. If a single, highly individuated snowflake were to precipitate itself from the grey forge of the December clouds, tumble down angle over unique angle, and expire, meltingly, on the thoughtfully combed expanse of one of these wide rakes, they would achieve transcendence. Mere lashes no longer, they would become Poetry. Unalloyed Poetry.

2   Elly May's eyes are brown and uncommonly wide. They may owe their preternatural dilation to the effort required to keep half a kilo of synthetic fur aloft. Or, it might be nothing more than one of the discreetly athletic requirements of voguing.

3   "Have you seen my Bette Davis?" she asks. I shake my head. We have only just met. I haven't had the chance to plumb her repertoire of tricks, which is evidently steppe-like in its expansiveness. It doesn't matter a jot that our acquaintance is so freshly minted. Elly May lowers her eyes to half-mast and lasers me with the same "where the hell have you been" regard she used when I asked her her name. It is surely no accident that avid is the mirror image of diva. As divas go, Elly May is the quintessence of avidity. She is accustomed to having her reputation parade before her, preceding even her hyperextended and feathery ocularia. She sighs the sigh of the worn-out and the righteous. In me, she sees, she has her work cut out for her.

4   "Then watch."

5   She stands, opens the full-length fur coat her mother gave her last year for Christmas. She squares her hands—her nails are magenta, her fingers festooned with gaudy, multifaceted glass bijoux—on her hips. They are so narrow, those hips! Even so, they are scarcely contained by the shiny vinyl swatch of her black miniskirt. It is a frock of her own design, and she says it began its life on earth as a tablecloth. No matter. It more than suits her. She looks like a million bucks. Elly May stretches her neck. Elly May angles her head. Elly May lifts her chin, and achieves the seemingly impossible by widening her eyes further still. She flares her nostrils to such cavernous good effect that I find myself momentarily thinking of the Chunnel. Every movement is acid-etched and arch. She lifts her fag to her lips, sucks, exhales both smoke and the inevitable camp expostulation.

6   "What a dump!"

Notice how animated this description is as we learn something about Elly May through Richardson's accumulation of detail. Richardson, with tongue in cheek, spends about one-third of the description on Elly May's false eyelashes before telling us anything about the person to whom the eyelashes are attached. We learn that Elly May is a diva, and this is reflected in the way she treats Richardson, whom she has just met and who is there to interview her. We also learn about her through her attire and posturing.

 Topics for Critical Thinking and Writing

1. In one paragraph, describe what you see from your window. Choose a particular time of day and describe only what you see (or might see) or otherwise sense within a moment or two.
2. In one paragraph, describe something that cannot be seen, or cannot be seen except by the effects it creates. (Something hot, or smelly, or loud?)
3. In one paragraph, describe something from the point of view of a child, or an old person, or someone of the opposite sex. (Note *person.* The point of view of a dog, or stone, or carrot is *out.*)
4. In one paragraph, describe a room—for example, a doctor's waiting room or an elementary school classroom—by showing something happening in it. Your description should reveal (without explicitly stating) your attitude toward it. The reader should be able to sense that the room is, for example, comfortable or sterile or pretentious or cozy or menacing, though no such words are used in the description.
5. Read this passage from a letter in which the writer blends description and narration, and answer the questions that follow.

> I have had a rather odd—or perhaps wacky and ludicrous would be more accurate—beginning to the new year. (Warning: this paragraph contains murder and mayhem, and so you may want to skip ahead.) I got up, had coffee with Mark, let the cats outside, did some dishes, and took a shower—the normal kinds of things for a relaxing morning at home on a holiday before going out for New Year's dinner. I looked outside to see if the cats, Chop and Suey, were ready to come in, and I realized that they were ganging up on a little mouse. I rushed outside, and as the mouse still moved spryly, I decided that it was fine, and so I brought the cats inside. Half an hour later, I figured enough time had passed, and it was safe to let the cats out again. Little did I know about the absolute stupidity of mice. I looked out a couple of minutes later to see a little mouse repeatedly trying to run up a tree. Mice, at least this one, can't climb trees; it just keeps running up a couple of feet and falling down again. As I close in on them, the mouse runs under Suey (the cat with brain damage from being hit by a car) and really confuses her, giving me a good opportunity to snag the cat. One down, one to go. The mouse makes a break for it; Chop follows. There I am in the middle of the road, slipping on the ice, carrying Suey, and chasing after Chop who is chasing after a mouse who is zigzagging and running around in circles on the road. I am, needless to say, somewhat amused by the situation and somewhat relieved that we don't own a video camera! I manage to grab Chop, and the mouse scampers into the bushes of a neighbour across the street. As I walk back across the road carrying my unhappy cats, I hear a noise behind me. I turn in time to see the mouse leave its cover in the bushes to make a break for it across the

back alley; a magpie swoops down and takes out the mouse. Is that a ridiculous and ironic tale or what!? I felt a bit like I had woken up on a corny sitcom! My only consolation after all that effort is that at least the bird finished off the poor mouse quickly because we all know what cats are like.

Questions: The word "I" appears nineteen times in this passage: what do you learn about the teller of the story from this description? How old, approximately, is she? Of what social or economic class? Who is Mark? What time of year is it? Where does the teller live? What is the teller's mood? How did you know all these things?

6. In one or two paragraphs, describe a person by showing him or her performing some action that takes less than five minutes. From the description the reader should be able to infer some of the following: the time of day; the weather; and the person's height, weight, age, sex, occupation, economic or educational background, and mood.

7. Describe and analyze an advertisement from a magazine or newspaper in about five hundred words. To do this, you will need a topic, such as "This advertisement appeals to male chauvinism," or "This advertisement plays on our fear that we may lack sex appeal." Include a copy of the advertisement with your essay.

8. Choose a recent political cartoon to describe and analyze. In your first paragraph identify the cartoon (cartoonist's name, and the place and date of publication) and describe the drawing (including any words in it) thoroughly enough so that someone who has not seen it can visualize or even draw it fairly accurately. In a second paragraph explain the political message. Don't inject your own opinion; present the cartoonist's point objectively. Submit a copy of the cartoon with your essay. Be sure to choose a cartoon of sufficient complexity to make the analysis worthwhile.

DESCRIPTION AT WORK

 **GINA MEN**

Gina Men wrote the following essay when she was a first-year college student.

Observing Mrs. Taylor

Every morning, she floats into the classroom with her red-striped bookbag cradled in her arms. Swiftly, she arranges her tools, with the textbook in the upper left corner of her table, the notebook in the center, and a mechanical pencil beside it. Explaining some problems from the previous day's assignment, she knows that no matter how hard she tries, her voice is never quite loud enough. And so she articulates each word by shaping her mouth to make sure that we at least <u>see</u> what she is trying to say. Occasionally, she even uses her arms, legs, and torso to construct a graph. For instance, she will uplift her arms to form a parabola (a graph which is symmetrical with respect to the y-axis) with her body acting as the y-axis. Using her stomach as the origin (the center of the graph), she will turn toward us sideways, with one arm uplifted to the left and one leg uplifted to the right in order to represent a tangent graph. (I remember, too, how she demonstrated that the quadratic equation fits perfectly into the melody of "Pop Goes the Weasel.") Although a difficult question from one of us sometimes causes a frown on her face, she always jots the question down immediately and promises to think it over in the evening. Finally, almost buried in the rustle of paper and book-packing, her meek voice rises: "<u>Girls, you ought to learn this lesson in your heart of hearts</u>." And she is out the door.

 ## Topics for Critical Thinking and Writing

1. How does Men establish her physical position and point of view? What is the effect of her use of the present tense? How does she organize the description?
2. The description depends largely on visual images. What other sense impressions are evoked?
3. What is Mrs. Taylor's subject? How does Men persuade you that she was an effective teacher?
4. Search your memory for the image of a teacher, family friend, or coach with a distinctive physical style. Then, in a paragraph, describe your subject at work.

 # LESLEY CHOYCE

Lesley Choyce, who emigrated to Canada in 1978, runs Pottersfield Press, works part-time in the English department of Dalhousie University, has hosted television shows, and has published numerous books. A writer of novels, poems, essays, history, and music, he is especially interested in literature of the Atlantic provinces and in creative writing.

Thin Edge of the Wedge

1   Wedge Island is barely discernible on a road map of Nova Scotia because there are no roads leading there. Although it is not truly an island, its tether to the eastern shore is so tenuous that it remains remote and seemingly adrift. Eroded by the forces of the North Atlantic, it is a mere fragment of what was once a formidable headland. Within a lifetime, it will most likely be reduced to a rubble of stone, an insignificant reef at high tide. But for now, the Wedge exists, a reminder that nothing is permanent on this shore. Geologists define it as a "drowned coast" because the sea is gradually engulfing it. It has been for a long time.

2   Something like a dinosaur's bony spine of boulders leads a wary hiker from the salt-bleached fish shacks on the mainland to the Wedge. If it's a fine July day— blue sky, big and bold above—the hiker might slide his hand along the silky beards of sea oats as he leaves solid land, then dance from rock to rock. Low tide is the best bet to make it there in one piece. Still, waves will spank the rocks from both sides, slap cold saltwater on his shoes and spit clean, frothy Atlantic into his face.

3   Wedge Island is a defeated drumlin, a dagger-shaped remnant of land stretching a good kilometre out to sea. Smashed lobster traps, shreds of polypropylene rope as well as bones of birds and beasts litter the rocks near the shore. Thirty metres up the red dirt cliff sits a parliament of herring gulls peering down at a rare visitor with some suspicion. If the visitor scurries up the side of crumbling dirt, the gulls will complain loudly at his intrusion, then take to the sky and let him pass.

4   At the top is a grassy peninsula a mere 60 centimetres wide where both sides have been sculpted away by rains and pounding seas. It's a place of vertigo and lost history. The land widens as it extends seaward onto this near-island of bull thistles, raspberry bushes and grass that seems cropped short as a putting green.

5   Farther out, at the very tip of the island, bare ribs of bedrock protrude into the sea. This is the same rock you'd find if you could make one giant leap from here across the Atlantic and step ashore on the edge of the Sahara. It is the very rock that was once part of the super-continent that drifted north to crash into this coast, then drag itself away to form Africa.

6   This island is a forgotten domain on the edge of the continent. It is easy to imagine that no man has ever been here before. But on the way back to the mainland, the truth reveals itself on the western shore. Not three metres from the edge of a cliff eight storeys high is a circle of lichen-covered rocks in the grass. A man-made well. The water is deep and long-legged insects skim along its obsidian surface. The well is full, nearly to the brim—it seems impossible given its elevation on this narrow wedge of land.

7   Nearby are two dents in the ground, as if some giant had punched down into a massive surface of dough. Those two dents were once the foundations of a farmhouse and barn. Nearby fields sprouted cabbage and turnips. A family lived on vegetables from the stony soil, cod, and mackerel from the sea. There were no roads, no cars, nothing but boats for commerce with Halifax. A way of life long gone.

8   The rains and seas will continue to conspire to undo the ribbon of land left between the well's fresh water and the sky. The well's stone walls will collapse. The drumlin's cliff will be pried by ice, and pocked by pelting rain. The sea will slip out stones from beneath the hill, the turf up above will tumble, and eventually the water of the farmer's well will gush out of the heart of the headland and race down to meet the sea.

Topics for Critical Thinking and Writing

1. What did Wedge Island used to look like? How has it changed? What has caused the changes?

2. How does Choyce describe Wedge Island? List at least five examples each of the vivid diction, figures of speech, unusual verbs, and alliteration that the author uses. What do these techniques tell you about how Choyce feels about the island he describes?

3. Using "Thin Edge of the Wedge" as a model, write a 500- to 750-word essay in which you describe a place and how time has changed it.

CHAPTER

11

Defining

THE NEED FOR DEFINITION

To argue a point or to explain an idea, writers frequently need to define words. Defining the terms of an argument is one of the persuasive writer's most useful strategies: a writer making an argument for or against abortion would be likely at some point in her essay to define the term "life." Even a primarily analytic essay may need to define its key terms. A writer analyzing a group of nineteenth-century Gothic stories, for example, might clarify his analysis by defining the term *Gothic tale*:

> Though it may be confused with the ghost story, the Gothic tale—
>
> despite its frequent reliance on supernatural elements—is quite distinct. A
>
> Gothic tale is one in which outdated and oppressive conventions confine a
>
> generally helpless victim, who is usually in some way associated with a
>
> decaying family line, and imprisoned in an isolated and deteriorating
>
> house, mansion, or castle.
>
> —CHAD HILL

The words may be *specialized* or unfamiliar to the writer's intended audience—for example, the words "venture capitalist" or "enterprise zones." Or, we might define a word that the audience thinks it knows but, in the writer's opinion, may be misunderstood. For instance, a writer might argue that the words "guerrilla" and "terrorist" are not synonyms, and then go on to define each word, showing the differences between them.

Often, however, providing a *synonym* is a reasonable strategy. In writing about the use of myths during war to dehumanize the opposing side, Michael Ignatieff writes of the "atrocity myth" and later calls it "this myth of inhuman otherness" (page 152). In Dey's article about her children growing up in small-town

Saskatchewan as the only black family for miles, the girls object to a school-mate's labelling of them as "black" in preference for "golden."

In addition to defining words because they are specialized ("venture capital-ist"), or because we want to distinguish them from other words ("guerrilla" and "terrorist"), or because we may think that synonyms will clarify them ("atrocity myth" and "myth of inhuman otherness"), we may define a word because the word has many meanings, and we want to make sure that readers take the word in a particular way. A word such as "ability," for example, may require defining in a discussion of the Scholastic Aptitude Test. To argue that a university entrance exam does or does not measure "academic ability," the writer and reader need, in a sense, to agree on a specific meaning for "ability." This kind of definition, where the writer specifies or stipulates a meaning, is called a *stipulative definition*.

The word "stipulate," by the way, comes from a Latin word meaning "to bar-gain." Explaining a word's *etymology*, its *history* or its *origin*, as we have just done, is often an aid in definition.

In short, in defining a word or term, writers have many options, and they need to take into account both their own purposes in writing and their readers' needs. Let's look at some examples.

KINDS OF DEFINITIONS

Inclusive/Exclusive Definitions

Here is a writer defining a *specialized* term for readers of a Central Florida newspaper:

> Enterprise zones are government-designated areas of severe poverty and high unemployment to which businesses are encouraged to relo-cate through tax breaks and other incentives. Where once there were vacant lots and boarded-up buildings, the theory goes, new companies attracted by the tax breaks would provide badly needed jobs, and the newly employed residents would spend their earnings on other local businesses, creating a ripple effect that revitalizes an entire community.
>
> —Max Friedman

Notice how Friedman defines "enterprise zones." In the first sentence, he places "enterprise zones" in a category or class, "government-designated areas." He next shows how they differ from other members of the class: they are areas "of severe poverty and high unemployment to which businesses are encour-aged to relocate through tax breaks and other incentives." Such a definition is sometimes called *inclusive/exclusive* because it *includes* the word in a relevant category (government-designated areas) and then *excludes* other members of that category (for example, "disaster zones" or "postal zones" or "war zones"). Notice too that Friedman's definition uses a parallel form, a noun for a noun: "zones" are "areas." (Avoid saying something like "Enterprise zones are when the government designates . . .")

Notice, also, that Friedman briefly describes "enterprise zones": they contain "vacant lots and boarded-up buildings." In the rest of the sentence he also describes, with a few details, the presumed effects of enterprise zones. (In the words "the theory goes," what does he imply about the actual effect of these zones?)

A definition of a specialized term can be very brief, for example: "Venture capitalists, *the specialized firms that raise money for new technological inventions . . .*" Here the definition is accomplished in a phrase (which we have italicized). A term can be defined in a paragraph, as Friedman does with "enterprise zones." But a writer might need the space of an essay to define a word. Notice how, in the following short essay—a book review—the writer begins with a whimsical definition of *caricature* as "a portrait with an attitude," but throughout the review she further defines caricature as "an acerbic and accessible form of social and political criticism" and "a savage mirror that confronts society."

> A caricature is a portrait with an attitude, a likeness meant to provoke recognition by its distortions. Although its purpose is often nothing more than to be a visual prank, caricature at its best has often been an acerbic and accessible form of social and political criticism. In *The Savage Mirror: The Art of Contemporary Caricature* (Watson-Guptil, paper, $29.95), Steven Heller, the art director of *The New York Times Book Review,* and Gail Anderson, the deputy art director of *Rolling Stone,* present an overview of contemporary caricature, tracing its evolution from 19th-century France through its powerful resurgence in the United States from the mid–1950's to the mid–1970's. The authors explain the roles that editorial preferences, design fads and technology have played in creating the current scene, which they seem, almost in spite of themselves, to find disappointing. For Ms. Anderson and Mr. Heller, caricaturists have great power—and perhaps even a duty—to address the issues of the day, to use their skills to rouse the public. Today the subjects of caricature are less likely to be political figures than celebrities, who menace our sensibilities more than our freedom. As the book amply illustrates, in changing from pen to airbrush, caricature has gone from inspired anger to dextrous hipness. Ms. Anderson and Mr. Heller clearly believe that a caricature should communicate an idea; as they survey contemporary caricature, they see "little gems of mild distortion" rather than a savage mirror that confronts society with its sorry reflection. This profusely illustrated book provides an excellent introduction to its subject, and the authors are persuasive in their arguments for the importance of caricature.
>
> —ROSEMARY RANCK

Stipulative Definitions

Now let's look at an example of a *stipulative definition.* In "The Morality and Rationality of Suicide," Richard B. Brandt asks his readers to agree on a *neutral* definition of suicide.

> "Suicide" is conveniently defined, for our purposes, as doing something which results in one's death, either from the intention of ending one's life or the intention to bring about some other state of affairs (such as relief from pain) which one thinks it certain or highly probable can be

achieved only by means of death or will produce death. It may seem odd to classify an act of heroic self-sacrifice on the part of a soldier as suicide. It is simpler, however, not to try to define "suicide" so that an act of suicide is always irrational or immoral in some way; if we adopt a neutral definition like the above we can still proceed to ask when an act of suicide in that sense is rational, morally justifiable, and so on, so that all evaluations anyone might wish to make can still be made.

Notice that Brandt concedes that there are apparent problems with this definition. It would, for example, include a soldier's self-sacrifice. But, he argues, if we adopt the definition he proposes, we can still evaluate a particular act as "rational, morally justifiable, and so on." In *stipulating* this definition of suicide we can see Brandt striking a bargain with his readers.

Striking such bargains is often necessary: although technical words have relatively stable meanings, many of the words that you will be defining—words such as *democracy, identity, family, society*—have so many meanings that your reader won't know what you mean until you explain which definition you are using.

Definition by Origin or History

The passage that follows, from a column called "The Word Watchers," is a *definition by origin and history* of the word "stonewall" used as a verb.

> "Stonewall" as a verb originated in the game of cricket, as a term for playing solely on the defensive. Australian political slang picked it up in the late nineteenth century, and it was adopted quickly by British politicians.
>
> In America, stonewalling was rarely used: the citation in *Webster's New International Unabridged Dictionary* is a James Reston column of the late fifties, "stonewalling for time in order to close the missile gap." But then Henry Kissinger picked up the term: I first heard him use it in late 1969 as, "The North Vietnamese are stonewalling us."
>
> As a needed figure of speech, the word's usage increased; more stones were added as a strategy of silence was adopted by the Watergaters, and when the President's tapes revealed him to have said "I want you to stonewall it," the word was sealed into the language.
>
> Stonewalling has a pejorative connotation today. But long before its scornful use by cricketers, politicians from Down Under and up above, the figure of speech was used in admiration during our Civil War about one of the Confederacy's greatest generals: "There stands Jackson, like a stone wall!"
>
> Might it be possible, someday, for stonewalling to regain an admirable connotation? The word-watchers will be watching.
>
> —WILLIAM SAFIRE

Safire's engaging discussion comes not only from his zeal for "word-watching" but also, we imagine, from the legwork of a staff of researchers, and an office wall of dictionaries and other reference books. But all writers must become word-watchers, to some degree, and it is fascinating as well as useful to learn word origins and histories. With nothing more than a good desk dictionary, we can learn that "yoga" derives from a Sanskrit word for union, or joining or yoking ("join" and "yoke" both come from this same root: yoga seeks to join or yoke the individual's consciousness to its spiritual source); that "Islam" is Arabic for "submission to God," and comes ultimately from an Arabic word for safety; that "science" comes from a Latin verb meaning "to know"; and that "holocaust" comes from a Greek word meaning "completely burnt." Here is the word history that accompanies the definition of "holocaust" in the third edition of *The American Heritage Dictionary of the English Language.*

> Totality of destruction has been central to the meaning of *holocaust* since it first appeared in Middle English in the 14th century and referred to the biblical sacrifice in which a male animal was wholly burnt on the altar in worship of God. *Holocaust* comes from Greek *holokauston* ("that which is completely burnt"), which was a translation of Hebrew *old* (literally "that which goes up," that is, in smoke). In this sense of "burnt sacrifice," *holocaust* is still used in some versions of the Bible. In the 17th century the meaning of *holocaust* broadened to "something totally consumed by fire," and the word eventually was applied to fires of extreme destructiveness. In the 20th century *holocaust* has taken on a variety of figurative meanings, summarizing the effects of war, rioting, storms, epidemic diseases, and even economic failures. Most of these usages arose after World War II, but it is unclear whether they permitted or resulted from the use of *holocaust* in reference to the mass murder of European Jews and others by the Nazis. This application of the word occurred as early as 1942, but the phrase *the Holocaust* did not become established until the late 1950's. Here it parallels and may have been influenced by another Hebrew word, *sho'ah* ("catastrophe"). In the Bible *sho'ah* has a range of meanings including "personal ruin or devastation" and "a wasteland or desert." *Sho'ah* was first used to refer to the Nazi slaughter of Jews in 1939, but its phrase *hasho'ah* ("the catastrophe") only became established after World War II. *Holocaust* has also been used to translate *hurban* ("destruction"), another Hebrew word used to summarize the genocide of Jews by the Nazis. This sense of *holocaust* has since broadened to include the mass slaughter of other peoples, but when capitalized it refers specifically to the destruction of Jews and other Europeans by the Nazis and may also encompass the Nazi persecution of Jews that preceded the outbreak of the war.

THE LIMITS OF DEFINITION BY SYNONYM

A Last Example

Paralyzed by illness, a professor of anthropology reflects on the meaning of the word "disabled." The passage is from his book, *The Body Silent:*

> I was badly damaged, yet just as alive as ever, and I had to make the best of it with my remaining capabilities. It then occurred to me that this is the universal human condition. We all have to muddle through life within our limitations, and while I had certain physical handicaps, I retained many strengths. My brain was the only part of the central cortex that still worked well, but that also is where I made my living.

Disability is an amorphous and relativistic term. Some people are unable to do what I do because they lack the mental equipment, and in this sense, they are disabled and I am not. Everybody is disabled in one way or another. And even though my growing paralysis would one day end my active participation in the affairs of the world, I could still sit back and watch them unfold.

—ROBERT F. MURPHY

Without calling attention to it, Murphy takes into account the *origin* of the word disability. "Dis" as a prefix (from Latin) means "not" or "deprived of." What does it mean, he seems to ask, to be deprived of or to not have ability? His discussion acknowledges that "damaged" and "handicapped" are *synonyms* for disabled. But, he argues, "*Disability* is an amorphous and relativistic term." Its meaning, he implies, needs to be *stipulated*. Above all, what his discussion makes clear is that he has a compelling reason to re-examine and explain how he defines the word "disability" and how we all should define it.

A NOTE ON USING A DICTIONARY

A dictionary is an invaluable resource for a writer. If you do not own a reliable recent dictionary, we advise you to buy one and to keep it handy as you read and write. You will use it to look up the meaning or several meanings of a word you are not sure of, to check its spelling or pronunciation, to see how its form changes in its various functions, to discover its origin. In some dictionaries, you will find usage notes that will tell you, for example, whether a word is considered slang, or obscene, or whether a usage is now generally accepted. We particularly recommend an extensive etymological dictionary. Any good bookstore will have several excellent dictionaries, such as *The Canadian Oxford Dictionary* or *Merriam-Webster's Collegiate Dictionary* (Eleventh Edition).

You should also become acquainted, in the library, with the great multi-volume *Oxford English Dictionary* (*OED*). In it you will find quotations illustrating the meanings of words over the centuries. It is an unparalleled source for shedding light on texts (especially poetry) written before our times.

The *OED* and other dictionaries are now available on CD-ROM; most colleges and universities provide online access to them as well. For information on accessing these resources, consult your institution's reference librarian.

The one use to which you ought *not* put a dictionary is this: Do not introduce an essay with the words "Webster says . . ." or "According to the dictionary . . ." Because the name Webster is no longer copyrighted, it appears on all sorts of dictionaries, bad as well as good. Besides, as we note in our discussion of introductory paragraphs, there is no staler opening.

A Checklist for Revising Definitions

✔ Do you give brief definitions, where needed—for example, of a specialized or technical term?

✔ Do you give sufficient examples to clarify the definition?

✔ Do you distinguish the term from a near synonym—for example, *communism* from *socialism, revolution* from *resistance, terrorism* from *guerrilla warfare*? Will a comparison help to define the term?

✔ Would it be helpful to mention the etymology or origin of the word?

✔ Do you make clear which meaning of a word you are using (stipulating), and why?

✔ Is the need for a definition implied or, in a long definition, do you explain the need?

 ## Topics for Critical Thinking and Writing

1. Define, for an audience unfamiliar with the terms, *bebop, rap, ska, hip hop, world music,* or *country music,* in 250 to 500 words.

2. Write one paragraph defining one of the following terms: *security blanket, twilight zone, holding pattern, stalking.* Your paragraph should disclose the origin of the term (if you cannot find it, make a reasonable guess) and some examples of current use distinct from its original meaning.

3. Write an opening paragraph for an essay in which you stipulate a meaning for *death* or *vegetarianism,* excluding one or two other meanings. Do not write the essay, just the opening paragraph.

4. In a paragraph explain the difference between "a reason" (for some action) and "an excuse." Provide a specific example, real or invented. Your audience is someone who expects you to offer an excuse.

5. If you are fluent in a language other than English, or in a dialect other than Standard English, write a paragraph defining for native speakers of Standard English a word that stands for some concept. Examples: Spanish *machismo* or *commoción,* Yiddish *haimish* or *chutzpah,* or Japanese *shibuih.*

6. Write an essay of approximately five hundred words on the word *natural* as it is used to advertise products such as cereals, yogurt, cosmetics, and cigarettes. Your essay should stipulate a definition of natural, and should have a thesis. An example of a thesis: "Yogurt may be a wholesome food, but most commercial yogurts are not as 'natural' as we are led to believe."

7. Write an essay defining the term *sexual harassment.* Explain the need for definition, what the term includes and excludes, and the relevance of the etymology of *harass.* Use examples of what is and is not sexual harassment to clarify your point.

8. Write an essay (about five hundred words) explaining one of the following terms: *horror film, situation comedy, soap opera, junk food, nostalgia, ethnic joke, yuppie.* Your essay will probably include a definition, reference to several examples, and perhaps an extended discussion of one example, explaining the reasons for its popularity or arguing its merits or lack of merits.

Definition at Work

 **LENA FLORA**

In the following brief essay, a student defines the term political correctness.

The Plight of the Politically Correct

Political correctness is a style of language, an attitude, and a standard of ethics that people have now been struggling with for years. Part of the reason for this struggle lies in the fact that no one is exactly sure what is and what is not politically correct. The phrase *political correctness* might be defined as "conformity to a body of liberal or radical opinion, especially on social matters." Political correctness also involves the avoidance of anything, even established vocabulary, that might be construed as discriminatory or pejorative. In effect, political correctness seems to mean taking every word in the English language, scrutinizing it for any way that it could possibly offend any one person, and using this criterion to ban its use in day-to-day speech. For example, I can no longer grow up and be a fireman, a policeman, a mailman, or a woman. I may not even be allowed to call myself female. Does this mean that I am fated to call myself testosteronally-challenged, or maybe x-chromosomally gifted? Am I a chauvinist pig if I like to be known as a woman, or if I refer to my daughter as my little girl? By some strict politically correct standards, yes. Also, political correctness forces me to refrain from using many adjectives I might use to describe myself. I am not Oriental, short, or near-sighted. Instead, I am Asian-American, vertically-challenged, and distant-visually-challenged person of feminine gender. I certainly don't feel challenged in any of these areas, only in the area of speaking with political correctness.

 Topics for Critical Thinking and Writing

1. Are you persuaded by Flora's definition of *political correctness*? What are two or three of the strongest points she makes in this paragraph? What points seem weak?
2. Would a person in favour of what Flora calls political correctness be likely to use the term *political correctness*? Why or why not?
3. If on the whole you disagree with Flora's definition of *political correctness,* write your own definition of the term.
4. If you agree with her definition, define the term *multiculturalism.*

 CHARLIE GILLIS

Charlie Gillis is a national correspondent for Maclean's. *He has previously written for the* National Post, Edmonton Journal, *and Canadian Press.*

Let's Redefine "Hero"

1   Daniel Francis's hour of greatness comes back to him in flashes—none of them especially pleasant. He's crawling down the hallway of a burning mobile home, holding his breath, as a desperate mother cries for help outside. "There was a kind of chemical smoke, and it was pretty thick," he says. "You couldn't see much." He remembers reaching out, and finding the elbow of a half-conscious 11-year-old girl who was crouched in the hallway. Tugging her backward, Francis worked his way to the trailer's rear door, pushing the girl to safety before tumbling out himself. Moments later, flames engulfed the home.

2   The night Francis saved Jocelyn Poulette in Millbrook, N.S., is one for the books: bravery and selflessness in the face of obvious danger. Throw in the then-23-year-old's knee-length cast (he'd broken his leg a couple of weeks earlier while play-wrestling with a pal), and you have something far beyond good citizenship. Francis was recently presented with a Governor General's Medal of Bravery, Canada's standard decoration for heroics. He's loath to blow his own horn, but it seems a pity the whole country wasn't able to attend his ceremony. We could use a refresher on what heroism really is.

3   Anyone who watches a supper-hour newscast knows what I mean. That word, once the preserve of the brave or visionary, has somehow become a default term for anyone from dearly missed accident victims to public employees who are, well, doing their jobs. One U.S. college newspaper I read recently declared their institution's groundskeepers "heroes" for keeping the campus free of litter; blood donors in Canada are "everyday heroes" for performing what is really a civic duty; all 2,749 innocent victims who died in the World Trade Center towers or on hijacked planes were repeatedly described as heroes following the 9/11 attacks—something I can't imagine sat well with the families of firefighters trapped in the collapsing buildings. If everyone's a hero, logic suggests, then no one's a hero, and our appreciation of the genuine article suffers for it.

4   The hyperbole can produce absurd results: last year, Toronto's transit authority launched a series of posters extolling the "heroic" deeds of its employees, with the laudable goal of engaging a cynical public. The acts, however, turned out to be little more than gestures of common decency—the kind we should be ashamed *not* to do. One driver (gasp!) stopped her streetcar after seeing a youngster wander into traffic and picked the child up. Another halted a subway train and had the power rail disconnected after spotting a boy on the tracks (instead of, one supposes, running the child down or watching him electrocute himself). The posters' attempts at irony only added to the satirical effect: "It's a bird! It's a plane!" one proclaimed. "It's . . . Deborah and Brad!?"

5   So how did this happen? Since when did the least we can do become grounds for civilization's most exalted status? Unfulfilled need is one explanation: few occasions any longer warrant the kind of bravery shown by Francis—not in our buttoned-down, seat-belted, gold-star-insured age. If we're throwing the label around a little, maybe it's because we *want* more heroes in our midst, which is hardly a sinful urge. Grief can play a role, too, in cases where the subject has been hurt or killed. It's a lot more comforting to think of bombing victims as heroes than hapless pawns in a terrorist war, even if circumstances suggest the latter.

6   But as George Orwell teaches, misuse of a word breeds doubt about it, and that point struck home for me last fall as I watched television coverage of the

death of Lieut. Chris Saunders, the submariner who succumbed to injuries suffered aboard HMCS *Chicoutimi*. Numerous reports depicted Saunders as a hero who died in the service of his country.

7   But it was hard to accept that application of the label at face value. Crew members' accounts would later suggest Saunders indeed acted selflessly, fighting an electrical fire aboard the ill-fated vessel after suffering severe smoke inhalation. Yet that wasn't widely known at the time, and conflating Saunders's death with a battlefield casualty played squarely into the hands of the current federal government's ends. The Liberals were about to come under heavy criticism for authorizing the cut-rate purchase of *Chicoutimi* and three other British-made subs, which have been plagued with problems since their delivery. Declaring Saunders a hero underscored the inherent risks of military service, rather than the specific risk of serving aboard leaky, dysfunctional vessels.

8   More subtle, but just as worrisome, is the willingness of intellectuals to play along—even play a part—in corrupting the hero ideal further. In a 1999 essay prepared for the Dominion Institute, writer and historian Charlotte Gray called on Canadians to "redefine" heroism according to national values, emphasizing such qualities as collective strength, quiet competence, respect for the land, humour, creative brilliance and something she calls "self-invention." Who, if anyone, that would exclude remains unclear (Lili St. Cyr, the famous Montreal stripper of the '40s and '50s, counts among Gray's self-inventors). But Gray does declare old-fashioned bravery passé. "Its only current manifestation," she says, "is in the nerves-of-steel takeover duels between the contemporary titans of capitalism."

9   As an unapologetic reactionary, I greet this with boos, and the few polls I've seen suggest that the rest of the country feels the same way. One taken in 1999 asked Canadians what values they associate most with heroism. Answers varied, but bravery/courage topped the list, with a 26 per cent rating, while honesty, honour and selflessness followed close behind. This suggests a gut-level affinity for traditional notions of heroism and gives lie to the stereotypical idea that Canadians are bent on reducing the heroic to the banal.

10   So why are some lowering the bar? If we know what makes a hero, why not protect the word from misuse and reserve the honour for its rightful owners? If there's a sad note to Daniel Francis's story, after all, it's that he seems unfazed when the designation is applied to him—as if heroism is something we all possess and need not take pride in. "It was just instinct kicking in, the spirit of the moment," he harrumphs when asked about his actions. "It was something anybody would have done."

11   Not true, by a long shot—though the world would be a better place if it were. Heroes, unfortunately, don't grow on trees, and nothing we say can change that.

 Topics for Critical Thinking and Writing

1   Are you persuaded that the term *hero* and its derivatives are overused?

2. How is *hero* used in everyday language, and how does Charlie Gillis redefine *hero*?

3. What effect does Gillis not using "heroics" until the end of the second paragraph and the word he is actually redefining until even later in his

essay have on your reading of his essay? Is it confusing? Does it add a subtle effect? Is it simply unnecessary given the clarity of his title?

4. Do you agree that part of the reason why *hero* is overused is, ironically, that there are fewer heroes around now, leaving people with an "unfulfilled need" in their safety-regulated lives?

5. We found ourselves nodding vigorous assent as we read "Let's Redefine 'Hero,'" and we were able to come up with a list of other words that are frustratingly overused and misused. What word provokes the kind of reaction in you that *hero* does for Gillis?

 # BARBARA LAWRENCE

Barbara Lawrence was educated at Connecticut College and at New York University, taught at the State University of New York at Old Westbury, and was an editor for Redbook *and* Harper's Bazaar. *This essay about the politics of language first appeared in* The New York Times.

Four-Letter Words Can Hurt You

1   Why should any words be called obscene? Don't they all describe natural human functions? Am I trying to tell them, my students demand, that the "strong, earthy, gut-honest"—or, if they are fans of Norman Mailer, the "rich, liberating, existential"—language they use to describe sexual activity isn't preferable to "phony-sounding, middle-class words like 'intercourse' and 'copulate'?" "Cop You Late!" they say with fancy inflections and gagging grimaces. "Now, what is *that* supposed to mean?"

2   Well, what is it supposed to mean? And why indeed should one group of words describing human functions and human organs be acceptable in ordinary conversation and another, describing presumably the same organs and functions, be tabooed—so much so, in fact, that some of these words still cannot appear in print in many parts of the English-speaking world?

3   The argument that these taboos exist only because of "sexual hangups" (middle-class, middle-age, feminist), or even that they are a result of class oppression (the contempt of the Norman conquerors for the language of their Anglo-Saxon serfs), ignores a much more likely explanation, it seems to me, and that is the sources and functions of the words themselves.

4   The best known of the tabooed sexual verbs, for example, comes from the German *ficken,* meaning "to strike"; combined, according to Partridge's etymological dictionary *Origins,* with the Latin sexual verb *futuere;* associated in turn with the Latin *fustis,* "a staff or cudgel"; the Celtic *buc,* "a point, hence to pierce"; the Irish *bot,* "the male member"; the Latin *battuere,* "to beat"; the Gaelic *batair,* "a cudgeller"; the Early Irish *bualaim,* "I strike"; and so forth. It is one of what etymologists sometimes call "the sadistic group of words for the man's part in copulation."

5   The brutality of this word, then, and its equivalents ("screw," "bang," etc.), is not an illusion of the middle class or a crotchet of Women's Liberation. In their origins and imagery these words carry undeniably painful, if not sadistic, implications, the object of which is almost always female. Consider, for example, what a "screw" actually does to the wood it penetrates; what a painful, even mutilating,

activity this kind of analogy suggests. "Screw" is particularly interesting in this context, since the noun, according to Partridge, comes from words meaning "groove," "nut," "ditch," "breeding sow," "scrofula" and "swelling," while the verb, besides its explicit imagery, has antecedent associations to "write on," "scratch," "scarify," and so forth—a revealing fusion of a mechanical or painful action with an obviously denigrated object.

6   Not all obscene words, of course, are as implicitly sadistic or denigrating to women as these, but all that I know seem to serve a similar purpose: to reduce the human organism (especially the female organism) and human functions (especially sexual and procreative) to their least organic, most mechanical dimension; to substitute a trivializing or deforming resemblance for the complex human reality of what is being described.

7   Tabooed male descriptives, when they are not openly denigrating to women, often serve to divorce a male organ or function from any significant interaction with the female. Take the word "testes," for example, suggesting "witnesses" (from the Latin *testis*) to the sexual and procreative strengths of the male organ; and the obscene counterpart of this word, which suggests little more than a mechanical shape. Or compare almost any of the "rich," "liberating" sexual verbs, so fashionable today among male writers, with that much-derided Latin word "copulate" ("to bind or join together") or even that Anglo-Saxon phrase (which seems to have had no trouble surviving the Norman Conquest) "make love."

8   How arrogantly self-involved the tabooed words seem in comparison to either of the other terms, and how contemptuous of the female partner. Understandably so, of course, if she is only a "skirt," a "broad," or a "chick," a "pussycat" or a "piece." If she is, in other words, no more than her skirt, or what her skirt conceals; no more than a breeder, or the broadest part of her; no more than a piece of a human being or a "piece of tail."

9   The most severely tabooed of all the female descriptives, incidentally, are those like a "piece of tail," which suggest (either explicitly or through antecedents) that there is no significant difference between the female channel through which we are all conceived and born and the anal outlet common to both sexes—a distinction that pornographers have always enjoyed obscuring.

10   This effort to deny women their biological identity, their individuality, their humanness, is such an important aspect of obscene language that one can only marvel at how seldom, in an era preoccupied with definitions of obscenity, this fact is brought to our attention. One problem, of course, is that many of the people in the best position to do this (critics, teachers, writers) are so reluctant today to admit that they are angered or shocked by obscenity. Bored, maybe, unimpressed, aesthetically displeased, but—no matter how brutal or denigrating the material—never angered, never shocked.

11   And yet how eloquently angered, how piously shocked many of these same people become if denigrating language is used about any minority group other than women; if the obscenities are racial or ethnic, that is, rather than sexual. Words like "coon," "kike," "spic," "wop," after all, deform identity, deny individuality and humanness in almost exactly the same way that sexual vulgarisms and obscenities do.

12   No one that I know, least of all my students, would fail to question the values of a society whose literature and entertainment rested heavily on racial or ethnic pejoratives. Are the values of a society whose literature and entertainment rest as heavily as ours on sexual pejoratives any less questionable?

Topic for Critical Thinking and Writing

In addition to giving evidence to support her view, what persuasive devices (for example, irony, analogy) does Barbara Lawrence use?

JAY INGRAM

Jay Ingram is best known as a co-host and producer of Daily Planet *on Discovery Channel and for his years as the host of* Quirks and Quarks *on CBC Radio. He is a science writer and broadcaster who makes complex scientific theories and knowledge comprehensible to the non-scientist. He has won many awards and has written several popular books on science. This piece originally apppeared as a column in* Equinox.

The Atom's Image Problem

1   What do you envision when you hear the word *atom*? I bet if you see anything at all it is a miniature solar system, with the nucleus of the atom as the sun, and tiny electrons whirling planetlike around it. And why not? A stylized version of this has long been synonymous with atomic power. It's probably the atom you saw in public school and is, indeed, a model rooted in science. The science is, however, a little out of date—by at least 70 years. If you try to redraw the atom as scientists imagine it today, it is transformed. What was solid becomes wispy and foggy, what was compact becomes vast, and, most important of all, what was predictable is not.

2   This revolution in the concept of the atom was largely accomplished in a few years of incredible scientific progress during the 1920s. So why are we non-scientists so out of date in our mental image of the atom? Is it because atomic science is so incompatible with everyday experience that we simply can't form and hold an image of it?

3   In his 1928 book *The Nature of the Physical World*, the great English astro-physicist Sir Arthur Eddington cast his eye back to the nineteenth century and said, "It was the boast of the Victorian physicist that he would not claim to understand a thing until he could make a model of it; and by a model he meant something constructed of levers, geared wheels, squirts, or other appliances familiar to an engineer." I suspect that most of us, if we are physicists at all, are Victorian. And I wonder if the Victorian physicists Eddington described weren't revealing something about human psychology that holds for most of us today.

4   By the time Eddington published his book, the solar-system model of the atom had already been out of favour for two years, replaced by the infinitely more challenging imagery of quantum mechanics. In fact, the solar-system atom, for all its hold on the popular imagination, held sway among scientists for little more than a decade. In that sense, it takes its place beside the cowboy: the Wild West has had much greater staying power in popular culture than it did in reality.

5   However brief the scientific reign of the solar-system atom, its beginnings were honest. In 1911 Ernest Rutherford made public the experiment that set the stage for its appearance. When he aimed highly energized subatomic particles at

thin sheets of gold foil, he was shocked to see that in some cases the particles bounced right back. Rutherford said, "It was almost as incredible as if you had fired a 15-inch shell at a piece of tissue paper and it came back and hit you." Rutherford concluded that the atoms of gold in the sheet couldn't be likened (as had been suggested) to miniature raisin buns—blobs of positive electrical charge stuffed with tiny negative charges. Instead, the positive charge had to be intensely concentrated at a point inside the atom. Only such a compact object could deflect the particles Rutherford had aimed at it. He didn't go so far as to limit the outer negative charges (the electrons) to precise orbits, and in that sense he was more in tune with the modern vision of the atom.

6   However, in 1912, shortly after this experiment, the Danish physicist Niels Bohr came to work with Rutherford, and by 1913 he put the electrons firmly in orbits about the nucleus. In doing so, Bohr solved what had been a major problem in previous theories: classical physics had predicted that as electrons circled in orbits, they would steadily radiate away their energy; as this happened, their orbits would decay and they would eventually spiral into the nucleus like satellites reentering the earth's atmosphere. In one scientist's words, "matter would incandesce and collapse." Bohr argued that continuous processes such as radiating energy and decaying orbits were out-of-date concepts, failing to capture the inner workings of the atom. He suggested that electrons were restricted to certain stable orbits, in which they could move without loss of energy, and could only jump from one to another by emitting or absorbing a packet, or quantum, of energy.

7   So by the beginning of World War I, the solar-system atom was in place, but by the mid-1920s, it was gone. It couldn't withstand the brilliant onslaught of experimentation and thought that swept through physics in Europe during that decade. A who's who of science repainted our portrait of the atom, even if we haven't noticed. Perhaps the most radical change was that, as seen from the quantum-theory point of view, such particles as electrons could behave as waves. So Erwin Schrödinger, an Austrian-born Irish physicist, was able to dispense with the precise orbits of the electrons, filling the same space with waves radiating outward from the nucleus, the peaks of which corresponded to the now-defunct orbits. Max Born, a theoretical physicist, altered that idea slightly by claiming that the waves' peaks didn't really show where electrons were but, rather, where they might be.

8   In 1927 German physicist Werner Heisenberg elevated that sense of uncertainty into a principle, called (guess what?) Heisenberg's Uncertainty Principle. He established that it was not just difficult but literally impossible to pinpoint both the position and the momentum (or velocity) of an electron at the same time—the very act of measurement would inevitably disturb the object being measured. In physics, the relationship has mathematical precision: you can know where the electron is, but then you don't know where it's going; if you endeavour to detect where it's going, you lose track of where it is. Is it any wonder that the solar-system model of the atom was trashed? It was replaced by a dissonant sort of picture—in tune with physicists' thinking but out of tune with the rest of us.

9   In today's atom, the electrons are still there outside the nucleus (although they often venture perilously close to it), but they are represented not by miniplanets but by probabilities, clouds of likelihood that suggest, "this is where you

might find it." Sometimes there are gaps in those clouds—places forbidden to electrons, yet these seem to present no barrier to the electrons' ability to materialize, first on one side of the gap, then on the other.

10   There's also the nucleus, the image of which has evolved from a tightly bound cluster of protons and neutrons to something that might be like a drop of liquid, spinning, pulsating, and quivering with the movements of the particles inside. Or it might be more like a series of Russian doll-like shells, nestled one inside the other. And as important as the nucleus is, it occupies only a minuscule fraction of the total size of the atom.

11   It has always struck me that physicists and chemists are, for the most part, perfectly happy to think of and talk about the atom as the sum of a set of equations. I'm sure they all believe these equations represent something in the real world, but it is probably not possible any more to say exactly what. The indeterminate and unknowable have replaced precision and prediction.

12   That's fine if you're a physicist—it's necessary—but it doesn't work very well for the rest of us. We don't have the language and skills to understand the atom as math; we need a model that squares with intuition. Clouds of probability don't; balls moving in orbits do.

13   Much is made these days of the idea that we are coping with the twentieth century equipped with only a Stone Age hunter-gatherer brain. It follows, then, that the brain should be particularly skilled at doing things useful for hunter-gatherers. Imagination is certainly one of those skills, but imagination of what? Of solid, substantial objects moving around each other in regular fashion? Or of pointlike particles that can't be localized and that behave like waves and move in strange and unpredictable ways?

14   And why should you care what the atom is like? If you are at all interested in the natural world, you have to care. The atom isn't just another feature of nature— it is nature. Unfortunately, the solar-system atom was likely about as much as we could handle in concrete conceptual terms. When scientists left the concept behind forever in the 1920s, it seems they left the rest of us behind too. They have their mathematical atom to contemplate. We have only our mental pictures.

 Topics for Critical Thinking and Writing

1. One of Ingram's purposes in this essay is to explode the analogy of the atom as a solar system. Is it ironic that he wants to erase the image used by atomic power?

2. In your own words, explain what Heisenberg's Uncertainty Principle is.

3. Ingram identifies himself with the lay reader rather than with the physicists by referring to the scientists as "they," and the non-scientists as "we" and "the rest of us." Is this kind of division effective? Is Ingram a "we"?

4. In his attempt to replace the solar-system image, Ingram uses a number of images, analogies, metaphors, and similes such as "clouds of likelihood," "like a drop of liquid, spinning, pulsating, and quivering," and "like a series of Russian doll-like shells." Are these accurate? Is it possible to provide a mental image of something so complex?

5. Do we need a mental image in order to understand atoms?

WILLIAM IAN MILLER

William Ian Miller is a professor of law at the University of Michigan Law School. The selection that follows is from his book The Anatomy of Disgust *(1997), which examines disgust from psychological, social, and political perspectives. Miller's more recent works include* Eye for an Eye *(2006),* Faking It *(2003), and* The Mystery of Courage *(2000).*

Darwin's Disgust

1   Modern psychological interest in disgust starts with Darwin, who centers it in the rejection of food and the sense of taste. Consider his account:

> The term "disgust," in its simplest sense, means something offensive to the taste. It is curious how readily this feeling is excited by anything unusual in the appearance, odour, or nature of our food. In Tierra del Fuego a native touched with his finger some cold preserved meat which I was eating at our bivouac, and plainly showed utter disgust at its softness; whilst I felt utter disgust at my food being touched by a naked savage, though his hands did not appear dirty. A smear of soup on a man's beard looks disgusting, though there is of course nothing disgusting in the soup itself. I presume that this follows from the strong association in our minds between the sight of food, however circumstanced, and the idea of eating it.[1]

Darwin is right about the etymology of disgust. It means unpleasant to the taste.[2] But one wonders whether taste would figure so crucially in Darwin's account if the etymology hadn't suggested it. The German *Ekel,* for instance, bears no easily discernible connection to taste. Did that make it easier for Freud to link disgust as readily with the anal and genital as with the oral zone?[3] I suspect that the English word is in some unquantifiable way responsible for the narrow focus on taste, oral incorporation, and rejection of food in psychological treatments of disgust.[4] Before the word disgust entered the English lexicon in the first quarter of the seventeenth century, taste figured distinctly less prominently than foul odors and loathsome sights. Disgust undoubtedly involves taste, but it also involves—not just by extension but at its core—smell, touch, even at times sight and hearing. Above all, it is a moral and social sentiment. It plays a motivating and confirming role in moral judgment in a particular way that has little if any connection with ideas of oral incorporation.[5] It ranks people and things in a kind of cosmic ordering.

[1]*The Expression of the Emotions in Man and Animals* 256–257.
[2]Disgust comes to English via French via Latin: *dis* (a negative prefix) + *gustus* (taste).
[3]See Susan Miller, "Disgust: Conceptualization, Development and Dynamics," 295; see Freud, *Three Essays* II 177–178.
[4]See, among others, the works of Tomkins, Izard, and Rozin in the list of Works Cited [not reproduced].
[5]The moral aspects of disgust have only very recently been recognized in academic psychological literature. See Haidt, McCauley, and Rozin, "Individual Differences in Sensitivity to Disgust," and Haidt, Rozin, et al., "Body, Psyche, and Culture." In the Freudian account disgust is distinctly moral or at least does much the same work as morality; Freud makes reaction formations a trinity of disgust, shame, and morality; see *Three Essays* II 177–178.

2   I use the word to indicate a complex sentiment that can be lexically marked in English by expressions declaring things or actions to be repulsive, revolting, or giving rise to reactions described as revulsion and abhorrence as well as disgust.[6] Disgust names a syndrome in which all these terms have their proper role. They all convey a strong sense of aversion to something perceived as dangerous because of its powers to contaminate, infect, or pollute by proximity, contact, or ingestion. All suggest the appropriateness, but not the necessity, of accompanying nausea or queasiness, or of an urge to recoil and shudder from creepiness.

3   Disgust, however, is not nausea. Not all disgust need produce symptoms of nausea, nor all nausea mark the presence of disgust. The nausea of the stomach flu is not a sign or consequence of disgust, although, should we vomit as a result, the vomiting and the vomit might themselves lead to sensations of disgust that would be distinguishable from the nausea that preceded it. The nausea of a hangover, however, is more complex, accompanied as it often is by feelings of contamination, poisoning, and self-disgust, as well as shame and embarrassment. On the other side, things or deeds we find disgusting put us in the world of disgust when we have the sense that we would not be surprised should we start feeling queasy or nauseated, whether or not we actually do so. Disgust surely has a feel to it; that feel, however, is not so much of nausea as of the uneasiness, the panic, of varying intensity, that attends the awareness of being defiled.

4   Let us put that aside for now and look more closely at the passage from Darwin. Is it food and taste that elicit disgust as a first-order matter?

> In Tierra del Fuego a native touched with his finger some cold preserved meat which I was eating at our bivouac, and plainly showed utter disgust at its softness; whilst I felt utter disgust at my food being touched by a naked savage, though his hands did not appear dirty.

In this passage, long before food ever reaches a mouth to raise the issue of its taste, we have suggestions of other categories that implicate disgust: categories of tactility as in cold (meat) vs. hot, soft vs. firm; overt categories of purity such as raw vs. cooked, dirty vs. clean; categories of bodily shame, naked vs. clothed; and broader categories of group definition, Tierra del Fuego vs. England, them vs. us. For the native, it is not ultimately the softness of the preserved meat so much as what eating it means about the person eating it. For Darwin, it is not just that someone touched his food (with clean hands no less), but that the person doing the touching was a *naked savage* who had already offended him. In the first clause the savage is merely a curious native in the two senses of curious: curious because strange and curious subjectively as a dispositional trait that makes him poke at Darwin's food. But once he finds Darwin's food disgusting, Darwin redescribes him downward as a naked savage capable of polluting his food. Before this interaction Darwin could look at the native with the contempt of bemusement or indifference or with a kind of benign contempt that often is

---

[6]Wierzbicka argues for the distinctiveness of the notions of revulsion, repulsiveness, and disgust ("Human Emotions," 588–591). Disgust, she supposes, refers to ingestion of, revulsion to contact with, and repulsiveness to proximity to the offensive entity. She underestimates the generality and easy interchangeability of these concepts. Disgust melds notions of ingestion, contact, and proximity.

itself a component of curiosity. The native, however, gets too close and gives real offense, and the inkling of threat is enough to transform a complacent contempt into disgust.

5   Would Darwin have been as disgusted by the native touching his food if the native had not insulted it by registering his revulsion? Or had the native already discerned Darwin's disgust for him and decided to use it to toy with him by touching his food? Would Darwin have been less disgusted if the native had touched him rather than his food? Food plays a role here, to be sure, and both actors share a deep belief that you pretty much are what you eat. The native recoils at the idea of what manner of man could eat such stuff, whereas Darwin fears ingesting some essence of savagery that has been magically imparted to his food by the finger of the naked savage. But oral ingestion is put in play here only because food is acting as one of a number of possible media by which pollution could be transferred. The issue is the doubts and fears each man's presence elicits in the other and the little battle for security and dominance by which they seek to resolve it; it is a battle of competing disgusts.

6   Less loaded with politics is the smear of soup on a man's beard, "though there is of course nothing disgusting in the soup itself." Again it is not food that is disgusting; Darwin's own explanation says it only becomes disgusting by the "strong association . . . between the sight of food . . . and the idea of eating it." But this can't be right. The sight of the man with his beard befouled is disgusting long before any idea of eating the soup on his beard ever would, if ever it could, occur to us. The association of ideas is not of seeing food in a beard and then imagining eating that food. If the soup is disgusting as food, it is so only because beard hair would be in it. Now that *is* disgusting. We could see this, in accordance with the structural theory of Mary Douglas, as a manifestation of things becoming polluting by being out of place.[7] That captures some of the problem but doesn't explain the sense that it is more the hair than the soup, more the man than the food, that elicits disgust. The soup on the beard reveals the man as already contaminated by a character defect, a moral failure in keeping himself presentable in accordance with the righteously presented demand that he maintain his public purity and cleanliness of person and not endanger us by his incompetence. It needn't have been soup or bread crumbs that incriminated him; it could just as well have been bits of lint or even soap residue. No doubt, however, the soup would be more disgusting than either lint or soap. The soup, after all, unlike lint or soap, might have fallen onto his beard from his mouth or from a spoon that had already been in his mouth. It is thus not our fear of oral incorporation that makes the soup disgusting to us but his failure to have properly orally incorporated it.

7   Yet suppose that it was not a naked savage who touched Darwin's meat but a cockroach that walked across it. Would the issue then be one primarily of ingesting food? Even here I think the matter is more complex. A roach walking across our arm would elicit disgust too and perhaps even more than if it walked across our food, and we are not about to eat our arm. The roach (and the naked savage) is disgusting before it touches our food; its contaminating powers come from some other source.

[7]*Purity and Danger.*

Topics for Critical Thinking and Writing

1. Miller quotes Darwin's definition of *disgust* at the beginning of the selection. To what end does he use that definition?
2. In the last sentence of the selection, Miller says that the "contaminating powers" of both the roach and the naked savage "come from some other source." According to Miller, what is that "other source"?
3. Miller distinguishes *disgust* from *nausea.* Look up *nausea* in the *Oxford English Dictionary,* and define the word in a brief essay of about three to four paragraphs. Give its etymology, distinguish it from a near synonym (perhaps *queasiness* or *revulsion*), and illustrate its proper use with an example.

Persuading

There are several ways to persuade. A threat may persuade you to hand over money; an emotional appeal may also persuade you to hand over money. But in this chapter we are concerned with persuading by means of *evidence* and *reasonable arguments.*

RHETORICAL ANALYSIS

The *Oxford English Dictionary* defines *rhetoric* as "the art of using language so as to persuade or influence others" and *analysis* as "the resolution or breaking up of anything complex into its various simple elements . . . the exact determination of the elements or components of anything complex." Thus, rhetorical analysis, like the forms of analysis discussed in Chapter 8, breaks the whole down into its parts, but here the emphasis is on the persuasive strategies used— or quite simply the "how" and "why" of the text. Rhetorical analysis interprets and discusses the methods used for explaining the argument presented in the text (rather than responding to the argument itself). The focus is on the dynamic relationship amongst the author, the audience, and the text, with an emphasis on how meaning is created: how the purpose is achieved, how the main points are made, how the reader is persuaded. (Before you investigate what the writer's purpose is and how he tries to influence his reader, you might find it helpful to review "Thinking about Purpose and Audience" from Chapter 1.)

What we now call rhetorical analysis or rhetorical criticism developed out of classic rhetoric, which is based upon the teachings of Aristotle (384–322 BCE), who emphasized how the text should be written to achieve the author's purpose of persuading, informing, and entertaining an audience (and sometimes also who the audience was and what skills they brought to their reading experience). From Aristotle's work on *ethos, pathos,* and *logos* in oratory, later rhetoricians developed the rhetorical triangle in order to visually express the idea that various aspects of writing should be given equal weight in any discussion of rhetoric (see Figure 12.1).

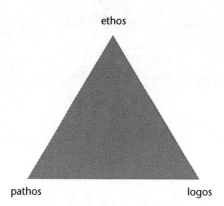

Figure 12.1 Classical Rhetorical Triangle

This triangle indicates the writer's authoritative stance and personal credibility (*ethos*), the reader's emotional response (*pathos*), and the text's effective argument and logical appeals (*logos*). (Sometimes this triad is discussed from the slightly different perspective of the writer's appeals within the text: ethical appeals to the reader's civic responsibilities [*ethos*], emotional appeals to the reader's feelings [*pathos*], and logical appeals to the reader's rationality [*logos*].) Rhetorical analysis retains the classic rhetorical emphasis on the elements used in and the function of the text, and on the concept of the fundamental relationship among the writer, text, and reader, as the updated rhetorical triangle shows (see Figure 12.2).

George A. Kennedy succinctly states that "The ultimate goal of rhetorical analysis, briefly put, is the discovery of the author's intent and of how that is transmitted through a text to an audience." While this definition is helpful, it does not recognize some of the complexities involved in this kind of analysis. First, there are problems with trying to establish authorial intention: we cannot know what was in the author's mind while he or she was writing, and the author often uses a *persona*, a narrative voice that may or may not actually be the author. Second, each reader brings a personal perspective, understanding, and knowledge to the reading experience, and the author's intended audience (the audi-

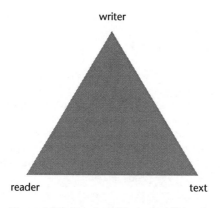

Figure 12.2 Standard Rhetorical Triangle

ence the writer had in mind) may not be the actual audience (you as a reader of his text). Your instructor may want to go over these complexities in more detail.

Recognition of the intricacies of authorial intention and reader-response has led to the more refined sense of the intent of the implied author (that is, the author as implied in the text) and shifts the emphasis so that the three elements are not always as evenly discussed as the equilateral triangles in Figures 12.1 and 12.2 suggest. The focus becomes the purpose of the text: what the text says, how the text says it, and what the indicators are in the text that suggest how the writer wants the audience to respond. For example, George Orwell first published "Shooting an Elephant" (reprinted in Part Five, "Readings"), about his experiences in Burma, in 1936. Obviously, his readers brought a different perspective to the text and to his shocking statements in the last paragraph than would a reader today. Nevertheless, we can still *infer* certain things about the author's purpose and intended audience by analyzing the structure, strategies, and style of the text itself—that is, by analyzing the evidence in the text and the historical context. Therefore, in addition to the triad, author–text–audience, the circumstances of the writing also play a role. To indicate this addition to the triad, the rhetorical triangle is sometimes enclosed within a circle to connote the rhetorical situation (see Figure 12.3).

The rhetorical situation includes addressing the reason for the writing, since persuasion implies that there may be a certain resistance on the part of the reader, and addressing the background of the writing. Background is the immediate context in which the text appears and, when relevant, the larger context such as the socio-cultural milieu of the writing. For example, for an article published in *Maclean's* in 1942 on conscription, you might consider the intended audience of the magazine, other articles in that issue, articles in other magazines on the same or similar topics, and the war in which the country was engaged.

Following are some questions to get you started with a rhetorical analysis, but remember that if you are writing an essay, you need to narrow your focus.

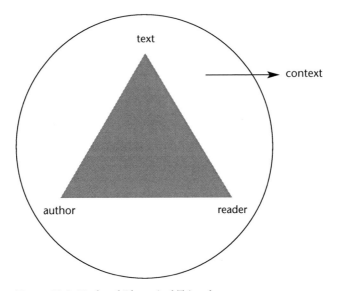

Figure 12.3 Updated Rhetorical Triangle

1. What is the rhetorical situation? What is the thesis and what are the main arguments?
2. What purpose and intended audience is implied by the text?
   a. What is the text trying to communicate? How does the author generate authority? Does the author use a persona? Is the intent to persuade? Dissuade? Defend? Assert? Call to action? Inform?
   b. How does the author try to influence or persuade the audience? What textual clues give you an idea of the intended audience? Is there a difference between the intended audience and the real audience?
3. How is the text organized and why might it be organized that way?
4. What strategies are used, how are they used, and what is their function?
   a. Does the author use analogy? Irony? Comparisons? Examples? Definitions? Statistics? Testimonials? Graphics? Charts? Why does the writer use these methods of development and what effect do they have?
   b. Comment upon the writer's style: use of quotations, transitions, sentence structure, technical jargon, irony, repetition, word choice, tone.
5. What does the writing tell you about the writer, about the culture that produced it? What values are being reinforced or countered? How do the strategies used reinforce and support the content and purpose? Are they effective?
6. How effective are the strategies and style? How effective is the text itself in achieving its implied purpose?

As you analyze texts for purpose, persona, implied audience, structure, strategies, tone, and context, remember that rhetorical analysis is a form of analytical thinking and reading. The basic purpose of rhetorical analysis is twofold: to encourage the reader to be aware of the response the writer is trying to effect and to provide the analyzer with writing strategies he can use in his own writing. For the rest of this chapter, we concentrate on *logos*, but keep in mind that while a persuasive or argumentation essay often foregrounds an appeal to the reader's reason, it most often also includes appeals to the reader's emotions and ethics.

 REBECCA TRAISTER

Rebecca Traister, a journalist, has written for numerous magazines, such as the New York Observer *and* New York Magazine, *and she is currently a staff writer at* Salon Life.

Thigh the Beloved Country

1   It was just a few weeks ago that the Dove "Campaign for Real Beauty" ads featuring recognizably curvy women got plastered on the walls of major metropolitan bus and subway stations.[1] Only days ago, the unexpected media storm about the campaign reached a late crescendo with an Op-Ed in the *New York Times.*

[1]Dove ran a series of ads using unretouched photographs of "real" women (rather than models) with bodies and faces of different shapes, sizes, colours, and ages. (Editor's note)

And now, seemingly out of nowhere, come the Nike Big Butts and Thunder Thighs, protruding from the pages of fashion magazines as part of the company's "Just Do It" campaign for fall.

2   One of the most provocatively placed posteriors shows itself a few pages into the September [2005] issue of *Glamour*, whose cover blares "800 Sexy Looks for Every Size!" Flip through a couple of images of actress Jennifer Connelly (who comes in one size: twig) and there it is: a big old can, clad in taut full-coverage underwear. Next to the image curve 19 lines of ad-copy verse:

My butt is big
And round like the letter C
And ten thousand lunges
Have made it rounder
But not smaller
And that's just fine.
It's a space heater
For my side of the bed
It's my ambassador
To those who walk behind me
It's a border collie
That herds skinny women
Away from the best deals
At clothing sales.
My butt is big
And that's just fine
And those who might scorn it
Are invited to kiss it.
Just do it.

3   It has to be said: The ad kicks ass. Sure, it's a little grrrrrrl-y, but that's a small bone to pick with two pages of advertising in a big fall-fashion issue of a major women's magazine, where we're traditionally treated to photographs of kohl-eyed consumptives peddling pencil skirts.

4   While the Dove "Real Beauty" campaign is riddled with contradictions (the "real" women celebrating their "real curves" are "really selling" cellulite cream, a balm for an imaginary flaw), the Nike ads are harder to fault. They seem to be selling Nike, the brand, rather than specific products. At the bottom of each ad is a link to Nikewomen.com, a Web site where viewers are asked the question "What story does your body tell?" and then shown the ads for each of the company's six anatomically specific celebrations of self. There are photos of knees, shoulders, hips, thighs, butts and legs, each with badass, and sometimes head-scratching, doggerel alongside. Web visitors can then view and purchase products—shorts and sports bras and shoes—made for that body part.

5   Nike spokeswoman Caren Bell said that the idea was conceived internally and by Nike's ad agency, Wieden & Kennedy. It launched this week in print ads in women's magazines, as well as in digital online publications such as Seventeen.com and Style.com. The body-part models, said Bell, are not professionals, but plucked from gyms around the country. "It's not about the ideal; it's about what's real," she said, adding, "We recognize that you can be fit and not be a model; you can be athletic and not be sample size."

6   Perhaps the Dove campaign and its attendant coverage have warmed us up for this vogue, which, according to Wednesday's *New York Times*, also includes a Chicken of the Sea tuna fish ad in which a svelte woman lets her gut hang out in an empty elevator. But it's still arresting to open up *InStyle* and see a pair of bulging, fleshy legs flatteringly photographed in black-and-white against a paint-splotchy background, next to the words, "I have thunder thighs."

7   It's especially breathtaking to see it amid the typical fall fashion ads. Besides *Glamour* and *InStyle*, this month's Nike campaign is running in *Lucky, Marie Claire, Self* and, surprisingly, that paean to emaciation *Vogue*. In each of the magazines, the Nike ads look downright subversive, nestled as they are between images of women with visible rib cages and exposed breasts, modeling thousand-dollar jackets and go-go boots. Neighboring pages carry pictures of languid amazon Uma Thurman caressing Louis Vuitton bags, while gaggles of anonymous babes who haven't seen sunlight—or hairbrushes—for weeks populate Marc Jacobs' pages. A Gap "favorite fits" campaign spotlights jeans "designed uniquely for your body" in "original," "curvy" and "straight" shapes (all of which look "skinny" in the photographs) but somehow fails to showcase "bloated" and "pear-shaped" fits.

8   But the most memorable—and funny—thing about the Nike ads isn't even the images, but the voice of the campaign, those little ditties that veer all over the map and often end up in crazy-land, beginning with those butt-as-border-collie and space-heater metaphors. But that's nothing. Booty appreciation is old hat since the J. Lo-ification of the American rear. It's a whole other ballgame to show pictures of sleek stems next to copy that reads "My legs were once two hairy sticks," but now "They are revered./ Envied for their strength/ Honored for their beauty/ Hairless for the most part . . ." This is the United States. Women don't grow hair on their legs. Especially in fashion magazines. Granted, the legs in the Nike ad look like they have never been inhabited by so much as a follicle. But the phrase "hairy sticks," even in reference to little-girl calves, is not one we imagine being bandied about on Madison Avenue as a savvy way to refer to gams.

9   And what about the shoulders, which "some say . . . are like a man's"? The verse continues, "I say, leave men out of it." There's a hips page that orgasmically asserts, "My hips return to puberty/ When I'm in dance class . . . And I don't understand them/ And sometimes they/ Don't understand themselves./ When the music stops/ They're still charged/ Don't touch me/ Sparks will fly." And the topper, the smoothly scarred knees, described in the ad as "tomboys." "My mother worries/ I will never marry/ With knees like that./ But I know there's someone out there/ Who will say to me:/ I love you/ And I love your knees./ I want the four of us/ To grow old together."

10   Huh. Banged-up knees and spinsterhood: the long-ignored connection. What's going *on* there? In part, the "leave men out of it, my well-used body does not inhibit my desirability" vibe makes a brawny statement about female empowerment. "It is about independence and being proud of who you are," said Bell.

11   Nike, a company named after the Greek goddess of victory, has a strong advertising history with women. Remember the 1995 campaign about athletic girls? "If you let me play sports/ I will like myself more/ I will have more self-confidence/ I'll be 50 percent less likely to get breast cancer/ I will suffer less depression/ I will be more likely to leave a man who beats me/ I'll be less likely to be pregnant before I want to/ I will learn to be strong." These ads tap the same vein—perhaps even some of the same girls who 10 years ago were itching to get on the soccer team.

12   But there's something less earnest about the "What story does your body tell?" campaign, something intoxicatingly bizarre, like reality television, or that "Saturday Night Live" chestnut, "Deep Thoughts With Jack Handy." Like Handy's musings, they're hilarious in a way that feels casually haphazard, but which has clearly been meticulously planned by the brains over at Nike and its longtime "Just Do It" advertising agency, Wieden & Kennedy.

13   The free-associative giddiness continues on Nike's Web site, which, like the Dove "Real Beauty" site, runs videos of the models talking about their bodies. The big-shouldered woman talks about how swimming has made her broad, but that she likes her shoulders anyway: "Who knows," she says, "one day maybe I'll fall in love with a bad swimmer and he'll be flailing around in the deep end calling my name and I'll swim over and I'll save him and I'll fling his wet body over my shoulders and I'll carry him home to bed." She pauses. "I've said too much." Uh-huh. The leg model speaks derisively about a "size 2 . . . maybe she was a size 4" woman at her gym whose "cat could have worn her workout bra as a collar." Oooh-kay.

14   There's something almost spooky about the frankness of the campaign, its willingness to attack the stereotypes—and body types—on which fashion and beauty merchandising is built. I'm enjoying these ads more than the Dove campaign, but both projects' outward denunciations of the perfection we've been programmed to strive for feel almost too healthy to be true. I've already written about the Dove contradictions, and I can't find a major problem with the Nike ads. Though I do have a vague fear that the media—from *Salon* to "The View" to the Associated Press and the *New York Times* and everyone else who has showered this mini-movement with attention—and all the women who are embracing these new advertising models are being laughed at.

15   Is this some sort of "Candid Camera" prank where advertisers trick consumers into believing that they really care about regular-size women? Will Alan Funt eventually emerge and cackle uproariously at how we fell for it, *actually wrote about* the possibility that this might herald a shift in the attitude toward what kinds of female shapes sell products? And will everyone then just go back to photographing underfed and over-coked Eastern European tweens?

16   Because if it's not a trick, then it feels like a sort of momentous, if carefully manipulated, moment: I'm watching a brief return to media health.

17   Not that it's perfect, far from it. For one thing, Nike's talking-model Web site makes clear what the print ads don't. That while these may be big, healthy women built like mighty brick houses, they all look to be under 25, if not under 22. It's a "real beauty" catch shared by the Dove campaign, in which the models, while cheerfully curvaceous, are also relative cubs compared to the free-spending mama tigers to whom they are pitching products. But Nike's sin in this regard is somehow less damaging. The company is, after all, selling athletic gear, not cellulite fixatives that women in their 20s would rarely need.

18   Then there's the fact that every woman celebrated in Nike's six ads sounds like one hell of an athlete. That's fine, and the company's prerogative as an athletic-wear manufacturer; it's certainly not *damaging*. But if, as Bell pointed out, the campaign is not about the ideal, but about what's real, it doesn't hurt to remember that for many American women, what's real is being out of shape. The idea of being physically fit, let alone being able to get beefy thighs from running a marathon, *is* a seemingly impossible ideal for many.

19   These butts and thunder thighs are mostly rock-hard muscle; there are no saddlebags. And while featuring them is surely a step in the right direction, real progress will be made when fashion plates share ad pages with women whose creases and folds and blemishes may be the product of triathlons . . . or nightly bags of Doritos. (*Salon*'s staff have already tried their hands at this and hope that you will too.)

20   In the meantime, there's nothing to do but enjoy the end of this particular summer, when those who get their back-to-school fashion tips from glossy tomes may do so with a modicum of self-worth, a smidgen less self-loathing about their un-wraithlike physiques. This year, they'll get to feast their eyes on some very big butts, spiritual space heaters, warming them with the reminder that not everyone can collar her cat with her sports bra. Whatever that means.

Topics for Critical Thinking and Writing

1. a. What methods of development does Traister employ in "Thigh the Beloved Country," her rhetorical analysis of the Nike ad campaign?
   b. Who is Traister's audience? What style and tone does she employ to appeal to that audience?
   c. What cultural assumptions do the ad campaigns and Traister challenge? Does Traister make any cultural assumptions?
2. Rhetorically analyze the Big Butt Nike ad in detail. You can find the ad at http://www.salon.com/mwt/feature/2005/08/18/nike_ads/index.html, at http://feministing.com/archives/001803.html, or at http://www. adrants.com/images/nike3_081205_big.jpg.
3. Choose a print ad, and write a 750- to 1000-word rhetorical analysis essay on it. Do a "close reading" of the ad itself and examine it in context. What is the company and the product? What is the context (in what magazine did you find the ad, and who is the target audience)? What methods of development does the ad use (e.g., setting, diction, photography, structure, style, tone)? Are there any inconsistencies, such as the one Traister notes about the Dove campaign? Or, analyze a whole campaign by a company (e.g., the variations used across different media such as print, billboard, website, and television).

MAKING REASONABLE ARGUMENTS

Persuasive writing that, in addition to offering other evidence, relies chiefly on reasoning (rather than on appeals to the emotions) is usually called *argument*. An argument here is not a wrangle but a *reasoned analysis*. What distinguishes argument from explanation (for instance, the explanation of a process) is this: whereas both consist of statements, in argument some statements are offered as *reasons* for other statements. Another way of characterizing argument is that argument assumes there is or may be substantial disagreement between informed readers. To overcome this disagreement, the writer tries to offer reasons that convince by their validity. Here, for example, is C. S. Lewis arguing against vivisection (experimentation on live animals for scientific research):

> A rational discussion of this subject begins by inquiring whether pain is, or is not, an evil. If it is not, then the case against vivisection falls. But then so does the case for vivisection. If it is not defended on the ground that it reduces human suffering, on what ground can it be defended? And if pain is not an evil, why should human suffering be reduced? We must therefore assume as a basis for the whole discussion that pain is an evil, otherwise there is nothing to be discussed.
>
> Now if pain is an evil then the infliction of pain, considered in itself, must clearly be an evil act. But there are such things as necessary evils. Some acts which would be bad, simply in themselves, may be excusable and even laudable when they are necessary means to a greater good. In saying that the infliction of pain, simply in itself, is bad, we are not saying that pain ought never to be inflicted. Most of us think that it can rightly be inflicted for a good purpose—as in dentistry or just and reformatory punishment. The point is that it always requires justification. On the man whom we find inflicting pain rests the burden of showing why an act which in itself would be simply bad is, in those particular circumstances, good. If we find a man giving pleasure it is for us to prove (if we criticize him) that his action is wrong. But if we find a man inflicting pain it is for him to prove that his action is right. If he cannot, he is a wicked man.

And here is U.S. Supreme Court Justice Louis Brandeis (before the terrorist attacks of September 11, 2001) concluding his justly famous argument that government may not use evidence illegally obtained by wiretapping:

> Decency, security and liberty alike demand that government officials shall be subjected to the same rules of conduct that are commands to the citizen. In a government of laws, existence of the government will be imperiled if it fails to observe the law scrupulously. Our Government is the potent, the omnipresent teacher. For good or for ill, it teaches the whole people by its example. Crime is contagious. If the Government becomes a lawbreaker, it breeds contempt for law; it invites every man to become a law unto himself; it invites anarchy. To declare that in the administration of the criminal law the end justifies the means—to declare that the Government may commit crimes in order to secure the conviction of a private criminal—would bring terrible retribution. Against that pernicious doctrine this Court should resolutely set its face.

Notice here that Brandeis's reasoning is highlighted by his forceful style. Note the resonant use of parallel constructions ("Decency, security and liberty," "For good or for ill," "it breeds . . . it invites," "To declare . . . to declare") and the variation between long and short sentences. Note too the wit in his comparisons: government is a teacher, crime is like a disease.

MAKING REASONABLE CLAIMS

You have only a little time—perhaps a few days, and even for a term paper at most a few weeks—to think about and to support your claim. You probably cannot come up with a comprehensive health-care program within that time, and you may not even be able to evaluate the evidence on whether our planet has or has not been undergoing a greenhouse effect, or whether or not elephants are so endangered that a ban on the sale of ivory is needed in order to preserve the species.

On the other hand, maybe you can. You may encounter a good collection of essays, pro and con, on a topic, and you will find that in the course of a day's reading you can become quite an expert. For instance, you may find, after reading a couple of dozen essays on abortion (or gun control, or euthanasia), that a few arguments on each side keep recurring, and you may rightly feel that you are in a position to offer your own point of view—that is, you may be in a position to make a reasonable and perhaps a novel claim.

Finally, we want to mention that what may at first seem to be an unreasonable claim may, after some reflection, become reasonable. Not much more than a century ago it seemed unreasonable to many otherwise intelligent people to argue that slavery was immoral. Issues such as those regarding same-sex marriage, women in the armed forces going into combat, gays in the military, and animal experimentation are still matters on which you can take a stand that your opponents regard as utterly unreasonable. It happens that on the day we are writing these pages, the newspaper includes an account of Andrew Martinez, the "Naked Guy," a junior at the University of California, Berkeley, who strolls the campus naked except for his peace sign, shoes and socks (and on cool days a sweatshirt), eats naked in the dining hall, and attends class naked. Campus police arrested the Naked Guy, but the state of California refused to prosecute him because nudity without "lewd behaviour" is not illegal. The university then passed a ban on campus nudity, addressed specifically at Martinez, and suspended him. He hopes to take the matter to the courts. The university's arguments include the charge that his behaviour constitutes sexual harassment of women and creates intolerable conditions for students in the "workplace." On the other hand, Martinez says that clothing is part of a middle-class, body-hating, repressive, consumerist society. Can one make a reasonable case for nudism? Can one make a reasonable case against nudism?

Claims of Fact

We can usually distinguish between two kinds of claims, claims of fact and claims of value, and we can sometimes distinguish these from a third kind, claims of policy. *Claims of fact* assert that something is or was or will be. They include, for instance, arguments about cause and effect, correlation, probability, and states of affairs. The following examples can be considered claims of fact:

Chocolate is the most popular flavour of ice cream for women.

Pornography stimulates violence against women.

Pornography reduces sexual tension and so reduces sexual violence.

Capital punishment reduces crime.

Capital punishment does not reduce crime.

To support a claim of this sort, you must provide information (probably after defining any terms that may be in doubt or that may be used in specific ways). Such information might, for instance, be testimony (for instance, your own experience or statements by men who have said that pornography stimulated them to violence), or it might be statistics (gathered from a report in a scholarly journal). Even if the claim has to do with the future—let's say the claim that gun control will not reduce crime—you try to offer information. For example, you might gather information about the experiences in Canada and the United States or of other countries with different strictures on regulations concerning the sale of guns.

Claims of Value

Claims of value concern what is right or wrong, good or bad, better or worse than something else:

> Country music deserves to be taken seriously.
>
> Rock is better than country music.
>
> Capital punishment is barbaric.
>
> Euthanasia is moral.

Some claims of value may be mere expressions of taste: "Vanilla is better than chocolate." It is hard to imagine how one could go about supporting such a claim—or refuting it. One probably can do no better than reply with the Latin proverb *"De gustibus non est disputandum"* (There is no disputing about taste). Notice, however, that the claim that vanilla is better than chocolate is quite different from the claim that most Canadians prefer vanilla to chocolate. The latter statement is a claim of fact, not of value, and it can be proved or disproved with information—for example, with information provided by the makers of ice cream.

Claims of value that go beyond the mere expression of taste—for instance, claims of morality or claims of artistic value—are usually supported by appeals to standards ("Such-and-such a proposal is bad *because* governments should not restrict the rights of individuals," or "Such-and-such music is good *because* it is complex," or because it is popular or because it is sincere or whatever). In supporting claims of value, writers usually appeal to standards that they believe are acceptable to their readers. Examples:

> Sex-education programs in schools are inappropriate *because* aspects of moral education should properly be given only by parents.
>
> Sex-education programs in schools are appropriate *because* society has a duty to provide what most parents obviously are reluctant to provide.
>
> Doctors should be permitted to end a patient's life if the patient makes such a request *because* each of us should be free to make the decisions that most concern us.
>
> Euthanasia is unacceptable *because* only God can give or take life.

In arguing a claim of value, be sure you have clearly in your mind the standards that you believe support the claim. You may find it appropriate to explain *why* you hold these standards and *how* adherence to these standards will be of benefit.

Claims of Policy

Claims of policy assert that a policy, law, or custom should be initiated, or altered, or dropped. Such claims usually are characterized by words such as "should," "must," and "ought."

Children should be allowed to vote, if they wish to.

A course in minority cultures ought to be required.

The federal tax on gasoline must be directed toward infrastructure.

In defending an unfamiliar claim of policy, you may want to begin by pointing out that there is a problem that is usually overlooked. For instance, if you urgently believe that children should have the right to vote—a view almost never expressed—you will probably first have to convince your audience that there really is an arguable issue here, an issue concerning children's rights, an issue that deserves serious thought.

In defending a claim of policy you will probably find yourself providing information, just as you would do in support of a claim of fact. For instance, if your topic is children and the vote, you might point out that until 1918 women could not vote in Canada, the usual arguments being that women were mentally unfit and that they would vote the way their men told them to vote. Experience has proved that these low estimates of the capabilities of the disenfranchised were absurd.

But in defending a claim of policy you will probably have to consider values as well as facts. Thus, in arguing for a specific use of the gasoline tax, you might want not only to provide factual information about how much money currently goes toward infrastructure and how much gas-tax money the government takes in annually, but also to argue that such use is *fairer* than an alternative such as having it placed in general revenue.

THREE KINDS OF EVIDENCE: EXAMPLES, TESTIMONY, STATISTICS

Writers of arguments seek to persuade by offering evidence. There are three chief forms of evidence used in argument:

- examples
- testimony, the citation of authorities
- statistics

We will briefly consider each of these.

Examples

Example is from the Latin *exemplum,* which means "something taken out." An example is the sort of thing, taken from among many similar things, that one selects and holds up for view, perhaps after saying "For example," or "For instance."

Three categories of examples are especially common in written arguments:

- real examples
- invented instances
- analogies

Real examples are just what they sound like, instances that have occurred. If, for example, we are arguing that gun control will work, we point to the gun-related crime rate in the United States and/or compare the number of children killed by guns in the home in Canada and America. Or, if we want to support the assertion that a woman can be a capable head of state, we may find ourselves pointing to women who actually served as heads of state, such as Golda Meir and Indira Gandhi (former prime ministers of Israel and India) and to Margaret Thatcher and Kim Campbell (former prime ministers of Britain and Canada).

The advantage of using real examples is, clearly, that they are real. Of course an opponent might stubbornly respond that Golda Meir, Indira Gandhi, and Margaret Thatcher for some reason or other could not function as the head of state in *our* country. Someone might argue, for instance, that the case of Golda Meir proves nothing, since the role of women in Israeli society is different from the role of women in Canada (a country in which a majority of the citizens are Christians). And another person might argue that much of Indira Gandhi's power came from the fact that she was the daughter of Nehru, an immensely popular Indian statesman. Even the most compelling real example inevitably will in some ways be special or particular, and in the eyes of some readers may not seem to be a fair example.

Consider, for instance, a student who is arguing that peer review should be part of the writing course. The student points out that he or she found it of great help in high school. An opponent argues that things in college are different—college students should be able to help themselves, even highly gifted college students are not competent to offer college-level instruction, and so on. Still, as the feebleness of these objections (and the objections against Meir and Gandhi) indicate, real examples can be compelling.

Invented instances are exempt from the charge that, because of some detail or other, they are not relevant as evidence. Suppose, for example, you are arguing against capital punishment on the grounds that if an innocent person is executed, there is no way of even attempting to rectify the injustice. If you point to the case of *X,* you may be met with the reply that *X* was not in fact innocent. Rather than get tangled up in the guilt or innocence of a particular person, it may be better to argue that we can suppose—we can imagine—an innocent person convicted and executed, and we can imagine that evidence later proves the person's innocence.

Invented instances have the advantage of presenting an issue clearly, free from all of the distracting particularities (and irrelevancies) that are bound up with any real instance. But invented instances have the disadvantage of being invented, and they may seem remote from the real issues being argued.

Analogies are comparisons pointing out several resemblances between two rather different things. For instance, one might assert that a government is like a ship, and in times of stress—if the ship is to weather the storm—the authority of the captain must not be questioned.

But do not confuse an analogy with proof. An analogy is an extended comparison between two things: it can be useful in exposition, for it explains the unfamiliar by means of the familiar: "A government is like a ship, and just as a ship has a captain and a crew, so a government has . . ."; "Writing an essay is like building a house; just as an architect must begin with a plan, so the writer must . . ." Such comparisons can be useful, helping to clarify what otherwise might be obscure, but their usefulness goes only so far. Everything is what it is, and not another thing. A government is not a ship, and what is true of a captain's power need not be true of a prime minister's power; and a writer is not an architect. Some of what is true about ships may be roughly true of governments, and some of what is true about architects may be (again, roughly) true of writers, but there are differences too. Consider the following analogy between a lighthouse and the death penalty:

> The death penalty is a warning, just like a lighthouse throwing its beams out to sea. We hear about shipwrecks, but we do not hear about the ships the lighthouse guides safely on their way. We do not have proof of the number of ships it saves, but we do not tear the lighthouse down.
>
> —J. EDGAR HOOVER

How convincing is Hoover's analogy as an argument, that is, as a reason for retaining the death penalty in the United States?

Testimony

Testimony, or the citation of authorities, is rooted in our awareness that some people are recognized as experts. In our daily lives we constantly turn to experts for guidance: we look up the spelling of a word in the dictionary, we listen to weather forecasts on the radio, we take an ailing cat to the vet for a checkup. Similarly, when we wish to become informed about controversial matters, we often turn to experts, first to help educate ourselves and then to help convince others.

Do not forget that *you* are an authority on many things. For example, today's newspaper includes an article about the cutback in funding for the teaching of the arts in elementary and secondary schools. Art educators are responding that the arts are not a frill and that the arts provide the analytic thinking, teamwork, motivation, and self-discipline that most people agree are needed to reinvigorate our schools. If you have been involved in the arts in school—for instance, if you studied painting or learned to play a musical instrument—you are in a position to evaluate these claims.

There are at least two reasons for offering testimony in an argument. The obvious one is that expert opinion does (and should) carry some weight with any audience; the less obvious one is that a change of voice (if the testimony is not your own) in an essay may afford the reader a bit of pleasure. No matter how engaging your own voice may be, a fresh voice—whether that of David Suzuki, Carol Shields, John Polanyi, or Joyce Wieland—may provide a refreshing change of tone.

But, of course, there are dangers: the chief one is that the words of authorities may be taken out of context or otherwise distorted, and the second is that the authorities may not be authorities on the present topic. Quite rightly we are concerned with what Suzuki says, but it is not entirely clear that his words can be fairly applied, on one side or the other, to such an issue as abortion. Quite rightly we are concerned with what Polanyi says, but it is not immediately clear that his eminence as a chemist constitutes him an authority on, say, world peace. In a moment, when we discuss errors in reasoning, we will have more to say about the proper and improper use of authorities.

Statistics

Statistics, another important form of evidence, are especially useful in arguments concerning social issues. If we want to argue for or against raising the driving age, we will probably do some research in the library and will offer statistics about the number of accidents caused by people in certain age groups.

But a word of caution: the significance of statistics may be difficult to assess. For instance, opponents of gun control legislation have pointed out, in support of the argument that such laws are ineffectual, that homicides in Florida *increased* after Florida adopted gun control laws. Supporters of gun control legislation cried foul, arguing that in the years after adopting these laws Miami became (for reasons having nothing to do with the laws) the cocaine capital of the United States, and the rise in homicide was chiefly a reflection of murders involved in the drug trade. That is, a significant change in the population has made a comparison of the figures meaningless. This objection seems plausible, and probably the statistics in this example therefore should carry little weight.

HOW MUCH EVIDENCE IS ENOUGH?

If you allow yourself ample time to write your essay, you probably will turn up plenty of evidence to illustrate your arguments, such as examples drawn from your own experience and imagination, from your reading, and from your talks with others. Examples will not only help to clarify and to support your assertions, but they will also provide a concreteness that will be welcome in a paper that might be on the whole fairly abstract. Your sense of your audience will have to guide you in making your selection of examples. Generally speaking, a single example may not fully illuminate a difficult point, and so a second example, a clincher, may be desirable. If you offer a third or fourth example, you probably are succumbing to a temptation to include something that tickles your fancy. If it is as good as you think it is, the reader probably will accept the unnecessary example and may even be grateful. But before you heap up examples, try to imagine yourself in your reader's place, and ask if the example is needed. If it is not needed, ask yourself if the reader will be glad to receive the overload.

One other point. On most questions, say on the value of bilingual education or on the need for rehabilitation programs in prisons, it's not possible to make a strictly logical case, in the sense of absolutely airtight proof. Don't assume that it is your job to make an airtight case. What you are expected to do is to offer a reasonable argument. Virginia Woolf put it this way: "When a subject is highly controversial . . . one cannot hope to tell the truth. One can only show how one came to hold whatever opinion one does hold."

AVOIDING FALLACIES

Let's further examine writing reasonable arguments by considering some obvious errors in reasoning. In logic these errors are called *fallacies* (from a Latin verb meaning "to deceive"). As Tweedledee says in *Through the Looking-Glass,* "If it were so, it would be; but as it isn't, it ain't. That's logic."

To persuade readers to accept your opinions you must persuade them that you are reliable; if your argument includes fallacies, thoughtful readers will not take you seriously. More important, if your argument includes fallacies, you are misleading yourself. When you search your draft for fallacies, you are searching for ways to improve the quality of your thinking.

1. False authority. Don't try to borrow the prestige of authorities who are not authorities on the topic in question—for example, a heart surgeon speaking on politics. Similarly, some former authorities are no longer authorities, because the problems have changed or because later knowledge has superseded their views. Pierre Elliott Trudeau, Nellie McClung, and Albert Einstein remain persons of genius, but an attempt to use their opinions when you are examining contemporary issues—even in their fields—may be questioned. Remember the last words of John B. Sedgwick, a Union Army general at the Battle of Spotsylvania in 1864: "They couldn't hit an elephant at this dist—." In short, before you rely on an authority, ask yourself if the person in question *is* an authority on the topic. And do not let stereotypes influence your idea of who is an authority. Remember the Yiddish proverb: "A goat has a beard, but that doesn't make him a rabbi."

2. False quotation. If you quote an authority, do not misquote. For example, you may find someone who grants that "there are strong arguments in favour of abolishing the policy of multiculturalism," but if she goes on to argue that, on balance, the arguments in favour of retaining it seem stronger to her, it is dishonest to quote her words so as to imply that she favours abolishing it.

3. Suppression of evidence. Do not neglect evidence that is contrary to your own argument. You owe it to yourself and your reader to present all the relevant evidence. Be especially careful not to assume that every question is simply a matter of *either/or*. There may be some truth on both sides. Take the following thesis: "Grades encourage unwholesome competition and should therefore be abolished." Even if the statement about the evil effect of grading is true, it may not be the whole truth, and therefore it may not follow that grades should be abolished. One might point out that grades do other things too: they may stimulate learning, and they may assist students by telling them how far they have progressed. One might nevertheless conclude, on balance, that the fault outweighs the benefits. But the argument will be more persuasive if the benefits of grades have been considered.

Concede to the opposition its due, and then outscore the opposition. Failure to confront the opposing evidence will be noticed; your readers will keep wondering why you do not consider this point or that and may consequently dismiss your argument. However, if you confront the opposition you will almost surely strengthen your own argument. As Edmund Burke said two hundred years ago, "He that wrestles with us strengthens our nerves, and sharpens our skill. Our antagonist is our helper."

4. Generalization from insufficient evidence. In rereading a draft of an argument that you have written, try to spot your own generalizations. Ask yourself if a reasonable reader is likely to agree that the generalization is based on an adequate sample.

A visitor to a college may sit in on three classes, each taught by a different instructor, and may find all three stimulating. That's a good sign, but can we generalize and say that the teaching at this college is excellent? Are three classes a sufficient sample? If all three are offered by the biology department, and if the biology department includes only five instructors, perhaps we can tentatively say that the teaching of biology at this institution is good. If the biology department contains twenty instructors, perhaps we can still say, though more tentatively, that this sample indicates that the teaching of biology is good. But what does the sample say about the teaching of other subjects at the college? It probably does say something—the institution may be much concerned with teaching across the board—but then again it may not say a great deal, since the biology department may be exceptionally concerned with good teaching.

5. The genetic fallacy. Do not assume that something can necessarily be explained in terms of its birth or origin. "He wrote the novel to make money, so it cannot be any good" is not a valid inference. The value of a novel does not depend on the author's motivations in writing it. Indeed, the value or worth of a novel needs to be established by reference to other criteria. Neither the highest nor the lowest motivations guarantee the quality of the product. Another example: "Capital punishment arose in days when society sought revenge, so now it ought to be abolished." Again an unconvincing argument: capital punishment may have some current value; for example, it may serve as a deterrent to crime. But that's another argument, and it needs evidence if it is to be believed. Be on guard, too, against the thoughtless tendency to judge people by their origins: Mr. X has a foreign accent, so he is probably untrustworthy or stupid or industrious.

6. Begging the question and circular reasoning. Do not assume the truth of the point that you should prove. The term "begging the question" is a trifle odd. It means, in effect, "You, like a beggar, are asking me to grant you something at the outset."

Examples: "The barbaric death penalty should be abolished"; "This senseless language requirement should be dropped." Both of these statements assume what they should prove—that the death penalty is barbaric and that the language requirement is senseless. You can of course make assertions such as these, but you must go on to prove them.

Circular reasoning is usually an extended form of begging the question. What ought to be proved is covertly assumed. Example: "X is the best-qualified candidate for the office, because the most informed people say so." Who are the most informed people? Those who recognize X's superiority. Circular reasoning, then, normally includes intermediate steps absent from begging the question, but the two fallacies are so closely related that they can be considered one.

"*Look, maybe you're right, but for the sake of argument let's assume you're wrong and drop it.*"

Drawing by Mankoff; © 1983 The New Yorker Magazine, Inc.

Another example: "I feel sympathy for her because I identify with her." Despite the "because," no reason is really offered. What follows "because" is merely a restatement, in slightly different words, of what precedes; the shift of words, from "feel sympathy" to "identify with" has misled the writer into thinking she is giving a reason. Other examples: "Students are interested in courses when the subject matter and the method of presentation are interesting"; "There cannot be peace in the Middle East because the Jews and the Arabs will always fight." In each case, an assertion that ought to be proved is reasserted as a reason in support of the assertion.

7. *Post hoc ergo propter hoc* (Latin for "after this, therefore because of this"). Don't assume that because *X* precedes *Y*, *X* must cause *Y*. For example: "He went to university and came back a boozer; university corrupted him." He might have taken up liquor even if he had not gone to university. Another example: "When a fifty-five-mile-per-hour (ninety-kilometre-per-hour) limit was imposed in the United States in 1974, after the Arab countries' embargo on oil, the number of vehicle fatalities decreased sharply, from 55 000 deaths in 1973 to 46 000 in 1974, so it is evident that a fifty-five-mile-per-hour limit—still adhered to in some states—saves lives." Not quite. Because gasoline was expensive after the embargo, the number of miles travelled decreased. The number of fatalities *per mile* remained constant. The price of gas, not the speed limit, seems responsible for the decreased number of fatalities. Moreover, the national death rate has continued to fall. Why? Several factors are at work: seat-belt and child-restraint laws, campaigns against drunk driving, improved car design, and improved roads. Medicine, too, may have improved so that today doctors can save accident victims who in 1974 would have died. In short, it probably is impossible to isolate this correlation between speed and safety.

8. *Argumentum ad hominem* (Latin for "argument toward the man"). Here the argument is directed toward the person rather than toward the issue. Do not shift from your topic to your opponent. A speaker argues in favour of legalizing abortions and her opponent, instead of facing the merits of the argument, attacks the character or the associations of the opponent: "You're a feminist, aren't you?"

9. False assumption. Consider the Scot who argued that Shakespeare must have been a Scot. Asked for his evidence, he replied, "The ability of the man warrants the assumption." Or take a statement such as "She goes to Yale, so she must be rich." Possibly the statement is based on faulty induction (the writer knows four Yale students, and all four are rich), but more likely the writer is just passing on a cliché. The Yale student in question may be on a scholarship, may be struggling to earn the money, or may be backed by parents of modest means who for eighteen years have saved money for her college education. Other examples: "I haven't heard him complain about French 101, so he must be satisfied"; "She's a writer, so she must be well read." A little thought will show how weak such assertions are; they *may* be true, but they may not.

The errors we have discussed are common. In revising, try to spot them and eliminate or correct them. You have a point to make, and you should make it fairly. If it can be made only unfairly, you do an injustice not only to your reader but also to yourself; you should try to change your view of the topic. You don't want to be like the politician whose speech had a marginal note: "Argument weak; shout here."

WIT

In addition to using sound argument and other evidence, writers often use wit, especially irony, to persuade. In irony, the words convey a meaning somewhat different from what they explicitly say. Wry understatement is typical. Here, for instance, is Thoreau explaining why in *Walden*, his book about his two years in relative isolation at Walden Pond, he will talk chiefly about himself:

> In most books, the *I*, or first person, is omitted; in this it will be retained; that, in respect to egotism, is the main difference. We commonly do not remember that it is, after all, always the first person that is speaking. I should not talk so much about myself if there were anybody else whom I knew as well. Unfortunately, I am confined to this theme by the narrowness of my experience.

Notice the wry apology in his justification for talking about himself: he does not know anyone else as well as he knows himself. Similarly, in "Unfortunately, I am confined to this theme by the narrowness of my experience," we hear a wry voice. After all, Thoreau knows, as we know, that *no one* has experience so deep or broad that he or she knows others better than himself or herself. Thoreau's presentation of himself as someone who happens not to have had the luck of knowing others better than himself is engagingly clever.

"Please forgive Edgar. He has no verbal skills."

Avoiding Sarcasm

Because writers must, among other things, persuade readers that they are humane, sarcasm has little place in persuasive writing. Although desk dictionaries usually define sarcasm as "bitter, caustic irony" or "a kind of satiric wit," if you think of a sarcastic comment that you have heard you will probably agree that "a crude, sneering remark" is a better definition. Lacking the wit of good satire and the carefully controlled mockery of irony, sarcasm usually relies on gross overstatement and intends simply to humiliate. *Sarcasm* is derived from a Greek word meaning "to tear flesh" or "to bite the lips in rage"—altogether an unattractive business. Sarcasm is unfair, for it dismisses an opponent's arguments with ridicule rather than with reason; it is also unwise, for it turns the reader against you. Readers hesitate to ally themselves with a writer who apparently enjoys humiliating the opposition. A sarcastic remark can turn the hearers against the speaker and arouse sympathy for the victim, and it often indicates a lack of reasoned argument. In short, sarcasm usually does not work.

ORGANIZING AN ARGUMENT

As we said earlier, writers find out what they think partly by means of the act of putting words on paper. But in presenting arguments for their readers, writers rarely duplicate their own acts of discovery. To put it another way, the process of setting forth ideas, and supporting them, does not follow the productive but untidy, repetitive, often haphazard process of preliminary thinking. For instance, a point that did not strike us until the middle of the third draft may, in the final version, appear in the opening paragraph. Or an example that seemed useful early in our thinking may, in the process of revision, be omitted in favour of a stronger example. Through a series of revisions, large and small, we try to work out the best strategy for persuading our readers to accept our reasoning as sound, our conclusion as valid. Unfortunately, we find, an argument cannot be presented either as it occurs to us or all at once.

Nor is there a simple formula that governs the organization of all effective argumentative essays. An essay may begin by announcing its thesis and then set forth the reasons that support the thesis. Or it may begin more casually, calling attention to specific cases and then broaden from these cases. Probably it will then go on to reveal an underlying unity that brings the thesis into view, and from here it will offer detailed reasoning that supports the thesis.

As the writer of a persuasive essay, you almost always have to handle, in some sequence or other, the following matters:

- The background (for instance, the need to consider the issue)
- The thesis (claim)
- The evidence that supports the thesis
- The counterevidence
- The response to counterclaims and counterevidence (either a refutation or a concession that there *is* merit to the counterclaims but not as much as to the writer's thesis)
- Some sort of reaffirmation, perhaps that the topic needs attention or that the thesis advanced is the most plausible or the most workable or the most moral or that the ball is now in the reader's court

Three methods of organizing arguments are fairly common, and one or another may suit an essay on which you are working.

1. Begin with the background, then set forth the thesis statement and work from the simplest argument up to the most complex. Such an arrangement will keep your reader with you, step by step.

2. After setting forth the background and your thesis, arrange the arguments in order of increasing strength. The danger in following this plan is that you may lose the reader from the start, because you begin with a weak argument. Avoid this problem by telling your reader that indeed the first argument is relatively weak (if it is terribly weak, it is not an argument at all, so scrap it), but that you offer it for the sake of completeness or because it is often given, and that you will soon give the reader far stronger arguments. Face the opposition to this initial argument, grant that opposition as much as it deserves, and salvage what is left of the argument. Then proceed to the increasingly strong arguments, devoting at least one paragraph to each. Introduce each argument with an appropriate transition ("another reason," "even more important," "most convincing of all"). State it briefly, summarize the opposing view, and then demolish this opposition. With this organization, your discussion of each of your own arguments ends affirmatively.

3. After sketching the background and stating your thesis in an introductory paragraph, mass all of the opposing arguments, and then respond to them one by one.

In short, when you (1) think you have done your initial thinking and your rethinking, (2) have, if appropriate, consulted published sources, (3) have talked with friends and perhaps with experts, and (4) have moved from random notes and lists to fairly full drafts, you are not quite done.

You still must check what you hope is your last draft to see if you have found the best possible order for the arguments, have given effective examples, and have furnished transitions. In short, you must check to see that you have produced an argument that will strike a reasonable reader as courteous, clear, and concrete.

A Checklist for Revising Drafts of Persuasive Essays

✔ Are the terms clearly defined?
✔ Is the thesis stated promptly and clearly?
✔ Are the assumptions likely to be shared by your readers? If not, are they reasonably argued rather than merely stated?
✔ Are the facts verifiable? Is the evidence reliable? (No out-of-date statistics, no generalizations from insufficient evidence?)
✔ Is the reasoning sound?
✔ Are the authorities really authorities on this matter?
✔ Are all of the substantial counter-arguments recognized and effectively responded to?
✔ Does the essay make use, where appropriate, of concrete examples?
✔ Is the organization effective? Does the essay begin interestingly, keep the thesis in view, and end interestingly?
✔ Is the tone appropriate? (Avoid sarcasm. Present yourself as fair-minded, and assume that those who hold a view opposed to yours are also fair-minded.)

Topics for Critical Thinking and Writing

1. Analyze and evaluate each of the following arguments. If any of the arguments contain fallacies, name the fallacies.

   a. The following paragraph is from a student essay titled "The Bias Inherent in Television News."

   > At first glance, it might seem as though the goal of those involved in the television news industry is to deliver accurate, relevant news stories to the general public. However, upon further examination it becomes apparent that the goal of the companies in this industry is the same as the goal of the companies in any other industry: profit. In order to reach this goal, television news is broadcast with the intent of receiving high ratings, which will in turn translate into revenue for those involved. However, with numerous news companies in existence, individual companies must compete for their portion of the viewing audience through the use of various devices. Some techniques used include the adoption of a personality to target an audience, the adherence to social and political prejudices in order to cater to the general opinion of the target audience, as well as the sensationalizing of stories. The competition for ratings among various television news companies creates a bias in the information broadcast, as truths in stories are altered to agree with the popular opinion of a specific group and factual evidence is often overshadowed by the dramatic elements of a story.

   b. To the Editor:

   > Your editorial last Wednesday arguing against censorship as an infringement on freedom is full of clever arguments but it overlooks an obvious fact. We have Pure Food and Drug laws to protect us against poison, and no one believes that such laws interfere with the freedom of those who produce food and drugs. The public is entitled, then, to laws that will similarly protect us from the poison that some movie-makers produce.

   c. To the Editor:

   > On Dec. 5 *The Times* published a story saying that colleges have come under pressure to improve the "quality of their teaching." Unfortunately, nobody knows what good teaching is, let alone how to evaluate it.
   >
   > Unlike scholarship, which has a visible product, namely published reports, the results of teaching are locked in the heads of students and are usually not apparent, even to the students themselves, for a very long period.
   >
   > One device which is frequently used is a poll of students, the so-called "student evaluation of teachers." This type of measure-

ment has been studied by Rodin and Rodin, who correlated it with how much the students learned, as demonstrated on tests. The correlation was highly negative (-.75). As the Rodins put it, "Students rate most highly instructors from whom they learn least."

What invariably happens is that attempts to reward "good teaching" turn out to reward good public relations.

d. The following paragraph was written by Walter Lippmann shortly after the United States entered World War II:

> The Pacific Coast is in imminent danger of a combined attack from within and from without. . . . It is [true] . . . that since the outbreak of the Japanese war there has been no important sabotage on the Pacific Coast. From what we know about the fifth column in Europe, this is not, as some have liked to think, a sign that there is nothing to be feared. It is a sign that the blow is well-organized and that it is held back until it can be struck with maximum effect. . . . I am sure I understand fully and appreciate thoroughly the unwillingness of Washington to adopt a policy of mass evacuation and internment of all those who are technically enemy aliens. But I submit that Washington is not defining the problem on the coast correctly. . . . The Pacific Coast is officially a combat zone: some part of it may at any moment be a battlefield. Nobody's constitutional rights include the right to reside and do business on a battlefield. And nobody ought to be on a battlefield who has no good reason for being there.

2. In his essay "Too Much Privacy Can Be Hazardous to the Person," Lawrence Solomon discusses concerns about the effects of electronic data collection and storage with respect to our sense of privacy. His conclusion is that despite the risk of abuses, this collection, storage, and sharing of information is really a good thing. Read this passage from his essay, and then list and evaluate the persuasive devices that he uses.

> Because the dangers—ranging from financial exploitation to, in the worst case, a police state—can be profound, legislation of various types is being proposed. Some argue that all personal information should be our own private property, to prevent marketers from storing and exchanging information about us without our consent; others would severely restrict or even prohibit the collection of sensitive personal data. These approaches miss the mark. The collection of data—the accumulation of knowledge—is almost always desirable. The relevant question is, when does the information belong in the public sphere and when in the private?
>
> The claim that we somehow have property rights to our personal information does not stand up to scrutiny. We all exchange information about others—"Did you see Andrea's new car?"; "I hear Jim got a promotion"—in our daily routines without requiring their consent, and a democratic society that respects free speech could not do otherwise. Even if we did enact laws to restrict or ban data banks from collecting information about us, it

would generally backfire. Junk mail is unwanted precisely because it is indiscriminate and useless. If marketing succeeds in sending us useful, targeted information, many of us would have our goal of restricting unwanted mail. In one survey, 71 percent of 18- to 20-year-olds wanted mail on products that interested them; in another, 52 percent of consumers wanted to be profiled if that would lead to special offers. Those who don't want the mail or the offers will only need to make their views heard: Few companies would defy their customers by selling their names.

3. Read the following passage, from George Will's *The Morning After.* Evaluate this selection as a piece of persuasive writing with attention to the aspects of good—or faulty—argumentation reviewed in this chapter.

   When a society becomes, like ours, uneasy about calling prisons penitentiaries or penal institutions, and instead calls them "correctional institutions," the society has lost its bearings. If prisoners are "corrected," that is nice but it is an ancillary outcome. The point of imprisonment is punishment. The idea of punishment is unintelligible if severed from the idea of retribution, which is inseparable from the concept of vengeance, which is an expression of anger. No anger, no justice.

4. Ruth Morris opens her essay "The Noose, the Chair and the Needle" (1986) with the following information:

   Polls show 68% of Canadians favour a return to hanging; soundings suggest about 2/3 of our present parliament, given a free vote, would endorse a return to capital punishment. Gloomy figures for those of us who don't want to see Canada join the US and Turkey as the only Western nations carrying out the death penalty.
       The good news is that the same polls show these beliefs to be based largely on the absence of accurate information:

   - 80% of Canadians have read nothing on the issue;
   - Canadians believe the violent crime rate to be seven times what it actually is, and that the murder rate has been increasing since 1976—it has not;
   - Most who advocate a return to capital punishment still believe deterrence works, and are unaware of extensive research which fails to show any evidence of the effectiveness of deterrence.

How effective is Morris in setting up and refuting arguments about capital punishment with reference to Canada? Does she include any fallacies of her own?

PERSUASION AT WORK

Erin Manning declares, "There are many ports of entry into the discourse of nationalism," and the following collection of essays provides a cross-cultural selection of those entries, representing various views on Canada and being

Canadian. Evaluate each of the following selections as a piece of persuasive writing with attention to the aspects of good—or faulty—argumentation reviewed in this chapter. For each essay, answer the following questions.

 Topics for Critical Thinking and Writing

1. What is the author's view of Canada and Canadians? Are you persuaded to agree with this view or at least to acknowledge it as valid?
2. What rhetorical and persuasive strategies does the writer use? Why might the writer use these strategies, and are they effective? How does the author organize his or her argument?
3. Who is the expected or intended audience? How do you know? How does the author appeal to his or her audience? What does each writer hope the audience takes away from their reading of the essay? Do you find the arguments compelling?
4. What cultural assumptions does the author challenge? What, if any, cultural assumptions does the author make during his or her argument?
   a. Write a rhetorical analysis essay responding to one of the following essays.
   b. Write a persuasive essay responding to one of the following essays.
5. Compare two of the following essays.
   a. Write a persuasive essay on Canada or on being Canadian: remember to narrow your focus.

 SHARON MORGAN BECKFORD

Sharon Morgan Beckford teaches in the English department of York University.

This Space Called Canada: Re-imagining the National Story

For we cannot forget how cultural life, above all in the West, but elsewhere as well, has been transformed in our lifetimes by the voicing of the margin.

—STUART HALL

In the final analysis, the established groups have only one choice: to make room in all spheres of life for the other groups. This way, everyone will live at a negotiated respectable level of harmony.

—CECIL FOSTER

Therefore we can see the necessity for the kind of education for critical consciousness that can enable those with power and privilege rooted in structures of domination to divest without having to see themselves as victims. Such thinking does not have to negate collective awareness that a culture of domination does seek to fundamentally distort and pervert the psyches of all citizens or that this perversion is wounding.

—BELL HOOKS

Introduction: Who Is a Canadian?

1   Last spring I had the opportunity to visit and learn about what Ruth Goldbloom, the Halifax philanthropist and principal backer of the Pier 21 Museum, saw as Canada's Ellis Island. Visual images are important in this old harbour terminus on the edge of the Atlantic Ocean and the easternmost beginning of Canada. This is a museum that chooses with care what items and artifacts it wants to collect from the past and carry forward into the future as representations of our heritage and part of our cultural mythology. On a strong foundation, which is the past, Pier 21 and its financial supporters want to help us build a strong and glorious present and future. For me, as a visitor to this museum, a question that stays long after I have left, and is the original impetus for this paper, is whether these backers also want to build and talk about a Canada that is inclusive.

2   The images preserved in museums like Pier 21 do not merely remain there. They become present right across Canada and in our imagining of who the early Canadians were and how they are related to the Canadians of today. We see many of these images in sixty-second mini-movies, a form of government- and corporate-sponsored advertising that is intended to bolster our sense of having a common heritage. One such example is the heritage minute commercials, produced by Historica, an agency whose mandate is "to provide Canadians with a deeper understanding of their history and its importance in shaping their future" ("About Historica"). We see these sixty-second mini-movies ubiquitously on television and in the cinema. In addition, the provincially-owned public education station, TV Ontario, has its own Trailblazer mini-movies, available to similarly owned provincial educators across the country. These docudramas of sorts all tell us about the great Canadians, the great things they have done and are doing, and how we should be proud of a collective greatness as Canadians.

3   In this version of the Canadian narrative, Pier 21 is possibly the most important beginning of Canada. It is also the beginning to a national story about those with an inalienable right to inhabit this social space and to jointly colonize the future in the name of a people simply called Canadians.

4   By gesturing to this landmark as Canada's Ellis Island, Goldbloom is hoping to return to a site that could be the start of one of the main narratives of how millions of people, born elsewhere, came to belong to this space called Canada. In American folklore, Ellis Island is the piece of land in the shadow of the Statue of Liberty where millions of immigrants, as the story goes, got their first glimpse of the United States of America and with that look began an inner social transformation that turned them into Americans. Ellis Island is part of the US mythology that speaks of giving "me your tired, your poor,/ your huddled masses yearning to breathe free,/ the wretched refuse of your teeming shore./ Send these, the homeless, tempest-tost to me,/ I lift my lamp beside the golden door!" (Lazarus). Ellis Island is part of the lore that "the land of the free and the home of the brave" takes the poor masses of the world, places them, figuratively, in the American melting pot, thus transforming them into Americans.

5   In Goldbloom's imaging, Pier 21 is the opening scene in the Canadian version of a similar story. This is a narrative of how so many of us became, and can become, Canadian citizens with an undisputable right of belonging. This is a story about Canada as "the true North, strong and free," a land which, purportedly, according to our official mantra, is a multicultural nation-state that draws from all the peoples

of the world the immigrants who are then fashioned into its citizens. And, as a story of transformation and belonging, it is a social construction of all of those who went through the crucible that changed them from outsiders into insiders, from strangers at the gate into full-fledged citizens, from immigrants into citizens.

6   But while walking through this museum, it soon became obvious to me that something was missing from what Pier 21 was offering as a full story of belonging. As the artifacts and images on display revealed, what was being presented was a narrative in the making that spoke only about some of us. This was a narrative of a new beginning that, depending on the gaze, can be noted not only for who it venerates and honours but also for who and what it leaves out. Indeed, in this narrative of the official beginning of Canada and its people, not all immigrants are recognized equally.

7   In a very short while it became significantly clear from the international and universal European representations—the national flags on display; the film on the reception of the immigrants from Europe; war brides from the European theatre of World War II; child evacuees from war-torn Europe; memorabilia, such as soldiers' uniforms, suitcases, passports, and letters attesting to European experiences—that this museum did not represent the plurality of Canadian identities. In this museum there were gaps and missing people that are meaningful to a full appreciation of what is Canada, and whether the story of its achievements and progress is a narrative, as Stuart Hall states in the first epigraph above, that is in any way voiced from the margins of society.

8   Missing were images and symbols that place people like me in the Canadian narrative. As Hall would say, missing were the tales from the margin—the non-European world not part of the accepted mainstream in Canada. For example, what of the images of the thousands of Caribbean Blacks who would have passed through Pier 21 at the beginning of the last century, when so many of them came to work the mines in Cape Breton and to live in and around Halifax? There was also nothing honouring or venerating any of those Blacks who arrived in Canada from the 1950s onwards through Halifax, or those who stayed on board the great ocean liner and got off in Montreal. There was nothing about my relatives who arrived in Canada just like so many of those immigrants who arrived from Europe. Indeed, there was nothing in the images on display that indicated that the Blacks who have been living in the Halifax area since the 1780s had a part to play in welcoming these Europeans to their Canada. Pier 21 had very little for me, an immigrant Black female from Jamaica. Its images were about Europeans and the privileged positions that some specially blessed immigrants occupy in Canada and its stories.

Images of Blackness and Belonging

9   As a museum, Pier 21 is a well-funded project that excludes a significant number of immigrants who came to Canada. Even if an argument could be made that certain ethnic groups did not arrive through the gateway of Pier 21, the Media Kit at the official website for Pier 21 states "Our mission is to preserve, present & celebrate the *authentic* Canadian immigration experience" (emphasis mine). This raises the question: if this is the "authentic" Canadian immigration experience, then, of what kind are all the experiences of immigrants not reflected in the narrative of Pier 21?

10   Furthermore, how have those responsible for promoting *Canadianness* found ways to include or represent other arrivals? The experience of the Underground Railroad and the notion of the "Promised Land," though important

and meaningful to who I am as a person of African descent, does not speak to my personal story or the stories of other Black immigrants who arrived since. Black people did not all arrive via the Underground Railroad, nor were our experiences of "welcome" a Jackie Robinson story.

11   I do not wish to be understood as suggesting that these stories do not matter, because they do; rather, the point I am making is that the stories of Black immigration are more than just narratives of "from slavery to freedom" in Canada, or about being welcomed from across the border. The story of Black immigration needs to include all the various waves of migrations of peoples of African descent. Finally, what is it that makes the experiences of Pier 21 *authentic,* what makes it necessary for those constructing the narrative to make a symbolic connection between those arriving via Pier 21 and those who arrived some 300 years earlier?

12   Rinaldo Walcott, also a Black immigrant to Canada, offers answers to these questions in his article "Rhetorics of Blackness, Rhetorics of Belonging." In challenging who gets automatic rights to be a Canadian, Walcott points to the Pier 21 Museum, refurbished and reopened on Canada Day 1999, as an example. In his examination of an article published in the *Toronto Star,* December 1998, he recalls the names of the many media personnel of the day—all white and mainstream—who entered through this "gateway to Canada." Canadians, such as Hanna Gartner, formerly the face and voice of *The National* and *The Nightly News Report* on CBC, Damiano Pietropaolo, then head of Drama for CBC-Radio National, Peter Newman, author and former editor of *Maclean's,* and former CBC president Anthony Manera all entered through Pier 21 (1928–1971). As Walcott rightly states, "These are people whose Canadian-ness is never questioned. Their ability to belong and become Canadian is not an issue of national concern" (13).

13   The point is that as a grand narrative of belonging in a country that is now officially multicultural, the story of the immigrants who entered via Pier 21 and went on to become outstanding Canadians is problematic. While it is important to acknowledge and legitimize our immigration experiences, the way the narrative is framed not only raises disturbing questions and issues about Canadianness and belonging but also demonstrates cultural invisibility at work. Even to think of the gateway as Canada's Ellis Island demands interrogation. Canada, as a plural society with an official multicultural policy, unlike the United States, does not need an Ellis Island. The narrative of Ellis Island is for the American "melting pot" ideal, not for a nation where multiculturalism is the official narrative. Canada, according to official proclamation, is not a melting pot and does not aspire to be one. Canada is, in the official narrative, a multicultural mosaic, perhaps a quilt of many distinctive colours, a garden of many different and diverse plants and flowers. In addition, Pier 21 Museum requires access to a great deal of funding, which is not readily available to many non-European immigrant groups who want to write themselves into the Canadian narrative. Those who hold power and privilege perhaps should reflect upon Canada's goal, both nationally and internationally.

14   A rethinking of what is Canada requires that those in control not see the images and representations of Canada solely as theirs or about themselves, or reflect a perspective of noninclusion they may hold of others. Re-visioning our collective identity, in all its diversity and difference, requires seeing the image of Canada as multicultural. This would allow diverse groups to determine the ways in which they are represented on the Canadian stage, both nationally and internationally. What is necessary is a reconceptualization of who and what is Canadian.

15   Canada may be better off educating the Canadians who create its images and representations to portray a multicultural sensibility; this would help to eliminate the practice of writing narratives of exclusion, erasure, or invisibility. As Walcott maintains, and a point that as a fellow Black Canadian I share:

> What is at stake is a whiteness which can become national and therefore Canadian, vis à vis other differences which cannot. The kind of people who came to Canada through Pier 21 are rarely, if ever, questioned about belonging to the national space by those who accept the official national narrative of nation-state formation. These folks are the natural inheritors of what Canada is, and they cannot only represent Canada in its national institutional spaces, but they can also speak for exactly what Canada is and means. They become ethnonationalist representatives of the nation-state. (14)

The important thing I want to draw from Walcott's discussion is his notion that Canadianness functions on the premise of an "ethnicity-free ethnicity." This is a logic, Walcott argues, that makes the Canadian phenotypically white, with little room outside of official multiculturalism for imagining blackness. And here, for the purpose of this essay, I want to extend the definition of blackness to include all other marginalized groups that are not considered as white.

16   The important symbolic value that should be elevated in this particular immigration narrative would be that of multiculturalism. For Will Kymlicka, multiculturalism has an important symbolic value for Canada, which "had a history of racial and ethnocentric bias in the selection of immigrants" (57). And while this symbolic value may come across as window-dressing, Kymlicka's point is significant; the symbolism lies in the recognition and affirmation "that Canada is a multiracial, polyethnic country, in which full citizenship does not depend on how close one's ethnic descent or cultural lifestyle is to that of the historically dominant group" (57).

17   Yet we find that the rhetoric of exclusion is prevalent in media representations in terms of their portrayal of minorities who are "othered" (marginalized) in society. In portraying the mainstream as "the standard by which to judge or accept" (Fleras and Elliott 171), the media cast "difference," as associated with minority men and women, as social deviancy. Alternately, minorities are stereotyped in various roles according to old prejudices. For example, minorities are at times labelled as outsiders by referring to them by their hyphenated Canadian identities, such as Jamaican-Canadian, or simply Jamaican, Tamil, or Filipino to name a few, even though the individual may very well be Canadian by birth. Marginalized groups are often cast as hostile and uncooperative with the police and involved in crime. "This reinforces the wedge between 'minority them' and 'mainstream us,' and too often demonizes an entire community for the sins of a few" (Fleras and Elliott 168).

18   The youths of marginalized groups suffer from this typecasting and the result for some is that they internalize the stereotypes circulated in the media and see themselves as second-class citizens or part of the underclass. Black youths, in particular, suffer from the stereotypes associated with crime and the ever-increasing, and perhaps misunderstood, *gangsta* tradition as popularized by hip hop culture imported from the United States. Images of Black youths in popular culture do not portray Black youths as being part of the "I am Canadian"

image. This issue of demonizing Black youths needs to be redressed. Criminal and deviant behaviour of a number of Black youths is partly the consequence of what Canadian multiculturalism policy is working against.

19   As the multicultural commitment reaffirms: "Beyond the inequity, suffering and social disruption that intolerance and racism causes, Canada cannot afford to have any of its citizens marginalized" (Canada). The social disruptions are a consequence of marginalization. A way of remedying this problem would be for the socially marginalized to see themselves as important to the Canadian body politick. As excluded individuals, they are alienated from society, yet they desire to find a sense or place to belong.

Cultural Identity, Cultural Representation, and the Multicultural Ideal

20   Since multiculturalism was declared as the official policy in Canada in 1971, the notion of what constitutes meaningful national identity continues to be challenged by groups designated as minorities, such as Blacks, Asians, and Aboriginals. Today, in Canada, national identity can no longer be framed in terms of biculturalism, where cultural heritage is focused on maintaining the myth of the two founding peoples, the British and the French; rather, national identity and, thus, issues of cultural heritage and cultural representation have become more complex. The mass media have been criticized for not presenting a more diverse Canadian image that is not problematized by minority images that are "tainted by overt prejudice, open discrimination, and racialized discourses" (Fleras and Elliott 175).

21   Consequently, "minority" groups continue to articulate their concerns about how they are being portrayed, if at all, in cultural representations designed to develop and sustain a diverse yet unified national image that supports the unity-in-diversity claim of multiculturalism. While they believe that Canadian identity is a multicultural one, so that we can speak of Canadian identities, many Canadians do not see themselves or their cultures reflected meaningfully in the national images or representations in the mass media. Portrayals of minority Canadians, when they do materialize, tend to be framed in terms of the spectacular, the stereotypical, and hyphenated Canadian, who is perhaps best understood as the non-Canadian, or immigrant, whether born in Canada or not. Yet, this is not the intention of Canada's commitment to multiculturalism. The official Canadian Multiculturalism website explains:

> Lessons learned through experience with bilingualism and multiculturalism have taught Canada that acceptance and understanding of differences between peoples make collective development possible. However, experience with diversity also shows that inequities must be acknowledged and addressed for a diverse people to move forward together. This is a slow and sometimes painful process, but it is essential if all Canadians are to enjoy the same sense of belonging and attachment to their country. (Canada)

Therefore, it is important for Canadians to challenge cultural representations that do not foster acceptance and belonging in ways that are worthy of our claim and international reputation of embracing diversity. As Fleras and Elliott remind us, "Central to Canadian multiculturalism is our commitment to improving the responsiveness of our institutions to minority needs and concerns" (159). It is also important, at this historical juncture, to work at displacing cultural hegemony to allow for a positive reflection of diversity.

22   A beginning to making a place for all Canadians in the dominant narrative, in ways that are meaningful to them, would be to find new ways of re-imagining our nation so that a rewriting of the grand narratives can take place. Finding ways to see the potential in our nation will allow us to create narratives that move beyond the immigrant stories, to establish stories of citizenship and belonging that are not framed in stereotypical or spectacular ways. Our responsibility is to "uncover" things Canadian (imbued with a Canadian sensibility) and to disseminate those stories that will begin a process of transformation in the minds of our citizens from tolerance for diversity to committed acceptance, and thus reflect all Canadians. Canada recognizes its shortcomings and has implemented policies to address them, as the commitment points out:

> As with official languages and multiculturalism, Canada has learned that constitutional measures and legislation alone are not enough to assure equal opportunity in a diverse society. To contribute fully and achieve their full potential, all peoples must have a voice in society and a chance to shape the future direction of the country of which they are a part. This requires mechanisms to enable individuals and groups to speak out and be heard, and to participate in national debates. It also requires programs that help equip individuals, communities, and organizations with the skills and tools they need to advance their interests. (Canada)

The question arises as to whether these mechanisms are accessible to all individuals and groups. We know that there are power structures in place, with access regulated by those with power, and we know that funds are limited and carefully awarded. Minorities do not have ready access to the institutional power that is often necessary to secure an award from a foundation such as the Historica Foundation. But for meaningful change to occur, the power relationships need to shift from time to time to accommodate a variety of voices and to allow all Canadians to share in the opportunities of a diverse society that has its pride of place on the international stage.

So Who IS Canadian?

23   As mentioned earlier, the images of Canadians in the media continue to be questioned and even challenged by minorities who do not see themselves represented appropriately, if at all. Fleras and Elliott maintain that "media representation of minorities border on the unacceptable" (170). Negativized representation of minorities is a systemic problem and although the media may not be deliberately disseminating negative images, "they accept, reflect, and do little to work against the ethnocentric assumptions of white superiority that are deeply ingrained in Western culture" (Fleras and Elliott 11).

24   A simple example is the Molson Breweries advertisements "I am Canadian," which depict groups of white males enjoying various social activities in Canada. How many visible minorities are reflected in the images projected of who is a Canadian? While it can be argued that Molson is appealing to a particular market segment, the symbolic value of "who is [a] Canadian" (or who is not a Canadian) cannot be ignored. This kind of advertising, Fleras and Elliott note, is "a symbolic and psychological form of violence" and is "based on certain assumptions about race and gender that are consistent with the notions that white males are superior . . . [and m]inority women and men are excluded from full Canadianness" (173).

25   As simple as advertisements may seem, they powerfully reinforce a particular ideology. Such representations need to be interrogated because of the messages they send. An inquiry into who chooses these images and why the absence of visible minorities is beyond conspicuous is necessary if the intent of multiculturalism is to be achieved. If members of the dominant group select representations of various ethnicities, then it stands to reason that various groups may argue about the ways in which they are represented or excluded from representations that lay claim to Canadianness. They may also disagree on how much the representations are "true" reflections of themselves.

26   Indeed, because minorities do not have the power to choose the images that best represent who they are, the images chosen by others for them become "inauthentic," leaving them with a sense of alienation. Rather than being the subject that constitutes the representations, the "marginalized" recognize themselves as the "object" of representation and rightfully become disillusioned with the intention of multiculturalism. As cultural theorist Stuart Hall reminds us, "it is only through the way in which we represent and imagine ourselves that we come to know how we are constituted and who we are" (261).

27   In *Distorted Mirror: Canada's Racist Face,* Foster invites readers to consider this question: "How can leaders succeed in convincing troubled youths there are no shortcuts when they cannot at the same time assure them of acceptance as full-fledged members of society, no matter how well qualified they might become?"(23). This question goes to the heart of the problem of social deviancy. Certainly, the representations of Black culture and Black youths do not suggest that there is, or can be, a place for them in Canada.

28   Black youths have been demonized and stereotyped as criminal. Often in the news, the reports linked with Black youths have been associated with drugs and violence. Fleras and Elliott also make the point that differences that are "threatening or dangerous are contained, controlled, normalized, stereotyped, idealized, marginalized, and reified" (171); one obvious result of this type of distancing of minorities from the mainstream core is that it "drives a psychological wedge between minorities and Canadians at large" (171). This results in cultural segregation, where the negativized images of the marginalized are popularized and made to represent the norm.

29   Indeed, acceptable forms of representation are not simple to construct because there are as many competing desires as there are ethnic groups. As Homi Bhabha argues in his essay "DissemiNation," the lived experience of all those who embody the nation is complicated by the perplexed histories of the living people, their cultures of survival and resistance that create a split in the narrative of the nation. More importantly, I would argue that this split results in the ways that Canada as a nation is imagined and how we are therefore represented.

Moving Forward: Toward the Transcendent

30   One of the things I would like to take away from Hall's essay is his notion that a culture in these postmodern times embraces popular culture, moving more toward everyday practices, toward local narratives, toward the decentring of old hierarchies and the grand narratives. This decentring or displacement opens up new spaces of contestation and, as he suggests, affects a "momentous shift" in the high culture of popular culture relations, thus presenting us with a strategic and important opportunity for intervention in the popular cultural field (256). Hall explains it this way:

> Within culture, marginality, though it remains peripheral to the broader
> mainstream, has never been such a productive space as it is now. And
> that is not simply the opening within the dominant of spaces that those
> outside it can occupy. It is also a result of the cultural politics of differ-
> ence, of the struggles around difference, of the production of new iden-
> tities, of the appearance of new subjects on the political and cultural
> stage. This move of difference . . . includes marginalized ethnicities, . . .
> feminism and sexual politics in the gay and lesbian movement. (256)

Thus, my argument should not be understood in terms of the either/or dichotomy,
displacing one grand narrative with several competing narratives. What I am advo-
cating is the shift in a balance of power, a struggle over cultural hegemony.

31   Cultural hegemony, according to Hall, "is always about shifting the balance
of power in the relations of culture; it is always about changing the dispositions
and the configurations of cultural power" (256). It is therefore important for the
marginalized not to lose sight of the opportunities open to them that can lead to
developing cultural strategies that can make a difference. This, of course, comes
with the knowledge of cost and the reality of underfunding or lack of funding, as
well as the approval of those needed to recognize and accept these new strategies
as a benefit to the whole polity, rather than as a threat. I believe that, in principle,
the Canadian government recognizes the importance of "shifting the balance."
Embracing diversity as strength would see an end to the practice of cultural marginalization that results in cultural invisibility. Since representation is socially constructed, and, as Hall points out, is an indication of who we are, those responsible
for shaping Canadian identity through representation need to work toward dis-
mantling ideologies that place minorities in subordinate positions in society and
label them as the marginalized others. Marlene Nourbese Philip maintains that
this is a form of management. Management, Philip says, is a way of controlling,
"putting the unmanageable into preordained places within society so that they
can be more easily controlled" (295). Philip observes: "Management works to
control that which is considered different and representative of Otherness" (295).
The "unmanaged" are those groups of people that European thought "has traditionally designated . . . not only as inferior but also, paradoxically, as threats to
their order, systems, and traditions of knowledge" (295).

32   Identifiable groups such as women, Africans, Asians, and Aboriginals, Philip
argues, at times accept and use words such as "marginalized" to describe themselves. In this sense, Philip is referring to the ways in which language is used to
control the way people who have been "Othered" are conditioned to think of
themselves. Thus, those considered as marginalized end up colluding with their
own management. Rather than thinking of themselves as centre stage, they
accept their position on the "margin."

33   Philip urges groups so positioned to think of themselves in more progressive terms, that is, consider themselves on the "frontier," and in so doing, resist
being placed or positioned or "managed." Resisting management means resisting
the imposition of limits, opening up new spaces of possibilities. Understanding
language as the underpinning of power enables the so-called "managed" to repo-
sition themselves outside of the relationship with the managers. As Philip puts it,

> From margin to frontier—is a deceptively simple act requiring no
> movement or change, but only a substitution of one word for another.
> It is an important and liberating step, this substitution of words and

meaning, but to make the authentic leap from margin to frontier demands nothing less than a profound revolution in thinking and metamorphosis of consciousness. (300)

This change in consciousness enables the so-called managed to seek and find new possibilities and ways of creating narratives that shape new ideologies to support our diversity. Fleras and Elliott make the point that "If we fail to unmask the ideologies that underpin representations, we will be further marginalizing the people those representations exclude. Visibility may not be the same as power; that being said, invisibility is decidedly disempowering" (182).

Conclusion

34 So while the Canadian government's efforts at putting Canadian multicultural policy in practice is commendable, it is not only important to "share our stories and perspectives," but also important to share power. The real change will come about when minorities are part of our political will, when they actively share power, in politics, in the boardrooms, and in various other positions of influence. Belonging is more than the "ethnic and the exotic" window dressings. Events such as Caribana, the Chinese Dragon Boat Race, Caravan, Black History "Month," the South Asian festivals, and other ethnic cultural events are now a Canadian way of life. These events are part of Canada's participation in the field of the "popular." While these differences enrich lives, the commitment to diversity should not end there. The commitment to diversity is most meaningful when it is reflected in who has power in the nation. Power is the main issue here, for "Until society sorts out who has power, and how it is used, and why it is used that way, and whose values will dominate, biases in representation will continue" (Fleras and Elliott 182). This essay is an invitation to reconceptualize who and what is Canadian and to advocate for constructions of cultural representations that reflect Canadian multicultural sensibilities. It is also about displacing cultural hegemony and a plea for Canadians and all media to value citizens as equals, entitled to the same sense of justice, belonging, and heritage. Marginalization runs counter to the unity-in-diversity claim of multiculturalism and disempowers some citizens.

35 Change can occur if we create a political culture in which there is more than just a willingness to understand the needs and interests of other groups. Just as important is the commitment to follow through with new projects that reflect our understanding of a multicultural sensibility. Yet, this type of change is not easy and can only occur with "changes to our education system, to the media portrayal of various groups, and to the political process" (Kymlicka 112). When Canadians look in the mirror of representation, they should recognize their diversity; there should be no strangers in the mirror.

36 In reflecting on the idea that in mythology the ending is merely a new beginning, it might be appropriate to return to Pier 21, this time wiser and with an intention to be inclusive. It may mean constructing a Canadian mosaic narrative, a quilt of sorts, that tells a wider story, not those carefully regulated segregated beginnings that we are passing on to the next generation, inculcating, subliminally, the idea that some immigration narratives have more social capital than others. Let's begin quilting, threading our stories to create a grand narrative of our Canadian mosaic.

Works Cited

"About Historica." *Histori.ca.* 2004. 8 September 2004 <www.histori.ca/ foundation/about.jsp>.

Bhabha, Homi K. "DissemiNation: Time, Narrative, and the Margins of the Modem Nation." *Nation and Narration.* Ed. Homi K. Bhabha. London: Routledge, 1999. 291-320.

Canada. Canadian Heritage. *Multiculturalism.* Ottawa: Government of Canada, 2004. 2 Aug. 2004 <www.canadianheritage.gc.ca/progs/multi/repect_e. cfm>.

Fleras, Augie and Jean Leonard Elliott. "Miscasting Minorities: Multiculturalism and the Mass Media." *Engaging Diversity: Multiculturalism in Canada.* Toronto: Nelson Thomson Learning, 2002. 157-92.

Foster, Cecil. *Distorted Mirror: Canada's Racist Face.* Toronto: Harper Collins, 1991.

Hall, Stuart. "What Is This 'Black' in Black Popular Culture?" *The Black Studies Reader.* Ed. Jacqueline Bobo, Cynthia Hudley, and Claudine Michel. New York: Routledge, 2004. 255-63.

hooks, bell. *Black Looks: Race and Representation.* Boston: South End, 1992.

Kymlicka, Will. "Renegotiating the Terms of Integration." *Finding Our Way: Rethinking Ethnocultural Relations in Canada.* Toronto: Oxford UP, 1998. 40-59.

Lazarus, Emma. "The New Colossus." Plaque. Available at <www.nps.gov/stli/ newcolossus>.

Philip, Marlene Nourbese. "Managing the Unmanageable." *Caribbean Women Writers: Essays from the First International Conference.* Ed. Selwyn R. Cudjoe. Wellesley, Massachusetts: Calaloux Publications, 1990. 295-300.

Pier 21. Media Kit. *Pier 21.* 2 Aug. 2004 <www.pier21.ca/fileadmin/whats_new_ images/Media Kit_info.pdf>.

Walcott, Rinaldo. "Rhetorics of Blackness, Rhetorics of Belonging: The Politics of Representation in Black Canadian Expressive Culture." *Canadian Review of American Studies* 29.2 (1999):1-24.

 **PIERRE DUBUC**

Pierre Dubuc is editor of l'aut'journal *and secretary of Syndicalistes et progressistes pour un Québec libre, a political club within the Parti Québécois. The following piece was written as an open letter in 2005.*

Quebec Separation Was Not Laid to Rest in 1995

1   Those of you outside Quebec who are inclined to reduce the sponsorship scandal[1] to a mere tempest in a teacup have a short-sighted and highly imprudent grasp of the political situation in Canada. If it were only a question of dollars and cents, the

---

[1]The sponsorship scandal refers to allegations investigated by commissioner Justice John H. Gomery that the federal government under Liberal Prime Minister Jean Chrétien misused funds. (Editors' note)

sponsorship scandal would no doubt appear almost insignificant compared to that of the firearms registry. However, this is above all a political scandal.

2   Judging from the English-Canadian press, it appears that the wake-up has been brutal for those who believed that the issue of Quebec separation had been laid to rest on October 30, 1995. Nightmare scenarios were evoked: a landslide win by the Bloc in the next election, followed by a victory by the Parti Québécois and the holding of a new referendum.

3   Seen from Quebec, we get the distinct impression that "a spectre is haunting Canada"—to paraphrase a famous expression—but rather than communism, that spectre is separatism. English-speaking Canada did not take the 1995 referendum too seriously, but that will never happen again now that it knows it could lose. So, the editorialists and columnists wheel out the heavy artillery: Plan B, the *Clarity Act*. The only thing they haven't done is brandish the threat of the partition of Quebec's territory, but that shouldn't be long in coming.

4   For those of you unable to closely follow the Quebec political scene, we can assure you that the sovereignty movement is once again on the march. Quebeckers are gleefully tuning in to RDI (Radio-Canada)—a television channel whose mandate is to "promote Canadian unity"—to hear the revelations of the Gomery Commission on the dirty sponsorship money that was intended to combat the "separatists." Not even all the imagination in the world could have invented such a boomerang effect.

5   But that is only one aspect—the least important—of what is going on in Quebec. Half-way through its term, the Charest [provincial Liberal] government is already one of the most unpopular in history. Its neo-liberal platform set out to weaken labour and social organizations and to dismantle the Quebec State through privatizations, thus crushing the backbone of the sovereignty movement.

6   But instead, the Charest government has succeeded in reinvigorating social movements in Quebec. One year ago, 100,000 workers took to the streets of Montreal to mark May 1 [2004]. This year, the confrontation increased a notch with the holding of a series of day-long strikes by public sector employees seeking the renewal of their collective agreements. On May 6, over 35,000 teachers marched in the streets of Quebec City.

7   This spring, nearly 200,000 CEGEP and university students held a strike to protest against the government's reform of the loans and bursaries program. It was the largest student strike in the history of Quebec, and this in a province with a rich history of student unrest.

8   The political character of these movements confirms Quebec's need to have its own social project, a project that can only be realized within an independent Quebec. Quebec sovereignty constitutes the most profound democratic demand of the Quebec populace and stands at the forefront of all its aspirations and struggles. This explains why, in a recent poll, 54 per cent of Quebeckers pronounced themselves in favour of sovereignty.

9   The social situation in Quebec against the backdrop of the current political crisis in Canada heralds a major confrontation, with all the risks that implies.

Canada Has Been Rendered Ungovernable

10   Since its creation in 1867, Canada has always been torn between powerful conflicting forces, both internal and external. While other federations have evolved toward greater centralization, Canada has always been too centralized for

Quebec and not enough for Ontario. Great Britain, and later the United States, supported the provinces' demands to weaken Canada, a competitor nation.

11 Historically, federal political parties have played a fundamental unifying role. This has been the case of the Liberal Party, which has traditionally dominated Canadian politics. Whenever the wearing effects of being in power became too obvious, the Conservatives moved in, giving the Liberal Party time to reinvent itself.

12 In order to move into power, the Conservatives had to ally themselves with Quebec nationalists. John Diefenbaker's Conservatives sought the support of Maurice Duplessis, while Brian Mulroney's Conservatives benefitted from René Lévesque's policy of "beau risque" (worthwhile risk).

13 But ever since the creation of the Bloc Québécois in 1990, following the failure of Meech Lake, whose aim was to repair Pierre Trudeau's 1982 constitutional coup de force by bringing Quebec into the Confederation "with honour and enthusiasm," there has no longer been the possibility of an alternative to the Liberals in the form of a majority Conservative government with a base in Quebec.

14 The struggle between Conservatives and Liberals—and the financial groups they represent—is now being waged within the Liberal Party, with the consequences we all know. The Liberal Party is in tatters and will be crushed in Quebec ridings with a francophone majority in the next election.

15 Consequently, Canada is at risk of winding up with an Italian-style government—that is, a succession of minority governments without a solid base in Quebec, that are prepared to sell out the country in order to stay in power—as [Prime Minister] Paul Martin is currently doing—thus feeding the centrifugal forces that are tearing this country apart.

16 Canada has been rendered ungovernable and only a major reform based on the hypothesis of the accession of Quebec to sovereignty can provide a possible way out of the current crisis. Canadian progressives outside Quebec must abandon all hope of satisfying Quebec's aspirations with vague constitutional reforms modelled on the Meech or Charlottetown accords. Instead, they should start reflecting on the possible shape of a Canada without Quebec and on the possible relations between the two countries.

Quebec and Canada vs. the United States—Same Struggle!

17 Of course, we are well aware that this approach is not presently on the rest of Canada's agenda, and it is with great concern that we apprehend a rise in "Quebec bashing" on the part of federal parties in a desperate bid to win a majority of seats in English-speaking Canada.

18 No one will be surprised if the Liberals decide to make the question of "national unity" a central issue in the next federal election, and we in Quebec recall very well that the Reform Party was the first to brandish the threat of Quebec partition.[2]

19 However, we have watched with some stupefaction as Jack Layton [Leader of the NDP] has climbed up on the Liberal battle horse and accused the Conservatives of allying themselves with the separatists. Is it because Buzz Hargrove [Canadian

[2]A group split from the Progressive Conservative party in 1987 creating the Reform Party (later the Canadian Alliance), which in 2003 reunited with the old Progressive Conservatives under the title Conservative Party of Canada. (Editors' note)

Auto Workers president] recommended that he leave Quebec to the Bloc Québécois that Mr. Layton now feels authorized to campaign in English Canada on the back of Quebec? The English-Canadian left should call Mr. Layton to order before his remarks poison relations between progressives in both nations.

20   We understand the complexity of the situation facing Canadian progressives outside Quebec and their concerns at the possibility of a Conservative win. We had the same concerns regarding the ADQ in Quebec. But we do not believe that the Liberals constitute an alternative, either directly or through the NDP.

21   We understand your desire to defend Canadian progressive values against the rise of the American-inspired right and to safeguard the independence of Canada against its absorption by the United States. In these times of globalization, the protection of Canadian identity is a just cause.

22   We know that progressives in English-speaking Canada still harbour a lot of resentment towards Quebec nationalists, whom they hold responsible for Canada's adherence to the Free Trade Agreement and NAFTA. It is true that this agreement would not have been possible without the Parti Québécois' support of the Mulroney government and that it subsequently rallied Quebec's nationalist elites.

23   But English-speaking Canada too easily forgets that this position was adopted out of vexation following the failure of the 1980 referendum. We must remember that, during this referendum, the government of René Lévesque had proposed "a new agreement with the rest of Canada, based on the equality of nations," in order to stand up to the United States. English-speaking Canada fought this sovereignty-association proposal tooth and nail, preferring to maintain Quebec in the same state of subjection it has been in since the conquest of 1760.

24   Today, Quebec is not pro-American, and it is certainly not pro-Bush. The massive demonstrations held in the streets of Montreal to protest against the war in Iraq made this clear in a spectacular way. On three occasions, in the dead of winter, over 150,000 people took to the streets of Montreal while tens of thousands more demonstrated elsewhere in Quebec. In proportion to the population, these were the largest protests in the world.

25   Some day, former Prime Minister Jean Chrétien's memoirs will no doubt reveal that these protests played a crucial role in his decision not to participate in the war. Mr. Chrétien feared that the government of Bernard Landry [PQ leader] would take advantage of the opportunity to bring the issue of Quebec independence to the table. Mr. Chrétien and Mr. Landry could not have been unaware that the first motion in favour of independence was tabled in the Quebec National Assembly by J.N. Francoeur during the conscription crisis in 1917.

Towards a Federalist Coup de Force?

26   We invite progressives in English-speaking Canada to undertake a careful analysis of the current political situation. Faced with the present impasse, we cannot exclude a federal coup de force. But this will only accelerate the course of history and raise the issue of Quebec independence with even greater intensity.

27   The hour of truth is near. And the crucial question is: what will the reaction of progressives in English-speaking Canada be if Quebec opts for national independence? Will they take the side of the repressive forces in English-speaking Canada or will they support the inalienable right of the people of Quebec to choose their future?

28   A progressive alternative is inconceivable without the sovereignty of Quebec, and the sovereignty of Quebec opens the door to this alternative.

 **JOHN GRUNDY**

John Grundy is a Ph.D. candidate in political science at York University.

Staging Queer Difference in the Entrepreneurial City: Marketing Diversity in Toronto

1   Queer Pride organizing in Toronto has undergone a radical transformation. According to Gary Kinsman, a former Pride organizer and a Professor of Sociology at Laurentian University, early Pride events mixed pleasure with politics: "Pride Day was consciously used as a day to build a movement, a day to build community organizations and to get people involved in political campaigns." In more recent years, however, Pride organizing reflects a very different set of priorities. While a number of political groups are still involved in the week-long festival, and while many people derive a sense of community from the parade, Pride events are no longer organized to advance queer social movement politics. Pride planners, along with local officials and business elites, seem much more concerned with reorganizing the event to bolster the local tourist industry.

2   Numerous studies have been conducted to assess the economic impact of the event (now estimated at $80 million including spin-offs) and to acquire detailed demographic information from spectators to assist corporations pursuing the heavily mythologized gay market. Pride organizers have stepped up marketing efforts this year by launching a cross-border advertising campaign to attract more American tourists to Toronto.

3   The evolution of Pride Toronto from a venue for lesbian and gay social movement politics to a marketing tool and tourist spectacle does not simply reflect the decisions made by organizers, but symbolizes much broader dynamics of the commodification of diversity in Toronto. Queerness, along with other forms of ethno-cultural diversity, has been conscripted into Toronto's economic development strategies. Toronto's gay district, much like Little Italy or Chinatown, now operates as a material and symbolic resource supporting Toronto's cosmopolitan image as well as the emergence of a local tourism industry based on the commodification of cultural difference.

4   This newfound appreciation for diversity should be regarded with suspicion. Beneath the glossy veneer of Toronto's official multicultural image lie persistent forms of marginalization.

Urban Entrepreneurialism and the Commodification of Difference

5   In the wake of globalization and the flight of manufacturing to cheaper regions, cities across North America have scrambled to devise new ways to attract and retain investment—and within these entrepreneurial schemes image is everything. Cities have sought to reinvent themselves through strategies of branding that sell the city like any other product. This involves the proliferation of spectacle in a variety of forms such as trophy architecture, revitalized waterfronts and historic districts, stadiums, and other forms of infrastructure development that channel money out of less-spectacular but much-needed services.

6   Urban branding also involves the marketing of diversity. Economic development policy star Richard Florida built a career by selling this strategy to cities.

In 2001, Florida began travelling the lecture circuit with his idea of "the gay index," a measurement of economic performance that links a thriving urban economy with a large gay (male) population. Florida (with associate Gary Gates) announced that "gays can be thought of as canaries of the knowledge economy. They signal a diverse and progressive environment that fosters the creativity and innovation necessary for success." In light of Florida's revelation, urban developers in cities across North America have rushed to make their respective locales attractive by staging diversity in the most theatrical and spectacular manner possible. They are taking stock of whatever cultural resources and ethnic enclaves may enhance urban branding strategies and function as "authentic" exotica for tourists and middle-class urban dwellers.

7   Toronto is no exception. Local urban imagineers have embarked on an urban branding campaign to repackage Toronto as a succession of tourist districts and ethnic enclaves. The *Economic Development Strategy Report* produced by the City in 2000 outlines the "branding of Toronto as the most ethnically, culturally, socially and economically diverse city in the world" as a strategic priority that will delineate Toronto's "unique identity." The report goes on to suggest that "Toronto will bolster its competitive position by finding new ways to creatively package previously overlooked aspects of the city . . . for tourists throughout the year."

8   The commodification of diversity in Toronto is rife with contradictions. While certain forms of cultural difference are incorporated into urban branding strategies, other forms of difference, those that don't help to consolidate Toronto's "unique identity," are subject to intensified surveillance and repression. New laws and policing practices, such as the Safe Streets Act, have served to further criminalize a broad section of Toronto's population including low-income people, people of colour, Aboriginal peoples, the homeless, youth, and psychiatric survivors. Moreover, numerous reports produced by the United Way and other agencies have exposed the disturbing underside of Toronto's multicultural image—the dramatic intensification of poverty among racialized communities in Toronto's under-resourced inner suburbs. Given these trends, Toronto's brand of celebratory multiculturalism appears to be more about civic-boosterism than equality.

(Ab)using Queer Culture

9   Toronto's queer culture is one of those "previously overlooked" resources to be packaged for tourists. Historically speaking, however, Toronto's queer communities were hardly "overlooked." For decades urban authorities viewed Toronto's burgeoning gay and lesbian presence as a sign of the city's moral decay. A number of viciously homophobic policing campaigns were mounted against gays and lesbians such as the "Clean Up Yonge Street" campaign in the late seventies and the infamous "Operation Soap" bathhouse raids of the early eighties that entailed the mass arrest of hundreds of gay men.

10   The same spaces once targeted by police are now targeted for commodification as part of an exotic identity-based entertainment district lending credence to the city's desired image as tolerant, diverse and "cool." Images of queer culture figure centrally in promotional literature to project, as one City of Toronto report puts it, "the sexiness of the city—new urban cool—young businessperson to young businessperson." A glossy tourist guide produced by Tourism Toronto touts the city's gay district as "a celebration of life, diversity, and . . . shopping. Sip a non-fat-extra-foamy latte in a café, install yourself in a restaurant window, or quaff a cold one on an outdoor patio . . . the Gay Village is sophisticated, spirited,

and . . . plays an essential role in making this a world class city. Be part of it!" Prospective gay male tourists are urged to "Grab a Speedo and water gun for outdoor water parties filled with hunky, mostly naked studs . . . and after the parties end, the fun doesn't stop! Toronto's seven centrally located bathhouses will be jam-packed featuring a smorgasbord of satisfaction."

11   Such over-the-top representations of queer commercial spaces accentuate the edgy urbanism that place marketers seek to project. Yet, the increasing visibility of Toronto's queer spaces and spectacles does nothing to challenge the persistent marginalization of queer people. While urban authorities began to exploit exotic images of queerness, agencies providing important services to queer people including the AIDS Committee of Toronto and the Toronto District School Board's Triangle Program had their budgets slashed. The situation also worsened for many queer youth in Toronto during the late nineties. Cuts to social assistance coupled with the lack of affordable housing impoverished many queer youth who had moved from smaller towns to Toronto in search of community and who were relying on welfare to establish themselves. A disproportionate number of queer youth became caught in the homeless shelter system.

12   Moreover, the organization of Toronto's queer district as an entertainment district further marginalizes those unable or unwelcome to consume in primarily white gay male commercial establishments including lesbians, transgender people, queers of colour, and queer youth. Clearly not all queers were empowered during the so-called gay nineties.

"We Are Not for Sale!"

13   The establishment of the Advisory Committee on Lesbian, Gay, Bisexual, and Transgender Issues in 1999 gave reason to hope things might change for vulnerable queers in Toronto. Mandated to advocate on behalf of lesbian, gay, bisexual and transgender people, the advisory committee provided Toronto's queer constituencies with a rare voice in the newly restructured municipality. Yet the under-resourced committee proved to be quite powerless, and before shutting down, began collaborating with Tourism Toronto to market the city's gay quarters as an identity-based entertainment district and tourist destination.

14   An entrepreneurial agenda now frames how queer issues are taken up within the local state. Within this agenda, Toronto's queer communities are depoliticized and re-conceived as a tourist attraction. This is cause for concern as it exacerbates inequalities within queer communities. The gay business class is empowered vis-a-vis the local state while the political grievances of severely marginalized queers are put on the back burner. We would do well to draw inspiration from a group of queer activists in Spain who recently blocked Barcelona's Pride Parade with shopping carts chanting, "We are not for sale!"

 **OVIDE MERCREDI**

Ovide Mercredi was the legal advisor for the Assembly of First Nations (AFN) (including during Meech Lake Accord dissent), then was the National Chief of AFN from 1991 to 1997 (including during the Charlottetown constitutional discussions) and is currently Grand Rapids First Nation Chief. He has taught Native Studies at University of Sudbury, University of Lethbridge, and McMaster University. He holds a law degree

and is a Native rights advocate and an advisor for treaty and Aboriginal rights. The
following piece is a speech given at Carleton University in the fall of 1990.

Indian Self-Government and Sovereignty in Canada

1   The issue of sovereignty in terms of self-rule for a people is not so much a legal
or constitutional issue, but a moral and political problem for all Canadians. I say
that not to be disrespectful to you, but to give you a perspective which you did
not see or hear in the constitutional process.

2   The structure of the constitutional talks was on the basis of the legal and
constitutional debate and did not address the primary issue, which in my view is
moral and political.

3   Let me explain it this way. You have a right to freedom which you cherish.
You understand it thoroughly in the context of individual freedom, and you will
do anything to defend it. More than that, what you tend to forget is that the individual right to freedom does not stand by itself. It derives from some collective
right of freedom that we have as equals, and when you look within your own
history in this country since Confederation, you have fought for and defended
your freedom in two world wars. But it wasn't the individual right that you
were defending, but the collective right of freedom to your institutions of government, to your democracy. What I fail to understand, as an aboriginal person,
is how you cannot somehow translate that passion which you have for freedom
into our context as aboriginal people.

4   What we are seeking is not so much recognition of an individual's freedom
within the context of Canada, although we know that we have to strive for our
civil and individual rights as well within your society, but essentially the collective expression of the freedom of the collectivity, the people themselves, to
decide through their own general will, the expression of their institutions, of
how they choose to live and where they choose to go collectively as a people. I
ask you what is so difficult about that?

5   All that we are looking for is what you already have, what you enjoy as a
people, which is your institutions that you collectively agree to, such as parliament, such as provincial legislatures, such as your judicial system. You take these
institutions, not for granted, but you accept them as the collective expression of
your freedom as a people. So when we talk about the right of self-government,
we are not talking about the right that you have to tell me, and my people, how
we are to conduct our affairs. I don't agree that you have the right to tell me, an
indigenous person, how I have to conduct my affairs. There lies the moral issue.
When we try to enter into dialogue with your governments, and we put forward
processes and ideas of how we might entertain negotiations or discussions, your
governments continually put obstructions in front of us and they rely on the rule
of law. They rely on the constitution, your constitution, as justification for refusing to sit down with us and engage in meaningful dialogue on how we could
express ourselves through our institutions of self-government in this country.
When your governments refuse to talk to us, it becomes a political issue.

6   Where we are heading right now in this country is a collision course where
you and I would lose, where there will be no winners. What we have to do is to
take lessons from our ancestors, yours and mine. Those who had at least a vision,
whether they believed it or not, that the proper way to deal with the aboriginal

people is through discussion, negotiations, and the making of treaties. In this country there was no Indian war between us and the government of Canada other than the resistance of the Métis people in Saskatchewan. There has never been a deployment of the army in this country against the aboriginal people until very recently in Kahnawake and Kanesatake.[1] That happened, in my view, because people have lost the vision that your ancestors and mine had—that we should resolve our differences through political discussion, and that we should come to some consensus on the issues that we face together.

7   We have a rich heritage in this country, a very rich heritage—the treaty-making process. Why is it that contemporary Canadians and their governments have forgotten about it? Is it because you are so ethnocentric in your views that you fail to see that the actions of your government amount to white supremacy? That is a strong suggestion, but think about it. From my perspective as an aboriginal person, when I am told, as I have been told by officials in the government, that they will not engage in discussions on the right to self-government until there is a constitutional amendment that recognizes explicitly our right to govern ourselves, then I know there is a great obstacle that I cannot do anything about. When we engage in discussions with them and we try to move issues forward, and I'll give you some examples, they place before you the suggestion that there are only two jurisdictions in this country, the provincial government and the federal government, and you wonder to yourself: at what point in your history as an indigenous person did your people surrender the right to govern themselves? Where in our history is there a document that tells you that I gave you the right to tell me how I am to live? Where in our entire history is there a scrap of paper that suggests that our people have abandoned their right to exist as a distinct people, or for that matter that they have relinquished their own self-government so they can adopt and embrace yours as superior forms of institutions of government?

8   I will tell you what sovereignty is not, so that you will have at least some understanding of why we also, like you, cherish our freedoms. First of all, it is not the *Indian Act*. It is not parliament sitting down deciding in assembly in one session to pass a law that tells me that I can do this but I can't do that. That is not sovereignty, that is not self-government and that is not self-rule. That is someone telling you what to do. Our people are operating under a system of government that is not traditional. The reason for that is that somewhere after Confederation some of your people decided in parliament that they would impose a system of government called the Chief and Council system, where they would delegate powers to the Indian people, but they would not recognize the law-making ability of the Indian people. They would just delegate some by-law making powers which would not become law until the Minister of Indian Affairs approved them. That is not sovereignty. That is delegated authority. That is the municipalization of our people's right to self-government, and has been rejected by our people.

---

[1]These Mohawk communities in Quebec were involved in the 1990 standoff, known as the Oka Crisis, with the Quebec provincial police and the Canadian Armed Forces. The three-month crisis, which began when the town of Oka tried to build a golf course on Native ancestral burial grounds, highlighted the need for federal and provincial governments to address Native constitutional concerns. (Editors' note)

9   When we had discussions during the constitutional process, many of the premiers, including the prime minister, were totally amazed at our assertion that we have a continuing right, a pre-existing right, to govern ourselves that does not derive from your parliament. The source of authority comes from our people, our own history, our own nations, our own culture. If you examine your own institutions and how you formed as a nation, you will understand what I am saying to you. All we want is to express ourselves in the same way that you are able to do, subsequent to Confederation throughout this country what Canadians were able to do as they formed provinces, and eventually we'll do in the northern parts of our country because Meech Lake did not pass.[2]

10   When we speak about self-government, our biggest problem in dealing with politicians, the premiers and the prime minister, is that somehow it is absurd for us to think that we can govern ourselves, that it is absurd for us to imagine or even dream about governmental powers equivalent to provincial powers. The reason why people feel, in my view, that it is not permissible for us to express ourselves through our own institutions is the conclusion that we are not ready to govern ourselves. That is a moral issue and has nothing to do with law or constitutional change. That has to do with attitudes, belief, morality. When you form opinions about us, as your government has done, that we are still not ready for self-government and that we need to be brought along a little more, that we still need a department of Indian Affairs to nudge us along, then you can appreciate what I am trying to say to you—that it is not a constitutional problem, it is not a legal problem, it is a moral problem.

11   If we can begin to address these issues and put aside these double standards that operate all the time—the double standard that tells me you can have your institutions of government but I cannot, the double standard that tells me you can elect your own representative to make laws for you but I cannot—if we can get rid of them we would have removed one major obstacle towards what we need to do.

12   What is it that we need to do? We need to come to some common understanding on how we are going to co-exist in this country. We need to talk about how we are going to share the resources of this country. We need to talk about how we are going to share power. We need to talk about how we are going to jointly deal with individual rights, but for us to get there, the moral issues have to be dealt with first, because otherwise, if we go back to the constitutional table, we will still be dealing with resistance to our rights, our freedoms.

13   You have a very rich heritage as a democracy. Many of us have studied your system of government. We know you much more than you know us because we are, just like you, a product of your educational system. We have studied Greek and Roman philosophy. We have studied Western civilization; we have memorized in your schools the historical events of your people. We know you exceedingly well, and we know that you cherish law and order, that you cherish the rule of law. We know that over the centuries your governments have evolved to where

[2]The Constitutional Amendment of 1987, agreed upon by all the premiers and commonly known as the Meech Lake Accord, would have brought about the full participation of Quebec in the Constitution of Canada. Native groups objected to not being included at the meetings and expressed concern about the devolution of powers from the federal government to the provinces. The accord failed in 1990 when Newfoundland and Manitoba refused to approve it. (Editors' note)

they are now, including your courts, and that throughout the history of your court system there have been periods when major developments took place, such as, for example, the recognition and protection of individual rights, concepts like due process and natural justice.

14   We were offended when the attorney-general of Ontario told the Indian lawyers in their assembly last year that it is not possible to have Indian tribal courts because of the *Charter of Rights and Freedoms*. I say to you: when did you become the standard for human rights? Perhaps we can do better if we create our own courts. Maybe we will interpret individual rights in a social context so that it is not possible for a person who is found guilty not to be accountable for the harm committed. Give us a chance to deal with issues like social problems. Give us a chance to deal with these problems in the courts, because the courts refuse to take on that added responsibility because your lawyers and judges are on a pedestal in your society, and they cannot condescend to deal with the social problems they find in court; they leave that to social workers and psychologists.

15   There is something to be said, even in the context of experimentation, for you to abandon your tendency to put obstacles in our path to self-government, because what might happen, very possibly, is that we might create laws, we might create courts, that would become models and new standards where human rights might have a different expression and meaning. So don't throw your *Charter of Rights and Freedoms* at us as an obstacle, because we will say to you that we will not accept that. To think there is only one way of looking at human rights is very ethnocentric.

16   When I went to Geneva on the rights of the child, when the convention was being drafted in its final stages, I was very surprised that the western civilizations are still bullying totally everybody in the world and imposing their concepts of the rights of the child without taking into account the different cultures that exist. What I saw was not an exchange as I expected in the United Nations between different cultures to develop standards of children's rights, but what exists here in this country, a western civilization imposing its political will on others. My question is how a dominant society can possibly justify continuing to bully the aboriginal people to toe the line and to be like everybody else because it is in their interest, and if they don't they will be held accountable for it.

17   I conclude by saying that we haven't given up on this country. We are looking for a way of arriving at consensual arrangements so that we can co-exist, where you can respect our collective rights as we respect yours, so that individual rights can be enjoyed by me in your society as you ought to be able to enjoy them within the context of my society as well. That is what we have to work for, that is where we have to go in the next 20–50 years.

18   We don't need confrontation, we don't need police officers enforcing the political will by force, because that is what happened in Oka in my view. We need processes, guidelines and discussion. We have to get away from these simple-minded politicians who talk about the rule of law. The rule of law has become a battle cry with the federal government and the premier of Quebec, and they think that Canadians are completely behind them now because they want law and order. But there is no law and order without justice, for justice is the foundation of law and order and what is absent in their battle cry is justice. Until your government begins to deal with justice for our people we will not make very much progress in this country.

19   I may have sounded preachy, sometimes I get that way, but let me tell you something that really struck me the other day. Like you, I have to get ready for winter and I was working outside. My daughter, who looks very much Indian, was playing with some children from the neighborhood—two white boys and a young lady, named Jill, who is very impressed with me. Every opportunity she gets she introduces me to her friends as one of *the* Indian leaders in Canada. On this occasion, she said to the boys, "He is one of the top Indian leaders in the world," and one of them asked, "How is he going to get out of jail?" I didn't interfere with them, but I heard one of the girls say, "You will never understand." What we have to do is make sure that we understand each other. We know you because we have studied you. It would be nice if somehow you would force yourselves to study us, to understand us, and maybe there's hope for this country so that a hundred years from now there is not another Indian leader, "the best in the world," standing here preaching to you, but proclaiming, not denouncing, the greatness of this country.

PART THREE

Some Forms of
Academic Writing

Outlining and Summarizing

Outlines come in several forms and serve several purposes. A scratch outline—a few phrases in a sequence that seems appropriate—can help you get started.

A paragraph outline—a topic sentence for each as-yet-unwritten paragraph—can help you shape and develop a work in progress. And a formal outline, presented at the beginning of a long piece of writing, can offer guidance to readers, helping them—and you—visualize the relationships among the parts of an essay or report, and functioning as a kind of table of contents.

The ability to write an accurate **summary** is necessary for writing essay examinations, laboratory reports, book reviews, and essays on literature; it is also essential for taking notes on research, for incorporating research into an essay or report, and for writing abstracts, which present in a paragraph or two the main ideas of a report, thesis, or dissertation.

We therefore begin Part Three, on academic writing, with a chapter on outlining and summarizing, skills central to much of the work we discuss in the next six chapters.

OUTLINING

When you write an outline, you do pretty much what artists do when they draw an outline: you give, without detail and shading, the general shape of your subject.

An outline is a kind of blueprint, a diagram showing the arrangement of the parts. It is, then, essentially an analysis of your essay, a classification of its parts. Not all writers use outlines, but those who use them report that an outline helps to make clear to them, before or while they labour through a first draft, what their thesis is, what the main points are, and what the subordinate points are. Outlines produced at later phases of the writing process can also help with organization and concision. Outlines can help writers subordinate what is subordinate; outlines can also help writers see if the development from part to part is clear, consistent, and reasonable.

An outline drafted before you write, however, is necessarily tentative. Do not assume that once you have constructed an outline your plan is fixed. If, as you begin to write, previously neglected points come to mind, or if you see that in any way the outline is unsatisfactory, revise or scrap the outline. One other caution: an outline does not indicate connections. In your essay be sure to use transitional words and phrases such as "thus," "however," "equally important," "less important but still worth mentioning," and "on the other hand" as well as transitional sentences and even paragraphs to make clear the relationships between your points.

Scratch Outline

The simplest outline is a *scratch outline,* half a dozen phrases jotted down, revised, rearranged, listing the topics to be covered in the most effective and logical order. As we suggest in Chapter 1, a scratch outline can help a writer get started. In the example shown here, for an essay on Alice Munro's short story "Boys and Girls," phrases serve as milestones rather than as a road map. Most writers do at least this much.

an initiation story

retrospective narration - adult narrator telling about childhood events and feelings

narrator a girl - nameless

initiation of girl (tomboy) into teenage girl/woman

changing perceptions of her surroundings - home, room, basement - and her appearance and her dreams

rebellious in nature (disobeying mother and grandmother, letting Flora go)

breaks the stereotype of being a "girl" only to conform to it eventually

changing relationship with her mother, father, and brother show her maturity

Paragraph Outline

A *paragraph outline* is more developed. It begins with a sentence or a phrase, stating the working thesis—this will ensure that you know where you are going—and then it gives the topic sentence or a phrase summarizing the topic idea of each paragraph. Thus a paragraph outline of Jeff Greenfield's "Columbo Knows the Butler Didn't Do It" (pages 177-79) might begin like this:

Thesis: *Columbo* is popular because it shows a privileged, undeserving elite brought down by a fellow like us.

I. *Columbo* is popular.
II. Its popularity is largely due to its hostility toward a social and economic elite.
III. The killers are all rich and white.
IV. Their lives are privileged.

And so on, one Roman numeral for each remaining paragraph. A paragraph outline has its uses, especially for papers under, say, a thousand words; it can help you to write unified paragraphs, and it can help you to write a reasonably organized essay. But after you write your essay, check to see if your paragraphs really are developments of what you assert to be the topic sentences, and check to see if you have made the organization clear to the reader, chiefly by means of transitional words and phrases (see pages 52–53). If your essay departs from your outline, the departures should be improvements.

As this last point suggests, your first paragraph outline, worked out after some preliminary thinking, should be a guide, not a straitjacket. As you jot down what you think may be your topic sentences, you will probably find that the jottings help you to get further ideas, but once you draft your essay you may find that the outline has served its initial purpose and has been superseded by a better organization than you had originally imagined. Of course, you should then sketch a new outline, one that corresponds to your draft, to make sure that the pattern of the essay as it now stands really is more effective than the earlier pattern.

Even if you do not write from an outline, when you complete your final draft you ought to be able to outline it—you ought to be able to sketch its parts. If you have trouble outlining the draft, your reader will certainly have trouble following your ideas. Even a paragraph outline made from what you hope is your final draft may help to reveal disproportion or faulty organization (for example, an anticlimactic arrangement of the material) that you can remedy before you write your final copy.

Formal Outline

For longer papers, such as a research paper (usually at least eight pages of double-spaced typing), a more complicated outline is usually needed. The *formal outline* shows relationships, distinguishing between major parts of the essay and subordinate parts. Major parts are indicated by capital Roman numerals. The parts should clearly bear on the thesis. Chief divisions within a major part are indicated by indented capital letters. Subdivisions within these divisions are indicated by Arabic numerals, farther indented. Smaller subdivisions are indicated by lower-case letters, indented still farther. Still smaller subdivisions—although they are rarely needed, because they are apt to provide too much detail for an outline—are indicated by small Roman numerals, again indented.

The point of indenting is to make the relationship among the parts visibly clear to yourself and to a reader. If you use I, II, and III, you are identifying three major points that are at least roughly equal. Under point I, A and B are parts roughly equal to each other, and so on. The outline is a sort of table of contents.

Note that you cannot have a single subdivision. In the example that follows, part I is divided into parts A and B; it cannot have only a part A. Similarly, part B cannot be "divided" into 1 without there being a 2. In effect, you can't say, as a naturalist did say, "The snakes in this district may be divided into one species—the venomous." If you have a single subdivision, eliminate it and work the material into the previous heading.

Here is a formal outline of Greenfield's "Columbo" essay. Other versions are, of course, possible. In fact, in order to illustrate the form of divisions and subdivisions, we have written a much fuller outline than is usual for such a short essay. We have also not hesitated to mix sentences and phrases, though some authorities require that an outline use only one form or the other.

Thesis: *Columbo* is popular because it shows the undeserving rich brought low by a member of the working class.

I. Popularity of *Columbo*
    A. What it is *not* due to
        1. Acting
        2. Clever detection of surprising criminal plot
    B. What it is due to
        1. Hostility to privileged elite
        2. Columbo is poor and shoddy.
        3. The high are brought low.
           a. No black (minority) villains
           b. The villains live far above us.
II. The hero
    A. Physical appearance
        1. Dress
        2. Hair
    B. Manner
    C. Success as an investigator
        1. Adversaries mistakenly treat him as negligible.
           a. They assume his lack of wealth indicates lack of intelligence.
           b. They learn too late.
         2. Columbo understands the elite.
           a. They are not superior mentally or in diligence.
           b. They are in a shaky position.
III. Our satisfaction with the program
    A. The villains do not deserve their privileges.
    B. Villains are undone by a man in the street.
    C. We look forward to an episode when Columbo visits the most privileged house.

There is, of course, no evidence that Greenfield wrote an outline before he wrote his essay. But he may have roughed out something along these lines, thereby providing himself with a ground plan or a road map. And while he looked at it he may have readjusted a few parts to give more emphasis here (changing a subdivision into a major division) or to establish a more reasonable connection there (say, reversing A and B in one of the parts).

SUMMARIZING

As we suggest above, the ability to write an accurate summary (abridgement, condensation) is central to much academic work: taking notes and writing research essays, as well as writing reviews, examinations, and even essays on literature.

The need to write summaries continues in professional life. Scientists usually begin a scientific paper with an abstract, lawyers write briefs (which are, as the name implies, documents that briefly set forth all the facts and points of law

pertinent to a case), and business executives must constantly reduce long mem-
oranda and reports to their essential points.

What a Summary Is

Writing a summary requires that you analyze the text you are summarizing, separating out the main points from the examples and details that support these points.
Here are a few principles that govern summaries.

1. A summary is much briefer than the original. It is not a paraphrase—a sen-
   tence-by-sentence translation of someone's words into your own. A summary is rarely longer than one-fourth the original, and often is much briefer.
   An entire essay may be summarized in a paragraph or two or even a sentence or two.
2. A summary usually omits almost all the concrete details of the original,
   presenting only the main points of the original.
3. A summary is accurate; it has no value if it misrepresents the point of the
   original.
4. The writer of a summary need not state the points in the same order as
   that of the original. If the writer of an essay has delayed revealing the
   main point until the end of the essay, the summary usually rearranges the
   order, stating the main point first. Occasionally, when the original author
   presents an argument in a disorderly or confusing sequence, a summary
   clarifies the argument by changing the order of statements.
5. A summary normally is written in the present tense because whether the
   author wrote the piece last year or a hundred years ago, we assume that
   the piece speaks to us today.

Here is a summary of Barnet, Stubbs, Bellanca, and Stimpson on "summary":

> A summary is a condensation or abridgement. Its chief characteristics
> are: (1) it is rarely more than one-fourth as long as the original; (2) its
> brevity is achieved by leaving out most of the details of the original; (3)
> it is accurate; (4) it may rearrange the organization of the original, espe-
> cially if rearrangement makes things clearer; (5) it is normally phrased
> in the present tense.

How to Write a Summary

With the text you intend to summarize before you—let's say a chapter of a book,
or an essay—get ready to take notes, on your computer or on a pad of paper.
Read the text quickly to get the gist of it, then begin rereading, slowly and
thoughtfully.

On rereading, jot down, after reading each paragraph, a sentence giving the
main point the paragraph makes, leaving out the details and examples that support the point. A very long paragraph may require two sentences; a series of
short paragraphs, each illustrating the same point, may require only one sentence. One sentence per paragraph is a rule of thumb.

Here is a student's summary of Michael Ignatieff's "Myth and Malevolence"
(pages 152-53):

1. In 1992 Serbs told reporters about Muslims killing Serbian children as a way to justify ethnic "cleansing."
2. Atrocity myths have been around for a long time in Western culture, from Romans accusing Christians to Christians accusing Jews through to Christians accusing Muslims.
3. These myths are used as justification and are worse in intrastate wars.
4. In the Serb war, the worst destruction took place in cities with high rates of ethnic intermarriage, to destroy neighbourly feelings by ingraining these myths in people's minds.
5. Atrocity myths—lies and propaganda—magnify small differences between groups and increase nationalistic sentiments by making one side seem blameless and the other side seem malevolent.
6. Name calling as a way to dehumanize the other side collapses the past into the present.
7. This renaming erases the identity and history of the other side and sometimes influences the outside world.
8. Activities of the outside world, such as war-crimes tribunals and human-rights commissions, can help by reclaiming the truth, because there is no peace without truth.

When you have written your sentence summarizing the last paragraph, you may have done enough if the summary is intended for your own private use—for example, if it is to help you review for an examination. But if you are going to use it as the basis of a summary within an essay you are writing, you will probably want to reshape it. In an essay of your own, you will seldom want to include a summary longer than three or four sentences, so your job will be to reduce and combine the sentences you have jotted down. Indeed, you may even want to reduce the summary to a single sentence. A student might summarize Ignatieff's essay thus:

Michael Ignatieff, in his essay "Myth and Malevolence," argues that

atrocity myths can so dehumanize the opposing side in a war, such as the

one in Serbia, that it makes horrors like genocide acceptable even to those

people not actively involved in promoting the war.

Notice that, since the summary is intended for a reader, the student has introduced the summary with Ignatieff's name and the title of the article.

A writer who wants to devote a little more space to summarizing Ignatieff's essay might come up with this summary:

Michael Ignatieff, in his essay "Myth and Malevolence," explains the

history and contemporary use of atrocity myths in war (such as claims

about the opposing side slaughtering innocent children). These myths

erase the identity and history of the opposing side to such an extent that it somehow makes their own atrocities like ethnic "cleansing" acceptable to the people by firing their sense of nationalism. The outside world needs to break these horrible myths by promoting truth and peace.

HOW MUCH SUMMARY IS ENOUGH?

As we suggest above, if you think that your reader needs a summary, you will also have to think about how long—that is, how detailed—the summary should be.

If you are writing a review of a book you read for your women's studies class, you probably should not assume that your reader has already read the book (readers tend not to read reviews of books they have already read!). You will therefore have to offer a fairly detailed summary of the text, probably at least a paragraph or two if the review is five to six paragraphs long. (To see how summary works in a review, see Jane Brox's review of Alexandra Johnson's book on pages 289-90.)

If you are analyzing a short story for a literature class, the matter is a bit trickier. In this case, you are probably writing about a text your classmates and instructor (that is to say, your audience) are at least somewhat familiar with. Nevertheless, you cannot simply launch into your analysis, because only readers who know the story *very* well would be able to follow your discussion. In this case, the best thing to do is to imagine that your readers are intelligent people who have read the text you are writing about, but that they read it some time ago, and need to be reminded—in passing—about who's who and what happens. (To see how writers use summary in essays on literature, see Beatrice Cody's essay on *The Awakening,* pages 323-32 and Aviva Geiger's essay on "The Yellow Wallpaper," pages 393-98.)

In general, your awareness of your reader's needs as well as your own purpose will guide you as you summarize the material you are writing about.

Exercises

1. If you have just completed a draft of an essay, outline it now, before beginning to revise. Doing so may enable you to see where you need to include more information, where the discussion veers off on a tangent, or where the parts of the argument or analysis need to be reorganized.
2. Read Beatrice Cody's essay on *The Awakening,* reprinted on pages 323-32, and then write a paragraph outline of the essay.
3. Summarize the following paragraph in one or two sentences:

   No society, whether human or animal, can exist without communication. Thoughts, desires, appetites, orders—these have to be conveyed from one brain to another, and they can rarely be conveyed directly. Only with telepathy do we find mind speaking straight to mind, without the intermediacy of signs, and this technique is still strange enough to seem a music-hall trick or a property of science fiction. The vast majority of sentient beings—men, women, cats, dogs, bees, horses—have to rely on signals, symbols of what we think and feel and want, and these signals can assume a vast variety of forms. There is, indeed, hardly any limit to the material devices we can use to express what is in our minds: we can wave our hands, screw up our faces, shrug our shoulders, write poems, write on walls, carve signs out of stone or wood, mould signs with clay or butter, scrawl sky-signs with an aircraft, semaphore, heliograph, telephone, run a pirate radio transmitter, stick pins in dolls. A dog will scratch at a door if it wants to be let in; a cat will mew for milk; a hostess will ring a bell for the course to be changed; a pub-customer will rap with a coin for service; a wolf will whistle; the people in the flat upstairs will bang with a stick if our party is too noisy. One can fill pages with such examples, bringing in the language of flowers and the signaling devices of honey-bees, but one will always end up with human speech as the most subtle, comprehensive, and exact system of communication we possess.

—ANTHONY BURGESS

4. Choose a current editorial and summarize it in about one-fourth its number of words. Include a copy of the editorial with your summary.
5. Using the outline of "Columbo Knows the Butler Didn't Do It" (page 283) and the essay itself (pages 177-79), write a summary of the essay, in about 250 words.

Reviewing

Readers turn to reviews when they want to decide on what movie to see or book to buy. But they also turn to reviews when they begin to gather information for a research project, as we discuss in Chapters 16 and 17 on the research essay. Because they are generally brief and written by experts in their disciplines, book reviews published in such academic journals as *Modern Fiction Studies* and *University of Toronto Quarterly,* for example, are excellent sources of information about recently published work in the fields of literature, cultural studies, and Canadian studies (see the *Book Review Index* in the reference section of your library).

Reviews serve other purposes as well. An engineer might write a review of a research proposal in order to help a committee decide on funding it; a publisher might ask a biologist to review a university biology textbook in order to help its authors make revisions. Editors of academic journals regularly ask experts in their fields to write reviews of articles submitted to them for publication.

Although there are many different kinds of reviews, they all share several features. In general, they

- describe or summarize the thing being reviewed
- point to its strengths and weaknesses, and
- make a judgment about its merit.

In this chapter we focus on writing book reviews. But the skills that you develop as you learn to review books will be of use in other kinds of reviews— and other kinds of writing—as well.

WRITING A BOOK REVIEW

Because book reviews in newspapers, magazines, and academic journals are usually about newly published works, reviewers normally assume that their readers will be unfamiliar with the books. The reviewer takes it as his or her job to acquaint readers with the book, its contents, and its value and to help them decide whether or not they wish to read it. Since most reviews are brief (500 to 1500 words) they cannot, like explications, comment on everything. On the other hand they cannot, like analyses, focus on one aspect of the writing; they usually attempt in some way to cover the book. Reviews, then, usually contain more summary and more evaluation than explications or analyses. Nevertheless, reviewers must approach the task analytically if they are to accomplish it in the relatively small space allotted. And if they are to be convincing, they must support their opinions with quotations (usually indispensable), examples, and specific references to the text so that readers may think and feel the way the reviewers think and feel.

A review commonly has a structure something like this:

1. An opening paragraph that names the author and the title, gives the reader some idea of the nature and scope of the work (a children's book; a book for the general reader; a book for specialists), and establishes the tone of the review (more about tone in a moment).
2. A paragraph or two of plot summary if the book is a novel; some summary of the contents if it is not.
3. A paragraph on the theme, purpose, idea, or vision embodied in the book, perhaps within the context of related works.
4. A paragraph or two on the strengths, if any (for instance, the book fulfills its purpose).
5. A paragraph or two on the weaknesses, if any.
6. A concluding paragraph in which the reviewer delivers his or her point—but the point in some degree has probably been implied from the beginning, because the concluding paragraph is a culmination rather than a surprise.

Tone, as we suggest elsewhere in this book (see pages 132-34), usually refers to the writer's attitude toward the subject, the readers, and the writer's self. The tone of a review is therefore somewhat dependent on the publication in which it will appear. A review in *Canadian Geographic* will have a different tone from one in *Ms.* Since you have not been commissioned to write your review and are essentially playing a game, you must *imagine* your reader. It is a reasonable idea to imagine that your classmates are your readers, forgetting of course that they may be reviewing the same book you are. And it is always productive to treat both your reader and your subject with respect. This does not mean you need to be solemn or boring; on the contrary, the best way to show your respect for your reader is to write something you would be interested in reading yourself.

Here is a book review from an academic journal. Although this review was published without a title, reviews often are given titles; if you are asked to write a review for one of your classes, you should be sure to title it.

 **JANE BROX**

Review of *The Hidden Writer: Diaries and the Creative Life* by Alexandra Johnson

1   "Whom do I tell when I tell a blank page?" Virginia Woolf asks her diary. In *The Hidden Writer: Diaries and the Creative Life,* Alexandra Johnson searches for

the complex and changeable answer as she traces women's diaries, always "the blank-faced old confidante," through two centuries as they work their way into the life of literature to become something for the public eye. An inveterate diarist herself, Johnson opens with a recollection of her own childhood interest in diaries, and ends—writer and teacher of writing—with selections from her adult journal. In between these chapters is a deft, intelligent examination of seven women's diaries beginning with the 1809 Edinburgh journal of Marjory Fleming: six years old, exuberant, testing out words, a nascent diarist. Fleming dies of meningitis just shy of her ninth birthday.

2   Johnson goes on to examine the private works and overshadowed ambitions of Sonya Tolstoy and Alice James, then continues with the competitive literary friendship of Virginia Woolf and Katherine Mansfield. Ambitions no longer closeted, Woolf's and Mansfield's diaries become companions to their literary accomplishments, pages where they not only set down daily thoughts and observations but sharpen technique and aim for style. Woolf writes in hers: "It strikes me that in this book I practice writing; do my scales; yes and work at certain effects . . . and shall invent my next book here." Her aspirations for a literature that would record "all the traces of the mind's passage through the world; & achieve in the end some kind of whole made of shivering fragments . . ." broadens the way for Anaïs Nin and May Sarton. Sarton, on the coast of Maine and late in her life, records just such fragments of solitude and aging in diaries she specifically intends for publication.

3   With Sarton's *Journal of a Solitude,* Johnson suggests, the diary has made a full journey from the hidden to the public, one that she subtly links to the journey of a more inclusive literature tunneling its way into the world. Diarists—observers, listeners, silent and ambitious—are kin to all those "haunting the corners of creative life . . . centuries of voices that have been lost forever. They are the shadow writers—male and female, white and black—voices beat back in the throat."

4   Whether she is describing Alice James' room in Leamington, the quiet broken only by the scratch of a pen, or the first meeting over dinner at Hogarth House of Katherine Mansfield, "sensual, wary, bohemian . . . the shock of the new about her," and Virginia Woolf, "tall, patrician, her skin fragile at the temples, her collar bones shimmering like ivory calligraphy," Johnson's clarifying prose, apt and evocative, is a pleasure to read. With each chapter, she sets forth an entire world, and you feel she has found just the right word, just the right phrase to recreate the atmosphere of the times. Her examinations of Sonya Tolstoy and the friendship between Woolf and Mansfield are feats of compression, encapsulating the complexities of these lives as well as the complexities of the place of these lives in the literature of their era.

5   From the private writings of these seven women, Johnson gleans "a time-lapse study of confidence." Her own comprehensive knowledge of diaries—those of her subjects, and those of well-known diarists such as Anne Frank and Sylvia Plath, and the lesser-known such as Etty Hillesum—gives added depth and continuity to her argument. In *The Hidden Writer* Alexandra Johnson weaves together a smart, graceful account that does honor to diaries, literature, and the creative life.

Topics for Critical Thinking and Writing

1. Characterize or describe the tone of the review.
2. Write a one-sentence summary of each paragraph. Your list of sentences should resemble an outline.
3. How well does your outline correspond with the structure we say reviews commonly have? (See page 289.)
4. If there are discrepancies between what we have said about reviews and the review by Brox, can you offer a reasonable explanation for these discrepancies? Or would you argue that we revise our discussion or that we choose a different review as an example?
5. Write a book review. Your instructor may give you a list of possibilities. If not, we recommend that you choose a book on a subject that you are familiar with. (In other words, if you are a fan of mystery fiction, you might review Gail Bowen's latest novel; if you are taking a course in the War of 1812, you might review a recent biography of one of the figures you are studying.)

WRITING OTHER REVIEWS

Our suggestions for writing a book review, with obvious modifications, can serve as guidelines for other reviews you may be assigned or choose to write: of an article, a proposal, a play, a film, a concert, or other performance. Again, it is the reviewer's job to acquaint readers, real or imagined, with a performance they are assumed to be unfamiliar with (although reviews are often read by readers who want to see their own judgments confirmed or their small talk improved). And again, you must adopt an appropriate tone, suggesting both your own expert knowledge of your topic and your respect for your readers' intelligence and taste.

Your best preparation for writing a review is to read reviews in publications you trust, consciously noting what you find informative, interesting, and persuasive. Then, if you are covering a live event, you will find it useful to ask to see in advance the promotional material usually in the hands of the organization sponsoring the event. You will want to be skeptical of some of the rave reviews you will find quoted (and of course you must not use them in your own review without acknowledging their sources), but you may well find biographical and other background information that will prepare you for the performance and make note-taking easier. And you must go prepared to take notes—often in the dark—and allow yourself sufficient time immediately after the event to type or rewrite your notes legibly.

Reviewing a CD or tape obviously has some advantages. You can listen to it many times, you may have access to the score or lyrics and previous recordings, and you can choose your own time and place for listening. Or perhaps the relaxed and witty style of the review we print below just makes it seem easier. The review was written by a student for a college newspaper.

 **JOSHUA DERMAN**

Deconstructing Pop: The Halo Benders

1   There's a piece of conventional wisdom regarding modern art that goes like this: creators of it have no appreciable skills, and they conceal this fact by creating art (music, books) that doesn't resemble anything (isn't tuneful, doesn't make sense).

2   This sentiment is particularly popular when applied to the scrawling, jagged genre of indie rock. Trace it back to the Sex Pistols, when bad music became chic; or even earlier to the Velvet Underground, whose aggressive feedback and guitar mutilation was so at odds with the bubblegum melodies of the day. In this music scene The Halo Benders' third album, *The Rebels Not In,* is a refreshing dose of accessible art rock. In it, they have created an album whose aural texture achieves musical ends you won't find anywhere in mainstream rock. After but a single hearing, you'll realize that indie rock is more than just about bad haircuts and funny T-shirts.

3   Judging by the press release that accompanied the album, being an indie rock star is akin to being a pedigree dog—your full name, when mentioned, must be accompanied by a lengthy musical genealogy. In the case of The Halo Benders, this could take pages: the Olympia, Washington-based band is actually a side-project, staffed by the frontmen of other indie groups. Calvin Johnson (Beat Happening), Doug Matsch (Built to Spill), Ralf Youtz (The Feelings), and Wayne Flower (Violent Green).

4   All the ingredients you've come to love or hate in lo-fi are here for the offer-ing: no verse-chorus structure, stop-and-start guitar solos, lyrics that sound as if they were excerpted from "The Jabberwocky," plus a general air of aggressive avant garde posture. But unlike some lo-fi outfits (i.e. Pavement), The Halo Benders actually sound like a band. There's a full, textured quality to their sound that one usually finds only on heavier-produced albums. Their lo-fi style isn't an affectation or an excuse, but a real aesthetic agenda. The marching of drums across a static soundscape, the simple polyphony of guitar and bass, organic song structure—these features are more expressive, more evocative than any slick Puff Daddy remix.

5   A critic once said of a Béla Bartók violin-and-piano sonata that the composer returned these instruments to their original functions: the violin is for scratch-ing, the piano for banging. The Halo Benders have done something similar for the electric guitar—you won't find any Hendrix-style guitar impersonations on this album, epic screech or distorted wah-wah. Doug Matsch embraces the jan-gly, plucky sound of the guitar and puts it to his purposes. His stop-and-go solos, breaking in waves over the drum and bass rhythm, owe more to Bach cantatas than to conventional alterna-rock.

6   The opening measures of the album's first track, "Virginia Reel Around the Fountain," pairs off a guitar and electric bass, whose low-frequency warblings sound like whale songs. "Love Travels Faster," a bitter-sweet spastic ballad, and the very VU-inspired "Turn It My Way" are also notably clever, well-wrought songs. One of the album's best songs is the haunting "Rebels Got a Hole in It"

(whatever that means), an epic instrumental that might make a good soundtrack for a post-apocalyptic road movie.

7   The vocal harmonies of Matsch and Calvin Johnson are an equally distinctive feature of The Halo Benders. Johnson's voice sounds much like that of an extremely bored, medicated Johnny Cash—his basso profundo is a little bit too deep to actually be believed. His singing is weird enough to be interesting at first, but after prolonged exposure its total lack of expression becomes unnerving. Thankfully, Matsch accompanies him on most songs in a higher register, and the resulting vocal harmonies are surprisingly satisfying, in a distinctly atonal kind of way.

8   As far as lyrics are concerned, *The Rebels Not In* is a mixed bag. The fact that none of the album's lyrics are really quotable out of context says something. (I am reminded of one verse from the first track: "Do a little dance on the kitchen table/Rub your tummy and show your navel.") I take it that the general idea behind this school of song-writing, as exemplified by Pavement's Stephen Malkmus, is that the words should conspire to produce a theme or feeling to accompany the music. If the music's not figurative, the words might as well not be either.

9   The fact that it's hard to say what the songs are about doesn't detract from the album, but it's sometimes difficult to distinguish lyrical avant garde from just plain laziness. It's hard to be taken seriously—which is what The Halo Benders deserve—when your lyrics are that far out in left field.

10   Despite its playfulness, this is an outstanding, inventive album. A far cry from their excellent but obscure 1994 release, *Don't Tell Me Now*, *The Rebels Not In* has serious cross-genre appeal. So dig the hyperactivity, put on your funny T-shirts, and revel in the cerebro-punk vibes.

 Topics for Critical Thinking and Writing

1. Characterize the writer's tone. Is it appropriate to his material and his audience? Explain.
2. On the basis of this review, would you buy *The Rebels Not In*? If you did not have to pay for the album, would you be interested, because of the review, in listening to it? Explain why or why not.
3. If you saw this writer's byline in your newspaper would you read the article? Explain.
4. Write a review of a current album. Or, attend a play or a concert and review it. In a note appended to your review, define your intended audience.

15

Interviewing

We have all been treated to the television interview with (and perhaps by) a celebrity. Question: "Which game was the toughest that you have ever lost?" Answer: "Uh, well, Marv, that's a tough question." Question: "When did you have your first sexual experience?" Answer: "Oh, Barbara, I knew you'd ask me that!" And we have read similarly inspiring transcriptions in popular magazines (while standing in the checkout line at a supermarket). But the interview is also an important tool of academic research and writing. Sociologists and psychologists regularly use interviews, and biographers and historians often rely heavily on interviews when they write about recent events. Interviews with poets and fiction writers in literary magazines help us to learn not only about the writers and their work but also about the craft of poetry or fiction. For the apprentice writer, interviews provide excellent sources for interesting essays about the person being interviewed or about issues and ideas.

WRITING AN ESSAY BASED ON AN INTERVIEW

A university campus is an ideal place to practise interviewing. Faculties are composed of experts in a variety of fields and distinguished visitors are a regular part of extracurricular life. In the next few pages, we will offer advice on conducting interviews and writing essays based on them. If you take our advice, you will acquire a skill you may well put to further, more specialized use in social science courses; at the same time you will be developing skills in asking questions and shaping materials relevant to all research and writing.

Before we list the steps for you to follow, we offer two examples, essays based largely on interviews. First read "The Einstein of Happiness," then answer the questions that follow it.

PATRICIA FREEMAN

The Einstein of Happiness

1   If the truth be known, being a professor of happiness is no picnic. People deride your research, trivialize your interests—then badger you for the secret of eternal bliss. Nevertheless, Allen Parducci, fifty-seven-year-old professor of psychology at UCLA, has been exploring the fabric of human felicity for over forty years.

2   Parducci became a happiness scholar because of his father, a stern architectural sculptor in Grosse Pointe, Michigan, who voiced a vexing conviction that "things balance out" between happiness and woe—or, as Mark Twain put it, "Every man is a suffering machine and a happiness machine combined, and for every happiness turned out in one department, the other stands ready to modify it with a sorrow or pain." Young Parducci, wondering why he ought to bother getting out of bed in the morning if that were true, set out to debunk the theory.

3   He conducted his research everywhere. He quizzed his college roommates as to the completeness of their contentment. He grilled his fellow sailors during World War II: "As the ship rolled back and forth and they retched, I'd ask them, 'How happy are you now? Are you really unhappy?'"

4   Eventually he received a graduate degree in psychology from Berkeley, where he could finally study the phenomenon scientifically. Today, he is known around the world for his work in "the relativism of absolute judgments"—a fancy phrase meaning that how we evaluate a thing depends on what we compare it to. (Though his work was an outgrowth of his search for the answers to human happiness, hardly anybody in academia has applied it that way.) To back up his ideas, he devised several studies to show that judgments of all kinds depend on the context in which they are made.

5   For one study, he gave a "test" of moral judgments to college students, who were asked to assign each item in a list of behaviors a ranking of from "1—not particularly bad or wrong" to "5—extremely evil." Half of the students were given a list of comparatively mild acts of wrongdoing, including such items as "cheating at solitaire," "wearing shorts on the street where it is illegal" and "stealing towels from a hotel room." The other half were given a much nastier list, including such acts as "selling to a hospital milk from diseased cattle." Both lists contained six of the same items. The crucial feature of the test was that the students were to judge the items according to their own personal values and not to judge them in comparison to one another. Nonetheless, the experiment showed that students' moral judgments depended on how the list was "skewed"—the six acts appearing on both lists were rated more leniently by students who judged them in the context of the nasty list than by those who encountered them on the mild list. "Poisoning a neighbor's barking dog," for example, got a rather harsh score of 4.19 when it appeared along with "playing poker on a Sunday" and a less disapproving 3.65 when it came just after "murdering your mother without justification or provocation."

6   According to the same principle, which Parducci calls a "negatively skewed distribution," our judgments of personal satisfaction depend on how often we experience the things we deem most satisfying. To demonstrate this, he devised

a study in which two groups of students selected cards from two different decks and won money based on the value assigned to each card. One group played with cards marked from 1 cent to 21 cents, with the higher values predominating, and the other groups with cards marked from 7 cents to 27 cents, with low sums predominating. Every player won the same total of money for the series, but group one, which garnered its winnings primarily from the higher end of the scale, reported themselves happier with their winnings.

7   What does all of this mean for us? It means, Parducci says, that just as the cardplayers were happiest when most of their winnings were close to the maximum that could be earned, we will likely be most satisfied if our lives are arranged so that the best of what we experience happens more frequently. The happy person, who finds "zest, fun and joy in life," says Parducci, is one for whom "the things he's experiencing are high relative to his standards." And conversely, the unhappy person—whose life is marked by "terror, anxiety and misery"—sets inappropriate standards for himself often comparing his life to an impossible ideal.

8   Parducci will venture a few tips on living the happy life, but only with prodding. If we want to be happy, he says, we ought not to live in the future, thinking that we'd be happy if only we could double our income, marry this person or get that job; instead we should learn to delight in what we have and look forward to things that happen every day. Above all, we should let go of what's impossible.

9   "We all know people who have had a great love affair break up and their friends say, 'Get it out of your head,' but they can't. But if they could, in effect, drop that relationship out of their context altogether, then the best of their experience with someone new would seem good and wonderful. They could experience the same high even with a lesser person."

10   The happiest person Parducci has ever known (though he doesn't think he's particularly good at telling whether people are happy or not) was a woman who died of cancer in her mid-thirties. "The six months before she died was like a party every night," he recalls. "Her friends would come over, her ex-husbands would visit, and everybody would have a great time. I asked her, 'Joanne, how do you feel about death?' and she said, 'I know I could die any time, but I'm very happy.'" Joanne was married approximately five times if you count both legal and informal spouses. "She'd meet these men anybody would say she shouldn't marry," Parducci says, "and it would be disastrous. She'd see virtues in people that no one else could see. It seemed that she was living in a dream world. I would have said, looking at her life, that she should see things the way they are. But sometimes I think some people are just born to be happy."

11   Most Americans, in fact, say that they are happy. According to national polls the average citizen gives himself a happiness rating of seven on a scale of one to ten. Parducci gives himself a six, a rating he believes actually makes him significantly more sanguine than most Americans. "People's reports of their own happiness show an astonishing positive bias," he says. He thinks people make themselves out to be happier than they really are because "there's the implication that there's something wrong with you if you can't somehow arrange your life to be satisfying."

12   In fact, unhappiness seems to be a national personality trait. "The success credo of American business is that you're supposed to always be setting higher standards," Parducci says. "And in setting inappropriately high standards, we can't help but doom ourselves to unhappiness. Society is pyramidal. There's only

one position at the top, and if everyone is pushing toward that one position, the great majority must inevitably fall by the wayside." But still we push our children to aim for medical school or sports superstardom.

13   Does Parducci hope, in some small way, to make the world a happier place to live? "I'm very skeptical about the possibility of doing that," he says. Still, there are those who would make him into a guru of good cheer. But, unlike Leo Buscaglia, psychologist to the masses and a fixture on the best-seller lists, Parducci is uninterested in providing road maps to felicity and pointers to pleasure. "I've been approached by several literary agents," he says. "There's always a pressure toward self-help. You know, 'The Ten Rules for Happiness.' But if it were that simple, it would have been discovered by now."

14   People tell him that he could make a fortune if only he would become at least a bit of a happiness hawker. "I ask myself, if lightning struck in that way, if I made a million dollars, would I be happier? But friends of mine who have made that kind of money say that it hasn't made them happy," he says.

15   Even though Parducci says he'd like to be "more happy," in the end there's something he considers more important—and that is, "being good." He will readily declare that religion—particularly Christianity—has fostered unhappiness by holding up an ideal of goodness that is impossible to live up to. Still, he says, "I think there are rules that people ought to follow, rules that may be difficult. Suppose Mephistopheles came and said, 'If you kill a few people I'll make you very happy.' I hope I would be strong enough to turn him down. I don't want to be identified with the 'me first' psychology that says we're all out for ourselves."

16   If he can't make people happier and he doesn't consider happiness the most important thing in the world anyway, why does Parducci press on with his work? "There's a satisfaction," he submits, "in just understanding things. We can understand how the planets move around the sun, though we can't affect them. We get satisfaction out of understanding happiness, even though we can't do much about it."

 ## Topics for Critical Thinking and Writing

1. What preparation do you think Patricia Freeman did for the interview?
2. List the questions Freeman might have posed to elicit the information in each paragraph or group of paragraphs. Were there any paragraphs for which you had difficulty imagining questions? Can you explain why? (Or, what information do you suppose did not come from Professor Parducci's own words? Who or what do you imagine to be the source of this information?)
3. Through much of the article we hear Parducci's voice, either paraphrased or directly quoted. Where do we hear the interviewer's voice as well?
4. Suppose you had begun with only the information that Allen Parducci is a professor of psychology at an American university. What library sources might tell you his age, education, major field of interest, publications, and current academic post? (See if you can find this information in your own library.)

Now read the second article and answer the questions following it.

EILEEN GARRED

Ethnobotanists Race against Time to Save Useful Plants

1   Although a white lab coat hangs on a bookshelf in his cramped office and an IBM personal computer sits on a nearby table, these are not the tools Mark Plotkin prefers to use. As an ethnobotanist, Plotkin has spent months in the tropical forests of South America, bringing along newspapers and moth balls to press and preserve plant specimens he then hauls back to the Botanical Museum at Harvard.

2   In annual visits over the past eight years, Plotkin has been patiently cultivating the trust of tribal medicine men in the Suriname jungle in order to learn how the native people use forest plants in their cultures. It is a race against time and the steadily increasing influences of civilization.

3   Tropical forests the world over are shrinking as deforestation escalates and development spurred by rapid population growth reaches further into the jungle. The Amazon region alone contains approximately 80,000 species of plants, a vast resource of living organisms, many of which are yet unknown to science. Plants of great potential value of medical, agricultural, and industrial uses are vanishing even before they are identified.

4   Perhaps more important, knowledge about plants long used by native Indians for beneficial purposes is dying out with the witch doctors. "Within one generation after civilization arrives, aboriginal peoples will forget most of their plant lore," predicts Richard Schultes, Director of the Botanical Museum.

5   The Westerners who arrive to build roads or preach the Gospel also bring with them Western medicines. "Our medicines are effective, cheap, and easy to get," Schultes adds. "The natives are not going to run through the forest to look for a leaf their ancestors used to alleviate sickness if they don't have to."

6   Few of the witch doctors today have young apprentices from the tribe because visiting missionaries have strongly discouraged shamanism. The last of the medicine men in the tribes must be coaxed to reveal their secrets to a new breed of botanist like Plotkin.

7   Last year, for example, Plotkin returned from Suriname with a small tree limb called doubredwa. The South American Indians scrape the bark into rum and claim the resulting drink is a powerful male aphrodisiac. "The world doesn't need more people," explains Plotkin. "What it needs is a treatment for impotence—and there it is in a woody vine from the Amazon."

8   Curare, a native arrow poison, has been used for a number of years in hospitals as an anesthetic and muscle relaxant during surgery. Another plant poison that stupefies fish and forces them to the water's surface where they are easy targets for spearfishers is the basis for the pesticide rotenone. Because it is biodegradable, rotenone is widely used in the United States.

9   Fruit from a common Amazonian palm produces oil that is very similar to olive oil, and the fruit from still another species is extremely rich in vitamins C and A.

10   "The so-called 'wonder drugs,' including penicillin, cortisone, and reserpine, that have revolutionized the practice of medicine came from plants that had some use in primitive societies that called the attention of a chemist to the plant," says Schultes.

11   According to Schultes, tribes of the northwest Amazon utilize just under 2000 different plant species for "medicinal" purposes. "In these plants there is a tremendous storehouse of new chemicals," he explains. "In the hands of a chemist, a naturally occurring chemical can be changed to form the basis of many new semisynthetic chemicals. So if you find in a plant one useful chemical, you are finding literally hundreds that chemists can make using that natural structure as a base. How can chemists hope to procure and analyze 80,000 species of plants?

12   "One shortcut for the chemist is to concentrate on the plants that native peoples by trial and error over thousands of years have found to have some biological activity," he says.

13   Although it often takes two decades or more of research from discovery of a plant to a packaged drug, ethnobotanists who provide chemists with the material must work quickly since the varieties of jungle plants and the numbers of medicine men who know how to identify and use them are disappearing at an alarming rate.

14   As a defined field of study, ethnobotany is more than a century old, but it has received greater attention only in recent years. Schultes, a pioneer in the field, lived and worked in Colombia and Peru from 1941 to 1954. During that time, he collected 24,000 plants and filled dozens of field notebooks, which he is still trying to put into publishable form.

15   "We call this work an 'ethnobotanical salvage operation,'" says Plotkin, "which just means that we are documenting the plants the Indians use and the ways in which they use them." The U.S. Division of the World Wildlife Fund is sponsoring Plotkin's work at the Harvard Botanical Museum. As part of the Tropical South American Conservation and Ethnobotany Project, Plotkin has compiled a catalog of more than 1000 useful plant species, which includes Latin and vernacular names, data on distribution, aboriginal use, chemical composition and economic potential. Previously, much of this information was widely scattered and not available to botanists, conservationists, and development planners.

16   Plotkin, whose initial interest in the beneficial uses of plants was cultivated by Schultes, is now primarily concerned with tying ethnobotany to conservation. Money, he says, is the bottom line. In fighting for preservation of the Amazon's tropical forest with its large reserve of natural resources, Plotkin aims to put conservation in economic terms.

17   "The ill-planned development in the tropics by local governments and transnational corporations is causing serious damage," he says. "But you can't tell Brazil, a country with the largest foreign debt in the world, 'Don't cut down the forest because you've got the cutest little monkey living there.' You have to explain that plant A is worth 'x' number of dollars and plant B, if you manage it right, will be worth 'y' number of dollars."

18   "You have to convince the government that it is worth more as a forest than as an agricultural area, which is probably going to fail anyway over the long term. Until you can put it in concrete economic terms, it's just talk."

19   As an example, Plotkin points to the irony that Brazil imports $20 million worth of olive oil a year, although there are millions of the palm trees that produce a similar edible oil within its borders.

20   One of the most common trees in the Amazon, the buriti palm, has a multitude of uses discovered by the Indians. Its fruit is rich in vitamins, an extract from the stem can be used to make bread, the fibers can be used to make twine, houses are built from its wood, and it grows only in swampy areas that could not

otherwise be used for agriculture. However, says Plotkin, the Brazilian government has yet to step in to look for high yielding strains of the buriti, or "tap into what is a potential gold mine" by putting it into plantations.

21   "Conservation works best if it's in that country's self-interest." says Plotkin. "Ethnobotany"—the study of the use of plants by native peoples who have intimate knowledge of forests and the useful products they contain—"is really in the forefront of international conservation efforts."

22   "For thousands of years, aboriginal peoples have been living with and depending on the native vegetation. Now civilization is destroying that knowledge," says Schultes. "Much more endangered than any species is the knowledge about plant lore. If we don't pick it up now, we'll never get it."

 Topics for Critical Thinking and Writing

1. Is the article primarily about Plotkin or about Schultes? If neither, what is it about?
2. What is ethnobotany? Where in the article is it defined? Should Garred have defined it earlier? Why or why not?
3. Garred is on the editorial staff of the *Harvard Gazette,* a weekly devoted to news of the Harvard community. How do you suppose Garred came upon her story? Reconstruct the steps she probably took to research her article.
4. From what office or offices at your institution might you learn of an activity of more than usual interest engaged in by a faculty member, an administrator, a student, an alumnus, or a trustee? (Check your university catalogue and directory for possible leads.)

GUIDELINES FOR CONDUCTING THE INTERVIEW AND WRITING THE ESSAY

As these two essays illustrate, writers use interviews in writing about people, and they also use interviews in writing about issues. For either purpose, an interview produces, and the writer reproduces, more than information. By skilful selection of the most interesting remarks for quotation and by reporting gestures and settings, the writer allows us to experience both the writer's and the speaker's interest in the topic under discussion.

Here are some steps to follow in conducting an interview and writing an essay based on it.

1. Finding a subject for an interview. As with all writing projects, the best place to start is with your own interest. If you are taking a course from a particularly interesting professor, you might end your search, and begin your research, there. Or, you might use an interview as a way of investigating a department you are thinking of majoring in. Your university catalogue website lists the names of all faculty members by department.

Skim the list in the department that interests you and begin to ask questions of more senior students. Then, with a name or two in mind, check your library for appropriate biographical reference works. The university website will likely also have bibliographies of faculty members, but also check various *Who's Who* volumes. In addition to *Canadian Who's Who*, you will find such works as *Who's Who in the West*, and similar titles for various countries, for religious communities, for women, and so forth. In addition, the circulation desk or the research librarian may have a list of current publications by faculty members. In some libraries, current publications by faculty and alumni are on display or you can look them up under "author" in the databases. Department administrators are good sources of information not only about the special interests of the faculty but also about guest speakers scheduled by the department in the near future. Investigate the athletic department if you are interested in sports or the departments of music, art, and drama for the names of resident or visiting performing artists. Other sources of newsworthy personalities or events are the publicity office, the president's office, the university newspaper. All are potential sources for information about recent awards, or achievements, or upcoming events that may lead you to a subject for an interview, and a good story.

2. Preliminary work. Find out as much as you can about your potential interviewee's work, from the sources we mentioned above. If the subject of your interview is a faculty member, ask the department secretary if you may see a copy of that person's vita (Latin for "life," and pronounced *vee-ta*). Many departments have these brief biographical sketches on file for publicity purposes. The vita will list, among other things, publications and current research interests.

3. Requesting the interview. In making your request, do not hesitate to mention that you are fulfilling an assignment, but also make evident your own interest in the person's work or area of expertise. (Showing that you already know something about the work, that you have done some preliminary homework, is persuasive evidence of your interest.) Request the interview, preferably in writing, at least a week in advance, and ask for ample time (probably an hour to an hour and a half) for a thorough interview.

4. Preparing thoroughly. If your subject is a writer, read and take notes on the publications that most interest you. Read book reviews, if available; read reviews of performances if your subject is a performing artist. As you read, write out the questions that occur to you. As you work on them, try to phrase your questions so that they require more than a yes or no answer. A "why" or "how" question is likely to be productive, but don't be afraid of a general question such as "Tell me something about . . ."

Revise your questions and put them in a reasonable order. Work on an opening question that you think your subject will find both easy and interesting to answer. "How did you get interested in . . ." is often a good start. Type your questions or write them boldly so that you will find them easy to refer to.

Think about how you will record the interview. Although a tape recorder may seem like a good idea, there are good reasons not to rely on one. First of all, your subject may be made uneasy by its presence and freeze up. Second, the recorder (or the operator) may malfunction, leaving you with a partial record, or nothing at all. Third, even if all goes well, when you prepare to write you will face a mass of material, some of it inaudible, and all of it daunting to transcribe.

If, despite these warnings, you decide (with your subject's permission) to tape, expect to take notes anyway. It is the only way you can be sure you will have a record of what was important to you out of all that was said. Think beforehand, then, of how you will take notes and, if you can, practise by interviewing a friend. You will probably find that you want to devise some system of short-hand, perhaps no more than using initials for names that frequently recur, dropping the vowels in words that you transcribe—whatever assists you to write quickly but legibly. But do not think you must transcribe every word. Be prepared to do a lot more listening than writing.

5. Presenting yourself for the interview. Dress appropriately, bring your prepared questions and a notebook or pad for your notes, and appear on time.

6. Conducting the interview. At the start of the interview, try to engage briefly in conversation, without taking notes, to put your subject at ease. Even important people can be shy. Remembering that will help keep you at ease, too. If you want to use a tape recorder, ask your subject's permission, and if it is granted, ask where the microphone may be conveniently placed.

As the interview proceeds, keep your purpose in mind. Are you trying to gain information about an issue or topic, or are you trying to get a portrait of a personality? Listen attentively to your subject's answers and be prepared to follow up with your own responses and spontaneous questions. Here is where your thorough preparation will pay off.

A good interview develops like a conversation. Keep in mind that your prepared questions, however essential, are not sacred. At the same time do not hesitate to steer your subject, courteously, from apparent irrelevancies (what one reporter calls "sawdust") to something that interests you more. "I'd like to hear a little more about . . ." you can say. Or, "Would you mind telling me about how you . . ." It is also perfectly acceptable to ask your subject to repeat a remark so that you can record it accurately, and if you do not understand something, do not be afraid to admit it. Experts are accustomed to knowing more than others do about their area of expertise and are particularly happy to explain even the most elementary parts of their lore to an interested listener.

7. Concluding the interview. Near the end of the time you have agreed upon, ask your subject if he or she wishes to add any material, or to clarify something said earlier. Express your thanks and, at the appointed time, leave promptly.

8. Preparing to write. As soon as possible after the interview, review your notes, amplify them with details you wish to remember but might have failed to record, and type them up. You might have discovered during the interview, or you might see now, that there is something more that you want to read by or about your subject. Track it down and take further notes.

9. Writing the essay. In writing your first draft, think about your audience. Unless a better idea occurs to you, consider your university newspaper or magazine, or a local newspaper, as the place you hope to publish your story. Write with the readers of that publication in mind. Thinking of your readers will help you to be clear—for instance to identify names that have come up in the interview but which may be unfamiliar to your readers.

As with other writing, begin your draft with any idea that strikes you, and write at a fast clip until you have exhausted your material (or yourself).

When you revise, remember to keep your audience in mind; your material should, as it unfolds, tell a coherent and interesting story. Interviews, like conversations, tend to be delightfully circular or disorderly. But an essay, like a story, should reveal its contents in a sequence that captures and holds attention.

If you have done a thorough job of interviewing you may find that you have more notes than you can reasonably incorporate without disrupting the flow of your story. Do not be tempted to plug them in anyway. If they are really interesting, save them, perhaps by copying them into your journal; if not, chuck them out. (For a wretched example of a story that ends with a detail the writer could not bear to let go, see "Fish Eat Brazilian Fisherman," page 72.)

In introducing direct quotations from your source, choose those that are particularly characteristic or vivid or memorable. Paraphrase or summarize the rest of what is usable. Although the focus of your essay is almost surely the person you interviewed, it is your story, and most of it should be in your own words. Even though you must keep yourself in the background, your writing will gain in interest if your reader hears your voice as well as your subject's.

You might want to use a particularly good quotation for your conclusion. (Notice that both essays we have chosen as examples conclude this way.) Now make sure that you have an attractive opening paragraph. Identifying the subject of your interview and describing the setting is one way to begin. (Again, look at the sample essays.) Give your essay an attractive title. Before you prepare your final draft, read your essay aloud. You are almost certain to catch phrases you can improve and places where a transition will help your reader to follow you without effort. Check your quotations for accuracy; check with your subject any quotations or other details you are in doubt about. Type your final draft, then edit and proofread carefully.

10. Going public. Make two copies of your finished essay, one for the person you interviewed, one for yourself. The original is for your instructor; hand it in on time.

 ## Topic for Writing

Write an essay based on an interview. You need not be limited in your choice of subject by the examples we have given. A very old person, a recent immigrant, the owner or manager of an interesting store or business, a veteran of a peace-keeping mission, or a gardener are only a few of the possibilities. If you can, include a few photographs of your subject, with appropriate captions.

16

Writing the Research Essay

*Knowledge is of two kinds. We know a subject ourselves, or we know
where we can find information upon it.*

—Samuel Johnson, in a
conversation in 1775

WHAT RESEARCH IS

Research consists of collecting information to support and develop ideas. Of course, this does not mean that you collect only the information that supports your initial ideas. Your ideas will develop, often in unexpected ways, as you gather information. The information can include facts, opinions, and the ideas of others, recorded in print or in bytes, and in the form of books, articles, lectures, reports, reviews, and interviews. Research essays are based in part on such material, and you will write them in many of your university courses.

Not everyone likes to do research, of course. There are hours spent reading books and articles that prove to be contradictory or irrelevant. There is never enough time to read all the material that is available—or even to get your hands on it. And some of the books are dull. The poet William Butler Yeats, though an indefatigable worker on projects that interested him, engagingly expressed an indifference to the obligation that confronts every researcher: to look carefully at all the available evidence. Running over the possible reasons why Jonathan Swift did not marry (that he had syphilis, for instance, or that he feared he would transmit hereditary madness), Yeats says: "Mr. Shane Leslie thinks that Swift's relation to Vanessa was not platonic, and that whenever his letters speak of a cup of coffee they mean the sexual act; whether the letters seem to bear him out I do not know, for those letters bore me."

Though research sometimes requires reading boring things, those who engage in it feel, at other times, an exhilaration, a sense of triumph at becoming expert on something. When you study a topic thoroughly, you are in a position to say, "Here is how other people have thought about this question; their ideas are all very interesting, but I see the matter differently: let me tell you what *I* think."

There can be great satisfaction in knowing enough about a topic to contribute to the store of knowledge and ideas about it. There can also be great satisfaction in simply learning to use the seemingly infinite resources now available to researchers—in print or electronic formats—as well as in learning to document and to acknowledge your research accurately and responsibly.

In this chapter and the next one we discuss

- how to find and evaluate sources, both print and electronic
- how to take useful notes
- how to use others' ideas to help you develop your own
- how to acknowledge your sources.

When you acknowledge sources, giving credit where credit is due for your use of the words *and* ideas of others, you provide a kind of road map for the researcher who comes after you and who may want to retrace some of your steps. And you publicly thank those who have helped you on your way.

PRIMARY AND SECONDARY MATERIALS

The materials of research are usually divided into two categories, primary and secondary. The primary materials or sources are the real subject of study; the secondary sources are critical and historical accounts written about these primary materials. For example, if you want to know whether Shakespeare's attitude toward Julius Caesar was highly traditional or highly original, or a little of each, you would read *Julius Caesar,* other Elizabethan writings about Caesar, and translations of Latin writings known to the Elizabethans; in addition to these primary materials you would read secondary material such as modern books on Shakespeare and on Elizabethan attitudes toward Rome and toward monarchs.

Similarly, the primary material for an essay on a novel by Kate Chopin, *The Awakening* (1899), is of course the novel itself; the secondary material consists of such things as biographies of Chopin and critical essays on the novel. But the line between these two kinds of sources is not always sharp. For example, if you are concerned with the degree to which *The Awakening* is autobiographical, primary materials include not only the novel and Chopin's comments on her writing, but perhaps also the comments of people who knew her. Thus the essays—based on interviews with Chopin—that two of her friends published in newspapers probably can be regarded as primary material because they were contemporary with the novel and because they give direct access to Chopin's views, while the writings of later commentators constitute secondary material.

SETTING A SCHEDULE

Writing a good research paper is likely to take longer than you think, and so it is important to set a schedule for yourself and give yourself lots of time for the work. Your schedule could look something like this:

Week 1 Prewriting stage: develop a research topic or question; go to the library and do a search of the library catalogue (databases) and journal indexes, and record bibliographical information as you go (the Internet can also be a good resource); begin narrowing the topic into a *working thesis*.

<u>Weeks 2–3</u> Read the material you gathered, making notes on each reading that you think will be helpful; arrange your notes and organize your ideas by writing a fairly detailed outline.

<u>Week 4</u> Write a first draft of your essay; go back to the library to search out any information to fill gaps that developed as your topic became more focused and specific.

<u>Week 5</u> Edit and revise your essay.

<u>Week 6</u> Let your essay sit for a couple of days, and then go back and read it as objectively as you can for problems with organization, introducing quotations, and so forth. Read it again for sentence-level writing errors such as comma splices and faulty parallelism. Then skim again the notes you made from reading secondary sources, and read your essay one last time to make sure that it contains no inadvertent plagiarism. And finally, hand in the essay.

DEVELOPING A RESEARCH TOPIC

Your instructor may assign a topic, in which case, you will be saved some work. (On the other hand, you may find yourself spending a lot of time with material you do not find exciting. Or you might become interested in something you would otherwise never have known about.) More likely, you will need to develop your own topic, a topic related to the subject of the course for which the research essay has been assigned. Some possibilities:

- Perhaps you have read Maxine Hong Kingston's *The Woman Warrior* (1976) for a women's studies course, and you have become interested in Confucian or Buddhist ideas that inform the narrative.
- Perhaps your government course has touched on the internment of Japanese Canadians during World War II, and you would like to know more about what happened and why.
- Perhaps you have read Chopin's *The Awakening* for a literature course, and you are wondering what readers thought about the novel when it was first published.

Any of these interests could well become a topic for a research essay. But how do you begin to find the relevant material?

Getting Started

There is no one right way to start, and of course different topics lend themselves to different kinds of approaches. Nevertheless, one good rule of thumb is to begin with what you already know, with what you already have at hand. For instance, the textbook for your government course may cite official documents on the relocation and internment of Japanese Canadians. Or your edition of Chopin's *The Awakening* may contain an introduction that references some critical essays on the novel; it is also likely to contain a selected bibliography, a list of books and articles about Chopin and her work. If you have already identified a few titles, you can go directly to your library's online catalogue and begin your search there. (We will have more to say about online searches in a moment.)

If, however, you know very little about the topic and have not yet identified any possible sources (let's say you know nothing or almost nothing about Confucianism, but Maxine Hong Kingston's *The Woman Warrior* has made you want to learn about it), it is not a bad idea to begin with an encyclopedia—the *Encyclopaedia Britannica*, perhaps—which you will find in the reference area of your college or university library. In addition to providing you with information about your topic, encyclopedia articles will usually include cross-references to other articles within the encyclopedia, as well as suggestions for further reading. These suggestions can help you begin to compose a list of secondary sources for your essay. And of course you need not limit yourself to this one encyclopedia: there are hundreds of invaluable specialized encyclopedias, such as *Encyclopedia of Anthropology, Encyclopedia of Crime and Justice, Encyclopedia of Psychology, Encyclopedia of Religion* (a good place to go for an introduction to Confucianism), and *Kodansha Encyclopedia of Japan*, and many of them are certain to be available in your library's reference area. Encyclopedias are also available online, in full-text versions you can access through your library's central information system.

THE LIBRARY'S CENTRAL INFORMATION SYSTEM

All libraries used to work in more or less the same way. Each one had a card catalogue, a set of hundreds of little drawers containing thousands (even millions) of alphabetically arranged note cards. When you wanted a book, you went to the card catalogue and looked it up by title, author, or subject. Because books would of course differ from library to library, the cards would also of course differ. But the system in every library was pretty much the same.

In recent years, online catalogues have replaced card catalogues in college and university libraries, and in most public libraries as well. And the online catalogue constitutes only a tiny fraction of the information available to you through your institution's library. From a computer terminal in your library (or from home via a telnet or World Wide Web connection), you can access bibliographies and indexes, full-text versions of encyclopedias and dictionaries and academic journals, the catalogues of *other* libraries—and much more.

Unlike card catalogues, each library's central information system is a bit different. Resources differ from one library to the next. And things change—literally—every day. For these reasons, our discussion of library resources in the following pages can only provide you with a sketch of what is available and a general sense of how to find it. The best advice we can give you about learning to find books and articles in your library is to go to your college or university's research or reference librarian and ask for help. Many libraries also offer on-site tutorials at the beginning of the term or post this information on their websites.

THE ONLINE CATALOGUE

Let's assume that you are at a computer terminal in the library. Let's also assume that you are taking a course in environmental studies, and as a result of one of the course lectures, you have become interested in researching the subject of food additives—that is, chemicals and other substances added to preserve desirable properties (colour, flavour, freshness) or to suppress undesirable properties in food. You want to do some reading, and you must now find the books, articles, and reports. Of course, as you do the reading, your focus may narrow, for instance to the potentially dangerous effects, in various foods, of sodium nitrate or to the controversy over the effects of aspartame (an artificial sweetener), or you may concentrate on so-called enriched bread, which is first robbed of many nutrients by refining and bleaching the flour and is then enriched by the addition of some of the nutrients in synthetic form. But at this point, you do not yet know what your focus will be, and you simply want to begin finding relevant material.

The steps required for searching the online catalogue vary from system to system, and so we cannot tell you exactly how you will perform a search at your library. Generally speaking, you will enter into the terminal some information about the source you are looking for (usually the author, title, or subject); the computer will perform the search, and the results will appear on the screen. **Author** and **title searches** are relatively straightforward. To find works by a particular author, you enter the author's name (beginning with the last name), and a list of his or her works will appear on the screen. To find a particular title, simply type in the title (omitting the initial "the," "an," or "a") at the appropriate prompt, and all the books with that title will likewise be listed on the screen.

Subject searches are more complicated because they often depend on highly structured language and very specific terms. (If you do not know what subject terms to use, consult the *Canadian Almanac and Directory,* the *Canadian Source Book,* or the *Library of Congress Subject Headings,* available

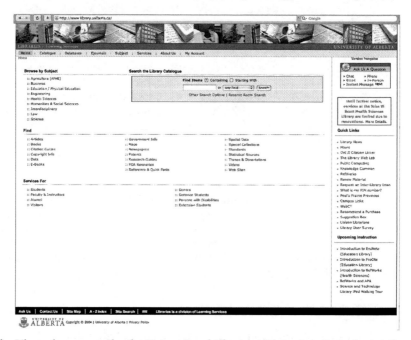

The Library home page for the University of Alberta at Edmonton. (A student at the University of Alberta might connect to this page from home and begin searching the library's resources here.) www.library.ualberta.ca.

in the reference area of your library.) To find material for the essay on food additives, you would begin with a subject search (since you don't have in mind the titles or authors of any particular books), typing the phrase "food additives"—which happens to be an accepted subject heading term—at the prompt on the computer screen. The computer will search the library's holdings, and a list of more detailed subject headings, such as the following list, will appear on the screen. (We reproduce an image of only the first screen that would appear in one specific library; the complete list of holdings for the subject "food additives" in this library contains ninety-four items.)

Note that the first line of this list says simply "food additives." The other entries are followed by phrases that indicate more specific subject categories, such as "Food additives—Israel—periodicals," categories that may be too specific for your purposes at the very beginning of your research on this topic. In this case, if you now were to enter "1," a second list of 42 items would appear, and this list would contain titles and authors of books on your subject. The first screen of this list, which contains the first 15 of the 42 items, appears on the next page.

HU GUIDE: SUBJECT HEADING LIST 94 items retrieved by your search:

FIND SU FOOD ADDITIVES

1	FOOD ADDITIVES
43	FOOD ADDITIVES —ANALYSIS
47	FOOD ADDITIVES —BIBLIOGRAPHY
50	FOOD ADDITIVES —CONGRESSES
55	FOOD ADDITIVES —DICTIONARIES
56	FOOD ADDITIVES —GREAT BRITAIN
57	FOOD ADDITIVES —HANDBOOKS MANUALS ETC
58	FOOD ADDITIVES —HEALTH ASPECTS
61	FOOD ADDITIVES —ISRAEL —PERIODICALS
62	FOOD ADDITIVES —LAW AND LEGISLATION
63	FOOD ADDITIVES —LAW AND LEGISLATION —AUSTRALIA
64	FOOD ADDITIVES —LAW AND LEGISLATION —CANADA
65	FOOD ADDITIVES —LAW AND LEGISLATION —DENMARK
66	FOOD ADDITIVES —LAW AND LEGISLATION —EUROPE—MISCELLANEA
67	FOOD ADDITIVES —LAW AND LEGISLATION —FRANCE
68	FOOD ADDITIVES —LAW AND LEGISLATION —GERMANY WEST

OPTIONS: ------------------- More - to see next page --------------------

GUide # - see guide at #th item   Help

index # - see list at #th item   Quit

Help COMMANDS   REDo - edit search   STORe # - save for email   COMment

COMMAND?

```
FIND SU FOOD ADDITIVES
----------------------------------------------------------------------
FOOD ADDITIVES
```

1	[retrieves related heading:	DIETARY SUPPLEMENTS]
2	[retrieves related heading:	ENRICHED FOODS]
3	[retrieves related heading:	FLAVOURING ESSENCES]
4	[retrieves related heading:	FOOD PRESERVATIVES]
5	[retrieves related heading:	SUCROSE POLYESTER]
6	[retrieves related heading:	SWEETENERS]

```
7       additives guide /hughes christopher c/ 1987 bks

8       alternatives to the current use of nitrite in foods/ 1982 bks

9       bugs in the peanut butter dangers in everyday food /weiner micha/ 1976 bks

10      chemical safety regulation and compliance proceeding /course on/ 1985 bks

11      chemicals we eat /benarde melvin a/ 1971 bks

12      chemicals we eat /benarde melvin a/ 1975 bks

13      eaters digest the consumers fact book of food additi /jacobson m/ 1972 bks

14      eating may be hazardous to your health how your gove /verrett ja/ 1974 bks

15      environmental poisons in our food /millichap j gordon/ 1993 bks

OPTIONS: ------------------- More - to see next page --------------------
                                                                   Help
GUide                   display # - see #th item                   Quit
Help COMMANDS           REDo - edit search  STORe # - save for email  COMment
COMMAND?
```

4-©	Sess-2	128.103.60.84

In addition to author, subject, and title searches, most online catalogues permit **keyword searches**. Searching by keyword allows you to search all fields and sometimes the texts themselves while avoiding the need to know the standardized subject headings and usually allows you to refine your search using "and," "or," and "not." To find material on food additives, for example, you might type in the words "chemicals and food" at the title keyword prompt; on the screen would appear a list of all the books in the library whose *titles* contain the words chemicals and food. (Note: the word "and" in this context is an *operator*; it tells the computer to look for books with *both* words in their title fields. Another option would be to use the word "or"; doing so would instruct the computer to locate titles containing either word.)

Why is a keyword search useful? Chiefly for two reasons. First, when you are just beginning your research you will not necessarily know all the right subject headings for the books you want, but you probably will already know some of the words likely to appear in their titles; performing a keyword search will quickly give you a sense of what is available. Second, a keyword search can be a kind of shortcut to finding a group of useful subject headings because the full bibliographic record for each book located by the keyword search will list all the subject headings under which the book is classified.

It is also usually possible to **limit an online search**. Let's say the list you retrieved during your initial subject search is very long—too long to browse through in the time you have available. You may be able to generate a shorter and more focused list by telling the computer to limit the search—for example, to books written in English or published during a particular range of years, or to books located in a particular part of your library (or in a library within your university's library system—the science library or the humanities library perhaps).

You may at this point decide to browse through the list you've generated, pausing to read the full catalogue record (or "long display") for titles that interest you. Your attention may have been caught, for example, by the title *Safe Food: Eating Wisely in a Risky World*. Reading the full record for this title, illustrated in our third screen image, will tell you the authors' names, the publisher, and the date and place of publication. (This information should enable you to decide if the book may be useful to you.)

The record also gives the book's length, call number, location, and availability—in addition to (as we note above) the subject headings under which it is listed. You will want to keep this information at hand: you will need the call number in order to find the book on the shelf; you will need the name of the author and the publication data when you make the Works Cited list or bibliog-

---

HU SHORT DISPLAY page 1 of 1   Item 36 of 94 retrieved by your search:

FIND SU FOOD ADDITIVES

--HU HOLLIS# ALM1510 /bks

AUTHOR:	Jacobson, Michael F.
TITLE:	Safe food : eating wisely in a risky world / Michael F. Jacobson, Lisa Y. Lefferts, Anne Witte Garland.
PUB. INFO:	Los Angeles, Calif. : Living Planet Press, c1991.
DESCRIPTION:	xvi, 234 p. : ill. ; 24 cm.
SUBJECTS:	*S1 Food—Toxicology.
	*S2 Food adulteration and inspection.
	*S3 Food additives.
LOCATION:	Hilles: RA1258.J32 1991x
	C2 - Enter DISPLAY C2 for circulation information
	Schlesinger: 641.5637 J17s

OPTIONS: ----------------------

Display Long		Next - next item	Help
LOCation	TRace *S1 (etc)	PRevious - prev item	Quit
Index	REDo - edit search	STORe - save for email	COMment
COMMAND?			

---

raphy for your essay. To record all this information you can (obviously) write it on a note card or piece of paper. But you may also be able simply to print it on one of the library's printers. Alternatively, you may be able to email it to yourself or download it onto a computer disk.

SKIMMING BOOKS AND BOOK REVIEWS

At this point you can begin to skim some of the books you have located, or you can put off looking at the books until you have found some relevant articles in periodicals. For the moment, let's postpone the periodicals.

Put a bunch of books in front of you, and choose one as an introduction. How do you choose one from half a dozen? Partly by its size—choose a thin one because it is less likely to bury you in details—and partly by other qualities. Roughly speaking, the book you choose should be among the more recent publications, and it should strike you as fair. A pamphlet published by a meat-packers association is desirably thin but you have a hunch that it may be biased. Roger John Williams's *Nutrition in a Nutshell* is published by a well-known commercial press (Doubleday), and it is only 171 pages, but because it was published in 1962 it may not reflect current food chemistry. The book *Safe Food,* published in 1991 and 243 pages long, might be a better place to start, or you may prefer the second edition of *Food Additives* (2005) available online through the catalogue.

When you have found the book that you think may serve as your introductory study, do the following:

- **Read the preface** in order to get an idea of the author's purpose and outlook.
- **Skim the table of contents** in order to get an idea of the organization and the coverage.
- **Skim the final chapter or the last few pages,** where you may be lucky enough to find a summary. (You are not reading a novel; skipping to the end is not against the rules.)

The index, too, may let you know if the book will suit your purpose by showing you what topics are covered and how much coverage they get. If the book still seems suitable, skim it.

At this stage it is acceptable to trust your hunches—you are only going to skim the book, not buy it or even read it—but you may want to look up some book reviews to assure yourself that the book has merit. There are a few especially useful general indexes to book reviews:

Book Review Digest (published from 1905 onward)

Book Review Index (1965–)

Canadian Periodical Index

Academic Search Premier

Given the topic of food additives, you might want to consult relevant business, health sciences, or general sciences indexes and abstracts; these are usually found online in the university library's databases, such as *Business Periodicals Index* (1958–) and *General Science Abstracts* (1978–).

Most reviews of a book will come out in the same year as the book, or within the next two years. We suggest beginning with *Book Review Digest* because it includes excerpts from and synopses of the reviews; if it has your book, the excerpts and synopses may be enough, and you won't have to dig out the reviews themselves. But *Book Review Digest* does not have as broad a coverage as the other indexes, and you may have to turn to them for citations, and then to the journals to which they refer you. (*Book Review Digest* covers about 200 periodicals; *Book Review Index* covers about 450.) Read the synopses in *Book Review Digest,* or some reviews in journals, and draw some conclusions about the merit of the book in question. Of course, you cannot assume that every review is fair, but a book that on the whole gets good reviews is probably at least good enough for a start.

By quickly reading such a book (take few or no notes at this stage) you will probably get an overview of your topic, and you will begin to see exactly what part of the topic you wish to pursue.

FINDING ARTICLES IN PERIODICALS

Your next step may be to locate articles in periodicals and academic journals. On some topics, especially recent happenings, there may be few or even no books, but there may well be many articles published in newspapers and magazines. Furthermore, scholars often publish their work in journals before it is published in book form. You could start thumbing through these publications at random, but such a procedure is monstrously inefficient. Fortunately, there are indexes to periodicals and databases—many available online—so you can quickly find the latest writing on your topic. Among the most widely used online indexes or databases on the library website are

Readers' Guide to Periodical Literature (1900–)

Arts and Humanities Abstracts

Social Science Abstracts

Science Citation Abstracts

Readers' Guide indexes more than 240 of the more familiar magazines— such as *Canadian Geographic, Good Housekeeping, Maclean's, Saturday Night, Scientific American, Sports Illustrated,* and *Time.* The other three indexes are guides to academic journals in the sciences and humanities. If you were looking for articles on literature, you might begin by doing a search in the *MLA* (Modern Language Association) *International Bibliography* found under humanities databases. If you wanted to find articles on food additives, you might check *Science Abstracts.* To search these indexes, at the prompt you simply type terms relevant to your topic. Many libraries also provide access to journals online, and so you may be able to access an article that interests you from your computer.

Keep in mind that indexes we discuss above are only a few of the many, many indexes available. Each discipline has its own specialized index, from *Accountant's Index* to *World Law Index.* To find the indexes most likely to help you find the articles you are looking for, search your library's electronic resources by keyword or subject—or consult a reference librarian.

FINDING BIBLIOGRAPHIES

Many researchers have published bibliographies, that is, lists of the works they have consulted. Sometimes the bibliographies appear as articles in scholarly journals or as appendices to books, or even as entire books. All of these kinds of bibliographies are listed in *Bibliographic Index,* a print resource that is issued three times a year and cumulates in an annual volume. Begin, of course, with the most recent issue, check it for your subject, and then work back for a few years. A recent bibliography will probably offer you as many sources as you will have time to consult. You may be able to locate a bibliography of works in your field by performing an online catalogue subject search (note the third item on the subject heading list on page 309): simply enter your subject heading, then a dash and the word "bibliography." You are also likely to find bibliographies in various disciplines when you consult the list of your library's electronic resources.

A WORD ON THE INTERNET

The Internet, a vast network of interconnected computers, can be a tremendous resource for researchers. But because anyone, anywhere, can post pretty much anything, the information available on the Internet can be difficult to evaluate. When you are working with secondary sources that have been published in journals or in book form, for the most part you are working with material that experts in that field have judged to be worth reading. Before it is published, an article in the journal *College English*, for example, will have been read by a number of reviewers (most or all of them college English professors), as well as by members of an advisory board and several editors. If *College English* is in your institution's library—and we bet it is—it is there in part because librarians have decided it is worth including in the serials collection. An article in *College English* may have weaknesses, but several experts have thought it was pretty good.

Information available on the Internet has not been similarly vetted. Advertisements coexist with course syllabi. One could (if one wanted to) access a chat-group on Leonardo DiCaprio as easily as one could find photographs of people's pets or an interview with Jamaica Kincaid or the full text of *Romeo and Juliet* or an essay on your research topic, written by your professor—or by the person who sits next to you in your biology class.

How do you judge what may be worth considering? In part by using the critical thinking skills we discuss elsewhere in this book. Ask questions of the material:

- Who is the author?
- For whom is the author writing? Who is the intended audience?
- Who sponsored the document?
- Can you tell if the author is an authority in the field? (Perhaps the document is linked to the author's home page.)
- Does he or she reference other critics or writers? Good ones?
- Is the text well written?
- Do arguments seem well supported, or is the document full of vague generalizations?
- Does the author point you toward other resources?
- How current is the piece?

For more on this matter, we recommend (appropriately enough) that you consult documents available on the Web, such as "Evaluating Information Found on the Internet" (http://milton.mse.jhu.edu:8001/research/education/net.html). It *should* still be available—but that's the other problem with Internet sources: what is here today may be gone tomorrow.

READING AND TAKING NOTES ON SECONDARY SOURCES

Almost all researchers—professionals as well as beginners—find that they end up with some notes that are irrelevant. On the other hand, when drafting the paper, they find that they vaguely remember certain material they now wish they had taken notes on. Especially in the early stages of your research, when the topic and thesis may still be relatively unfocused, it's hard to know what is noteworthy and what is not. You simply have to flounder a bit.

As we have suggested, it may be helpful to read (or skim) an article or book all the way through the first time around without taking notes. By the time you reach the end, you may find it is not noteworthy. Or you may find a useful summary near the end that will contain most of what you can get from the piece. Or you will find that, having a sense of the whole, you can now quickly reread the piece and take notes on the chief points.

Even if you do follow this procedure, a certain amount of inefficiency is inevitable; therefore plenty of time should be allowed. And it is worth keeping in mind that different people really do work differently. We list three strategies; we suspect that, over time, you will develop your own.

- Take notes using note cards, writing on one side only, because material on the back of a card is usually neglected when you come to write the paper. (Taking notes by hand offers several advantages—not least of which is that you do not need access to a computer to do it.) You may prefer to use loose-leaf paper for sources with lots of helpful information.

- Take notes on your computer, keeping a separate file for each book or article. Material can be easily moved from one file to another as the organization of the essay begins to take shape.
- Do not take notes—or take very few notes. Photocopy secondary material you think you might use, and underline and annotate that material as you read and think about it. (Material from electronic sources can be downloaded and later printed out and annotated as well.) The disadvantage here is obvious: this method uses a lot of paper. But there are two big advantages: passages from the sources are transcribed (or, in the case of downloaded material, moved) only once, into the draft itself, so there's less risk of mistakes and distortions; and the research—the collecting of information—can go very quickly. **A word of caution** though: it is crucial that you think carefully about the material you are collecting and that you annotate it thoroughly. If you do not, you will find yourself with a pile of paper, and no idea of what to do with it. Or, you may find that underlining rather than summarizing leads to over-reliance on the words and ideas of others.

A Guide to Note Taking

1. Be sure to record the title and author of the source. If you're using note cards, specify the source in an abbreviated form in the upper-left corner; if you're taking notes on your computer, make a separate file for each book or article, and use the author's name and the first significant word of the title to identify the file. If you are using photocopies, make sure that you also photocopy the bibliographic information—which usually appears in full on the title pages of books and often (but not always) appears on the first page of a journal article. (And be sure to make a record of the full span of the article, not just the pages that you have copied.)

2. Write summaries, not paraphrases (that is, write abridgements rather than restatements, which in fact may be as long as or longer than the original). There is rarely any point to paraphrasing. Generally speaking, either quote exactly (and put the passage in quotation marks, with a notation of the source, including the page number or numbers) or summarize, reducing a page or even an entire article or chapter of a book to a few sentences that can be written on a note card, typed into your computer, or squeezed into the margin of a photocopied page. Even when you summarize, record your source (including the page numbers), so that you can give appropriate credit in your essay.

3. Quote sparingly. Of course in your summary you will sometimes quote a phrase or a sentence—putting it in quotation marks—but quote sparingly. You are not simply transcribing what you read; rather you are assimilating knowledge, and you are thinking, and so for the most part your source should be digested rather than engorged whole. Thinking now, while taking notes, will also help you later to avoid plagiarism. If, on the other hand, when you take notes you mindlessly copy material at length, later when you are writing the essay you may be tempted to copy it yet again, perhaps without giving credit. Similarly, if you simply photocopy pages from articles or books, and then merely underline some passages without annotating your reading, you probably will not be thinking; you will just be underlining. But if you make a terse summary you will be forced to think and to find your own words for the idea. Quote directly only those passages that are particularly effective, or crucial, or memorable. In your finished essay these quotations will provide authority and emphasis.

4. Quote accurately. After copying a quotation, check your transcription against the original, and correct any misquotation. Verify the page number also. If a quotation runs from the bottom of, say, page 306 to the top of 307, make a distinguishing mark (for instance two backslashes after the last word of the first page), so that if you later use only part of the quotation, you will know the page on which it appeared.

5. Use ellipses (three spaced periods) to indicate the omission of any words within a sentence. If the omitted words are at the end of the quoted sentence, put a period immediately at the point where you end the sentence, and then add three spaced periods to indicate the omission. Example:

> If the . . . words were at the end of the quoted sentence, put a period

immediately at the end. . . .

Use square brackets to indicate your additions to the quotation. Here is an example.

> Here is an [uninteresting] example.

6. *Never* copy a passage by changing an occasional word, under the impression that you are thereby putting it into your own words. Notes of this sort may find their way into your essay, your reader will sense a style other than your own, and suspicions (and perhaps even charges) of plagiarism will follow. (For a detailed discussion of plagiarism, see below.)

7. Comment on your notes. Again, consider it your obligation to *think* about the material as you make your notes, evaluating it and using it as a stimulus to further thought. For example, you may want to say "Tyler seems to be generalizing from insufficient evidence," or "Corsa made the same point five years earlier"; but make certain that later you will be able to distinguish between these comments and the notes summarizing or quoting your source. A suggestion: surround all comments recording your responses with double parentheses, thus: ((. . .)).

8. Write a keyword on each card or at the beginning of each section of notes in your computer file. A brief key—for example "effect on infants' blood"—can help you to tell at a glance what is on the card or in the file.

9. Do not be tempted to simply cut and paste large quantities of the original text into your notes. Sloppy cutting and pasting can lead to inadvertent plagiarism.

ACKNOWLEDGING SOURCES

Borrowing without Plagiarizing

As we suggested earlier, respect for your readers and for your sources requires that you acknowledge your indebtedness for material when

1. you quote directly from a work, or
2. you paraphrase or summarize someone's words (the words of your paraphrase or summary are your own, but the points are not), or
3. you appropriate an idea that is not common knowledge.

Most commonly, the words, ideas, and information that you cite in a research essay will come from printed and electronic sources. But you must also acknowledge the advice of peer editors and ideas that come from lectures and class discussions (unless your instructor tells you not to do so). We give the form for acknowledging peer editors on pages 28–29; we will tell you how to document all these other sources in the pages that follow.

Let us suppose you are going to make use of William Bascom's comment on the earliest responses of Europeans to African art:

> The first examples of African art to gain public attention were the bronzes and ivories which were brought back to Europe after the sack of Benin by a British military expedition in 1897. The superb technology of the Benin bronzes won the praise of experts like Felix von Luschan who wrote in 1899, "Cellini himself could not have made better casts, nor anyone else before or since to the present day." Moreover, their relatively realistic treatment of human features conformed to the prevailing European aesthetic standards. Because of their naturalism and technical excellence, it was at first maintained that they had been produced by Europeans—a view that was still current when the even more realistic bronze heads were discovered at Ife in 1912. The subsequent discovery of new evidence has caused the complete abandonment of this theory of European origins of the bronzes of Benin and Ife, both of which are cities in Nigeria.

—WILLIAM BASCOM, *AFRICAN ART IN CULTURAL PERSPECTIVE*
(NEW YORK: NORTON, 1973), P. 4

1. Acknowledging a direct quotation. You may want to use some or all of Bascom's words, in which case you will write something like this:

As William Bascom says, when Europeans first encountered Benin and Ife works of art in the late nineteenth century, they thought that Europeans had produced them, but the discovery of new evidence "caused the complete abandonment of this theory of European origins of the bronzes of Benin and Ife, both of which are cities in Nigeria" (4).

Normally, at the end of an essay a page headed Works Cited will give bibliographic information (author, title, place of publication, name of the publisher, date of publication, and page numbers if relevant) for each work cited within the essay. The point here is not that you must use detailed footnotes but that you must give credit. Not to give credit is to plagiarize, which is a serious breach of the rules governing academic work.

2. Acknowledging a paraphrase or summary. Summaries (abridgements) are usually superior to paraphrases (rewordings, of approximately the same length as the original) because summaries are briefer, but occasionally you may find that you cannot abridge a passage in your source and yet you don't want to quote it word for word—perhaps because it is too technical or because it is poorly written. Even though you are changing some or all of the words, you must give credit to the source because the idea is not yours, nor, probably, is the sequence of the presentation.

Here is an example of a summary:

William Bascom, in <u>African Art</u>, points out that the first examples of

African art- -Benin bronzes and ivories- -brought to Europe were thought

by Europeans to be of European origin, because of their naturalism and

their technical excellence, but evidence was later discovered that caused

this theory to be abandoned.

Not to give Bascom credit is to plagiarize, even though the words are yours. The offence is just as serious as not acknowledging a direct quotation. And, of course, if you say something like the following and do not give credit, you are also plagiarizing, even though almost all of the words are your own:

The earliest examples of African art to become widely known in Europe

were bronzes and ivories that were brought to Europe in 1897. These works

were thought to be of European origin, and one expert said that Cellini

could not have done better work. Their technical excellence, as well as their

realism, fulfilled the European standards of the day. The later discovery of

new evidence at Benin and Ife, both in Nigeria, refuted this belief.

It is pointless to offer this sort of rewording: if there is a point, it is to conceal the source and to take credit for thinking that is not your own.

3. Acknowledging an idea. Let us say that you have read an essay in which Irving Kristol argues that journalists who pride themselves on being tireless critics of national policy are in fact irresponsible critics because they have no policy they prefer. If this strikes you as a new idea and you adopt it in an essay—even though you set it forth entirely in your own words and with examples not offered by Kristol—you should acknowledge your debt to Kristol. *Not to acknowledge such borrowing is plagiarism.* Your readers will not think the less of you for naming your source; rather, they will be grateful to you for telling them about an interesting writer.

Fair Use of Common Knowledge

If in doubt as to whether or not to give credit (either with formal documentation or merely in a phrase such as "Carol Gilligan says . . ."), give credit. But as you begin to read widely in your field or subject, you will develop a sense of what is considered common knowledge.

Unsurprising definitions in a dictionary can be considered common knowledge, and so there is no need to say, "According to *Webster*, a novel is a long narrative in prose." (That is weak in three ways: it is unnecessary, it is uninteresting, and it is inexact since "Webster" appears in the titles of several dictionaries, some good and some bad.)

Similarly, the date of Freud's death can be considered common knowledge. Few can give it when asked, but it can be found out from innumerable sources, and no one need get the credit for providing you with the date. Again, if you simply *know,* from your reading of Freud, that Freud was interested in literature, you need not cite a specific source for an assertion to that effect, but if you know only because some commentator on Freud said so, and you have no idea whether the fact is well known or not, you should give credit to the source that gave you the information. Not to give credit—for ideas as well as for quoted words—is to plagiarize.

"But How Else Can I Put It?"

If you have just learned—say from an encyclopedia—something that you sense is common knowledge, you may wonder, "How can I change into my own words the simple, clear words that this source uses in setting forth this simple fact?" For example, if before writing about the photograph of the Oka Crisis (page 171), you look up the event in *The Canadian Encyclopedia* (online), you will find this statement about the confrontation: "A land dispute between the reserve and the municipality was brought to national attention in 1990 when the Mohawk Warriors Society set up a blockade." You cannot use this statement as your own, word for word, without feeling uneasy. But to put in quotation marks such a routine statement of what can be considered common knowledge, and to cite a source for it, seems pretentious. After all, Spotlight Canada (www.geocities.com/av_team2001/oka.html) says much the same thing: "In the 1990s, a crisis happened that was important for the Aboriginal nations in Canada. The Mohawk Community began with the standoff at Oka, Quebec. The reason why the Mohawk native people created a barricade . . . was because the government was going to expand a golf course in Oka which would invade the ancestral burial grounds of the Mohawks." It may be that the words "barricade" and "blockade" are simply the most obvious and most accurate words, and perhaps you will end up using one of them. Certainly to change "blockade" or "barricade" to "obstruction on the road" in an effort to avoid plagiarizing would be to make a change for the worse and still to be guilty of plagiarism. But you will not get yourself into this mess of wondering whether to change clear, simple wording into awkward wording if in the first place, when you take notes, you *summarize* your sources, thus: "1990: Oka Crisis, Mohawks and Oka municipality, dispute over land claims, widespread publicity" or "Oka, 1990, confrontation over land dispute, road blockade, media attention." Later (even if only thirty minutes later), when drafting your paper, if you turn this nugget—probably combined with others—into the best sentence you can, you will not be in danger of plagiarizing, even if the word "organized" turns up in your sentence.

Of course, even when dealing with material that can be considered common knowledge—and even when you have put it into your own words—you probably *will* cite your source if you are drawing more than just an occasional fact from the source. If, for instance, your paragraph on the Oka Crisis uses half a dozen facts from a source, cite the source. You do this both to avoid charges of plagiarism and to protect yourself in case your source contains errors of fact.

WRITING THE ESSAY

When you use sources, you are not merely dumping on the table the contents of a shopping cart filled at the scholar's supermarket, the library. You are cooking a meal. You must have a point, an opinion, a thesis; you are working toward a conclusion, and your readers should always feel they are moving toward that conclusion (by means of your thoughtful argument and use of sources) rather than reading an anthology of commentary on the topic. You have become an expert on your topic; you now know what others have to say about it, but if you have been *thinking* about what the secondary sources have said about your primary material, it is likely that you have noticed contradictions and gaps, that you agree with some opinions and arguments (and disagree with others), that you have begun to develop your *own* ideas about your topic.

There remains the difficult job of writing the essay. Beyond referring you to the rest of this book, we can offer only seven pieces of advice.

1. With a tentative thesis in mind, begin by rereading your notes and sorting them by topic. Put together what belongs together. Do not hesitate to reject material that—however interesting—now seems irrelevant or redundant. After sorting, resorting, and rejecting, you will have a kind of first draft without writing a draft.

2. From your notes you can make a first outline. Although you cannot yet make a paragraph outline, you may find it useful to make a fairly full outline, indicating, for example, not only the sequence of points but also the quotations that you will use. In sketching the outline, of course you will be guided by your working *thesis*. As you worked, you probably modified your tentative ideas in the light of what your further research produced, but by now you ought to have a relatively firm idea of what you want to say. Without a thesis you will have only the basis for a *report*, not a potential essay.

3. Transcribe or download quotations, even in the first draft, exactly as you want them to appear in the final version. Of course this takes some time, and the time will be wasted if, as may well turn out, you later see that the quotation is not really useful. (On the other hand, the time has not really been wasted, since it helped you ultimately to delete the unnecessary material.)

If at this early stage you just write a note reminding yourself to include the quotation—something like "here quote Jackson on undecided voters"—when you reread the draft you will not really know how the page sounds. You will not, for instance, know how much help your reader needs by way of a lead-in to the quotation or how much discussion should follow. Only if you actually see the quotation are you in the position of your audience—and all good writers try to imagine their audience.

4. Include, right in the body of the draft, all of the relevant citations so that when you come to revise you don't have to start hunting through your notes to find who said what and where. You can, for the moment, enclose these citations within diagonal lines, or within double parentheses—anything at all to remind you that they will be your documentation.

5. Resist the urge to include every note in your essay. As we suggest in Chapter 1, writing is a way of discovering ideas. Consequently, as you write your first draft, your thesis will inevitably shift, and notes that initially seemed important will now seem irrelevant. Do not stuff them into the draft, even if you are concerned about meeting a page requirement: readers know padding when they see it.

6. Resist the urge to do more research. As you draft, you may also see places where another piece of evidence, another reference to a source, or another example would be useful. And you may feel compelled to head back to the library. We think that for now you should resist that urge too: it may simply be procrastination in disguise. Continue writing this first draft if possible, and plan to incorporate new material in a later draft.

7. As you revise your draft, make sure that you do not merely tell the reader "A says . . . B says . . . C says . . ." Rather, by using such expressions as "A claims," "B provides evidence that," "C gives the usual view," "D concedes that," you help the reader to see the role of the quotation in your paper. Let your reader know why you are quoting or how the quotation fits into your organization.

A Checklist for Reading Drafts

✔ Is the tentative title informative and focused?
✔ Does the paper make a point, or does it just accumulate other people's ideas?
✔ Does it reveal the thesis early?
✔ Are general statements supported by evidence?
✔ Are all the *words* and *ideas* of the sources accurately attributed?
✔ Are quotations introduced adequately?
✔ Are all of the long quotations necessary, or can some of them be effectively summarized or shortened using ellipsis?
✔ Are quotations discussed adequately?
✔ Does the paper advance in orderly stages? Can your imagined reader easily follow your thinking?
✔ Is the documentation in the correct form?

TWO SAMPLE RESEARCH ESSAYS BY STUDENTS

Here are two essays in which students have drawn on the writing of others in developing their ideas. The first, "Politics and Psychology in *The Awakening*," by Beatrice Cody, uses the MLA form of in-text citations, which are clarified by a list headed "Works Cited." The second, Jacob Alexander's "Nitrite: Preservative or Carcinogen?," uses the APA form of in-text citations, which are clarified by a list headed "References." (These samples have been updated to the most recent documentation styles.) For more on documenting sources, see Chapter 17, "Documenting the Research Essay."

MLA STYLE

1.3 cm (1/2″)

Cody 1

Beatrice Cody

Ms. Bellanca

Writing 125

1 April 99

Politics and Psychology in <u>The Awakening</u>

Title announces focus and scope of essay.

At first glance, Kate Chopin's novel <u>The Awakening</u> (1899) poses no problem to the feminist reader. It is the story of Edna Pontellier, a woman living at the turn of the century who, partly through a half-realized summer romance, discovers that sensual love, art, and individuality mean more to her than marriage or motherhood. When she concludes that there can be no compromise between her awakened inner self and the stifling shell of her outer life as a wife and mother, she drowns herself. In such a summary, Edna appears to be yet another victim of the "Feminine Mystique" described by Betty Friedan in the 1950's, a mind-numbing malaise afflicting the typical American housewife whose husband and society expected her to care for family at the expense of personal freedom and fulfillment. However, it is possible that the events leading to Edna's tragic death were not caused solely by the expectations of a sexist society pre-dating Friedan's model, in which a wife was not only dutiful to but also the "property" of her husband (Culley 117), and a mother not only stayed home but also sacrificed even the "essential" for her children (Chopin <u>Awakening</u> 48). Perhaps Edna's suicide resulted from the torments of her individual psyche, her inability to cope with the patriarchal expectations, which most women in fact were able to tolerate.

Plot summary helps orient readers unfamiliar with novel.

←—2.5 cm—→

←2.5 cm (1″)→

Citation includes title because there are two works by Chopin in Works Cited list.

Clear statement of thesis.

2.5 cm

Cody 2

It is difficult to say how Chopin wished <u>The Awak-</u>

<u>ening</u> to be interpreted. Heroines who explore their own

individuality (with varying degrees of success and failure)

abound in her work (Shinn 358); Chopin herself, though

married, was a rather nontraditional wife who smoked

cigarettes, and, like Edna Pontellier, took walks by herself

(Nissenbaum 333-34). One might think therefore that

Chopin was making a political statement in <u>The Awak-</u>

<u>ening</u> about the position of women in society based on her

own rejection of that position. But aside from slim bio-

graphical evidence and the assertions of some critics such

as Larzer Ziff and Daniel S. Rankin that Chopin sympa-

thized with Edna, we have no way of knowing whether

she regarded this protagonist as a victim of sexist

oppression or simply, to quote her family doctor in the

novel itself, as "a sensitive and highly organized woman

. . . [who] is especially peculiar" (66). It is therefore

necessary to explore the two possibilities, using evidence

from the novel to determine whether Edna Pontellier's

awakening is political or peculiarly personal in nature.

It does not take a deeply feminist awareness to

detect the dominant, controlling stance Edna's husband,

Leonce, assumes in their marriage. Throughout the novel

Chopin documents the resulting injustices, both great and

small, which Edna endures. In one instance Leonce comes

home late at night after Edna has fallen asleep, and, upon

visiting their sleeping children, concludes that both of

them are feverish. He wakes Edna so that she may check

on them, despite her assertion that the children are

perfectly well. He chides her for her "inattention" and "ha-

bitual neglect of the children" (7)--rather than respecting

her ability as their mother to judge the state of their

Cody 3

health or attending to them himself--and reduces her to
tears. She defers to his judgment, looking at the boys as
he had asked, and, finding them entirely healthy, goes

*Ellipsis
(three spaced
periods)
indicate that
words have
been omitted
from sentence.*

out to the porch where "an indescribable oppression . . .
filled her whole being with a vague anguish" (8). Though
in some ways inconsequential, actions such as these
epitomize Leonce Pontellier's attitude toward women and
particularly toward his wife. It is his belief that she has a
certain role and specific duties (those of a woman) which
must be done well--according to his (a man's) standards.
Although he would probably claim to love Edna, he does
not seem to regard her as an autonomous individual; she
is the mother of his children, the hostess of such "callers"
as he deems appropriate (i.e., the ones who will bring him
influence and esteem) (51) and essentially another
decoration in his impeccably furnished house (50). When
Edna's awakening leads her to abandon household chores
in favor of painting, Chopin exposes Leonce's sexism:

*Prose
quotations
longer than
four typed
lines are
indented
2.5 cm from
the left
margin and
double-spaced.*

> Mr. Pontellier had been a rather courteous
> husband so long as he met a certain tacit
> submissiveness in his wife. But her new
> and unexpected line of conduct completely
> bewildered him . . . her absolute disregard
> for her duties as a wife angered him. (57)

*Block
quotations
do not need
quotation
marks. Note
that the
period
precedes the
parenthetic
citation in a
block
quotation.*

It would seem from such evidence that Chopin
intended <u>The Awakening</u> to depict the wrongs that women
suffered at the hands of men in her society. Taking this
cue from Chopin, many twentieth-century critics choose
to view it in a political light. Larzer Ziff, for example,
claims that the novel "rejected the family as the automatic equivalent of feminine self-fulfillment, and on the very
eve of the twentieth century it raised the question of what

Cody 4

woman was to do with the freedom she struggled toward" (175). Winfried Fluck, noting Edna's "preference for semi-conscious states of being . . . sleeping, dreaming, dozing, or the moment of awakening" (435), argues that she is enacting a "a radical retreat from the imprison- ment of all social roles" (435). Marie Fletcher states that "[Edna's] suicide is the last in a series of rebellions which structure her life, give it pathos, and make of the novel . . . an interpretation of the 'new woman'" (172)--"the emerging suffragist/woman professional of the late nineteenth century" (Culley 118). Even in 1899 an anonymous reviewer in the <u>New Orleans Times- Democrat</u> noticed the political implications of the novel, declaring in his own conservative way that

> a woman of twenty-eight, a wife and twice a mother who is pondering upon her relations to the world about her, fails to perceive that the relation of a mother to her children is far more important than the gratification of a passion which experience has taught her is . . . evanes- cent, can hardly be said to be fully awake. (150)

These critics lead us to focus on the socio-political implications of the novel, and on the questions it raises about woman's role and responsibility: when if ever does a woman's personal life become more important than her children? Or, how does Edna embody the emancipated woman? But I believe that more than just the social pressure and politics of the late nineteenth century were acting on Edna. It was the inherent instability of her own psyche, exacerbated by the oppression she suffered as a woman, that drove her to swim out to her death at the end of <u>The Awakening</u>.

Cody 5

*Clear
transition
("despite").*

Despite the feminist undertones discernible in
Chopin's work, a strong sense prevails that Edna's
tragedy is unique, a result of her own psychology, not
only of societal oppression. Throughout the novel Chopin
describes Edna's agitated state of mind and drops hints
about her upbringing and family life before marriage.
Upon piecing all the clues to her personality together one
gets a troubling, stereotypical picture. Edna's widowed
father is a stern colonel from Kentucky who "was perhaps
unaware that he had coerced his own wife into her grave"
(71). From the scenes in which he appears one deduces
that he is harsh and authoritative with his family; the
narrator's comment about his wife implies that perhaps
he was abusive (no doubt psychologically, possibly physically) as well. He gambles compulsively on horseracing
(69), which denotes an addictive personality. He also
makes his own very strong cocktails--"toddies"--which he
drinks almost all day long (71). He retains the appearance
of sobriety, however, which indicates a high tolerance
built up over much time. From this evidence one may
assume that he suffers from alcoholism.

*In this
paragraph
and the next,
Cody develops
her argument
by analyzing
the text of the
novel.*

The rest of Edna's family--two sisters--fit the mold
of the dysfunctional family that a violent, alcoholic parent
tends to create. Her oldest sister seems to be the hyper-
responsible, over-functioning "perfect" daughter. She
served as a surrogate mother to Edna and her younger
sister, and is described by Edna's husband as the only
daughter who "has all the Presbyterianism undiluted"
(66). Edna's younger sister is, predictably, exactly the
opposite: Leonce Pontellier describes her as a "vixen" (66).
She has rebelled against all of the rules and expectations
that the eldest daughter obeys and fulfills. Edna,

Cody 6

the middle child, is hence a curious case. Chopin tells us
that "even as a child she had lived her own small life all
within herself" (15). In such family situations the middle
child is usually rather introverted. Where the two other
siblings strive compulsively either to correct or create
problems, the sibling in the middle passively escapes
from her painful family situation by withdrawing into
herself (Seixas and Youcha 48-49).

Evidence from experts offered in support of thesis.

So far this simplistic but relatively reliable delin-
eation of personalities works for Edna's character. Later
in life she perpetuates the patterns of her dysfunctional
family by marrying a man who almost mirrors her
father in personality; he is simply a workaholic rather
than an alcoholic. Edna gives birth to two children,
"a responsibility which she had blindly assumed" (20)
in her typically passive way. The first time she truly
examines her role in this marriage and indeed in the
world at large occurs on Grand Isle, a resort island where
she and her family are vacationing for the summer.
There she begins to spend a great deal of time with a
young man named Robert Lebrun, and a mutual desire
gradually arises between them. This desire, and the
general sensuality and openness of the Creole community
to which she is exposed, bring about Edna's sexual,
artistic, and individual awakening. Although the reader is
excited and inspired by this awakening in Edna--a woman
learning to shed the fetters of both her oppressive
marriage and society in general--the way it takes control
of her life is disturbingly reminiscent of mental illness.
She becomes infatuated with Robert, devotes an inordinate
amount of time to painting, and seeks out classical music,
which wracks her soul in a torturous ecstasy.

Cody 7

Throughout her awakening, she experiences myriad moods and feelings that she had never felt before in her docile, passive state. Many of these moods manifest themselves in the form of mysterious, troubling voices: "the voices were not soothing that came to her from the darkness and the sky above and the stars" (53); "she felt like one who has entered and lingered within the portals of some forbidden temple in which a thousand muffled voices bade her begone" (84). Behind the veil of metaphor here one can detect hints of an almost schizoid character. Chopin even describes Edna as two selves, which naturally befits a woman undergoing an emotional transformation, but which also denotes a distinctly schizophrenic state of mind: "she was becoming herself and daily casting aside that fictitious self which we assume like a garment with which to appear before the world" (57); "she could only realize that she herself--her present self--was in some way different from the other self" (41). Chopin phrases her descriptions of Edna in such a way that they could in fact describe either a woman gaining her emotional autonomy or a woman losing her mind.

As compelling as I find the suggestion of Edna's insanity, I must admit that her struggle between self-hood and motherhood is one too common to all women to be passed off as the ravings of a madwoman. As to which interpretation she preferred, Chopin offered few clues. For example, in February 1898 Chopin responded to a question, posed by the society page of the <u>St. Louis Post-Dispatch</u>, about the possible motives for a recent rash of suicides among young high-society women. Rather than the pressure of society as a likely motive, she suggests a "highly nervous" disposition (qtd. in Toth 120). Indeed, she asserts that "leadership in society is a business . . .

Parenthetic reference to an indirect source. (The quotation from Chopin appears on page 120 of Toth's book.)

there is nothing about it that I can see that would tend to produce an unhealthy condition of mind. On the contrary, it prevents women from becoming morbid, as they might, had they nothing to occupy their attention when at leisure" (qtd. in Toth 120). Perhaps, then, we are to suppose that a combination of psychic instability and extensive leisure, rather than the oppression of her society, caused Edna to take her own life. And yet this same response in the Post-Dispatch includes a counter-question to the editor: "Business men commit suicide every day, yet we do not say that suicide is epidemic in the business world. Why should we say the feeling is rife among society women, because half a dozen unfortunates, widely separated, take their own lives?" (qtd. in Toth 120). Her implicit criticism of the double standard suggests that Chopin was aware of the politics of gender relations in her own society in addition to the existence of an "hysterical tendency" in some women (qtd. in Toth 120). One cannot therefore discount the possibility that Chopin meant Edna's suicide to be in part a reaction to her society's rigid and limiting expectations of women.

Chopin received such harsh criticism of Edna Pontellier's sexual freedom and attitude toward family that, when The Awakening was published, if not before, she must have had some idea of how controversial the issue of her protagonist's personal freedom really was: her hometown library banned the book, and Chopin herself was banned from a St. Louis arts club (Reuben). Her critics tend to believe that she sympathized unreservedly with her headstrong heroine; but even the retraction she published soon after her novel does not reveal whether she viewed Edna as oppressed or mentally ill. Apparently written for the benefit of her scandalized reviewers, the

Citation of online source. (Source is unpaginated, so citation gives only the author's name.)

Cody 9

retraction ironically relieves Chopin of all responsibility for Edna's "making such a mess of things and working out her own damnation" (159). Again, as in her ambiguous response to the <u>Post-Dispatch</u>, Chopin leaves curious readers unsatisfied, and the motive of Edna's suicide unclear.

It is left to the reader therefore to decide whether Edna is a martyr to a feminist cause--the liberation of the American housewife–or the victim of a psychological disturbance that drives her to suicide. I believe that it is best not to dismiss either possibility. To begin with, one cannot deny that in the nineteenth century few options other than marriage and child-rearing were open to women. These narrow options were the result of a societal structure in which men socially, economically, and sexually dominated women. In the late twentieth century we can look back at Chopin's time and feel confident in condemning this state of affairs, but from contemporary criticism of <u>The Awakening</u> alone, it is clear that this political view was not so widely accepted at the turn of the century. Perhaps Chopin had an unusually clear and untimely insight into what we now consider the sexism of her society, but she chose to condemn it only implicitly by portraying it as a fact of life against which her unbalanced heroine must struggle and perish. As Larzer Ziff puts it, "Edna Pontellier is trapped between her illusions and the condition which society arbitrarily establishes to maintain itself, and she is made to pay" (175). Chopin fused the political and the personal in Edna Pontellier, who, like most women in the world, suffers not only from the pressures of a society run by and for men, but also from her own individual afflictions.

Sources are listed in alphabetical order by author.

"Works Cited" is centred.

Three hyphens indicate another work by the author cited immediately above.

Second and subsequent lines of entry are indented five spaces.

Signed entry in a reference work with alphabetically arranged entries.

Journal article.

Begin Works Cited list on new page. Continue pagination.

Short form of citation. Articles by Culley and Fletcher are reprinted in the Norton edition of The Awakening. The full citation for the volume appears under Chopin.

Online source (paginated).

Online source (unpaginated).

Works Cited

Chopin, Kate. <u>The Awakening</u>. 1899. Ed. Margaret Culley. New York: Norton, 1976.

– – –. "Retraction." 1899. Rpt. in <u>The Awakening</u>. By Kate Chopin. 159.

Culley, Margaret. "The Context of <u>The Awakening</u>." In <u>The Awakening</u>. By Kate Chopin. 17-19.

Fletcher, Marie. "The Southern Woman in the Fiction of Kate Chopin." Rpt. in <u>The Awakening</u>. By Kate Chopin. 170-73.

Fluck, Winfried. "'The American Romance' and the Changing Functions of the Imaginary." <u>New Literary History</u> 27.3 (1996): 415-457. <u>Project Muse</u>. JHU. 1 May 1998. <http://muse:jhu.edu:80/ journals/new literary_history /v27/27.3fluck.html>.

"New Publications." <u>New Orleans Times-Democrat</u>. Rpt. in <u>The Awakening</u>. By Kate Chopin. 150.

Nissenbaum, Stephen. "Chopin, Kate O'Flaherty." <u>Notable American Women</u>. 1971 ed.

Rankin, Daniel S. "Influences Upon the Novel." Rpt. in <u>The Awakening</u>. By Kate Chopin. 163-65.

Reuben, Paul P. "Chapter 6: 1890-1910: Kate Chopin (1851-1904)." <u>PAL: Perspectives in American Literature--A Research and Reference Guide</u>. 20 Mar. 1998. <www.csustan.edu/english/ reuben/pal/chap6/chopin.html>.

Seixas, Judith S., and Geraldine Youcha. <u>Children of Alcoholism: A Survivor's Manual</u>. New York: Harper, 1985.

Shinn, Thelma J. "Kate O'Flaherty Chopin." <u>American Women Writers</u>. 1979 ed.

Toth, Emily. "Kate Chopin on Divine Love and Suicide: Two Rediscovered Articles." <u>American Literature</u>. 63 (1991): 115-21.

Ziff, Larzer. Excerpt from <u>The American 1890s: Life and Times of a Lost Generation</u>, 279-305. Rpt. in <u>The Awakening</u>. By Kate Chopin. 173-75.

APA STYLE

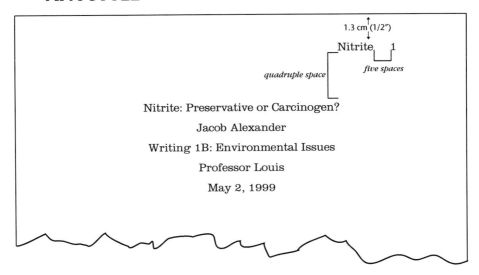

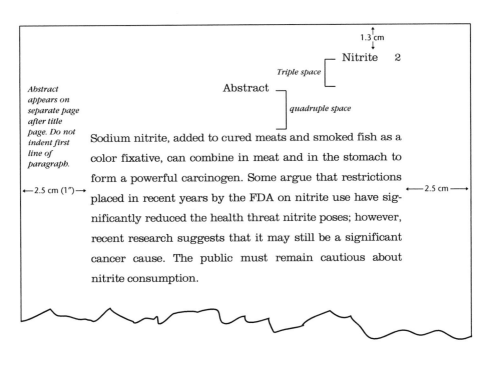

Page number and short form of title appear on every page

Nitrite: Preservative or Carcinogen?

According to Julie Miller Jones, a professor of food and nutrition and the author of *Food Safety*, "average Americans eat their weight in food additives every year" (cited in Murphy, 1996, p. 140). There are approximately fifteen thousand additives currently in use (National Cancer Institute Fact Sheet [NCI], 1996); many of them are known to be dangerous. Of these, nitrites may be among the most hazardous of all. In this country, ham, bacon, corned beef, salami, bologna, lox, and other cold cuts and smoked fish almost invariably contain sodium nitrite. In fact, one-third of the federally inspected meat and fish we consume–more than seven billion pounds of it every year–contains this chemical (Jacobson, 1987, p. 169).

An indirect reference. Alexander consulted Murphy, who quotes Jones.

Just how dangerous are nitrites, and why–if they really are dangerous–does the food industry still use them? Both questions are difficult to answer. Some experts say that nitrites protect consumers from botulism, a deadly disease that can be caused by spoiled food, and that "the benefits of nitrite additives outweigh the risks" (Edlefsen & Brewer, no date). Others argue that the dangers nitrites once posed have been significantly reduced–even eliminated–by restrictions placed on their use by the Food and Drug Administration. Nevertheless, the evidence has long suggested that nitrites are linked to stomach cancer; recent research has linked nitrites to leukemia and brain tumors as well (Warrick, 1994; Legator & Daniel, 1995). Perhaps the only certain conclusions one can reach are that the effects of nitrite on the human body are still to some degree uncertain--and that to protect themselves, consumers must be cautious and informed.

Citation gives author because Jacobson is not named in the text. Note format: author, date of publication, and page number preceded by a "p."

A reference to two sources. The writer is summarizing whole works, so no page numbers are given.

Clear statement of thesis.

Nitrite   4

That nitrite is a poison has been clear for almost three decades. In 1974, Jacqueline Verrett, who worked for the FDA for fifteen years, and Jean Carper reported on several instances of people poisoned by accidental overdoses of nitrites in cured meats:

Quotations of more than forty words must be indented 2.5 cm from the left margin.

> In Buffalo, New York, six persons were hospitalized with "cardiovascular collapse" after they ate blood sausage which contained excessive amounts of nitrites. . . . In New Jersey, two persons died and many others were critically poisoned after eating fish illegally loaded with nitrites. In New Orleans, ten youngsters between the ages of one and a half and five became seriously ill . . . after eating wieners or bologna overnitrited by a local meat-processing firm; one wiener that was obtained later from the plant was found to contain a whopping 6,570 parts per million. In Florida, a three-year-old boy died after eating hot dogs with three times greater nitrite concentration than the government allows. (pp. 138-139)

The chemical has the unusual and difficult-to-replace quality of keeping meat a fresh-looking pink throughout the cooking, curing, and storage process (Assembly of Life Science, 1982, p. 3). The nitrous acid from the nitrite combines with the hemoglobin in the blood of the meat, fixing its red color so that the meat does not turn the tired brown or gray natural to cured meats.

Unfortunately, it does much the same thing in humans. Although most of the nitrite passes through the body unchanged, a small amount is released into the bloodstream. This combines with the hemoglobin in the blood to form a pigment called methemoglobin, which cannot carry oxygen. If enough oxygen is incapacitated, a person dies. The allowable amount of nitrite in a quarter pound of meat has the potential to incapacitate between 1.4 and 5.7 percent of the hemoglobin in an average-sized adult (Verrett & Carper, 1974, pp. 138-39). One of the problems with nitrite poisoning is that infants under a year, because of the quantity and makeup of their blood, are especially susceptible to it.

If the consumer of nitrite isn't acutely poisoned (and granted, such poisonings are rare), his or her blood soon returns to normal and this particular danger passes: the chemical, however, has long-term effects, as research conducted in the 1970s clearly established. Nitrite can cause headaches in people who are especially sensitive to it, an upsetting symptom considering that in rats who ate it regularly for a period of time it has produced lasting "epileptic like" changes in the brain-- abnormalities which showed up when the rats were fed only a little more than an American fond of cured meats might eat (Wellford, 1973, p. 173). Experiments with chickens, cattle, sheep, and rats have shown that nitrite, when administered for several days, inhibits the ability of the liver to store vitamin A and carotene (Hunter, 172, p. 90). And finally, Nobel laureate Joshua Lederberg points out that, in microorganisms, nitrite enters the DNA. "If it does the same thing in humans," he says, "it will cause mutant genes." Geneticist Bruce Ames adds, "If out of one million people, one person's genes are mutant, that's a serious problem. . . . If we're filling ourselves now with mutant genes, they're going to be around for generations" (cited in Zwerdling, 1971, pp. 34-35).

By far the most alarming characteristic of nitrite,

Nitrite   6

however, is that in test tubes, in meats themselves, in animal stomachs, and in human stomachs--wherever a mildly acidic solution is present--it can combine with amines to form nitrosamines. And nitrosamines are carcinogens. Even the food industry and the agencies responsible for allowing the use of nitrite in foods admit that nitrosamines cause cancer. Edlefsen and Brewer, writing recently for the National Food Safety Database, note that "over 90 percent of the more than 300 known nitrosamines in foods have been shown to cause cancer in laboratory animals." They continue: "No case of human cancer has been shown to result from exposure to nitrosamines," but they acknowledge that "indirect evidence indicates that humans would be susceptible" (no date).

An online source. (The authors and title are named in the sentence; the source has no date or page numbers.)

It is important to note that nitrite alone, when fed to rats on an otherwise controlled diet, does not induce cancer. It must first combine with amines to form nitrosamines. Considering, however, that the human stomach has the kind of acidic solution in which amines and nitrites readily combine, and considering as well that amines are present in beer, wine, cereals, tea, fish, cigarette smoke, and a long list of drugs including antihistamines, tranquilizers, and even oral contraceptives, it is hardly surprising to find that nitrosamines have been found in human stomachs.

When animals are fed amines in combination with nitrite, they developed cancer with a statistical consistency that is frightening, even to scientists. Verrett and Carper report that after feeding animals 250 parts per million (ppm) of nitrites and amines, William Lijinsky, a scientist at Oak Ridge National Laboratory,

found malignant tumors in 100 percent of the test animals within six months. . . . "Unheard

Nitrite   7

of," he says. . . . "You'd usually expect to find
50 percent at the most. And the cancers are all
over the place–in the brain, lung, pancreas,
stomach, liver, adrenals, intestines. We open
up the animals and they are a bloody mess."
[He] believes that nitrosamines, because of
their incredible versatility in inciting cancer,
may be the key to an explanation for the mass
production of cancer in seemingly dissimilar
populations. In other words, nitrosamines
may be a common factor in cancer that has
been haunting us all these years. (1974, p. 136)

Verrett and Carper (1974, pp. 43-46) list still more
damning evidence. Nitrosamines have caused cancer in
rats, hamsters, mice, guinea pigs, dogs, and monkeys. It
has been proven that nitrosamines of over a hundred
kinds cause cancer. Nitrosamines have been shown to
pass through the placenta from the mother to cause
cancer in the offspring. Even the lowest levels of
nitrosamines ever tested have produced cancer in
animals. When animals are fed nitrite and amines
separately over a period of time, they develop cancers
of the same kind and at the same frequency as animals
fed the corresponding nitrosamines already formed.

To address these problems (and in response to
intense public concern), in 1978, the FDA ruled that a
reducing agent, such as ascorbic acid, must be added
to products containing nitrite; the reducing agent
inhibits the formation of nitrosamines (Edlefsen &
Brewer, no date). And in the last two decades, at least, the
furor over nitrite seems as a consequence to have abated.
In fact, an anonymous Internet posting, dated August
1997, entitled "Nitrite: Keeping Food Safe" celebrates

*This online
source did not
provide a date
of publication.*

Nitrite   8

nitrite as a "naturally-derived" substance that, according
to the American Academy of Science, has never been
found to cause cancer. On the contrary, the anonymous
author states, nitrite does many good things for
consumers; it may even help to fight cancer: "it
safeguards cured meats against the most deadly
foodborne bacterium known to man" and helps with
"promoting blood clotting, healing wounds and burns
and boosting immune function to kill tumor cells."

No citation is
given here
because all
information is
included in
the sentence
itself.

Other experts are less certain that reducing agents
have entirely solved the nitrosamine problem. The
Consumer's Dictionary of Food Additives notes that one
common agent, sodium ascorbate, which is added to the
brine in which bacon is cured, "offers only a partial
barrier because ascorbate is soluble in fatty tissues"
(Winter, 1994, p. 282). But in the wake of several studies
reported in the March 1993 *Cancer Causes and Control*,
it is unclear that "inhibiting" the formation of
nitrosamines actually makes nitrites safe to consume.

The Los Angeles Times reports that one of these
studies, conducted by John Peters, an epidemiologist at
USC, found that "children who eat more than 12 hot dogs
per month have nine times the normal risk of developing
childhood leukemia" (Warrick, 1994). Interestingly,
the study was focused not on nitrites, but rather on
electromagnetic fields. "'Dietary exposure to processed or
cured meats was part of a little side questionnaire to our
study on (electro)magnetic fields,'" Peters said. "'We were
as surprised as anyone by the hot dogs findings. . . . It was
the biggest risk for anything we saw in the study–about
four times the risk for EMF's'" (cited in Warrick, 1994).

An indirect
reference.

In another of these recent studies, hot dogs were
linked to brain tumors: researchers found that "children

born to mothers who ate at least one hot dog per week
while pregnant have twice the risk of developing brain
tumors, as do children whose fathers ate too many hot
dogs before conception" (Warrick, 1994). Dr. M. Legator
and Amanda Daniel comment that "these studies confirm
thirty years worth of scientific research on the cancer
causing properties of preserved meats and fish" (1995).

The question, then, is why nitrite continues to be
used in so much of the meat Americans consume.
Although nitrite adds a small amount to flavor, it is used
primarily for cosmetic purposes. Food producers are of
course also quick to point out that nitrite keeps people
safe from botulinum in cured meats, an argument to
which the public may be particularly susceptible because
of a number of recent and serious food scares.
Nevertheless, some evidence suggests that the protection
nitrite offers is both unnecessary and ineffective.

Michael Jacobson explains the preservative action
of nitrite:

> Nitrite makes botulinum spores sensitive to
> heat. When foods are treated with nitrite and
> then heated, any botulinum spores that may
> be present are killed. In the absence of nitrite,
> spores can be inactivated only at temperatures
> that ruin the meat products. . . . Nitrite's
> preservative action is particularly important
> in foods that are not cooked after they leave
> the factory, such as ham, because these offer
> an oxygen-free environment, the kind in
> which botulinum can grow. The toxin does
> not pose a danger in foods that are always
> well cooked, such as bacon, because the toxin
> would be destroyed in cooking.

Nitrite   10

> Laboratory studies demonstrate clearly
> that nitrite can kill botulinum, but whether it
> actually does in commercially processed meat
> has been called into question. Frequently, the
> levels used may be too low to do anything but
> contribute to the color. (1987, p. 165)

Bratwurst and breakfast sausage are manufactured now
without nitrite because they don't need to be colored pink;
bacon is always cooked thoroughly enough to kill off
any botulinum spores present. Certainly there are other
ways of dealing with botulism. High or low temperature
prevents botulism. What nitrite undoubtedly does lower,
however, is the level of care and sanitation necessary in
handling meat.

Clearly, the use of nitrite adds immeasurably to the
profit-making potential of the meat industry, but why
does the federal government allow this health hazard in
our food? In the first place, nitrite and nitrate have been
used for so long that it is hard for lawmakers to get past
their instinctive reaction, "But that's the way we've
always done it." Indeed, the Romans used saltpeter, a
nitrate, to keep meat and, as early as 1899, scientists
discovered that the nitrate breaks down into nitrite and
that it is the nitrite which actually preserves the red color

Note that a reference to a single page is preceded by "p." and that a reference to two or more pages is preceded by "pp."

in meats (Jacobson, 1987, pp. 164-65). Thus, by the time
the U.S. Department of Agriculture and the Food and
Drug Administration got into the business of regulating
food, they tended to accept nitrite and nitrate as givens.

A second reason for the inadequacy of regulation is
that government mechanisms for protecting the consumer
are full of curious loopholes. In 1958 Congress passed the
Food Additive Amendment, including the Delaney Clause,
which clearly states that additives should be banned if

they induce cancer in laboratory animals. Unfortunately, however, the amendment does not apply to additives that were in use before it was passed, so, since nitrite and nitrate had already been in use for a long time, they were automatically included on the list of chemicals "Generally Recognized as Safe." To complicate matters further, nitrite in meat is regulated by the USDA, while nitrite in fish is under the jurisdiction of the FDA. And these agencies generally leave it to industry--the profit-maker-- to establish whether or not an additive is safe. The final irony in this list of governmental errors is that the FDA depends heavily, for "independent" research and advice, on the food committees of the National Academy of Sciences which Daniel Zwerdling claims are "like a Who's

Because the author is named in the sentence, the citation gives only the date and page number.

Who of the food and chemical industry" (1971, p. 34). (This, of course, is the organization cited in the anonymous web posting quoted above, the organization that holds that "nitrite levels in cured meat have not been linked to the development of human cancers.")

Clearly, consumers need to be informed; clearly, it is unwise to count on government agencies for protection against the dangers food additives may pose. Some experts continue to argue that nitrite is safe enough; Edelfson and Brewer, for example, cite a 1992 study by J. M. Jones that suggests that drinking beer exposes a consumer to more nitrite than does eating bacon—and that new car interiors are a significant source of nitrite as well.[1] Others recommend caution. One expert advises: "If you must eat nitrite-laced meats, include a food or drink high in vitamin C at the same time--for example,

An explanatory footnote.

[1]Presumably the exposure here results from contact, not ingestion.

Nitrite   12

orange juice, grapefruit juice, cranberry juice, or lettuce" (Winter, 1994, p. 282). And, in fact, a study by a committee organized by the National Academy of Science strongly implies (Assembly, 1982, p. 12) that the government should develop a safe alternative to nitrites.

In the meantime, the chemical additive industry doesn't seem very worried that alternatives, such as biopreservatives, will pose a threat to its profits. An industry publication, "Chemical Marketing Reporter," recently reassured its readers by announcing that "around 82.5 million pounds of preservatives, valued at $133 million, were consumed in the US in 1991." The report also stated that "though the trend toward phasing out controversial preservatives like sulfites, nitrates and nitrites continues, natural substitutes remain expensive and often less than effective, making biopreservatives a distant threat" (Tollefson, 1995).

References

References begin on new page.

Assembly of Life Science. (1982). *Alternatives to the current use of nitrite in food*. Washington: National Academy Press.

Second and subsequent lines of entries are indented five spaces.

Edlefsen, M. & Brewer, M. S. (n.d.). *The national food safety database*. Nitrates/Nitrites. Retrieved May 6, 1998 from: www.foodsafety.org/il/il089.htm

A book. Capitalize only the first word in book and article titles.

Hunter, B. T. (1972). *Fact/book on food additives and your health*. New Canaan, Conn.: Keats.

Jacobson, M. F. (1987). *Eater's digest*. Washington: Center for Science in the Public Interest.

An online version of a printed newspaper article.

Legator, M. & Daniel, A. Reproductive systems can be harmed by toxic exposure. *Galveston County Daily News*. Retrieved May 6, 1998 from: www.utmb.edu/toxics/newsp.htm#canen

Capitalize the initial letter of all important words in newspaper and periodical titles.

Murphy, K. (1996, May 6). Do food additives subtract from health? *Business Week* [online], p. 140. Retrieved July 30, 1998 from: Lexis-Nexis.

An online version of a printed magazine article. Note that the year precedes the month and date in the parentheses following the author.

National Cancer Institute. (1996, June). *NCI fact sheet*. Food additives. Retrieved May 4, 1998 from: http://nisc8a.upenn.edu/pdghtml/6/eng/ 600037.html

Tollefson, C. (1995, May 29). Stability preserved; preservatives; food additives '95. *Chemical Marketing Reporter* 247(22), [online], p. SR28. Retrieved May 6, 1998 from Lexis-Nexis.

A book by two authors. Note use of ampersand between authors' names.

Verritt, J. & Carper, J. (1974). *Eating may be hazardous to your health*. New York: Simon and Schuster.

Warrick, P. (1994, June 8). A frank discussion. *Los Angeles Times* [online], p. E1. Retrieved May 6, 1998 from Lexis-Nexis.

Winter, R. (1994). *A consumer's dictionary of food additives* (Updated Fourth Edition). New York. Crown.

Use "p." or "pp." when citing books or newspapers, but not periodicals. Ramparts is a periodical.

Zwerdling, D. (1971, June). Food pollution. *Ramparts* 9(11), 31-37, 53-54.

Exercises

1. If you have trouble finding material in the library, don't hesitate to ask a librarian for assistance. But you will soon learn to solve many of the most common problems yourself. Here are a few.

   a. You want to do some research for a paper on the environmental impact of gold mining in Canada. You perform a keyword search of the online catalogue, entering the phrase "gold mines and mining and Canada and environmental impact" at the prompt, and find no citations. When you try a more general search by entering the phrase "gold mines and mining and Canada" at the prompt, you find 171 entries. How do you go about limiting your search to find other relevant books on the subject?

   b. You want to do a paper on Thomas King's short stories, and the online catalogue lists several relevant books, but when you check the stacks you find none of these books is on the shelf. What might you do next, short of abandoning the topic or going to another library?

   c. You need reviews of a film released a few months ago. How might you use electronic resources to locate them?

   d. You are looking for an issue of a journal published a few months ago. It is not on the shelf with the current issues, and it is not on the shelf with the bound volumes. Where is it? What might you do next to locate the article you want?

   e. You want to write a paper on bilingual education, or, more exactly, on bilingual education in Nova Scotia. How do you locate books on this subject in the online catalogue? To locate articles on this subject, what indexes might you consult?

2. Read the following paragraph, by Mark Edmundson, from his book *Nightmare on Main Street: Angels, Sadomasochism, and the Culture of the Gothic* (1997).

   Gothic is the art of haunting, and in two senses. Gothic shows time and again that life, even at its most ostensibly innocent, is possessed, that the present is in thrall to the past. All are guilty. All must, in time, pay up. And Gothic also sets out to haunt its audience, possess them so they can think of nothing else. They have to read it—or see it—again and again to achieve some peace. (Repetition, Freud claimed, is the way we attempt to master a trauma.) For a work to be Gothic, the critic Chris Baldick says, it "should combine a fearful sense of inheritance in time with a claustrophobic sense of enclosure in space, these two dimensions reinforcing one another to produce an impression of sickening descent into disintegration." When a culture teems with such work and cannot produce persuasive alternatives, its prognosis is anything but favorable.

   a. Write a paragraph in which you imitate someone who is plagiarizing the passage.

   b. Write a paragraph that acknowledges the author but nevertheless illustrates plagiarism.

   c. Write a paragraph in which you quote from and acknowledge Edmundson, but distort his point or otherwise misrepresent what he says. (The paragraph need not contain plagiarism.)

   d. Write a paragraph in which you make honest use of Edmundson's material.

CHAPTER

17

Documenting the Research Essay

This chapter provides instruction for documenting research essays using the two most common academic styles. Remember that when you use secondary sources, you must document those sources. If your instructor does not make it clear when handing out the assignment, make sure you ask which style is preferred in that discipline.

One purpose of documentation is to enable your readers to retrace your steps, to find your sources, and to read what you read—whether you read it in the library, on the Internet, or in today's newspaper. To make this possible, you must give your readers enough information to locate and identify each source you cite. For printed sources, this information generally includes:

- the author
- the title
- the publisher
- the date and place of publication
- page number(s).

And for electronic sources, this information includes (at minimum):

- the site address
- the date on which you accessed the information.

The way this information is presented varies from discipline to discipline: sociologists, for example, present the date of publication more prominently than do historians; at the end of a research work, engineers usually list their sources by number (in order of their appearance in the text) while literary critics list sources alphabetically by author name. In the following pages we discuss in detail two systems of documentation: the Modern Language Association (or MLA) style is often used in the humanities; and the American Psychological Association (or APA) style is frequently used in the social sciences, education, and business.

MLA FORMAT

Citations within the Text

Brief parenthetic citations within the body of the essay are made clear by a list of your sources, titled Works Cited, appended to the essay. Thus, an item in your list of Works Cited will clarify a sentence in your essay like this one:

> According to Angeline Goreau, Aphra Behn in her novels continually contradicts "the personal politics she had defended from the outset of her career as a writer" (252).

This citation means that the words inside the quotation marks appear on page 252 of a source written by Goreau which will be listed in Works Cited. More often than not the parenthetic citation (page reference) appears at the end of a sentence, as in the example just given, but it can appear elsewhere in the sentence. Its position will depend in part on your ear, and in part on the requirement that you point clearly to the place where your source's idea ends and your own point begins. In the following example, the idea that follows the parenthetic citation is not Gardiner's, but the writer's own.

> Judith Kegan Gardiner, on the other hand, acknowledges that Behn's work "displays its conflicts with patriarchal authority" (215), conflicts that appear most notably in the third volume of <u>Love Letters</u>.

Seven points must be made about these citations:

1. Quotation marks. The closing quotation mark appears after the last word of the quotation, *not* after the parenthetic citation. Since the citation is not part of the quotation, the citation is not included within the quotation marks.

2. Omission of words (ellipsis). If the quoted words are obviously a complete phrase, as in the example above, you do not need to indicate by ellipsis (three spaced periods) that you are omitting material before or after the quotation, but if the quotation is longer than a phrase and is not a complete sentence, you must indicate that you are omitting material. If you are omitting material from the beginning of the sentence, after the opening quotation mark insert three spaced periods, and then give the quotation. If you are omitting material from the end of the sentence, insert three spaced periods after the quoted words, or four periods if you are ending your sentence, one immediately after the last quoted word, the last three spaced, and then close with a quotation mark. (For more on ellipses, see pages 317 and 479.)

3. Addition of words. On occasion, you will need to add a word or two to a quotation in order to clarify its meaning or to make it flow with the rest of the sentence. If you must make such an addition—and such additions should be kept to a minimum because they can be distracting—enclose the word or words in square brackets, *not* parentheses. If the quotation contains a misspelling or other error, transcribe it as it appears in the source, and insert the word "*sic*" (Latin for "thus," as in "thus the word appears in the source; it's not *my* error") in italics and in square brackets, thus: [*sic*].

4. Punctuation with parenthetic citations. Look again at the two examples just given. Notice that if you follow a quotation with a parenthetic citation, any necessary period, semicolon, or comma *follows* the parenthetic citation. In the first example, a period follows the citation; in the second, a comma. In the next example, notice that the comma follows the citation.

Johnson insists that "these poems can be interpreted as Tory

propaganda" (72), but his brief analysis is not persuasive.

If, however, the quotation itself uses a question mark or an exclamation mark, this mark of punctuation appears *within* the closing quotation mark; even so, a period follows the parenthetic citation.

Jenkins-Smith is the only one to suggest doubt: "How can we accept

such a superficial reading of these works?" (178). He therefore rejects the

entire argument.

5. Two or more titles by one author. If your list of Works Cited includes more than one work by an author, you will have to give additional information (either in your sentence or within the parentheses) to indicate *which* of the titles you mean. We will go into this further on page 349.

6. Long (or "block") quotations. We have been talking about short quotations, which are not set off but are embedded within your own sentences with quotation marks to indicate quoted words. Long quotations, usually defined as more than four prose lines of type in your paper, are set off, as in the example below *without* quotation marks.

Janet Todd explains Behn's reverence for the Stuart monarchy:

> She was a passionate supporter of both Charles II and James II
>
> as not simply rulers but as sacred majesties, god-kings on earth,
>
> whose private failings in no way detracted from their high
>
> office. . . . For her, royalty was not patriarchal anachronism as
>
> it would be for liberated women writers a hundred years on, but
>
> a mystical state. (73)

While it is true that Behn expressed "passionate support" in a poem

written in praise of James II (Todd 73), her novels suggest that her

attitude toward the Stuarts was much more complicated.

In introducing a long quotation, keep in mind that a reader will have trouble reading a sentence that consists of a lead-in, a long quotation, and then a continuation of your own sentence. It is better to have a short lead-in ("Janet Todd explains Behn's reverence for the Stuart monarchy"), and then set off a long quotation that is a complete sentence or group of sentences and therefore ends with a period. The quotation that is set off begins on a new line, is double-spaced and indented ten spaces (2.5 cm or one inch) from the left margin, and, we repeat, is *not* enclosed within quotation marks. Put a period at the end of the quotation (since the quotation is a complete sentence or group of sentences and is not embedded within a longer sentence of your own), hit the space bar twice, and give the citation in parentheses on the same line. Do *not* put a period after the parenthetic citation that follows a long quotation.

    7. Citing a summary or a paraphrase. Even if you do not quote a source directly, but use its point in a paraphrase or a summary, you will give a citation:

> Goreau notes that Behn participated in public life and in politics not
>
> only as a writer: in the 1660s she went to Antwerp as a spy for Charles II
>
> (89-90).

The basic point, then, is that the system of in-text citation gives the documentation parenthetically. Notice that in all but one of the previous examples the author's name is given in the text (rather than within the parenthetic citation). But there are several other ways of giving the citation, and we shall now look at them.

Author and Page Number in Parenthetic Citation

> Heroines who explore their own individuality (with varying degrees of
>
> success and failure) abound in Chopin's work (Shinn 358).

It does not matter whether you summarize (as in this example) or quote directly; the parenthetic citation means that your source is page 358 of a work by Shinn, listed in Works Cited, at the end of your essay. Notice there is no comma between the author's name and the page number.

Title and Page Number in Parentheses

If, as we mentioned earlier, your list of Works Cited includes two or more titles by the same author, you cannot in the text simply give a name and a page reference; the reader would not know to which of the titles you are referring. Let's assume that Works Cited includes two items by Larzer Ziff. If in a sentence in your essay you do not specify one title—that is, if you do not say something like, "For example, Larzer Ziff, in *The American 1890's,* claims . . ."—you will have to give the title in a shortened form in the parenthetic citation:

> Larzer Ziff, for example, claims that the novel "rejected the family as
>
> the automatic equivalent of feminine self-fulfillment . . ." (<u>American</u> 175).

Notice in this example that *American* is a short title for Ziff's book *The American 1890's: Life and Times of a Lost Generation.* The full title is given in Works Cited, as is the title of another work by Ziff, but the short title in the parenthetic citation is enough to direct the reader to page 175 of the correct source in Works Cited.

Notice also that, when a short title and a page reference are given in parentheses, a comma is *not* used after the title.

Author, Title, and Page Number in Parentheses

We have just seen that if Works Cited includes two or more works by an author, and if in your lead-in you do not specify which work you are at the moment making use of, you will have to give the title as well as the page number in parentheses. Similarly, if for some reason you do not in your lead-in mention the name of the author, you will have to add this bit of information to the parenthetic citation, thus:

> At least one critic has claimed that the novel "rejected the family as the
>
> automatic equivalent of feminine self-fulfillment . . ." (Ziff, <u>American</u> 175).

Notice that, as in the previous example, a comma does *not* separate the title from the page reference; but notice, too, that a comma *does* separate the author's name from the title. (Don't ask us why; ask the Modern Language Association. Or just obey orders.)

A Government Document or a Work of Corporate Authorship

Treat the issuing body as the author. Thus, you will probably write something like this:

> The Commission on Food Control, in <u>Food Resources Today</u>, concludes
>
> that there is no danger (36-37).

A Work by Two or More Authors

If a work is by *two authors,* give the names of both, either in the parenthetic citation (the first example below) or in a lead-in (the second example):

> Where the two other siblings strive compulsively either to correct or
>
> create problems, the sibling in the middle passively escapes from her painful
>
> family situation by withdrawing into herself (Seixas and Youcha 48-49).

or

> Seixas and Youcha note that where the two other siblings strive
>
> compulsively either to correct or create problems, the sibling in the middle
>
> passively escapes from her painful family situation by withdrawing into
>
> herself (48-49).

If there are more than *three authors,* give the last name of the first author, followed by "et al." (an abbreviation for *et alii,* Latin for "and others"), thus:

Gardner et al. found that . . .

or

Sometimes even higher levels are found (Gardner et al. 83).

Parenthetic Citation of an Indirect Source (That Is, Material That Was Quoted or Summarized in the Source You Used)

Suppose you are reading a book by Jones, and she quotes Smith, and you wish to use Smith's material. Your lead-in will be to Smith but your citation will be to Jones—the source you are using. You will have to make it clear that you are quoting not Jones but Smith, and so your parenthetic citation will look like this:

(qtd. in Jones 84-85)

Parenthetic Citation of Two or More Works

In microorganisms, nitrite enters the blood (Hervey 72; Lederer 195).

Note that a semicolon followed by a space separates the two sources.

A Work in More Than One Volume

This is a bit tricky.

1. If you have used only one volume, in Works Cited you will specify the volume, and so in your parenthetic in-text citation you will need to give only a page number—as illustrated by most of the examples that we have been giving.
2. If you have used more than one volume, your parenthetic citation will have to specify the volume as well as the page, thus:

   Landsdale points out that nitrite combines with hemoglobin to

   form a pigment which cannot carry oxygen (2: 370).

   The reference is to page 370 of volume 2 of a work by Landsdale.
3. If, however, you are citing not a page but an entire volume—let's say volume 2—your parenthetic citation would be

   (vol. 2)

   Or, if you did not name the author in your lead-in, it would be

   (Landsdale, vol. 2)

Notice that

- in citing a volume and page, the volume number, like the page number, is given in Arabic (not Roman) numerals;
- the volume number is followed by a colon, then a space, then the page number;

- abbreviations such as "vol." and "p." and "pg." are *not* used, except when citing a volume number without a page number, as illustrated in the last two examples.

An Anonymous Work

For an anonymous work, give the title in your lead-in, or give it in a shortened form in your parenthetic citation:

Official Guide to Food Standards includes a statistical table on

nitrates (362).

or

A statistical table on nitrates is available (Official Guide 362).

But double-check to make sure that the work is truly anonymous. Some encyclopedias, for example, give the authors' names. If initials follow the article, these are the initials of the author's name. Check the alphabetic list of authors given at the front or at the back of the encyclopedia.

A Literary Work

You will specify the edition of a literary work in Works Cited—let's say an edition of Conrad's *Heart of Darkness* with a preface by Albert Guerard, or Alvin Kernan's edition of *Othello*. But because classic works of literature are widely available, and your reader may have at hand an edition different from the one that you have read, it is customary to use the following forms.

1. A novel. In parentheses give the page number of the edition you specify in Works Cited, followed by a semicolon, a space, and helpful additional information, thus:

(181; ch. 6)

or

(272; part 1, ch. 7).

2. A play. Most instructors want the act, scene, and (if the lines are numbered) the line numbers, rather than a page reference. Thus,

(2.4.18-23)

would refer to lines 18–23 of the fourth scene of the second act.

If you are quoting a few words within a sentence of your own, immediately after closing the brief quotation give the citation (enclosed within parentheses), and, if your sentence ends with the quotation, put the period after the closing parenthesis.

That Macbeth fully understands that killing Duncan is not a manly act but a villainous one is clear from his words to Lady Macbeth: "I dare do all that may become a man" (1.7.46). Moreover, even though he goes on to kill Duncan, he does not go on to deceive himself into thinking that his act was noble.

If, however, your sentence continues beyond the citation, after the parenthetic citation put whatever punctuation may be necessary (for instance, a comma may be needed), complete your sentence, and end it with a period.

This is clear from his words, "I dare do all that may become a man" (1.7.46), and he never loses his awareness of true manliness.

3. A poem. Preferences vary, and you cannot go wrong in citing the page, but for a poem longer than, say, a sonnet (fourteen lines), most instructors find it useful if students cite the line numbers, in parentheses, after the quotations. In your first use, preface the numerals with "line" or "lines" (not in quotation marks, of course); in subsequent citations simply give the numerals. For very long poems that are divided into books, such as Homer's *Odyssey,* give the page, a semicolon, a space, the book number, and the line number(s). The following example refers to page 327 of a title listed in Works Cited; it goes on to indicate that the passage occurs in the ninth book of the poem, lines 130–35.

(327; 9.130-35)

Long quotations (more than three lines of poetry) are indented ten spaces (2.5 cm). As we explained on pages 348–49, if you give a long quotation, try to give one that can correctly be concluded with a period. After the period, hit the space bar twice, and then, on the same line, give the citation in parentheses.

A Personal Interview

Probably you will not need a parenthetic citation, because you will say something like

Cyril Jackson, in an interview, said . . .

or

According to Cyril Jackson, . . .

and when your readers turn to Works Cited, they will see that Jackson is listed, along with the date of the interview. But if you do not mention the source's name in the lead-in, you will have to give it in the parentheses, thus:

It has been estimated that chemical additives earn the drug companies well over five hundred million dollars annually (Jackson).

A Lecture

If your research essay includes a distinctive phrase, idea, or piece of information from a class lecture or discussion, you will want to give the speaker credit for it. If you give a signal phrase, the parenthetic citation should include only the date of the lecture; if you do not give a signal phrase, include the speaker's name, followed by a comma, followed by the date. For example:

> (Stimpson, Sept. 20, 1999)

(The entry for the lecture on the Works Cited list will contain the title of the lecture—if there is one—and the place where it was given.)

Electronic Sources

Follow the format for print sources. In some cases, page numbers will be available; in others, paragraphs will be numbered; in still others, no number will be given. Use what you have, indicating the author's name or title where necessary, as determined by context. When giving paragraph numbers, use the abbreviation "pars." (Use a comma to separate the abbreviation from the author's name or title.)

> Reuters reported internationally that a pie was thrown in Jean
>
> Chrétien's face during the prime minister's visit to Charlottetown (pars. 1–2).

A Note on Footnotes in an Essay Using Parenthetic Citations

There are two reasons for using footnotes in an essay that chiefly uses parenthetic citations.

1. In a research paper you will of course draw on many sources, but in other kinds of papers you may be using only one source, and yet within the paper you may often want to specify a reference to a page or (for poetry) to a line number, or (for a play) to an act, scene, and line number. In such a case, to append a page headed Work Cited, with a single title, is silly; it is better to use a single footnote when you first allude to the source. Such a note can run something like this:

> [1]All references are to Mary Shelley, <u>Frankenstein</u>, afterword by Harold
>
> Bloom (New York: Signet, 1965).

Here's another example of this sort of footnote:

> [2]All experiments described in this paper were performed in January
>
> 1999 in the laboratory of Dr. Jan Pechenik, of Tufts University.

2. Footnotes can also be used in another way in a paper that documents sources by giving parenthetic citations. If you want to include some material that might seem intrusive in the body of the essay, you may relegate it to a footnote. For example, in a footnote you might translate a quotation given in a foreign language, or in a footnote you might write a paragraph in which you offer an amplification of some point. By putting the amplification in a footnote you are signalling to the reader that it is dispensable or tangential; it is, so to speak, thrown in as something extra, something relevant but not essential to your argument.

A raised Arabic numeral indicates in the body of your text that you are adding a footnote at this point. (The "insert" function of your word processing program will insert both the raised numeral and the text of your footnote in the appropriate places in your essay; simply click "insert" and "footnote" at the point in the text where you want the footnote to appear, and follow the program's instructions.)

Joachim Jeremias's The Parables of Jesus is probably the best example

of this sort of book.[1]

Usually the number is put at the end of a sentence, immediately after the period, but put it in earlier if clarity requires you to do so.

Helen Cam[1] as well as many lesser historians held this view.

The List of Works Cited

Your parenthetic documentation consists of references that become meaningful when the reader consults your list of Works Cited. We give sample entries below, but see also the list of Works Cited at the end of a student's documented paper, on page 332.

The list of Works Cited continues the pagination of the essay; if the last page of text is 10, then the list begins on page 11. Your last name and the page number or just the page number will appear in the upper-right corner, 1.3 cm (half an inch) from the top of the sheet. Next, type "Works Cited," centred, 2.5 cm (one inch) from the top, then double-space and type the first entry. Here are the governing conventions.

Alphabetic Order

1. Arrange the list alphabetically by author, with the author's last name first.
2. List an anonymous work alphabetically under the first word of the title, or under the second word if the first word is *A, An,* or *The,* or a foreign equivalent.
3. If your list includes two or more works by one author, the work whose title comes earlier in the alphabet precedes the work whose title comes later in the alphabet. Use three hyphens (- - -) in place of the author's name in the second entry.

Form on the Page

1. Begin each entry flush with the left margin, but if an entry runs to more than one line, indent five spaces for each succeeding line of the entry.
2. Double-space each entry, and double-space between entries.

Here is the basic MLA style for types of sources:

Books

Author, Ann, and Ben Author. Title of Book. Place of Publication: Publisher, date.

Articles

Author, Ann. "Title of Article." <u>Title of Journal</u> vol #. issue # (date): page–page.

Internet Sites

Author, Ann. "Title of Piece." Date posted. Publication information if there is any. Source if there is one. Date you accessed the site <address of the Web site>.

From here on, things get complicated. Over the next few pages, we provide more detail on MLA style and go through different source types in detail. We begin with books and then move on to other types of sources.

Books

The Author's Name

Note that the last name is given first, but otherwise the name is given as on the title page. Do not substitute initials for names written out on the title page.

If your list includes two or more works by an author, the author's name is not repeated for the second title, but is represented by three hyphens followed by a period and two spaces. When you give two or more works by the same author, the sequence is determined by the alphabetic order of the titles, as in the example below, listing two books by Pierson, where "Canadian" precedes "They're."

Colman, Penny. <u>Where the Action Was: Women War Correspondents in</u>

<u>World War II</u>. New York: Crown Publishers, 2002.

Pierson, Ruth Roach. <u>Canadian Women and the Second World War</u>.

Ottawa: Canadian Historical Association, 1983.

- - -. <u>They're Still Women After All: The Second World War and Canadian</u>

<u>Womanhood</u>. Toronto: McClelland and Stewart, 1986.

Wicks, Ben. <u>Promise You'll Take Care of My Daughter: The Remarkable</u>

<u>War Brides of World War II</u>. Toronto: Stoddart, 1992.

We have already discussed the treatment of an anonymous work; on the following pages we will discuss books by more than one author, government documents, and works of corporate authorship.

The Title

Take the title from the title page, not from the cover or the spine, but disregard any unusual typography—for instance, the use of only capital letters, or the use of & for *and*. Italicize or underline the title and subtitle. (The MLA recommends underlining rather than italicizing in texts submitted in courses or for publication because underlining may be more visible to readers.) If you choose to underline the title, use one continuous underline, but do not underline the period that concludes this part of the entry. Example:

<u>Frankenstein: Or, The Modern Prometheus</u>.

A peculiarity: italicizing can be used to indicate the title of a book, but if a title of a book itself includes the title of a book (for instance, a book about Mary Shelley's *Frankenstein* might include the title of her novel in its own title), the title-within-the-title is neither italicized nor underlined. Thus the title would be given as (if italicized)

> *The Endurance of* Frankenstein

If it were underlined, it would be

> <u>The Endurance of</u> Frankenstein.

Place of Publication, Publisher, and Date

For the place of publication, give the name of the city (you can usually find it either on the title page or on the copyright page, which is the reverse of the title page). If several cities are listed, give only the first. If the city is not likely to be widely known, or if it may be confused with another city of the same name (for instance, London, Ontario, and London, England), add the name of the province or country.

The name of the publisher is abbreviated. Usually the first word is enough (Random House becomes Random; Little, Brown and Co. becomes Little), but if the first word is a first name, such as in Alfred A. Knopf, the last name (Knopf) is used instead. University presses are abbreviated thus: Yale UP, U of Toronto P, State U of New York P.

The date of publication of a book is given when known; if no date appears on the book, write (but do *not* enclose in quotation marks) "n.d." to indicate "no date."

Here are sample entries, illustrating the points we have covered thus far:

Early, Gerald. <u>One Nation Under a Groove: Motown and American Culture</u>.

Hopewell, N.J.: Echo, 1995.

Feitlowitz, Marguerite. <u>A Lexicon of Terror: Argentina and the Legacies of</u>

<u>Torture</u>. New York: Oxford UP, 1998.

Frye, Northrop. <u>Fables of Identity: Studies in Poetic Mythology</u>. New York:

Harcourt, 1963.

---. <u>Fools of Time: Studies in Shakespearean Tragedy</u>. Toronto: U of

Toronto P, 1967.

Kennedy, Paul. <u>Preparing for the Twenty-First Century</u>. New York:

Random, 1993.

Savage, Candace. <u>Witch: The Wild Ride from Wicked to Wicca</u>. Vancouver:

Greystone Books, 2000.

Notice that a period follows the author's name, and another period follows the title. If a subtitle is given, as it is for Feitlowitz's book, it is separated from the title by a colon and a space. A colon follows the place of publication, a comma follows the publisher, and a period follows the date.

A Book by More Than One Author

The book is alphabetized under the last name of the first author named on the title page. If there are *two or three authors,* the names of these are given, after the first author's name, in the normal order, *first name first.*

Carroll, William K., and R. S. Ratner. <u>Challenges and Perils: Social</u>

    <u>Democracy in Neoliberal Times</u>. Black Point, NS: Fernwood, 2005.

Notice, again, that although the first author's name is given *last name first,* the second author's name is given in the normal order. Notice, too, that a comma (and the word "and") is put after the first name of the first author, separating the authors.

    If there are *more than three authors,* give the name of only the first, and then add (but *not* enclosed within quotation marks) "et al."

Belenky, Mary Field, et al. <u>Women's Ways of Knowing: The Development</u>

    <u>of the Self, Voice, and Mind</u>. New York: Basic Books, 1986.

Government Documents

If the writer is not known, treat the government and the agency as the author.

Canada. Natural Resources Canada. <u>Values and Ethics Review</u>. Ottawa:

    Natural Resources Canada, Audit and Evaluation Branch, 2002.

Works of Corporate Authorship

Begin the citation with the corporate author, even if the same body is also the publisher, as in the first example:

Canadian Psychiatric Association. <u>Mental Illness and Work</u>. Ottawa:

    Canadian Psychiatric Association, 2005.

Carnegie Council on Policy Studies in Higher Education. <u>Giving Youth a</u>

    <u>Better Chance: Options for Education, Work, and Service</u>. San

    Francisco: Jossey, 1980.

A Reprint, for Instance a Paperback Version of an Older Hardback

After the title, give the date of original publication (it can usually be found on the copyright page of the reprint you are using), then a period, and then the place, publisher, and date of the edition you are using. The example indicates that the University of Toronto Press book was originally published in 1949 and that the student is using the reprint of 1989.

Dawson, R. MacGregor, and W. F. Dawson. <u>Democratic Government in</u>

    <u>Canada</u>. 1949. Revised by Norman Ward. Toronto: U of Toronto P, 1989.

A Book in Several Volumes

Gillmor, Don, and Pierre Turgeon. Canada: A People's History. 2 vols.

McClelland and Stewart, 2000.

If you have used more than one volume, in your essay you will (as has been explained on page 351) indicate a reference to, say, page 250 of volume 2 thus: (2: 250).

If, however, you have used only one volume of the set—let's say volume 1—in your entry in Works Cited write, after the period following the date, "Vol. 1," as in the next entry:

Gillmor, Don, and Pierre Turgeon. Canada: A People's History. 2 vols.

McClelland and Stewart, 2000. Vol. 1.

In this case, the parenthetic citation would be to the page only, not to the volume and page, since a reader will understand that the page reference must be to this volume. But notice that in Works Cited, even though you say you used only volume 1, you also give the total number of volumes.

One Book with a Separate Title in a Set of Volumes

Sometimes a set of volumes with an overall title also uses a separate title for each book in the set. If you are listing such a book, use the following form:

Churchill, Winston. The Age of Revolution. Vol. 3 of A History of the

English-Speaking Peoples. New York: Dodd, 1957.

A Book with an Author and an Editor

Churchill, Winston, and Franklin D. Roosevelt. The Complete

Correspondence. 3 vols. Ed. Warren F. Kimball. Princeton: Princeton

UP, 1985.

Hardy, W. G. From Sea unto Sea: Canada 1850-1910, The Road to

Nationhood. Ed. Thomas B. Costain. Toronto: Popular Library, 1960.

If a book has one editor, the abbreviation is "ed."; if two or more editors, "eds."

If you are making use of the editor's introduction or other editorial material, rather than the author's work, list the book under the name of the editor, rather than the author, following the form we give later for "An Introduction, Foreword, or Afterword."

A Revised Edition of a Book

Barnet, Sylvan, et al. The Practical Guide to Writing with Readings and

Handbook. 2nd ed. Toronto: Pearson, 2006.

A Translated Book

Franqui, Carlos. <u>Family Portrait with Fidel: A Memoir</u>. Trans. Alfred

     MacAdam. New York: Random, 1984.

But if you are discussing the translation itself, as opposed to the book, list the work under the translator's name. Thus

MacAdam, Alfred, trans. <u>Family Portrait with Fidel: A Memoir</u>. By Carlos

     Franqui. New York: Random, 1984.

An Introduction, Foreword, or Afterword

Richeson, David. Foreword. <u>The New North: An Account of a Woman's</u>

     <u>1908 Journey through Canada to the Arctic</u>. 1909. By Agnes Deans

     Cameron. Saskatoon: Western Producer, 1986. vii-xi.

Usually a book with an introduction or some such comparable material is listed under the name of the author of the book (here Cameron), rather than under the name of the writer of the foreword (here Richeson), but if you are referring to the apparatus rather than to the book itself, use the form just given. The words Introduction, Preface, Foreword, and Afterword are neither enclosed within quotation marks nor underlined.

A Book with an Editor but No Author

Although anthologies of literature fit this description, here we have in mind a book of stories written by various people but collected by editors, whose names appear on the collection.

Beardy, Flora and Robert Coutts, eds. <u>Voices from Hudson Bay: Cree</u>

     <u>Stories from York Factory</u>. Montreal: McGill UP, 1996.

A Work in a Volume of Works by One Author

The following entry indicates that a short work by Thomas King—a short story called "One Good Story, That One"—appears in a book by King titled *One Good Story, That One*. Notice that the inclusive page numbers of the short work are cited—not merely the numbers of pages that you may have referred to, but *the page numbers of the entire work*.

King, Thomas. "One Good Story, That One." In <u>One Good Story, That One</u>.

     Harper, 1993. 3-10.

A Work in an Anthology—That Is, in a Collection of Works by Several Authors

There are several possibilities here. Let's assume, for a start, that you have made use of one work in an anthology. In Works Cited, begin with the author (last name first) and title of the work you are citing, not with the name of the anthologist or the title of the anthology. Here is an entry for Coleridge's poem "Kubla

Khan," found on pages 501–03 in the second volume of a two-volume anthology edited by David Damrosch and several others.

Coleridge, Samuel Taylor. "Kubla Khan." The Longman Anthology of

British Literature. Ed. David Damrosch, et al. 2 vols. New York:

Longman, 1999. 2: 501-03.

Now let's assume that during the course of your essay you refer to several, rather than to only one, work in this anthology. You can, of course, list each work in the form just given. Or you can have an entry in Works Cited for Damrosch's anthology, under Damrosch's name, and then in each entry for a work in the anthology you can eliminate some of the data by simply referring to Damrosch, thus:

Coleridge, Samuel Taylor. "Kubla Khan." Damrosch 2: 501-03.

Again, this requires that you also list Damrosch's volume, thus:

Damrosch, David, et al., eds. The Longman Anthology of British

Literature. 2 vols. New York: Longman, 1999. Vol. 2.

The advantage of listing the anthology separately is that if you are using a dozen works from it, you can shorten the dozen entries in Works Cited merely by adding one entry, that of the anthology itself. Notice, of course, that in the body of the essay you would still refer to Coleridge and to your other eleven authors, not to the editor of the anthology—but the entries in Works Cited will guide the reader to the book you have used.

A Book Review

Dyer, Alison. Rev. of Wolfe and Montcalm: Their Lives, Their Times and

the Fate of a Continent. By Joy Carroll. The Beaver. 85.2 (April/May

2005): 46-47.

If a review is anonymous, list it under the first word of the title, or under the second word if the first word is *A, An,* or *The*. If an anonymous review has no title, begin the entry with "Rev. of" and then give the title of the work reviewed; alphabetize the entry under the title of the work reviewed. If the review has a title, give it between the period following the reviewer's name and "Rev."

An Article or Essay—Not a Reprint—in a Collection

A book may consist of a collection (edited by one or more persons) of new essays by several authors. Here is a reference to one essay in such a book. (The essay, by Carpenter, occupies pages 109–25 in a collection edited by Moon and Obe.)

Carpenter, David. "Hoovering to Byzantium." Taking Risks: Literary

Journalism from the Edge. Ed. Barbara Moon and Don Obe. Banff:

Banff Centre Press, 1998. 109-125.

An Article or Essay Reprinted in a Collection

The previous example (Carpenter's essay in Moon and Obe's collection) involves an essay written for a collection. But some collections reprint earlier material, for example essays from journals, or chapters from books. The following example cites an essay that was originally printed in *The New York Times*. This essay has been reprinted in a later collection of essays edited by the author, and it is Nunberg's collection that the student used.

Nunberg, Geoffrey. "As Google Goes, So Goes the Nation." <u>The New York</u>

<u>Times</u>. 18 May 2003, Week in Review, 16-17. Rpt. in <u>Going Nucular:</u>

<u>Language, Politics, and Culture in Confrontational Times</u>. Ed.

Geoffrey Nunberg. New York: PublicAffairs, 2005. 227-30.

The student has read Nunberg's article, but not the original in *The New York Times*, where it occupied pages 16–17. The material was actually read on pages 227–30 in a collection of writings by Nunberg published by PublicAffairs. Details of the original publication—title, date, page numbers, and so forth—were found in the collection *Going Nucular*. Almost all editors will include this information, either on the copyright page or at the foot of the reprinted essay, but sometimes they do not give the original page numbers. In such a case, the original numbers need not be included in the entry.

Notice that the entry begins with the author and the title of the work you are citing (here, Nunberg's articles), not with the name of the editor of the collection or the title of the collection. In the following example, the student used an essay by Arthur Sewell; the essay was originally on pages 53–56 in a book by Sewell titled *Character and Society in Shakespeare,* but the student encountered the piece on pages 36–38 in a collection of essays edited by Leonard Dean, on Shakespeare's *Julius Caesar.* Here is how the entry should run:

Sewell, Arthur. "The Moral Dilemma in Tragedy: Brutus." <u>Character and</u>

<u>Society in Shakespeare</u>. Oxford: Clarendon, 1951. 53-56. Rpt. in

<u>Twentieth Century Interpretations of Julius Caesar</u>. Ed. Leonard F.

Dean. Englewood Cliffs: Prentice, 1968. 36-38.

An Encyclopedia or Other Alphabetically Arranged Reference Work

The publisher, place of publication, volume number, and page number should be included for less familiar reference books, but do *not* have to be given for familiar ones. For such works, list only the edition (if it is given) and the date.

For a *signed* article, begin with the author's last name. (If the article is signed with initials, check the volume for a list of contributors—it is usually near the front, but it may be at the back—which will say who the initials stand for.) Use the following form:

Messer, Thomas. "Picasso." <u>Encyclopedia Americana</u>. 1998 ed.

For an *unsigned article,* begin with the title of the article.

"Picasso, Pablo (Ruiz y)." Encyclopaedia Britannica: Macropaedia. 1985 ed.

"Automation." The Business Reference Book. 1977 ed.

Films, Television and Radio Programs

A Film
Begin with the director's name (last name first), followed by "dir." Next give the title of the film, underlined, then a period, two spaces, the name of the studio, the date, and a period.

Cronenberg, David, dir. A History of Violence. New Line Cinema, 2005.

A Television or Radio Program

Corner Gas. CTV. 10 Oct 2005.

Articles in Journals and Newspapers

An Article in a Scholarly Journal
The title of the article is enclosed within quotation marks, and the title of the journal is underlined (or italicized).

Some journals are paginated consecutively—the pagination of the second issue begins where the first issue leaves off; other journals begin each issue with page 1. The forms of the citations differ slightly. First, an article in a *journal that is paginated consecutively*:

Purdon, James John. "John Aubrey's 'Discourse in Paper'." Essays in

    Criticism 55 (2005): 226-47.

Purdon's article occupies pages 226–47 of volume 55, which was published in 2005. (Note that the volume number is followed by a space, and then by the year, in parentheses, and then by a colon, a space, and the page numbers of the entire article.) Because the journal is paginated consecutively, the issue number does *not* need to be specified.

For a *journal that begins each issue with page 1* (there will be four page 1s each year if such a journal is a quarterly), the issue number must be given. After the volume number, type a period and (without hitting the space bar) the issue number, as in the next example.

Helleiner, Eric. "A Fixation with Floating: The Politics of Canada's

    Exchange Rate Regime." Canadian Journal of Political Science 38.1

    (March 2005): 23-44.

Helleiner's article appeared in the first issue of volume 38 of *Canadian Journal of Political Science.*

An Article in a Weekly, Biweekly, or Monthly Publication
The date and page numbers are given, but volume numbers and issue numbers are usually omitted for these publications. This example is for an article in a monthly publication:

Gillis, Charlie. "Let's Redefine 'Hero'." <u>Maclean's</u> February 28, 2005: 32-33.

An Article in a Newspaper
Because a newspaper usually consists of several sections, a section number or a capital letter may precede the page number (e.g., A1). The example indicates that an article begins on page 1 of section 1 and is continued on a later page.

Bennet, James. "Judge Cites Possible Breaches of Ethics Guidelines by

 Starr." <u>New York Times</u> 8 Aug. 1998. Sec. 1: 1+.

Other Types of Sources

An Interview
The citation gives the name of the person you interviewed, the form of the interview (e.g., personal, telephone, or email), and the date.

Facundo, Alan. Personal interview. 10 Aug. 2005.

A Lecture
In addition to the date of the lecture and the name of the speaker, the citation should include the title of the presentation (if there is one) and the place it was given. If there is no title, use a descriptive word or phrase such as "class lecture" (do not use quotation marks). If the lecture was sponsored by a particular organization or group, give that information before the date.

Cavell, Richard. "McLuhan in Space." Made in Canada Speaking Series.

 University of Alberta, Edmonton. 25 Oct. 2001.

DeFehr, Wayne. Class lecture on Michael Ondaatje's poetry. University of

 New Brunswick. 20 Sept. 2005.

Portable Database Sources
Material obtained from a portable database, such as a CD-ROM, magnetic tape, or diskette, is treated like print material, but with one important difference: you must specify the physical form of the source. This information comes after the underlined title of the source and before the city of publication.

<u>Canadian Radio Circuits Database, 1938-1948</u>. CD-ROM. Whirlwind

 Software, 2002.

Gates, Henry Louis, and Kwame Anthony Appiah, eds. <u>Encarta Africana</u>.

 CD-ROM. Redmond, WA: Microsoft, 1999.

If the database is periodically published and updated, additional information is required. You must include the original date of publication of the material you're using, as well as the date of publication for the database. And if the source of the information is not also the distributor (the MLA publishes the CD-ROM version of the MLA International Bibliography, for example, but SilverPlatter distributes it), you must include the distributor (or vendor's) name as well.

Odygaard, Floyd D. P. "California's Collodion Artist: The Images of

William Dunniway." <u>Military Images</u> 16.5 1995: 14-19. <u>America:</u>

<u>History and Life on Disc</u>. CD-ROM. ABC-Clio. Winter 1997-98.

Electronic Sources

Online Sources
Online sources are treated like books and articles, with four major (and many minor) exceptions:
- The **Internet address** of the source is given in angle brackets at the end of the entry.
- The **date accessed**—the date on which *you* found the source—is included in the citation.
- **Page numbers** are included in the citation *only* if the source is paginated. (This is often the case with full-text online versions of books and journal articles, in which case the pagination follows that of the print source.)
- Sometimes paragraphs are numbered; the citation gives **paragraph numbers** when the sources provide them.

The basic format for an online source follows that of a print source. You give, in the following order,
- author
- title
- publication information (including date of original publication, if applicable)
- page or paragraph numbers if available.

Then you give additional information—as much as is applicable and available—in the following order.
- name of database, project, periodical, or site (underlined)
- number of volume, issue, or version
- date of posting
- name of site sponsor (if applicable)
- date *you* consulted the material
- electronic address (or URL) in angle brackets.

Again, keep in mind that one purpose of documentation is to enable your readers to retrace your steps. It may also be useful to keep in mind that, like the Internet itself, guidelines for citing electronic sources are continually evolving. Our guidelines are based on the format given in *MLA Handbook for Writers of Research Papers*, Sixth Edition (2003).

Here are some examples.

1. Novel

Jewett, Sarah Orne. <u>The Country of the Pointed Firs</u>. 1910. <u>Bartleby Archive</u>.

Columbia U. 3 June 1999 <www.cc.columbia.edu/acis/bartleby/jewett>.

2. Journal Article

Stewart, Susan. "Thoughts on the Role of the Humanities in Contemporary

Life." <u>New Literary History</u> 36.1 (2005): 97-103. <u>Project Muse</u>. JHU. 1

May 2005 <http://muse:jhu.edu:80/journals/new literary_history/

v27/27.3fluck.html>.

While the URL of the document should be provided in full, if the URL is long, you may, instead, choose to provide the URL of the site's search page if there is one.

3. Magazine and Newspaper Article (from a Print Source)

Harvey, John. "Re-refined Oil Blunts the Pain of Costly Crude." <u>Toronto</u>

<u>Star</u>. 24 Sept 2005 <u>Lexis-Nexis</u>. 4 Oct. 2005 <http://lexisnexis.com>.

4. Magazine and Newspaper Article (No Print Source)

Green, Laura. "Sexual Harassment Law: Relax and Try to Enjoy It." <u>Salon</u>

3 March 1998. 14 Aug. 1998 <www.salon1999.com/mwt/feature/1998/

03/cov_03featurea.html>.

5. Article in a Reference Work

"Chopin, Kate." <u>Britannica Online</u>. Vers 98.1.1. June 1998. Encyclopaedia

Britannica. 14 Aug. 1998 <www.eb.com:180/cgi-bin/g?DocF=micro/

125/57.html>.

Reuben, Paul P. "Chapter 6: 1890-1910: Kate Chopin (1851-1904)."

<u>PAL: Perspectives in American Literature--A Research and Reference</u>

<u>Guide</u> 20 March 1998 <www.csustan.edu/english/reuben/pal/chap6/

chopin.html>.

6. Personal Website

Jamail, Dahr. Home page. 8 Dec. 2004. 17 Jan. 2005

<http://darhjamailiraq.com>.

7. Email

Maphet, Mercedes. "Re: Kate Chopin Diaries." Email to author. 4 May 1998.

8. Posting to a Discussion List, Online Forum, or Blog

Boyle, Laurel. "Girls' Education in Afghanistan." Online posting. 20 May

2005. UNICEF Discussion Group. 1 April 2005 <http://forum.unicef.ca/

SOWC>.

Riverbend. "The Raid." Weblog. 11 Feb. 2006. Baghdad Burning. 12 Feb.

2006 <http://riverbendblog.blogspot.com/>.

Although we have covered the most common sources, it is entirely possible that you will come across a source that does not fit any of the categories that we have discussed. For several hundred pages of explanation of these matters, covering the proper way to cite all sorts of troublesome and unbelievable (but real) sources, see Joseph Gibaldi, *MLA Handbook for Writers of Research Papers,* Sixth Edition (New York: Modern Language Association of America, 2003). Numerous websites also provide additional information about and discussion of documenting online sources. The research skills you have developed will enable you to locate and evaluate these sites.

APA FORMAT

The MLA style is used chiefly by writers in the humanities. Writers in the social sciences and in business, education, and psychology commonly use a style developed by the American Psychological Association. In the following pages we give the chief principles of the APA style, but for full details the reader should consult the fifth edition (2001) of *Publication Manual of the American Psychological Association.*

An Overview of the APA Format

A paper that uses the format prescribed by the American Psychological Association will contain brief parenthetic citations within the text and will end with a page headed "References," which lists all of the author's sources. This list of sources begins on a separate page, continuing the pagination of the last page of the essay itself. Thus, if the text of the essay ends on page 8, the first page of references is page 9.

Here are some general guidelines for formatting both citations within the text and the list of references at the end of the essay.

Citations within the Text

The APA style emphasizes the date of publication; the date appears not only in the list of references at the end of the paper, but also in the paper itself wherever you give a brief parenthetic citation of a source that you have quoted, summarized, or used in any other way. Here is an example:

Income, education, and occupation are indicators used in society's ranking

system (Hiller, 2000, p. 84).

The title of Hiller's book or article will be given in your list of references. By turning to the list, the reader will learn in what publication Hiller made this point.

A Summary of an Entire Work

Hiller (2000) concluded the opposite.

or

Similar views are easily found (Hiller, 2000; Phillips, 1993).

A Reference to a Page or Pages

Hiller (2000, p. 84) states that in Canada the number of middle-income

families and unattached individuals is "slipping (from 18.3% in 1951 to

16.3% in 1996)."

A Reference to an Author Represented by More Than One Work in the References

As we explain under "Form for Authors" in the list of References, if you list two or
more works published by an author in the same year, the works are listed in alphabetic order by the first letter of the title. The first work is labelled *a,* the second *b,*
and so on. Here is a reference to the second work that Hiller published in 1982:

S. D. Clark writes about the development of Canadian sociology (Hiller,

1982b).

The List of References

Form on the Page

1. Begin each entry flush with the left margin, but if an entry runs to more
   than one line, indent five spaces for each succeeding line of the entry.
2. Double-space within each entry, and double-space between entries.

Although we will go over the APA style in more detail on the following pages,
here is the basic format for books, periodicals (items published on a regular basis
such as journals, newspapers, and newsletters), and online documents:

Books
Author, A.A. (Date of publication). *Title of book: subtitle if available.* Place of
Publication: Publisher.

Articles
Author, A.A., Author, B.B., & Author, C.C. (Date of publication). Title of article.
Title of Periodical, #.#, page-page.

Internet Sites

Author, A.A. & Author, B.B. (Date of publication). Title of article if there is one. *Title of whole work*, publication information if there is any. Retrieved month day, year, from source.

Books and Periodicals

Form for Authors

1. Arrange the list **alphabetically by author.**

2. Give the **author's last name first,** followed by the initials *only* of the first and of the middle name (if any). The publication date follows the name; if there is no publication date, write n.d.

3. **If there is more than one author,** invert all the names (last name first) and give only initials for the first and middle names. List up to and including six authors; when there are seven or more, the seventh and subsequent authors are abbreviated as "et al." ("and others"). (But do not invert the editor's name when the entry begins with the name of an author who has written an article in an edited book. See the example on page 370, illustrating "A Work in a Collection of Essays.") When there are two or more authors, use an ampersand (&) before the name of the last author. Here is an example of an article in the book *Issues in Canadian Business*.

Foster, M. K. & Pickard, L. (1994). *Issues in Canadian business*. Toronto:

Dryden.

4. **If there is more than one work by an author,** list the works in the order of publication, the earliest first.

If two works by an author were published in the same year, give them in alphabetic order by the first letter of the title, disregarding *A, An,* or *The,* and their foreign equivalents. Designate the first work as *a,* the second as *b.* Repeat the author's name at the start of each entry.

If the author of a work or works is also the co-author of other works listed, list the single-author entries first, arranged by date. Following these, list the multiple-author entries, in a sequence determined alphabetically by the second author's name. Thus, in the example below, notice that the works Bem wrote unassisted are listed first, arranged by date, and when two works appear in the same year they are arranged alphabetically by title. These single-author works are followed by the multiple-author works, with the work written with Lenney preceding the work written with Martyna and Watson.

Bem, S. L. (1974). The measurement of psychological androgyny. *Journal of*

Consulting and Clinical Psychology, 42, 155-62.

Bem, S. L. (1981a). The BSRI and gender schema theory: A reply to Spence

and Helmreich. *Psychological Review, 88,* 369-71.

Bem, S. L. (1981b). Gender schema theory: A cognitive account of sex

typing. *Psychological Review, 88,* 354-64.

Bem, S. L. & Lenney, E. (1976). Sex-typing and the avoidance of cross-sex

behavior. *Journal of Personality and Social Psychology, 33*, 48-54.

Bem, S. L., Martyna, W., & Watson, C. (1976). Sex-typing and androgyny:

Further exploration of the expressive domain. *Journal of Personality and*

Social Psychology, 34, 1016-23.

Form of Title

In references to books, capitalize only the first letter of the first word of the title (and of the subtitle, if any) and capitalize proper nouns. *Italicize* the complete title and type a period after it.

In references to articles in periodicals or in edited books, capitalize only the first letter of the first word of the article's title (and subtitle, if any) and all proper nouns. Do not put the title within quotation marks. Type a period after the title of the article. For the title of the journal, and the volume and page numbers, see the next instruction.

In references to periodicals, capitalize all important words, as you would usually do. (Note that the rule for the titles of periodicals differs from the rule for books and articles.) Give the volume number in *italicized* Arabic numerals. Do not use *vol.* before the number. Use *p.* or *pp.* before the page numbers for parts of books and for magazine and newspaper articles, but *not* for journal articles.

Sample References

A Book by One Author

Abella, I. (1999). *A coat of many colours: Two centuries of Jewish life in*

Canada. Toronto: Key Porter Books.

A Book by More than One Author

Spence, J. T., & Helmreich, R. L. (1978). *Masculinity and femininity.* Austin:

University of Texas Press.

A Collection of Essays

Ross, J. I. (Ed.) (1995). *Violence in Canada: Sociopolitical perspectives.* Don

Mills: Oxford University Press.

A Work in a Collection of Essays

Tunnell, K. D. (1995). Worker insurgency and social control: Violence by

and against labour in Canada. In J. I. Ross (Ed.) *Violence in Canada:*

Sociopolitical perspectives. (pp. 78-96). Don Mills: Oxford University Press.

Government Documents

If the writer is not known, treat the government and the agency as the author. Canadian Government Publishing is the official publisher of the Government of Canada.

Government of Canada. Office of Foreign Affairs and International Trade.

(2000). *Diplomatic, consular and other representatives in Canada*. Ottawa:

Canadian Government Publishing.

An Article in a Journal That Paginates Each Issue Separately

Swinton, E. (1993, Winter). New wine in old casks: Sino-Japanese and

Russo-Japanese war prints. *Asian Art, 27*-49.

The publication is issued four times a year, each issue containing a page 27. It is necessary, therefore, to tell the reader that this article appears in the winter issue.

An Article in a Journal with Continuous Pagination

Herdt, G. (1991). Representations of homosexuality. *Journal of the History of*

Sexuality, 1, 481-504.

An Article from a Monthly or Weekly Magazine

Swerdlow, L. (1999, August). Global culture. *National Geographic*. pp. 2-5.

An Article in a Newspaper

Mahoney, I. (2001, Nov 15). Klein to push PM on health disputes. *Globe*

and Mail. p. A17.

(*Note:* If no author is given, simply begin with the article title, followed by the date in parentheses.)

A Book Review

Bayme, S. (1993). Tradition or modernity? [Review of Neil Gillman, *Sacred*

fragments: Recovering theology for the modern Jew]. *Judaism, 42*, 106-13.

Bayme is the reviewer, not the author of the book. The book under review is called *Sacred Fragments: Recovering Theology for the Modern Jew,* but the review, published in volume 42 of a journal called *Judaism*, had its own title, "Tradition or Modernity?"

If the review does not have an author title, type the material in square brackets, then two spaces, then the date (given in parentheses), and proceed as in the example just given.

Electronic Sources

References to electronic sources generally follow the format for printed sources. Include

- the author
- the year of publication in parenthesis, followed by a period
- the title (and edition and page numbers, if applicable) and a period

then

- the word "Retrieved" and then the month, day, and year you accessed the source
- the word "from" and then the Internet address of the database name or supplier

For more information see the APA website: www.apastyle.org/elecref.html.

Professional or Government Site

Government of Canada (2001). Minister of Public Works and Government

  Services. *Facts on Canada: British Columbia*. Retrieved Nov 10, 2001

  from http://www.communication.gc.ca/facts/bc_e.html.

Edlefsen, M., & Brewer, M.S. (n.d.). The National Food Safety Database.

  Nitrates/Nitrites. Retrieved May 6, 2000 from http://www.foodsafety.

  org/il/il089.htm.

Encyclopedia Article

Muckraker (journ.). (1994-1998). In *Britannica Online*. Retrieved Jan 2,

  2000 from www.eb.com:180cgibin/g?DocF=index/mu/ckr.html

Newspaper Article

Stevenson, J. (2001, Nov 15). Looming global oil price war could wreak

  collateral damage in Canada. *National Post*. Retrieved Nov 15, 2001

  from http://www.nationalpost.com.

Warrick, P. (1994, June 8). A frank discussion. *Los Angeles Times*, p. E1.

  Retrieved Aug 12, 1995 from Lexis-Nexis database.

Journal Article

Tollefson, C. (1995, May 29). Stability preserved: preservatives; food

additives '95. *Chemical Marketing Reporter*, 247.22, SR28. Retrieved

May 6, 1998 from Lexis-Nexis database.

Book

Hiis. J. (1890). *How the other half lives*. New York: Charles Scribner's Sons.

David Phillips (ed.). Retrieved Sept 14, 1998 from http://www.cis.edu/

amstud/inforev/riis/ch#3/html.

A NOTE ON OTHER SYSTEMS OF DOCUMENTATION

The MLA style is commonly used in the humanities, and the APA style is commonly used in the social sciences, business, and education, but many other disciplines use their own styles. The Chicago style, used in many disciplines, is available in *The Chicago Manual of Style*, 15th edition (2003). What follows is a list of handbooks that give the systems used in some other disciplines.

Biology

Council of Biology Editors, Style Manual Committee. *Scientific Style and Format: CBE Style Manual for Authors, Editors, and Publishers in the Biological Sciences.* 6th ed. New York: Cambridge University Press, 1994.

Chemistry

American Chemical Society. *ACS Style Guide: A Manual for Authors and Editors.* 2nd ed. Washington, D.C.: American Chemical Society, 1997.

Geology

U.S. Geological Survey. *Suggestions to Authors of the Reports of the United States Geological Survey.* 8th ed. Washington: GPO, Department of the Interior, 1997.

Law

The Bluebook: A Uniform System of Citation. 18th ed. Cambridge: Harvard Law Review Association, 2005.

Mathematics

American Mathematical Society, *A Manual for Authors of Mathematical Papers.* 8th ed. Providence, R.I.: American Mathematical Society, 1990.

Medicine

American Medical Association. *Manual of Style.* 9th ed. Baltimore: Williams and Wilkins, 1998.

Physics
American Institute of Physics. *AIP Style Manual*. 4th ed. New York: American Institute of Physics, 1990.

Exercises

1. Using the MLA form, list the following items in Works Cited.
   a. A book titled *Areas of Challenge for Soviet Foreign Policy*, with an introduction by Adam B. Ulam. The book, published in 1985 by the Indiana University Press, in Bloomington, is written by three authors: Gerrit W. Gong, Angela E. Stent, and Rebecca V. Strode. Write *two* entries for Works Cited, the first entry indicating that you referred only to Ulam's introduction, the second entry indicating that you referred to material written by the three authors of the book.
   b. *Journal of Political and Military Strategy* paginates its issues continuously; the second issue takes up where the first issue leaves off. The issues of 1984 constitute volume 12. Issue number 2 (the fall issue) contains an article that runs from page 229 to page 241. The article, written by James Burke, is titled "Patriotism and the All-Volunteer Force."
   c. *International Security* begins the pagination of each issue with page 1. The issues of 1985 constitute volume 9. Issue number 4 (the spring issue) contains an article that runs from page 79 to page 98. The article, written by Klaus Knorr, is titled "Controlling Nuclear War."
   d. On page 257 of the book you are now holding in your hand, you will find an essay by Sharon Morgan Beckford. How would you list the essay in Works Cited?
2. Go to your library and prepare entries for Works Cited for any five of the following:
   A signed article in a recent issue of a journal devoted to some aspect of psychology.
   A signed article in a newspaper.
   A signed article in a recent issue of *Quill & Quire.*
   A signed journal article retrieved with an information service.
   An unsigned article in a recent issue of *Maclean's.*
   A signed article in an online version of a recent issue of *Maclean's.*
   An unsigned article from the Macropaedia portion of *Encyclopaedia Britannica.*
   A signed article from the Micropaedia portion of *Encyclopaedia Britannica.*
   An unsigned article from *Britannica Online.*
   A catalogue from your university.
   An email message.
   A website.

Writing about Literature

RESPONDING TO LITERARY TEXTS

One important difference between literary and non-literary texts is the literary author's concern with presenting experience concretely, with *showing* rather than with *telling*. Let's consider the briefest literary form, the proverb. Take this example: "A rolling stone gathers no moss." Of course the statement says something—it offers an assertion—but its concreteness helps to make it memorable.

Compare the original, for instance, with this unmemorable **paraphrase** or restatement, "If a stone is always moving around, vegetation won't have a chance to grow on it." The original version seems more real, more present, more convincing; it offers a small but complete world, hard (stone) and soft (moss), inorganic and organic, at rest and in motion.

The shapeliness of the proverb also makes it memorable. This shapeliness is perhaps *felt* rather than consciously recognized, but a close look reveals that each of the nouns in the sentence (*stone* and *moss*) has one syllable, and each of the two words of motion (*rolling, gathers*) has two syllables, with the accent on the first of the two. The world of the proverb is complex but it is also unified into a whole by such relationships as these.

And generally speaking, this is the way most poets, fiction writers, and dramatists work. They present scenes (for instance, a lover eagerly anticipating a meeting with the beloved) that are memorable for their vividness, their shapeliness, and their rich implications. "John loves Mary," written on a wall, is information—mere *telling* rather than *showing*. Literature is something else; it is, as Robert Frost said, "a performance in words."

Although literary texts are especially compact or rich and dense, and are especially shapely (interestingly patterned or organized), when you respond to a literary text you are not doing something essentially different from what you do when you respond to *any* text—for instance, a psychology textbook or an argument about same-sex marriage. You experience a variety of responses; you agree or disagree, you feel pleasure or irritation or puzzlement or boredom. And since your writing will be in large measure a report of your responses, your first reading of a work (which starts the responses) is the beginning of the writing process.

READING FICTION

Fiction can range from the short story of a page or two to the thousand-page novel. Let's begin with a very short story, an anonymous tale from nineteenth-century Japan.

 MUDDY ROAD

1 Two monks, Tanzan and Ekido, were once travelling together down a muddy road. A heavy rain was still falling.

2   Coming around a bend, they met a lovely girl in a silk kimono and sash, unable to cross the intersection.

3   "Come on, girl," said Tanzan at once. Lifting her in his arms, he carried her over the mud.

4   Ekido did not speak again until that night when they reached a lodging temple. Then he no longer could restrain himself. "We monks don't go near females," he told Tanzan, "especially not young and lovely ones. It is dangerous. Why did you do that?"

5   "I left the girl there," said Tanzan. "Are you still carrying her?"

A superb story. The opening paragraph, though simple and matter-of-fact, conveys the sense that something interesting is going to happen during this journey along a muddy road on a rainy day. The references to the mud and the rain seem to suggest as well that the journey itself rather than the travellers' destination will be the heart of the story. The first paragraph of this **third-person narrative** also of course introduces the two **characters** (Tanzan and Ekido) and the **setting** (a muddy road); the second paragraph introduces a **complication** (the encounter with the girl) into the **plot** (the sequence of events or happenings). Still, there is apparently no **conflict,** though "Ekido did not speak again until that night" suggests an unspoken conflict, an action (or, in this case, an inaction) that must be explained, an imbalance that must be righted before the story can end. At last Ekido, no longer able to contain his thoughts, lets his indignation burst out: "We monks don't go near females . . . especially not young and lovely ones. It is dangerous. Why did you do that?" His words reveal not only his moral principles but also his insecurity and the anger that grows from it. And now, when the conflict is out in the open, comes the brief reply that reveals Tanzan's very different character as clearly as the outburst revealed Ekido's. This reply—though initially, perhaps, surprising—feels exactly right, bringing the story to a satisfying end. It provides the **denouement** (literally, the "unknotting"), or resolution. A longer story might offer **foreshadowing**—hints of what is to come, or early details that later gain in significance—but "Muddy Road" is so brief that there is hardly space or need for such significant anticipations. (When you read Charlotte Perkins Gilman's "The Yellow Wallpaper" later in this chapter, you probably will be surprised by the ending, but if you then reread it you will notice that the narrator's first description of the wallpaper in her bedroom, and perhaps even the way she discusses her illness in the beginning of the story, serve as foreshadowing.)

    What is the story about, what is its **theme**? We do not want to reduce the story to a neat moral, but we can say that some idea holds it together. There is plenty of room for a difference of opinion about what that idea is; probably no two people will use exactly the same words in discussing what a given literary text is about. But perhaps we can say this story concerns the difference between living according to the spirit of the monastic law (free from attachment to things of this world) and, on the other hand, living according to the letter of the law (complying only outwardly with the law). More briefly, we might say that the story concerns spirituality. Or perhaps its theme is understanding, understanding others and oneself.

What does the story add up to, what is its point or **meaning**? This is a somewhat different question. To ask it is to begin to develop an **argument** about the text, the kind of argument that usually forms the **thesis** or main point of an analytic essay on a work of literature. To put the question another way, we might ask: What is the story *saying about* the theme with which it is concerned? What is it saying about spirituality, or about understanding, or about living by the spirit (versus the letter) of the law? Again, different readers may answer this question in different ways, but one might say that the point of "Muddy Road" is to suggest the limitations of purely legalistic behaviour, of living by the letter of the law.

That interpretation would probably seem right, even natural, to a reader familiar with the New Testament precept "The letter [of the law] killeth, the spirit giveth life." It is worth noting, though, that "Muddy Road" is a Zen story and that a Zen interpretation, while harmonious with what we have said above, would be significantly different. Zen emphasizes "nothingness," "a state of no-mind." A Zen interpretation of "Muddy Road" would probably note that one monk brings rational or categorical thinking (rules, women, monks) to the encounter with the lovely girl. The other, bringing "no-mind" to the encounter, is unaffected by it; after helping the woman, he leaves, as he came, in a state of "no-mind."

Is one interpretation better or more right than the other? No. Evidence supports both readings; both readings are grounded in the details of the text. But each interpretation of "Muddy Road" is shaped by the context within which the story is read. Your sense of the meaning of the texts you are asked to write about will likewise be shaped by your background, beliefs, and experiences; how you interpret what you read may also be affected by the ideas you have begun to explore in your reading for other courses (psychology, perhaps, or history or women's studies) and by the influence of your teachers in both high school and university. To help you begin to develop some perspective on the literary interpretation you will be doing in your university courses, we offer on pages 404-06 of this chapter a very brief overview of some of the most important current approaches to literary criticism. For an example of student writing that uses several different kinds of critical material, see Beatrice Cody's essay on Kate Chopin's novel *The Awakening*, reprinted in Chapter 16, "Writing the Research Essay," pages 323-32.

But first, let's look at another story.

 # CHARLOTTE PERKINS GILMAN

First published in New England Magazine *in 1892, "The Yellow Wallpaper" is based in part on Gilman's own experience with depression in the years following the birth of her daughter Katharine. Her physician, Dr. Weir Mitchell, prescribed bed rest for female patients suffering from what was then called "nervous prostration." "In some cases," he wrote, "for four or five weeks, I do not permit the patient to sit up, or to sew or write or read, or to use the hands in any active way except to clean the teeth." As the story suggests, Gilman did not find his treatment effective.*

The Yellow Wallpaper

1   It is very seldom that mere ordinary people like John and myself secure ancestral halls for the summer.

2   A colonial mansion, a hereditary estate, I would say a haunted house, and reach the height of romantic felicity—but that would be asking too much of fate!

3   Still I will proudly declare that there is something queer about it.

4   Else, why should it be let so cheaply? And why have stood so long untenanted?

5   John laughs at me, of course, but one expects that in marriage.

6   John is practical in the extreme. He has no patience with faith, an intense horror of superstition, and he scoffs openly at any talk of things not to be felt and seen and put down in figures.

7   John is a physician, and *perhaps*—(I would not say it to a living soul, of course, but this is dead paper and a great relief to my mind)—*perhaps* that is one reason I do not get well faster.

8   You see he does not believe I am sick!

9   And what can one do?

10   If a physician of high standing, and one's own husband, assures friends and relatives that there is really nothing the matter with one but temporary nervous depression—a slight hysterical tendency—what is one to do?

11   My brother is also a physician, and also of high standing, and he says the same thing.

12   So I take phosphates or phosphites—whichever it is, and tonics, and journeys, and air, and exercise, and am absolutely forbidden to "work" until I am well again.

13   Personally, I disagree with their ideas.

14   Personally, I believe that congenial work, with excitement and change, would do me good.

15   But what is one to do?

16   I did write for a while in spite of them; but it *does* exhaust me a good deal—having to be so sly about it, or else meet with heavy opposition.

17   I sometimes fancy that in my condition if I had less opposition and more society and stimulus—but John says the very worst thing I can do is to think about my condition, and I confess it always makes me feel bad.

18   So I will let it alone and talk about the house.

19   The most beautiful place! It is quite alone, standing well back from the road, quite three miles from the village. It makes me think of English places that you read about, for there are hedges and walls and gates that lock, and lots of separate little houses for the gardeners and people.

20   There is a *delicious* garden! I never saw such a garden—large and shady, full of box-bordered paths, and lined with long grape-covered arbors with seats under them.

21   There were greenhouses, too, but they are all broken now.

22   There was some legal trouble, I believe, something about the heirs and coheirs; anyhow, the place has been empty for years.

23   That spoils my ghostliness, I am afraid, but I don't care—there is something strange about the house—I can feel it.

24   I even said so to John one moonlight evening, but he said what I felt was a *draught,* and shut the window.

25   I get unreasonably angry with John sometimes. I'm sure I never used to be so sensitive. I think it is due to this nervous condition.

26   But John says if I feel so, I shall neglect proper self-control; so I take pains to control myself—before him, at least, and that makes me very tired.

27   I don't like our room a bit. I wanted one downstairs that opened on the piazza and had roses all over the window, and such pretty old-fashioned chintz hangings! but John would not hear of it.

28   He said there was only one window and not room for two beds, and no near room for him if he took another.

29   He is very careful and loving, and hardly lets me stir without special direction.

30   I have a schedule prescription for each hour in the day; he takes all care from me, and so I feel basely ungrateful not to value it more.

31   He said we came here solely on my account, that I was to have perfect rest and all the air I could get. "Your exercise depends on your strength, my dear," said he, "and your food somewhat on your appetite; but air you can absorb all the time." So we took the nursery at the top of the house.

32   It is a big, airy room, the whole floor nearly, with windows that look all ways, and air and sunshine galore. It was nursery first and then playroom and gymnasium, I should judge; for the windows are barred for little children, and there are rings and things in the walls.

33   The paint and paper look as if a boys' school had used it. It is stripped off— the paper—in great patches all around the head of my bed, about as far as I can reach, and in a great place on the other side of the room low down. I never saw a worse paper in my life.

34   One of those sprawling flamboyant patterns committing every artistic sin.

35   It is dull enough to confuse the eye in following, pronounced enough to constantly irritate and provoke study, and when you follow the lame uncertain curves for a little distance they suddenly commit suicide—plunge off at outrageous angles, destroy themselves in unheard of contradictions.

36   The color is repellent, almost revolting; a smouldering unclean yellow, strangely faded by the slow-turning sunlight.

37   It is a dull yet lurid orange in some places, a sickly sulphur tint in others.

38   No wonder the children hated it! I should hate it myself if I had to live in this room long.

39   There comes John, and I must put this away,—he hates to have me write a word.

40   We have been here two weeks, and I haven't felt like writing before, since that first day.

41   I am sitting by the window now, up in this atrocious nursery, and there is nothing to hinder my writing as much as I please, save lack of strength.

42   John is away all day, and even some nights when his cases are serious.

43   I am glad my case is not serious!

44   But these nervous troubles are dreadfully depressing.

45   John does not know how much I really suffer. He knows there is no *reason* to suffer, and that satisfies him.

46   Of course it is only nervousness. It does weigh on me so not to do my duty in any way!

47   I meant to be such a help to John, such a real rest and comfort, and here I am a comparative burden already!

48   Nobody would believe what an effort it is to do what little I am able,—to dress and entertain, and order things.

49   It is fortunate Mary is so good with the baby. Such a dear baby!

50   And yet I *cannot* be with him, it makes me so nervous.

51   I suppose John never was nervous in his life. He laughs at me so about this wall-paper!

52   At first he meant to repaper the room, but afterwards he said that I was letting it get the better of me, and that nothing was worse for a nervous patient than to give way to such fancies.

53   He said that after the wall-paper was changed it would be the heavy bedstead, and then the barred windows, and then that gate at the head of the stairs, and so on.

54   "You know the place is doing you good," he said, "and really, dear, I don't care to renovate the house just for a three months' rental."

55   "Then do let us go downstairs," I said, "there are such pretty rooms there."

56   Then he took me in his arms and called me a blessed little goose, and said he would go down to the cellar, if I wished, and have it whitewashed into the bargain.

57   But he is right enough about the beds and windows and things.

58   It is an airy and comfortable room as any one need wish, and, of course, I would not be so silly as to make him uncomfortable just for a whim.

59   I'm really getting quite fond of the big room, all but that horrid paper.

60   Out of one window I can see the garden, those mysterious deep-shaded arbors, the riotous old-fashioned flowers, and bushes and gnarly trees.

61   Out of another I get a lovely view of the bay and a little private wharf belonging to the estate. There is a beautiful shaded lane that runs down there from the house. I always fancy I see people walking in these numerous paths and arbors, but John has cautioned me not to give way to fancy in the least. He says that with my imaginative power and habit of story-making, a nervous weakness like mine is sure to lead to all manner of excited fancies, and that I ought to use my will and good sense to check the tendency. So I try.

62   I think sometimes that if I were only well enough to write a little it would relieve the press of ideas and rest me.

63   But I find I get pretty tired when I try.

64   It is so discouraging not to have any advice and companionship about my work. When I get really well, John says we will ask Cousin Henry and Julia down for a long visit; but he says he would as soon put fireworks in my pillow-case as to let me have those stimulating people about now.

65   I wish I could get well faster.

66   But I must not think about that. This paper looks to me as if it *knew* what a vicious influence it had!

67   There is a recurrent spot where the pattern lolls like a broken neck and two bulbous eyes stare at you upside down.

68   I get positively angry with the impertinence of it and the everlastingness. Up and down and sideways they crawl, and those absurd, unblinking eyes are everywhere. There is one place where two breadths didn't match, and the eyes go all up and down the line, one a little higher than the other.

69   I never saw so much expression in an inanimate thing before, and we all know how much expression they have! I used to lie awake as a child and get more entertainment and terror out of blank walls and plain furniture than most children could find in a toy-store.

70   I remember what a kindly wink the knobs of our big, old bureau used to have, and there was one chair that always seemed like a strong friend.

71   I used to feel that if any of the other things looked too fierce I could always hop into that chair and be safe.

72   The furniture in this room is no worse than inharmonious, however, for we had to bring it all from downstairs. I suppose when this was used as a playroom they had to take the nursery things out, and no wonder! I never saw such ravages as the children have made here.

73   The wall-paper, as I said before, is torn off in spots, and it sticketh closer than a brother—they must have had perseverance as well as hatred.

74   Then the floor is scratched and gouged and splintered, the plaster itself is dug out here and there, and this great heavy bed which is all we found in the room, looks as if it had been through the wars.

75   But I don't mind it a bit—only the paper.

76   There comes John's sister. Such a dear girl as she is, and so careful of me! I must not let her find me writing.

77   She is a perfect and enthusiastic housekeeper, and hopes for no better profession. I verily believe she thinks it is the writing which made me sick!

78   But I can write when she is out, and see her a long way off from these windows.

79   There is one that commands the road, a lovely shaded winding road, and one that just looks off over the country. A lovely country, too, full of great elms and velvet meadows.

80   This wall-paper has a kind of sub-pattern in a different shade, a particularly irritating one, for you can only see it in certain lights, and not clearly then.

81   But in the places where it isn't faded and where the sun is just so—I can see a strange, provoking, formless sort of figure, that seems to skulk about behind that silly and conspicuous front design.

82   There's sister on the stairs!

83   Well, the Fourth of July is over! The people are all gone and I am tired out. John thought it might do me good to see a little company, so we just had mother and Nellie and the children down for a week.

84   Of course I didn't do a thing. Jennie sees to everything now.

85   But it tired me all the same.

86   John says if I don't pick up faster he shall send me to Weir Mitchell in the fall.

87   But I don't want to go there at all. I had a friend who was in his hands once, and she says he is just like John and my brother, only more so!

88   Besides, it is such an undertaking to go so far.

89   I don't feel as if it was worth while to turn my hand over for anything, and I'm getting dreadfully fretful and querulous.

90   I cry at nothing, and cry most of the time.

91   Of course I don't when John is here, or anybody else, but when I am alone.

92   And I am alone a good deal just now. John is kept in town very often by serious cases, and Jennie is good and lets me alone when I want her to.

93   So I walk a little in the garden or down that lovely lane, sit on the porch under the roses, and lie down up here a good deal.

94   I'm getting really fond of the room in spite of the wall-paper. Perhaps *because* of the wall-paper.

95   It dwells in my mind so!

96   I lie here on this great immovable bed—it is nailed down, I believe—and follow that pattern about by the hour. It is as good as gymnastics, I assure you. I start, we'll say, at the bottom, down in the corner over there where it has not

been touched, and I determine for the thousandth time that I *will* follow that pointless pattern to some sort of a conclusion.

97   I know a little of the principle of design, and I know this thing was not arranged on any laws of radiation, or alternation, or repetition, or symmetry, or anything else that I ever heard of.

98   It is repeated, of course, by the breadths, but not otherwise.

99   Looked at in one way each breadth stands alone, the bloated curves and flourishes—a kind of "debased Romanesque" with *delirium tremens*—go waddling up and down in isolated columns of fatuity.

100   But, on the other hand, they connect diagonally, and the sprawling outlines run off in great slanting waves of optic horror, like a lot of wallowing seaweeds in full chase.

101   The whole thing goes horizontally, too, at least it seems so, and I exhaust myself in trying to distinguish the order of its going in that direction.

102   They have used a horizontal breadth for a frieze, and that adds wonderfully to the confusion.

103   There is one end of the room where it is almost intact, and there, when the crosslights fade and the low sun shines directly upon it, I can almost fancy radiation after all,—the interminable grotesques seem to form around a common center and rush off in headlong plunges of equal distraction.

104   It makes me tired to follow it. I will take a nap I guess.

105   I don't know why I should write this.

106   I don't want to.

107   I don't feel able.

108   And I know John would think it absurd. But I *must* say what I feel and think in some way—it is such a relief!

109   But the effort is getting to be greater than the relief.

110   Half the time now I am awfully lazy, and lie down ever so much.

111   John says I mustn't lose my strength, and has me take cod liver oil and lots of tonics and things, to say nothing of ale and wine and rare meat.

112   Dear John! He loves me very dearly, and hates to have me sick. I tried to have a real earnest reasonable talk with him the other day, and tell him how I wish he would let me go and make a visit to Cousin Henry and Julia.

113   But he said I wasn't able to go, nor able to stand it after I got there; and I did not make out a very good case for myself, for I was crying before I had finished.

114   It is getting to be a great effort for me to think straight. Just this nervous weakness I suppose.

115   And dear John gathered me up in his arms, and just carried me upstairs and laid me on the bed, and sat by me and read to me till it tired my head.

116   He said I was his darling and his comfort and all he had, and that I must take care of myself for his sake, and keep well.

117   He says no one but myself can help me out of it, that I must use my will and self-control and not let any silly fancies run away with me.

118   There's one comfort, the baby is well and happy, and does not have to occupy this nursery with the horrid wall-paper.

119   If we had not used it, that blessed child would have! What a fortunate escape! Why, I wouldn't have a child of mine, an impressionable little thing, live in such a room for worlds.

120   I never thought of it before, but it is lucky that John kept me here after all, I can stand it so much easier than a baby, you see.

121   Of course I never mention it to them any more—I am too wise,—but I keep watch of it all the same.

122   There are things in that paper that nobody knows but me, or ever will.

123   Behind that outside pattern the dim shapes get clearer every day.

124   It is always the same shape, only very numerous.

125   And it is like a woman stooping down and creeping about behind that pattern. I don't like it a bit. I wonder—I begin to think—I wish John would take me away from here!

126   It is so hard to talk with John about my case, because he is so wise, and because he loves me so.

127   But I tried it last night.

128   It was moonlight. The moon shines in all around just as the sun does.

129   I hate to see it sometimes, it creeps so slowly, and always comes in by one window or another.

130   John was asleep and I hated to waken him, so I kept still and watched the moonlight on that undulating wall-paper till I felt creepy.

131   The faint figure behind seemed to shake the pattern, just as if she wanted to get out.

132   I got up softly and went to feel and see if the paper *did* move, and when I came back John was awake.

133   "What is it, little girl?" he said. "Don't go walking about like that—you'll get cold."

134   I thought it was a good time to talk, so I told him that I really was not gaining here, and that I wished he would take me away.

135   "Why darling!" said he, "our lease will be up in three weeks, and I can't see how to leave before."

136   "The repairs are not done at home, and I cannot possibly leave town just now. Of course if you were in any danger, I could and would, but you really are better, dear, whether you can see it or not. I am a doctor, dear, and I know. You are gaining flesh and color, your appetite is better, I feel really much easier about you."

137   "I don't weigh a bit more," said I, "nor as much; and my appetite may be better in the evening when you are here, but it is worse in the morning when you are away!"

138   "Bless her little heart!" said he with a big hug, "she shall be as sick as she pleases! But now let's improve the shining hours by going to sleep, and talk about it in the morning!"

139   "And you won't go away?" I asked gloomily.

140   "Why, how can I, dear? It is only three weeks more and then we will take a nice little trip of a few days while Jennie is getting the house ready. Really dear you are better!"

141   "Better in body perhaps—" I began, and stopped short, for he sat up straight and looked at me with such a stern, reproachful look that I could not say another word.

142   "My darling," said he, "I beg of you, for my sake and for our child's sake, as well as for your own, that you will never for one instant let that idea enter your

mind! There is nothing so dangerous, so fascinating, to a temperament like yours. It is a false and foolish fancy. Can you not trust me as a physician when I tell you so?"

143   So of course I said no more on that score, and we went to sleep before long. He thought I was asleep first, but I wasn't, and lay there for hours trying to decide whether that front pattern and the back pattern really did move together or separately.

144   On a pattern like this, by daylight, there is a lack of sequence, a defiance of law, that is a constant irritant to a normal mind.

145   The color is hideous enough, and unreliable enough, and infuriating enough, but the pattern is torturing.

146   You think you have mastered it, but just as you get well underway in following, it turns a back-somersault and there you are. It slaps you in the face, knocks you down, and tramples upon you. It is like a bad dream.

147   The outside pattern is a florid arabesque, reminding one of a fungus. If you can imagine a toadstool in joints, an interminable string of toadstools, budding and sprouting in endless convolutions—why, that is something like it.

148   That is, sometimes!

149   There is one marked peculiarity about this paper, a thing nobody seems to notice but myself, and that is that it changes as the light changes.

150   When the sun shoots in through the east window—I always watch for that first long, straight ray—it changes so quickly that I never can quite believe it.

151   That is why I watch it always.

152   By moonlight—the moon shines in all night when there is a moon—I wouldn't know it was the same paper.

153   At night in any kind of light, in twilight, candle light, lamplight, and worst of all by moonlight, it becomes bars! The outside pattern I mean, and the woman behind it is as plain as can be.

154   I didn't realize for a long time what the thing was that showed behind, that dim sub-pattern, but now I am quite sure it is a woman.

155   By daylight she is subdued, quiet. I fancy it is the pattern that keeps her so still. It is so puzzling. It keeps me quiet by the hour.

156   I lie down ever so much now. John says it is good for me, and to sleep all I can.

157   Indeed he started the habit by making me lie down for an hour after each meal.

158   It is a very bad habit I am convinced, for you see I don't sleep.

159   And that cultivates deceit, for I don't tell them I'm awake—O no!

160   The fact is I am getting a little afraid of John.

161   He seems very queer sometimes, and even Jennie has an inexplicable look.

162   It strikes me occasionally, just as a scientific hypothesis,—that perhaps it is the paper!

163   I have watched John when he did not know I was looking, and come into the room suddenly on the most innocent excuses, and I've caught him several times *looking at the paper!* And Jennie too. I caught Jennie with her hand on it once.

164   She didn't know I was in the room, and when I asked her in a quiet, a very quiet voice, with the most restrained manner possible, what she was doing with the paper—she turned around as if she had been caught stealing, and looked quite angry—asked me why I should frighten her so!

165   Then she said that the paper stained everything it touched, that she had

found yellow smooches on all my clothes and John's, and she wished we would be more careful!

166 Did not that sound innocent? But I know she was studying that pattern, and I am determined that nobody shall find it out but myself!

167 Life is very much more exciting now than it used to be. You see I have something more to expect, to look forward to, to watch. I really do eat better, and am more quiet than I was.

168 John is so pleased to see me improve! He laughed a little the other day, and said I seemed to be flourishing in spite of my wall-paper.

169 I turned it off with a laugh. I had no intention of telling him it was *because* of the wall-paper—he would make fun of me. He might even want to take me away.

170 I don't want to leave now until I have found it out. There is a week more, and I think that will be enough.

171 I'm feeling ever so much better! I don't sleep much at night, for it is so interesting to watch developments; but I sleep a good deal in the daytime.

172 In the daytime it is tiresome and perplexing.

173 There are always new shoots on the fungus, and new shades of yellow all over it. I cannot keep count of them, though I have tried conscientiously.

174 It is the strangest yellow, that wall-paper! It makes me think of all the yellow things I ever saw—not beautiful ones like buttercups, but old foul, bad yellow things.

175 But there is something else about that paper—the smell! I noticed it the moment we came into the room, but with so much air and sun it was not bad. Now we have had a week of fog and rain, and whether the windows are open or not, the smell is here.

176 It creeps all over the house.

177 I find it hovering in the dining-room, skulking in the parlor, hiding in the hall, lying in wait for me on the stairs.

178 It gets into my hair.

179 Even when I go to ride, if I turn my head suddenly and surprise it—there is that smell!

180 Such a peculiar odor, too! I have spent hours in trying to analyze it, to find what it smelled like.

181 It is not bad—at first, and very gentle, but quite the subtlest, most enduring odor I ever met.

182 In this damp weather it is awful, I wake up in the night and find it hanging over me.

183 It used to disturb me at first. I thought seriously of burning the house—to reach the smell.

184 But now I am used to it. The only thing I can think of that it is like is the *color* of the paper! A yellow smell.

185 There is a very funny mark on this wall, low down, near the mopboard. A streak that runs round the room. It goes behind every piece of furniture, except the bed, a long, straight, even *smooch,* as if it had been rubbed over and over.

186 I wonder how it was done and who did it, and what they did it for. Round and round and round—round and round and round—it makes me dizzy!

187   I really have discovered something at last.

188   Through watching so much at night, when it changes so, I have finally found out.

189   The front pattern *does* move—and no wonder! The woman behind shakes it!

190   Sometimes I think there are a great many women behind, and sometimes only one, and she crawls around fast, and her crawling shakes it all over.

191   Then in the very bright spots she keeps still, and in the very shady spots she just takes hold of the bars and shakes them hard.

192   And she is all the time trying to climb through. But nobody could climb through that pattern—it strangles so; I think that is why it has so many heads.

193   They get through, and then the pattern strangles them off and turns them upside down, and makes their eyes white!

194   If those heads were covered or taken off it would not be half so bad.

195   I think that woman gets out in the daytime!

196   And I'll tell you why—privately—I've seen her!

197   I can see her out of every one of my windows!

198   It is the same woman, I know, for she is always creeping, and most women do not creep by daylight.

199   I see her on that long road under the trees, creeping along, and when a carriage comes she hides under the blackberry vines.

200   I don't blame her a bit. It must be very humiliating to be caught creeping by daylight!

201   I always lock the door when I creep by daylight. I can't do it at night, for I know John would suspect something at once.

202   And John is so queer now, that I don't want to irritate him. I wish he would take another room! Besides, I don't want anybody to get that woman out at night but myself.

203   I often wonder if I could see her out of all the windows at once.

204   But, turn as fast as I can, I can only see out of one at one time.

205   And though I always see her, she *may* be able to creep faster than I can turn!

206   I have watched her sometimes away off in the open country, creeping as fast as a cloud shadow in a high wind.

207   If only that top pattern could be gotten off from the under one! I mean to try it, little by little.

208   I have found out another funny thing, but I shan't tell it this time! It does not do to trust people too much.

209   There are only two more days to get this paper off, and I believe John is beginning to notice. I don't like the look in his eyes.

210   And I heard him ask Jennie a lot of professional questions about me. She had a very good report to give.

211   She said I slept a good deal in the daytime.

212   John knows I don't sleep very well at night, for all I'm so quiet!

213   He asked me all sorts of questions, too, and pretended to be very loving and kind.

214   As if I couldn't see through him!

215   Still, I don't wonder he acts so, sleeping under this paper for three months.

216   It only interests me, but I feel sure John and Jennie are secretly affected by it.

217   Hurrah! This is the last day, but it is enough. John is to stay in town over night, and won't be out until this evening.

218   Jennie wanted to sleep with me—the sly thing! but I told her I should undoubtedly rest better for a night all alone.

219   That was clever, for really I wasn't alone a bit! As soon as it was moonlight and that poor thing began to crawl and shake the pattern, I got up and ran to help her.

220   I pulled and she shook, I shook and she pulled, and before morning we had peeled off yards of that paper.

221   A strip about as high as my head and half around the room.

222   And then when the sun came and that awful pattern began to laugh at me, I declared I would finish it to-day!

223   We go away to-morrow, and they are moving all my furniture down again to leave things as they were before.

224   Jennie looked at the wall in amazement, but I told her merrily that I did it out of pure spite at the vicious thing.

225   She laughed and said she wouldn't mind doing it herself, but I must not get tired.

226   How she betrayed herself that time!

227   But I am here, and no person touches this paper but me,—not *alive!*

228   She tried to get me out of the room—it was too patent! But I said it was so quiet and empty and clean now that I believed I would lie down again and sleep all I could; and not to wake me even for dinner—I would call when I woke.

229   So now she is gone, and the servants are gone, and the things are gone, and there is nothing left but that great bedstead nailed down, with the canvas mattress we found on it.

230   We shall sleep downstairs tonight, and take the boat home tomorrow.

231   I quite enjoy the room, now it is bare again.

232   How those children did tear about here!

233   This bedstead is fairly gnawed!

234   But I must get to work.

235   I have locked the door and thrown the key down into the front path.

236   I don't want to go out, and I don't want to have anybody come in, till John comes.

237   I want to astonish him.

238   I've got a rope up here that even Jennie did not find. If that woman does get out, and tries to get away, I can tie her!

239   But I forgot I could not reach far without anything to stand on!

240   This bed will *not* move!

241   I tried to lift and push it until I was lame, and then I got so angry I bit off a little piece at one corner—but it hurt my teeth.

242   Then I peeled off all the paper I could reach standing on the floor. It sticks horribly and the pattern just enjoys it! All those strangled heads and bulbous eyes and waddling fungus growths just shriek with derision!

243   I am getting angry enough to do something desperate. To jump out of the window would be admirable exercise, but the bars are too strong even to try.

244   Besides I wouldn't do it. Of course not. I know well enough that a step like that is improper and might be misconstrued.

245   I don't like to *look* out of the windows even—there are so many of those creeping women, and they creep so fast.

246   I wonder if they all come out of that wall-paper as I did?

247   But I am securely fastened now by my well-hidden rope—you don't get *me* out in the road there!

248   I suppose I shall have to get back behind the pattern when it comes night, and that is hard!

249   It is so pleasant to be out in this great room and creep around as I please!

250   I don't want to go outside. I won't, even if Jennie asks me to.

251   For outside you have to creep on the ground, and everything is green instead of yellow.

252   But here I can creep smoothly on the floor, and my shoulder just fits in that long smooch around the wall, so I cannot lose my way.

253   Why there's John at the door!

254   It is no use, young man, you can't open it!

255   How he does call and pound!

256   Now he's crying for an axe.

257   It would be a shame to break down that beautiful door!

258   "John dear!" said I in the gentlest voice, "the key is down by the front steps, under a plantain leaf!"

259   That silenced him for a few moments.

260   Then he said—very quietly indeed, "Open the door, my darling!"

261   "I can't," said I. "The key is down by the front door under a plantain leaf!"

262   And then I said it again, several times, very gently and slowly, and said it so often that he had to go and see, and he got it of course, and came in. He stopped short by the door.

263   "What is the matter?" he cried. "For God's sake, what are you doing!"

264   I kept on creeping just the same, but I looked at him over my shoulder.

265   "I've got out at last," said I, "in spite of you and Jane. And I've pulled off most of the paper, so you can't put me back!"

266   Now why should that man have fainted? But he did, and right across my path by the wall, so that I had to creep over him every time!

A Student's Response to "The Yellow Wallpaper": Aviva Geiger's Preliminary Exercises and Final Draft

In the final weeks of her composition class, Geiger was asked to write a critical analysis and interpretation of "The Yellow Wallpaper." The first step of the process was a brief exercise: students were asked to summarize the story and to identify its themes, to say what the story seemed to be about; then they were to write down their questions about the story—to articulate what puzzled them or disturbed them, to try to say what did not make sense or add up. The second step required students to choose one of the questions they had formulated—the question that seemed most interesting after they had read the story several times—and then to begin gathering passages from the text that might help them to answer the question they had chosen. (As we suggest on pages 398–99, asking questions and answering them is one way to begin to shape an initial response into an essay topic.) Here is what Aviva wrote for the first exercise.

Exercise #1: Thoughts on "The Yellow Wallpaper"

by Charlotte Perkins Gilman

The story is a first-person account of a woman's decline into insanity, brought on by the confinement she feels from a male-dominated society. One of its themes is the narrowness of a woman's role in society; the story suggests the harm that is done by enforcing that role. It also deals with the issue of insanity and the repercussions insanity can have for an entire family when it touches any one member of the family.

Questions:

Why does the narrator repeatedly refer to the act of creeping as she sinks into insanity? What does the creeping symbolize to her?

> She first brings it up while describing the wallpaper at night, when she says: "Behind that outside pattern the dim shapes get clearer every day . . . [I]t is like a woman stooping down and creeping about behind that pattern. I don't like it a bit" (383). Later on, she starts to hallucinate about a woman creeping around outdoors, saying: "I can see her out of every one of my windows! It is the same woman, I know, for she is always . . . creeping along, and when a carriage comes she hides . . . I don't blame her a bit. It must be very humiliating to be caught creeping by daylight!" (386). Finally, at the end of the story, the narrator "becomes" the woman in the wallpaper and creeps around as well. The question is why the narrator uses the verb "to creep" over and over again, and eventually feels compelled to start creeping herself.

Why does the narrator ignore her own baby throughout the story?

> She refers to her inability to mother her child when she says, "It is fortunate Mary is so good with the baby. Such a dear baby! And yet I <u>cannot</u> be with him, it makes me so nervous" (380). In fact, even at the beginning of the story before her delusions start, the narrator seems much more preoccupied with inanimate objects

such as furniture and wallpaper than she is with her own child. Nevertheless, the narrator appears to care about her baby. She says later on: "There's one comfort, the baby is well and happy, and does not have to occupy this nursery with the horrid wallpaper. . . . Why, I wouldn't have a child of mine, an impressionable little thing, live in such a room for worlds" (382). Even in this statement, however, the narrator refers to her child in the abstract ("a child of mine").

Throughout the entire story, she never even mentions its name.

So perhaps the real question is: why does the narrator seem incapable of dealing with the idea of being a mother?

Geiger has made a good start. She has identified some important themes: the story, she says, is about "confinement" and "insanity" brought on by "male-dominated society," and about the consequences of insanity on all the members of a family. (Note, though, that Geiger's sense of what the story is about will change as she continues to ponder it. She comes to realize, for example, that "The Yellow Wallpaper" does not actually say much about how the narrator's insanity affects the rest of her family, and so she drops that point in the next exercise.) And she asks two main questions—the first about why the narrator "creeps," and the second about why she is incapable of taking care of her child. Both are good questions, in part because the story *does not* offer clear and easy answers to them. (If the questions were easy to answer, anyone could answer them, and there would not be much reason to analyze the story or to write the essay.) In the next stage of the sequence, Geiger chooses to explore the second question and begins considering more passages, passages that help to complicate and to focus her sense of what the story is saying about the narrator's relationship to her child.

Exercise #2: Topic for Essay on "The Yellow Wallpaper"

Why does the narrator keep mentioning children while she can hardly bring herself to think about her own child? From the first time she mentions children, when describing the bedroom and the wallpaper, the narrator's words imply that she identifies herself with children. The narrator tells us the bedroom "was nursery first and then playroom and gymnasium, I should judge; for the windows are barred for little children . . ." (379). Furthermore, she says of the wallpaper: "No wonder the children hated it! I should hate it myself if I had to live in this room long" (379). Of course, the narrator is only guessing that the room was ever inhabited by children, and she projects her own dislike of the wallpaper onto the children she has imagined.

The question is why the narrator subconsciously projects her own emotions onto children in particular. Her comment about barred windows in the above passage provides a possible explanation. The narrator identifies with children because they are restricted and confined in much the same way that she is by her husband John. For example, she describes how John patronizes her and restricts her freedom when she says:

> Dear John! He loves me very dearly, and hates to have me sick. I tried to have a real earnest reasonable talk with him the other day, and tell him how I wish he would let me go and make a visit to Cousin Henry and Julia.
>
> But he said I wasn't able to go, nor able to stand it after I got there; and I did not make out a very good case for myself, for I was crying before I had finished. (382)

In several other passages, she tells of how John supervises her and "hardly lets me stir without special direction" (379). Therefore, it seems likely that the narrator keeps mentioning children because she feels she is treated like a child by her husband.

In a larger sense, however, it is not John who restricts and confines the narrator as much as a male-dominated society that defines an extremely narrow role for wives. This role basically consists of acting as a companion for the husband, organizing the household, and mothering the children. In the following passage, the narrator describes how she cannot bring herself to fulfill any one of these three wifely duties:

>   I meant to be such a help to John, such a real rest and
> comfort, and here I am a comparative burden already!
>
>   Nobody would believe what an effort it is to do what little I am
> able,—to dress and entertain, and order things.
>
>   It is fortunate Mary is so good with the baby. Such a dear
> baby!
>
>   And yet I <u>cannot</u> be with him, it makes me so nervous. (379–80)

Thus, the narrator's inability to deal with her own child seems to be a
symptom of her inability to perform the general tasks expected of a wife. It
is not that the narrator dislikes her child, but allowing herself to be a good
mother would symbolize her submission to the behavioral constraints of
society placed on married women.

The narrator clearly expresses her love for the baby when she says:

>   There's one comfort, the baby is well and happy, and does not
> have to occupy this nursery with the horrid wall-paper. . . .
>
>   Why, I wouldn't have a child of mine, an impressionable little
> thing, live in such a room for worlds.
>
>   I never thought of it before, but it is lucky that John kept me
> here after all, I can stand it so much easier than a baby, you see.
> (382–83)

This passage shows that the narrator truly is concerned for her child's
welfare despite the lack of attention she seems to pay him. It also
reinforces the idea that the narrator unconsciously equates her own
marital situation with an adult's treatment of a child. She tries to kid
herself that she can stand the constraints placed on her "so much easier
than a baby," but at the same time, she describes how John <u>kept</u> her in the
nursery instead of the baby. Thus, John's treatment of his wife and his
treatment of his child are basically interchangeable. However, John does

not do this out of cruelty; he is merely acting as his society dictates a husband should act. In the end, the narrator's loss of touch with reality shows that society's restrictive treatment is actually much harder on a rational adult than it would be on a child. Through the narrator's references to children, therefore, the author conveys the message that children should be treated as children but grown women should not.

This exercise gave Geiger the basis for the draft of her essay. It does not yet contain the main point or thesis that will be developed in the final revision (that "the inherent conflict between the needs of the narrator's child and the expectations of her husband precipitates her eventual decline into madness"), and it lacks the focus of the revision (the last sentence of the exercise, for example, is a bit flat). Nevertheless, it does contain some of the main points and a good deal of the evidence found in the revision, reprinted below.

The Narrator's Dilemma in

Charlotte Perkins Gilman's "The Yellow Wallpaper"

Charlotte Perkins Gilman's short story "The Yellow Wallpaper" appears to be a straightforward feminist critique of the oppression of married women in the nineteenth century. Reported by an unnamed first-person narrator, "The Yellow Wallpaper" tells the story of a depressed woman whose husband, John, keeps her so confined that she becomes obsessed with the wallpaper in her bedroom and experiences a mental breakdown. But a careful reading of Gilman's references to children and childhood throughout the story suggests that her critique of women's oppression is much more focused and complex than it would at first seem. Although the narrator hardly mentions her own newborn baby at all, her mind returns to the notion of children in the abstract again and again. Gradually it becomes clear that her attitude toward children actually illustrates a paradox in the unstated duties of a married woman. She realizes that, as a mother, she can serve no greater purpose than to act as a caretaker and protector for her child, but in order to fulfill her role as a wife, she is required to act like a child herself. The inherent conflict between the needs of the narrator's child and the expectations of her husband precipitates her eventual decline into madness.

Although the narrator only mentions her baby twice, the two references clearly convey the anxiety and guilt that motherhood has created for her. She sighs: "It does weigh on me so not to do my duty in any way! . . . It is fortunate Mary is so good with the baby. Such a dear baby! And yet I <u>cannot</u> be with him, it makes me so nervous." (379–80)[1] The narrator understands that as a new mother, she should naturally want to love and nurture her son, but for some reason, she seems to find the prospect of acting like a mother too frightening to face. Later in the story, she attempts to overcome these qualms by asserting:

> There's one comfort, the baby is well and happy, and does not have to occupy this nursery with the horrid wall-paper. . . .
>
> Why, I wouldn't have a child of mine, an impressionable little thing, live in such a room for worlds.
>
> I never thought of it before, but it is lucky that John kept me here after all, I can stand it so much easier than a baby. . . .
>
> (382–83)

The narrator's tone here suggests that she is trying to convince herself that she <u>can</u> fill the role of a proper mother and that she <u>does</u> look out for her child's welfare. Despite all her attempts at maternal sentiment, however, her concern for her son seems insincere. She still only thinks of her baby in the abstract- -"a child of mine"- -and she sounds more like she is reciting from a script than speaking from the heart.

Perhaps the narrator has difficulty with behaving like a mother because she is treated like a child herself throughout the story. From the

---

[1] All page references are to Charlotte Perkins Gilman, "The Yellow Wallpaper," reprinted in <u>The Practical Guide to Writing</u>, Second Canadian Edition (Pearson Education, 2006), 377-88.

very first page, the narrator's husband, John, consistently exhibits the philosophy that a man can expect no more logic or self-knowledge from his wife than he could from a small child. Accordingly, John dictates nearly every aspect of the narrator's daily life. In one instance, she describes how her husband and her brother take responsibility for her health. She says she takes, on their orders, "phosphates or phosphites— whichever it is, and tonics, and journeys, and air, and exercise, and am absolutely forbidden to 'work' until I am well again" (378), even though she maintains: "Personally, I disagree with their ideas. Personally, I believe that congenial work, with excitement and change, would do me good" (378). Her words give the impression that John would brazenly proceed according to his own theories of mental health care in the face of any protest that the narrator might put forth.

The temptation, of course, is to blame John for the fact that his regime fails to pull the narrator out of her depression and, instead, drives her deeper into mental illness. However, at some points in the story, the narrator's childish behavior seems to justify his patronizing attitude toward her. The narrator reports a conversation, for example, in which her own conduct could have done nothing but confirm John's suspicions about the irrational nature of womankind:

> I tried to have a real earnest reasonable talk with him the other day, and tell him how I wish he would let me go and make a visit to Cousin Henry and Julia.
>
> But he said I wasn't able to go, nor able to stand it after I got there; and I did not make out a very good case for myself, for I was crying before I had finished. (382)

Although John does come across as dictatorial in his control of his wife's activities, this exchange also demonstrates the narrator's childishly inconsistent behavior. Only the page before, she had complained: "I don't feel as if it was worth while to turn my hand over for anything" (381), describing how the company of visitors tired her. No wonder, then, that John believes his wife will change her mind and wish to return home again if he allows her to visit her friends. The narrator's own indecisiveness creates the need for John to make decisions on her behalf.

Furthermore, the narrator herself seems to believe in her husband's notions about the similarities between wives and children. She mentions children repeatedly over the course of the story, and each time, she gives the impression that she identifies with them. When first describing her bedroom, she says: "It was nursery first and then playroom and gymnasium, I should judge; for the windows are barred for little children . . ." (379), and of the wallpaper she exclaims: "No wonder the children hated it! I should hate it myself if I had to live in this room long" (379). Although the narrator really only assumes that children ever inhabited her room, her mind wanders back to images of children again and again. More important, the narrator seems to project her own instinctual distaste for the wallpaper onto the children she has imagined, suggesting she agrees with her husband's implicit belief that the opinions and thought processes of a woman are as immature and irrational as those of small children.

To some extent, then, the narrator's behavior does confirm her husband's expectations. Nevertheless, her increasingly severe delusions, which contain clear symbols of restraint and confinement, show that she feels terribly constrained by her husband's domineering attitude. In her description of the bedroom, she mentions that "the windows are barred for little children" (379), and she reiterates the image of the bars later on through her hallucinations about the wallpaper. While watching the paper at night, she says of its pattern: "by moonlight, it becomes bars! The outside pattern I mean, and the woman behind it is as plain as can be" (384). Clearly, the bars symbolize the narrator's own feeling of confinement at the hands of her husband. Of course, the previous owners of the house put bars in their windows to protect their children, not to confine them, and John is equally well-intentioned in the constraints he places on his wife. Nevertheless, despite the narrator's apparent willingness to conform to her husband's image of a child-like wife, her delusions surrounding the bars reveal the long-buried resentment that has resulted from John's patronizing treatment.

Thus, the narrator feels torn between the two conflicting roles that marriage and motherhood have created for her. She finds the prospect of maturing into a loving and responsible caretaker for her baby so frightening that she cannot stand to spend any time with him, but at the same time, she seems to know that by continuing to act like a child herself, she will never be permitted the freedom for which she yearns. It is this baffling conflict to which she addresses the refrain: "But what is one to do?" (378). Stripped of the distractions that writing and social interaction once provided, the narrator finds herself confronted with an intractable dilemma. The reader can only guess whether a character with more mental toughness could have successfully wrangled with this dilemma; for, instead of taking on the struggle, the narrator loses herself in a new distraction: the yellow wallpaper of her nursery/bedroom.

For this reason, it seems that Gilman does not find John's demeaning treatment entirely at fault in the narrator's mental breakdown. While John's insistence on coddling the narrator does create a difficult paradox for her to face as a new mother, it is the narrator's inability to cope with the paradox that eventually leads her to insanity. In this way, Gilman's theme takes the form of a double-edged sword. She condemns John and the male-dominated society he represents for their patronizing attitude toward married women. Nevertheless, she also suggests that wives must take responsibility for their own well-being and force themselves to face the painful conflicts that marriage and motherhood create.

GETTING IDEAS FOR WRITING ABOUT FICTION

Here are some questions that may help to stimulate responses and therefore ideas about stories. Not every question is, of course, relevant to every story, but if after reading a story and thinking about it, you then run your eye over this checklist, you will probably find some questions that will help you to think further about the story—in short, that will help you to get ideas.

It is best to do your thinking with a pen or pencil in hand or in front of your word processor. If some of the following questions seem to you to be especially relevant to the story you will be writing about, jot down—freely, without worrying about spelling—your initial responses, interrupting your writing only to glance again at the story when you feel the need to check the evidence.

 A Checklist: Asking Questions about Fiction

✔ What happens in the story? Summarize the **plot**. (Think about what your summary *leaves out*.)
✔ Is the story told in chronological order or are there flashbacks or flashforwards? On rereading, what **foreshadowing** of events do you detect?
✔ What **conflicts** does the story include?
✔ With which **character** or characters do you sympathize? How does the writer reveal character? How does the author create sympathy for some characters but not for others? Are the characters and their actions plausible? What motivates them? Do their names suggest anything about their characters or functions in the story? What do minor characters contribute to the story?
✔ Who tells the story? Is the story narrated by a **first-person narrator** (as was the case in "The Yellow Wallpaper")? If so, is that narrator the main character or **protagonist**? If the narrator is a character in the story, how reliable does he or she appear to be? Or is the story told by a **third-person narrator** (as was the case in "Muddy Road")? If so, does the narrator represent the action primarily through the thoughts and actions of one of the characters? Or does the narrator seem to stand entirely outside the characters, to be neutral? Try to assess your response to or the effect on you of the **point of view.**
✔ Where and when does the story take place? What is the relation of the **setting** to the **plot** and **characters**?
✔ Do certain characters seem to you to stand for something in addition to themselves; that is, are they **symbolic**? Does the **setting**—a house, a

farm, a landscape, a town, a period—have an extra dimension? (Trust your responses to a story. If you don't sense a symbolic overtone in a character or action, move on. Don't let a hunt for symbols distract you from enjoying and thinking about the story.)

✔ Is the **title** informative? Did its meaning seem to change after you read the story?

✔ What do you especially like or dislike about the story? Do you think your responses are in large degree unique, or do you think that most readers share them? Why?

✔ What is the story about? What is its **theme**? Does the theme concern values you hold, or does it challenge them?

✔ What does the story seem to be *saying about* its theme? What point does the author seem to be making? (About what?) What is the **meaning** of the story?

READING POETRY

Let's begin with an example. The following short poem, first published in 1951, provided Lorraine Hansberry with the title of her well-known play, *A Raisin in the Sun*.

 LANGSTON HUGHES

Langston Hughes (1902-67) was a prolific writer of poetry, short stories, plays, essays, and novels. He became known as a poet during the Harlem Renaissance (1920s). He earned a B.A. at Lincoln University in 1929 and was later awarded a Guggenheim Fellowship and a Rosenwald Fellowship. "Harlem" was first published in The Montage of a Dream Deferred *(1951).*

Harlem

What happens to a dream deferred?

>Does it dry up
>like a raisin in the sun?
>Or fester like a sore—
>And then run?
>Does it stink like rotten meat?
>Or crust and sugar over—
>like a syrupy sweet?

>Maybe it just sags
>like a heavy load.

>*Or does it explode?*

Reread the poem, this time thinking about its effect on you. Are there words or ideas that puzzle you, please you, displease you, or what?

Of course, different readers will respond at least somewhat differently to any work. On the other hand, poets and storytellers, like psychologists, historians, and all other writers, want to communicate, and so they try to control their readers' responses. They count on their readers to understand the meanings of words as the writers themselves understand them. Thus Hughes could assume that his readers knew that Harlem was the site of a large African-American community in New York City, and further, that the phrase "dream deferred" refers to the unfulfilled hopes of African Americans who live in a predominantly white society. But Hughes does not say (as we have just said) "hopes"; rather, he says "dream." And he does not say "unfulfilled"; rather, he says "deferred." You might ask yourself exactly what differences there are between these words. Next, when you reread the poem, you might think about which expression is better in the context, "unfulfilled hopes" or "dream deferred," and why?

This sort of questioning of the words of the text, or, rather, questioning your responses to the words of the text, is at the heart of writing about literature—just as it is at the heart of writing about any sort of complicated text. If after a second reading of a literary text you still feel short of responses—but don't forget that being puzzled is itself a response worth studying—you will almost surely be able to generate responses by using the invention devices that we mention in our first chapter: freewriting, listing, clustering, keeping a journal, and asking questions. (At the end of this section, we will suggest some additional strategies for generating responses to poetry.)

A Student Thinks about "Harlem": Richard Taub's Annotations, Journal Entries, Notes, and Final Draft

Let's turn to an analysis of the poem, an examination of how the parts fit. As you look at the poem, think about the parts, and jot down whatever thoughts come to mind. After you have written your own notes, consider the annotations of one student, Richard Taub.

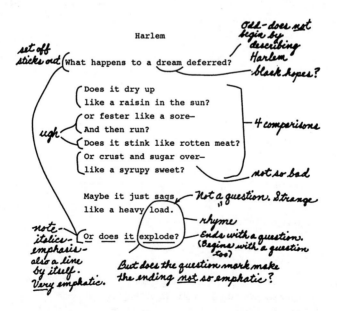

Taub's annotations chiefly get at the **structure** of the poem, the relationship of the parts. He notices that the poem begins with a line set off by itself and ends with a line set off by itself, and he also notices that each of these lines is a question. Further, he indicates that each of these two lines is emphasized in other ways: the first begins farther to the left than any of the other lines—as though the other lines are subheadings or are in some way subordinate—and the last is italicized.

Taub later wrote entries in his journal:

Feb. 18. Since the title is "Harlem," it's obvious that the "dream" is by African-American people. Also, obvious that Hughes thinks that if the "dream" doesn't become real there may be riots ("explode"). I like "raisin in the sun" (maybe because I like the play), and I like the business about "a syrupy sweet"--much more pleasant than the festering sore and the rotten meat. But if the dream becomes "sweet," what's wrong with that? Why should something "sweet" explode?

Feb. 21. Prof. McCabe said to think of structure or form of a poem as a sort of architecture, a building with a foundation, floors, etc. topped by a roof--but since we read a poem from top to bottom, it's like a building upside down. Title or first line is foundation (even though it's at top); last line is roof, capping the whole. As you read, you add layers. Foundation of "Harlem" is a question (first line). Then, set back a bit from foundation, or built on it by white space, a tall room (7 lines high, with 4 questions); then, on top of this room, another room (two lines, one statement, not a question). Funny; I thought that in poems all stanzas are the same number of lines. Then--more white space, so another unit--the roof. Man this roof is going to fall in--"explode." Not just the roof, maybe the whole house.

Feb. 21, p.m. I get it; one line at start, one line at end; both are questions, but the last sort of says (because it is in italics) that it is the most likely answer to the question of the first line. The last line is also a question, but it's still an answer. The big stanza (7 lines) has 4 questions: 2 lines, 2 lines, 1 line, 2 lines. Maybe the switch to 1 line is to give some variety, so as not to be dull? It's exactly in the middle of the poem. I get the progress from raisin in the sun (dried, but not so terrible), to festering sore and to stinking meat, but I still don't see what's so bad about "a syrupy sweet." Is Hughes saying that after things are very bad they will get better? But why, then, the explosion at the end?

Feb. 23. "Heavy load" and "sags" in next-to-last stanza seems to me to suggest slaves with bales of cotton, or maybe poor cotton pickers dragging big sacks of cotton. Or maybe people doing heavy labor in Harlem. Anyway, very tired. Different from running sore and stinking meat earlier; not disgusting, but pressing down, deadening. Maybe worse than a sore or rotten meat--a hard, hopeless life. And then the last line. Just one line, no fancy (and disgusting) simile. Boom! Not just pressed down and tired, like maybe some racist whites think (hope?) blacks will be? Bang! Will there be survivors?

Drawing chiefly on these notes, Taub jotted down some key ideas to guide him through a draft of an analysis of the poem. In organizing his draft, Taub followed the organization of the poem. On the following pages we give his notes and final draft.

11 lines; short, but powerful; explosive
Question (first line)
Answers (set off by space, & also indented)
"raisin in the sun": shrinking
"sore"   } *disgusting*
"rotten meat"
"syrupy sweet": relief from disgusting comparisons
Final question (last line): explosion?
explosive (powerful) because:
short, condensed, packed
in italics
stands by self — like first line
no fancy comparison; very direct

An Analysis of Langston Hughes's "Harlem"

"Harlem" is a poem that is only eleven lines long, but it is charged

with power. It explodes. Hughes sets the stage, so to speak, by telling us in

the title that he is talking about Harlem, and then he begins by asking

"What happens to a dream deferred?" The rest of the poem is set off by

being indented, as though it is the answer to his question. This answer is

in three parts (three stanzas, of different lengths).

In a way, it's wrong to speak of the answer, since the rest of the poem

consists of questions, but I think Hughes means that each question (for

instance, does a "deferred" hope "dry up / like a raisin in the sun?") really is

an answer, something that really has happened and that will happen again.

The first question, "Does it dry up / like a raisin in the sun?" is a famous

line. To compare hope to a raisin dried in the sun is to suggest a terrible

shrinking. The next two comparisons are to a "sore" and to "rotten meat."

These comparisons are less clever, but they are very effective because they

are disgusting. Then, maybe because of the disgusting comparisons, he gives a comparison that is not at all disgusting. In this comparison he says that maybe the "dream deferred" will "sugar over- - / like a syrupy sweet."

The seven lines with four comparisons are followed by a stanza of two lines with just one comparison:

> Maybe it just sags
>
> like a heavy load.

So if we thought that this postponed dream might finally turn into something "sweet," we were kidding ourselves. Hughes comes down to earth, in a short stanza, with an image of a heavy load, which probably also calls to mind images of people bent under heavy loads, maybe of cotton, or maybe just any sort of heavy load carried by African-Americans in Harlem and elsewhere.

The opening question ("What happens to a dream deferred?") is followed by four questions in seven lines, but now, with "Maybe it just sags / like a heavy load" we get a statement, as though the poet at last has found an answer. But at the end we get one more question, set off by itself and in italics: "Or does it explode?" This line itself is explosive for three reasons: it is short, it is italicized, and it is a stanza in itself. It's also interesting that this line, unlike the earlier lines, does not use a simile. It's almost as though Hughes is saying, "O.K., we've had enough fancy ways of talking about this terrible situation; here it is, straight."

Getting Ideas for Writing about Poetry

If you are going to write about a fairly short poem (say, under thirty lines), copy out the poem, writing or typing it double-spaced. By writing it out you will be forced to notice details, down to the punctuation. After you have copied the poem, proofread it carefully against the original. Catching an error—even the addition or omission of a comma—may help you to notice a detail in the original that you might otherwise have overlooked. And of course, now that you have the poem with ample space between the lines, you have a worksheet with room for jottings.

A good essay is based on a genuine response to a poem; a response may be stimulated in part by first reading the poem aloud and then considering the following questions.

A Checklist: Asking Questions about Poems

✔ What was your first response? On rereading, what parts interest or puzzle you? What words seem especially striking or unusual? (Consult a dictionary for the several meanings of words you're unsure of.)

✔ How would you describe the **speaker** of the poem? What persona or voice is suggested? What **tone** or emotion do you detect—for example, remorse, regret, affection, irony, sorrow?

✔ What is the **structure** of the poem? Are there stanzas? Are there rhymes or repeated sounds? Do the lines vary in length or echo each other? Are there unexpected stresses or pauses? How do they affect you?

✔ What is the poem about? Is the **theme** stated or implied? How might you state it in a sentence?

✔ What **images** do you find? (An image recalls a sensation of sight, sound, taste, touch, or smell.) What does the poem suggest **symbolically** as well as literally?

✔ What do you especially like or dislike about the poem? Do you think your responses are in large degree unique, or do you think that most readers share them? Why?

A RANGE OF CRITICAL APPROACHES

It is probably impossible to write an essay on a piece of literature without writing from some critical position, even if that position is not explicit or acknowledged.* An essay might concern a short story, say, and make no reference to the author's gender or biography, or to the time and place of its writing, or to the economic conditions that influenced its production; even so, that essay would still be informed by certain assumptions about how literature works and about how it ought to be read. In fact, **formalist criticism**—also known as the **New Criticism** of the 1930s to 1970s—takes precisely the approach outlined above, emphasizing the work as a self-contained unity to be studied in itself, not as part of a historical context or an author's life. Formalist critics emphasize the *form* of the work, the relationships between the parts: the construction of the plot, the contrasts between characters, the functions of rhymes, the point of view, and so on.

Critics since the 1970s have challenged the principles of formalist criticism, especially the idea that a work can be read in isolation. (Even so, students are

---

*The discussion that follows draws on Chapter 16, "Writing about Literature: An Overview," in Barnet et al., *Literature for Composition: Essays, Fiction, Poetry, and Drama,* Fourth Edition (New York: HarperCollins, 1996), pages 430-52. Theory is dynamic and constantly shifting; it involves different perspectives even within each critical approach and overlaps among the various approaches.

often asked to do just that—especially at the beginning of the semester in first-year literature courses—in part because such assignments can focus on the close-reading skills at the heart of all literary analysis.) For example, **reader-response criticism** focuses on the relationship between texts and readers, arguing that meaning is not something that an author embeds in a work, but that it is something that a reader creates in responding to a work. Early **feminist criticism**, which grew out of the women's movement of the 1960s, challenged the principles of formalism from another direction. Feminist critics have emphasized and explored the differences between women and men, and (generally speaking) argued that literature written by men is different from literature written by women, which is seen to embody the experiences of a group marginalized by the dominant patriarchal culture. Feminist criticism has been concerned with the depiction of women and men in a male-determined literary canon and with women's responses to these images; it has also been concerned with women's writing and the connections between the woman writer's biography and her work. When it explores such connections, it is making use of a form of **historical criticism** (see below) known as **biographical criticism**, which interprets a given work in the context of its author's life as revealed through autobiographies, diaries, journals, letters, and the like. Contemporary feminism, sometimes called third-wave feminism or post-feminism, has broadened its scope into a number of interrelated fields, but is still primarily concerned with the political and the social; feminists tend to focus on pluralism and difference, and on the subject as multiply positioned across a number of categories of analysis such as gender, race/ethnicity, class, and sexuality. **Psychological** or **psychoanalytic criticism** is related to biographical criticism: the psychoanalytic critic examines the author and his or her work through the lens of psychology, usually Freudian; works of art, like dreams, are interpreted as disguised versions of repressed wishes. Lacanian psychoanalytic theory rewrites the Freudian and emphasizes the notion of the subject, or the self, as fragmented, as repressing desires, and as constructed primarily through language. Since language is symbolic, we can never get at the true meaning of a text because it always contains gaps and fissures through which the unconscious of both the writer and the reader affect interpretation.

   Lesbian criticism, gay criticism, and (more recently) **queer theory** all have their roots in feminist theory. Lesbian and gay criticism addresses such questions as: (1) How have straight writers portrayed lesbians and gays, and how have lesbian and gay writers portrayed straight women and men? (2) What strategies did lesbian and gay writers use to make their work acceptable to a general public in an age when lesbian and gay behaviour was unmentionable? Whereas lesbian and gay criticism has tended to examine the effects of an author's—or a character's—sexual identity, queer theorists question the concept of sexual identity itself; Judith Butler, for example, argues that various categories of identity ("heterosexual," "homosexual") are socially constructed and represent ways of defining human beings that are distinct to particular cultures and historical periods.

   Like all the approaches discussed above, **historical criticism** and **New Historicism** also consider the literary text in context, but these two critical approaches differ greatly from each other. Historical criticism assumes that an understanding of how people thought and felt in the past can contribute to an understanding of a particular work. (**Marxist criticism**, a form of historical criticism, sees history primarily as a struggle between socioeconomic classes, and literature as the product of the economic forces of the period, a product of work that also *does* work—serving to assure the society that produces it that the society's values are solid, even universal.) New Historicism, which emerged in the 1980s and is especially associated with Stephen Greenblatt, insists that there is no "history" in the sense of a narrative of indisputable past events, and suggests that an understanding of how people thought and felt in the past is not really possible to achieve. Rather, New Historicism holds that there is only *our* version—our narrative, our representation—of the past. Each age projects its own preconceptions on the past. **Post-colonial criticism,** sharing with New Historicism and Marxism a concern with history and politics, is linked with the work of Edward Said and Gayatri Spivak. Its focus is twofold: (1) on texts written about colonized places by writers from colonizing nations, where it challenges certain cultures' (mis)representations of other cultures; and (2) on work produced in former European colonies, where it expands the notion of European literature to include writing produced by subaltern (or marginalized) peoples. At the other end of the spectrum, more or less, is **deconstruction** or **post-structural criticism**, which (like formalist criticism) pays rigorous attention to the text, but which (unlike formalist criticism) assumes that the world is unknowable and that language is unstable, elusive, unfaithful. Deconstructionists hold that literary "texts" inevitably are self-contradictory and therefore open to multiple interpretations; they also believe that authors are "socially constructed" from the "discourses of power" or "signifying practices" that surround them. Despite the differences between deconstruction and other critical approaches, deconstructionist thinking has powerfully influenced literary criticism since the 1960s. Jacques Derrida's *Of Grammatology* (1967, trans. 1976) is the seminal document, an influence on perhaps all the theory and criticism that came after it.

For a student essay that makes use of a range of critical approaches—biographical, feminist, psychological, historical—see Beatrice Cody's "Politics and Psychology in *The Awakening*," reprinted in Chapter 16, "Writing the Research Essay."

THREE SHORT WORKS OF FICTION

 ## THOMAS KING

Thomas King is a prolific writer of short stories, poems, novels, and screen and radio plays. He has been shortlisted for the Governor General's Literary Award for Green Grass, Running Water *and won the Canadian Authors Association Award for fiction. Although King was born and raised in California, he considers himself a Canadian writer. He currently teaches at Guelph University.*

One Good Story, That One

1   Alright.

2   You know, I hear this story up north. Maybe Yellowknife, that one, somewhere. I hear it maybe a long time. Old story this one. One hundred years, maybe more. Maybe not so long either, this story.

3   So.

4   You know, they come to my place. Summer place, pretty good place, that one. Those ones, they come with Napiao, my friend. Cool. On the river. Indians call him Ka-sin-ta, that river, like if you did nothing but stand in one place all day and maybe longer. Ka-sin-ta also call Na-po. Napiao knows that one, my friend. Whiteman call him Saint Merry, but I don't know what that mean. Maybe like Ka-sin-ta. Maybe not.

5   Napiao comes with those three. Whiteman, those.

6   No Indianman.

7   No Chinaman.

8   No Frenchman.

9   Too bad, those.

10   Sometimes the wind come along say hello. Pretty fast, that one. Blow some things down on the river, that Ka-sin-ta. Sometimes he comes up too, pretty high. Moves things around, that Ka-sin-ta.

11   Three men come to my summer place, also my friend Napiao. Pretty loud talkers, those ones. One is big. I tell him maybe looks like Big Joe. Maybe not.

12   Anyway.

13   They come and Napiao, too. Bring greetings, how are you, many nice things they bring to says. Three.

14   All white.

15   Too bad, those.

16   Ho, my friend says, real nice day. Here is some tobacco.

17   All those smile. Good teeth.

18   Your friend Napiao, they says, that one says you tell a good story, you tell us your good story.

19   They says, those ones.

20   I tell Napiao, sit down, rest, eat something. Those three like to stand. Stand still. I think of Ka-sin-ta, as I told you. So I says to Napiao, Ka-sin-ta, in our language and he laugh. Those three laugh, too. Good teeth. Whiteman, white teeth.

21   I says to them, those ones stand pretty good. Napiao, my friend, says tell these a good story. Maybe not too long, he says. Those ones pretty young, go to sleep pretty quick. Anthropologist, you know. That one has a camera. Maybe.

22   Okay, I says, sit down.

23   These are good men, my friend says, those come a long ways from past Ta-pe-loo-za. Call him Blind Man Coulee, too. Ta-pe-loo-za means like a quiet place where the fish can rest, deep quiet place. Blind man maybe comes there later. To that place. Maybe fish.

24   Alright.

25   How about a story, that one says.

26   Sure, I says. Maybe about Jimmy runs the store near Two Bridges. His brother become dead and give Jimmy his car. But Jimmy never drives.

27   Napiao hold his hand up pretty soft. My friend says that good story, Jimmy and his car. These ones don't know Jimmy.

28   Okay, I says. Tell about Billy Frank and the dead-river pig. Funny story, that one, Billy Frank and the dead-river pig. Pretty big pig. Billy is real small, like Napiao, my friend. Hurt his back. Lost his truck.

29   Those ones like old stories, says my friend, maybe how the world was put together. Good Indian story like that, Napiao says. Those ones have tape recorders, he says.

30   Okay, I says.

31   Have some tea.

32   Stay awake.

33   Once upon a time.

34   Those stories start like that, pretty much, those ones, start on time. Anyway. There was nothing. Pretty hard to believe that, maybe.

35   You fellows keep listening, I says. Watch the floor. Be careful.

36   No water, no land, no stars, no moon. None of those things. Must have a sun someplace. Maybe not. Can't say. No Indians are there once upon a time. Lots of air. Only one person walk around. Call him god.

37   So.

38   They look around, and there is nothing. No grass. No fish. No trees. No mountains. No Indians, like I says. No whiteman, either. Those come later, maybe one hundred years. Maybe not. That one god walk around, but pretty soon they get tired. Maybe that one says, we will get some stars. So he does. And then he says, maybe we should get a moon. So, they get one of them, too.

39   Someone write all this down, I don't know. Lots of things left to get.

40   Me-a-loo, call her deer.

41   Pa-pe-po, call her elk.

42   Tsling-ta, call her Blue-flower-berry.

43   Ga-ling, call her moon.

44   So-see-ka, call her flint.

45   A-ma-po, call her dog.

46   Ba-ko-zao, call her grocery store.

47   Pe-to-pa-zasling, call her television.

48   Pretty long list of things to get, that. Too many, maybe those ones say, how many more that one needs for world. So. Pretty soon that one can fix up real nice place. Not too hot. Not too cold. Like here, we sit here. My summer place is like that one.

49   I call my summer place O-say-ta-he-to-peo-teh. Means cool sleeping place. Other place, they call her Evening's garden. Good time to fish, that. Evening. Cool, not so hot. That Evening's garden like here.

50   Two human beings that one puts there. Call the man Ah-damn. Call the woman, Evening. Same as garden.

51   Okay.

52   She looks around her garden. Pretty nice place, that one. Good tree. Good deer. Good rock. Good water. Good sky. Good wind. No grocery store, no television.

53   Ah-damn and Evening real happy, those ones. No clothes, those, you know. Ha, Ha, Ha, Ha. But they pretty dumb, then. New, you know.

54   Have some tea.

55   Stay awake.

56   Good part is soon here.

57   That woman, Evening, she is curious, nosy, that one. She walk around the garden and she look everywhere. Look under rock. Look in grass. Look in sky. Look in water. Look in tree.

58   So.

59   She find that tree, big one. Not like now, that tree. This one have lots of good things to eat. Have potato. Have pumpkin. Have corn. Have berries, all kind. Too many to say now.

60   This good tree also have some mee-so. Whiteman call them apples. This first woman look at the tree with the good things and she gets hungry. Make a meal in her head.

61   Leave that mee-so alone. Someone says that. Leave that mee-so alone. Leave that tree alone. The voice says that. Go away someplace else to eat!

62   That one, god. Hello, he's back.

63   Hey, says Evening, this is my garden.

64   You watch out, says that one, pretty loud voice. Sort of shout. Bad temper, that one. Maybe like Harley James. Bad temper, that one. Always shouting. Always with pulled-down mean look. Sometimes Harley come to town, drives his truck to town. Gets drunk. Drives back to that house. That one goes to town, get drunk, come home, that one, beat his wife. His wife leave. Goes back up north. Pretty mean one, that one. You boys know Harley James? Nobody there to beat up, now. Likes to shout, that one. Maybe you want to hear about Billy Frank and the dead-river pig?

65   Boy, my friend says, I can taste those mee-so. These boys pretty excited about those mee-so, I think.

66   Okay, I says.

67   Keep your eyes open, look around.

68   Evening, that one says, look pretty good, these. So she eat one, that mee-so. Boy, not bad, real juicy, that one. She is generous, Evening, good woman, that one. Brings mee-so to Ah-damn. I think he is busy then, writing things down. All the animals' names he writes somewhere, I don't know. Pretty boring that.

69   Deer come by, says Me-a-loo.

70   Elk come by, says Pa-pe-o.

71   Blue-flower-berry come by, says Tsling-ta.

72   Ah-damn not so smart like Evening, that one thinks Blue-flower-berry is animal, maybe.

73   Dog come by, says A-ma-po.

74   Raven come by, says Ne-co-tah.

75   Coyote come by, says Klee-qua.

76   Snail come by, says E-too.

77   Squirrel come by, says Qay-tha.

78   Owl come by, says Ba-tee-po-tah.

79   Weasel come by, says So-tha-nee-so.

80   Rabbit come by, says Klaaa-coo.

81   Flint come by, says So-see-ka.

82   Fish come by, says Laa-po.

83   Crayfish come by, says Tling.

84   Beaver come by, says Khan-yah-da.

85   Boy, all worn out. All those animals come by. Coyote come by maybe four, maybe eight times. Gets dressed up, fool around.

86   Says Piisto-pa.

87   Says Ho-ta-go.

88   Says Woho-i-kee.

89   Says Caw-ho-ha.

90   Ha, ha, ha, ha.

91   Tricky one, that coyote. Walks in circles. Sneaky.

92   That Ah-damn not so smart. Like Harley James, whiteman, those. Evening, she be Indian woman, I guess.

93   Evening come back. Hey, she says, what are all these coyote tracks come around in a circle. Not so smart, Ah-damn, pretty hungry though. Here, says Evening, mee-so, real juicy. So they do. Ah-damn, that one eat three mee-so. Ah-damn, says Evening, I better get some more mee-so.

94   Pretty soon that one, god, come by. He is pretty mad. You ate my mee-so, he says.

95   Don't be upset, says Evening, that one, first woman. Many more mee-so back there. Calm down, watch some television, she says.

96   But they are upset and that one says that Evening and Ah-damn better leave that good place, garden, Evening's garden, go somewhere else. Just like Indian today.

97   Evening says, okay, many good places around here. Ah-damn, that one wants to stay. But that fellow, god, whiteman I think, he says, you go too, you ate those mee-so, my mee-so.

98   Ah-damn is unhappy. He cry three times, ho, ho, ho, I only ate one, he says.

99   No, says that god fellow, I see everything. I see you eat three of my mee-so.

100   I only ate two, says Ah-damn but pretty quick that one throw him out.

101   Ha!

102   Throw him out on his back, right on those rocks. Ouch, ouch, ouch, that one says. Evening, she have to come back and fix him up before he is any good again. Alright.

103   There is also a Ju-poo-pea, whiteman call him snake. Don't know what kind. Big white one maybe, I hear, maybe black, something else. I forgot this part. He lives in tree with mee-so. That one try to get friendly with Evening so she stick a mee-so in his mouth, that one. Crawl back into tree. Have trouble talking, hissss, hissss, hissss, hissss. Maybe he is still there. Like that dead-river pig and Billy Frank lose his truck.

104   So.

105   Evening and Ah-damn leave. Everybody else leave, too. That tree leave, too. Just god and Ju-poo-pea together.

106   Ah-damn and Evening come out here. Have a bunch of kids.

107   So.

108   That's all. It is ended.

109   Boy, my friend says, better get some more tea. One good story, that one, my friend, Napiao says.

110   Those men push their tape recorders, fix their cameras. All of those ones smile. Nod their head around. Look out window. Shake my hand. Make happy noises. Say goodbyes, see you later. Leave pretty quick.

111   We watch them go. My friend, Napiao, put the pot on for some tea. I clean up all the coyote tracks on the floor.

 Topics for Critical Thinking and Writing

1. Thomas King tells modern stories for modern purposes and readers; however, he clearly uses patterns and purposes of oral tradition. King has said that he is developing "ways in which oral literature and written literature can merge." Discuss King's narrative strategies: digressions of the story-within-a-story; the narrator as a character; the allegorical, non-confrontational manner of speaking to the audience (both inside the

story and to us as readers); and the use of humour, repetition, analogy, and any other strategies that you can identify.

2. This story becomes many stories through the use of a story-within-a-story and shifting audiences. What is King's story "about"? What story does the narrator tell the anthropologists? What story would the narrator prefer to tell? Who is the narrator really telling the story to?

3. Are the anthropologists fooled? Do they smile and shake hands at the end because they are satisfied that they have attained what they came for? Or, are they embarrassed and retreat hastily because they realize they were being gulled?

4. Discuss the title. What is the "good story"? How is the title ironic?

5. How does King use the Trickster figure (in this case Coyote)?

6. King wrote, "Assumptions are a dangerous thing." In "One Good Story, That One," what assumptions is King challenging?

 ERNEST HEMINGWAY

Ernest Hemingway (1899–1961) was born in Oak Park, Illinois. After graduating from high school in 1917 he worked on the Kansas City Star, *but left to serve as a volunteer ambulance driver in Italy, where he was wounded in action. He worked briefly in Toronto for the* Toronto Star Weekly *and then as the European correspondent for the* Toronto Daily Star. *He settled in Paris, where he moved in a circle of American expatriates that included Ezra Pound, Gertrude Stein, and F. Scott Fitzgerald. It was in Paris that he wrote stories and novels about what Gertrude Stein called a "lost generation" of rootless Americans in Europe. Hemingway won both the Pulitzer Prize and the Nobel Prize in Literature.*

Cat in the Rain

1 There were only two Americans stopping at the hotel. They did not know any of the people they passed on the stairs on their way to and from their room. Their room was on the second floor facing the sea. It also faced the public garden and the war monument. There were big palms and green benches in the public garden. In the good weather there was always an artist with his easel. Artists liked the way the palms grew and the bright colors of the hotels facing the gardens and the sea. Italians came from a long way off to look up at the war monument. It was made of bronze and glistened in the rain. It was raining. The rain dripped from the palm trees. Water stood in pools on the gravel paths. The sea broke in a long line in the rain and slipped back down the beach to come up and break again in a long line in the rain. The motor cars were gone from the square by the war monument. Across the square in the doorway of the café a waiter stood looking out at the empty square.

2 The American wife stood at the window looking out. Outside right under their window a cat was crouched under one of the dripping green tables. The cat was trying to make herself so compact that she would not be dripped on.

3 "I'm going down and get that kitty," the American wife said.

4 "I'll do it," her husband offered from the bed.

5 "No, I'll get it. The poor kitty out trying to keep dry under a table."

6 The husband went on reading, lying propped up with the two pillows at the foot of the bed.

7   "Don't get wet," he said.

8   The wife went downstairs and the hotel owner stood up and bowed to her as she passed the office. His desk was at the far end of the office. He was an old man and very tall.

9   "Il piove," the wife said. She liked the hotel-keeper.

10   "Si, si, Signora, brutto tempo. It is very bad weather."

11   He stood behind his desk in the far end of the dim room. The wife liked him. She liked the deadly serious way he received any complaints. She liked his dignity. She liked the way he wanted to serve her. She liked the way he felt about being a hotel-keeper. She liked his old, heavy face and big hands.

12   Liking him she opened the door and looked out. It was raining harder. A man in a rubber cape was crossing the empty square to the café. The cat would be around to the right. Perhaps she could go along under the eaves. As she stood in the doorway an umbrella opened behind her. It was the maid who looked after their room.

13   "You must not get wet," she smiled, speaking Italian. Of course, the hotel-keeper had sent her.

14   With the maid holding the umbrella over her, she walked along the gravel path until she was under their window. The table was there, washed bright green in the rain, but the cat was gone. She was suddenly disappointed. The maid looked up at her.

15   "Ha perduto qualque cosa, Signora?"

16   "There was a cat," said the American girl.

17   "A cat?"

18   "Si, il gatto."

19   "A cat?" the maid laughed. "A cat in the rain?"

20   "Yes," she said, "under the table." Then, "Oh, I wanted it so much. I wanted a kitty."

21   When she talked English the maid's face tightened.

22   "Come Signora," she said. "We must get back inside. You will be wet."

23   "I suppose so," said the American girl.

24   They went back along the gravel path and passed in the door. The maid stayed outside to close the umbrella. As the American girl passed the office, the padrone bowed from his desk. Something felt very small and tight inside the girl. The padrone made her feel very small and at the same time really important. She had a momentary feeling of being of supreme importance. She went on up the stairs. She opened the door of the room. George was on the bed, reading.

25   "Did you get the cat?" he asked, putting the book down.

26   "It was gone."

27   "Wonder where it went to," he said, resting his eyes from reading.

28   She sat down on the bed.

29   "I wanted it so much," she said. "I don't know why I wanted it so much. I wanted that poor kitty. It isn't any fun to be a poor kitty out in the rain."

30   George was reading again.

31   She went over and sat in front of the mirror of the dressing table looking at herself with the hand glass. She studied her profile, first one side and then the other. Then she studied the back of her head and her neck.

32   "Don't you think it would be a good idea if I let my hair grow out?" she asked, looking at her profile again.

33   George looked up and saw the back of her neck, clipped close like a boy's.

34   "I like it the way it is."

35   "I get so tired of it," she said. "I get so tired of looking like a boy."

36   George shifted his position in the bed. He hadn't looked away from her since she started to speak.

37   "You look pretty darn nice," he said.

38   She laid the mirror down on the dresser and went over to the window and looked out. It was getting dark.

39   "I want to pull my hair back tight and smooth and make a big knot at the back that I can feel," she said. "I want to have a kitty to sit on my lap and purr when I stroke her."

40   "Yeah?" George said from the bed.

41   "And I want to eat at a table with my own silver and I want candles. And I want it to be spring and I want to brush my hair out in front of a mirror and I want a kitty and I want some new clothes."

42   "Oh, shut up and get something to read," George said. He was reading again.

43   His wife was looking out of the window. It was quite dark now and still raining in the palm trees.

44   "Anyway, I want a cat," she said, "I want a cat. I want a cat now. If I can't have long hair or any fun, I can have a cat."

45   George was not listening. He was reading his book. His wife looked out of the window where the light had come on in the square.

46   Someone knocked at the door.

47   "Avanti," George said. He looked up from his book.

48   In the doorway stood the maid. She held a big tortoise-shell cat pressed tight against her and swung down against her body.

49   "Excuse me," she said, "the padrone asked me to bring this for the Signora."

 Topics for Critical Thinking and Writing

1. One reader has argued that the cat represents the child that the girl wants to have. Do you think there is something to this idea? How might you support or refute it?

2. Would it make any difference if the animal were a dog instead of a cat?

3. Can we be certain that the cat at the end of the story is the cat that the woman saw in the rain? (When we first hear about the cat in the rain we are not told anything about its colour, and at the end of the story we are not told that the tortoise-shell cat is wet.) Does it matter if there are two cats?

4. What do you suppose Hemingway's attitude was toward each of the three chief characters? How might you support your hunch?

5. Hemingway wrote the story in Italy, when his wife Hadley was pregnant. In a letter to F. Scott Fitzgerald he said,

   Cat in the Rain wasn't about Hadley. . . . When I wrote that we were at Rapallo but Hadley was 4 months pregnant with Bumby. The Inn Keeper was the one at Cortina D'Ampezzo. . . . Hadley never made a speech in her life about wanting a baby because she had been told various things by her doctor and I'd—no use going into all that. (*Earnest Hemingway: Selected Letters, 1917-1961.* Ed. Carlos Baker. New York: Scribner's, 180)

According to some biographers, the story shows that Hemingway knew his marriage was heading for the rocks (Hemingway and Hadley divorced). Does knowing that Hemingway's marriage turned out unhappily help you to understand the story? Does it make the story more interesting? And do you think that the story tells a biographer something about Hemingway's life?

6. It is sometimes said that a good short story does two things at once: it provides a believable picture of the surface of life, and it also illuminates some moral or psychological complexity that we feel is part of the essence of human life. This dual claim may not be true, but for the moment accept it. Do you think that Hemingway's story fulfills either or both of these specifications? Support your view.

 ## ISABEL ALLENDE

Isabel Allende, when not living in Chile, spent time studying and working in many countries in Latin America, Europe, and the Middle East. After being exiled from Chile in 1973 following a CIA-assisted military coup of her uncle, President Salvador Allende, she lived in Venezuela and then settled in the United States. She has worked for the United Nations and as a journalist, college professor, and writer. Allende, who is considered one of the foremost Latin American writers, has published numerous short stories and novels and two non-fiction books; her work has been translated into twenty-seven languages.

If You Touched My Heart

1 Amadeo Peralta was raised in the midst of his father's gang and, like all the men of his family, grew up to be a ruffian. His father believed that school was for cissies; you don't need books to get ahead in life, he always said, just balls and quick wits, and that was why he trained his boys to be rough and ready. With time, nevertheless, he realized that the world was changing very rapidly and that his business affairs needed to be more firmly anchored. The era of undisguised plunder had been replaced by one of corruption and bribery; it was time to administer his wealth by using modern criteria, and to improve his image. He called his sons together and assigned them the task of establishing friendships with influential persons and of learning the legal tricks that would allow them to continue to prosper without danger of losing their impunity. He also encouraged them to find sweethearts among the old-line families and in this way see whether they could cleanse the Peralta name of all its stains of mud and blood. By then Amadeo was thirty-two years old; the habit of seducing girls and then abandoning them was deeply ingrained; the idea of marriage was not at all to his liking but he did not dare disobey his father. He began to court the daughter of a wealthy landowner whose family had lived in the same place for six generations. Despite her suitor's murky reputation, the girl accepted, for she was not very attractive and was afraid of ending up an old maid. Then began one of those tedious provincial engagements. Wretched in a white linen suit and polished boots, Amadeo came every day to visit his fiancée beneath the hawk-like eye of his future mother-in-law or some aunt, and while the young lady served coffee

and *guayabá* sweets he would peek at his watch, calculating the earliest moment to make his departure.

2   A few weeks before the wedding, Amadeo Peralta had to make a business trip through the provinces and found himself in Agua Santa, one of those towns where nobody stays and whose name travellers rarely recall. He was walking down a narrow street at the hour of the siesta, cursing the heat and the oppressive, cloying odour of mango marmalade in the air, when he heard a crystalline sound like water purling between stones; it was coming from a modest house with paint flaked by the sun and rain like most of the houses in that town. Through the ornamental iron grille he glimpsed an entryway of dark paving stones and whitewashed walls, then a patio and, beyond, the surprising vision of a young girl sitting cross-legged on the ground and cradling a blond wood psaltery on her knees. For a while he stood and watched her.

3   "Come here, sweet thing," he called, finally. She looked up, and despite the distance he could see the startled eyes and uncertain smile in a still-childish face. "Come with me," Amadeo asked—implored—in a hoarse voice.

4   She hesitated. The last notes lingered like a question in the air of the patio. Peralta called again. The girl stood up and walked towards him; he slipped his hand through the iron grille, shot the bolt, opened the gate, and seized her hand, all the while reciting his entire repertoire of seduction: he swore that he had seen her in his dreams, that he had been looking for her all his life, that he could not let her go, and that she was the woman fate had meant for him—all of which he could have omitted because the girl was simple and even though she may have been enchanted by the tone of his voice she did not understand the meaning of his words. Hortensia was her name and she had just turned fifteen; her body was tuned for its first embrace, though she was unable to put a name to the restlessness and tremors that shook it. It was so easy for Peralta to lead her to his car and drive to a nearby clearing that an hour later he had completely forgotten her. He did not recognize her even when a week later she suddenly appeared at his house, one hundred and forty kilometres away, wearing a simple yellow cotton dress and canvas espadrilles, her psaltery under her arm, and inflamed with the fever of love.

5   Forty-seven years later, when Hortensia was rescued from the pit in which she had been entombed and newspapermen travelled from every corner of the nation to photograph her, not even she could remember her name or how she had got there.

6   The reporters accosted Amadeo Peralta: 'Why did you keep her locked up like a miserable beast?'

7   'Because I felt like it,' he replied calmly. By then he was eighty, and as lucid as ever; he could not understand this belated outcry over something that had happened so long ago.

8   He was not inclined to offer explanations. He was a man of authority, a patriarch, a great-grandfather; no one dared look him in the eye; even priests greeted him with bowed head. During the course of his long life he had multiplied the fortune he inherited from his father; he had become the owner of all the land from the ruins of the Spanish fort to the state line, and then had launched himself on a political career that made him the most powerful cacique in the territory. He had married the landowner's ugly daughter and sired nine legitimate descendants with her and an indefinite number of bastards with other women, none of whom he remembered since he had a heart hardened to love. The only woman

he could not entirely discard was Hortensia; she stuck in his consciousness like a persistent nightmare. After the brief encounter in the tall grass of an empty lot, he had returned to his home, his work, and his insipid, well-bred fiancée. It was Hortensia who had searched until she found *him;* it was she who had planted herself before him and clung to his shirt with the terrifying submission of a slave. This is a fine kettle of fish, he had thought; here I am about to get married with all this hoopla and to-do, and now this idiot girl turns up on my doorstep. He wanted to be rid of her, and yet when he saw her in her yellow dress, with those entreating eyes, it seemed a waste not to take advantage of the opportunity, and he decided to hide her while he found a solution.

9   And so, by carelessness, really, Hortensia ended up in the cellar of an old sugar mill that belonged to the Peraltas, where she was to remain for a lifetime. It was a large room, dank, and dark, suffocating in summer and in the dry season often cold at night, furnished with a few sticks of furniture and a straw pallet. Amadeo Peralta never took time to make her more comfortable, despite his occasionally feeding a fantasy of making the girl a concubine from an oriental tale, clad in gauzy robes and surrounded with peacock feathers, brocade tented ceilings, stained-glass lamps, gilded furniture with spiral feet, and thick rugs where he could walk barefoot. He might actually have done it had Hortensia reminded him of his promises, but she was like a wild bird, one of those blind guacharos that live in the depths of caves: all she needed was a little food and water. The yellow dress rotted away and she was left naked.

10   "He loves me; he has always loved me," she declared when she was rescued by neighbours. After being locked up for so many years she had lost the use of words and her voice came out in spurts like the croak of a woman on her deathbed.

11   For a few weeks, Amadeo had spent a lot of time in the cellar with her, satisfying an appetite he thought insatiable. Fearing that she would be discovered, and jealous even of his own eyes, he did not want to expose her to daylight and allowed only a pale ray to enter through the tiny hole that provided ventilation. In the darkness, they coupled frenziedly, their skin burning and their hearts impatient as carnivorous crabs. In that cavern all odours and tastes were heightened to the extreme. When they touched, each entered the other's being and sank into the other's most secret desires. There, voices resounded in repeated echoes; the walls returned amplified murmurs and kisses. The cellar became a sealed flask in which they wallowed like playful twins swimming in amniotic fluid, two swollen, stupefied foetuses. For days they were lost in an absolute intimacy they confused with love.

12   When Hortensia fell asleep, her lover went out to look for food and before she awakened returned with renewed energy to resume the cycle of caresses. They should have made love to each other until they died of desire; they should have devoured one another or flamed like mirrored torches, but that was not to be. What happened instead was more predictable and ordinary, much less grandiose. Before a month had passed, Amadeo Peralta tired of the games, which they were beginning to repeat; he sensed the dampness eating into his joints, and he began to feel the attraction of things outside the walls of that grotto. It was time to return to the world of the living and to pick up the reins of his destiny.

13   "You wait for me here. I'm going out and get very rich. I'll bring you gifts and dresses and jewels fit for a queen," he told her as he said goodbye.

14   "I want children," said Hortensia.

15   "Children, no; but you shall have dolls."

16   In the months that followed, Peralta forgot about the dresses, the jewels, and the dolls. He visited Hortensia when he thought of her, not always to make love, sometimes merely to hear her play some old melody on her psaltery; he liked to watch her bent over the instrument, strumming chords. Sometimes he was in such a rush that he did not even speak; he filled her water jugs, left her a sack filled with provisions, and departed. Once he forgot about her for nine days, and found her on the verge of death; he realized then the need to find someone to help care for his prisoner, because his family, his travels, his business, and his social engagements occupied all his time. He chose a tight-mouthed Indian woman to fill that role. She kept the key to the padlock, and regularly came to clean the cell and scrape away the lichens growing on Hortensia's body like pale delicate flowers almost invisible to the naked eye and redolent of tilled soil and neglected things.

17   "Weren't you ever sorry for that poor woman?" they asked when they arrested her as well, charging her with complicity in the kidnapping. She refused to answer but stared straight ahead with expressionless eyes and spat a black stream of tobacco.

18   No, she had felt no pity for her; she believed the woman had a calling to be a slave and was happy being one, or else had been born an idiot and like others in her situation was better locked up than exposed to the jeers and perils of the street. Hortensia had done nothing to change her jailer's opinion; she never exhibited any curiosity about the world, she made no attempt to be outside for fresh air, and she complained about nothing. She never seemed bored; her mind had stopped at some moment in her childhood, and solitude in no way disturbed her. She was, in fact, turning into a subterranean creature. There in her tomb her senses grew sharp and she learned to see the invisible; she was surrounded by hallucinatory spirits who led her by the hand to other universes. She left behind a body huddled in a corner and travelled through starry space like a messenger particle, living in a dark land beyond reason. Had she had a mirror, she would have been terrified by her appearance; as she could not see herself, however, she was not witness to her deterioration: she was unaware of the scales sprouting from her skin, or the silkworms that had spun a nest in her long, tangled hair, or the lead-coloured clouds covering eyes already dead from peering into shadows. She did not feel her ears growing to capture external sounds, even the faintest and most distant, like the laughter of children at school recess, the ice-cream vendor's bell, birds in flight, or the murmuring river. Nor did she realize that her legs, once graceful and firm, were growing twisted as they adjusted to moving in that confined space, to crawling, nor that her toenails were thickening like an animal's hooves, her bones changing into tubes of glass, her belly caving in, and a hump forming on her back. Only her hands, forever occupied with the psaltery, maintained their shape and size, although her fingers had forgotten the melodies they had once known and now extracted from the instrument the unvoiced sob trapped in her breast. From a distance, Hortensia resembled a tragic circus monkey; on closer view, she inspired infinite pity. She was totally ignorant of the malignant transformations taking place; in her mind she held intact the image of herself as the young girl she had last seen reflected in the window of Amadeo Peralta's automobile the day he had driven her to this lair. She believed she was as pretty as ever, and continued to act as if she were; the memory of beauty crouched deep inside her and only if someone approached very close would he have glimpsed it beneath the external façade of a prehistoric dwarf.

19   All the while, Amadeo Peralta, rich and feared, cast the net of his power across the region. Every Sunday he sat at the head of a long table occupied by his sons and nephews, cronies and accomplices, and special guests such as politicians and generals whom he treated with a hearty cordiality tinged with sufficient arrogance to remind everyone who was master here. Behind his back, people whispered about his victims, about how many he had ruined or caused to disappear, about bribes to authorities; there was talk that he had made half his fortune from smuggling, but no one was disposed to seek the proof of his transgressions. It was also rumoured that Peralta kept a woman prisoner in a cellar. That aspect of his black deeds was repeated with more conviction even than stories of his crooked dealings; in fact, many people knew about it, and with time it became an open secret.

20   One afternoon on a very hot day, three young boys played hookey from school to swim in the river. They spent a couple of hours splashing around on the muddy bank and then wandered off towards the old Peralta sugar mill that had been closed two generations earlier when cane ceased to be a profitable crop. The mill had the reputation of being haunted; people said you could hear sounds of devils, and many had seen a dishevelled old witch invoking the spirits of dead slaves. Excited by their adventure, the boys crept onto the property and approached the mill. Soon they were daring enough to enter the ruins; they ran through large rooms with thick adobe walls and termite-riddled beams; they picked their way through weeds growing from the floor, mounds of rubbish and dog shit, rotted roof tiles, and snakes' nests. Making jokes to work up their courage, egging each other on, they came to the huge roofless room that contained the ruined sugar presses; here rain and sun had created an impossible garden, and the boys thought they could detect a lingering scent of sugar and sweat. Just as they were growing bolder they heard, clear as a bell, the notes of a monstrous song. Trembling, they almost retreated, but the lure of horror was stronger than their fear, and they huddled there, listening, as the last note drilled into their foreheads. Gradually, they were released from their paralysis; their fear evaporated and they began looking for the source of those weird sounds so different from any music they had ever known. They discovered a small trap door in the floor, closed with a lock they could not open. They rattled the wood planks that sealed the entrance and were struck in the face by an indescribable odour that reminded them of a caged beast. They called but no one answered; they heard only a hoarse panting on the other side. Finally they ran home to shout the news that they had discovered the door to hell.

21   The children's uproar could not be stilled, and thus the neighbours finally proved what they had suspected for decades. First the boys' mothers came to peer through the cracks in the trap door; they, too, heard the terrible notes of the psaltery, so different from the banal melody that had attracted Amadeo Peralta the day he had paused in a small alley in Agua Santa to dry the sweat from his forehead. The mothers were followed by throngs of curious and, last of all, after a crowd had already gathered, came the police and firemen, who chopped open the door and descended into the hole with their lamps and equipment. In the cave they found a naked creature with flaccid skin hanging in pallid folds; this apparition had tangled grey hair that dragged the floor, and moaned in terror of the noise and light. It was Hortensia, glowing with a mother-of-pearl phosphorescence under the steady beams of the firefighters' lanterns; she was nearly blind, her teeth had rotted away, and her legs were so weak she could barely stand. The only sign of her human origins was the ancient psaltery clasped to her breast.

22   The news stirred indignation throughout the country. Television screens and newspapers displayed pictures of the woman rescued from the hole where she had spent her life, now, at least, half-clothed in a cloak someone had tossed around her shoulders. In only a few hours, the indifference that had surrounded the prisoner for almost half a century was converted into a passion to avenge and succour her. Neighbours improvised lynch parties for Amadeo Peralta; they stormed his house, dragged him out, and had the Guard not arrived in time, would have torn him limb from limb in the plaza. To assuage their guilt for having ignored Hortensia for so many years, everyone wanted to do something for her. They collected money to provide her a pension, they gathered tons of clothing and medicine she did not need, and several welfare organizations were given the task of scraping the filth from her body, cutting her hair, and outfitting her from head to toe, so she looked like an ordinary old lady. The nuns offered her a bed in a shelter for indigents, and for several months kept her tied up to prevent her from running back to her cellar, until finally she grew accustomed to daylight and resigned to living with other human beings.

23   Taking advantage of the public furore fanned by the press, Amadeo Peralta's numerous enemies finally gathered courage to launch an attack against him. Authorities who for years had overlooked his abuses fell upon him with the full fury of the law. The story occupied everyone's attention long enough to see the former caudillo in prison, and then faded and died away. Rejected by family and friends, a symbol of all that is abominable and abject, harassed by both jailers and companions-in-misfortune, Peralta spent the rest of his days in prison. He remained in his cell, never venturing into the courtyard with the other inmates. From there, he could hear the sounds from the street.

24   Every day at ten in the morning, Hortensia, with the faltering step of a madwoman, tottered down to the prison where she handed the guard at the gate a warm saucepan for the prisoner.

25   "He almost never left me hungry," she would tell the guard in an apologetic tone. Then she would sit in the street to play her psaltery, wresting from it moans of agony impossible to bear. In the hope of distracting her or silencing her, some passers-by gave her money.

26   Crouched on the other side of the wall, Amadeo Peralta heard those sounds that seemed to issue from the depths of the earth and course through every nerve in his body. This daily castigation must mean something, but he could not remember what. From time to time he felt something like a stab of guilt, but immediately his memory failed and images of the past evaporated in a dense mist. He did not know why he was in that tomb, and gradually he forgot the world of light and lost himself in his misfortune.

 ## Topics for Critical Thinking and Writing

1. Why does Amadeo Peralta imprison Hortensia in the cellar?
2. Why doesn't Hortensia try to leave?
3. What passages suggest that Allende holds the townspeople to some degree responsible for what happens to Hortensia?
4. Hortensia brings Amadeo food when he is imprisoned at the end of the story; she also plays her psaltery ("wresting from it moans of agony impossible to bear"). How do you explain these actions?

THREE POEMS

 ## WILLIAM SHAKESPEARE

William Shakespeare (1564–1616) is widely regarded as the world's greatest drama-tist, but he also wrote non-dramatic poetry, including 154 sonnets. The sonnets were published in 1609 but probably were written from about 1598 to 1605 or so. The fourteen lines of Shakespeare's sonnets can be divided into three quatrains (units of four lines each) and a couplet (a pair of rhyming lines). In each quatrain, the first and third lines rhyme with each other, and the second and fourth lines rhyme. The rhyme scheme thus may be formulated as abab cdcd efef gg.

Sonnet 73

That time of year thou mayst in me behold
When yellow leaves, or none, or few, do hang
Upon those boughs which shake against the cold,
Bare ruined choirs[1] where late the sweet birds sang.   4
In me thou see'st the twilight of such day
As after sunset fadeth in the west,
Which by-and-by black night doth take away,
Death's second self that seals up all in rest,   8
In me thou see'st the glowing of such fire
That on the ashes of his youth doth lie,
As the deathbed whereon it must expire,
Consumed with that which it was nourished by.   12
　　This thou perceiv'st, which makes thy love more strong,
　　To love that well which thou must leave ere long.

 ## Topics for Critical Thinking and Writing

1. Paraphrase—that is, put into your own words—the entire poem.
2. To what does the narrator compare himself in the first quatrain? In the second? In the third?
3. What would be gained or lost if the sequence of quatrains were reversed, that is, if the poem began with the last quatrain and ended with the first?

 ## MARJORIE PICKTHALL

Marjorie Pickthall (1883–1922) was born in England and emigrated to Toronto in 1889. She moved back to England from 1912 to 1919 and participated in World

---

[1]The part of the church where services were sung.

War I as an ambulance driver, farm labourer, and library clerk. She eventually settled on Vancouver Island. Before her early death from an embolus, Pickthall wrote about two hundred short stories, one hundred poems, and five novels.

The Wife

Living, I had no might
To make you hear,
Now, in the inmost night,
I am so near
No whisper, falling light,   5
Divides us, dear.

Living, I had no claim
On your great hours.
Now the thin candle-flame,
The closing flowers,   10
Wed summer with my name,—
And these are ours.

Your shadow on the dust,
Strength, and a cry,
Delight, despair, mistrust,—   15
All these am I.
Dawn, and the far hills thrust
To a far sky.

Living, I had no skill
To stay your tread,   20
Now all that was my will
Silence has said.
We are one for good and ill
Since I am dead.

 Topics for Critical Thinking and Writing

1. Who is the narrator of "The Wife"? What is the situation in the poem? What do you make of the last two lines?
2. Analyze the structure of the poem. What is the rhyme scheme? How many lines are there per stanza? What word is repeated as the first word of three out of four of the stanzas? What do you notice about line length? How does the structure of the poem work with the content?
3. What does Pickthall imply about voice and silence in her poem?

 **PAT MORA**

Pat Mora did her undergraduate work at Texas Western College, and then earned a master's degree at the University of Texas at El Paso, where she subsequently served as assistant to the vice-president for academic affairs, director of the university museum, and from 1981 to 1989 assistant to the president. She has published essays on Hispanic culture as well as books for children and teens, but she is best known for her books of poetry. Mora has received several literary and academic awards.

Immigrants

Immigrants
wrap their babies in the American flag,
feed them mashed hot dogs and apple pie,
name them Bill and Daisy,
buy them blonde dolls that blink blue   5
eyes or a football and tiny cleats
before the baby can even walk,
speak to them in thick English,
    hallo, babee, hallo.
whisper in Spanish or Polish   10
when the babies sleep, whisper
in a dark parent bed, that dark
parent fear, "Will they like
our boy, our girl, our fine american
boy, our fine american girl?"

 Topics for Critical Thinking and Writing

1. To say that someone—for example, a politician—"wraps himself in the American flag" is to suggest disapproval or even anger or contempt. What behaviour does the phrase usually describe? What does Mora mean when she says that immigrants "wrap their babies in the American flag"?

2. What do you suppose is Mora's attitude toward the immigrants? Do you think the poet fully approves of their hopes? On what do you base your answer? Speaking generally, do they seek to assimilate to an Anglo-American culture?

3. Does Mora's description of the behaviour of immigrants ring true of the immigrant group you are part of or know best? Speaking generally, do such groups seek to assimilate to the dominant culture? What is your attitude toward these efforts or their efforts to retain their culture?

4. Taking into consideration views on Canada and being Canadian expressed from a variety of cultural perspectives in the essays in Chapter 12, and the ideas contained in Mora's poem, write an essay of 750 to 1000 words on a subject related to multiculturalism, the melting pot/mosaic, and immigration in Canada and/or the United States. Be sure to narrow your topic's focus.

Writing Essay Examinations

WHAT EXAMINATIONS ARE

An examination not only measures learning and thinking but also stimulates both of these processes. Even the short-answer quiz—chiefly a device to coerce the student to do the assigned reading—is a sort of push designed to move the student forward. Of course, internal motivation is far superior to external, but even such crude external motivation as a quiz can have a beneficial effect. Students know this; indeed they often seek external compulsion, choosing a course "because I want to know something about it, and I know that I won't do the reading on my own." (Teachers often teach a new course for the same reason; we want to become knowledgeable about, say, communism in China, and we know that despite our lofty intentions we may not seriously confront the subject unless we are under the pressure of facing a class.) In short, however ignoble it sounds, examinations force the student to acquire learning and then to convert learning into thinking.

Sometimes it is not until preparing for the final examination that the student—rereading the chief texts and classroom notes—sees what the course is really about; until this late stage, the trees obscured the forest, but now, as the student reviews and sorts things out, a pattern emerges. The experience of reviewing and then of writing an examination, though fretful, can be highly exciting as connections are made and ideas take on life. Such discoveries about the whole subject matter of a course can almost never be made by writing critical essays on topics of the student's own construction, for such topics rarely require a view of the whole. Furthermore, most of us are more likely to make imaginative leaps when trying to answer questions that other people pose to us than when we are trying to answer questions we pose to ourselves. And although questions posed by others cause anxiety, when students confront and respond to them in an examination they often make yet another discovery—a self-discovery, a sudden and satisfying awareness of powers they did not know they had.

WRITING ESSAY ANSWERS

We assume that before the examination you have read the assigned material, made notes in the margins of your books, made summaries of the reading and of the classroom comments, reviewed all of this material, and had a decent night's sleep. Now you are facing the examination sheet.

Here are eight obvious but important practical suggestions.

1. Take a moment to jot down, as a kind of outline or source of further inspiration, a few ideas that strike you after you have thought a little about the question. You may at the outset realize there are three points you want to make: unless you jot these down—three key words will do—you may spend all the allotted time on only one.

2. Do not bother to copy the question in the examination booklet, but if you have been given a choice of questions do indicate the question number, or write a word or two that will serve as a cue to the reader.

3. Answer the question. Consider this question: "Fromm and Lorenz try to explain aggression. Compare their theories, and discuss the extent to which they assist us in understanding the Israeli–Palestinian conflict." Notice that you must compare—not just summarize—two theories, and that you must also evaluate their relevance to a particular conflict. In short, take seriously such words as *compare, define, evaluate,* and *summarize.* And do not waste time generalizing about aggression; again, answer the question.

4. You can often get a good start merely by turning the question into an affirmation, for example by turning "In what ways is the poetry of Allen Ginsberg influenced by Whitman?" into "The poetry of Ginsberg is influenced by Whitman in at least . . . ways."

5. Do not waste time summarizing at length what you have read, unless asked to do so—but of course occasionally you may have to give a brief summary in order to support a point. The instructor wants to see that you can *use* your reading, not merely that you have done the reading.

6. Budget your time. Do not spend more time on a question than the allotted time—at least, not *much* more.

7. Be concrete. Illustrate your arguments with examples and facts—names, dates, and quotations or paraphrases or summaries if possible.

8. Leave space for last-minute additions. Either skip a page between essays or write only on the right-hand pages or double-space your answers so that on rereading you can add material at the appropriate place on the left-hand pages.

Beyond these general suggestions, we can best talk about essay examinations by looking at specific types of questions.

Questions on Literature

The most common questions encountered in literature examinations can be sorted into five categories:

1. A passage to explicate
2. A historical question, such as "Trace Leonard Cohen's religious development," "Trace the development of Shakespeare's conception of the tragic hero," or "What are Virginia Woolf's contributions to feminist criticism?"

3. A critical quotation to be evaluated
4. A comparison, such as "Compare the dramatic monologues of Browning with those of T. S. Eliot"
5. A wild question, such as "What would Dickens think of Stephen King?" or "What would Juliet do if she were in Ophelia's position?"

A few remarks on each of these types may be helpful:

1. An explication is a commentary describing what is going on in a poem or in a short passage of prose. As a short rule, look carefully at the tone (speaker's attitude toward self, subject, and audience) and at the implications of the words (the connotations or associations), and see if there is a pattern of imagery. For example, religious language ("adore," "saint") in a secular love poem may define the nature of the lover and the beloved. Remember, *an explication is not a paraphrase* (a putting into other words) but an attempt to show the relations of the parts, especially by calling attention to implications. Organization of such an essay is rarely a problem, since most explications begin with the first line and go on to the last.

2. A good essay on a historical question will offer a nice combination of argument and evidence; the thesis will be supported by concrete details (names, dates, perhaps even brief paraphrases or summaries). A discussion of Cohen's movement toward Buddhism cannot be convincing if it does not specify certain works as representative of Cohen in certain years. If you are asked to relate a writer or a body of work to an earlier writer or period, list the chief characteristics of the earlier writer or the period and then show *specifically* how the material you are discussing is related to these characteristics. And if you can quote some relevant lines from the works, your reader will feel that you know not only titles and stock phrases but also the works themselves.

3. If you are asked to evaluate a critical quotation, read it carefully and in your answer take account of *all* of the quotation. If the critic has said, "Eliot in his plays always . . . but in his poems rarely . . ." you will have to write about both the plays and the poems; it will not be enough to talk only about the plays (unless, of course, the instructions on the examination ask you to take only as much of the quotation as you wish). Watch especially for words such as "always," "for the most part," "never"; although the passage may on the whole approach the truth, you may feel that important qualifications are needed. This is not being picky; true thinking involves making subtle distinctions, yielding assent only so far and no further. And, again, be sure to give concrete details and support your argument with evidence.

4. Comparisons are discussed on pages 156–63. Because comparisons are especially difficult to write, be sure to take a few moments to jot down a sort of outline so that you can know where you will be going. A comparison of Browning's and Eliot's monologues might treat two poems by each, devoting alternate paragraphs to one author; or it might first treat one author's poems and then turn to the other. But if it adopts this second strategy, the essay may break into two parts. You can guard against this weakness by announcing at the outset that you will treat the authors separately, then by reminding your reader during your treatment of the first author that certain points will be picked up when you get to the second author, and again by briefly reminding your reader during the second part of the essay of certain points already made.

5. Curiously, a wild question such as "What would Dickens think of Stephen King?" or "What would Juliet do in Ophelia's position?" usually produces tame answers: a half-dozen ideas about Dickens or Juliet are neatly applied to King or Ophelia, and the gross incompatibilities are thus revealed. But, as the previous paragraph suggests, it may be necessary to do more than to set up bold and obvious oppositions. The interest in such a question and in the answer to it may largely be in the degree to which superficially different figures *resemble* each other in some important ways. And remember that the wildness of the question does not mean that all answers are equally acceptable; as usual, a good answer will be supported by concrete details.

A Sample Answer

Here is a sample exam question and student answer for a first-year final exam in English.

The exam question was as follows (although we provide only one quotation here):

> Write on TWO of the following three quotations [for our purposes, only one quotation is provided here]. You will need to include the following information for each: the title and author or poet; an explication of the quotation itself; and an explanation of the significance of the quotation to the work as a whole (/6 each):

>> So much for endings. Beginnings are always more fun. True connoisseurs, however, are known to favour the stretch in between, since it's the hardest to do anything with.
>> That's about all that can be said for plots, which anyway are just one thing after another, a what and a what and a what.
>> Now try How and Why.

The student's answer was as follows:

> This quotation is from Margaret Atwood's metafictional short story "Happy Endings." The story criticizes the happy endings that occur in sentimental fiction, saying that the endings of most stories are fake and unrealistic; they lack the reality of real life. This quotation points out that it is not the ending that is important, but rather how you get there. In Atwood's words, it is the "How and Why" that is really important. The author plays with this notion by not really providing the reader with plots at all, but rather with plot outlines. Atwood begins this story with a description of the standard story with a happy ending—man and woman meet, fall in love, and live happily ever after. But, she then goes on to set up a series of different middles for the story. Each starts at more or less

the same point, but each takes a very different turn in the plot. Ironically,

each scenario arrives at the same ending, death, proving Atwood's point

that it really is the how and why that matter.

Questions on the Social Sciences

First, an obvious statement: courses in the social sciences almost always require lots of reading. Do the reading when it is assigned, rather than try to do it the night before the examination. Second, when confronted with long reading assignments, you probably will read more efficiently if you skim the table of contents of a book to see the layout of the material, and then read the first and last chapters, where the authors usually summarize their theses. Books and articles on history, psychology, and sociology are not whodunits; there is nothing improper about knowing at the start how it will all turn out. Indeed, if at the start you have a clear grasp of the author's thesis, you may have the pleasure of catching the author perpetrating the crime of arguing from insufficient evidence. The beginning and the end of an article in a journal also may offer summaries that will assist you to read the article with relative ease. But only a reading of the entire work (perhaps with a little skimming) will offer you all the facts and—no less important—the fully developed view or approach that the instructor believes is essential to an understanding of the course.

The techniques students develop in answering questions on literature may be transferred to examinations in the social sciences. A political science student, for example, can describe through explication the implicit tone or attitude in some of the landmark decisions of the Supreme Court. Similarly, the student of history who has learned to write an essay with a good combination of argument and evidence will not simply offer generalizations or present a list of facts unconnected by some central thesis, but will use relevant facts to support a thesis. The student who is able to evaluate a critical quotation or to compare literary works can also evaluate and compare documents in all the social sciences. Answers to wild questions can be as effective or as trite in the social sciences as in literature. "You are the British ambassador in Petrograd in November 1918. Write a report to your government about the Bolshevik revolution of that month" is to some instructors and students an absurd question; to others it is an interesting and effective way of ascertaining whether a student has not only absorbed the facts of an event but has also learned how to interpret them.

Questions on the Physical Sciences and Mathematics

Although the answer to an examination question in the physical sciences usually requires a mathematical computation, a few sentences may be useful in explaining the general plan of the computation, the assumptions involved, and perhaps the results.

It is particularly valuable to set down at the outset in a brief statement, probably a single sentence, your plan for solving the problem posed by the examination question. The statement is equivalent to the topic sentence of a paragraph. For instance, if the examination question is "What is the time required for an object to fall from the orbit of the moon to the earth?" the statement of your plan might be: "The time required for an object to fall from the orbit of the moon to the earth can be obtained by integration from Newton's law of motion, taking account of the increasing gravitational force as the object approaches the earth." Explicitly setting down your plan in words is useful first in clarifying your thought: is the plan a complete one leading to the desired answer? Do I know what I need to know to implement the plan? If your plan makes no sense, you can junk it right away before wasting more time on it.

The statement of plan is useful also in communicating with the instructor. Your plan of solution, although valid, may be a surprise to the instructor (who may have expected a solution to the problem posed above starting from Kepler's laws without any integration). When this is so, the instructor will need your explanation to become oriented to your plan, and to properly assess its merits. Then if you botch the subsequent computation or cannot remember how the gravitational force varies with the distance, you will still have demonstrated that you have some comprehension of the problem. If on the other hand you present an erroneous computation without any explanation, the instructor will see nothing but chaos in your effort.

It may also be useful to explain assumptions or simplifications: "I assume the body is released with zero velocity and accordingly set $b = 0$," or "The third term is negligible and I drop it."

Finally, the results of your computation should be summarized or interpreted in words to answer the question asked. "The object will fall to the earth in five days." (The correct answer, for those who are curious.) Or, if you arrive at the end of both your computation and the examination hour and find you have a preposterous result, you can still exit gracefully (and increase your partial credit) with an explanation: "The answer of fifty-three days is clearly erroneous since the fall time of an object from the moon's orbit must be less than the seven days required for the moon to travel a quarter orbit."

PART FOUR

A Writer's Handbook

Punctuation

Speakers can raise or lower the volume or pitch of their voices; they can speak a phrase slowly and distinctly and then (making a parenthetical remark, perhaps) quicken the pace. They can wave their arms, pound a table, or pause meaningfully. Because they are physically removed from their audience, writers can do none of these things. Nevertheless, they can embody some of the tones and gestures of speech in the patterns of their written sentences, and in the dots, hooks, and dashes of punctuation that clarify those patterns.

Punctuation clarifies, first of all, by removing or reducing ambiguity. Consider this headline from a story in a newspaper:

SQUAD HELPS DOG BITE VICTIM

Of course, there is no real ambiguity here—only a laugh—because the stated meaning is so clearly absurd, and on second reading we supply the necessary hyphen in *dog-bite*.

Here is another example:

Woman without her man is lost.

The sentence obviously implies that a woman who does not have a man is lost. However, with a few flicks of the wrist, we add some punctuation *et voilà*:

Woman: without her, man is lost.

The sentence now says the opposite of what it did with no punctuation. Neither version has a legitimate meaning, but as a pair they humorously reinforce the point that punctuation is important.

Other ill-punctuated sentences may be troublesome rather than entertaining. Take the following sentence:

He arrived late for the rehearsal did not end until midnight.

Almost surely you stumbled in the middle of the sentence, thinking that it was about someone arriving tardily at a rehearsal, and then, since what followed made no sense, you probably went back and mentally added the comma (by pausing) at the necessary place:

> He arrived late, for the rehearsal did not end until midnight.

Punctuation helps to keep the reader on the right path. And the path is your train of thought. If your punctuation is faulty, you unintentionally direct the reader off your path.

Even when punctuation is not the key to meaning, it usually helps you get your meaning across neatly. Consider the following sentence:

> There are two kinds of feminism—one is the growing struggle of women to understand and change the shape of their lives and the other is a narrow ideology whose adherents are anxious to clear away whatever does not conform to their view.

The sentence is clear enough, but we could sharpen it by changing the punctuation. Because a dash usually indicates an abrupt interruption—it usually precedes a sort of afterthought—a colon would be better. The colon, usually the signal of an amplification of what precedes it, here would suggest that the two classifications are not impromptu thoughts but carefully considered ones. Second, and more important, in the original version the two classifications are run together without any intervening punctuation, but since the point is that the two are utterly different, it is advisable to separate them by inserting a comma or semicolon, indicating a pause. A comma before "and the other" would do, but probably a semicolon (without the "and") is preferable because it gives a heavier pause, thereby making the separation clearer. Here is the sentence, revised:

> There are two kinds of feminism: one is the growing struggle of women to understand and change the shape of their lives; the other is a narrow ideology whose adherents are anxious to clear away whatever does not conform to their view.

The proper punctuation enables the reader to move easily through the sentence.

The rules of punctuation are not always intended to contribute to meaning or to make reading easier, however. Sometimes they are stylistic conventions. For example, in Canadian usage a period never comes immediately after quotation marks; it precedes quotation marks, thus:

> "If you put the period inside the closing quotation mark," the writing instructor said, "I will give you an A."

If you put the period after the closing quotation mark, the meaning remains the same, but you are also informing your reader that you do not know the conventions of Canadian usage—conventions all writers in Canada are expected to adhere to. A pattern of such errors will diminish your authority as a writer: your reader, noticing that you do not know where to put the period in relation to the quotation mark, may well begin to wonder what else you don't know. Conversely, demonstrating that you know the rules will help to gain your reader's confidence and establish your authority as a writer.

A Word on Computer Grammar and Punctuation Checks

Word-processing programs include a tool that can check grammar and punctuation. At your request, the program will flag sentences that look faulty and offer suggestions for correcting mistakes. These programs can be helpful: they can draw your attention to sentence fragments, to problems with plurals and possessives, and even to passive verbs. They don't catch everything, however, and they do not always know how to fix the problems they identify: there are forty-nine faulty sentences in the first nine exercises at the end of this chapter; a computer check of these sentences flagged fourteen of them and offered correct editing suggestions on only six.

Our advice: use the tool if you have it, but do not let it do your editing for you. Check the program's suggestions against your own knowledge and the advice offered in this book.

THREE COMMON ERRORS: FRAGMENTS, COMMA SPLICES, AND RUN-ON SENTENCES

Fragments and How to Correct Them

A fragment is a part of a sentence set off as if it were a complete sentence: *Because I didn't care. Being an accident. Later in the week. For several reasons. My oldest sister.* Fragments are common in speech, but they are used sparingly in writing, for particular effects (see page 127). A fragment used carelessly in writing often looks like an afterthought—usually because it *was* an afterthought, that is, an explanation or other addition that belongs to the previous sentence.

With appropriate punctuation (and sometimes with no punctuation at all) a fragment can usually be connected to the previous sentence.

Incorrect

> Many nineteenth-century horror stories have been made into films. Such as *Dracula* and *Frankenstein.*

Correct

> Many nineteenth-century horror stories have been made into films, such as *Dracula* and *Frankenstein.*

Incorrect

> Many schools are putting renewed emphasis on writing. Because of increased concerns about literacy levels.

Correct

> Many schools are putting renewed emphasis on writing because of increased concerns about literacy levels.

Incorrect

> She wore only rope sandals. Being a strict vegetarian.

Correct

Being a strict vegetarian, she wore only rope sandals.
She wore only rope sandals because she was a strict vegetarian.

Incorrect

A fragment often looks like an afterthought. Perhaps because it *was* an afterthought.

Correct

A fragment often looks like an afterthought—perhaps because it *was* an afterthought.

Incorrect

He hoped to get credit for two summer courses. Batik and Hang-Gliding.

Correct

He hoped to get credit for two summer courses: Batik and Hang-Gliding.

Notice in the preceding examples that, depending upon the relationship between the two parts, the fragment and the statement before it can be joined by a comma, a dash, a colon, or by no punctuation at all.

Notice also that unintentional fragments often follow subordinating conjunctions, such as *because* and *although*. Subordinating conjunctions introduce a subordinate (dependent) clause; such a clause cannot stand as a sentence. Here is a list of the most common subordinating conjunctions.

after	though
although	unless
because	until
before	when
if	where
provided	whereas
since	while

Fragments also commonly occur when the writer, as in the third example, mistakenly uses *being* as a main verb.

Comma Splices and Run-on Sentences, and How to Correct Them

An error known as a *comma splice* (or *comma fault*) results when a comma is mistakenly placed between two independent clauses that are not joined by a coordinating conjunction: *and, or, nor, but, for, yet, so.* Two independent clauses written as one sentence with no punctuation or coordinating conjunction between them are known as a *run-on sentence* (or a *fused sentence*).

Examples of the two errors:

- *Comma splice*: In the second picture the man leans on the woman's body, he is obviously in pain.

- *Run-on sentence:* In the second picture the man leans on the woman's body he is obviously in pain.

Comma splices and run-on sentences may be corrected in five principal ways:

1. Use a period to create two sentences.

In the second picture the man leans on the woman's body. He is obviously in pain.

2. Use a semicolon.

In the second picture the man leans on the woman's body; he is obviously in pain.

3. Use a comma and a coordinating conjunction (*and, or, nor, but, for, yet, so*).

In the second picture the man leans on the woman's body, and he is obviously in pain.

4. Make one of the clauses dependent (subordinate). **Use a subordinating conjunction** such as *after, although, because, before, if, provided, since, though, unless, until, when, where, whereas, while.*

In the second picture the man leans on the woman's body because he is obviously in pain.

5. Reduce one of the independent clauses to a phrase, or even to a single word.

In the second picture the man, obviously in pain, leans on the woman's body.

Comma splices and run-on sentences are especially common in sentences containing transitional words or phrases such as the following:

also	however
besides	indeed
consequently	in fact
for example	nevertheless
furthermore	therefore
hence	whereas

When these words join independent clauses, the clauses cannot be linked by a comma.

Incorrect

She argued from faulty premises, however the conclusions happened to be correct.

Correct

Here are five correct revisions, following the five rules we have just given. (In the first two revisions we place "however" after, rather than before, "the conclusions" because we prefer the increase in emphasis, but the grammatical point is the same.)

1. She argued from faulty premises. The conclusions, however, happened to be correct. (Two sentences)
2. She argued from faulty premises; the conclusions, however, happened to be correct. (Semicolon)
3. She argued from faulty premises, but the conclusions happened to be correct. (Coordinating conjunction)
4. Although she argued from faulty premises, the conclusions happened to be correct. (Subordinating conjunction)
5. She argued from faulty premises to correct conclusions. (Reduction of an independent clause to a phrase)

Correct the comma splice in the following sentence:

The man is not pleased, in fact, he is embarrassed.

THE PERIOD

1. Periods are used to mark the ends of sentences (or intentional sentence fragments) other than questions and exclamations.

A sentence normally ends with a period.

She said, "I'll pass."

Yes.

Once more, with feeling.

But a sentence within a sentence is punctuated according to the needs of the longer sentence. Notice, in the following example, that a period is *not* used after "pass."

She said, "I'll pass," but she said it without conviction.

2. Periods are used with abbreviations of titles and terms of reference.

Dr., Mr., Mrs., Ms.

p., pp. (for "page" and "pages"), i.e., e.g., etc.

But when the capitalized initial letters of the words naming an organization are used in place of the full name, the periods are commonly omitted:

CBC, CORE, IBM, CFL, UCLA, UNICEF, USAF

3. Periods are also used to separate chapter from verse in the Bible, and an act from a scene in a play.

Genesis 3.2, Mark 6.10, Hamlet II.iv

For further details on references to the Bible, see page 480.

THE QUESTION MARK

Use a question mark after a direct question:

Did Bacon write Shakespeare's plays?

Do not use a question mark after an indirect question or after a polite request:

He asked if Bacon wrote Shakespeare's plays.

Would you please explain what the support for Bacon is really all about.

THE COLON

The colon has four uses:

- to introduce a list or series of examples
- to introduce an amplification or explanation of what precedes the colon
- to introduce a quotation (though a quotation can be introduced by other means)
- to indicate time.

Now let's look at each of these four uses.

1. The colon may introduce a list or series.

Students are required to take one of the following sciences: biology, chemistry, geology, or physics.

2. The colon may introduce an explanation. It is almost equivalent to *namely,* or *that is.* What follows the colon usually explains or amplifies what precedes the colon, though sometimes the two parts are more or less equal. The material on either side of the colon can usually stand as a separate sentence but sometimes what follows the colon is a phrase, clause, or fragment.

She explained her fondness for wrestling: she did it to shock her parents.

The forces which in China created a central government were absent in Japan: farming had to be on a small scale, there was no need for extensive canal works, and a standing army was not required to protect the country from foreign invaders.

When I let it slip among ordinary company that I am a professor of English, you can guess what the reaction is: "Oh-oh," they say with nervous smiles, "I'd better watch my language."

—MICHAEL HORNYANSKY

Notice in this last example that the writer uses a capital letter after the colon; the usage is acceptable when a complete sentence follows the colon, as long as that style is followed consistently throughout a paper. But most students find it easier to use lower-case letters after colons, the prevalent style in writing today.

3. The colon, like the comma, may be used to introduce a quotation as long as the introductory part is an independent clause or you want particular emphasis. It is more formal than the comma, setting off the quotation to a greater degree.

On December 26, 1999, the *Calgary Herald* quoted Alberta Premier Ralph Klein: "I used to literally get thousands of people out to protests and rallies."

4. A colon is used to separate the hour from the minutes when the time is given in figures.

9:15, 12:00

Colons (like semicolons) go outside of closing quotation marks if they are not part of the quotation.

"There is no such thing as a free lunch": the truth of these words is confirmed every day.

THE SEMICOLON

There are four main uses of the semicolon. Sheridan Baker (in *The Practical Stylist*) summed them up in this admirable formula: "Use a semicolon where you could also use a period, unless desperate." Correctly used, the semicolon can add precision to your writing; it can also help you out of some tight corners.

1. You may use a semicolon instead of a period between closely related independent clauses not joined by a coordinating conjunction.

All happy families resemble one another; every unhappy family is unhappy in its own fashion.

—LEO TOLSTOY

The demands that men and women make on marriage will never be fully met; they cannot be.

—JESSIE BERNARD

In our fractured culture, we cannot agree on morals; we cannot even agree that moral matters should come before literary ones when there is a conflict between them.

—FLANNERY O'CONNOR

When a cat washes its face it does not move its paw; it moves its face.

In each of the examples the independent clauses might have been written as sentences separated by periods; the semicolon pulls the statements together, emphasizing their relationship. Alternatively, the statements might have been linked by a comma plus a coordinating conjunction (*and, or, nor, but, for, yet, so*). For example:

The demands made upon marriage will never be fully met, *for* they cannot be.

When a cat washes its face it does not move its paw, *but* it moves its face.

The sentences as originally written, using semicolons, have more bite.

2. You *must* use a semicolon (rather than a comma) if you use a *conjunctive adverb* to connect independent clauses. (A conjunctive adverb is a transitional word such as *also, consequently, furthermore, however, moreover, nevertheless, therefore.*)

> His hair was black and wavy; however, it was fake.
>
> We don't like to see our depressed relative cry; nevertheless, tears can provide a healthy emotional outlet.
>
> She said "I do"; moreover, she repeated the words.

Take note of the following three points:

- A comma goes after the conjunctive adverb.
- Semicolons (like colons) go outside closing quotation marks if they are not part of the quotation.
- A conjunctive adverb requires a semicolon to join independent clauses. A comma produces a comma splice.

How is the following sentence incorrect?

> This book may be used to train your black lab to retrieve or to assess your posture while walking back and forth like royalty, however, if all else fails, it may also be read.

3. You may use a semicolon to separate a series of phrases with internal punctuation.

> He had a car, which he hadn't paid for; a wife, whom he didn't love; and a father, who was unemployed.

4. Use a semicolon between independent clauses linked by coordinating conjunctions if the sentence would otherwise be difficult to read, because it is long and complex or because it contains internal punctuation.

> In the greatest age of painting, the nude inspired the greatest works; and even when it ceased to be a compulsive subject, it held its position as an academic exercise and a demonstration of mastery.

THE COMMA

The comma (from a Greek word meaning "to cut") indicates a relatively slight pause within a sentence. If after checking the rules you are still uncertain of whether or not to use a comma in a given sentence, read the sentence aloud and see if it sounds better with or without a pause; you can then add or omit the comma. A women's shoe store in New York has a sign on the door:

> NO MEN PLEASE.

If the proprietors would read the sign aloud, they might want to change it to

> NO MEN, PLEASE

When you are typing, always follow a comma with a space.

For your reference, here is an outline for the following pages, which summarize the correct uses of the comma:

1. Independent clauses (unless very short) joined by a coordinating conjunction *(and, or, nor, but, for, yet, so)* take a comma before the conjunction.

Most students see at least a few football games, and many go to every game of the season.

Most students seem to have an intuitive sense of when to use a comma, but in fact the "intuition" is the result of long training.

If the introductory independent clause is short, the comma can be omitted:

She dieted but she continued to gain weight.

2. An introductory subordinate clause or long phrase of more than five words is usually followed by a comma.

Having revised his manuscript for the third time, he went to bed.

In order to demonstrate her point, the instructor stood on her head.

If the introductory subordinate clause or phrase is short, say five words or fewer, the comma may be omitted, provided no ambiguity results from the omission.

Having left the instructor soon forgot.

But compare this last example with the following:

Having left, the instructor soon forgot.

If the comma is omitted, the sentence is misread. Where are commas needed in the following sentences and why?

Instead of discussing the book she wrote a summary.

When Shakespeare wrote comedies were already popular.

While he ate his poodle would sit by the table.

As we age small things become killers.

3. A subordinate clause or long modifying phrase placed at the end of a sentence as an afterthought is usually preceded by a comma.

The first amusement-park rides began appearing in recreational locations in the 1840s, although it is possible that portable versions made their way to Canadian exhibitions and fairs before this.

Buster Keaton fell down a flight of stairs without busting, thereby gaining his nickname from Harry Houdini.

By the time he retired, Hank Aaron had 755 home runs, breaking Babe Ruth's record by 41.

With afterthoughts, the comma may be omitted if there is a clear sequence of cause and effect, signalled by such words as *because, for,* and *so.* Compare the following examples:

In 1601 Shakespeare wrote *Hamlet,* probably his best-known play.

In 1601 Shakespeare wrote *Hamlet* because revenge tragedy was in demand.

4. A pair of commas can serve as a *pair* of unobtrusive parentheses. Be sure not to omit the second comma.

Doctors, I think, have an insufficient knowledge of acupuncture.

The earliest known paintings of Christ, dating from the third century, are found in the catacombs outside Rome.

For a province world-renowned for its agricultural activity, particularly grain production, Saskatchewan includes a vast amount of both forest land and wood volume.

Under this heading we can include a conjunctive adverb (a transitional adverb such as *also, besides, consequently, however, likewise, nevertheless, therefore)* inserted within a sentence. These transitional words are set off between a pair of commas.

Her hair, however, was stringy.

If one of these words begins a sentence, the following comma is optional. Notice, however, that the presence of such a word as "however" is not always a safeguard against a run-on sentence or comma splice; if the word occurs between two independent clauses and it goes with the second clause, you need a semicolon before it and a comma after it.

His hair was black and wavy; however, it was fake.

(See the discussion of comma splices on pages 433–35.)

5. Use a comma to set off a non-restrictive modifier. A non-restrictive modifier, as the following examples will make clear, is a sort of parenthetical addition; it gives supplementary information about the subject, but it can be omitted without changing the subject. A restrictive modifier, on the other hand, is not supplementary but essential and so is not enclosed between commas; if a restrictive modifier is omitted, the subject becomes more general:

Men seldom make passes

At girls who wear glasses.

— DOROTHY PARKER

In Parker's celebrated poem, "who wear glasses" is a restrictive modifier, narrowing or restricting the subject down from "girls" to a particular group of girls: "girls who wear glasses."

Here is a *non*-restrictive modifier:

For the majority of immigrants, who have no knowledge of English, language is the chief problem.

Now a restrictive modifier:

For the majority of immigrants who have no knowledge of English, language is the chief problem.

The first version says—in addition to its obvious message that language is the chief problem—that the majority of immigrants have no knowledge of English. The second version makes no such assertion; it talks not about the majority of immigrants but only about a more restricted group: those immigrants who have no knowledge of English.

Other examples:

Shakespeare's shortest tragedy, *Macbeth,* is one of his greatest plays.

In this sentence, *"Macbeth"* is non-restrictive because the subject is already as restricted as possible; Shakespeare can have written only one "shortest tragedy." That is, *"Macbeth"* is merely an explanatory equivalent of "Shakespeare's shortest tragedy," and it is therefore enclosed in commas. (A noun or noun phrase serving as an explanatory equivalent to another, and in the same syntactical relation to other elements in the sentence, is said to be "in apposition.") But compare

Shakespeare's tragedy *Macbeth* is one of his greatest plays.

with the misleadingly punctuated sentence,

Shakespeare's tragedy, *Macbeth,* is one of his greatest plays.

The first of these is restrictive, narrowing or restricting the subject "tragedy" down to one particular tragedy, and so it rightly does not separate the modifier from the subject by a comma. The second, punctuated so that it is non-restrictive, falsely implies that *Macbeth* is Shakespeare's only tragedy. Here is an example of a non-restrictive modifier correctly punctuated:

Women, who constitute 51.3 percent of the population and 53 percent of the electorate, constitute only 2.5 percent of the U.S. House of Representatives and 1 percent of the Senate.

In the next three examples, the first two illustrate the correct use of commas after a non-restrictive appositive, and the third illustrates the correct omission of commas after a restrictive appositive.

> The Queen's Plate horse race, North America's oldest annual sports event, has been staged in Canada since 1860.
>
> North America's oldest annual sports event, the Queen's Plate horse race, has been staged in Canada since 1860.
>
> North America's horse race the Queen's Plate has been staged in Canada since 1860.

6. Words, phrases, and clauses in series (a list of three or more) take a comma after each item except the last.

> Photography is a matter of eyes, intuition, and intellect.
>
> She wrote plays, poems, and stories.
>
> When you're in trouble in the mountains and you don't have a flare, a smoke signal, a radio, a cellphone, or a Collie named Lassie, you have to improvise.

But adjectives in a series may cause difficulty. The next two examples correctly omit the commas.

> a funny silent film
>
> a famous French professor

In both examples, the noun and the adjective immediately before it form a compound that is modified by the earlier adjective. That is, the adjectives are not a coordinate series (what is funny is not simply a film but a silent film, what is famous is not simply a professor but a French professor) and so commas are not used. Compare:

> a famous French professor
>
> a famous, arrogant French professor

In the second example, only "famous" and "arrogant" form a coordinate series. If in doubt, see if you can replace the commas with "and"; if you can, the commas are correct. In the example given, you could insert "and" between "famous" and "arrogant," but not between "arrogant" and "French."

Commas are not needed if all the members of the series are connected by conjunctions.

> He ate steak for breakfast and lunch and supper.

7. Use a comma to set off direct discourse.

> "It's a total failure," she said.
>
> She said, "It's a total failure."

But do not use a comma for indirect discourse.

She said that it is a total failure.

She said it is a total failure.

8. Use a comma to set off "yes" and "no."

Yes, he could take Writing 125 at ten o'clock.

9. Use a comma to set off words of direct address (person or group being spoken to).

Look, Bill, you can take Writing 125 at ten o'clock.

My fellow Canadians, we must join to fight intolerance.

10. Use a comma to separate a geographical location within another geographical location.

She was born in Victoria, British Columbia, in 1895.

Another way of putting it is to say that a comma is used after each unit of an address except between the postal code and the province named immediately before it.

11. Use a comma to set off the year from the month or day.

Canada became a country on July 1, 1867.

No comma is needed if you use the form "1 July 1867."

12. Note the position of the comma when used with other punctuation: if a comma is required with parenthetic material, it follows the second parenthesis.

Because Japan was secure from invasion (even the Mongols were beaten back), its history is unusually self-contained.

The only time a comma may precede a parenthesis is when parentheses surround a digit or letter used to enumerate a series.

Questions usually fall into one of three categories: (1) true or false, (2) multiple choice, (3) essay.

A comma always goes inside closing quotation marks unless the quotation is followed by a parenthesis.

"The trouble with talking about the United States in confident generalities is that it is a kind of Jekyll and Hyde phenomenon," writes John W. Holmes, "except that it is rarely seen as Jekyllian as Americans like to think and very rarely as Hydean as its critics allege" (41).

THE DASH

A dash is made by typing two hyphens without hitting the space-bar before, between, or after. It indicates an abrupt break or pause.

1. The material within dashes may be something like parenthetic material (material that is not essential), though by setting it within dashes—an emphatic form of punctuation—the writer gives the material more emphasis than it would get within parentheses.

> The bathroom—that private place—has rarely been the subject of scholarly study.

> The Great Wall of China forms a continuous line more than 2200 kilometres long—the distance from Banff to Winnipeg—running from Beijing to the edge of the mountains of Central Asia.

> A favourite wildlife species for park visitors and locals alike has got to be the loveable little mosquito—the skeeter's aerial acrobatics, soothing music, and feisty personality have ensured it a special place in our hearts.

Notice that if the words between two dashes are deleted the remaining words still form a grammatical sentence.

2. A dash can serve, somewhat like a colon, as a pause before a series. It is more casual than a colon.

> The earliest Shinto holy places were natural objects—trees, boulders, mountains, islands.

> Each of the brothers had his distinct comic style—Groucho's double-talk, Chico's artfully stupid malapropisms, Harpo's horseplay.
>
> —GERALD MAST

A dash is never used next to a comma in the middle of a sentence. When a dash appears at the end of direct speech, it indicates interrupted speech and is not followed by a period.

> "Oh, no, he's—" she screamed, as gunshots split the air.

Overuse of the dash—even only a little overuse—gives writing an unpleasantly agitated—even explosive—quality.

PARENTHESES

Let's begin with a caution: avoid using parentheses to explain pronouns, such as: "In his speech he (Hamlet) says . . ." If "he" needs to be explained by "Hamlet," omit the "he" and just say "Hamlet."

1. Use parentheses around subordinate material. What is in parentheses is less essential to the meaning of the sentence than similar material set off in commas and less vigorously expressed than similar material set off in dashes; rather, it is almost a casual aside.

> No exhibit of Canadian painting would be complete without Truncheon's *The Leave-Taking* (with its image of a boy hesitantly boarding the CPR *Flyer* at Washbowl, Manitoba, as he prepares to set off for Toronto).

Avoid an abundance of these interruptions, and avoid a long parenthesis within a sentence (you are now reading a simple example of this annoying but common habit of writers who have trouble sticking to the point), because the reader will lose track of the main sentence.

2. Use parentheses to enclose digits or letters in a list that appears in running text.

The exhibition included: (1) decorative screens, (2) ceramics, (3) ink paintings, (4) kimonos.

3. Do not confuse parentheses with square brackets, which are used around material you add to a quotation. See page 479.

4. For the use of parentheses in documentation, see Chapter 17, "Documenting the Research Essay."

5. Note the position of other punctuation with a parenthesis: the example under rule number 2, of commas preceding parentheses around digits or letters in a list within running text, is the rare exception to the rule that punctuation other than quotation marks never immediately precedes an opening parenthesis. Sometimes, it *follows* the closing parenthesis, as the comma does in this example:

While guest curator for the Whitney (he has since returned to the Denver Art Museum), Feder assembled a magnificent collection of masks, totems, paintings, clothing, and beadwork.

(If an entire sentence is in parentheses, put the final punctuation—period, question mark, or exclamation mark—inside the closing parenthesis.)

ITALICS

In typewritten material <u>underlining</u> is the equivalent of *italic* type.

This sentence is printed in italic type.

<u>This sentence is understood to be printed in italic type.</u>

1. Italicize the name of a plane, ship, train, film, radio or television program, CD, musical composition, statue, painting, play, pamphlet, or book. Do not underline names of sacred works such as the Bible, the Koran, and Acts of the Apostles, or political documents such as the Magna Carta and the Declaration of Independence. Notice that when you write of *The New York Times,* you italicize *New York* because it is part of the title, but when you write of the London *Times,* you do not italicize "London" because "London" is not part of the title, only information added for clarity. Similarly, when you refer to *Maclean's* magazine do not italicize "magazine."

2. Use italics only sparingly for emphasis. Sometimes, however, this method of indicating your tone of voice is *exactly right.*

3. Use italics for foreign words that have not become part of the English language.

Acupuncture aims to affect the *ch'i,* a sort of vital spirit that circulates through the bodily organs.

But:

He ate a pizza.

She behaved like a prima donna.

Avoid clichés.

4. You may use italics in place of quotation marks to identify a word.

Honolulu means "safe harbour."

5. You may also use italics to identify a word or term to which you wish to call special attention.

Claude Lévi-Strauss tells us that one of the great purposes of art is *miniaturization.* He points out that most works of art are miniatures, being smaller (and therefore more easily understood) than the objects they represent.

CAPITAL LETTERS

Certain obvious conventions—the use of a capital for the first word in a sentence, for names (of days of the week, holidays, months, people, countries), and for words derived from names (such as pro-French)—will not be discussed here.

1. Titles of works in English are usually given according to the following formula. Use a capital for the first letter of the first word, for the first letter of the last word, and for the first letter of all other words that are not articles, conjunctions, or prepositions.

The Merchant of Venice

A Midsummer Night's Dream

"Boys and Girls"

"The Short Happy Life of Francis Macomber"

Fire with Fire

2. Use a capital for a quoted sentence within a sentence, but not for a quoted phrase (unless it is at the beginning of your sentence) and not for indirect discourse.

He said, "You can even fool some of the people all of the time."

He said you can fool some people "all of the time."

He said that you can even fool some of the people all of the time.

3. Use a capital for a rank or title preceding a proper name or for a title substituting for a proper name.

> She said she was Dr. Perez.
>
> Prime Minister Lester Pearson won the Nobel Peace Prize in 1957 for his diplomacy during the Suez Crisis in 1956.

But:

> Why would anyone wish to be prime minister?
>
> Macdonald was the first prime minister.

4. Use a capital when the noun designating a family relationship is used as a substitute for a proper noun.

> If Mother is busy, ask Tim.

But:

> Because my mother was busy, I asked Tim.

5. Formal geographical locations (but not mere points on the compass) are capitalized.

> North America
>
> Southeast Asia
>
> In the Southwest, rain sometimes evaporates before touching the ground.
>
> Have you been to the West Coast lately?
>
> The North has its share of racism.

But:

> The wind came from the south.
>
> Farther south, the hazardous Strait of Belle Isle was the first gateway to North America for sailors from Europe.

Do *not* capitalize the names of the seasons.

> spring, summer, winter, fall

THE HYPHEN

The hyphen has five uses, all drawing on the etymology of the word *hyphen*, which comes from the Greek for "in one," "together."

1. Use a hyphen to attach certain prefixes to root words. *All-, pro-, ex-,* and *self-* are the most common of these ("all-powerful," "ex-wife," "pro-labour," "self-made"), but note that even these prefixes are not always followed by a hyphen. If in doubt, check a dictionary. Prefixes before proper names are always followed by a hyphen:

anti-Semite, pro-NATO, un-Canadian

Prefixes ending in *i* are hyphenated before a word beginning with *i:*

anti-intellectual, semi-intelligible

A hyphen is normally used to break up a triple consonant resulting from the addition of a prefix:

ill-lit

2. Use a hyphen to tie compound adjectives into a single unit.

out-of-date theory, twenty-three well-written books, no-smoking area, sixth-century play

The sea-tossed raft was a common nineteenth-century symbol of the tragic human condition.

But if a compound modifier follows the modified term, it is usually not hyphenated, thus:

The theory was out of date.

In the nineteenth century, novels were a popular genre.

3. Use a hyphen to join some compound nouns.

Scholar-teacher, philosopher-poet

4. Use a hyphen to indicate a span of dates or page numbers.
(If you look closely at date ranges in books, you will see that publishers often use the longer en-dash: 1957–59.)

1957-59, pp. 162-68

THE APOSTROPHE

Use an apostrophe to indicate the possessive, to indicate a contraction, and to form certain unusual plurals.

1. The most common way to indicate the possessive of a singular noun is to add an apostrophe followed by s.

A dog's life, a week's work, a mouse's tail

For a proper noun that ends in *s* or another sibilant (-*cks*, -*x*, -*z*), also add an apostrophe followed by *s*.

Sophocles's plays, Chavez's ideas, Marx's doctrines

Possessive pronouns, such as *his, hers, its, theirs, ours,* do not take an apostrophe:

his book, its fur

The book is hers, not ours.

The book is theirs.

(*Exception:* indefinite pronouns take an apostrophe, as in "one's hopes" and "others' opinions.")

For plurals ending in *s,* add only an apostrophe to indicate the possessive:

the boys' father, the Smiths' house, the Joneses' car

If the plural does not end in *s,* add an apostrophe and an *s.*

women's clothing, moose's eyes

Don't try to form the possessive of the title of a work (for example, of a play, a book, or a film): write "the imagery in *The Merchant of Venice*" rather than "*The Merchant of Venice*'s imagery." Using an apostrophe gets you into the problem of whether or not to italicize the *s;* similarly, if you use an apostrophe for a work normally enclosed in quotation marks (for instance, a short story), you cannot put the apostrophe and the *s* after the quotation marks, but you cannot put it inside either.

2. Use an apostrophe to indicate the omitted letters or numbers in contractions.

She won't.

It's time to go.

the class of '87

3. Until recently an apostrophe was used to make plurals of words that do not usually have a plural, and (this is optional) to make the plurals of digits and letters.

Her speech was full of if's and and's and but's.

Ph.D.'s don't know everything.

Mind your p's and q's. I got two A's and two B's.

He makes his 4's in two ways.

the 1920's

This use of the apostrophe is no longer standard, but it remains acceptable.

ABBREVIATIONS

In general, avoid abbreviations except in footnotes and except for certain common ones listed below. And do not use an ampersand (&) unless it appears in material you are quoting or in a title. Abundant use of abbreviations makes an essay sound like a series of newspaper headlines. Usually, for example, *United States* is better than *U.S.,* but it is acceptable to write *CBC* rather than *Canadian Broadcasting Corporation.*

1. Abbreviations of titles, with the first letter capitalized, are used before a name.

Dr. Bellini, Ms. Smith, St. Thomas

But:

The doctor took her temperature and eighty dollars.

2. Degrees that follow a name are abbreviated. Our style is to use periods, although they may be omitted.

B.A., D.D.S., M.D., Ph.D.

3. Other acceptable abbreviations include:

BCE, CE, a.m., p.m., e.g., i.e.

(By the way, *e.g.* means *for example; i.e.* means *that is.* The two ought not to be confused. See pages 462 and 464.)

4. The name of an agency or institution may be abbreviated by using the initial letters, capitalized and usually without periods, but it is advisable to give the name in full when first mentioning it (not everyone knows that CAA means Canadian Automobile Association, for instance) and to use the abbreviation in subsequent references. Some examples are: the Congress of Racial Equality (CORE), International Business Machines (IBM), and University of Prince Edward Island (UPEI).

NUMBERS

1. Write numbers out if you can do so in one or two words; otherwise, use numerals. Remember to hyphenate two-word numbers from twenty-one to ninety-nine.

sixteen, seventy-two, ten thousand, one sixth
10 200; 10 200 000
There are 336 dimples on a golf ball.

But write out round millions and billions, to avoid a string of zeroes.

a hundred and ten million

For large round numbers you can also use a combination of figures and words.

The cockroach is about 250 million years old.

Do not mix figures and spelled-out words.

Prince Edward Island has a population per square kilometre of 23.8 persons; the national figure is 3.

Note, however, that because a figure cannot be capitalized, if a number begins a sentence it should always be written out:

Two hundred and fifty million years ago the cockroach first appeared on earth.

2. Use figures in dates, addresses, decimals, percentages, page numbers, and hours followed by a.m. or p.m.

February 29, 1900; 0.06 percent; 6 percent; 8:16 a.m.

But hours unmodified by minutes are usually written out, followed by *o'clock.*

Fireworks on Canada Day typically begin at ten o'clock.

3. Use an apostrophe to indicate omitted figures.

class of '98

the '90s (but: "the nineties")

4. In listing inclusive numbers, give the second number in full for the numbers up through ninety-nine:

2-5, 8-11, 28-34

For larger numbers, give only the last two digits of the second number (101-06; 112-14) unless the full number is necessary (198-202).

5. Dates can be given with the month first, followed by numerals, a comma, and the year

February 10, 1999

or they can be given with the day first, then the month and then the year (without a comma after the day or month)

10 February 1999

6. BC (no periods and no space between the letters) follows the year, but AD precedes it. (Remember, though, that it is becoming more common to use BCE and CE, with both following the year.)

1000 BC, 1000 BCE

AD 200, 200 CE

7. Roman numerals are less popular than they used to be. Capitalized roman numerals were used to indicate a volume number, but these are now commonly given in Arabic numerals. Capital Roman numerals still are used, however, for the names of individuals in a series (Elizabeth II) and for the primary divisions of an outline; lower-case Roman numerals are used for the pages in the front matter (table of contents, foreword, preface, etc.) of a book. The old custom of citing acts and scenes of a play in Roman numerals and lines in Arabic numerals (II.iv.17-25) is still preferred by many instructors, but the use of Arabic numerals throughout (2.4.17-25) is gaining acceptance.

Exercises

1. Correct the following sentence fragments. You may join fragments to independent clauses, or you may recast them as complete sentences.
   a. He left the sentence fragments in the final version of his essay. Instead of trying to fix them.
   b. Her associate left the country. Although their project was unfinished.
   c. Walter S. Allward of Toronto won the bid to build a war memorial. That of the Canadian War Memorial at Vimy Ridge.
   d. He made corrections on the final copy of his essay by hand. Being unwilling to print out the whole paper again.
   e. She spent three hours waiting in line in the rain to buy tickets to the Tragically Hip concert. Since she was an irrepressible fan.
2. Determine which of the following sentences are run-ons and which contain comma splices. Label them accordingly and correct them appropriately—using any of the five methods shown on pages 433–35.
   a. Findley's *Headhunter* is one of Jim's favourite books, he is reading it now for the fifth time.
   b. Don't write run-on sentences they are not acceptable.
   c. The quarterback was intercepted on fourteen consecutive passes, he was traded the following season.
   d. Ambiguously punctuated sentences are usually confusing often they are humorous.
   e. There are those who warn that computers are dehumanizing students, however such people have produced no verifiable evidence.
3. Correct the following sentences, inserting the necessary colons and semicolons.
   a. I signed up for four courses this semester calculus, geology, women's studies, and English.
   b. "Every dark cloud has a silver lining" I've found that the cliché does not always hold true.
   c. The semicolon is tricky it can be effective, but it is often misused.
   d. I finished my final papers three weeks early consequently, I had nothing to do while everyone else was working.
   e. The case for nuclear power has always rested on two claims that reactors were reasonably safe and that they were indispensable as a source of energy.
   f. Dinner was a disaster he broiled fish, which he burned he steamed broccoli, which came out soggy and he baked a soufflé, which fell.
4. In these sentences insert commas where necessary to set off phrases and clauses.
   a. While she was cooking the cat jumped onto the refrigerator.
   b. Geometry is a prerequisite for trigonometry and calculus is a prerequisite for physics.
   c. He wanted to go to Europe in the summer so he had to take a part-time job.
   d. Although she's aware of the dangers of smoking it seems impossible for her to quit.

    e. Final exams they thought were a waste of time.

    f. One of the best-selling books in Canada in the 1990s *Boom, Bust & Echo* was written by David K. Foot and Daniel Stoffman.

5. Insert commas to make the restrictive elements in the following sentences non-restrictive. Be prepared to explain how changing the punctuation changes each sentence's meaning.

    a. My uncle who owns a farm breeds racehorses.

    b. The circus which returns to Vancouver every winter is attended by thousands.

    c. Teachers who are the ones chiefly entrusted with educating people formally should concentrate more heavily on developing their students' analytical skills.

    d. Athletes who ought to know better sometimes play while injured.

6. Punctuate these sentences using the instructions given in items 6–11 on pages 442–43 as guidelines.

    a. Mount Logan Yukon is Canada's highest peak at 5959 metres.

    b. Yes it's a sentimental story but I like it.

    c. "You have no taste" he said.

    d. The plot of his detective novel was flimsy weak and unoriginal.

    e. I would prefer not to receive a partridge in a pear tree two French hens three turtle doves and all that other stuff again this Christmas.

7. Place commas correctly in the following sentences.

    a. "Don't write sentence fragments" the instructor said "they are unacceptable."

    b. Arguing with him was useless (he was most stubborn when he was wrong) so she decided to drop the subject.

    c. To revise Mrs. Beeton's famous recipe you must: (1) find your hare (2) catch it (3) cook it.

    d. "A Good Man Is Hard to Find" "The Watcher" and "A Rose for Emily" are three of his favourite short stories.

8. Correct the following sentences, adding apostrophes where needed. Label each word you correct to indicate whether it is a possessive, a contraction, or an unusual plural.

    a. Its easy to learn to use apostrophes.

    b. The boys books are on their shelves, under their beds, and in their closets.

    c. There are three copies of Davies *Fifth Business* in the professors office.

    d. My copys falling apart.

    e. In the 1940s ones dollars went further.

9. In the following sentences, decide what punctuation is needed, and then add it. If the sentence is correctly punctuated, place a check mark to the left of it.

    a. Around his neck is a scarf knotted in front and covering his head is a wide brimmed hat.

    b. Amelia Hall playing Queen Anne in *Richard III* was the first Canadian and the first woman to speak on the stage at Stratford.

    c. The demands that men and women make on marriage will never be fully met they cannot be.

d. The Polish painter Oskar Kokoschka once said to a man who had posed for a portrait those who know you wont recognize you but those who dont will.

e. Neverendum coined in the 1990s is the popular name for recurrent discussion of the Quebec referendum.

f. Archibald Lampman stated I am not a great poet and I never was.

g. Shlomo a giraffe in the Tel Aviv Zoo succumbed to the effects of falling down after efforts to raise him with ropes and pulleys were unsuccessful.

h. Character like a photograph develops in darkness.

i. In a grief reaction especially when the person has suffered a loss crying comes easily and produces a healthy release from pent up emotion.

10. Identify and correct the multiple errors in the following sentences.

a. The CBC ran a special debuting on Oct 17 2004. Called The Greatest Canadian.

b. The competition started with names submitted to the CBC which were narrowed down to a top 10 list each of the top ten were given an advocate to speak on his behalf and convince Canadians to vote for that person as the greatest Canadian.

c. The special averaged 500 000 and seven-hundred thousand viewers per episode, some views found the show to be uncanadian because Quebec was not included and because the selection process resulted in many famous rather than "great" people

d. Tommy Douglas who is credited with being the father of medicare being the winner.

e. The runners up were as follows Terry Fox, Marathon of Hope runner, Pierre Elliott Trudeau, PM, and Frederick Banting, discoverer of insulin. The following Canadians also made it into the top 10 David Suzuki, Lester Pearson, Don Cherry, John A. Macdonald, Alexander Graham Bell and Wayne Gretzky.

f. According to CBCs website, "At one point, CBC commentator Rex Murphy—who championed Trudeau—got into a heated verbal tussle with George Stroumboulopoulos, who argued that Douglas was the source of Trudeaus idea's. "There is a difference between the fertilizer and the tree", Murphy said pointedly."

g. The show, not surprisingly, spawned a website parody called The Most Embarrassing Canadian, the website states that as our national broadcaster embarks on its questionable quest to elect the greatest Canadian, you are invited to participate in an equally dubious endeavour, and one that speaks much more directly to the Canadian psyche: poking fun at famous Canadians [The Most Embarrassing Canadian].

11. Here is an excerpt from Lynne Truss's *Eats, Shoots & Leaves: The Zero Tolerance Approach to Punctuation* with, ironically enough, the punctuation omitted from within each sentence. Mark in the correct punctuation.

Part of ones despair of course is that the world cares nothing for the little shocks endured by the sensitive stickler. While we look in horror at a badly punctuated sign the world carried on around us blind to our plight. We are like the little boy in The Sixth Sense who can see dead people except that we can see dead punctuation. Whisper it in petrified little boy tones dead punctuation is invisible to everyone else yet we see it all the time. No one understands us seventh sense people. They regard us as freaks.

12. We reprint below the fourth paragraph of Jeff Greenfield's essay "Columbo Knows the Butler Didn't Do It," but without punctuation and capitalization. Go through the paragraph, adding the punctuation you find necessary. Check your work against the original paragraph on page 178. If you find differences between your punctuation and Greenfield's, try to explain why Greenfield made the choices he did and why you made the choices you did.

columbos villains are not simply rich they are privileged they live the lives that are for most of us hopeless daydreams houses on top of mountains with pools servants and sliding doors parties with women in slinky dresses and endless food and drink plush enclosed box seats at professional sports events the envy and admiration of the crowd while we choose between johnny carson and *invasion of the body snatchers* they are at screenings of movies the rest of us wait in line for on third avenue three months later.

13. Here are the first two paragraphs—but without punctuation and capitalization—from the dust jacket of Donald Jack's *Rogues, Rebels, and Geniuses: The Story of Canadian Medicine*. Add the necessary punctuation and capitalization.

this is the story of canadas contribution to the glory of the independent spirit and to the progress of medicine as told through the lives of its passionate crude roistering neurotic brilliant doctors so begins this lively and absorbing account of more than 400 years of medicine in canada from the indian shamans to the present day canadian doctors have made an enormous contribution to world medicine their achievements range from the discovery of insulin to the development of the cobalt bomb and the famous names are here grenfell archibald osler bethune penfield selye banting but as pierre berton points out in his foreword to the book rogues rebels and geniuses is more than a history of canadian medicine in a curious way it is also a history of the canadian nation in his monumental examination of the place of doctors in our history donald jack makes it clear that since cartiers day medical men have been bound up in the development of the country not only as practitioners but also as politicians explorers gadflies soldiers community leaders

Usage

Some things are said or written and some are not. More precisely, anything can be said or written, but only some things are acceptable to the ears and minds of many readers. "I don't know nothing about it" has been said and will be said again, but many hearers who encounter this expression are likely to judge the speaker as a person with nothing of interest to say—and immediately tune out.

Although such a double negative is not acceptable today, it used to be: Chaucer's courteous Knight never spoke no baseness, and Shakespeare's courtly Mercutio, in *Romeo and Juliet*, "will not budge for no man." But things have changed; what was acceptable in the Middle Ages and the Renaissance (for example, emptying chamber pots into the gutter) is not always acceptable now. And some of what was once unacceptable has become acceptable. At the beginning of the twentieth century, grammarians suggested that one cannot use *drive* in speaking of a car; one drives (forces into motion) an ox, or even a person ("He drove her to distraction"), but not a machine. A century of usage, however, has erased all objections.

This chapter presents a list of expressions that, although commonly used, set many teeth on edge. Seventy years from now some of these expressions may be as acceptable as "drive a car"; but we are writing for today, and we might as well try to hold today's readers by following today's taste in language.

A NOTE ON IDIOMS

An idiom (from a Greek word meaning "peculiar") is a fixed group of words, peculiar to a given language. Thus in English we say, "I took a walk," but Germans "make a walk," Spaniards "give a walk," and Japanese "do a walk." (If we think the German, Spanish, and Japanese expressions are odd, we might well ask ourselves where it is that we take a walk to.) If a visitor from Argentina says, in English, that she "gave a walk," she is using *un*idiomatic English, just as anyone who says he knows a poem "at heart" instead of "by heart" is using unidiomatic English.

Probably most unidiomatic expressions use the wrong preposition. Examples:

Unidiomatic	*Idiomatic*
comply to	comply with
superior with	superior to

Sometimes while we write, or even while we speak, we are unsure of the idiom and we pause to try an alternative—"parallel with?" "parallel to?"—and we don't know which sounds more natural, more idiomatic. At such moments, more often than not, either is acceptable, but if you are in doubt, check a dictionary. (*The Canadian Oxford Dictionary* would have been helpful in the quandary over parallel with or to.)

In any case, if you are a native speaker of English, when you read your draft you will probably detect unidiomatic expressions such as *superior with;* that is, you will hear something that sounds odd, and so you will change it to something that sounds familiar, idiomatic—here, *superior to.* If any unidiomatic expressions remain in your essay, the trouble may be that an effort to write impressively has led you to use unfamiliar language. A reader who sees such unidiomatic language may sense that you are straining for an effect. Try rewriting the passage in your own voice.

If English is not your first language and you are not yet fluent in it, plan to spend extra time revising and editing your work. Check prepositional phrases with special care. In addition to using a modern Canadian dictionary such as the *Canadian Oxford*, consult reference works designed with the international or bilingual student in mind. One compact book our students find particularly useful is Michael Swan's *Practical English Usage,* published by Oxford University Press. But don't neglect another invaluable resource: students who are native speakers. They will usually be able to tell you whether or not a phrase "sounds right," though they may not know why.

A GLOSSARY OF DICTION USAGE

a, an Use *a* before words beginning with a consonant ("a book") or with a vowel sounded as a consonant ("a one-way ticket," "a university"). Use *an* before words beginning with a vowel or a vowel sound, including those beginning with a silent *b* ("an egg," "an hour"). If an initial *b* is pronounced but the accent is not on the first syllable, *an* is acceptable, as in "*an* historian" (but "*a* history course").

Aboriginal, Native peoples Both terms are acceptable for the First Peoples of Canada, although *Aboriginal peoples* is more widely preferred when referring collectively to the First Nations, Inuit, and Métis.

above Try to avoid writing *for the above reasons, in view of the above,* or *as above.* These expressions sound unpleasantly legalistic. Substitute *for these reasons,* or *therefore,* or some such expression or word.

academics Only two meanings of this noun are widely accepted: (1) "members of an institution of higher learning," and (2) "persons who are academic in background or outlook." Avoid using it to mean "academic subjects," as in "A student should pay attention not only to academics but also to recreation."

accept, except *Accept* means "to receive with consent." *Except* means "to exclude" or "excluding."

affect, effect *Affect* is usually a verb, meaning (1) "to influence, to produce an effect, to impress," or (2) "to pretend, to put on," as in "He affected an English accent." (Psychologists use it as a noun for "feeling," e.g., "The patient experienced no affect.") *Effect,* as a verb, means "to bring about" ("The workers effected the rescue in less than an hour"). As a noun, *effect* means "result" ("The effect was negligible").

African Canadian, African-Canadian Both forms are used to denote a Canadian of African ancestry. In recent years these words have been preferred to *black,* and hyphen-free Canadians are now often seen as preferable to the hyphenated variety, especially for the noun usage.

aggravate "To worsen, to increase for the worse," as in "Smoking aggravated the irritation." Although it is widely used to mean "annoy" ("He aggravated me"), many readers are annoyed by such a use.

all ready, already *All ready* means "everything is ready." *Already* means "by this time."

all right, alright The first of these is the preferable spelling; for many Canadian readers it is the only acceptable spelling.

all together, altogether *All together* means that members of a group act or are gathered together ("They voted all together"); *altogether* is an adverb meaning "entirely," "wholly" ("This is altogether unnecessary").

allusion, illusion An *allusion* is an implied or indirect reference. "As Trudeau says" is a reference to Trudeau, but "As a great politician has said," along with a quoted comment about the state's place in the bedrooms of the nation, constitutes an *allusion* to Trudeau. *Allusion* has nothing to do with *illusion* (a deception). Note the spelling (especially the second *i*) in *disillusioned* ("left without illusions," "disenchanted").

almost See *most.*

a lot Two words (not *alot*).

among, between See *between.*

amount, number *Amount* refers to bulk or quantity: "A small amount of gas was still in the tank." Use *number,* not *amount,* to refer to separate (countable) units: "A large number of people heard the lecture" (not "a large amount of people"). Similarly, "an amount of money," but "a number of dollars."

analyzation Unacceptable; use *analysis.*

and etc. Because *etc.* is an abbreviation for *et cetera* ("and others"), the *and* in *and etc.* is redundant. (See also the entry on *et cetera.*)

and/or Acceptable, but a legalism and unpleasant-sounding. Often *or* by itself will do, as in "students who know Latin or Italian." When *or* is not enough ("The script was written by Groucho and/or Harpo") it is better to recast ("The script was written by Groucho or Harpo, or both").

ante-, anti- The prefix *ante-* means "before" (*antenatal,* "before childbirth"); *anti-* means "against" (*antivivisectionist*). Hyphenate *anti-* before capitals (*anti-Semitism*) and before *i* (*anti-intellectual*).

anxious Best reserved for uses that suggest anxiety ("He was anxious before the examination"), though some authorities now accept it in the sense of "eager" ("He was anxious to serve the community").

anybody One word ("Do you know anybody here?"). If two words (*any body*), you mean any corpse ("Several people died in the fire, but the police cannot identify any body").

any more, anymore *Any more* is used as an adjective: "I don't want any more meat" (here *any more* says something about meat). *Anymore* (one word) can be used as an adverb: "I don't eat meat anymore" (here *anymore* says something about eating), though in Canada *any more* is often preferable for this usage too.

anyone One word ("Why would anyone think that?"), unless you mean "any one thing," as in "Here are three books; you may take any one." *Anyone* is an indefinite singular pronoun meaning *any person:* "If anyone has a clue, he or she should call the police." In one poorly written advertisement, the writer moved from *anyone* (singular) to *their* (third person plural) to *your* (second person): "Anyone who thinks a Yonex racquet has improved their game, please raise your hand."

area of Like *field of* and *topic of* ("the field of literature," "the topic of politics"), *area of* can usually be deleted. "The area of marketing" equals "marketing."

around Avoid using *around* in place of *about:* "He wrote it in about three hours." See also *centres on.*

as, like *As* is a conjunction; use it in forming comparisons, to introduce clauses. (A clause has a subject and a verb.)

You can learn to write, as you can learn to swim.
Huck speaks the truth as he sees it.

Like is a preposition; use it to introduce prepositional phrases:

He looks like me.

Like Hamlet, Laertes has lost a father.
She thinks like a lawyer.

A short rule: use *like* when it introduces a noun *not* followed by a verb: "Nothing grabs people like *People.*"

Writers who are fearful of incorrectly using *like* resort to cumbersome evasions: "He eats in the same manner that a pig eats." But there's nothing wrong with "He eats like a pig."

Asian, Oriental *Asian* as a noun and as an adjective is the preferred word. *Oriental* (from *oriens,* "rising sun," "east") is in disfavour because it implies a Eurocentric view—that is, that things "oriental" are east of the European colonial powers who invented the term. Similarly, **Near East, Middle East,** and **Far East** are terms that are based on a Eurocentric view. No brief substitute has been agreed on for *Near East* and *Middle East,* but *East Asia* is now regarded as preferable to *Far East.*

as of now Best deleted, or replaced by *now.* Not "As of now I don't smoke" but "Now I don't smoke" or "I don't smoke now" or "I don't smoke."

aspect Literally, "a view from a particular point," but it has come to mean *topic,* as in "There are several aspects to be considered." Try to get a sharper word; for example, "There are several problems to be considered," or "There are several consequences to be considered."

as such Often meaningless, as in "Tragedy as such evokes pity."

as to Usually *about* is preferable. Not "I know nothing as to the charges," but "I know nothing about the charges."

bad, badly *Bad* used to be only an adjective ("a bad movie"), and *badly* was an adverb ("she sings badly"). In "I felt bad," *bad* describes the subject, not the verb. (Compare "I felt happy," or "I felt good about getting a raise." After verbs of appearing, such as "feel," "look," "seem," "taste," an adjective, not an adverb, is used. If you are in doubt, substitute a word for *bad,* for instance *sad,* and see what you say. Since you would say "I feel sad about his failure," you can say "I feel bad . . .") But "badly" is acceptable and even preferred by many. Note, however, this distinction: "This meat smells bad" (an adjective describing the meat), and "Because I have a stuffed nose I smell badly" (an adverb describing my ability to smell something).

being   Do not use *being* as a main verb, as in "The trouble being that his reflexes were too slow." The result is a sentence fragment. See pages 432–33.

being that, being as   A sentence such as "Being that she was a stranger . . ." sounds like an awkward translation from the Latin. Use *because.*

beside, besides   *Beside* means "at the side of." Because *besides* can mean either "in addition to" or "other than," it is ambiguous, as in "Something besides TB caused his death." It is best, then, to use *in addition to* or *other than,* depending on what you mean.

between   Only English teachers who have had a course in Middle English are likely to know that between comes from *by twain.* And only English teachers and editors are likely to object to its use (and to call for *among*) when more than two are concerned, as in "among the three of us." Note, too, that even conservative usage accepts *between* in reference to more than two when the items are at the moment paired: "Negotiations *between* Israel and Egypt, Syria, and Lebanon seem stalled." *Between,* a preposition, takes an object ("between you and me" not "between you and I").

biannually, bimonthly, biweekly   Every two years, every two months, every two weeks (*not* twice a year, etc.). Twice a year is *semi-annually.* Because *biannually, bimonthly,* and *biweekly* are commonly misunderstood, it is best to avoid them and to say "every two . . ."

Black, black   Some publishers capitalize the word when it refers to race; others use a lower-case letter, making it consistent with *white,* which is never capitalized. See also *African Canadian,* which is the preferred term now.

can, may   When schoolchildren asked "Can I leave the room?" their teachers used to correct them thus: "You *can* leave the room if you have legs, but you *may not* leave the room until you receive permission." In short, *can* indicates physical possibility, *may* indicates permission. But because "you may not" and "why mayn't I?" sound not merely polite but stiff, *can* is usually preferred except in formal contexts.

centres on, centres around   Use *centres on,* because *centre* refers to a point, not to a movement around.

collective nouns   A collective noun, singular in form, names a collection of individuals. Examples: *audience, band, committee, crowd, jury, majority, minority, team.* When you are thinking chiefly of the whole as a unit, use a singular verb (and a singular pronoun, if any): "The majority rules"; "The jury is announcing its verdict." But when you are thinking of the individuals, use a plural verb (and pronoun, if any): "The majority are lawyers"; "The jury are divided and they probably cannot agree." If the plural sounds odd, you can usually rewrite: "The jurors are divided and they probably cannot agree."

compare, contrast   To *compare* is to note likenesses and differences: "Compare a motorcycle with a bicycle." To *contrast* is to emphasize differences. When professors ask students to "compare," they often mean "compare and contrast."

compare with, compare to   *Compare with* means to examine things together looking for similarities and differences: "compared with her classmate's interpretation of the poem, Gale's is more thorough and valid." *Compare to* means to show that two things are similar or belong in the same category: "In interest, computer science class compares to biology class." *Compare to* is also used in metaphorical comparisons (e.g., The poet compares his lady's cheeks *to* roses).

complement, compliment *Complement* as a noun means "that which completes"; as a verb, "to fill out, to complete." *Compliment* as a noun is an expression of praise; as a verb it means "to offer praise."

comprise "To include, contain, consist of": "The university comprises two colleges and a medical school" (not "is comprised of"). Conservative authorities hold that "to be comprised of" is always incorrect, and they reject the form that is often heard: "Two colleges and a medical school comprise the university." Here the word should be *compose,* not *comprise.*

concept Should often be deleted. For "The concept of the sales tax is regressive" write "The sales tax is regressive."

contact Because it is vague, avoid using *contact* as a verb. *Not* "I contacted him" but "I spoke with him" or "I wrote to him," or whatever.

continual, continuous Conservative authorities hold that *continuous* means "uninterrupted," as in "It rained continuously for six hours"; *continually* means "repeated often, recurring at short intervals," as in "For a year he continually wrote letters to her."

contrast, compare See *compare.*

could have, could of See *of.*

criteria Plural of *criterion;* hence it is always incorrect to speak of "a criteria," or to say "The criteria is . . ."

data Plural of *datum.* Although some social scientists speak of "this data," "these data" is preferable: "These data are puzzling." Because the singular, *datum,* is rare and sounds odd, it is best to substitute *fact* or *figure* for *datum.*

different from Prefer it to *different than,* unless you are convinced that in a specific sentence *different from* sounds terribly wrong, as in "These two books are more different than I had expected." (In this example, "more," not "different," governs "than." But this sentence, though correct, is awkward and therefore it should be revised: "These two books differ more than I had expected.")

dilemma A situation requiring a choice between equally undesirable alternatives; not every difficulty or plight or predicament is a *dilemma.* Not "Her dilemma was that she had nowhere to go," but "Her dilemma was whether to go out or to stay home: one was frightening, the other was embarrassing." And note the spelling (two *m*'s, no *n*).

disinterested, uninterested *Disinterested* means impartial. "A judge should be disinterested." *Uninterested* means indifferent, unconcerned, not interested in: "I am uninterested in gossip about movie stars."

due to Some people, holding that *due to* cannot modify a verb (as in "He failed due to illness"), tolerate it only when it modifies a noun or pronoun ("His failure was due to illness"). They also insist that it cannot begin a sentence ("Due to illness, he failed"). In fact, however, daily usage accepts both. But because it almost always sounds stiff, try to substitute *because of,* or *through.*

due to the fact that Wordy for *because.*

each Although many authorities hold that *each,* as a subject, is singular, even when followed by "them" ("Each of them is satisfactory"), the plural is gaining acceptance in some quarters ("Each of them are satisfactory"). But it is usually better to avoid the awkwardness by substituting *all* for *each:* "All of them are satisfactory." When *each* refers to a plural subject, the verb must be plural: "They each have a book"; "We each are trying." *Each* cannot be made into a possessive; you cannot say "Each's opinion is acceptable."

effect See *affect.*

e.g. Abbreviation for *exempli gratia,* meaning "for example." It is thus different from *i.e.* (an abbreviation for *id est,* meaning "that is"). E.g. (not italicized) introduces an example; i.e. (also not italicized) introduces a definition. Because these two abbreviations of Latin words are often confused, it may be preferable to avoid them and use their English equivalents.

either . . . or, neither . . . nor If the subjects are singular, use a singular verb: "Either the boy or the girl is lying." If one of the subjects joined by *or* or *nor* is plural, most grammarians say that the verb agrees with the nearer subject, thus: "Either a tree or two shrubs are enough," or "Neither two shrubs nor a tree is enough." But because the singular verb in the second of these sentences may sound odd, follow the first construction; that is, put the plural subject nearer to the verb and use a plural verb. Another point about *either . . . or:* in this construction, "either" serves as advance notice that two equal possibilities are in the offing. Beware of putting "either" too soon, as in "Either he is a genius or a lunatic." Better: "He is either a genius or a lunatic."

enthuse Objectionable to many readers. For "He enthused," say "He was enthusiastic." Use *enthuse* only in the sense of "to be excessively enthusiastic," "to gush."

et cetera, etc. Latin for "and other things"; if you mean "and other people," you need *et al.,* short for *et alii.* Because *etc.* is vague, its use is usually inadvisable. Not "He studied mathematics, etc." but "He studied mathematics, history, economics, and French." Or, if the list is long, cut it by saying something a little more informative than *etc.*—for example, "He studied mathematics, history, and other liberal arts subjects." Even *and so forth* or *and so on* is preferable to *etc.* Confine *etc.* (and most other abbreviations, including *et al.*) to footnotes, and even in footnotes try to avoid it.

Eurocentric language Language that reveals a European perspective (although the term is mostly used to refer to a North American perspective, as well). An example is the word *Hispanic* when used to refer not to persons from Spain but to persons from Mexico and Central and South America who may not be descended from Spaniards. (The Latin name for Spain was Hispania.) Similarly, the terms *Near East* and *Far East* represent a European point of view (near to and far from Europe), and are objectionable to persons of non-European heritage. See also *Asian.*

everybody, everyone These take a singular verb ("Everybody is here"), and a pronoun referring to them is usually singular ("Everybody thinks his problems are suitable topics of conversation"), but use a plural pronoun if the singular would seem unnatural ("Everybody was there, weren't they?"). To avoid the sexism of "Everybody thinks his problems . . ." revise to "All people think their problems . . ."

examples, instances   See *instances.*

except   See *accept.*

exists   Often unnecessary and a sign of wordiness. Not "The problem that *exists* here is" but "The problem here is."

expound   Usually pretentious for *explain* or *say.* To *expound* is to give a methodical explanation of theological matters.

facet   Literally "little face," especially one of the surfaces of a gem. Don't use it (and don't use *aspect* or *factor* either) to mean "part" or "topic." It is most acceptable when, close to its literal meaning, it is used to suggest a new appearance, as when a gem is turned: "Another *facet* appears when we see this law from the taxpayer's point of view."

the fact that   Usually wordy. "Because of the fact that boys played female roles in Elizabethan drama" can be reduced to "Because boys played female roles in Elizabethan drama."

factor   Strictly speaking, a *factor* helps to produce a result. Although *factor* is often used in the sense of "point" ("Another factor to be studied is . . . "), such use is often wordy. "The possibility of plagiarism is a factor that must be considered" simply adds up to "The possibility of plagiarism must be considered." *Factor* is almost never the precise word: "the factors behind Gatsby's actions" are, more precisely, "Gatsby's motives."

famous, notorious   See *notorious.*

Far East   See *Asian.*

farther, further   Purists say that *farther* always refers to physical distance and *further* to time ("The gymnasium is farther than the library"; "Let us think further about this").

fatalistic, pessimistic   *Fatalistic* means "characterized by the belief that all events are predetermined and therefore inevitable"; *pessimistic* means "characterized by the belief that the world is evil," or, less gloomily, "expecting the worst."

fewer, less   See *less.*

field of   See *area of.*

firstly, secondly   Acceptable, but it is better to use *first, second.*

former, latter   These words are acceptable, but they are often annoying because they force the reader to reread earlier material in order to locate what *the former* and *the latter* refer to. The expressions are legitimately used in order to avoid repeating lengthy terms, but if you are talking about an easily repeated subject—say, Paul Martin and Stephen Harper—don't hesitate to replace *the former* and *the latter* with their names. The repetition will clarify rather than bore.

good, well   *Good* is an adjective ("a good book"). *Well* is usually an adverb ("She writes well"). Standard English does not accept "She writes good." But Standard English requires *good* after verbs of appearing, such as "seems," "looks," "sounds," "tastes": "it looks good," "it sounds good." *Well* can also be an adjective meaning "healthy": "I am well."

graduate, graduate from   Use *from* if you name the institution or if you use a substitute word as in "She graduated from high school"; if the institution (or substitute) is not named, *from* is omitted: "She graduated in 1983." The use of the passive ("She was graduated from high school") is acceptable but sounds fussy to many.

he or she, his or her, he/she, his/her   These expressions are awkward, but the implicit sexism in the generic use of the male pronoun ("A citizen should exercise his right to vote") may be more offensive than the awkwardness of *he or she* and *his or her*. Moreover, sometimes the male pronoun, when used for males and females, is ludicrous, as in "The more violence a youngster sees on television, regardless of his age or sex, the more aggressive he is likely to be." Do what you can to avoid the dilemma. Sometimes you can use the plural *their:* "Students are expected to hand in their papers on Monday" (instead of "The student is expected to hand in his or her paper on Monday"). Or eliminate the possessive: "The student must hand in a paper on Monday." See also *man, mankind.*

hopefully   Commonly used to mean "I hope" or "It is hoped" ("*Hopefully,* the rain will stop soon"), but it is best to avoid what some consider a dangling modifier. After all, the rain itself is not hopeful. If you mean "I hope the rain will stop soon," say exactly that. Notice, too, that *hopefully* is often evasive; if the president of the college says, "Hopefully tuition will not rise next year," don't think you've heard a promise to fight against an increase; you've only heard someone evade making a promise. In short, confine *hopefully* to its adverbial use, meaning "in a hopeful manner": "Hopefully he uttered a prayer."

however   Independent clauses (for instance, "He tried" and "He failed") should not be linked with a *however* preceded by a comma. *In*correct: "He tried, however he failed." What is required is a period ("He tried. However, he failed") or a semicolon before *however* ("He tried; however, he failed").

the idea that   Usually dull and wordy. Not "The idea that we grow old is frightening," but "That we grow old is frightening," or (probably better) "Growing old is frightening."

identify   When used in the psychological sense, "to associate oneself closely with a person or an institution," it is preferable to include a reflexive pronoun, thus: "He identified himself with Hamlet," *not* "He identified with Hamlet."

i.e.   Latin for *id est,* "that is." The English words are preferable to the Latin abbreviation. On the distinction between *i.e.* and *e.g.,* see *e.g.*

immanent, imminent   *Immanent,* "remaining within, intrinsic"; *imminent,* "likely to occur soon, impending."

imply, infer   The writer or speaker *implies* (suggests); the perceiver *infers* (draws a conclusion): "Karl Marx implied that . . . but his modern disciples infer from his writings that . . ." Although *infer* is widely used for *imply,* preserve the distinction.

incidence, incident   *Incidence* is the extent or frequency of an occurrence: "The incidence of violent crime in Tokyo is very low." The plural, *incidences,* is rarely used: "The incidences of crime and of fire in Tokyo. . . ." An *incident* is one occurrence: "The incident happened yesterday." The plural is *incidents:* "The two incidents happened simultaneously."

individual   Avoid using the word to mean only "person": "He was a generous individual." But it is precise when it implicitly makes a contrast with a group: "In a money-mad society, he was a generous individual"; "Although the faculty did not take a stand on this issue, faculty members as individuals spoke out."

instances   Instead of *in many instances* use *often.* Strictly speaking an *instance* is not an object or incident in itself but one offered as an example. Thus "another instance of his failure to do his duty" (not "In three instances he failed to do his duty").

irregardless Unacceptable; use *regardless.*

it is Usually this expression needlessly delays the subject: "It is unlikely that many students will attend the lecture" could just as well be "Few students are likely to attend the lecture."

its, it's The first is a possessive pronoun ("The flock lost its leader"); the second is a contraction of *it is* ("It's a wise father that knows his child"). You will have no trouble if you remember that the possessive pronoun *its,* like other possessive pronouns such as *our, his, their,* does *not* use an apostrophe.

kind of Singular, as in "That kind of movie bothers me." (*Not* "Those kind of movies bother me.") If, however, you are really talking about more than one kind, use *kinds* and be sure that the demonstrative pronoun and the verb are plural: "Those kinds of movies bother me." Notice also that the phrase is *kind of,* not *kind of a.* Not "What *kind of a* car does she drive?" but "What *kind of* car does she drive?"

latter See *former.*

lay, lie *To lay* means "to put, to set, to cause to rest." It takes an object: "May I lay the coats on the table?" The past tense and the participle are *laid:* "I laid the coats on the table"; "I have laid the coats on the table." *To lie* means "to recline," and it does not take an object: "When I am tired I lie down." The past tense is *lay,* the participle is *lain:* "Yesterday I lay down"; "I have lain down hundreds of times without wishing to get up."

lend, loan The usual verb is *lend:* "Lend me a pen." The past tense and the participle are both *lent. Loan* is a noun: "This isn't a gift, it's a loan." But, curiously, *loan* as a verb is acceptable in past forms: "I loaned him my bicycle." In its present form ("I often loan money") it is used chiefly by bankers.

less, fewer *Less* (as an adjective) refers to bulk amounts (also called mass nouns): less milk, less money, less time. *Fewer* refers to separate (countable) items: fewer glasses of milk, fewer dollars, fewer hours.

lifestyle, life-style, life style All three forms are acceptable, but because many readers regard the expression as imprecise, try to find a substitute such as *values.*

like, as See *as.*

literally It means "strictly in accord with the primary meaning; not metaphorically." It is not a mere intensive. "He was literally dead" means that he was a corpse; if he was merely exhausted, *literally* won't do. You cannot be "literally stewed" (except by cannibals), "literally tickled pink," or "literally head over heels in love."

loose, lose *Loose* is an adjective ("The nail is loose") meaning not tight; *lose* is a verb ("Don't lose the nail") meaning to misplace.

the majority of Usually a wordy way of saying *most.* Of course if you mean "a bare majority," say so; otherwise *most* will usually do. Certainly "The majority of the basement is used for a cafeteria" should be changed to "Most of the basement is used for a cafeteria." *Majority* can take either a singular verb or a plural verb. When *majority* refers to a collection—for example, a group acting as a body—the verb is singular, as in "The majority has withdrawn its support from the mayor." But when *majority* refers to members of a group acting as individuals, as in "The majority of voters in this district vote Liberal," a plural verb (here, "vote") is usually preferred. If either construction sounds odd, use "most," with a plural verb: "Most voters in this district vote Liberal."

man, mankind The use of these words in reference to males and females sometimes is ludicrous, as in "Man, being a mammal, breastfeeds his young." But even when not ludicrous the practice is sexist, as in "man's brain" and "the greatness of mankind." Consider using such words as *human being, person, humanity, people.* Similarly, for "man-made," *artificial* or *synthetic* may do.

may, can See *can.*

me The right word in such expressions as "between you and me" and "They gave it to John and me." It is the object of verbs and of prepositions. In fact, *me* rather than *I* is the usual form after any verb, including the verb *to be;* "It is me" is nothing to be ashamed of. See the entry on *myself.*

medium, media *Medium* is singular, *media* is plural: "TV is the medium to which most children are most exposed. Other media include film, radio, and magazines." It follows, then, that *mass media* takes a plural verb: "The mass media exert an enormous influence."

Middle East See *Asian.*

might of, might have; must of, must have *Might of* and *must of* are colloquial for *might have* and *must have.* In writing, use the *have* form: "He might have cheated; in fact, he must have cheated."

more Avoid writing a false (incomplete) comparison such as: "His essay includes several anecdotes, making it more enjoyable." Delete "more" unless there really is a comparison with another essay. On false comparisons see also the entry on *other.*

most, almost Although it is acceptable in speech to say "most everyone" and "most anybody," it is preferable in writing to use "almost everyone," "almost anybody." But of course: "Most students passed."

myself *Myself* is often mistakenly used for *I* or *me,* as in "They praised Tony and myself," or "Professor Chen and myself examined the dead rat." In the first example, *me* is the word to use; after all, if Tony hadn't been there the sentence would say, "They praised me." (No one would say, "They praised myself.") Similarly, in the second example if Professor Chen were not involved, the sentence would run, "I examined the dead rat," so what is needed here is simply "Professor Chen and I examined. . . ."

In general, use *myself* only when (1) it refers to the subject of the sentence ("I look out for myself"; "I washed myself") or (2) when it is an intensive: ("I myself saw the break-in"; "I myself have not experienced racism").

Native see *Aboriginal.*

nature You can usually delete *the nature of,* as in "The nature of my contribution is not political but psychological."

Near East See *Asian.*

needless to say The reader may well wonder why you go on to say it. Of course this expression is used to let readers know that they are probably familiar with what comes next, but usually *of course* will better serve as this sign.

neither . . . nor See *either . . . or.*

nobody, no one, none *Nobody* and *no one* are singular, requiring a singular verb ("Nobody believes this," "No one knows"), but they can be referred to by a plural pronoun: "Nobody believes this, do they?" "No one knows, do they?" *None,* though it comes from *no one,* almost always requires a plural verb when it refers to people ("Of the ten people present, none are students") and a singular verb when it refers to things ("Of the five assigned books, none is worth reading").

not only . . . but also Keep in mind these two points: (1) many readers object to the omission of "also" in such a sentence as "She not only brought up two children but practised law," and (2) all readers dislike a faulty parallel, as in "She not only is bringing up two children but practises law." ("Is bringing up" needs to be paralleled with "is also practising.")

notorious Widely and unfavourably known; not merely famous, but famous for some discreditable trait or deed.

not un- Such an expression as "not unfamiliar" is useful only if it conveys something different from the affirmative. Compare the frostiness of "I am not unfamiliar with your methods" with "I am familiar with your methods." If the negative has no evident advantage, use the affirmative.

number, amount See *amount.*

a number of Requires a plural verb: "A number of women are presidents of corporations." But when *number* is preceded by *the* it requires a singular verb: "The number of women who are presidents is small." (The plural noun after *number* of course may require a plural verb, as in "women are," but *the number* itself remains singular; hence its verb is singular, as in "is small.")

of Be careful not to use *of* when *have* is required. Not "He might of died in the woods," but "He might have died in the woods." Note that what we often hear as "would've" or "should've" or "must've" or "could've" is "would have" or "should have" or "must have" or "could have," *not* "would of," etc.

off of Use *off* or *from:* "Take if off the table"; "He jumped from the bridge."

often-times Use *often* instead.

old-fashioned, old-fashion Only the first is acceptable.

one British usage accepts the shift from *one* to *he* in "One begins to die the moment he is born," but North American usage prefers "One begins to die the moment one is born." A shift from *one* to *you* ("One begins to die the moment you are born") is unacceptable. As a pronoun, *one* can be useful in impersonal statements, such as the sentence about dying at the beginning of this entry, where it means "a person," but don't use it as a disguise for yourself ("One objects to Smith's argument"). Try to avoid *one; one one* usually leads to another, resulting in a sentence that, in James Thurber's words, "sounds like a trombone solo" ("If one takes oneself too seriously, one begins to . . ."). See also *you.*

one of Takes a plural noun, and if this is followed by a clause, the preferred verb is plural: "one of those students who are," "one of those who feel." Thus, in such a sentence as "One of the coaches who have resigned is now seeking reinstatement," notice that "have" is correct; the antecedent of "who" (the subject of the verb) is "coaches," which is plural. Coaches have resigned, though "one . . . is seeking reinstatement." But in such an expression as "one out of a hundred," the following verb may be singular or plural ("One out of a hundred is," "One out of a hundred are").

only Be careful where you put it. The classic textbook example points out that in the sentence "I hit him in the eye," *only* can be inserted in seven places (beginning in front of "I" and ending after "eye") with at least six different meanings. Try to put it just before the expression it qualifies. Thus, not "Prime ministerial aides are only responsible to one person," but "Prime ministerial aides are responsible to only one person" (or "to one person only").

oral, verbal   See *verbal.*

Oriental   see *Asian.*

other   Often necessary in comparisons. "No Canadian country music star is as controversial as k. d. lang" falsely implies that k. d. lang is not a Canadian country music star. The sentence should be revised to "No other Canadian country music star is as controversial as k. d. lang."

per   Usually it sounds needlessly technical ("twice per hour") or disturbingly impersonal ("as per your request"). Preferable: "twice an hour," "according to your request," or "as you requested."

per cent, percent, percentage   The first two of these are interchangeable; both mean "per hundred," "out of a hundred," as in "Ninety per cent (or percent) of the students were white." *Per cent* and *percent* are always accompanied by a number (written out or in figures). It is usually better to write out *per cent* or *percent* than to use a percent sign (12%), except in technical or statistical papers. *Percentage* means "a proportion or share in relation to the whole," as in "A very large percentage of the student body is white." Many authorities insist that *percentage* is never preceded by a number. Do not use *percentage* to mean "a few," as in "Only a percentage of students attended the lecture"; a percentage can be as large as 99.99. It is usually said that with *per cent, percent,* and *percentage,* whether the verb is singular or plural depends on the number of the noun that follows the word, thus: "Ninety percent of his books are paperbacks"; "Fifty percent of his library is worthless"; "A large percentage of his books are worthless." But some readers (including the authors of this book) prefer a singular verb after *percentage* unless the resulting sentence is as grotesque as this one: "A large percentage of the students is unmarried." Still, rather than say a "percentage . . . are," we would recast the sentence: "A large percentage of the student body is unmarried," or "Many [or "Most," or whatever] of the students are unmarried."

per se   Latin for "by itself." Usually sounds legalistic or pedantic, as in "Metre per se has an effect."

pessimistic   See *fatalistic.*

phenomenon, phenomena   The plural is *phenomena;* thus, "these phenomena" but "this phenomenon."

plus   Unattractive and imprecise as a noun meaning "asset" or "advantage" ("When he applied for the job, his appearance was a plus"), and equally unattractive as a substitute for *moreover* ("The examination was easy, plus I had studied") or as a substitute for *and* ("I studied the introduction plus the first chapter").

politics   Preferably singular ("Ethnic politics has been a strong force for a century"), but a plural verb is acceptable.

precede, proceed   To *precede* is to go before or ahead ("*X* precedes *Y*"). To *proceed* is to go forward ("The spelling lesson proceeded smoothly").

prejudice, prejudiced   *Prejudice* is a noun: "It is impossible to live entirely without prejudice." But use the past participle *prejudiced* as an adjective: "He was prejudiced against me from the start."

preventative, preventive Both are acceptable but the second form is the one now used by writers on medicine ("preventive medicine"); *preventative* has come to sound awkward to North American ears.

principal, principle *Principal* is (1) an adjective meaning "main," "chief," "most important" ("The principal arguments against IQ testing are three"), and (2) a noun meaning "the chief person" ("Ms. Murphy was the principal of Jefferson High") or "the chief thing" ("She had so much money she could live on the interest and not touch the principal"). *Principle* is always a noun meaning "rule" or "fundamental truth" ("It was against his principles to eat meat").

prior to Pretentious for *before.*

protagonist Literally, the first actor, and, by extension, the chief actor. It is odd, therefore, to speak of "the protagonists" in a single literary work or occurrence. Note also that the prefix is *proto,* "first," not *pro,* "for"; it does *not* mean one who strives for something.

quite Usually a word to delete, along with *definitely, pretty, rather,* and *very. Quite* used to mean "completely" ("I quite understand") but it has come also to mean "to a considerable degree," and so it is ambiguous as well as vague.

quotation, quote Quotation is a noun, quote is a verb. "I will quote Churchill" is fine, but not "these quotes from Churchill." And remember, you may *quote* one of Hamlet's speeches, but Hamlet does not *quote* them; he says them.

rather Avoid use with strong adjectives. "Rather intelligent" makes sense, but "rather tremendous" does not. "Rather brilliant" probably means "bright"; "rather terrifying" probably means "frightening," "rather unique" probably means "unusual." Get the right adjective, not *rather* and the wrong adjective.

the reason . . . is because Usually *because* is enough (not "The reason they fail is because they don't study," but simply "They fail because they don't study"). Similarly, *the reason why* can usually be reduced to *why.* Notice, too, that because *reason* is a noun, it cannot neatly govern a *because* clause: not "The reason for his absence is because he was sick," but "The reason for his absence was illness."

rebut, refute To rebut is to argue against, but not necessarily successfully. If you mean "to disprove," use *disprove* or *refute.*

in regard to, with regard to Often wordy for *about, concerning,* or *on,* and sometimes even these words are unnecessary. Compare: "He knew a great deal in regard to jazz"; "He knew a great deal about jazz." Compare: "Hemingway's story is often misunderstood with regard to Robert Wilson's treatment of Margot Macomber"; "In Hemingway's story, Robert Wilson's treatment of Margot Macomber is often misunderstood."

relate to Usually a vague expression, best avoided, as in "I can relate to Hedda Gabler." Does it mean "respond favourably to," "identify myself with," "interact with" (and how can a reader "interact with" a character in a play?)? Use *relate to* only in the sense of "have connection with" (as in "How does your answer relate to my question?"); even in such a sentence a more exact expression is preferable.

repel, repulse Both verbs mean "to drive back," but only *repel* can mean "to cause distaste," "to disgust," as in "His obscenities repelled the audience."

respectfully, respectively *Respectfully* means "with respect, showing respect" ("Japanese students and teachers bow respectfully to each other").

Respectively means "each in turn" ("Professors Arnott, Bahktian, and Cisneros teach, respectively, chemistry, business, and biology").

sarcasm Heavy, malicious sneering ("Oh, you're really a great friend, aren't you?" addressed to someone who won't lend the speaker ten dollars). If the apparent praise, which really communicates dispraise, is at all clever, conveying, say, a delicate mockery or wryness, it is irony, not sarcasm.

seem Properly it suggests a suspicion that appearances may be deceptive: "He seems honest (but . . .)." Don't say "The book seems to lack focus" if you believe it does lack focus.

semi-annually, semi-monthly, semi-weekly See *biannually.*

sexist language Language that takes males as the norm. For example, the use of *he* with reference to females as well as to males ("When a legislator votes, he takes account of his constituency"), like the use of *man* for all human beings ("Man is a rational animal"), is now widely perceived as subtly (or not so subtly) erasing females. See the entries on *he or she, man, mankind,* and *s/he.*

shall, will, should, would The old principle held that in the first person *shall* is the future indicative of *to be* and *should* the conditional ("I shall go," "We should like to be asked"); and that *will* and *would* are the forms for the second and third persons. When the forms are reversed ("I will go," "Government of the people . . . shall not perish from the earth"), determination is expressed. But today hardly anyone adheres to these principles. Indeed, *shall* (except in questions) sounds stilted to many ears.

s/he This new gender-free pronoun ("As soon as the student receives the forms, s/he should fill them out") is sometimes used in place of *he or she* or *she or he,* which is used to avoid the sexism implied when the male pronoun "he" is used to stand for women as well as men ("As soon as the student receives the forms, he should fill them out"). Other, less noticeable ways of avoiding sexist writing are suggested under *he or she.*

simplistic Means "falsely simplified by ignoring complications." Do not confuse it with *simplified,* whose meanings include "reduced to essentials" and "clarified."

since, because Traditional objections to *since,* in the sense of "because," have all but vanished. Note, however, that when *since* is ambiguous and could also refer to time ("Since he joined the navy, she found another boyfriend"), it is better to say *because* or *after,* depending on which you mean.

situation Overused, vague, and often unnecessary. "His situation was that he was unemployed" adds up to "He was unemployed." And "an emergency situation" is probably an emergency.

split infinitives The infinitive is the verb form that merely names the action, without indicating when or by whom performed ("walk," rather than "walked" or "I walk"). Grammarians, however, developed the idea that the infinitive was "to walk," and they held that we cannot separate or split the two words, as in "to quickly walk." It is generally incorrect to split infinitives, but there are exceptions: it would sound odd to say "to go boldly" instead of "to boldly go." Notice, however, that often the inserted word can be deleted ("to really understand" is "to understand"), and that it is unacceptable to place several words between *to* and the verb (as in "to quickly and in the remaining few pages before examining the next question conclude").

stanza   See *verse.*

subjunctive   For the use of the subjunctive with conditions contrary to fact (for instance, "If I were you"), see the entry on *was/were.* The subjunctive is also used in *that* clauses followed by verbs demanding, requesting, or recommending: "He asked that the students be prepared to take a test." This last sort of sentence sounds stiff, though, so it is better to use an alternative construction, such as "He asked the students to prepare for a test."

than, then   *Than* is used chiefly in making comparisons ("German is harder than French"), but also after "rather," "other," and "else" ("I'd rather take French than German"; "He thinks of nothing other than sex"). *Then* commonly indicates time ("She took German then, but now she takes French"; "Until then, I'll save you a seat"), but it may also mean "in that case" ("It's agreed, then, that we'll all go"), or "on the other hand" ("Then again, she may find German easy"). The simplest guide: use *than* after comparisons and after "rather," "other," "else"; otherwise use *then.*

that, which, who   Many pages have been written on these words; opinions differ, but you will offend no one if you observe the following principles. (1) Use *that* in restrictive (that is, limiting) clauses: "The rocking chair that creaks is on the porch." (2) Use *which* in non-restrictive (in effect, parenthetic) clauses: "The rocking chair, which creaks, is on the porch." (See pages 440–42.) The difference between these two sentences is this: in the first, one rocking chair—the one that creaks—is singled out from several; in the second, the fact that the rocking chair creaks is simply tossed in, and is not added for the purpose of identifying the one chair out of several. (3) Use *who* for people, in restrictive and in non-restrictive clauses: "The men who were playing poker ignored the women"; "The men, who were playing poker, ignored the women." But note that often *that, which,* and *who* can be omitted: "The creaky rocking chair is on the porch"; "The men, playing poker, ignored the women." In general, omit these words if the sentence remains clear. See pages 86–87.

their, there, they're   The first is a possessive pronoun: "Chaplin and Keaton made their first films before soundtracks were developed." The second, *there,* sometimes refers to a place ("Go there," "Do you live there?"), and sometimes is what is known in grammar as an introductory expletive ("There are no solutions to this problem"). The third, *they're,* is a contraction of "they are" ("They're going to stay for dinner").

this   Often used to refer vaguely to "what I have been saying." The reader is usually left wondering whether "this" refers to what was said in the previous sentence, the previous paragraph, or the previous page. Try to be specific: "This last point is invalid"; "This clue gave the police all they needed."

thusly   Unacceptable; *thus* is an adverb and needs no adverbial ending.

till, until   Both are acceptable, but *until* is preferable because *till*—though common in speech—looks literary in print. (The following are *not* acceptable in formal writing: *til, 'til; 'till* is always incorrect.

to, too, two   *To* is toward; *too* is either "also" ("She's a lawyer, too") or "excessively" ("It's too hot"); *two* is one more than one ("Two is company").

topic of   See *area of.*

toward, towards   Both are standard English; *toward* is more common in North America, *towards* in Great Britain.

type   Often colloquial (and unacceptable in most writing) for *type of,* as in "this type teacher." But *type of* is not especially pleasing either. Better to write "this kind of teacher." And avoid using *type* as a suffix: "essay-type examinations" are essay examinations; "natural-type ice cream" is natural ice cream. Sneaky manufacturers make "Italian-type cheese," implying that their domestic cheese is imported and at the same time protecting themselves against charges of misrepresentation.

unique   The *only* one of its kind. Someone or something cannot be "rather unique" or "very unique" or "somewhat unique," any more than a woman can be somewhat pregnant. Instead of saying "rather unique," say something like *rare* or *unusual* or *extraordinary.*

U.S., United States   Generally, *United States* is preferable to *U.S.*

usage   Don't use *usage* where *use* will do, as in "Here Richards completes his usage of dark images." *Usage* properly implies a customary practice that has created a standard: "Usage has eroded the difference between 'shall' and 'will.'"

use of   The use of *use of* is usually unnecessary. "Through the use of setting he conveys a sense of foreboding" may be reduced to "The setting conveys . . ." or "His setting conveys . . ."

utilize, utilization   Often inflated for *use* and *using,* as in "The infirmary has noted that it is second-year students who have most utilized the counselling service." But when one means "find an effective use for," *utilize* may be the best word, as in "The man was unable to utilize his new Blackberry" where *use* might wrongly suggest that he could not operate the device.

verbal   Often used where *oral* would be more exact. *Verbal* simply means "expressed in words," and thus a *verbal agreement* may be either written or spoken. If you mean spoken, call it an *oral agreement.*

verse, stanza   A *verse* is a single line of a poem; a *stanza* is a group of lines. But in speaking or writing about songs, usage sanctions *verse* for *stanza,* as in "Second verse, same as the first."

viable   A term from physiology, meaning "capable of living" (for example, referring to a fetus at a stage of its development). Now pretentiously used and overused, especially by politicians and journalists, to mean "workable," as in "a viable presidency." Avoid it.

was, were   Use the subjunctive form—*were* (rather than *was*)—in expressing a wish ("I wish I were younger") and in "if" clauses that are contrary to fact ("If I were rich," "If I were you . . .").

we   If you mean *I,* say *I.* Not "The first fairy tale we heard" but "the first fairy tale I heard." (But of course *we* is appropriate in some statements: "We have all heard fairy tales"; "If we look closely at the evidence, we can agree that . . .") The rule: don't use *we* as a disguise for *I.* See page 105.

well   See *good.*

well known, widely known   Athletes, performers, politicians, and such folk are not really *well known* except perhaps by a few of their friends and their relatives; use *widely known* if you mean they are known (however slightly) to many people.

which   Often can be deleted. "Students are required to fill out scholarship applications which are lengthy" can be written "Students are required to fill out lengthy scholarship applications." Another example: "*The Tempest,* which is Shakespeare's last play, was written in 1611"; "*The Tempest,*

Shakespeare's last play, was written in 1611," or "Shakespeare wrote his last play, *The Tempest,* in 1611." For the distinction between *which* and *that,* see the entry on *that.*

while Best used in a temporal sense, meaning "during the time": "While I was speaking, I suddenly realized that I didn't know what I was talking about." While it is not wrong to use *while* in a non-temporal sense, meaning "although" (as at the beginning of this sentence), it is better to use *although* in order to avoid any ambiguity. Note the ambiguity in: "While he was fond of movies he chiefly saw westerns." Does it mean "Although he was fond of movies," or does it mean "During the time when he was fond of movies"? Another point: do not use *while* if you mean *and;* "First-year students take English 101, while second-year students take English 201" (substitute *and* for *while*).

who, whom Strictly speaking, *who* must be used for subjects, even when they look like objects: "He guessed who would be chosen." (Here *who* is the subject of the clause "who would be chosen.") *Whom* must be used for the objects of a verb, verbal (gerund, participle), or preposition: "Whom did he choose?"; "Whom do you want me to choose?"; "To whom did he show it?" We may feel stuffy in writing "Whom did he choose?" or "Whom are you talking about?" but to use *who* is certain to annoy some readers. Often you can avoid the dilemma by rewriting: "Who was chosen?"; "Who is the topic of conversation?" See also the entry on *that.*

whoever, whomever The second of these is the objective form, as in "He will appoint whomever he chooses." *Whomever* is often incorrectly used as the subject of a clause. "She will open the class to whomever wants to take it" is incorrect. The object of "to" is not "whomever"; it is the entire clause— "whoever wants to take it"—and "whoever" is the subject of "wants."

who's, whose The first is a contraction of *who is* ("I'm everybody who's nobody"). The second is a possessive pronoun: "Whose book is it?" "I know whose it is."

will, would See *shall* and also *would.*

would "I would think that" is a wordy version of "I think that." (On the mistaken use of *would of* for *would have,* see also the entry on *of.*)

you In relatively informal writing, *you* is ordinarily preferable to the somewhat stiff *one:* "If you are addicted to cigarettes, you may find it helpful to join SmokEnders." (Compare: "If one is addicted to cigarettes, one may . . .") But because the direct address of *you* may sometimes descend into nagging, it is usually better to write: "Cigarette addicts may find it helpful . . ." Certainly a writer (you?) should not assume that the reader is guilty of vices ("You should not molest children") unless the essay is clearly aimed at an audience that admits to these vices, say a pamphlet directed at child molesters who are seeking help. Thus, it is acceptable to say, "If you are a poor speller," but it is not acceptable to say, to the general reader, "You should improve your spelling"—the reader's spelling may not need improvement. And avoid *you* when the word cannot possibly apply to the reader: "A hundred years ago you were faced with many diseases that now have been eradicated." Something like "A hundred years ago people were faced . . ." is preferable.

your, you're The first is a possessive pronoun ("your book"); the second is a contraction of *you are* ("You're mistaken").

Manuscript Form

BASIC MANUSCRIPT FORM

When you submit a piece of writing to your instructor (or to anyone else), make sure it looks good. You want to convey the impression that you care about what you have written, that you have invested yourself and your time in it, that the details matter to you.

Much of what follows is ordinary academic procedure. Unless your instructor specifies something different, you can adopt these principles as a guide.

1. Print your essay on 21.5-by-28-cm (8½-by-11-inch) paper of good weight.

2. Make certain that the printer has enough ink and that the print is dark and clear. One sure way to irritate your instructor is to turn in an essay with nearly invisible print.

3. Do not use a fancy font. Unless your instructor specifies something else, stick to Times or Courier. And use a reasonable point size: generally a 12-point font will do.

4. Print your essay on one side of the paper only. If for some reason you have occasion to submit a handwritten copy, use lined paper and write on every other line in black or dark blue ink.

5. Set the line spacing at "double." The essay (even the heading—see item 6 below) should be double-spaced, not single- or triple-spaced.

6. In the upper-left corner, 2.5 cm (1 inch) from the top, put your name, your instructor's name, the course number, and the date. And put your last name before the page number (in the top-right corner) of each subsequent page, so the instructor can easily reassemble your essay if somehow a page gets detached and mixed with other papers.

7. Titles. Use this form for your title: hit the "enter" (or "return") key *once* after the date and then centre the title of your essay. We give instructions for punctuating titles in Chapter 20, but we will reiterate the most important points here. Capitalize the first letter of the first and last words of your title, the first word after a semicolon or colon if you use either one, and the first letter of all the other words except articles, conjunctions, and prepositions, thus:

Two Kinds of Symbols in *To Kill a Mockingbird*

Notice that the title of your writing is not underlined, italicized, or enclosed in quotation marks. (If, as here, your title includes words that would normally be underlined or italicized or in quotation marks, those words are so treated.) If the title runs more than one line, double-space the lines.

8. Begin the essay just below the title. (Again, hit "enter" or "return" only once.) If your instructor prefers a title page, start the essay on the next page and number it 1. The title page is not numbered.

9. Margins. Except for page numbers, which should appear 1.3 cm (1/2 inch) from the top of the page, leave a 2.5-cm (1 inch) margin at top, bottom, and sides of the text.

10. Number the pages consecutively, using Arabic numerals in the upper-right corner, 1.3 cm (1/2 inch) from the top. Do not put a period or a hyphen after the numeral, and do not precede the numeral with "page" or "p." (Again, if you give the title on a separate sheet, the page that follows it is page 1. Do not number the title page.)

11. Paragraphs. Indent the first word of each paragraph five spaces from the left margin.

12. Proofreading. Check for typographical errors, and check spelling. Use your word processor's spell checker—but do not rely on it exclusively. This program will flag words that are not in its dictionary and offer suggestions for correcting mistakes. (A misspelled word is of course not in the dictionary and is thus flagged.) But a word flagged is not necessarily misspelled; it may simply not be in the program's dictionary. Proper names, for example, regularly get flagged. Keep in mind also that most programs cannot distinguish between homophones *(to, too, two; there, their; alter, altar),* nor can they tell you that you should have written *accept* instead of *except.*

13. Keep a copy of your essay for yourself until the original has been returned. It is a good idea to keep notes and drafts too. They may prove helpful if you are asked to revise a page, substantiate a point, or supply a source you omitted.

14. Fasten the pages of your paper with a paper clip or staple in the upper-left corner. Stiff binders are unnecessary; indeed, they are a nuisance to the instructor, adding bulk and making it awkward to write annotations.

2.5 cm (1")

Your Name

Double-
space

Your Instructor's Name

Font is Times

Writing 127

April 1, 2006

Capitalize main words in title

Formatting Your Essays: The Right Way to Do It

Centre title

Print your essay on 21.5-x-28-cm (8 1/2 x 11-inch) paper of good weight, and make sure that the printer has enough ink and that the print is dark and clear. Do not use a fancy font. Unless your instructor specifies something else, stick to Times or Courier. And use a reasonable point size: generally a 12-point font will do. The essay (even the heading) should be double-spaced--not single-spaced, not triple-spaced--and it should be printed on one side of the paper only.

5 spaces, or tab

In the upper-left-hand corner, 2.5 cm from the top, put your name, your instructor's name, the course number, and the date, all on separate lines. Put your last name before the page number (in the upper-right-hand corner) of each subsequent page, so the instructor can easily reassemble your essay if somehow a page gets detached and mixed with other papers. Hit the "enter" (or "return") key *once* after the date and then centre the title of your essay. Capitalize the first letter of the first and last words of your title, the first word after a semicolon or colon if you use either one, and the first letter of all the other words except articles, conjunctions, and prepositions. Notice that your own title is neither underlined nor enclosed in quotation marks. If the title runs more than one line, double-space the lines. Begin the essay just below the title. (Again, you'll hit "enter" or "return" only once.) If your instructor prefers a title page, begin the essay on the next page and number it 1.

Except for page numbers, which should appear 1.3 cm from the top of the page, leave a 2.5-cm margin at top, bottom, and sides of text. Number the pages consecutively, using Arabic numerals in the

—2.5 cm—

2.5 cm

1.3 cm (1/2″)
Your name 2

upper-right-hand corner, 1.3 cm from the top. Do not put a period or

a hyphen after the numeral, and do not precede the numeral with

"page" or "p."

    Indent the first word of each paragraph five spaces from the

left margin.

    Fasten the pages of your paper with a staple or paper clip in the

upper-left-hand corner. Stiff binders are unnecessary; indeed, they are

a nuisance because they add bulk and make essays difficult to

annotate. Spell-check your essay and proofread it carefully; make a

copy for yourself, and then turn the essay in.

USING QUOTATIONS (AND PUNCTUATING QUOTATIONS CORRECTLY)

If you are writing about a text, or about an interview, quotations from your material or subject are indispensable. They not only let your readers know what you are talking about, they also give your readers the material you are responding to, thus letting them share your responses. But quote sparingly and quote briefly. Use quotations as evidence, not as padding. If the exact wording of the original is crucial, or especially effective, quote it directly, but if it is not, don't bore the reader with material that can be effectively reduced either by summarizing or by cutting. And make sure, by a comment before or after a quotation, that your reader understands why you find the quotation relevant. Do not count on a quotation to make your point for you.

Here are some additional matters to keep in mind, especially as you revise.

1. Identify the speaker or writer of the quotation. Usually this identification (e.g., "Smith explains,") precedes the quoted material in accordance with the principle of letting readers know where they are going. But occasionally it may follow the quotation, especially if the name will provide a meaningful surprise. For example, in a discussion of a proposed tax reform, you might quote a remark that is hostile to the idea and then reveal that the author of the proposal was also the author of the remark.

2. When you introduce a quotation, consider using verbs other than "says." Depending on the context—that is, on the substance of the quotation and its place in your essay—it might be more accurate to say "Smith argues," "adds," "contends," "points out," "admits," or "comments." Or, again with just the right verb, you might introduce the quotation with a transitional phrase: "In another context, Smith had observed that . . ." or "To clarify this point, Smith refers to . . ." or "In an apparent contradiction, Smith suggests . . ." But avoid such inflated words as "opines," "avers," and "is of the opinion that." The point is not to add "elegant variation" (see page 114) to your introduction of someone else's words, but accuracy and grace. A verb often used *in*accurately is "feels." Ralph Linton does not "feel" that "the term *primitive art* has come to be used with at least three distinct meanings." He "points out," "writes," "observes," or "says" so.

3. Distinguish between short and long quotations and treat each appropriately. Enclose *short quotations,* four (or fewer) lines of prose type, within quotation marks:

> Anne Lindbergh calls the harrowing period of the kidnapping and
>
> murder of her first child the "hour of lead." "Flying," she wrote, "was
>
> freedom and beauty and escape from crowds" (qtd. in Smith 68).

Set off *long quotations* (more than four lines of prose type). Do *not* enclose them within quotation marks. To set off a quotation, begin a new line, indent ten spaces from the left margin, and double-space the quotation:

> The last paragraph of <u>Five Years of My Life</u> contain Dreyfus's words
>
> when he was finally freed:
>
>> The Government of the Republic gives me back my liberty. It is
>>
>> nothing to me without honor. Beginning with today, I shall
>>
>> unremittingly strive for the reparation of the frightful judicial
>>
>> error of which I am still the victim. I want all France to know by a
>>
>> final judgment that I am innocent. (238)
>
> But he was never to receive that judgment.

Note that long quotations are usually introduced by a sentence ending with a colon (as in the above example) or by an introductory phrase, such as "Dreyfus wrote:"

4. Do not try to introduce a long quotation into the middle of one of your own sentences. It is too difficult for the reader to come out of the quotation and to pick up your thread. Instead, as in the preceding example about the Dreyfus case, introduce the quotation, set it off, and then begin a new sentence of your own.

5. An embedded quotation (that is, a quotation embedded into a sentence of your own) must fit grammatically into the sentence of which it is a part. For example, suppose you want to use Othello's line "I have done the state some service."

Incorrect

> Near the end of the play Othello says that he "have done the state some
>
> service."

Correct

Near the end of the play Othello says that he has "done the state some service."

Correct

Near the end of the play, Othello says, "I have done the state some service."

6. Quote exactly. Check your quotation for accuracy at least twice. If you need to edit a quotation—for example, in order to embed it grammatically, or to inform your reader of a relevant point—observe the following rules:

    a. To add or to substitute words, enclose the words in square brackets—not parentheses.

"In the summer of 1816 [Mary Wollstonecraft and Percy Bysshe Shelley] visited Switzerland and became the neighbours of Lord Byron."

Trotsky became aware that "Stalin would not hesitate a moment to organize an attempt on [his] life."

    b. Indicate the omission of material with ellipses—three periods, with a space between periods and before and after each period.

<u>The New York Times</u> called it "the most intensive manhunt . . . in the country's history" (3 March 1932).

    c. If your sentence ends with the omission of the last part of the original sentence, use four periods: one immediately after the last word quoted, and three (spaced) to indicate the omission.

The manual says, "If your sentence ends with the omission of the last part of the original sentence, use four spaced periods. . . ."

    d. Notice that if you begin the quotation with the beginning of a sentence (in the example we have just given "If your" is the beginning of a quoted sentence), you do *not* indicate that material preceded the words you are quoting. Similarly, if you end your quotation with the end of the quoted sentence, you give only a single period, not an ellipsis, although of course the material from which you are quoting may have gone on for many more sentences. However, if you begin quoting from the middle of a sentence, or end quoting before you reach the end of a sentence in your source, it is customary to indicate the omissions. But even such omissions need not be indicated when the quoted material is obviously incomplete—when, for instance, it is a word or phrase.

7. Use punctuation accurately. There are three important rules to observe:
a.   Commas and periods go inside the quotation marks (if there is no reference).

"The land," Nick Thompson observes, "looks after us."

b.   Commas and periods go after a page reference.

Mark Abby describes a mild day: "A damp February afternoon in

Montreal, mild enough for smokers to huddle in small groups outside

McGill University's tobacco-free arts building" (283).

c.   Semicolons and colons go outside quotation marks.

He turned and said, "Learn the names of all these places"; it sounded

like an order.

d.   Question marks, exclamation points, and dashes go inside if they are part
of the quotation, outside if they are your own.

Amanda ironically says to her daughter, "How old are you, Laura?"

(The question mark is part of the quotation and therefore goes inside the quotation marks.)
In the following example, why is the question mark placed outside the quotation marks?

Is it possible to fail to hear Laura's weariness in her reply, "Mother,

you know my age"?

8. Use single quotation marks for a quotation within a quotation.

The student told the interviewer, "I ran back to the dorm and I called

my boyfriend and I said, 'Listen, this is just incredible,' and I told him all

about it."

9. Enclose titles of short works in quotation marks. Short works
include chapters in books, short stories, essays, short poems, songs, lectures,
speeches, and unpublished works (even if long).
Underline (or use italic type) for titles of long works. Underlining indicates
italics, used in print and available on computers but ordinarily not available on
typewriters. Underline (or italicize) titles of published book-length works: novels, plays, periodicals, collections of essays, anthologies, pamphlets, textbooks,
and long poems (such as *Paradise Lost*). Underline (or italicize) also titles of
films, CDs, videos, television programs, ballets, operas, and works of art, and the
names of planes, ships, and trains.
Exception: titles of sacred works (for example, the New Testament, the
Hebrew Bible, Genesis, Acts, the Gospels, the Koran) are neither underlined nor

enclosed within quotation marks. To cite a book of the Bible with chapter and verse, give the name of the book, then a space, then an Arabic numeral for the chapter, a period, and an Arabic numeral (*not* preceded by a space) for the verse, thus: Exodus 20.14–15. Standard abbreviations for the books of the Bible (for example, Chron.) are permissible in footnotes and in parenthetic citations within the text.

10. Use quotation marks to identify a word or term that you wish to spotlight. (Italics or underlining may be used instead of quotation marks.)

By "comedy" I mean not only a funny play, but any play that ends

happily.

11. Do not use quotation marks to enclose slang or a term that you fear is too casual. Use the term or do not use it; don't apologize by putting it in quotation marks.

Incorrect

Because of "red tape" it took three years.

Incorrect

At last I was able to "put in my two cents."

In both of these sentences the writers are signalling their uneasiness; in neither is there any cause for uneasiness.

12. Do not use quotation marks to convey sarcasm, as in the following sentence:

These "politicians" are nothing but thieves.

Sarcasm, usually a poor form of argument, is best avoided. But of course there are borderline cases when you may want to convey your dissatisfaction with a word used by others.

African sculpture has a long continuous tradition, but this tradition

was jeopardized by the introduction of "civilization" to Africa.

Perhaps the quotation marks here are acceptable, because the writer's distaste has not yet become a sneer and because she is, in effect, quoting. But it is probably better to change "civilization" to "Western culture," omitting the quotation marks.

13. Do not enclose the title of your own essay in quotation marks, and do not underline or italicize it.

CORRECTIONS IN THE FINAL COPY

Extensive revisions should have been made in your drafts, but minor last-minute changes may be made on the finished copy. Proofreading may catch some typographical errors, and you may notice some small weaknesses. You can make corrections with the proofreader's symbols that follow the triangles. If you fail to find an error in each triangle, look again.

1. *Changes* in printed wording may be made by crossing through words and rewriting just above them.

When I first moved to Canada at the age of nine, I had ~~few~~ ^{no} doubts as to

my identity.

2. *Additions* should be made above the line, with a caret (^) below the line at the appropriate place:

When I first moved to Canada at the age ^of^ nine, I had no doubts as to my

identity.

3. *Transpositions* of letters or words may be made thus:

When I frist moved to Canada at the age of nine, I had no doubts as to

my identity.

4. *Deletions* are indicated by a horizontal line through the word or words to be deleted. Delete a single letter by drawing a vertical or diagonal line through it.

When I first moved to Canada at ~~at~~ the age of nine, I had no doubts as

to my identity.

5. *Separation* of words accidentally run together is indicated by a vertical line, *closure* by a curved line connecting the things to be closed up.

When I first/moved to Canada at the age of nine, I had no dou bts as to

my identity.

6. *Paragraphing* may be indicated by the paragraph symbol before the word that is to begin the new paragraph.

When I first moved to Canada at the age of nine, I had no doubts as to

my identity. ¶Within a year, however . . .

PART FIVE

Readings

MARGARET ATWOOD

Margaret Atwood, born in 1939 in Ottawa, did her undergraduate work at Victoria College and graduate work at Radcliffe College and Harvard. She has worked as a cashier, waiter, film writer, and teacher, but she began writing as a child and established herself as a writer before she was thirty. In addition to writing stories, novels, poetry, criticism, and films, she has edited anthologies of Canadian literature. She has won numerous national and international awards. The essay that we reprint was commissioned for a collection entitled The Writer on Her Work *(1992, vol. 2) in which writers give their responses to questions about writing.*

Nine Beginnings

1   1. *Why do you write?*

2   I've begun this piece nine times. I've junked each beginning.

3   I hate writing about my writing. I almost never do it. Why am I doing it now? Because I said I would. I got a letter. I wrote back *no*. Then I was at a party and the same person was there. It's harder to refuse in person. Saying *yes* had something to do with being nice, as women are taught to be, and something to do with being helpful, which we are also taught. Being helpful to women, giving a pint of blood. With not claiming the sacred prerogatives, the touch-me-not self-protectiveness of the artist, with not being selfish. With conciliation, with doing your bit, with appeasement. I was well brought up. I have trouble ignoring social obligations. Saying you'll write about your writing is a social obligation. It's not an obligation to the writing.

4   2. *Why do you write?*

5   I've junked each of nine beginnings. They seemed beside the point. Too assertive, too pedagogical, too frivolous or belligerent, too falsely wise. As if I had some special self-revelation that would encourage others, or some special knowledge to impart, some pithy saying that would act like a talisman for the driven, the obsessed. But I have no such talismans. If I did, I would not continue, myself, to be so driven and obsessed.

6   3. *Why do you write?*

7   I hate writing about my writing because I have nothing to say about it. I have nothing to say about it because I can't remember what goes on when I'm doing it. That time is like small pieces cut out of my brain. It's not time I myself have lived. I can remember the details of the rooms and places where I've written, the circumstances, the other things I did before and after, but not the process itself. Writing about writing requires self-consciousness; writing itself requires the abdication of it.

8   4. *Why do you write?*

9   There are a lot of things that can be said about what goes on around the edges of writing. Certain ideas you may have, certain motivations, grand designs that don't get carried out. I can talk about bad reviews, about sexist reactions to my writing, about making an idiot of myself on television shows. I can talk about

books that failed, that never got finished, and about why they failed. The one that had too many characters, the one that had too many layers of time, red herrings that diverted me when what I really wanted to get at was something else, a certain corner of the visual world, a certain voice, an inarticulate landscape.

10　I can talk about the difficulties that women encounter as writers. For instance, if you're a woman writer, sometime, somewhere, you will be asked: *Do you think of yourself as a writer first, or as a woman first?* Look out. Whoever asks this hates and fears both writing and women.

11　Many of us, in my generation at least, ran into teachers or male writers or other defensive jerks who told us women could not really write because they couldn't be truck drivers or Marines and therefore didn't understand the seamier side of life, which included sex with women. We were told we wrote like housewives, or else we were treated like honorary men, as if to be a good writer was to suppress the female.

12　Such pronouncements used to be made as if they were the simple truth. Now they're questioned. Some things have changed for the better, but not all. There's a lack of self-confidence that gets instilled very early in many young girls, before writing is even seen as a possibility. You need a certain amount of nerve to be a writer, an almost physical nerve, the kind you need to walk a log across a river. The horse throws you and you get back on the horse. I learned to swim by being dropped into the water. You need to know you can sink, and survive it. Girls should be allowed to play in the mud. They should be released from the obligations of perfection. Some of your writing, at least, should be as evanescent as play.

13　A ratio of failures is built into the process of writing. The wastebasket has evolved for a reason. Think of it as the altar of the Muse Oblivion, to whom you sacrifice your botched first drafts, the tokens of your human imperfection. She is the tenth Muse, the one without whom none of the others can function. The gift she offers you is the freedom of the second chance. Or as many chances as you'll take.

14　*5. Why do you write?*

15　In the mid-eighties I began a sporadic journal. Today I went back through it, looking for something I could dig out and fob off as pertinent, instead of writing this piece about writing, but it was useless. There was nothing in it about the actual composition of anything I've written over the past six years. Instead there are exhortations to myself—to get up earlier, to walk more, to resist lures and distractions. *Drink more water,* I find. *Go to bed earlier.* There were lists of how many pages I'd written per day, how many I'd retyped, how many yet to go. Other than that, there was nothing but descriptions of rooms, accounts of what we'd cooked and/or eaten and with whom, letters written and received, notable sayings of children, birds and animals seen, the weather. What came up in the garden. Illnesses, my own and those of others. Deaths, births. Nothing about writing.

16　*January 1, 1984. Blakeny, England. As of today, I have about 130 pp. of the novel done and it's just beginning to take shape & reach the point at which I feel that it exists and can be finished and may be worth it. I work in the bedroom of the big house, and here, in the sitting room, with the wood fire in the fireplace and the coke fire in the dilapidated Roeburn in the kitchen. As usual I'm too cold, which is better than being too hot—today is grey, warm for the time of year, damp. If I got up earlier maybe I would work more, but I might just spend more time procrastinating—as now.*

17   And so on.

18   *6. Why do you write?*

19   You learn to write by reading and writing, writing and reading. As a craft it's acquired through the apprentice system, but you choose your own teachers. Sometimes they're alive, sometimes dead.

20   As a vocation, it involves the laying on of hands. You receive your vocation and in your turn you must pass it on. Perhaps you will do this only through your work, perhaps in other ways. Either way, you're part of a community, the community of writers, the community of storytellers that stretches back through time to the beginning of human society.

21   As for the particular human society to which you yourself belong—sometimes you'll feel you're speaking for it, sometimes—when it's taken an unjust form—against it, or for that other community, the community of the oppressed, the exploited, the voiceless. Either way, the pressures on you will be intense; in other countries, perhaps fatal. But even here—speak "for women," or for any other group which is feeling the boot, and there will be many at hand, both for and against, to tell you to shut up, or to say what they want you to say, or to say it a different way. Or to save them. The billboard awaits you, but if you succumb to its temptations you'll end up two-dimensional.

22   Tell what is yours to tell. Let others tell what is theirs.

23   *7. Why do you write?*

24   Why are we so addicted to causality? *Why do you write?* (Treatise by child psychologist, mapping your formative traumas. Conversely: palm-reading, astrology and genetic studies, pointing to the stars, fate, heredity.) *Why do you write?* (That is, why not do something useful instead?) If you were a doctor, you could tell some acceptable moral tale about how you put Band-Aids on your cats as a child, how you've always longed to cure suffering. No one can argue with that. But writing? What is it *for?*

25   Some possible answers: *Why does the sun shine? In the face of the absurdity of modern society, why do anything else? Because I'm a writer. Because I want to discover the patterns in the chaos of time. Because I must. Because someone has to bear witness. Why do you read?* (This last is tricky: maybe they don't.) *Because I wish to forge in the smithy of my soul the uncreated conscience of my race. Because I wish to make an axe to break the frozen sea within.*[1] (These have been used, but they're good.)

26   If at a loss, perfect the shrug. Or say: *It's better than working in a bank.* Or say: *For fun.* If you say this, you won't be believed, or else you'll be dismissed as trivial. Either way, you'll have avoided the question.

27   *8. Why do you write?*

28   Not long ago, in the course of clearing some of the excess paper out of my workroom, I opened a filing cabinet drawer I hadn't looked into for years. In it was a bundle of loose sheets, folded, creased, and grubby, tied up with leftover string. It consisted of things I'd written in the late fifties, in high school and the early years of university. There were scrawled, inky poems, about snow, despair,

---

[1]The passage about the smithy is from the end of James Joyce's novel, *A Portrait of the Artist as a Young Man* (1916). The next sentence, about an axe to break the frozen sea within us, is from a letter (1904) by Franz Kafka. Each passage is offered by the author as an explanation of why he writes. (Editors' note)

and the Hungarian Revolution. There were short stories dealing with girls who'd had to get married, and dispirited, mousy-haired high-school English teachers—to end up as either was at that time my vision of Hell—typed finger-by-finger on an ancient machine that made all the letters half-red.

29   There I am, then, back in grade twelve, going through the writers' magazines after I'd finished my French Composition homework, typing out my lugubrious poems and my grit-filled stories. (I was big on grit. I had an eye for lawn-litter and dog turds on sidewalks. In these stories it was usually snowing damply, or raining; at the very least there was slush. If it was summer, the heat and humidity were always wiltingly high and my characters had sweat marks under their arms; if it was spring, wet clay stuck to their feet. Though some would say all this was just normal Toronto weather.)

30   In the top right-hand corners of some of these, my hopeful seventeen-year-old self had typed, "First North American Rights Only." I was not sure what "First North American Rights" were; I put it in because the writing magazines said you should. I was at that time an aficionado of writing magazines, having no one else to turn to for professional advice.

31   If I were an archeologist, digging through the layers of old paper that mark the eras in my life as a writer, I'd have found, at the lowest or Stone Age level—say around ages five to seven—a few poems and stories, unremarkable precursors of all my frenetic later scribbling. (Many children write at that age, just as many children draw. The strange thing is that so few of them go on to become writers or painters.) After that there's a great blank. For eight years, I simply didn't write. Then, suddenly, and with no missing links in between, there's a wad of manuscripts. One week I wasn't a writer, the next I was.

32   Who did I think I was, to be able to get away with this? What did I think I was doing? How did I get that way? To these questions I still have no answers.

33   *9. Why do you write?*

34   There's the blank page, and the thing that obsesses you. There's the story that wants to take you over and there's your resistance to it. There's your longing to get out of this, this servitude, to play hooky, to do anything else: wash the laundry, see a movie. There are words and their inertias, their biases, their insufficiencies, their glories. There are the risks you take and your loss of nerve, and the help that comes when you're least expecting it. There's the laborious revision, the scrawled-over, crumpled-up pages that drift across the floor like spilled litter. There's the one sentence you know you will save.

35   Next day there's the blank page. You give yourself up to it like a sleepwalker. Something goes on that you can't remember afterwards. You look at what you've done. It's hopeless.

36   You begin again. It never gets any easier.

 ## Topics for Critical Thinking and Writing

1. In her first try, Atwood doesn't answer the question "Why do you write?" What question does she answer and how does she answer it?
2. The beginning of her second try, like the beginning of her first, tells us that she began nine times and "junked each of nine beginnings." But we

can see that there are nine beginnings here. What is going on? Why has she not "junked" these?

3. Atwood says in her third try, "Writing about writing requires self-consciousness; writing itself requires the abdication of it." What does it mean to abdicate self-consciousness? How do you think abdicating self-consciousness affects or would affect your writing?

4. In her sixth try, Atwood says, "You learn to write by reading and writing, writing and reading." To what extent do you agree? What have you learned about writing by reading or by writing? What have you learned about writing—and writers—from reading "Nine Beginnings"?

5. Why does Atwood write?

 SISSELA BOK

Sissela Bok has taught courses in philosophy at Brandeis and in medical ethics and in decision making at the Harvard Medical School. A scholar with wide-ranging interests, she is currently a Distinguished Fellow at the Harvard Center for Population and Development Studies. Her most recent book is Mayhem: Violence as Public Entertainment. *The following selection is from* Lying: Moral Choice in Public and Private Life *(1978), a book concerned with such problems as whether or not to lie to people for their own good.*

To Lie or Not to Lie?—The Doctor's Dilemma

1   Should doctors ever lie to benefit their patients—to speed recovery or to conceal the approach of death? In medicine as in law, government, and other lines of work, the requirements of honesty often seem dwarfed by greater needs: the need to shelter from brutal news or to uphold a promise of secrecy; to expose corruption or to promote the public interest.

2   What should doctors say, for example, to a forty-six-year-old man coming in for a routine physical checkup just before going on vacation with his family who, though he feels in perfect health, is found to have a form of cancer that will cause him to die within six months? Is it best to tell him the truth? If he asks, should the doctors deny that he is ill, or minimize the gravity of the prognosis? Should they at least conceal the truth until after the family vacation?

3   Doctors confront such choices often and urgently. At times, they see important reasons to lie for the patient's own sake; in their eyes, such lies differ sharply from self-serving ones.

4   Studies show that most doctors sincerely believe that the seriously ill do not want to know the truth about their condition, and that informing them risks destroying their hope, so that they may recover more slowly, or deteriorate faster, perhaps even commit suicide. As one physician wrote: "Ours is a profession which traditionally has been guided by a precept that transcends the virtue of uttering the truth for truth's sake, and that is 'as far as possible do no harm.'"

5   Armed with such a precept, a number of doctors may slip into deceptive practices that they assume will "do no harm" and may well help their patients. They may prescribe innumerable placebos, sound more encouraging than the facts warrant, and distort grave news, especially to the incurably ill and the dying.

6   But the illusory nature of the benefits such deception is meant to bestow is now coming to be documented. Studies show that, contrary to the belief of many physicians, an overwhelming majority of patients do want to be told the truth, even about grave illness, and feel betrayed when they learn that they have been misled. We are also learning that truthful information, humanely conveyed, helps patients cope with illness: helps them tolerate pain better, need less medication, and even recover faster after surgery.

7   Not only do lies not provide the "help" hoped for by advocates of benevolent deception; they invade the autonomy of patients and render them unable to make informed choices concerning their own health, including the choice of whether to *be* a patient in the first place. We are becoming increasingly aware of all that can befall patients in the course of their illness when information is denied or distorted.

8   Dying patients especially—who are easiest to mislead and most often kept in the dark—can then not make decisions about the end of life: about whether or not to enter a hospital, or to have surgery; about where and with whom to spend their remaining time; about how to bring their affairs to a close and take leave.

9   Lies also do harm to those who tell them: harm to their integrity and, in the long run, to their credibility. Lies hurt their colleagues as well. The suspicion of deceit undercuts the work of the many doctors who are scrupulously honest with their patients; it contributes to the spiral of litigation and of "defensive medicine," and thus it injures, in turn, the entire medical profession.

10   Sharp conflicts are now arising. Patients are learning to press for answers. Patients' bills of rights require that they be informed about their condition and about alternatives for treatment. Many doctors go to great lengths to provide such information. Yet even in hospitals with the most eloquent bill of rights, believers in benevolent deception continue their age-old practices. Colleagues may disapprove but refrain from remonstrating. Nurses may bitterly resent having to take part, day after day, in deceiving patients, but feel powerless to take a stand.

11   There is urgent need to debate this issue openly. Not only in medicine, but in other professions as well, practitioners may find themselves repeatedly in straits where serious consequences seem avoidable only through deception. Yet the public has every reason to be wary of professional deception, for such practices are peculiarly likely to become ingrained, to spread, and to erode trust. Neither in medicine, nor in law, government, or the social sciences can there be comfort in the old saw, "What you don't know can't hurt you."

 Topics for Critical Thinking and Writing

1. Is there anything in Bok's opening paragraph that prepares the reader for Bok's own position on whether or not lying is ever justifiable?

2. List the reasons Bok offers on behalf of telling the truth to patients. Are some of these reasons presented more convincingly than others? If any are unconvincing, rewrite them to make them more convincing.

3. Suppose Bok's last sentence was revised to read thus: "In medicine, law, government, and the social sciences, what you don't know *can* hurt you." Which version do you prefer, and why?

4. "What you don't know can't hurt you." Weigh the truth of this assertion in your own life. Were there instances of a truth being withheld from you that did hurt you? Were there occasions when you were told a truth that you now judge would have been better withheld? On the whole, do you come out in favour of the assertion, against it, or somewhere in between?
5. How much should adopted children be told about their biological parents? Consider reasons both for and against telling all. Use not only your own experiences and opinions but those of others, such as friends and classmates.

 DEBRA DICKERSON

A former officer in the U.S. Air Force and a graduate of Harvard Law School, Debra Dickerson has published articles in The Nation, Good Housekeeping, Washington Post Book World, *and other periodicals. "Who Shot Johnny?" originally appeared in* The New Republic; *it was reprinted in* The Best American Essays 1997.

Who Shot Johnny?

1   Given my level of political awareness, it was inevitable that I would come to view the everyday events of my life through the prism of politics and the national discourse. I read *The Washington Post, The New Republic, The New Yorker, Harper's, The Atlantic Monthly, The Nation, National Review, Black Enterprise,* and *Essence* and wrote a weekly column for the Harvard Law School *Record* during my three years just ended there. I do this because I know that those of us who are not well-fed white guys in suits must not yield the debate to them, however well-intentioned or well-informed they may be. Accordingly, I am unrepentant and vocal about having gained admittance to Harvard through affirmative action; I am a feminist, stoic about my marriage chances as a well-educated, thirty-six-year-old black woman who won't pretend to need help taking care of herself. My strength flags, though, in the face of the latest role assigned to my family in the national drama. On July 27, 1995, my sixteen-year-old nephew was shot and paralyzed.

2   Talking with friends in front of his house, Johnny saw a car he thought he recognized. He waved boisterously—his trademark—throwing both arms in the air in a full-bodied, hip-hop Y. When he got no response, he and his friends sauntered down the walk to join a group loitering in front of an apartment building. The car followed. The driver got out, brandished a revolver, and fired into the air. Everyone scattered. Then he took aim and shot my running nephew in the back.

3   Johnny never lost consciousness. He lay in the road, trying to understand what had happened to him, why he couldn't get up. Emotionlessly, he told the story again and again on demand, remaining apologetically firm against all demands to divulge the missing details that would make sense of the shooting but obviously cast him in a bad light. Being black, male, and shot, he must apparently be involved with gangs or drugs. Probably both. Witnesses corroborate his version of events.

4   Nearly six months have passed since that phone call in the night and my nightmarish headlong drive from Boston to Charlotte. After twenty hours behind the wheel, I arrived haggard enough to reduce my mother to fresh tears and to find my nephew reassuring well-wishers with an eerie sang-froid.

5   I take the day shift in his hospital room; his mother and grandmother, a clerk and cafeteria worker, respectively, alternate nights there on a cot. They don their uniforms the next day, gaunt after hours spent listening to Johnny moan in his sleep. How often must his subconscious replay those events and curse its host for saying hello without permission, for being carefree and young while a would-be murderer hefted the weight of his uselessness and failure like Jacob Marley's chains? How often must he watch himself lying stubbornly immobile on the pavement of his nightmares while the sound of running feet syncopate his attacker's taunts?

6   I spend these days beating him at gin rummy and Scrabble, holding a basin while he coughs up phlegm and crying in the corridor while he catheterizes himself. There are children here much worse off than he. I should be grateful. The doctors can't, or won't, say whether he'll walk again.

7   I am at once repulsed and fascinated by the bullet, which remains lodged in his spine (having done all the damage it can do, the doctors say). The wound is undramatic—small, neat, and perfectly centered—an impossibly pink pit surrounded by an otherwise undisturbed expanse of mahogany. Johnny has asked me several times to describe it but politely declines to look in the mirror I hold for him.

8   Here on the pediatric rehab ward, Johnny speaks little, never cries, never complains, works diligently to become independent. He does whatever he is told; if two hours remain until the next pain pill, he waits quietly. Eyes bloodshot, hands gripping the bed rails. During the week of his intravenous feeding, when he was tormented by the primal need to masticate, he never asked for food. He just listened while we counted down the days for him and planned his favorite meals. Now required to dress himself unassisted, he does so without demur, rolling himself back and forth valiantly on the bed and shivering afterward, exhausted. He "ma'am"s and "sir"s everyone politely. Before his "accident," a simple request to take out the trash could provoke a firestorm of teenage attitude. We, the women who have raised him, have changed as well; we've finally come to appreciate those boxer-baring, over-sized pants we used to hate—it would be much more difficult to fit properly sized pants over his diaper.

9   He spends a lot of time tethered to rap music still loud enough to break my concentration as I read my many magazines. I hear him try to soundlessly mouth the obligatory "mothafuckers" over-laying the funereal dirge of the music tracks. I do not normally tolerate disrespectful music in my or my mother's presence, but if it distracts him now . . .

10 "Johnny," I ask later, "do you still like gangster rap?" During the long pause I hear him think loudly, I'm paralyzed, Auntie, not stupid. "I mostly just listen to hip-hop," he says evasively into his *Sports Illustrated.*

11 Miserable though it is, time passes quickly here. We always seem to be jerking awake in our chairs just in time for the next pill, his every-other-night bowel program, the doctor's rounds. Harvard feels a galaxy away—the world revolves around Family Members Living with Spinal Cord Injury class, Johnny's urine output, and strategizing with my sister to find affordable, accessible housing. There is always another long-distance uncle in need of an update, another church member wanting to pray with us, or Johnny's little brother in need of some attention.

12 We Dickerson women are so constant a presence the ward nurses and cleaning staff call us by name and join us for cafeteria meals and cigarette breaks. At Johnny's birthday pizza party, they crack jokes and make fun of each other's hus-

bands (there are no men here). I pass slices around and try not to think, Seventeen with a bullet.

13   Oddly, we feel little curiosity or specific anger toward the man who shot him. We have to remind ourselves to check in with the police. Even so, it feels pro forma, like sending in those $2 rebate forms that come with new pantyhose: you know your request will fall into a deep, dark hole somewhere, but still, it's your duty to try. We push for an arrest because we owe it to Johnny and to ourselves as citizens. We don't think about it otherwise—our low expectations are too ingrained. A Harvard aunt notwithstanding, for people like Johnny, Marvin Gaye was right that only three things are sure: taxes, death, and trouble. At least it wasn't the second.

14   We rarely wonder about or discuss the brother who shot him because we already know everything about him. When the call came, my first thought was the same one I'd had when I'd heard about Rosa Parks's beating: a brother did it. A non-job-having, middle-of-the-day malt-liquor-drinking, crotch-clutching, loud-talking brother with many neglected children born of many forgotten women. He lives in his mother's basement with furniture rented at an astronomical interest rate, the exact amount of which he does not know. He has a car phone, an $80 monthly cable bill, and every possible phone feature but no savings. He steals Social Security numbers from unsuspecting relatives and assumes their identities to acquire large TV sets for which he will never pay. On the slim chance that he is brought to justice, he will have a colorful criminal history and no coherent explanation to offer for his act. His family will raucously defend him and cry cover-up. Some liberal lawyer just like me will help him plea-bargain his way to yet another short stay in a prison pesthouse that will serve only to add another layer to the brother's sociopathology and formless, mindless nihilism. We know him. We've known and feared him all our lives.

15   As a teenager, he called, "Hey, baby, gimme somma that boodie!" at us from car windows. Indignant at our lack of response, he followed up with, "Fuck you, then, 'ho!" He called me a "white-boy-lovin' nigger bitch oreo" for being in the gifted program and loving it. At twenty-seven, he got my seventeen-year-old sister pregnant with Johnny and lost interest without ever informing her that he was married. He snatched my widowed mother's purse as she waited in predawn darkness for the bus to work and then broke into our house while she soldered on an assembly line. He chased all the small entrepreneurs from our neighborhood with his violent thievery and put bars on our windows. He kept us from sitting on our own front porch after dark and laid the foundation for our periodic bouts of self-hating anger and racial embarrassment. He made our neighborhood a ghetto. He is the poster fool behind the maddening community knowledge that there are still some black mothers who raise their daughters but merely love their sons. He and his cancerous carbon copies eclipse the vast majority of us who are not sociopaths and render us invisible. He is the Siamese twin who has died but cannot be separated from his living, vibrant sibling; which of us must attract more notice? We despise and disown this anomalous loser, but for many he *is* black America. We know him, we know that he is outside the fold, and we know that he will only get worse. What we didn't know is that, because of him, my little sister would one day be the latest hysterical black mother wailing over a fallen child on TV.

16   Alone, lying in the road bleeding and paralyzed but hideously conscious, Johnny had lain helpless as he watched his would-be murderer come to stand

over him and offer this prophecy: "Betch'ou won't be doin' nomo' wavin', mothafucker."

17   Fuck you, asshole. He's fine from the waist up. You just can't do anything right, can you?

 Topics for Critical Thinking and Writing

1. Characterize Dickerson's tone in the last lines of the essay.
2. Upon hearing that her nephew had been shot, Dickerson says (paragraph 14) she knew immediately that "a brother did it." She goes on to describe the shooter as a "non-job-having, middle-of-the-day malt-liquor-drinking, crotch-clutching, loud-talking brother with many neglected children born of many forgotten women." Is this description racist? Why or why not?
3. Do you think that this essay perpetuates racial stereotypes—or not?
4. This essay, a narrative account, does not contain an explicit argument or thesis. What is its *implicit* argument?

 JOAN DIDION

Joan Didion was born in California in 1934 and educated at the University of California, Berkeley. While she was a senior in college she wrote a prize-winning essay for a contest sponsored by Vogue, *and soon she became an associate features editor for* Vogue. *As a freelance writer, Didion has written novels, essays, and screenplays. This piece is from her first non-fiction collection,* Slouching Towards Bethlehem *(1966).*

On Keeping a Notebook

1   "'That woman Estelle,'" the note reads, "'is partly the reason why George Sharp and I are separated today.' *Dirty crepe-de-Chine wrapper, hotel bar, Wilmington RR, 9:45 a.m. August Monday morning.*"

2   Since the note is in my notebook, it presumably has some meaning to me. I study it for a long while. At first I have only the most general notion of what I was doing on an August Monday morning in the bar of the hotel across from the Pennsylvania Railroad station in Wilmington, Delaware (waiting for a train? missing one? 1960? 1961? why Wilmington?), but I do remember being there. The woman in the dirty crepe-de-Chine wrapper had come down from her room for a beer, and the bartender had heard before the reason why George Sharp and she were separated today. "Sure," he said, and went on mopping the floor. "You told me." At the other end of the bar is a girl. She is talking, pointedly, not to the man beside her but to a cat lying in the triangle of sunlight cast through the open door. She is wearing a plaid silk dress from Peck & Peck, and the hem is coming down.

3   Here is what it is: the girl has been on the Eastern Shore, and now she is going back to the city, leaving the man beside her, and all she can see ahead are the viscous summer sidewalks and the 3 a.m. long-distance calls that will make her lie awake and then sleep drugged through all the steaming mornings left in August (1960? 1961?). Because she must go directly from the train to lunch in New York, she wishes that she had a safety pin for the hem of the plaid silk

dress, and she also wishes that she could forget about the hem and the lunch and stay in the cool bar that smells of disinfectant and malt and make friends with the woman in the crepe-de-Chine wrapper. She is afflicted by a little self-pity, and she wants to compare Estelles. That is what that was all about.

4   In fact I have abandoned altogether that kind of pointless entry; instead I tell what some would call lies. "That's simply not true," the members of my family frequently tell me when they come up against my memory of a shared event. "The party was *not* for you, the spider was *not* a black widow, *it wasn't that way at all.*" Very likely they are right, for not only have I always had trouble distinguishing between what happened and what merely might have happened, but I remain unconvinced that the distinction, for my purposes, matters. The cracked crab that I recall having for lunch the day my father came home from Detroit in 1945 must certainly be embroidery, worked into the day's pattern to lend verisimilitude; I was ten years old and would not now remember the cracked crab. The day's events did not turn on cracked crab. And yet it is precisely that fictitious crab that makes me see the afternoon all over again, a home movie run all too often, the father bearing gifts, the child weeping, an exercise in family love and guilt. Or that is what it was to me. Similarly, perhaps it never did snow that August in Vermont; perhaps there never were flurries in the night wind, and maybe no one else felt the ground hardening and summer already dead even as we pretended to bask in it, but that was how it felt to me, and it might as well have snowed, could have snowed, did snow.

5   *How it felt to me:* that is getting closer to the truth about a notebook. I sometimes delude myself about why I keep a notebook, imagine that some thrifty virtue derives from preserving everything observed. See enough and write it down, I tell myself, and then some morning when the world seems drained of wonder, some day when I am only going through the motions of doing what I am supposed to do, which is write—on that bankrupt morning I will simply open my notebook and there it will all be, a forgotten account with accumulated interest, paid passage back to the world out there: dialogue overheard in hotels and elevators and at the hat-check counter in Pavillon (one middle-aged man shows his hat check to another and says, "That's my old football number"); impressions of Bettina Aptheker and Benjamin Sonnenberg and Teddy ("Mr. Acapulco") Stauffer; careful *aperçus* about tennis bums and failed fashion models and Greek shipping heiresses, one of whom taught me a significant lesson (a lesson I could have learned from F. Scott Fitzgerald, but perhaps we all must meet the very rich for ourselves) by asking, when I arrived to interview her in her orchid-filled sitting room on the second day of a paralyzing New York blizzard, whether it was snowing outside.

6   Why did I write it down? In order to remember, of course, but exactly what was it I wanted to remember? How much of it actually happened? Did any of it? Why do I keep a notebook at all? It is easy to deceive oneself on all those scores. The impulse to write things down is a peculiarly compulsive one, inexplicable to those who do not share it, useful only accidentally, only secondarily, in the way that any compulsion tries to justify itself. I suppose that it begins or does not begin in the cradle. Although I have felt compelled to write things down since I was five years old, I doubt that my daughter ever will, for she is a singularly blessed and accepting child, delighted with life exactly as life presents itself to her, unafraid to go to sleep and unafraid to wake up. Keepers of private notebooks are a different breed altogether, lonely and resistant rearrangers of things, anxious malcontents, children afflicted apparently at birth with some presentiment of loss.

7   My first notebook was a Big Five tablet, given to me by my mother with the sensible suggestion that I stop whining and learn to amuse myself by writing down my thoughts. She returned the tablet to me a few years ago; the first entry is an account of a woman who believed herself to be freezing to death in the Arctic night, only to find, when day broke, that she had stumbled onto the Sahara Desert, where she would die of the heat before lunch. I have no idea what turn of a five-year-old's mind could have prompted so insistently "ironic" and exotic a story, but it does reveal a certain predilection for the extreme which has dogged me into adult life; perhaps if I were analytically inclined I would find it a truer story than any I might have told about Donald Johnson's birthday party or the day my cousin Brenda put Kitty Litter in the aquarium.

8   So the point of my keeping a notebook has never been, nor is it now, to have an accurate factual record of what I have been doing or thinking. That would be a different impulse entirely, an instinct for reality which I sometimes envy but do not possess. At no point have I ever been able successfully to keep a diary; my approach to daily life ranges from the grossly negligent to the merely absent, and on those few occasions when I have tried dutifully to record a day's events, boredom has so overcome me that the results are mysterious at best. What is this business about "shopping, typing piece, dinner with E, depressed"? Shopping for what? Typing what piece? Who is E? Was this "E" depressed, or was I depressed? Who cares?

9   I imagine, in other words, that the notebook is about other people. But of course it is not. I have no real business with what one stranger said to another at the hat-check counter in Pavillon; in fact I suspect that the line "That's my old football number" touched not my own imagination at all, but merely some memory of something once read, probably "The Eighty-Yard Run." Nor is my concern with a woman in a dirty crepe-de-Chine wrapper in a Wilmington bar. My stake is always, of course, in the unmentioned girl in the plaid silk dress. *Remember what it was to be me:* that is always the point.

10   It is a difficult point to admit. We are brought up in the ethic that others, any others, all others, are by definition more interesting than ourselves; taught to be diffident, just this side of self-effacing. ("You're the least important person in the room and don't forget it," Jessica Mitford's governess would hiss in her ear on the advent of any social occasion: I copied that into my notebook because it is only recently that I have been able to enter a room without hearing some such phrase in my inner ear.) Only the very young and the very old may recount their dreams at breakfast, dwell upon self, interrupt with memories of beach picnics and favorite Liberty lawn dresses and the rainbow trout in a creek near Colorado Springs. The rest of us are expected, rightly, to affect absorption in other people's favorite dresses, other people's trout.

11   And so we do. But our notebooks give us away, for however dutifully we record what we see around us, the common denominator of all we see is always, transparently, shamelessly, the implacable "I." We are not talking here about the kind of notebook that is patently for public consumption, a structural conceit for binding together a series of graceful *pensées;* we are talking about something private, about bits of the mind's string too short to use, an indiscriminate and erratic assemblage with meaning only for its maker.

12   And sometimes even the maker has difficulty with the meaning. There does not seem to be, for example, any point in my knowing for the rest of my life that, during 1964, 720 tons of soot fell on every square mile of New York City, yet there it is in my notebook, labeled "FACT." Nor do I really need to remember

that Ambrose Bierce liked to spell Leland Stanford's name "£eland $tanford" or that "smart women almost always wear black in Cuba," a fashion hint without much potential for practical application. And does not the relevance of these notes seem marginal at best?:

> In the basement museum of the Inyo County Courthouse in Independence, California, sign pinned to a mandarin coat: "This Mandarin Coat was often worn by Mrs. Minnie S. Brooks when giving lectures on her TEAPOT COLLECTION."

> Redhead getting out of car in front of Beverly Wilshire Hotel, chinchilla stole, Vuitton bags and tags reading:
> MRS. LOU FOX
> HOTEL SAHARA
> VEGAS

13   Well, perhaps not entirely marginal. As a matter of fact, Mrs. Minnie S. Brooks and her MANDARIN COAT pull me back into my own childhood, for although I never knew Mrs. Brooks and did not visit Inyo County until I was thirty, I grew up in just such a world, in houses cluttered with Indian relics and bits of gold ore and ambergris and the souvenirs my Aunt Mercy Farnsworth brought back from the Orient. It is a long way from that world to Mrs. Lou Fox's world, where we all live now, and is it not just as well to remember that? Might not Mrs. Minnie S. Brooks help me to remember what I am? Might not Mrs. Lou Fox help me to remember what I am not?

14   But sometimes the point is harder to discern. What exactly did I have in mind when I noted down that it cost the father of someone I know $650 a month to light the place on the Hudson in which he lived before the Crash? What use was I planning to make of this line by Jimmy Hoffa: "I may have my faults, but being wrong ain't one of them"? And although I think it interesting to know where the girls who travel with the Syndicate have their hair done when they find themselves on the West Coast, will I ever make suitable use of it? Might I not be better off just passing it on to John O'Hara? What is a recipe for sauerkraut doing in my notebook? What kind of magpie keeps this notebook? "*He was born the night the* Titanic *went down.*" That seems a nice enough line, and I even recall who said it, but is it not really a better line in life than it could ever be in fiction?

15   But of course that is exactly it: not that I should ever use the line, but that I should remember the woman who said it and the afternoon I heard it. We were on her terrace by the sea, and we were finishing the wine left from lunch, trying to get what sun there was, a California winter sun. The woman whose husband was born the night the *Titanic* went down wanted to rent her house, wanted to go back to her children in Paris. I remember wishing that I could afford the house, which cost $1,000 a month. "Someday you will," she said lazily. "Someday it all comes." There in the sun on her terrace it seemed easy to believe in someday, but later I had a low-grade afternoon hangover and ran over a black snake on the way to the supermarket and was flooded with inexplicable fear when I heard the checkout clerk explaining to the man ahead of me why she was finally divorcing her husband. "He left me no choice," she said over and over as she punched the register. "He has a little seven-month-old baby by her, he left me no choice." I would like to believe that my dread then was for the human

condition, but of course it was for me, because I wanted a baby and did not then have one and because I wanted to own a house that cost $1,000 a month to rent and because I had a hangover.

16   It all comes back. Perhaps it is difficult to see the value in having one's self back in that kind of mood, but I do see it: I think we are well advised to keep on nodding terms with the people we used to be, whether we find them attractive company or not. Otherwise they turn up unannounced and surprise us, come hammering on the mind's door at 4 a.m. of a bad night and demand to know who deserted them, who betrayed them, who is going to make amends. We forget all too soon the things we thought we could never forget. We forget the loves and the betrayals alike, forget what we whispered and what we screamed, forget who we were. I have already lost touch with a couple of people I used to be: one of them, a seventeen-year-old, presents little threat, although it would be of some interest to me to know again what it feels like to sit on a river levee drinking vodka-and-orange-juice and listening to Les Paul and Mary Ford and their echoes sing "How High the Moon" on the car radio. You see I still have the scenes, but I no longer perceive myself among those present, no longer could even improvise the dialogue. The other one, a twenty-three-year-old, bothers me more. She was always a good deal of trouble, and I suspect she will reappear when I least want to see her, skirts too long, shy to the point of aggravation, always the injured party, full of recriminations and little hurts and stories I do not want to hear again, at once saddening me and angering me with her vulnerability and ignorance, an apparition all the more insistent for being so long banished.

17   It is a good idea, then, to keep in touch, and I suppose that keeping in touch is what notebooks are all about. And we are all on our own when it comes to keeping those lines open to ourselves: your notebook will never help me, nor mine you. "*So what's new in the whiskey business?*" What could that possibly mean to you? To me it means a blonde in a Pucci bathing suit sitting with a couple of fat men by the pool at the Beverly Hills Hotel. Another man approaches, and they all regard one another in silence for a while. "So what's new in the whiskey business?" one of the fat men finally says by way of welcome, and the blonde stands up, arches one foot and dips it in the pool, looking all the while at the cabaña where Baby Pignatari is talking on the telephone. That is all there is to that, except that several years later I saw the blonde coming out of Saks Fifth Avenue in New York with her California complexion and a voluminous mink coat. In the harsh wind that day she looked old and irrevocably tired to me, and even the skins in the mink coat were not worked the way they were doing them that year, not the way she would have wanted them done, and there is the point of the story. For a while after that I did not like to look in the mirror, and my eyes would skim the newspapers and pick out only the deaths, the cancer victims, the premature coronaries, the suicides, and I stopped riding the Lexington Avenue IRT because I noticed for the first time that all the strangers I had seen for years—the man with the Seeing Eye dog, the spinster who read the classified pages every day, the fat girl who always got off with me at Grand Central— looked older than they once had.

18   It all comes back. Even that recipe for sauerkraut: even that brings it back. I was on Fire Island when I first made that sauerkraut, and it was raining, and we drank a lot of bourbon and ate the sauerkraut and went to bed at ten, and I listened to the rain and the Atlantic and felt safe. I made the sauerkraut again last night and it did not make me feel any safer, but that is, as they say, another story.

Topics for Critical Thinking and Writing

1. In the sixth paragraph, beginning "Why did I write it down?" Didion says that "it is easy to deceive oneself" about the reasons for keeping a notebook. What self-deceptive reasons does she go on to give? What others can be added? And exactly why *does* she keep a notebook? (Didion in her last three paragraphs—and especially in the first two of these—makes explicit her reasons, but try to state her reasons in a paragraph of your own.)

2. In paragraph 5 Didion refers to a lesson she might have learned from F. Scott Fitzgerald and goes on to say, "but perhaps we all must meet the very rich for ourselves." If you have read a book by Fitzgerald, explain (in a paragraph) the point to someone who doesn't get it.

3. In paragraph 13 Didion says, "It is a long way from that world to Mrs. Lou Fox's world, where we all live now." What does she mean?

4. If you keep a notebook (or diary or journal), explain in one to three paragraphs why you keep it. Following Didion's example, use one entry or two to illustrate the notebook's usefulness to you. If you don't keep a notebook, explain in one to three paragraphs why you don't, and explain what effect, if any, Didion's essay had on you. Do you now think it would be a good idea to keep a notebook? Or did the essay reinforce your belief that there's nothing useful in it for you? Explain.

 ## STEPHEN JAY GOULD

Stephen Jay Gould (1941–2002) was a professor of geology at Harvard University, where he taught paleontology, evolutionary biology, geology, and the history of science. The essays he wrote for the magazine Natural History *have been collected in a series of highly readable books.*

Women's Brains

1 In the Prelude to *Middlemarch,* George Eliot lamented the unfulfilled lives of talented women:

> Some have felt that these blundering lives are due to the inconvenient indefiniteness with which the Supreme Power has fashioned the natures of women: if there were one level of feminine incompetence as strict as the ability to count three and no more, the social lot of women might be treated with scientific certitude.

2 Eliot goes on to discount the idea of innate limitation, but while she wrote in 1872, the leaders of European anthropometry were trying to measure "with scientific certitude" the inferiority of women. Anthropometry, or measurement of the human body, is not so fashionable a field these days, but it dominated the human sciences for much of the nineteenth century and remained popular until intelligence testing replaced skull measurement as a favored device for making invidious comparisons among races, classes, and sexes. Craniometry, or mea-

surement of the skull, commanded the most attention and respect. Its unquestioned leader, Paul Broca (1824–80), professor of clinical surgery at the Faculty of Medicine in Paris, gathered a school of disciples and imitators around himself. Their work, so meticulous and apparently irrefutable, exerted great influence and won high esteem as a jewel of nineteenth-century science.

3   Broca's work seemed particularly invulnerable to refutation. Had he not measured with the most scrupulous care and accuracy? (Indeed, he had. I have the greatest respect for Broca's meticulous procedure. His numbers are sound. But science is an inferential exercise, not a catalog of facts. Numbers, by themselves, specify nothing. All depends upon what you do with them.) Broca depicted himself as an apostle of objectivity, a man who bowed before facts and cast aside superstition and sentimentality. He declared that "there is no faith, however respectable, no interest, however legitimate, which must not accommodate itself to the progress of human knowledge and bend before truth." Women, like it or not, had smaller brains than men and, therefore, could not equal them in intelligence. This fact, Broca argued, may reinforce a common prejudice in male society, but it is also a scientific truth. L. Manouvrier, a black sheep in Broca's fold, rejected the inferiority of women and wrote with feeling about the burden imposed upon them by Broca's numbers:

> Women displayed their talents and their diplomas. They also invoked philosophical authorities. But they were opposed by *numbers* unknown to Condorcet or to John Stuart Mill. These numbers fell upon poor women like a sledge hammer, and they were accompanied by commentaries and sarcasms more ferocious than the most misogynist imprecations of certain church fathers. The theologians had asked if women had a soul. Several centuries later, some scientists were ready to refuse them a human intelligence.

4   Broca's argument rested upon two sets of data: the larger brains of men in modern societies, and a supposed increase in male superiority through time. His most extensive data came from autopsies performed personally in four Parisian hospitals. For 292 male brains, he calculated an average weight of 1,325 grams; 140 female brains averaged 1,144 grams for a difference of 181 grams, or 14 percent of the male weight. Broca understood, of course, that part of this difference could be attributed to the greater height of males. Yet he made no attempt to measure the effect of size alone and actually stated that it cannot account for the entire difference because we know, a priori, that women are not as intelligent as men (a premise that the data were supposed to test, not rest upon):

> We might ask if the small size of the female brain depends exclusively upon the small size of her body. Tiedemann has proposed this explanation. But we must not forget that women are, on the average, a little less intelligent than men, a difference which we should not exaggerate but which is, nonetheless, real. We are therefore permitted to suppose that the relatively small size of the female brain depends in part upon her physical inferiority and in part upon her intellectual inferiority.

5   In 1873, the year after Eliot published *Middlemarch,* Broca measured the cranial capacities of prehistoric skulls from L'Homme Mort cave. Here he found a difference of only 99.5 cubic centimeters between males and females, while modern populations range from 129.5 to 220.7. Topinard, Broca's chief disciple,

explained the increasing discrepancy through time as a result of differing evolutionary pressures upon dominant men and passive women:

> The man who fights for two or more in the struggle for existence, who has all the responsibility and the cares of tomorrow, who is constantly active in combating the environment and human rivals, needs more brain than the woman whom he must protect and nourish, the sedentary woman, lacking any interior occupations, whose role is to raise children, love, and be passive.

6   In 1879, Gustave Le Bon, chief misogynist of Broca's school, used these data to publish what must be the most vicious attack upon women in modern scientific literature (no one can top Aristotle). I do not claim his views were representative of Broca's school, but they were published in France's most respected anthropological journal. Le Bon concluded:

> In the most intelligent races, as among the Parisians, there are a large number of women whose brains are closer in size to those of gorillas than to the most developed male brains. This inferiority is so obvious that no one can contest it for a moment; only its degree is worth discussion. All psychologists who have studied the intelligence of women, as well as poets and novelists, recognize today that they represent the most inferior forms of human evolution and that they are closer to children and savages than to an adult, civilized man. They excel in fickleness, inconstancy, absence of thought and logic, and incapacity to reason. Without doubt there exist some distinguished women, very superior to the average man, but they are as exceptional as the birth of any monstrosity, as, for example, of a gorilla with two heads; consequently, we may neglect them entirely.

7   Nor did Le Bon shrink from the social implications of his views. He was horrified by the proposal of some American reformers to grant women higher education on the same basis as men:

> A desire to give them the same education, and, as a consequence, to propose the same goals for them, is a dangerous chimera. . . . The day when, misunderstanding the inferior occupations which nature has given her, women leave the home and take part in our battles; on this day a social revolution will begin, and everything that maintains the sacred ties of the family will disappear.

Sound familiar?[1]

8   I have reexamined Broca's data, the basis for all this derivative pronouncement, and I find his numbers sound but his interpretation ill-founded, to say the least. The data supporting his claim for increased difference through time can be easily dismissed. Broca based his contention on the samples from L'Homme Mort alone—only seven male and six female skulls in all. Never have so little data yielded such far ranging conclusions.

[1]When I wrote this essay, I assumed that Le Bon was a marginal, if colorful, figure. I have since learned that he was a leading scientist, one of the founders of social psychology, and best known for a seminal study on crowd behavior, still cited today (*La psychologie des foules,* 1895), and for his work on unconscious motivation.

9   In 1888, Topinard published Broca's more extensive data on the Parisian hospitals. Since Broca recorded height and age as well as brain size, we may use modern statistics to remove their effect. Brain weight decreases with age, and Broca's women were, on average, considerably older than his men. Brain weight increases with height, and his average man was almost half a foot taller than his average woman. I used multiple regression, a technique that allowed me to assess simultaneously the influence of height and age upon brain size. In an analysis of the data for women, I found that, at average male height and age, a woman's brain would weigh 1,212 grams. Correction for height and age reduces Broca's measured difference of 181 grams by more than a third, to 113 grams.

10   I don't know what to make of this remaining difference because I cannot assess other factors known to influence brain size in a major way. Cause of death has an important effect: degenerative disease often entails a substantial diminution of brain size. (This effect is separate from the decrease attributed to age alone.) Eugene Schreider, also working with Broca's data, found that men killed in accidents had brains weighing, on average, 60 grams more than men dying of infectious diseases. The best modern data I can find (from American hospitals) records a full 100-gram difference between death by degenerative arteriosclerosis and by violence or accident. Since so many of Broca's subjects were very elderly women, we may assume that lengthy degenerative disease was more common among them than among the men.

11   More importantly, modern students of brain size still have not agreed on a proper measure for eliminating the powerful effect of body size. Height is partly adequate, but men and women of the same height do not share the same body build. Weight is even worse than height, because most of its variation reflects nutrition rather than intrinsic size—fat versus skinny exerts little influence upon the brain. Manouvrier took up this subject in the 1880s and argued that muscular mass and force should be used. He tried to measure this elusive property in various ways and found a marked difference in favor of men, even in men and women of the same height. When he corrected for what he called "sexual mass," women actually came out slightly ahead in brain size.

12   Thus, the corrected 113-gram difference is surely too large; the true figure is probably close to zero and may as well favor women as men. And 113 grams, by the way, is exactly the average difference between a 5 foot 4 inch and a 6 foot 4 inch male in Broca's data. We would not (especially us short folks) want to ascribe greater intelligence to tall men. In short, who knows what to do with Broca's data? They certainly don't permit any confident claim that men have bigger brains than women.

13   To appreciate the social role of Broca and his school, we must recognize that his statements about the brains of women do not reflect an isolated prejudice toward a single disadvantaged group. They must be weighed in the context of a general theory that supported contemporary social distinctions as biologically ordained. Women, blacks, and poor people suffered the same disparagement, but women bore the brunt of Broca's argument because he had easier access to data on women's brains. Women were singularly denigrated but they also stood as surrogates for other disenfranchised groups. As one of Broca's disciples wrote in 1881: "Men of the black races have a brain scarcely heavier than that of white women." This juxtaposition extended into many other realms of anthropological argument, particularly to claims that, anatomically and emotionally, both women and blacks were like white children—and that white children, by the theory of recapitulation,

represented an ancestral (primitive) adult stage of human evolution. I do not regard as empty rhetoric the claim that women's battles are for all of us.

14   Maria Montessori did not confine her activities to educational reform for young children. She lectured on anthropology for several years at the University of Rome, and wrote an influential book entitled *Pedagogical Anthropology* (English edition, 1913). Montessori was no egalitarian. She supported most of Broca's work and the theory of innate criminality proposed by her compatriot Cesare Lombroso. She measured the circumference of children's heads in her schools and inferred that the best prospects had bigger brains. But she had no use for Broca's conclusions about women. She discussed Manouvrier's work at length and made much of his tentative claim that women, after proper correction of the data, had slightly larger brains than men. Women, she concluded, were intellectually superior, but men had prevailed heretofore by dint of physical force. Since technology has abolished force as an instrument of power, the era of women may soon be upon us: "In such an epoch there will really be superior human beings, there will really be men strong in morality and in sentiment. Perhaps in this way the reign of women is approaching, when the enigma of her anthropological superiority will be deciphered. Woman was always the custodian of human sentiment, morality and honor."

15   This represents one possible antidote to "scientific" claims for the constitutional inferiority of certain groups. One may affirm the validity of biological distinctions but argue that the data have been misinterpreted by prejudiced men with a stake in the outcome, and that disadvantaged groups are truly superior. In recent years, Elaine Morgan has followed this strategy in her *Descent of Woman*, a speculative reconstruction of human prehistory from the woman's point of view—and as farcical as more famous tall tales by and for men.

16   I prefer another strategy. Montessori and Morgan followed Broca's philosophy to reach a more congenial conclusion. I would rather label the whole enterprise of setting a biological value upon groups for what it is: irrelevant and highly injurious. George Eliot well appreciated the special tragedy that biological labeling imposed upon members of disadvantaged groups. She expressed it for people like herself—women of extraordinary talent. I would apply it more widely— not only to those whose dreams are flouted but also to those who never realize that they may dream—but I cannot match her prose. In conclusion, then, the rest of Eliot's prelude to *Middlemarch:*

> The limits of variation are really much wider than anyone would imagine from the sameness of women's coiffure and the favorite love stories in prose and verse. Here and there a cygnet is reared uneasily among the ducklings in the brown pond, and never finds the living stream in fellowship with its own oary-footed kind. Here and there is born a Saint Theresa, foundress of nothing, whose loving heartbeats and sobs after an unattained goodness tremble off and are dispersed among hindrances instead of centering in some long-recognizable deed.

Topics for Critical Thinking and Writing

1. In paragraph 3, what does Gould mean when he says, "But science is an inferential exercise, not a catalog of facts"?

2. Gould quotes (paragraph 5) Topinard's explanation for the increasing discrepancy in the size of brains. Given your own understanding of evolution, what do you think of Topinard's explanation?
3. In paragraph 9 Gould says, "Brain weight decreases with age." Do you believe this? Why? How would one establish the truth or falsity of the assertion?
4. In paragraph 12 Gould says, "Thus, the corrected 113-gram difference is surely too large; the true figure is probably close to zero and may as well favor women as men." Why "thus"? What evidence or what assumptions prompt Gould to say that the figure is surely too large?
5. In paragraph 13 Gould says, "I do not regard as empty rhetoric the claim that women's battles are for all of us." What does this mean?
6. Also in paragraph 13 Gould refers to the "social role of Broca and his school." What does he mean by that? On the basis of this essay (and other essays of Gould's you may have read), try to formulate in a sentence or two the social role of Gould.

 # MARTIN LUTHER KING JR.

Martin Luther King Jr. (1929–68), U.S. clergyman and civil rights leader, achieved national fame in the mid-1950s when he led the boycott against segregated bus lines in Montgomery, Alabama; reprinted here is an excerpt from his memoir about this time, Stride Toward Freedom *(1958). In 1964 he was awarded the Nobel Peace Prize, but he continued to encounter strong opposition. On April 4, 1968, while in Memphis to support striking sanitation workers, he was shot and killed.*

Nonviolent Resistance

1 Oppressed people deal with their oppression in three characteristic ways. One way is acquiescence: the oppressed resign themselves to their doom. They tacitly adjust themselves to oppression, and thereby become conditioned to it. In every movement toward freedom some of the oppressed prefer to remain oppressed. Almost 2800 years ago Moses set out to lead the children of Israel from the slavery of Egypt to the freedom of the promised land. He soon discovered that slaves do not always welcome their deliverers. They become accustomed to being slaves. They would rather bear those ills they have, as Shakespeare pointed out, than flee to others that they know not of. They prefer the "fleshpots of Egypt" to the ordeals of emancipation.

2 There is such a thing as the freedom of exhaustion. Some people are so worn down by the yoke of oppression that they give up. A few years ago in the slum areas of Atlanta, a Negro guitarist used to sing almost daily: "Ben down so long that down don't bother me." This is the type of negative freedom and resignation that often engulfs the life of the oppressed.

3 But this is not the way out. To accept passively an unjust system is to cooperate with that system; thereby the oppressed become as evil as the oppressor. Noncooperation with evil is as much a moral obligation as is cooperation with good. The oppressed must never allow the conscience of the oppressor to slumber. Religion reminds every man that he is his brother's keeper. To accept injustice or segregation passively is to say to the oppressor that his actions are morally

right. It is a way of allowing his conscience to fall asleep. At this moment the oppressed fails to be his brother's keeper. So acquiescence—while often the easier way—is not the moral way. It is the way of the coward. The Negro cannot win the respect of his oppressor by acquiescing; he merely increases the oppressor's arrogance and contempt. Acquiescence is interpreted as proof of the Negro's inferiority. The Negro cannot win the respect of the white people of the South or the peoples of the world if he is willing to sell the future of his children for his personal and immediate comfort and safety.

4   A second way that oppressed people sometimes deal with oppression is to resort to physical violence and corroding hatred. Violence often brings about momentary results. Nations have frequently won their independence in battle. But in spite of temporary victories, violence never brings permanent peace. It solves no social problem; it merely creates new and more complicated ones.

5   Violence as a way of achieving racial justice is both impractical and immoral. It is impractical because it is a descending spiral ending in destruction for all. The old law of an eye for an eye leaves everybody blind. It is immoral because it seeks to humiliate the opponent rather than win his understanding; it seeks to annihilate rather than to convert. Violence is immoral because it thrives on hatred rather than love. It destroys community and makes brotherhood impossible. It leaves society in monologue rather than dialogue. Violence ends by defeating itself. It creates bitterness in the survivors and brutality in the destroyers. A voice echoes through time saying to every potential Peter, "Put up your sword." History is cluttered with the wreckage of nations that failed to follow this command.

6   If the American Negro and other victims of oppression succumb to the temptation of using violence in the struggle for freedom, future generations will be the recipients of a desolate night of bitterness, and our chief legacy to them will be an endless reign of meaningless chaos. Violence is not the way.

7   The third way open to oppressed people in their quest for freedom is the way of nonviolent resistance. Like the synthesis in Hegelian philosophy, the principle of nonviolent resistance seeks to reconcile the truths of two opposites—acquiescence and violence—while avoiding the extremes and immoralities of both. The nonviolent resister agrees with the person who acquiesces that one should not be physically aggressive toward his opponent; but he balances the equation by agreeing with the person of violence that evil must be resisted. He avoids the nonresistance of the former and the violent resistance of the latter. With nonviolent resistance, no individual or group need submit to any wrong, nor need anyone resort to violence in order to right a wrong.

8   It seems to me that this is the method that must guide the actions of the Negro in the present crisis in race relations. Through nonviolent resistance the Negro will be able to rise to the noble height of opposing the unjust system while loving the perpetrators of the system. The Negro must work passionately and unrelentingly for full stature as a citizen, but he must not use inferior methods to gain it. He must never come to terms with falsehood, malice, hate, or destruction.

9   Nonviolent resistance makes it possible for the Negro to remain in the South and struggle for his rights. The Negro's problem will not be solved by running away. He cannot listen to the glib suggestion of those who would urge him to migrate en masse to other sections of the country. By grasping his great opportunity in the South he can make a lasting contribution to the moral strength of the nation and set a sublime example of courage for generations yet unborn.

10   By nonviolent resistance, the Negro can also enlist all men of good will in his struggle for equality. The problem is not a purely racial one, with Negroes set against whites. In the end, it is not a struggle between people at all, but a tension between justice and injustice. Nonviolent resistance is not aimed against oppressors but against oppression. Under its banner consciences, not racial groups, are enlisted.

11   If the Negro is to achieve the goal of integration, he must organize himself into a militant and nonviolent mass movement. All three elements are indispensable. The movement for equality and justice can only be a success if it has both a mass and militant character; the barriers to be overcome require both. Nonviolence is an imperative in order to bring about ultimate community.

12   A mass movement of militant quality that is not at the same time committed to nonviolence tends to generate conflict, which in turn breeds anarchy. The support of the participants and the sympathy of the uncommitted are both inhibited by the threat that bloodshed will engulf the community. This reaction in turn encourages the opposition to threaten and resort to force. When, however, the mass movement repudiates violence while moving resolutely toward its goal, its opponents are revealed as the instigators and practitioners of violence if it occurs. Then public support is magnetically attracted to the advocates of nonviolence, while those who employ violence are literally disarmed by overwhelming sentiment against their stand.

 ## Topics for Critical Thinking and Writing

1. Analysis is a term from science, and to some people it suggests coldness, a dispassionate clinical examination. Point to passages in this essay where King communicates his warmth or sympathy or passion.

2. In the first paragraph the passage about Moses and the children of Israel is not strictly necessary; the essential idea of the paragraph is stated in the previous sentence. Why, then, does King add this material? And why the quotation from Shakespeare?

3. Pick out two or three sentences that seem to you to be especially effective, and analyze the sources of their power. You can choose either isolated sentences or (because King often effectively links sentences with repetition of words or of constructions) consecutive ones.

4. In a paragraph, set forth your understanding of what nonviolent resistance is. Use whatever examples from your own experience or reading you find useful.

 ## STEPHEN KING

Stephen King, with more than 100 million copies of his books in print, is one of the world's most popular authors. King was born in Portland, Maine, in 1947. After graduating from the University of Maine, he taught high-school English until he was able to devote himself full-time to writing. In addition to writing stories and novels—some of which have been made into films—he has written Danse Macabre, *a book that, like the essay reprinted here, discusses the appeal of horror.*

Why We Crave Horror Movies

1   I think that we're all mentally ill; those of us outside the asylums only hide it a little better—and maybe not all that much better, after all. We've all known people who talk to themselves, people who sometimes squinch their faces into horrible grimaces when they believe no one is watching, people who have some hysterical fear—of snakes, the dark, the tight place, the long drop . . . and, of course, those final worms and grubs that are waiting so patiently underground.

2   When we pay our four or five bucks and seat ourselves at tenth-row center in a theater showing a horror movie, we are daring the nightmare.

3   Why? Some of the reasons are simple and obvious. To show that we can, that we are not afraid, that we can ride this roller coaster. Which is not to say that a really good horror movie may not surprise a scream out of us at some point, the way we may scream when the roller coaster twists through a complete 360 or plows through a lake at the bottom of the drop. And horror movies, like roller coasters, have always been the special province of the young; by the time one turns 40 or 50, one's appetite for double twists or 360-degree loops may be considerably depleted.

4   We also go to re-establish our feelings of essential normality; the horror movie is innately conservative, even reactionary. Freda Jackson as the horrible melting woman in *Die, Monster, Die!* confirms for us that no matter how far we may be removed from the beauty of a Robert Redford or a Diana Ross, we are still light-years from true ugliness.

5   And we go to have fun.

6   Ah, but this is where the ground starts to slope away, isn't it? Because this is a very peculiar sort of fun, indeed. The fun comes from seeing others menaced— sometimes killed. One critic has suggested that if pro football has become the voyeur's version of combat, then the horror film has become the modern version of the public lynching.

7   It is true that the mythic, "fairy-tale" horror film intends to take away the shades of gray. . . . It urges us to put away our more civilized and adult penchant for analysis and to become children again, seeing things in pure blacks and whites. It may be that horror movies provide psychic relief on this level because this invitation to lapse into simplicity, irrationality and even outright madness is extended so rarely. We are told we may allow our emotions a free rein . . . or no rein at all.

8   If we are all insane, then sanity becomes a matter of degree. If your insanity leads you to carve up women like Jack the Ripper or the Cleveland Torso Murderer, we clap you away in the funny farm (but neither of those two amateur-night surgeons was ever caught, heh-heh-heh); if, on the other hand, your insanity leads you only to talk to yourself when you're under stress or to pick your nose on your morning bus, then you are left alone to go about your business . . . though it is doubtful that you will ever be invited to the best parties.

9   The potential lyncher is in almost all of us (excluding saints, past and present; but then, most saints have been crazy in their own ways), and every now and then, he has to be let loose to scream and roll around in the grass. Our emotions and our fears form their own body, and we recognize that it demands its own exercise to maintain proper muscle tone. Certain of these emotional muscles are accepted—even exalted—in civilized society; they are, of course, the emotions that tend to maintain the status quo of civilization itself. Love, friendship, loyalty, kindness—these are all the emotions that we applaud, emotions

that have been immortalized in the couplets of Hallmark cards and in the verses (I don't dare call it poetry) of Leonard Nimoy.

10 When we exhibit these emotions, society showers us with positive reinforcement; we learn this even before we get out of diapers. When, as children, we hug our rotten little puke of a sister and give her a kiss, all the aunts and uncles smile and twit and cry, "Isn't he the sweetest little thing?" Such coveted treats as chocolate-covered graham crackers often follow. But if we deliberately slam the rotten little puke of a sister's fingers in the door, sanctions follow—angry remonstrance from parents, aunts and uncles; instead of a chocolate-covered graham cracker, a spanking.

11 But anticivilization emotions don't go away, and they demand periodic exercise. We have such "sick" jokes as, "What's the difference between a truckload of bowling balls and a truckload of dead babies?" (You can't unload a truckload of bowling balls with a pitchfork . . . a joke, by the way, that I heard originally from a ten-year-old.) Such a joke may surprise a laugh or a grin out of us even as we recoil, a possibility that confirms the thesis: If we share a brotherhood of man, then we also share an insanity of man. None of which is intended as a defense of either the sick joke or insanity but merely as an explanation of why the best horror films, like the best fairy tales, manage to be reactionary, anarchistic, and revolutionary all at the same time.

12 The mythic horror movie, like the sick joke, has a dirty job to do. It deliberately appeals to all that is worst in us. It is morbidity unchained, our most base instincts let free, our nastiest fantasies realized . . . and it all happens, fittingly enough, in the dark. For those reasons, good liberals often shy away from horror films. For myself, I like to see the most aggressive of them—*Dawn of the Dead,* for instance—as lifting a trap door in the civilized forebrain and throwing a basket of raw meat to the hungry alligators swimming around in that subterranean river beneath.

13 Why bother? Because it keeps them from getting out, man. It keeps them down there and me up here. It was Lennon and McCartney who said that all you need is love, and I would agree with that.

14 As long as you keep the gators fed.

 ## Topics for Critical Thinking and Writing

1. In paragraph 6 King, paraphrasing an unnamed critic, suggests that "the horror film has become the modern version of the public lynching." In your opinion, why did some people find excitement in a lynching? Does the horror film offer somewhat similar excitement(s)?

2. King suggests in paragraph 11 that we have within us a stock of "anticivilization emotions [that] don't go away, and they demand periodic exercise." What, if any, evidence are you aware of that supports this view?

3. In paragraph 11 King tells a joke about dead babies. He suggests that jokes of this sort "may surprise a laugh or a grin out of us even as we recoil." Analyze your own response to the joke, or to similar jokes. Did you laugh or grin? Or was your response utterly different? If so, what was it?

4. In paragraphs 12 and 13, King says that horror movies serve a valuable social purpose. Do you think he has proved this point? What are the strengths (if any) and the weaknesses (if any) of his argument?

STEPHEN LEACOCK

Stephen Leacock (1869–1944) was a Canadian writer best known as a humorist;
beginning in 1910, he published approximately one humorous book a year for the rest
of his life. He trained as an economist and worked as a lecturer and then department
head in the Department of Political Economy at McGill University. Leacock published
many works about political science, history, and literary criticism. The Stephen Leacock
Medal for Humour, established in 1947, is awarded annually for the best humorous
book by a Canadian author. This essay is from his first collection of comic writings,
Literary Lapses *(1910), which received popular and critical acclaim.*

A, B, and C: The Human Element in Mathematics

1   The student of arithmetic who has mastered the first four rules of his art, and
successfully striven with money sums and fractions, finds himself confronted by
an unbroken expanse of questions known as problems. These are short stories of
adventure and industry with the end omitted, and though betraying a strong family resemblance, are not without a certain element of romance.

2   The characters in the plot of a problem are three people called A, B, and C.
The form of the question is generally of this sort:

3   "A, B, and C do a certain piece of work. A can do as much work in one hour
as B in two, or C in four. Find how long they work at it."

4   Or thus:

5   "A, B, and C are employed to dig a ditch. A can dig as much in one hour as B
can dig in two, and B can dig twice as fast as C. Find how long, etc. etc."

6   Or after this wise:

7   "A lays a wager that he can walk faster than B or C. A can walk half as fast
again as B, and C is only an indifferent walker. Find how far, and so forth."

8   The occupations of A, B, and C are many and varied. In the older arith-
metics they contented themselves with doing "a certain piece of work." This
statement of the case, however, was found too sly and mysterious, or possibly
lacking in romantic charm. It became the fashion to define the job more clearly
and to set them at walking matches, ditch-digging, regattas, and piling cord
wood. At times, they became commercial and entered into partnership, having
with their old mystery a "certain" capital. Above all they revel in motion. When
they tire of walking-matches—A rides on horseback, or borrows a bicycle and
competes with his weaker-minded associates on foot. Now they race on loco-
motives; now they row; or again they become historical and engage stage-
coaches; or at times they are aquatic and swim. If their occupation is actual
work they prefer to pump water into cisterns, two of which leak through holes
in the bottom and one of which is watertight. A, of course, has the good one; he
also takes the bicycle, and the best locomotive, and the right of swimming with
the current. Whatever they do they put money on it, being all three sports. A
always wins.

9   In the early chapters of the arithmetic, their identity is concealed under the
names John, William, and Henry, and they wrangle over the division of marbles.
In algebra they are often called X, Y, Z. But these are only their Christian names,
and they are really the same people.

10   Now to one who has followed the history of these men through countless pages of problems, watched them in their leisure hours dallying with cord wood, and seen their panting sides heave in the full frenzy of filling a cistern with a leak in it, they become something more than mere symbols. They appear as creatures of flesh and blood, living men with their own passions, ambitions, and aspirations like the rest of us. Let us view them in turn. A is a full-blooded blustering fellow, of energetic temperament, hot-headed and strong-willed. It is he who proposes everything, challenges B to work, makes the bets, and bends the others to his will. He is a man of great physical strength and phenomenal endurance. He has been known to walk forty-eight hours at a stretch, and to pump ninety-six. His life is arduous and full of peril. A mistake in the working of a sum may keep him digging a fortnight without sleep. A repeating decimal in the answer might kill him.

11   B is a quiet, easy-going fellow, afraid of A and bullied by him, but very gentle and brotherly to little C, the weakling. He is quite in A's power, having lost all his money in bets.

12   Poor C is an undersized, frail man, with a plaintive face. Constant walking, digging, and pumping has broken his health and ruined his nervous system. His joyless life has driven him to drink and smoke more than is good for him, and his hand often shakes as he digs ditches. He has not the strength to work as the others can; in fact, as Hamlin Smith has said, "A can do more work in one hour than C in four."

13   The first time that I ever saw these men was one evening after a regatta. They had all been rowing in it, and it had transpired that A could row as much in one hour as B in two, or C in four. B and C had come in dead fagged and C was coughing badly. "Never mind, old fellow," I heard B say, "I'll fix you up on the sofa and get you some hot tea." Just then A came blustering in and shouted, "I say, you fellows, Hamlin Smith has shown me three cisterns in his garden and he says we can pump them until to-morrow night. I bet I can beat you both. Come on. You can pump in your rowing things, you know. Your cistern leaks a little, I think, C." I heard B growl that it was a dirty shame and that C was used up now, but they went, and presently I could tell from the sound of the water that A was pumping four times as fast as C.

14   For years after that I used to see them constantly about town and always busy. I never heard of any of them eating or sleeping. Then owing to a long absence from home, I lost sight of them. On my return I was surprised to no longer find A, B, and C at their accustomed tasks; on inquiry I heard that work in this line was now done by N, M, and O, and that some people were employing for algebraical jobs, four foreigners called Alpha, Beta, Gamma, and Delta.

15   Now it chanced one day that I stumbled upon old D, in the little garden in front of his cottage, hoeing in the sun. D is an aged labouring man who used occasionally to be called in to help A, B, and C. "Did I know 'em, sir?" he answered, "why, I knowed 'em ever since they was little fellows in brackets. Master A, he were a fine lad, sir, though I always said, give me Master B for kind-heartedness-like. Many's the job as we've been on together, sir, though I never did no racing nor aught of that, but just the plain labour, as you might say. I'm getting a bit too old and stiff for it nowadays, sir—just scratch about in the garden here and grow a bit of a logarithm, or raise a common denominator or two. But Mr. Euclid[1] he use me still for them propositions, he do."

---

[1]Euclid (c. 325–265 BCE), a famous mathematician from antiquity, is best known for his treatise *The Elements*. (Editors' note)

16   From the garrulous old man I learned the melancholy end of my former acquaintances. Soon after I left town, he told me, C had been taken ill. It seems that A and B had been rowing on the river for a wager, and C had been running on the bank and then sat in a draught. Of course the bank had refused the draught and C was taken ill. A and B came home and found C lying helpless in bed. A shook him roughly and said, "Get up, C, we're going to pile wood." C looked so worn and pitiful that B said, "Look here, A, I won't stand this, he isn't fit to pile wood to-night." C smiled feebly and said, "Perhaps I might pile a little if I sat up in bed." Then B, thoroughly alarmed, said, "See here, A, I'm going to fetch a doctor; he's dying." A flared up and answered, "You've no money to fetch a doctor." "I'll reduce him to his lowest terms," B said firmly, "that'll fetch him." C's life might even then have been saved but they made a mistake about the medicine. It stood at the head of the bed on a bracket, and the nurse accidentally removed it from the bracket without changing the sign. After the fatal blunder C seems to have sunk rapidly. On the evening of the next day, as the shadows deepened in the little room, it was clear to all that the end was near. I think that even A was affected at the last as he stood with bowed head, aimlessly offering to bet with the doctor on C's laboured breathing. "A," whispered C, "I think I'm going fast." "How fast do you think you'll go, old man?" murmured A. "I don't know," said C, "but I'm going at any rate."—The end came soon after that. C rallied for a moment and asked for a certain piece of work that he had left downstairs. A put it in his arms and he expired. As his soul sped heavenward A watched its flight with melancholy admiration. B burst into a passionate flood of tears and sobbed, "Put away his little cistern and the rowing clothes he used to wear, I feel as if I could hardly ever dig again."—The funeral was plain and unostentatious. It differed in nothing from the ordinary, except that out of deference to sporting men and mathematicians, A engaged two hearses. Both vehicles started at the same time, B driving the one which bore the sable parallelepiped containing the last remains of his ill-fated friend. A on the box of the empty hearse generously consented to a handicap of a hundred yards, but arrived first at the cemetery by driving four times as fast as B. (Find the distance to the cemetery.) As the sarcophagus was lowered, the grave was surrounded by the broken figures of the first book of Euclid.—It was noticed that after the death of C, A became a changed man. He lost interest in racing with B, and dug but languidly. He finally gave up his work and settled down to live on the interest of his bets.— B never recovered from the shock of C's death; his grief preyed upon his intellect and it became deranged. He grew moody and spoke only in monosyllables. His disease became rapidly aggravated, and he presently spoke only in words whose spelling was regular and which presented no difficulty to the beginner. Realizing his precarious condition he voluntarily submitted to be incarcerated in an asylum, where he abjured mathematics and devoted himself to writing the History of the Swiss Family Robinson in words of one syllable.

Topics for Critical Thinking and Writing

1. a. How does Leacock achieve his comic effect in "A, B, and C: The Human Element in Mathematics"? You may wish to consider, among other things, plot line, characterization, and use of language. Illustrate your answer with specific references to the essay.

b. In "American Humour" (*Essays and Literary Studies.* New York: John Lane, 1916), Leacock discusses various types of humour in the spectrum from low-brow to high-brow: does Leacock achieve in his essay what he describes in the following passage as a "higher plane [of] humour"?

> The final stage of the development of humour is reached when amusement no longer arises from a single "funny" idea, meaningless contrast, or odd play upon words, but rests upon a prolonged and sustained conception of the incongruities of human life itself. The shortcomings of our existence, the sad contrast of our aims and our achievements, the little fretting aspiration of the day that fades into the nothingness of to-morrow kindle in the mellowed mind a sense of gentle amusement from which all selfish exultation has been chastened by the realisation of our common lot of sorrow. On this higher plane humour and pathos mingle and become one.

2. a. Why does he write about something abstract as if it were concrete? Why might he choose to create "short stories" out of mathematical problems?

   b. In a couple of paragraphs, compare Leacock's and Ingram's (Chapter 11) essays.

 # C. S. LEWIS

C[live] S[taples] Lewis (1898–1963) taught medieval and Renaissance literature at Oxford and later at Cambridge. In addition to writing about literature, he wrote fiction (including the children's classic The Chronicles of Narnia*), poetry, and numerous essays and books on moral and religious topics, including* God in the Dock *(1970) from which this essay is taken.*

Vivisection

1 It is the rarest thing in the world to hear a rational discussion of vivisection. Those who disapprove of it are commonly accused of "sentimentality," and very often their arguments justify the accusation. They paint pictures of pretty little dogs on dissecting tables. But the other side lies open to exactly the ·same charge. They also often defend the practice by drawing pictures of suffering women and children whose pain can be relieved we are assured only by the fruits of vivisection. The one appeal, quite as clearly as the other, is addressed to emotion, to the particular emotion we call pity. And neither appeal proves anything. If the thing is right—and if right at all, it is a duty—then pity for the animal is one of the temptations we must resist in order to perform that duty. If the thing is wrong, then pity for human suffering is precisely the temptation which will most probably lure us into doing that wrong thing. But the real question—*whether* it is right or wrong—remains meanwhile just where it was.

2 A rational discussion of this subject begins by inquiring whether pain is, or is not, an evil. If it is not, then the case against vivisection falls. But then so does the case for vivisection. If it is not defended on the ground that it reduces human suffering, on what ground can it be defended? And if pain is not an evil, why should human suffering be reduced? We must therefore assume as a basis for the whole discussion that pain is an evil, otherwise there is nothing to be discussed.

3   Now if pain is an evil then the infliction of pain, considered in itself, must clearly be an evil act. But there are such things as necessary evils. Some acts which would be bad, simply in themselves, may be excusable and even laudable when they are necessary means to a greater good. In saying that the infliction of pain, simply in itself, is bad, we are not saying that pain ought never to be inflicted. Most of us think that it can rightly be inflicted for a good purpose—as in dentistry or just and reformatory punishment. The point is that it always requires justification. On the man whom we find inflicting pain rests the burden of showing why an act which in itself would be simply bad is, in those particular circumstances, good. If we find a man giving pleasure it is for us to prove (if we criticize him) that his action is wrong. But if we find a man inflicting pain it is for him to prove that his action is right. If he cannot, he is a wicked man.

4   Now vivisection can only be defended by showing it to be right that one species should suffer in order that another species should be happier. And here we come to the parting of the ways. The Christian defender and the ordinary "scientific" (i.e., naturalistic) defender of vivisection, have to take quite different lines.

5   The Christian defender, especially in the Latin countries, is very apt to say that we are entitled to do anything we please to animals because they "have no souls." But what does this mean? If it means that animals have no consciousness, then how is this known? They certainly behave as if they had, or at least the higher animals do. I myself am inclined to think that far fewer animals than is supposed have what we should recognize as consciousness. But that is only an opinion. Unless we know on other grounds that vivisection is right we must not take the moral risk of tormenting them on a mere opinion. On the other hand, the statement that they "have no souls" may mean that they have no moral responsibilities and are not immortal. But the absence of "soul" in that sense makes the infliction of pain upon them not easier but harder to justify. For it means that animals cannot deserve pain, nor profit morally by the discipline of pain, nor be recompensed by happiness in another life for suffering in this. Thus all the factors which render pain more tolerable or make it less totally evil in the case of human beings will be lacking in the beasts. "Soullessness," in so far as it is relevant to the question at all, is an argument against vivisection.

6   The only rational line for the Christian vivisectionist to take is to say that the superiority of man over beast is a real objective fact, guaranteed by Revelation, and that the propriety of sacrificing beast to man is a logical consequence. We are "worth more than many sparrows,"[1] and in saying this we are not merely expressing a natural preference for our own species simply because it is our own but conforming to a hierarchical order created by God and really present in the universe whether any one acknowledges it or not. The position may not be satisfactory. We may fail to see how a benevolent Deity could wish us to draw such conclusions from the hierarchical order He has created. We may find it difficult to formulate a human right of tormenting beasts in terms which would not equally imply an angelic right of tormenting men. And we may feel that though objective superiority is rightly claimed for men, yet that very superiority ought partly to *consist in* not behaving like a vivisector: that we ought to prove ourselves better than the beasts precisely by the fact of acknowledging duties to them which they do not acknowledge to us. But on all these questions different opinions can be honestly held. If on grounds of our real, divinely ordained, superiority a Christian pathologist thinks it right to vivisect, and does so with scrupu-

[1]Matthew 10.31

lous care to avoid the least dram or scruple of unnecessary pain, in a trembling awe at the responsibility which he assumes, and with a vivid sense of the high mode in which human life must be lived if it is to justify the sacrifices made for it, then (whether we agree with him or not) we can respect his point of view.

7 But of course the vast majority of vivisectors have no such theological background. They are most of them naturalistic and Darwinian. Now here, surely, we come up against a very alarming fact. The very same people who will most contemptuously brush aside any consideration of animal suffering if it stands in the way of "research" will also, on another context, most vehemently deny that there is any radical difference between man and the other animals. On the naturalistic view the beasts are at bottom just the same *sort* of thing as ourselves. Man is simply the cleverest of the anthropoids. All the grounds on which a Christian might defend vivisection are thus cut from under our feet. We sacrifice other species to our own not because our own has any objective metaphysical privilege over others, but simply because it is ours. It may be very natural to have this loyalty to our own species, but let us hear no more from the naturalists about the "sentimentality" of antivivisectionists. If loyalty to our own species, preference for man simply because we are men, is not a sentiment, then what is? It may be a good sentiment or a bad one. But a sentiment it certainly is. Try to base it on logic and see what happens!

8 But the most sinister thing about modern vivisection is this. If a mere sentiment justifies cruelty, why stop at a sentiment for the whole human race? There is also a sentiment for the white man against the black, for a *Herrenvolk*[2] against the non-Aryans, for "civilized" or "progressive" peoples against "savages" or "backward" peoples. Finally, for our own country, party or class against others. Once the old Christian idea of a total difference in kind between man and beast has been abandoned, then no argument for experiments on animals can be found which is not also an argument for experiments on inferior men. If we cut up beasts simply because they cannot prevent us and because we are backing our own side in the struggle for existence, it is only logical to cut up imbeciles, criminals, enemies or capitalists for the same reasons. Indeed, experiments on men have already begun. We all hear that Nazi scientists have done them. We all suspect that our own scientists may begin to do so, in secret, at any moment.

9 The alarming thing is that the vivisectors have won the first round. In the nineteenth and eighteenth centuries a man was not stamped as a "crank" for protesting against vivisection. Lewis Carroll protested, if I remember his famous letter correctly, on the very same ground which I have just used.[3] Dr. Johnson— a man whose mind had as much *iron* in it as any man's—protested in a note on *Cymbeline* which is worth quoting in full. In Act I, scene v, the Queen explains to the Doctor that she wants poisons to experiment on "such creatures as We count not worth the hanging,—but none human."[4] The Doctor replies:

Your Highness
Shall from this practice but make hard your heart.[5]

[2]German for "master race." (Editors' note)

[3]"Vivisection as a Sign of the Times," *The Works of Lewis Carroll,* ed. Roger Lancelyn Green (London, 1965), pp. 1089–92. See also "Some Popular Fallacies about Vivisection," *ibid.,* pp. 1092–1100.

[4]Shakespeare, *Cymbeline,* I. v. 19–20.

[5]*Ibid.,* 23.

Johnson comments: "The thought would probably have been more amplified, had our author lived to be shocked with such experiments as have been published in later times, by a race of men that have practised tortures without pity, and related them without shame, and are yet suffered to erect their heads among human beings."[6]

10   The words are his, not mine, and in truth we hardly dare in these days to use such calmly stern language. The reason why we do not dare is that the other side has in fact won. And though cruelty even to beasts is an important matter, their victory is symptomatic of matters more important still. The victory of vivisection marks a great advance in the triumph of ruthless, non-moral, utilitarianism over the old world of ethical law; a triumph in which we, as well as animals, are already the victims, and of which Dachau and Hiroshima mark the more recent achievements. In justifying cruelty to animals we put ourselves also on the animal level. We choose the jungle and must abide by our choice.

11   You will notice I have spent no time in discussing what actually goes on in the laboratories. We shall be told, of course, that there is surprisingly little cruelty. That is a question with which, at present, I have nothing to do. We must first decide what should be allowed: after that it is for the police to discover what is already being done.

Topics for Critical Thinking and Writing

1. What purpose does Lewis's first paragraph serve? Is his implied definition of sentimentality adequate for his purpose?

2. By the end of the second paragraph are you willing to agree, at least for the sake of argument, that pain is an evil?

3. In the third paragraph Lewis gives two examples (dentistry and reformatory punishment) to prove that the infliction of pain "always requires justification." Are these two examples adequate and effective?

4. By the end of the fifth paragraph (the paragraph beginning "The Christian defender") are we more or less convinced that Lewis is fully aware of both sides of the argument? Do we feel he is fairly presenting both sides?

5. Characterize the tone (Lewis's attitude) implied in "The position may not be satisfactory" (paragraph 6). Notice also the effect of the repetition (in the same paragraph) of "We may fail to see," "We may find it difficult," and "And we may feel. . . ." How tentative do you think Lewis really is?

6. The eighth paragraph begins, "But the most sinister thing about modern vivisection is this." How surprising is the word "sinister"? And why does Lewis bring in (drag in?) racial and religious persecution?

7. Late in his essay (paragraph 9) Lewis quotes Lewis Carroll, Shakespeare, and Dr. Johnson. Except for a phrase from the Bible, these are the first quotations he uses. Should he have introduced these quotations, or others, earlier?

8. Analyze the final paragraph. Is Lewis correct in dismissing the question of how much cruelty there is in laboratories? Characterize the tone of the last sentence.

---

[6]*Johnson on Shakespeare: Essays and Notes Selected and Set Forth with an Introduction* by Sir Walter Raleigh (London, 1908), p. 181.

 **STEVE MARTIN**

Steve Martin (b. 1945) is a stand-up comedian and movie actor as well as a prolific writer of books, plays, essays, short stories, and screenplays. This essay originally appeared in The New Yorker *in 1998.*

Studies in the New Causality

> *A 27-year-old Michigan man, who complained that a rear-end auto collision had turned him into a homosexual, has been awarded $200,000 by a jury.*
>
> —"Ann Landers," July 30, 1998

1   Recent discoveries in the legal profession have left scientists, many of whom still linger romantically in the Newtonian world, scrambling to catch up in the field of New Causality. In a case last month, a judge in Sacramento ruled in favor of changing the value of pi, thus acquitting a tire manufacturer of making tires that were not fully round. An appeal by scientists was thrown out for lack of evidence when the small courtroom could not physically accommodate a fully expressed representation of pi. The oblong tires in question were produced at the retrial, the judge said they looked round to him, the defense played the race card, and the value of pi was changed to 2.9.

2   Cause and effect have traditionally been expressed by the example of one billiard ball hitting another billiard ball, the striking billiard ball being the "cause" and the struck billiard ball being the "effect." However, in the new legal parlance the cause of the second billiard ball's motion is unclear, depending on whether you're prosecuting or defending the first billiard ball. If you are suing the first billiard ball, it is entirely conceivable that striking the second billiard ball harmed your chances of becoming Miss Paraguay. If you're defending the first billiard ball, the motion of the second billiard ball could be an unrelated coincidence.

3   It's easy to understand how one physical thing can influence another physical thing: my car hit your car because I was blinded by your shiny hair barrette. But what about emotional causality? Can my harsh words affect your mood, costing you millions of dollars that you would have earned behind the counter at Burger King? Apparently so. Several months ago, a male office worker was awarded sixty-seven thousand dollars because a female co-worker asked him if he would like her to drop his "package" off at the post office; he was further awarded fifty thousand dollars after arguing that she was also in constant possession of a vagina, the knowledge of which rendered him unable to concentrate.

4   A more difficult causality to prove, however, is physical to emotional. Can being struck from behind in a car accident cause someone to become a homosexual? Obviously the answer is yes, evidenced by the large award in the lawsuit cited above. Even more interesting is a little-known case in which a man was awarded thirty-six thousand dollars after a driver *failed* to collide with his car, causing him to become a *latent* homosexual.

5   The New Causality guidelines have redefined many of the basic concepts with which the scientific world has struggled for centuries. They are:

6   The "Ninety-seven Steps" Rule: It used to be accepted that one event caused another one event to happen. No longer so. It is now acceptable to have up to ninety-seven causality links:

Your dog ate my philodendron which depressed my mother who in a stupor voted for Marion Barry causing an upswing in crack sales that allowed Peru to maintain an embassy and accumulate parking tickets, encouraging me to stay a meter maid rather than become an Imagineer. And so on.

7   SEMANTIC CAUSALITY: Semantic causality occurs when a word or phrase in the cause is the same as a word or phrase in the effect. "You failed to install my client's *sink* properly, causing her to *sink* into a depression." In the case cited earlier, the plaintiff's lawyer might say that the "party" driving the Camaro collided with his client's car, and isn't a "party" where homosexuals gather and socialize with one another?

8   AFTER-THE-FACT CAUSALITY: This simple law states that having sex with an intern can cause a financial misdealing to occur twenty years prior.

9   UNIVERSAL CAUSALITY: This is the law that has the legal world most excited. It rests on the proposition that "anything can cause anything," or, more simply put, the "Bill Gates gave my dog asthma" principle. If the law of Universal Causality bears out, the economy will receive an invigorating boost when everyone sues everyone else for everything. Everything actionable that ever happened to you will be the fault of your next-door neighbor, who, in turn, will sue Bill Gates, who, in turn, will sue himself.

10   These advancements in the legal world mean for science that a large stellar object is no longer the *cause* of the bending of light rays that pass nearby but its *blame*. Scientists everywhere are scurrying to make sense of the New Causality, with Newtonians turning into Einsteinians, and Einsteinians turning into Cochranians. Meanwhile, astronomers have discovered new and distant objects in the farthest reaches of the universe. Are they protogalaxies forming near the beginning of time? The courts will decide.

 ## Topics for Critical Thinking and Writing

1. At what point, exactly, do you realize that the essay is satirical?
2. Who or what is Martin's primary target?
3. As precisely as possible, explain what makes "Studies in the New Causality" funny.
4. In paragraphs 6 to 9 Martin lists four basic concepts of the New Causality: "The 'Ninety-seven Steps' Rule," "Semantic Causality," "After-the-Fact Causality," and "Universal Causality." In a paragraph or so, set out a fifth concept of your own.

 ## ERIC McLUHAN

Eric McLuhan teaches at the University of Toronto and lectures extensively throughout the world. He is the author of The Role of Thunder at Finnegan's Wake *(1997) and* Electric Language: Understanding the Present *(1998), in which this reading appears. He is also co-editor of the* McLuhan Studies Journal *and director of McLuhan Program International. Like his father, Marshall McLuhan, with whom he co-authored* The City as Classroom *(1977) and* Laws of Media *(1998), Eric McLuhan researches the social effects of new technologies and media.*

Arachne or Penelope: Queen of the Net, Mistress of the Web?

The age demanded an image
Of its accelerated grimace,
Something for the modern stage,
Not, at any rate, an Attic grace;

Not, not certainly, the obscure reveries
Of the inward gaze;
Better mendacities
Than the classics in paraphrase!

—EZRA POUND, "HUGH SELWYN MAUBERLY," II

1   Homer, Hesiod, and the preliterate poets encoded in their verses the full encyclopedia of their arts and sciences. By the word recited and sung, a hypnotic and mimetic spell bound culture and society. Memories were strong and vigorous. Precisely the same conditions apply today among the young with their songs and costumes, minus the encyclopedic knowledge.

2   But comes the written, alphabetic word: memory decays. The goddess Athena takes over as governess of social and intellectual affairs, and also her city, Athens, where the civilized gather and prosper. Outside the gates live the *barbaroi*, those who lack articulate speech and can only howl "*bar-bar-bar.*" Athena was patroness of sweet reason; under her tutelage, Western civilization grew amid rhetoric and writing. The great epic poets give place to the theatrical poets and lyrical poets with their private voices. Abstract philosophical thought was the latest technology.

3   Although Athena's sway has held for twenty-four centuries, the electric age demands a new image. Rational detachment and abstraction have lost their appeal and their cogency. No longer is the city—or any mere place—"where the action is." In the age of the Internet, the center is no-where and now-here, everywhere at once. Everywhere is both center and periphery, placeless and boundless. We live "in the broadest way immarginable." What kind of patroness would suit this virtual world of the net and the web?

4   Many today have decided on the ancient web-crawler, Arachne, the maiden renowned for her skill at spinning and weaving. Ovid gives this account of her:

Neither for place of birth nor birth itself had [Arachne] fame, but only for her skill.
   Her father, Idmon of Colophon, used to dye the absorbent wool for her with Phocaean purple. Her mother was now dead; but she was low-born herself, and had a husband of the same degree. Nevertheless the girl, Arachne, had gained fame for her skill throughout the Lydian towns, although she herself had sprung from a humble home and dwelt in the hamlet of Hypaepa. Often, to watch her wondrous skill, the nymphs would leave their own vineyards on Timolus' slopes, and the water-nymphs of Pactolus would leave their waters. And 'twas the pleasure not alone to see her finished work, but to watch her as she worked; so graceful and deft was she. Whether she was winding the rough yarn into a new ball, or shaping the stuff with her fingers, reaching back to the distaff for more wool, fleecy as a cloud, to draw into long soft threads, or giving a twist with practised thumb to the graceful

spindle, or embroidering with her needle: you could know that Pallas [Athena] had taught her. Yet, she denied it, and, offended at the suggestion of a teacher ever so great, she said, "Let her but strive with me; and if I lose there is nothing which I would not forfeit."

—OVID, *METAMORPHOSES* TRANS. FRANK JUSTUS MILLER.
LOEB CLASSICAL LIBRARY. (CAMBRIDGE, MASS.
HARVARD UNIVERSITY PRESS, 1916. RPT., 1971), VI. 7-25

5   Athena herself hears of the challenge and takes it up. They hold a competition. Athena weaves an image of the gods in their glory. Arachne, imprudently, weaves one of mortals being gulled by the gods: Europa, Asterie, Leda, and many others. And she had the bad taste (and worse judgment) to beat Athena:

Not Pallas nor Envy himself, could find a flaw in [Arachne's] work. The golden-haired goddess [Athena] was indignant at her success, and rent the embroidered web with its heavenly crimes; and as she held a shuttle of Cytorian boxwood, thrice and again she struck Idmonian Arachne's head. The wretched girl could not endure it, and put a noose about her bold neck.

As she hung, Pallas lifted her in pity, and said: "live on, indeed, wicked girl, but hang thou still; and let this same doom of punishment (that thou mayest fear for future times as well) be declared upon thy race, even to remote posterity." So saying, as she turned to go she sprinkled her with the juices of Hecate's herb; and forthwith her hair, touched by the poison, fell off, and with it both nose and ears, and the head shrank up; the whole body also was small; the slender fingers clung to her side as legs; the rest was belly. Still, from this she ever spins a thread; and now, as a spider, she exercises her old-time weaver-art.

—*METAMORPHOSES*, VI. 129-145

6   How appropriate to have Arachne as muse and patroness of the *content* of the electric circuit, the telephone system, the World Wide Web, and the Internet! With her, the governing sense is not the eye, as during Athena's reign, but the gut sense, the visceral and proprioceptive forms of deep awareness. The various webs and nets serve for keeping in touch; each thrilling thread presages a new bit or byte. Instantaneous, unreasoning, participational knowing works here, finding our Western accustomed detachment cumbersome and ponderous.

7   Yet, while there is a great deal to be said for assigning this matriarch as guiding spirit of the *content* of the net and the web, I think there is another, even better suited to the task of patroness of the circuit and the net.

8   Electricity is a monarchical form, not democratic: for patroness it requires not a commoner but a queen. Besides, Arachne, after all, made something from her spinning and weaving. She transformed matter, in a way, and was in turn herself transformed because of her impudence and imprudence.

9   But the World Wide Web is not in the process of becoming some other thing; the Internet is not about to finally realize its real nature as a product, a thing apart. Both the WWW and the Internet ARE. They exist. If they change, they change in size only, by growing and shrinking, for they already have attained their essential natures. They need, then, a deity that combines concern for weaving and so on with an emphasis on being rather than on becoming.

10   Homer gives us one such: the wife of King Odysseus, Queen Penelope.

11   Penelope personifies constancy and circumspection: often Homer bestows upon her the epithet "circumspect Penelope." She emphasizes duration, that is, being, transformation without direction or goal. Several times Homer describes her stratagem, always with the same words. Here, for example, one of the suitors narrates:

> She set up a great loom in her palace, and set to weaving a web of threads long and fine. Then she said to us, "Young men, my suitors now that the great Odysseus has perished, wait, though you are eager to marry me, until I finish this web, so that my weaving will not be useless and wasted. This is a shroud for the hero Laertes, for when the destructive doom of death, which lays men low, shall take him lest any Achaian woman in this neighborhood hold it against me that a man of many conquests lies with no sheet to wind him.
>
> So she spoke, and the proud heart in us was persuaded. Thereafter in the daytime she would weave at her great loom, but in the night she would have torches set by, and undo it. So for three years she was secret in her design, convincing the Achaians, but when the fourth year came, with the seasons returning, and the months waned, and many days had been brought to completion, one of her women, who knew the whole of the story, told us, and we found her in the act of undoing her glorious weaving. So against her will and by force she had to finish it. Then she displayed the great piece of weaving that she had woven. She had washed it and it shone like the sun or the moon.
>
> —*The Odyssey of Homer* Trans. Richard Lattimore.
> (New York: Harper and Row, 1963, 1967. Rpt., 1977),
> XXIV. 129-148

12   No matter that Penelope was eventually forced to finish her weaving: by then the story was over. Her role in it had been to personify constancy, faithfulness, prudence, and resourcefulness. Moreover, she found a technique of passive resistance for deflecting the attacks by the suitors on her marriage and the kingdom. So she, too, undergoes a siege, one that echoes her husband's siege of Troy (and Poseidon's siege of him). Troy fell because of Odysseus' cunning and skill; Penelope is forced to capitulate because of her servant's selfishness and stupidity. Penelope personifies waiting as the isometric modality of being.

13   Another significant difference between our rival patronesses: Arachne entered a contest, the outcome (win or lose) uncertain. Penelope, on the other hand, knows the future (Odysseus will return eventually); she decides to concern herself with the present, with defending and preserving a citadel, and with preserving a state of suspension. Besides a spider's web has a focus or center; a net does not.

14   Let Arachne, then, serve as patroness and guide to those nomadic hunters who wander or surf the webs and nets. She spins tales and casts eloquent images to seize the gaze and stun her prey. She is the huntress and the patroness of those who would seek to exploit the net for a goal, profit. She is the left side of the brain on the net; Penelope is the right side. Let Penelope reign as patroness of this new state itself, not a city-state but a global state with the gossipaceous character of a small village, even as the kingdom of Ithaka was small, but no less royal. Urban and orbal.

15   Finally, what is the significance of what Penelope was doing—weaving a shroud? In the *Odyssey*, she is weaving it for Laertes, son of Arkesios and father of her husband, Odysseus. Laertes, brought back to life by Athena, fought in the last battle in the story (XXIV. 513-525). Fighting alongside his son, he throws the last spear with deadly accuracy and force.

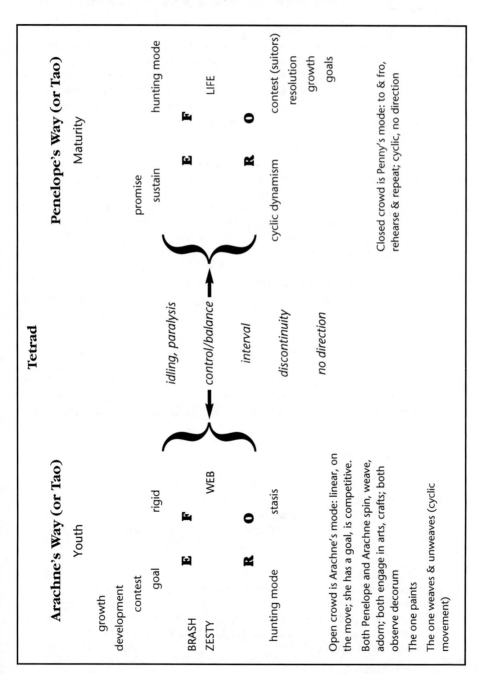

Tetrad

Arachne's Way (or Tao)
Youth

growth
development
contest
goal   **E   F**   rigid   WEB

R   O   stasis

hunting mode

Open crowd is Arachne's mode: linear, on the move; she has a goal, is competitive.

Both Penelope and Arachne spin, weave, adorn; both engage in arts, crafts; both observe decorum

The one paints

The one weaves & unweaves (cyclic movement)

BRASH
ZESTY

idling, paralysis

control/balance

interval

discontinuity

no direction

Penelope's Way (or Tao)
Maturity

promise   hunting mode
sustain   **E   F**   LIFE

R   O   contest (suitors)
cyclic dynamism   resolution
growth
goals

Closed crowd is Penny's mode: to & fro, rehearse & repeat; cyclic, no direction

16   Today, once again, Penelope weaves her shroud, a shroud for the growing millions of disembodied users of the net. This shroud enfolds the world, the World Wide Shroud. And it is never finished, just like the essay thrown out on the net which the author and readers can tinker with, and elaborate on, and comment on, and undo and redo endlessly. And it resembles the net itself, which also shrinks by night and expands by day. The net and the web are themselves encyclopedias, culture-poems of corporate—anonymous, unanimous—authorship.

17   So today, we find ourselves in just such a mythic world of encyclopedic simultaneity: the net and web yield at every moment the living circle of cliché human knowledge, not the shop-worn one-thing-at-a-time narrative laden with archetypes. Our mode now has to be epic, not lyric or dramatic. Not tragic (for finding a private identity), but instead decidedly comic, for the job facing us is that of the beachhead, that of founding a community.

 ## Topics for Critical Thinking and Writing

1. Why does McLuhan look to ancient mythology for an image of the contemporary age, the "electric age . . . the age of the Internet" (especially in a book entitled *Electric Language: Understanding the Present*)?
2. Why might he choose to look for a "patroness" rather than a patron?
3. Search the Internet for more information on Athena, Arachne, and Penelope. (You might start with a search of classical mythology.) What does your search tell you about these ancient figures? Why might McLuhan have chosen them? Do you agree or disagree that these figures are appropriate images, and why or why not?
4. Why does McLuhan assert that Arachne is appropriate as "muse and patroness of the *content* of the electric circuit, the telephone system, the World Wide Web, and the Internet" and then assert that Penelope is even more appropriate? Why might he state that "[Arachne] is the left side of the brain on the net; Penelope is the right side"?
5. What does the title mean? And, why might McLuhan write "Arachne and Penelope" and then "Queen of the Net, Mistress of the Web" when Penelope is the queen? What is the effect of this reversal?
6. Ultimately, McLuhan does not write much directly about the Internet and the Web in this chapter of his book: what is he saying indirectly about these features of the electric age?
7. What different writing strategies does he use (see Part Two of this textbook) and to what effect?

 ## MARSHALL MCLUHAN

Canadian Marshall McLuhan (1911–80), who has been referred to as the "Oracle of the Electronic Age," was a leading authority on culture and technology and coined the phrase "The medium is the message." As a communications theorist, he is best known for his books The Gutenberg Galaxy *(1962),* Understanding Media *(1964), and* The Medium Is the Massage *(1967).*

The Role of New Media in Social Change

1 From the Neolithic age until the advent of electromagnetic technology men have been busy extending their bodies technologically. The fragmentation of work and social action that results from specialized extensions of the body has been given close study by Lynn White, in his *Medieval Technology and Social Change*. He opens with a consideration of the stirrup as it modified social organization in the early Middle Ages. As an extension of the foot, the stirrup enabled men to wear armor on horseback. Man became a sort of tank. But armor was expensive. It required the work and skill of a craftsman for a year to turn out a full suit of armor. The small farmer could not pay for such armor. The result was a change in the entire landholding pattern. The Feudal System was spurred into existence by the stirrup, the mere extension of the foot.

2 The extensions of hand and arm and back that made up the industrial complex of the eighteenth and nineteenth centuries were meshed with Gutenberg technology[1] to create the great team efforts of assembly-line patterns of work and production. But the industrial complex was based on specialist fragmentation of tasks and extensions of the body which carried to an extreme the division of labor that had begun in the Neolithic period in about 3000 B.C.

3 A totally different kind of extension occurred with the application of electromagnetism to social organization. Electricity enabled us to extend the central nervous system itself. It is a biological kind of event that creates maximal involvement of each of us in the total social process. Electric speed tends to abolish time and space in human awareness. There is no delay in the effect of one event upon another. The electric extension of the nervous system creates the unified field of organically interrelated structures that we call the present Age of Information. With the reduction of time and space in the pattern of events there is not only a great increase in the amount of data for daily experience, but action and reaction tend to become fused. Whereas in the previous technologies of fragmented extensions of the body there had been typically a considerable gap in time between social action and the ensuing consequences and reactions, this gap of time has almost disappeared. We are confronted with a situation that invites simultaneous or configurational and ecological awareness instead of the older awareness of sequential and linear cause and effect. In the mechanical age of the wheel and the lever, acceleration had expanded and enlarged the sphere of action. At electric or instant speeds the same sphere contracts almost to the dimensions of a single consciousness. Listening to a concert with an eminent psychologist, I happened to mention the highly tactile character of orchestral strings as compared with the other instruments. He seemed quite surprised and asked: "Do you mean that an auditory experience can have a tactile component?" Discussing the matter with him later, it became apparent that many psychologists assume that not only is auditory experience merely auditory, but so with the other senses. Visual experience is merely visual, etc. Thus, in such a view, there would be little difference in the experience and effects of TV and movies. And indeed many students of the media assume that it is the content of media, whether of the sung word, the spoken word, the written word, that really matters. It is this sort of assumption that has tended to divert attention away from

[1]Johannes Gutenberg (1397–1468) invented the modern printing press in 1440, and he produced the first book using movable type. (Editors' note)

the forms and parameters of the media themselves. The sensory modalities of the media as such have not been studied. The very idea of "content" which obsesses us, on the other hand, is unknown to non-literate societies. Our Western divisions between form and content occur with literacy and because of literacy. Literacy is itself a work of intense visual stress in a culture. When men begin to translate the speech complex into a visual code they have already opted for a division of labor that affects the whole society. They have become settled and have begun to specialize. Writing is impossible for man the food-gatherer but it is inevitable for Neolithic man, the agriculturalist.

4   In his monumental study of *The Beginnings of Architecture*, Siegfried Giedion has many occasions to comment on the fact that before script there is no architecture. Until man intensifies the visual parameters of his life by writing, he cannot *enclose* space. Before writing, man resorts to hollowed-out spaces. The parameters of hollowed-out space are mainly tactile, kinetic, and auditory. The visual components of the cave are minimal. Such proprioceptive space is almost like that of clothing, an immediate extension of our bodies. In our own electric age, space for the physicist has become a non-visual thing of complex stresses. It is no longer uniform and continuous but diverse and heterogeneous. On the other hand, when Newton's physics first entered the European ken, Pascal moaned: "The eternal silence of these infinite spaces terrifies me." Before Newton our Western space orientation had had a much smaller visual parameter but the auditory components of space-structure had been very high. With the advent of the printed word, the visual modalities of Western life increased beyond anything experienced in any previous society. The parameters of the visual as such are continuity, uniformity, and connectedness. These are not the notes or modes of any of our other senses. Today, when our electric technologies have extended far more than our visual faculties, the parameters of sense experience in the Western world have been radically altered. Our new media—the telephone, the telegraph and radio and television—are extensions of the nervous system.

5   I suggest that the sensory typology of an entire population is directly altered by each and every new extension of the body or of the senses. Each extension is an amplification that in varying but measurable degrees, alters the hierarchy of sensory preference in ordering daily experience and environment for whole populations.

6   Thus, it is an ancient observation, that was repeated by Henri Bergson, that speech is a technology of extension that amplified man's power to store and exchange perceptual knowledge; but it interrupted the sharing of a unified collective consciousness experienced by pre-verbal man. Before speech, it is argued, men possessed a large measure of extra-sensory perceptions which was fragmented by speech technology.

7   Until electro-magnetism over a century ago, all the extensions of man appear as fragmentary. Tools and weapons, clothing and housing, as much as the wheel, or letters, are direct, specialist extensions of our bodies that amplify and channel energies in a specialist and fragmented way. Today much study is being devoted to the micro-climates created for our bodies by clothing. Some measurements indicate that unclad societies eat 40 percent more than those that are clad. As a technology of physical extensions, clothing channels time and energies for special tasks. It also changes the patterns of sensory perception and awareness; and nudity has very different meanings in different cultures. So it is with all the other extensions of ourselves.

8   The problem of dichotomy between form and content, that troubles and con-
fuses our Western perception of media today, is now beginning to yield to new
awareness of structures, of total fields in interplay, and to ecological approaches
in general. We still need to develop awareness of the pervasive visual parameters
and assumptions that phonetic literacy had imposed upon Western culture for
2000 years. Today, even the physicist is often hampered by his unconscious visual
bias. This bias is utterly inhibiting to the physicist since his data are almost
entirely non-visual. It is thus not at all accidental that physics is mainly cultivated
by men from cultural areas in which visual values are at a minimum. The unfortunate effects of highly literate culture on the state of the physical sciences is a
theme of Milic Capek's *The Philosophical Impact of Contemporary Physics*. In
the West our intense visual bias and our habit of considering form and content as
quite separate derives from the structure of the phonetic alphabet. There is only
one such alphabet, among the many kinds of scripts. And the unique property of
our alphabet that is unknown to the Chinese or to the Egyptian is its power to
separate sound, sight, and meaning. The letters of our alphabet are semantically
neutral. They can translate the words of any language. But they translate them by
semantically meaningless sounds into semantically meaningless visual symbols.
This divorce between the visual code and the semantic structure has gradually
permeated and shaped all the perceptions of Western literate man.

9   We have long stressed content and ignored form in communication. But this
visual and literate structuring of our perceptions has provided us with very little
accompanying immunity to the effects of non-visual form. We were amused in
1900 when the Chinese protested that vertical telegraph poles would upset the
psychic equilibrium of their people. We still imagine that the effects of radio
depend upon radio programs. Yet such literate assumptions were no protection
against Fascism. When radio began in Europe it awakened the ancient tribal
energies in their auditory depths, as radio does today in backward countries. The
auditory form of radio has, of course, a quite different effect in literate societies
from its effect in oral and auditory cultures. Intensely visual and industrial cultures like England and America had few remaining tribal roots and vestiges to be
re-energized by the tribal drum of radio. Where such roots still existed as in
Ireland, Wales, and Scotland, there were marked tribal stirrings and revivals. In
the more urban and industrialized England and America radio was mainly felt as
a resurgence of the folk arts of jazz and song and dancing. In areas like Germany,
where tribal experience had been retained by many linguistic and artistic means,
radio meant a revival of mystic forms of togetherness and depth involvement
that has not been forgotten.

10   In the same way, the effect of TV has been very different in Europe and in the
U.S.A. The TV image of "mosaic," as it is named by the TV engineers, has a quite different sensory character and effect from the movie and photographic image. The
mosaic of the TV image provides, structurally, an experience of what J. J. Gibson
calls "active or exploratory touch" as opposed to passive or cutaneous touch.

11   The TV mosaic created by the "scanning finger" is visually of low definition, making for maximal involvement of the viewer. The painters after
Cézanne, in the 1860s, deliberately set about to endow the retinal impression
with tactual values. In order to involve their audience maximally they resorted
to various low-definition visual effects, many of which anticipated the typical
form of the TV image. They achieved an effect described by J. J. Gibson in his
experiments when he reports, "The paradox is even more striking, for tactual

perception corresponds well to the form of the object when the stimulus is almost formless, and less well when the stimulus is a stable representation of the form of the object. A clear unchanging perception arises when the flow of sense impressions changes most."

12   At the same time as Monet and Seurat and Rouault were dimming the visual parameters of art in order to achieve maximal audience participation, the symbolists were demonstrating the superiority of suggestion over statement in poetry. The same principle obtains on the telephone as compared with radio. The auditory image of the telephone is of low definition. It elicits maximal attention and cannot be used as background. All the senses rally to strengthen the weak sound of the phone. We even feel the need to be kinetically involved via doodling or pacing. And whereas we complete the strong auditory image of radio by visualizing, we only slightly visualize on the phone.

13   Dr. Llewellyn-Thomas has used the Mackworth head-camera to study the eye-movements of children watching TV. There is great significance in his discovery that the eyes of the child never waiver [*sic*] from the faces of the actors even in scenes of violence. Maximal involvement is experienced not in the action of the scene but in the *reactions* of the actors in the scenes. The result is the same as the one recorded by J. J. Gibson concerning tactual perception as most adequate when the stimulus was almost formless. That is, exploratory touch comes into play as the visual parameter is dimmed. It is a normal feature of the comics. Cartoons and comics are visually very dim affairs. The amount of visual data provided is small. But involvement or exploratory touch is at a maximum. Leo Bogart's study of "comic strips and their Adult Readers" observes how comic strip humor seems to produce a grim, unsmiling kind of amusement for the most part. "Genuine hearty laughs seem to be few and far between." Once more, the involvement is high in these forms just in proportion as the intensity of the stimulus is vague and weak. The same comic scenes projected in high visual definition on a movie screen would evoke much more overt response.

14   Most people were struck by the TV coverage of the Kennedy assassination. We were all conscious of great depth of involvement, but there was no excitement, no sensationalism. When involvement is maximal, we are nearly numb.

15   One of the notable effects of the TV image on those in the primary grades seems to be the development of near-point reading. The average distance from the page of children in the first three grades has recently been measured in Toronto by Dr. W.A. Hurst. The average distance is 6 1/2 inches. The children seem to be striving to do a psychomimetic version of their relation to the TV image. They seem to be trying to read by proprioception and exploratory touch. The printed page, however, is of high definition visually and cannot so be apprehended.

16   It isn't only the act of reading that conflicts with habits of TV perception. I wish to suggest that the depth involvement characteristic of TV viewing discourages the traditional habit and need of "seeing ahead." The TV child today cannot see ahead, in a motivational sense, just because he is so deeply involved. He needs a totally new pedagogy and a new curriculum that will accommodate his shifting sensory ratios and his natural drive towards depth participation since TV. This returns us to the theme that our Western preference for considering the content of media instead of their configurational features is itself a bias of perception derived from the form of phonetic literacy. I do not need to be reminded of how much we owe to literacy. It has given us our way of life. It separated the individual from the tribal horde. I suggest that if we value this legacy of literacy,

we shall need to take steps to maintain its existence by a fuller understanding of the role of new media in social change. Autonomy and freedom are best secured by a grasp of the new parameters of our condition. I would meet you upon this exponentially, as the mathematicians put it.

Topics for Critical Thinking and Writing

1. Why does McLuhan write, "Our new media—the telephone, the telegraph, and radio and television—are extensions of the nervous system" (paragraph 4)? Do you agree or disagree? Why?
2. Jay Ingram argues in "The Atom's Image Problem" (Chapter 11) that we need a visual representation of the atom even if physicists do not; McLuhan argues that many physicists have a visual bias that hampers them in their work. Compare the arguments made about the visual in these two essays.
3. Which sentence in the essay do you think best exemplifies McLuhan's thesis (see pages 14–16 for a review of the thesis)? Why did you choose that particular sentence? Where does it appear in the essay?
4. a. In a 750- to 1000-word essay, apply what McLuhan says about the role of new media to our pervasive use of the computer; how do email and the Internet extend our bodies, integrate form and content, and/or effect social change in the way we think and behave? *Or,*
   b. In a 750- to 1000-word essay, compare Eric McLuhan's "Arachne and Penelope" (previous essay) and Marshall McLuhan's "The Role of New Media in Social Change," using Marshall McLuhan's famous idea "The medium is the message" to focus your analysis.

 ## SEAN MILLS

Sean Mills is a doctoral student at Queen's University, studying the political and intellectual history of Quebec during the 1960s.

Modern, Postmodern, and Post-Postmodern

1   "And what is it that you do, son?" a friend's father asked me in a friendly tone. When I explained to him that I was working on a Ph.D. in Canadian history, he briefly hesitated, then responded: "Interesting . . . but, isn't there something more relevant that you can spend your time doing?"

2   Becoming a historian at the beginning of the twenty-first century is a daunting task. For a student slowly making his or her way through the long and solitary journey of graduate school, the fractured field of Canadian history is both exhilarating and destabilizing. In scholarly journals, debates rage about the significance of history, about the merits of long-accepted approaches to studying the past, and about new methods and theoretical orientations.

3   Yet, alongside this excitement and energy sits a growing uneasiness: as historians have been honing their skills and developing even more nuanced and sophisticated understandings of the past, the role that history plays in the lives of

regular individuals is in sharp decline. One of the most eerie phenomena of our era, Eric Hobsbawm states in his masterful history *Age of Extremes: The Short Twentieth Century, 1914–1991,* is the "destruction of the past." Most young people, he argues, now "grow up in a sort of permanent present lacking any organic relation to the public past of the times they live in."

4   The feeling of living in a perpetual present, with little knowledge of or interest in the past, forms a part of what many theorists have described as the "conditions of postmodernity," the lived experience of the changing social and economic realities of the last forty years. If the modern period could be characterized by a faith in Progress and the triumph of Reason, then the postmodern age is exemplified by a growing skepticism and distrust of grand narratives that once explained both the past and the present and helped orient us towards the future.

5   This mood of skepticism, this distrust of totalizing explanations, this celebration of the partial and fractured nature of all knowledge, made quick inroads into the social sciences and the humanities. A new term, *postmodernism,* quickly emerged as a catchall phrase that sought to give coherence to a wide variety of artistic and philosophical trends.

6   No single essay could possibly explain the many ways in which the term *postmodernism* is used (and abused), but it can generally be said to refer to attacks on the belief that any objective truth can be known about the world. Postmodernists have therefore challenged the very foundations of social thought. They have sought, for example, to discard the idea that the individual self is autonomous and therefore capable of rationally choosing his or her destiny: rather than being innate or chosen, human identity is constructed through discourses. And they have challenged the belief that language can transparently and accurately describe the outside world: rather than presenting a one-to-one relationship with the objects it seeks to describe, language is always multireferential, always open to multiple readings and interpretations.

7   Postmodernists have also aimed their sights directly at historians' claims of objectivity. The past, many claim, does not come to us in the form of a story, with a clear beginning, middle, and an end. Rather, it is historians who decide which facts are included into history and which are left out. Following this logic, any historical study merely represents the perspective of its author, and displaces other equally "true" versions of the past. We therefore need to allow the flourishing of many perspectives, wide varieties of readings, multiple voices.

8   Postmodernism slowly made its way into academic history, not as a specific program or doctrine, but as a change in tone or a new mood. From the end of the 1960s to the end of the 1980s, social history had dominated academic studies of the past. The basic premise of this social history, or "history from the bottom up," was that the material world, and not the world of ideas, acted as the motor force behind historical change. But just when social history seemed to be living its hour of glory, this confidence in the material world, and in the possibility of objective history, slowly began to wane. In the late 1980s, many historians began challenging the social-history consensus. Drawing on postmodernist theories, historians started analyzing the hidden meanings in language, and began articulating the need for a new, more complicated understanding of the workings of power.

9   Not all social historians gave in easily to the new trends, and many forcefully defended both their methods and their belief in the centrality of the material world in history. By the mid-1990s, however, it became clear that postmodernist-inspired historians had opened an important fracture in the foundations that had

previously sustained social history. Out of the cracks emerged new questions, new methods, and new approaches to the past.

10   For one, postmodernism forced historians to be more aware of their own sub-jectivities. They were forced to recognize that writing from a particular position shaped what one saw in the past, and therefore influenced the type of history that an author produced. Historians also acquired the tools to recognize the constructed nature of words and classifications that they had previously taken for granted. Seemingly self-evident categories like "men" and "women," or "white" and "black," were shown to have been constructed in various ways at different points in history. Rather than being self-evident, the categories themselves became subject to histori-cal scrutiny, and researchers generally found ample evidence to support their claims that the terms of reference were by no means natural or stable.

11   It is now almost twenty years since postmodernism first rippled the tranquil waters of academic history. While it is clear that it has brought us a great number of tools and methods that help us understand the past, postmodernist-inspired history is not without its flaws. While social historians often placed too much weight on the material world and too little on politics and ideology, the new his-tory sometimes reverses the problem, seeing the entire world through the lens of language and representation and downplaying the role that economic condi-tions played in people's lives in the past (and present). Also, the jargon-laden lan-guage in which much of the new history is written seriously limits its appeal to a wider audience, having the unintended side effect of ensuring that this "democ-ratic" history is often only understood by a small circle of specialists.

12   In hindsight, however, it is clear that, if nothing else, postmodernism has had an important impact on the world of academic history in that it provoked much rethinking of established methods and theories. Historians are now humbly resigned to the fact that they will never be able to come up with a defin-itive history, one that never needs to be revised. They know that a new genera-tion will see things in the historical record that they could not, and that their his-tories will always remain partial and incomplete.

13   Perhaps because of historians' humbled aspirations, or because of the dimin-ished role of the scholar, or even because of the lingering social-history tradition, historians today no longer ask the "big" questions that they once did. Under the conditions of postmodernity, historians have more modest goals. For a genera-tion that cut its teeth in reaction to the conservative national history that came before it, this is perhaps unavoidable. Over the past forty years, historians have researched and discovered the incredible richness of the country's past. We now know more than we once thought possible about the lives of ordinary men and women, about their social conditions and about the subjective ways in which they formed their multifaceted identities. What we have largely lost, however, is any picture of the whole, any larger portrait that can give coherence to people's everyday experiences.

14   The new generation of emerging historians will not be able to avoid these larger questions. But when they turn their attention to the larger picture, follow-ing the lead of a few members of the older generation, they will not do so by repudiating either the social or the postmodernist-inspired history that went before them. The insights are too many, the evidence too compelling, the argu-ments too profound. Rather, they will build on their foundations, explore their strengths, and question their weaknesses.

15 Under the conditions of postmodernity, we know that history is, and always will be, an imperfect tool for understanding the past. But admitting that it is imperfect is not the same as claiming that it is useless. History is certainly a flawed tool for understanding the world around us, for giving coherence to the seeming incoherence of everyday life, but it is still the best tool that we have.

 ## Topics for Critical Thinking and Writing

1. a. Write a summary of Mills's explanation both of modern/modernism and of postmodern/postmodernism. (You might find it helpful to review the relevant sections of this textbook; to find these, see "summary" in the Index at the back of this book.)
   b. In your own words, explain what the approach of postmodernism is.
   c. Why might Mills have chosen *not* to refer directly to "post-postmodern," the third term in his title, in the essay? What does Mills implicitly say about "the post-postmodern" or post-postmodernism?
2. What does Mills mean by "the subjective ways in which [men and women] formed their multifaceted identities" (paragraph 13)? You may find it helpful to review "A Range of Critical Approaches," Chapter 18, to help you answer this question.
3. In light of Thomas King's claim that "the truth about stories is that that's all we are" (meaning that we can't understand the world without telling stories), compare and discuss Mills's essay about different ways of viewing and studying history and Thomas King's short story "One Good Story, That One" (Chapter 18) about perspectives on stories and history.

 # BHARATI MUKHERJEE

Bharati Mukherjee was born into a wealthy and traditional family in Calcutta, India, where, as a young child, she experienced the violence that resulted from the Indian Independence Act in 1947, which partitioned India and Pakistan. Raised and educated in India and England, Mukherjee moved to Iowa to attain a master's degree and a Ph.D. She moved to Canada in 1966, becoming a naturalized citizen in 1972. Preferring to live in the United States, citing the difficulty she experienced as a "visible minority" in Canada, she moved back there in 1980 and took out American citizenship. Mukherjee is a professor of creative writing, and she is a well-known writer of fiction and non-fiction; this essay originally appeared in Saturday Night *(1981).*

An Invisible Woman

1 This story begins in Calcutta and ends in a small town in New York State called Saratoga Springs. The very long, fifteen-year middle is set in Canada. In this story, no place or person fares well, but Canada comes off poorest of all.

2 I was born in Calcutta, that most Victorian and British of post-independence Indian cities. It was not the Calcutta of documentary films—not a hell where beggars fought off dying cattle for still-warm garbage—but a gracious, green,

subtropical city where Irish nuns instructed girls from better families on how to hold their heads high and how to drop their voices to a whisper and still be heard and obeyed above the screams of the city.

3   There was never a moment when we did not know that our city and our country were past their prime. We carried with us the terrible knowledge that while our lives were comfortable, they would be safer somewhere else. Ambition dictated emigration. In the 1950s everyone was waiting for the revolution. "The first thing the Communists do," my best friend told me when we were fifteen, "is feel your hands. If your hands are soft, it's *kaput* for you." In our school every girl had soft hands. But when Stalin died, the nuns prayed for his soul: this was known as "fair play," an example for us pliant, colonial girls to follow.

4   In a city continually blistered with revolutionary fervour, we plodded through our productions of *The Mikado*.[1] At least twice I was escorted by van loads of police past striking workers outside the gates of my father's factory so that I could go to school and dance a quadrille or play a walk-on part. "Our girls can take their places with the best anywhere in the world," Mother John-Baptist, the headmistress, had promised my father on my first day of school. (And we have, all over India and the English-speaking, even German-speaking, world.) On a sticky August night in 1961, when my younger sister, who was going to Vassar College, and I, on my way to the University of Iowa, left by Air India for New York, I felt that I could.

5   Great privilege had been conferred upon me; my struggle was to work hard enough to deserve it. And I did. This bred confidence, but not conceit. I never doubted that if I wanted something—a job, a scholarship—I could get it. And I did. I had built-in advantages: primarily those of education, secondarily those of poise and grooming. I knew that if I decided to return to India after my writing degree at Iowa was finished, my father would find me a suitable husband. I would never work, never be without servants and comfort, and I could dabble in the arts until they bored me. My daughters would attend the same school as I had, my sons a similar school. It was unthinkable that they would not be class leaders, then national leaders, and that they would not perpetuate whatever values we wished to give them. Such is the glory, and the horror, of a traditional society, even at its tattered edges.

6   I had no trouble at Iowa, and though I learned less about those Vietnam and assassination years than I might have, I liked the place well enough to stay on and arrange for extensions of my scholarship. I married an American, Clark Blaise, whose parents had come from Canada and then divorced, and whose mother had returned to Winnipeg. I stayed on for a PhD, thus cutting off forever the world of passive privilege I had come from. An MA in English is considered refined, but a doctorate is far too serious a business, indicative more of brains than beauty, and likely to lead to a quarrelsome nature. We had a son, and when that son was almost two we moved to Canada. Clark had dreamed restless dreams of Canada, especially of Montréal. Still unformed at twenty-five, he felt it was the place that would let him be himself.

7   It is now the summer of 1966, and the three of us cross at Windsor in a battered VW van. Our admission goes smoothly, for I have a lecturer's position at McGill. I say "smoothly," but I realize now there was one curious, even comic

[1]*The Mikado* (1880) is an operetta written by Gilbert and Sullivan. (Editors' note)

event that foreshadowed the difficulties faced by Indians in Canada. A middle-aged immigration officer, in filling out my application, asked me the year of my birth. I told him, in that private-school accent of which I was once so proud. Mishearing, he wrote down "1914" and remarked, "Ah, we're the same age." He happened to be exactly twice my age. He corrected his error without a fuss. Ten minutes inside Canada, and I was already invisible.

8   The oldest paradox of prejudice is that it renders its victims simultaneously invisible and over-exposed. I have not met an Indian in Canada who has not suffered the humiliations of being overlooked (in jobs, in queues, in deserved recognition) and from being singled out (in hotels, department stores, on the streets, and at customs). It happened to me so regularly in Canada that I now feel relief, just entering Macy's in Albany, New York, knowing that I won't be followed out by a security guard. In America, I can stay in hotels and *not* be hauled out of elevators or stopped as I enter my room. It's perhaps a small privilege in the life of a North American housewife—not to be taken automatically for a shoplifter or a whore—but it's one that my years in Canada, and especially my two years in Toronto, have made me grateful for. I know objections will be raised; I know Canadians all too well. Which of us has *not* been harassed at customs? On a summer's night, which of us *can* walk down Yonge Street without carloads of stoned youths shouting out insults? We have all stood patiently in bakery lines, had people step in front of us, we've all waved our plastic numbers and wailed, "But I was next—"

9   If we are interested in drawing minute distinctions, we can disregard or explain away nearly anything. ("Where did it happen? Oh, *Rosedale.*[2] Well, no wonder . . ." Or, "Were you wearing a sari? No? Well, no wonder . . ." Or, "Oh, *we* wouldn't do such a thing. He must have been French or something . . .") And I know the pious denials of hotel clerks. In a Toronto hotel I was harassed by two house detectives who demanded to see my room key before allowing me to go upstairs to join my family—harassed me in front of an elevator-load of leering, elbow-nudging women. When I complained, I extracted only a "some of my best friends are Pakis" from the night manager, as he fervently denied that what I had just experienced was in fact a racial incident.

10   And I know the sanctimonious denials of customs officers, even as they delight in making people like me dance on the head of a bureaucratic pin. On a return from New York to Toronto I was told, after being forced to declare a $1 valuation on a promotional leaflet handed out by a bookstore, that even a book of matches had to be declared. ("I didn't ask if you *bought* anything. Did you hear me ask about purchases? Did you? I'll ask you again in very clear English. *Are you bringing anything into the country?*")

11   Do not think that I enjoy writing this of Canada. I remain a Canadian citizen. This is the testament of a woman who came, like most immigrants, confident of her ability to do good work, in answer to a stated need. After the unsophisticated, beer-swilling rednecks of Iowa, British-Commonwealth Canada, and Montréal in particular, promised a kind of haven. At the road-stops in Iowa and Illinois, when I entered in a sari, silverware would drop, conversations cease; it was not the kind of attention I craved. It was never a hostile reaction (it might have been, in the Deep South, but I avoided that region). It was innocent, dumbfounded stupefaction, and I thought I would be happy enough to leave it behind. As we drove past Toronto on the 401, we picked up the strains of sitar music on

[2]Rosedale is a wealthy Anglo area of Toronto. (Editors' note)

the radio; Montréal had spice shops and was soon to have Indian restaurants. It should have been a decent country, and we should have been happy in it.

12   I have been in America, this time, for only a few months, but in that time I've been attacked by a streaker on Sixth Avenue in New York; my purse has been snatched on Fifth Avenue; our car has been rammed and our insurance defrauded in Saratoga Springs; a wallet has been stolen and our children have complained of the drinking and dope-smoking even in their schoolrooms. Yes, it's America: violent, mindlessly macho, conformist, lawless. And certainly no dark-skinned person has the right to feel comfortable inside American history. Yet I do. If I am not exempt from victimization here, neither are Clark or my sons, and neither am I exempt from redress. I am less shocked, less outraged and shaken to my core, by a purse-snatching in New York City in which I lost all of my dowry-gold—everything I'd been given by my mother in marriage—than I was by a simple question asked of me in the summer of 1978 by three high-school boys on the Rosedale subway station platform in Toronto. Their question was, "Why don't you go back to Africa?"

13   It hurt because of its calculation, its calm, ignorant satisfaction, its bland assumption of the right to break into my privacy. In New York, I was violated because of my suspected affluence (a Gucci purse) and my obviously foreign, heedless non-defensiveness. Calcutta equipped me to survive theft or even assault; it did not equip me to accept proof of my unworthiness. (Friends say, "Rosedale? Well . . ." or "Teenagers, well . . ." and I don't dispute them. But I owe it to my friends, and I have many friends in Canada, to dig deeper.)

14   Thanks to Canadian rhetoric on the highest level, I have learned several things about myself that I never suspected. The first is that I have no country of origin. In polite company, I am an "East Indian" (the opposite, presumably, of a "West Indian"). The East Indies, in my school days, were Dutch possessions, later to become Indonesia. In impolite company I'm a "Paki" (a British slur unknown in America, I'm happy to say). For an Indian of my generation, to be called a "Paki" is about as appealing as it is for an Israeli to be called a Syrian. In an official Green Paper on Immigration and Population,[3] I learn that I'm something called a "visible minority" from a "non-traditional area of immigration" who calls into question the "absorptive capacity" of Canada. And that big question (to which my contribution is really not invited) is, "What kind of society do we really want?"

15   A spectre is haunting Canada: the perfidious "new" (meaning "dark" and thus, self-fulfillingly, "non-assimilatable") immigrant, coming to snatch up jobs, welfare cheques, subway space, cheap apartments, and blue-eyed women.

16   The Green Paper in 1975—which seemed an admirable exercise in demographic planning, an open invitation to join in a "debate"—was really a premeditated move on the part of the government to throw some bones (some immigrants) to the howling wolves. The "we" of that open question was understood to mean the Anglo-Saxon or Québec-French "founding races"; it opened up the sewers of resentment that polite, British-style forbearance had kept a lid on. My kind of

[3]The Green Paper on Immigration and Population was published in 1975 to encourage "informed and constructive debate" on Canada's immigration policies. Some say it caused unprecedented debate and led to a more thorough, comprehensive policy; however, others contend that the federal government did not wait for the public debate before drafting legislation. Either way, the Immigration Act of 1976 was generally lauded. (Editors' note)

Canadian was assumed, once again, not to exist, not to have a legitimate opinion to offer. ("Well, you could have made an official deposition through the proper multicultural channel whenever hearings were held in your community . . .")

17   Most Indians would date the new up-front violence, the physical assaults, the spitting, the name-calling, the bricks through the windows, the pushing and shoving on the subways—it would be, by this time, a very isolated Indian who has not experienced one or more of those reactions—from the implied consent given to racism by that infamous document. I cannot describe the agony and the betrayal one feels, hearing oneself spoken of by one's own country as being somehow exotic to its nature—a burden, a cause for serious concern. It may have been rhetorically softened, it may have been academic in tone, but in feeling it was Nuremberg, and it unleashed its own mild but continuing *Kristallnacht.*[4] In that ill-tempered debate, the government itself appropriated the language, the reasoning, the motivation that had belonged—until then—to disreputable fringe groups. Suddenly it was all right, even patriotic, to blame these non-assimilatable Asian homes for urban crowding, unemployment, and welfare burdens. And the uneducated, unemployed, welfare-dependent, native-born *lumpen* teenagers leaped at the bait.

18   It is not pleasant to realize your own government has betrayed you so coldly.

19   What about the "absorptive capacity" of the ambitious immigrant to take in all these new, startling descriptions of himself? It creates double-vision when self-perception is so utterly at odds with social standing. We are split from our most confident self-assumptions. We must be blind, stupid, or egomaniacal to maintain self-respect or dignity when society consistently undervalues our contribution. In Montréal, I was, simultaneously, a full professor at McGill, an author, a confident lecturer, and (I like to think) a charming and competent hostess and guest—*and* a house-bound, fearful, aggrieved, obsessive, and unforgiving queen of bitterness. Whenever I read articles about men going berserk, or women committing suicide, and read the neighbours' dazed pronouncements ("But he was always so friendly, so outgoing, never a problem in the world . . ."), I knew I was looking into a mirror. Knowing that the culture condescended toward me, I needed ways of bolstering my self-respect—but those ways, at least to politely raised, tightly disciplined women of my age and origin, can only be achieved in society, in the recognition of our contributions.

20   And there, of course, I am up against another Canadian dilemma. I have always been struck by an oddity, call it a gap, in the cultural consciousness of the Canadian literary establishment. For fifteen years I was a professor of English and of creative writing at McGill. I published novels, stories, essays, reviews. In a land that fills its airports with itinerant poets and story-tellers, I was invited only once to give a reading by myself (after *Days and Nights in Calcutta* appeared, Clark and I, who had written it together, were frequently invited together). On that one occasion, I learned, after arriving in a mining town at three in the morn-

[4]After the Nuremberg Laws of 1935 denied German citizenship to Jews, the rights of Jews were increasingly restricted in Germany. On the night of November 9, 1938, Nazi youth carried out a pogrom known as *Kristallnacht* or "The Night of Broken Glass." The violence and looting resulted in a number of Jews being murdered and thousands being deported, as well as the destruction of hundreds of Jewish homes, businesses, and synagogues. It was a harbinger of what the Nazis called "The Final Solution" and we call the Holocaust. (Editors' note)

ing, that I'd been invited from the jacket photo and was expected to "come across." ("The others did.") No provisions had been made for my stay, except in my host's bachelor house. ("Oh, you let him meet you at the airport at three a.m.? And you went back to his house thinking there was a wife?") Friends explained to me that really, since nothing happened (except a few shoves and pushes), I shouldn't mention it again. Until now, I haven't.

21   Of course, it is possible to interpret everything in a different light. While no one likes to be pawed, isn't it nice to be acknowledged, even this way? (Don't laugh, it was suggested.) My point is simply this: an Indian slips out of invisibility in this culture at considerable peril to body and soul. I've alluded briefly (in *Days and Nights*) to the fact that I was not invited to join the Writers' Union of Canada, back at its founding, even though at that particular moment I was a Canadian and Clark was not (my Indian citizenship conferred special dispensations that his American one did not). The first explanation for the oversight was that the invitation extended to Clark was "assumed" to include me. While even a low-grade feminist might react uncomfortably to such a concoction, another, and I think truthful, explanation was offered. "We didn't know how to spell your name, and we were afraid of insulting you," a well-known writer later wrote me. She's right; I would have been insulted (just as I'm mildly insulted by Canada Council letters to "Mr. Bharati Blaise"). And then, with a tinge of self-justification, she continued: "Your book was published by an American publisher and we couldn't get hold of it, so . . ."

22   Well, it's an apology and an explanation and it's easy to forgive as an instance of the persistent amateurism in the Canadian soul. But if you scrutinize just a little harder, and if you've dipped into the well of forgiveness far too often, you see a very different interpretation. *If you don't have a family compact name, forget about joining us.* If you don't have Canadian content, forget about publishing here. "The only Canadian thing about the novel is that it was written by a woman who now lives in Montréal," said a reviewer of my second novel, *Wife*, in *Books in Canada* (she was herself a feminist and emerging ethnicist), not even recognizing a book aimed right at her. "How can you call yourself a Canadian writer if you didn't play in snow as a child?" asked a CBC television interviewer. And more severely: "How do you justify taking grants and then not writing about Canada?"

23   The answer to all that is that I do write about Canada, perhaps not as directly as I am writing now, but that I refuse to capitulate to the rawness of Canadian literature—and, more to the point, I refuse to set my work in Canada because to do so would be to reduce its content to the very subject of this essay: politics and paranoia and bitter disappointment. The condition of the Indian in Canada is a sociological and political subject. We've not yet achieved the ease that would permit us to write of the self and of the expanding consciousness. To set my work in Canada is necessarily to adopt an urgent and strident tone; I would find irony an ill-considered option in any such situation. I advocate, instead, fighting back.

24   In case anyone finds a copy of *Wife*, it should be read in the following way: the nominal setting is Calcutta and New York City. But in the mind of the heroine, it is always Toronto.

25   Fifteen years ago, the Indian was an exotic in America, except in university towns and maybe New York City. Now I doubt if there's a town in America without its Indian family—even Saratoga Springs has Indian dentists and pediatricians. I am no longer an exotic butterfly (people used to stagger up to me, quite unconscious that there was a young woman inside the folds of brilliant cloth,

just to feel the material, and then walk away). Nor am I a grubby, dishonest, smelly, ignorant, job-snatching, baby-breeding, unassimilatable malcontent. For the first time in my adult life, I am unemployed—the price I was obliged to pay for immigration to the United States. Clark this year is teaching in the local college. Our income is less than a third of what it has been, and dark times are coming. Next year, I can take the job Clark is filling now; the college has made us an interesting proposal, though it leaves many questions unanswered. Will Clark then stay here or return? He doesn't know.

26   America trusts confrontation; its rough sense of justice derives from slugging it out. It tolerates contradictions that seem, in retrospect, monstrous. Perhaps it trusts to the Constitution and the knowledge that somehow, someday, that document will resolve all difficulties. This is not the British style, not the Canadian style, in which conflict is viewed as evidence of political failure. In Canada, Parliament's sacred duty is the preservation of order; its mandate, at least in recent years, is to anticipate disorder. I can appreciate that, and if I were a white mainstream Canadian I'd probably endorse it wholeheartedly. Toronto really is a marvellous, beautiful city, as I tell all my American friends. Good God, if ever there was a city I should have been happy in, it was Toronto.

27   But when you are part of the Canadian and Toronto underbelly, invisible and nakedly obvious, you can't afford a white man's delusions. It's in Canada that a columnist can write a glib and condescending book, attack the frail, ineffective civil liberties legislation in the country, and be called a brilliant and daring intellectual. It's Canada that struggles against a constitution of its own, and its premiers who downgrade the concept of a human rights charter.

28   While preparing to write this account, I interviewed dozens of people, mostly of Indian and Pakistani origin, in many parts of Canada. I read until I grew sick—of the assaults, the recommendations, the testimonies. I attended meetings, I talked to grandparents, and I talked to high-schoolers. I walked with the police down the troubled streets of east-end Toronto; I pursued some of the more lurid stories of the past year in Toronto. I turned down collaboration on some other stories; I did not feel Canadian enough to appear on a TV programme celebrating the accomplishments of new Canadians; nor did I wish to take part in a TV show that set out to ascribe suicides among Indo-Canadian women solely to community pressures to have male children. Friends who supported this research will probably not find their observations in this piece; they will find, instead, that I turned it all inside out.

29   To a greater or lesser extent those friends and I share a common history. We came in the mid-1960s for professional reasons. We saw scope and promise, and we were slow to acknowledge the gathering clouds. Some of us have reacted positively, working with the local or provincial governments, serving as consultants, as organizers, as impresarios of understanding. Others have taken hockey sticks on vigilante patrols to protect their people. Many, including myself, have left, unable to keep our twin halves together.

Topics for Critical Thinking and Writing

1. What contrasts does Mukherjee develop between Canada and the United States?
2. Do you agree with Mukherjee that Canada, the multicultural nation, is a monolith, and the United States, the melting pot, is diverse? Does this

view of the two nations depend upon where she lived and travelled in each country?

3. What is the significance of the title "An Invisible Woman"?
4. Mukherjee advocates "fighting back," and yet she chose to move to the United States. Is this a capitulation or a reflection of just how difficult she found it to live in Canada?
5. Have you or people you know experienced the insidious violence of subtle racism or the physical violence of overt racism?
6. Research the historical events that occurred in India when Mukherjee lived there (1940–1961) or in Canada when she lived here (1966–80). How is her writing influenced by these events?

 NICHOLAS NEGROPONTE

Nicholas Negroponte, born in 1943, holds degrees in architecture from the Massachusetts Institute of Technology, where he founded the renowned Media Lab and where he now teaches. He is a co-creator and was a regular contributor to Wired *magazine. He also helped to found a charity that provides hundred-dollar laptops for children in developing countries. Among his influential books are* The Architecture Machine *(1970) and (the source of the following brief essay)* Being Digital *(1995), in which Negroponte discusses human–computer interfaces and the connections among the entertainment, information, and interactive worlds.*

Being Asynchronous

1   A face-to-face or telephone conversation is real time and synchronous. Telephone tag is a game played to find the opportunity to be synchronous. Ironically, this is often done for exchanges, which themselves require no synchrony whatsoever, and could just as well be handled by non-real-time message passing. Historically, asynchronous communication, like letter writing, has tended to be more formal and less off-the-cuff exchanges. This is changing with voice mail and answering machines.

2   I have met people who claim they cannot understand how they (and we all) lived without answering machines at home and voice mail at the office. The advantage is less about voice and more about off-line processing and time shifting. It is about leaving messages versus engaging somebody needlessly in on-line discussion. In fact, answering machines are designed slightly backward. They should not only activate when you are not there or don't want to be there, but they should *always* answer the telephone and give the caller the opportunity to simply leave a message.

3   One of the enormous attractions of e-mail is that it is not interruptive like a telephone. You can process it at your leisure, and for this reason you may reply to messages that would not stand a chance in hell of getting through the secretarial defenses of corporate, telephonic life.

4   E-mail is exploding in popularity because it is *both* an asynchronous and a computer-readable medium. The latter is particularly important, because interface agents will use those bits to prioritize and deliver messages differently. Who sent the message and what it is about could determine the order in which you see it—no different from the current secretarial screening that allows a call from

your six-year-old daughter to go right through, while the CEO of the XYZ Corporation is put on hold. Even on a busy workday, personal e-mail messages might drift to the top of the heap.

5   Not nearly as much of our communications need to be contemporaneous or in real time. We are constantly interrupted or forced into being punctual for things that truly do not merit such immediacy or promptness. We are forced into regular rhythms, not because we finished eating at 8:59 p.m., but because the TV program is about to start in one minute. Our great-grandchildren will understand our going to the theater at a given hour to benefit from the collective presence of human actors, but they will not understand the synchronous experiencing of television signals in the privacy of our home—until they look at the bizarre economic model behind it.

 ## Topics for Critical Thinking and Writing

1. Do you agree with Negroponte that "answering machines . . . should *always* answer the telephone"? Explain.
2. Whom is Negroponte addressing in paragraph 3? Does the attraction of email he cites apply to anyone else? Explain.
3. When did you start to use email? How do you currently use it? What advantages or disadvantages do you find in "being asynchronous"?
4. Think about technological developments over the past five or ten years. Choose one and discuss its advantages and disadvantages.

 # GEORGE ORWELL

George Orwell (1903–50), an Englishman, adopted this name; he was born Eric Blair, in India. He was educated at Eton, in England, but in 1921 he went to Burma, where he served for five years as a police officer, about which he published the following piece in 1936. He then returned to Europe, doing odd jobs while writing novels and stories, of which the most well-known are Animal Farm *(1945) and* 1984 *(1949). In 1936 he fought in the Spanish Civil War on the side of the Republicans, an experience reported in* Homage to Catalonia *(1938). His last years were spent writing in England.*

Shooting an Elephant

1   In Moulmein, in Lower Burma, I was hated by large numbers of people—the only time in my life that I have been important enough for this to happen to me. I was sub-divisional police officer of the town, and in an aimless, petty kind of way anti-European feeling was very bitter. No one had the guts to raise a riot, but if a European woman went through the bazaars alone somebody would probably spit betel juice over her dress. As a police officer I was an obvious target and was baited whenever it seemed safe to do so. When a nimble Burman tripped me up on the football field and the referee (another Burman) looked the other way, the crowd yelled with hideous laughter. This happened more than once. In the end the sneering yellow faces of young men that met me everywhere, the insults hooted after me when I was at a safe distance, got badly on my nerves. The

young Buddhist priests were the worst of all. There were several thousands of them in the town and none of them seemed to have anything to do except stand on street corners and jeer at Europeans.

2   All this was perplexing and upsetting. For at that time I had already made up my mind that imperialism was an evil thing and the sooner I chucked up my job and got out of it the better. Theoretically—and secretly, of course—I was all for the Burmese and all against their oppressors, the British. As for the job I was doing, I hated it more bitterly than I can perhaps make clear. In a job like that you see the dirty work of Empire at close quarters. The wretched prisoners huddling in the stinking cages of the lockups, the grey, cowed faces of the long-term convicts, the scarred buttocks of the men who had been flogged with bamboos—all these oppressed me with an intolerable sense of guilt. But I could get nothing into perspective. I was young and ill-educated and I had had to think out my problems in the utter silence that is imposed on every Englishman in the East. I did not even know that the British Empire is dying, still less did I know that it is a great deal better than the younger empires that are going to supplant it. All I knew was that I was stuck between my hatred of the empire I served and my rage against the evil-spirited little beasts who tried to make my job impossible. With one part of my mind I thought of the British Raj as an unbreakable tyranny, as something clamped down, in *saecula saeculorum,*[1] upon the will of prostrate peoples; with another part I thought that the greatest joy in the world would be to drive a bayonet into a Buddhist priest's guts. Feelings like these are the normal by-products of imperialism; ask any Anglo-Indian official, if you can catch him off duty.

3   One day something happened which in a roundabout way was enlightening. It was a tiny incident in itself, but it gave me a better glimpse than I had had before of the real nature of imperialism—the real motives for which despotic governments act. Early one morning the sub-inspector at a police station at the other end of the town rang me up on the 'phone and said that an elephant was ravaging the bazaar. Would I please come and do something about it? I did not know what I could do, but I wanted to see what was happening and I got onto a pony and started out. I took my rifle, an old .44 Winchester and much too small to kill an elephant, but I thought the noise might be useful *in terrorem.*[2] Various Burmans stopped me on the way and told me about the elephant's doings. It was not, of course, a wild elephant, but a tame one which had gone "must." It had been chained up, as tame elephants always are when their attack of "must" is due, but on the previous night it had broken its chain and escaped. Its mahout, the only person who could manage it when it was in that state, had set out in pursuit, but had taken the wrong direction and was now twelve hours' journey away, and in the morning the elephant had suddenly reappeared in the town. The Burmese population had no weapons and were quite helpless against it. It had already destroyed somebody's bamboo hut, killed a cow and raided some fruit-stalls and devoured the stock; also it had met the municipal rubbish van and, when the driver jumped out and took to his heels, had turned the van over and inflicted violences upon it.

4   The Burmese sub-inspector and some Indian constables were waiting for me in the quarter where the elephant had been seen. It was a very poor quarter, a

[1]For world without end.
[2]As a warning.

labyrinth of squalid bamboo huts, thatched with palmleaf, winding all over a steep hillside. I remember that it was a cloudy, stuffy morning at the beginning of the rains. We began questioning the people as to where the elephant had gone and, as usual, failed to get any definite information. That is invariably the case in the East; a story always sounds clear enough at a distance, but the nearer you get to the scene of events the vaguer it becomes. Some of the people said that the elephant had gone in one direction, some said that he had gone in another, some professed not even to have heard of any elephant. I had almost made up my mind that the whole story was a pack of lies, when we heard yells a little distance away. There was a loud, scandalized cry of "Go away, child! Go away this instant!" and an old woman with a switch in her hand came round the corner of a hut, violently shooing away a crowd of naked children. Some more women followed, clicking their tongues and exclaiming; evidently there was something that the children ought not to have seen. I rounded the hut and saw a man's dead body sprawling in the mud. He was an Indian, a black Dravidian coolie, almost naked, and he could not have been dead many minutes. The people said that the elephant had come suddenly upon him round the corner of the hut, caught him with its trunk, put its foot on his back and ground him into the earth. This was the rainy season and the ground was soft, and his face had scored a trench a foot deep and a couple of yards long. He was lying on his belly with arms crucified and head sharply twisted to one side. His face was coated with mud, the eyes wide open, the teeth bared and grinning with an expression of unendurable agony. (Never tell me, by the way, that the dead look peaceful. Most of the corpses I have seen look devilish.) The friction of the great beast's foot had stripped the skin from his back as neatly as one skins a rabbit. As soon as I saw the dead man I sent an orderly to a friend's house nearby to borrow an elephant rifle. I had already sent back the pony, not wanting it to go mad with fright and throw me if it smelt the elephant.

5   The orderly came back in a few minutes with a rifle and five cartridges, and meanwhile some Burmans had arrived and told us that the elephant was in the paddy fields below, only a few hundred yards away. As I started forward practically the whole population of the quarter flocked out of the houses and followed me. They had seen the rifle and were all shouting excitedly that I was going to shoot the elephant. They had not shown much interest in the elephant when he was merely ravaging their homes, but it was different now that he was going to be shot. It was a bit of fun to them, as it would be to an English crowd; besides they wanted the meat. It made me vaguely uneasy. I had no intention of shooting the elephant—I had merely sent for the rifle to defend myself if necessary—and it is always unnerving to have a crowd following you. I marched down the hill, looking and feeling a fool, with the rifle over my shoulder and an ever-growing army of people jostling at my heels. At the bottom, when you got away from the huts, there was a metalled road and beyond that a miry waste of paddy fields a thousand yards across, not yet ploughed but soggy from the first rains and dotted with coarse grass. The elephant was standing eight yards from the road, his left side towards us. He took not the slightest notice of the crowd's approach. He was tearing up bunches of grass, beating them against his knees to clean them and stuffing them into his mouth.

6   I had halted on the road. As soon as I saw the elephant I knew with perfect certainty that I ought not to shoot him. It is a serious matter to shoot a working elephant—it is comparable to destroying a huge and costly piece of machinery—and obviously one ought not to do it if it can possibly be avoided. And at

that distance, peacefully eating, the elephant looked no more dangerous than a cow. I thought then and I think now that his attack of "must" was already passing off; in which case he would merely wander harmlessly about until the mahout came back and caught him. Moreover, I did not in the least want to shoot him. I decided that I would watch him for a little while to make sure that he did not turn savage again, and then go home.

7   But at that moment I glanced round at the crowd that had followed me. It was an immense crowd, two thousand at the least and growing every minute. It blocked the road for a long distance on either side. I looked at the sea of yellow faces above the garish clothes—faces all happy and excited over this bit of fun, all certain that the elephant was going to be shot. They were watching me as they would watch a conjurer about to perform a trick. They did not like me, but with the magical rifle in my hands I was momentarily worth watching. And suddenly I realized that I should have to shoot the elephant after all. The people expected it of me and I had got to do it; I could feel their two thousand wills pressing me forward, irresistibly. And it was at this moment, as I stood there with the rifle in my hands, that I first grasped the hollowness, the futility of the white man's dominion in the East. Here was I, the white man with his gun, standing in front of the unarmed native crowd—seemingly the leading actor of the piece; but in reality I was only an absurd puppet pushed to and fro by the will of those yellow faces behind. I perceived in this moment that when the white man turns tyrant it is his own freedom that he destroys. He becomes a sort of hollow, posing dummy, the conventionalized figure of a sahib. For it is the condition of his rule that he shall spend his life in trying to impress the "natives," and so in every crisis he has got to do what the "natives" expect of him. He wears a mask, and his face grows to fit it. I had got to shoot the elephant. I had committed myself to doing it when I sent for the rifle. A sahib has got to act like a sahib; he has got to appear resolute, to know his own mind and do definite things. To come all that way, rifle in hand, with two thousand people marching at my heels, and then to trail feebly away, having done nothing—no, that was impossible. The crowd would laugh at me. And my whole life, every white man's life in the East, was one long struggle not to be laughed at.

8   But I did not want to shoot the elephant. I watched him beating his bunch of grass against his knees, with that preoccupied grandmotherly air that elephants have. It seemed to me that it would be murder to shoot him. At that age I was not squeamish about killing animals, but I had never shot an elephant and never wanted to. (Somehow it always seems worse to kill a *large* animal.) Besides, there was the beast's owner to be considered. Alive, the elephant was worth at least a hundred pounds; dead, he would only be worth the value of his tusks, five pounds, possibly. But I had got to act quickly. I turned to some experienced-looking Burmans who had been there when we arrived, and asked them how the elephant had been behaving. They all said the same thing: he took no notice of you if you left him alone, but he might charge if you went too close to him.

9   It was perfectly clear to me what I ought to do. I ought to walk up to within, say, twenty-five yards of the elephant and test his behavior. If he charged, I could shoot; if he took no notice of me, it would be safe to leave him until the mahout came back. But also I knew that I was going to do no such thing. I was a poor shot with a rifle and the ground was soft mud into which one would sink at every step. If the elephant charged and I missed him, I should have about as much chance as a toad under a steam-roller. But even then I was not thinking particularly of my

own skin, only of the watchful yellow faces behind. For at that moment, with the crowd watching me, I was not afraid in the ordinary sense, as I would have been if I had been alone. A white man mustn't be frightened in front of "natives"; and so, in general, he isn't frightened. The sole thought in my mind was that if anything went wrong those two thousand Burmans would see me pursued, caught, trampled on and reduced to a grinning corpse like that Indian up the hill. And if that happened it was quite probable that some of them would laugh. That would never do. There was only one alternative. I shoved the cartridges into the magazine and lay down on the road to get a better aim.

10   The crowd grew very still, and a deep, low, happy sigh, as of people who see the theatre curtain go up at last, breathed from innumerable throats. They were going to have their bit of fun after all. The rifle was a beautiful German thing with cross-hair sights. I did not then know that in shooting an elephant one would shoot to cut an imaginary bar running from ear-hole to ear-hole. I ought, therefore, as the elephant was sideways on, to have aimed straight at his ear-hole; actually I aimed several inches in front of this, thinking the brain would be further forward.

11   When I pulled the trigger I did not hear the bang or feel the kick—one never does when a shot goes home—but I heard the devilish roar of glee that went up from the crowd. In that instant, in too short a time, one would have thought, even for the bullet to get there, a mysterious, terrible change had come over the elephant. He neither stirred nor fell, but every line of his body had altered. He looked suddenly stricken, shrunken, immensely old, as though the frightful impact of the bullet had paralysed him without knocking him down. At last, after what seemed a long time—it might have been five seconds, I dare say—he sagged flabbily to his knees. His mouth slobbered. An enormous senility seemed to have settled upon him. One could have imagined him thousands of years old. I fired again into the same spot. At the second shot he did not collapse but climbed with desperate slowness to his feet and stood weakly upright, with legs sagging and head drooping. I fired a third time. That was the shot that did for him. You could see the agony of it jolt his whole body and knock the last remnant of strength from his legs. But in falling he seemed for a moment to rise, for as his hind legs collapsed beneath him he seemed to tower upward like a huge rock toppling, his trunk reaching skywards like a tree. He trumpeted, for the first and only time. And then down he came, his belly towards me, with a crash that seemed to shake the ground even where I lay.

12   I got up. The Burmans were already racing past me across the mud. It was obvious that the elephant would never rise again, but he was not dead. He was breathing very rhythmically with long rattling gasps, his great mound of a side painfully rising and falling. His mouth was wide open. I could see far down into caverns of pale pink throat. I waited a long time for him to die, but his breathing did not weaken. Finally I fired my two remaining shots into the spot where I thought his heart must be. The thick blood welled out of him like red velvet, but still he did not die. His body did not even jerk when the shots hit him, the tortured breathing continued without a pause. He was dying, very slowly and in great agony, but in some world remote from me where not even a bullet could damage him further. I felt I had got to put an end to that dreadful noise. It seemed dreadful to see the great beast lying there, powerless to move and yet powerless to die, and not even to be able to finish him. I sent back for my small rifle and poured shot after shot into his heart and down his throat. They seemed to make no impression. The tortured gasps continued as steadily as the ticking of a clock.

13   In the end I could not stand it any longer and went away. I heard later that it took him half an hour to die. Burmans were bringing dahs and baskets even before I left, and I was told they had stripped his body almost to the bones by the afternoon.

14   Afterwards, of course, there were endless discussions about the shooting of the elephant. The owner was furious, but he was only an Indian and could do nothing. Besides, legally I had done the right thing, for a mad elephant has to be killed, like a mad dog, if its owner fails to control it. Among the Europeans opinion was divided. The older men said I was right, the younger men said it was a damn shame to shoot an elephant for killing a coolie, because an elephant was worth more than any damn Coringhee coolie. And afterwards I was very glad that the coolie had been killed; it put me legally in the right and it gave me a sufficient pretext for shooting the elephant. I often wondered whether any of the others grasped that I had done it solely to avoid looking a fool.

 ## Topics for Critical Thinking and Writing

1. How does Orwell characterize himself at the time of the events he describes? What evidence in the piece suggests that he wrote it some years later?
2. a. Orwell says the incident was "enlightening." What does he mean? Picking up this clue, state in a sentence or two the thesis or main point.
   b. What persuasive, rhetorical, and literary techniques does Orwell use? Provide examples.
3. Compare Orwell's description of the dead coolie (in paragraph 4) with his description of the elephant's death (in paragraphs 11 and 12). Why does Orwell devote more space to the death of the elephant?
4. How would you describe the tone of the last paragraph, particularly of the last two sentences? Do you find the paragraph to be an effective conclusion? Explain.

 ## KATHA POLLITT

Katha Pollitt (b. 1949) writes chiefly on literary, political, and social topics for such publications as The Nation, The Atlantic, Harper's, *and* The New York Times. *In addition to essays, she writes poetry; her first collection of poems,* Antarctic Traveller *(1982), won the National Book Critics Circle Award. This article originally appeared in* The New York Times *in 1995.*

Why Boys Don't Play with Dolls

1   It's twenty-eight years since the founding of NOW,[1] and boys still like trucks and girls still like dolls. Increasingly, we are told that the source of these robust preferences must lie outside society—in prenatal hormonal influences, brain chem-

---

[1]National Organization for Women. (Editors' note)

istry, genes—and that feminism has reached its natural limits. What else could possibly explain the love of preschool girls for party dresses or the desire of toddler boys to own more guns than Mark from Michigan?

2   True, recent studies claim to show small cognitive differences between the sexes: He gets around by orienting himself in space; she does it by remembering landmarks. Time will tell if any deserve the hoopla with which each is invariably greeted, over the protests of the researchers themselves. But even if the results hold up (and the history of such research is not encouraging), we don't need studies of sex-differentiated brain activity in reading, say, to understand why boys and girls still seem so unalike.

3   The feminist movement has done much for some women, and something for every woman, but it has hardly turned America into a playground free of sex roles. It hasn't even got women to stop dieting or men to stop interrupting them.

4   Instead of looking at kids to "prove" that differences in behavior by sex are innate, we can look at the ways we raise kids as an index to how unfinished the feminist revolution really is, and how tentatively it is embraced even by adults who fully expect their daughters to enter previously male-dominated professions and their sons to change diapers.

5   I'm at a children's birthday party. "I'm sorry," one mom silently mouths to the mother of the birthday girl, who has just torn open her present—Tropical Splash Barbie. Now, you can love Barbie or you can hate Barbie, and there are feminists in both camps. But *apologize* for Barbie? Inflict Barbie, against your own convictions, on the child of a friend you know will be none too pleased?

6   Every mother in that room had spent years becoming a person who had to be taken seriously, not least by herself. Even the most attractive, I'm willing to bet, had suffered over her body's failure to fit the impossible American ideal. Given all that, it seems crazy to transmit Barbie to the next generation. Yet to reject her is to say that what Barbie represents—being sexy, thin, stylish—is unimportant, which is obviously not true, and children know it's not true.

7   Women's looks matter terribly in this society, and so Barbie, however ambivalently, must be passed along. After all, there are worse toys. The Cut and Style Barbie styling head, for example, a grotesque object intended to encourage "hair play." The grown-ups who give that probably apologize, too.

8   How happy would most parents be to have a child who flouted sex conventions? I know a lot of women, feminists, who complain in a comical, eyeball-rolling way about their sons' passion for sports: the ruined weekends, obnoxious coaches, macho values. But they would not think of discouraging their sons from participating in this activity they find so foolish. Or do they? Their husbands are sports fans, too, and they like their husbands a lot.

9   Could it be that even sports-resistant moms see athletics as part of manliness? That if their sons wanted to spend the weekend writing up their diaries, or reading, or baking, they'd find it disturbing? Too antisocial? Too lonely? Too gay?

10   Theories of innate differences in behavior are appealing. They let parents off the hook—no small recommendation in a culture that holds moms, and sometimes even dads, responsible for their children's every misstep on the road to bliss and success.

11   They allow grown-ups to take the path of least resistance to the dominant culture, which always requires less psychic effort, even if it means more actual work: Just ask the working mother who comes home exhausted and nonetheless finds it easier to pick up her son's socks than make him do it himself. They let families buy

for their children, without *too* much guilt, the unbelievably sexist junk that the kids, who have been watching commercials since birth, understandably crave.

12   But the thing the theories do most of all is tell adults that the *adult* world— in which moms and dads still play by many of the old rules even as they question and fidget and chafe against them—is the way it's supposed to be. A girl with a doll and a boy with a truck "explain" why men are from Mars and women are from Venus, why wives do housework and husbands just don't understand.

13   The paradox is that the world of rigid and hierarchical sex roles evoked by determinist theories is already passing away. Three-year-olds may indeed insist that doctors are male and nurses female, even if their own mother is a physician. Six-year-olds know better. These days, something like half of all medical students are female, and male applications to nursing school are inching upward. When tomorrow's three-year-olds play doctor, who's to say how they'll assign the roles?

14   With sex roles, as in every area of life, people aspire to what is possible, and conform to what is necessary. But these are not fixed, especially today. Biological determinism may reassure some adults about their present, but it is feminism, the ideology of flexible and converging sex roles, that fits our children's future. And the kids, somehow, know this.

15   That's why, if you look carefully, you'll find that for every kid who fits a stereotype, there's another who's breaking one down. Sometimes it's the same kid—the boy who skateboards *and* takes cooking in his afterschool program; the girl who collects stuffed animals *and* A-pluses in science.

16   Feminists are often accused of imposing their "agenda" on children. Isn't that what adults always do, consciously and unconsciously? Kids aren't born religious, or polite, or kind, or able to remember where they put their sneakers. Inculcating these behaviors, and the values behind them, is a tremendous amount of work, involving many adults. We don't have a choice, really, about *whether* we should give our children messages about what it means to be male and female—they're bombarded with them from morning till night.

 Topics for Critical Thinking and Writing

1. In a paragraph, summarize Pollitt's answer to the question her title raises.
2. In paragraph 7 Pollitt says, "Women's looks matter terribly in this society." Do you agree with this generalization? If they do matter "terribly," do they matter more than men's? What evidence can you give, one way or the other? Set forth your answer in an essay of about 250 words.
3. In paragraph 14 Pollitt says that "the ideology of flexible and converging sex roles" is the one that "fits our children's future." What would be examples of "flexible and converging sex roles"? And do you agree that this ideology is the one that suits the immediate future? Why?
4. Do you believe that you have been influenced by Barbie or by any other toy? Explain.
5. In her final paragraph Pollitt says that adults always impose an "agenda" on their children, consciously or unconsciously. What agenda did your parents, or other adults charged with your upbringing, impose or try to impose? What was your response? As you think back on it, were the

agenda and the responses appropriate? Present your answer in an essay of 500 to 750 words.

6. If you have heard that "brain chemistry" or "genes" (paragraph 1) account for "innate differences in behavior" (paragraph 10) in boys and girls, in a paragraph set forth the view, and in another paragraph evaluate it, drawing perhaps on your reading of Pollitt's essay.

 ## HEATHER PRINGLE

Heather Pringle was born in Edmonton, and after studying history and Victorian literature at university and working at the Provincial Museum of Alberta, she moved to Vancouver. She is primarily a science writer in the fields of archeology, anthropology, and history. She writes for such magazines as Science, Discover, New Scientist, Geo, Omni, Canadian Geographic, *and* Saturday Night, *and she has authored three books. This essay first appeared in* Equinox *in 1993.*

The Way We Woo

1   Helen Fisher slips into a ringside seat, amusement stirring in her dark eyes. It's just after eight on a steamy Friday night at the Mad Hatter Restaurant and Pub, one of dozens of softly lit singles bars on Manhattan's prosperous Upper East Side. A bevy of young businessmen, ties loosened and beer glasses in hand, lean against the railings, sizing up each female who walks in the door. On the street outside, barhoppers stream by the plate-glass windows like tropical fish. "There's constant motion here," says Fisher. "It looks like a real good pickup bar."

2   Elegantly dressed in a black skirt and sweater set, Fisher looks more like a society columnist than someone about to settle down for an evening in a singles bar. But the 48-year-old anthropologist has spent the past decade deciphering the mysteries of human mating behaviour, and she still relishes the odd evening in the field. "Men and women have no idea the amount of sexual signals they are sending out to each other," she says, angling her chair for a better view. "They'd be amazed."

3   Fisher, a research associate in the department of anthropology at the American Museum of Natural History in New York, is one of a new scientific breed seeking out the biological and genetic roots of our love lives. Unwilling to accept traditional views, she and her colleagues have begun taking a fresh look at human romance—from the first twinges of physical attraction to the heady flush of courtship and the bitter acrimony of divorce. Taking clues from the animal kingdom and anthropology, they are turning up answers to some of the most enduring mysteries of romance: why men fall for pretty faces and women pine for men of means; why males roam from bed to bed, while females dream of Mr. Right; and why love is so intoxicating and divorce so commonplace.

4   As she glances across the room, Fisher begins pointing out some of the subtleties of human courtship, patterns of behaviour that seem to stem from a distant past. Those men by the railing, for example? Fisher grins. Singles bars, she explains, work much like the mating grounds of sage grouse and other birds. After staking out individual territories in the most prominent area in the bar, the men are now attempting to attract females with simple courtship displays: stretching, exaggerating simple movements, and laughing heartily. "One of

them is even swinging from side to side, which is a real gesture of approachability," she says.

5   Fisher points out a miniskirted woman deep in conversation with a man at the bar. "See how she's gesturing and swaying and preening?" Fisher asks. "She keeps on touching her eyes, her nose, and her mouth." Stroking her face as if stroking that of her companion, she is flashing a series of intention cues—messages that she wants to touch him. But he remains strangely impassive, refusing to turn even his shoulders toward her. The conversation may be flowing, says Fisher, but the courtship ritual is rapidly stalling. As we watch, shameless voyeurs, the animated discussion slowly sputters and dies. "The pickup runs on messages," concludes Fisher, shaking her head, "and every one of them has to be returned." Turning to the bartender, the woman asks for her bill, then hurries out into the night.

6   What is ultimately going on here? Beyond the rejected advances and the private humiliations, Fisher sees the workings of an age-old ritual. After years of study and debate, she and other evolutionary anthropologists now suggest that human romance has been shaped by biology and the forces of natural selection. According to this controversial line of thought, humans conduct their love lives in much the same manner around the world. From the singles bars of North America to the marriage brokers of Asia, we attract, court, and discard mates in ways that subtly but surely promote the survival of our species.

7   It's a theory that challenges decades of entrenched thinking. Historians have long insisted that love itself was a cultural invention, an emotion first conceived by the courtly poets of Europe some eight hundred years ago and subsequently passed on to Europe's idle rich. In time, went this thinking, the idea of romantic love percolated to the lower classes, who in turn carried it to colonies far and wide. Such views dovetailed nicely with modern anthropological thought. Since the 1920s, when American scientist Margaret Mead returned from fieldwork on the South Seas islands of Samoa, most anthropologists believed that human behaviour was shaped largely by culture. Children, they noted, were as impressionable as clay. "It's a view that there is basically no human nature," says David Buss, a professor of psychology at the University of Michigan in Ann Arbor, "that humans are simply a product of their environment."

8   Over the past two decades, however, serious cracks have appeared in those theoretical walls. Influenced by Charles Darwin, a small but vocal group of social scientists now suggest that natural selection, not culture, has shaped certain key human behaviours. Over hundreds of thousands of years, they theorize, evolution has moulded not only anatomy but the human psyche itself, favouring certain social behaviours, certain states of mind, that promote survival and reproductive success. In other words, biology lies just beneath the surface of much human psychology. Could our romances, they ask, be guided by certain evolved mechanisms? Could the human heart be unconsciously governed by the ancient encodings of our genes?

9   Psychologists Martin Daly and Margo Wilson think the answers are in little doubt. After fifteen years of research, the husband-and-wife team at McMaster University in Hamilton, Ontario, conclude that love runs a remarkably similar course around the world. Wilson smiles as she observes that men tend to be attracted to the same qualities in women everywhere—even in traditional Islamic cultures, where females are veiled from head to shoulder. "The fact that you have these flirtatious eyes looking out from a whole black garb must just

stimulate the imagination far beyond what is beneath the veil," she laughs. "Mystery is sexually exciting."

10   Wilson's interest in human romance first arose in the mid-1970s, when she and Daly came across the writings of those investigating the evolutionary basis of social behaviour in animals. After examining the life histories of animals as diverse as the dung fly, the Jamaican lizard, and the elephant seal, researchers had noted that males and females often approached the mating game very differently as a result of basic reproductive biology. Among most mammal species, for instance, females slave away much of their adult lives caring for their young—nurturing embryos, nursing infants, and often protecting litters alone. Absorbed by maternal duties, they are physically incapable of producing as many young as their male counterparts are. With a greater investment in their young, females tend to pick mates carefully, selecting those best able to help their brood survive. Most males, on the other hand, are spared such intensive parental labour. Serving largely as sperm donors, they take a different tactic, favouring quantity over quality in mating and inseminating as many fertile females as possible.

11   Intrigued, Daly and Wilson wondered how the behaviour of *Homo sapiens* fit into this pattern. Like other mammalian females, women invest long months in pregnancy, breast-feeding, and early childcare, keeping their families small. Men, however, are less burdened. (One eighteenth-century Moroccan emperor reputedly fathered seven hundred sons and more than three hundred daughters before celebrating his fiftieth birthday.) Could such radical biological differences shape human romance? Would men the world over, for example, be more promiscuous than women?

12   While comprehensive statistics were scarce, the team soon began piecing together an astonishing case. In an American study of middle-aged couples published in 1970, one social scientist reported that twice as many males as females had committed adultery. In a German study of young working-class singles, 46 percent of the males, compared with only 6 percent of the females, were interested in casual sex with an attractive stranger. All around the world, from the Amazonian rainforest to the Kalahari Desert, field accounts of anthropologists lined up on this point: men of all ages craved far more sexual variety than women. Quips Wilson, "Male sexual psychology seems to be that you're willing to do it with, you know, chickens or anything."

13   Daly and Wilson found one other sweeping pattern in the anthropological literature: in every society, men and women entered into marriages—formal, long-standing unions that gave legitimacy to the resulting children. Had basic biology also shaped wedlock? If the biologists were right, women would marry men most capable of contributing to their children's well-being, while men would marry the most fertile females they could find.

14   In fact, the psychologists discovered, men generally wed younger women—a finding that squared well with evolution-minded predictions. As Wilson points out, women in their early twenties are much more fertile than those in their thirties; older men are far more likely to have acquired the kind of wealth and social status that could shelter their children from harm. And, notes Wilson, research shows that the attractiveness of a male in most cultures is judged more by his maturity, skills, and status than by a square-cut jaw and fine features. "Like Henry Kissinger," says Wilson of the former US Secretary of State. "People used to say he was really handsome. He was in a high-status position, a very powerful position."

Passion Play: A Step-by-Step Script

After spending long, smoky evenings observing couples in North American singles bars, researchers have discerned several steps in human courtship:

Approach: As a rule, it is the female who begins the mating ritual, walking up to a male or taking a seat beside him. If he reciprocates her interest by turning and looking, a conversation ensues.

Talk: As the two chat, accents and manner of speech are highly revealing. "Talking is an enormous escalation point," notes Helen Fisher. "How many people have opened their mouth and had a horrible accent, and you just realized, no way? A lot of pickups end there." But if a man and a woman successfully negotiate that hurdle, they slowly turn to face each other, moving first their heads, then their shoulders and, finally, their entire bodies.

Touch: Generally, the woman will touch first, brushing her hand briefly along a man's arm or shoulder. If the man responds in kind, touching becomes more frequent.

Gaze: As the conversation becomes more intense and pleasurable, the couple begin glancing into each other's eyes, until they are finally unable to look away. Researchers call this the "copulatory gaze."

Body Synchrony: Mesmerized by talk and touch, the couple begin moving in harmony. If the female lifts her glass for a sip, the mate does too. If he slouches in his chair to the right, she mirrors his movement. "I would like to speculate," writes Timothy Perper in his book *Sex Signals: The Biology of Love*, "that by the time they are fully synchronized, each person is physiologically prepared for intercourse."

15   To study human tastes in mates in more detail, David Buss drew up a list of thirty-one attributes and arranged for men and women in Africa, Asia, Europe, and South America to grade them by importance. "The results amazed me in that they basically confirmed the evolutionary predictions that others had speculated about," he notes. In the thirty-seven cultures polled, responses were strongly consistent, suggesting a universal, biological truth honed over millennia of evolution. While both sexes graded traits such as intelligence and kindness highly, they diverged sharply in two areas. "Women place a premium on status, older age and maturity, and resources," says Buss. "Men place a premium on youth and physical attractiveness."

16   Buss suggests that the male predilection for beauty is informed by sound biological logic. How else could a man judge the potential fertility of his mate? "The capacity of a woman to bear children is not stamped on her forehead," he writes in a recent paper. "It is not part of her social reputation, so no one is in a position to know. Even the woman herself lacks direct knowledge of her fertility and reproductive value." But certain visual cues, he explains, could serve as rough measures. Shapely legs, shiny hair, lustrous eyes, and a clear, unblemished complexion in a female all signal health and youth. And some researchers have suggested that symmetrical facial features—particularly eyes of well-matched colour and alignment—could indicate mutation-free genes. Ancestral males drawn to such qualities, notes Buss, would have likely fathered more children than men attracted to other physical traits.

17   The differing biological goals of the sexes also have profound effects on human relations and courtship behaviour. While women need time to size up a man's finances and social status, men can measure beauty and youth with a mere

flicker of an eye. Consider the recently published results of a study at the Florida State University at Tallahassee. Psychologists Russell Clark and Elaine Hatfield dispatched young men to different corners of the campus, instructing each to pitch one of three questions to female strangers: "Would you go out with me tonight?" "Would you come over to my apartment tonight?" or "Would you go to bed with me tonight?" While 56 percent of the females consented to a date, only 6 percent agreed to visit the male's apartment—and not one consented to sex. But when a female approached male strangers with the same questions, 50 percent of the men agreed to a date, 69 percent consented to an apartment visit— and 75 percent offered to go to bed with her that night.

18   As Buss and other psychologists slowly piece together the evolution of physical attraction, other researchers examine the biological and genetic origins of the emotion of love itself. At the University of Nevada, Las Vegas, just a short stroll away from the rotund cupids and neon hearts adorning the city's all-night wedding chapels, anthropologist William Jankowiak is sweeping aside earlier cultural theories. Passionate attachments, he suggests, "must have evolved for some sense of adaptation. [They] must have helped *Homo sapiens* survive in the battle against the cockroach."

19   A soft-spoken but intense scholar, Jankowiak became interested in the evolution of love some six years ago while conducting fieldwork in Inner Mongolia. During casual reading of ancient Chinese folktales, he was amazed to discover descriptions of passionate love that could have been penned today. "I said, 'My God, I wonder if this has been universal in Chinese history,' and it was. And then I started wondering if this was universal all over."

20   Turning to the scientific literature, Jankowiak unearthed two studies published in the 1960s by American psychologist Paul Rosenblatt. Interested in the emergence of love as a basis for marriage, Rosenblatt had pored over anthropological reports for dozens of human cultures, concluding that less than two-thirds had any concept of the emotion of love. As Jankowiak read the studies, however, he could see that Rosenblatt had missed a key source of information—the folklore of tribal peoples. Troubled by the omission, Jankowiak decided to start from scratch, eager to see whether love was an emotion present in all cultures.

21   With graduate student Edward Fischer, Jankowiak settled into the work, searching for love songs, tales of elopement, and other signs of romantic entanglements. In cultures where no trace of passion could be found in the literature, Jankowiak called up the anthropologists themselves to enquire whether any relevant evidence had been left out. In the end, the two researchers recorded romantic love in a resounding 88.5 percent of the 166 cultures they studied. For Jankowiak, the results strongly suggested that love is a common part of the human condition, an experience owing more to biology than to culture.

22   Still, some scholars puzzled over the small number of societies where no sign of romantic love had been uncovered. If love was a universal condition, how had inhabitants of these cultures mustered such resistance? At the University of California, Santa Barbara, doctoral candidate Helen Harris decided to take a closer look at one such society—the Mangaians of the South Pacific. According to anthropological reports, the inhabitants of Mangaia had developed a highly sexual culture. At the age of thirteen or so, boys on the island were trained by older women to bring female partners to orgasm several times before reaching climaxes of their own. The craft perfected, the young men began court-

Harlequin's Lock on Our Hearts

Every month, Harlequin Enterprises Limited ships its purple prose around the globe—from Abu Dhabi to Zimbabwe and from Iceland to Tonga. Selling more than two hundred million books a year, the Canadian firm claims to have made "the language of love universal, crossing social, cultural, and geographical borders with an ease unrivalled by any other publisher." What is its secret of success?

As it turns out, Harlequin editors understand human desire pretty well. According to company guidelines for the Harlequin Regency line of novels, for example, heroines must be attractive and quick-witted and range in age between eighteen and twenty-eight years old. The objects of their affections, on the other hand, must be virile and prosperous, possess high societal positions—"we prefer peers," say the editors—and range in age from twenty-four to thirty-five years old.

Such matches are made in heaven, according to mate-preference studies conducted by Douglas Kenrick and an associate at Arizona State University in Tempe. As Kenrick notes, females are strongly drawn to men who possess leadership skills and occupy the top rungs of a hierarchy. Moreover, they crave mates up to eight or nine years older than themselves. Men, on the other hand, are not particularly charmed by leadership. Instead, they hanker after beautiful females in their twenties—something that Harlequin editors seem to have known all along.

ing the favours of island women—averaging three orgasms a night, seven nights a week. But according to an anthropologist who lived among the Mangaians in the 1950s, neither sex ever experienced the emotion of love. "He said that when he talked about it, the Mangaians didn't understand," notes Harris.

23   Perplexed, Harris began her own fieldwork, interviewing males and females who had been adolescents during the 1950s. As her research proceeded, she could see that the sensational tales of sexual prowess had obscured the rich emotional life of Mangaia. Now middle-aged, the men and women recounted tales of deep passion, even love at first sight. "One of the women said she was in one of the stores on the island, she turned around, and she saw this man," recalls Harris. "She did not know him, but feelings just came over her that she had never felt before. . . . She analyzed it and said, 'I think it was just God's way of getting two people together. It's natural for people to feel this way.' And she and this man finally married after some years."

24   While it seems likely that romantic love arose in all human cultures, from the lean reindeer herders of Lapland to the now silent scholars of the Sung Dynasty, it is less clear just when and why this emotional state evolved. Researchers have yet to discern any convincing evidence of such strong emotions in the animal kingdom, for instance. And surveys have shown that intimate, long-lasting associations between a male and a female are strikingly rare even among our close primate relatives. "Yet the hallmark of the human animal is that we form these pair bonds," says Helen Fisher, sitting down with a glass of iced tea in her small Manhattan apartment. "So how come?"

25   In search of clues, Fisher turned to the zoological literature, studying several species that form such intimate bonds. In foxes, she found a clear biological imperative. Bearing some five helpless kits at a time, female red foxes become virtual prisoners of their broods. Equipped with only thin, low-fat milk, mothers

must nurse each of their young every two to three hours. Without a male to help feed her, a female would soon starve to death. "But when the kits begin to wander off," says Fisher, "the pair bond breaks up. It lasts only long enough to raise those kits through infancy."

26   As Fisher sees it, hominid females may have become similarly vulnerable some four million years ago. With climatic change, our simian ancestors were forced from the receding forests of Africa onto vast grassy plains, where stealthy predators stalked. "What I think," says Fisher, who has just published her theories in a new book, *Anatomy of Love: The Natural History of Monogamy, Adultery, and Divorce,* "is that we came down from the trees and we were forced onto two legs instead of four. Females suddenly needed to carry their babies in their arms instead of on their backs. What a huge reproductive burden," she says with a wince. "They also had to start carrying sticks and stones for tools and weapons in this dangerous place. So women needed a mate to help rear their young."

27   As they roamed farther onto the grasslands, early human males also found compelling reasons to pair off with females. Along the vast savannas, food sources such as cashew trees, berry patches, and the occasional meaty carcass were widely scattered. Constantly roaming, males were unable to feed or defend large harems. "Polygyny was almost impossible for men," says Fisher, "and pair bonding was critical for women." So males who fell in love and formed pairs with females were more successful in passing on their genes, thus perpetuating the penchant for intimacy.

28   Setting down her iced tea, Fisher points out that science has yet to prove her theories conclusively. No one, for instance, has located specific genes capable of turning love on or off in the human psyche. Even so, some medical research supports her contention. At the New York State Psychiatric Institute in New York City, researcher Michael Liebowitz suggests that the powerful emotion of love is created by a tidal wave of certain naturally produced chemicals in the brain. And others have suggested that the taps for these chemicals might be directly controlled by our genes.

29   A psychiatrist who specializes in the treatment of anxiety and depression, Liebowitz first began to suspect the chemical basis of love in the early 1980s after noticing the profound effects of particular antidepressants on patients who were addicted to the thrill of new relationships. After researching the matter carefully, he now suggests that the sheer intoxication of love—the warm, reckless euphoria that sweeps over us and drives away all other thoughts—may be caused by certain chemical excitants flooding into brain structures thought to control love and emotional arousal.

30   One of the most likely chemical candidates, he says, is phenylethylamine, a natural amphetamine-like substance that has been found by other researchers to have some powerful effects on the behaviour of certain laboratory animals. Mice injected with the substance squeal exuberantly and leap into the air like popcorn, and rhesus monkeys given a closely related compound make kissing sounds. And there is evidence that humans are highly susceptible too. When Liebowitz and colleague Donald Klein treated romance junkies with antidepressants that raise the levels of phenylethylamine in the brain, the patients gradually gave up their hungry search for new mates. "They could settle down and accept life with more stable and appropriate partners," explains Liebowitz.

The Universal Seven-Year Itch

While North Americans vow at the altar to forsake all others, less than 50 percent make good on their promise. But Canadians and Americans are not alone in their adulteries; infidelity is the rule rather than the exception around the world.

The Kuikuru of the Amazonian rainforest, for example, often seek out lovers just a few months after marriage. Kuikuru men and women have been known to juggle as many as twelve extra partners at a time, and their affairs are discussed with great openness and delight in the Amazonian society.

Among traditional Hindu communities in India, adultery is strongly discouraged. But infidelity clearly flourishes anyway. Notes one Sanskrit proverb: "Only when fire will cool, the moon burn, or the ocean fill with tasty water will a woman be pure."

In Japan, specially designated love hotels cater to adulterous couples. Furnished with such exotica as wall-to-wall mirrors, video recorders, whips and handcuffs, rooms are rented by the hour and enjoy a brisk trade during the day and early evening.

31   Impressed by such evidence, he suggests that neural chemicals play a key part in sparking the giddy excitement of attraction. But the effects of such chemicals are temporary. As time passes, Liebowitz theorizes, nerve endings in the brain may cease to respond to phenylethylamine and a second chemical system kicks into place. Based on such natural narcotics as endorphins, it can endow lovers with the warm, comfortable feelings of a secure attachment. "Unfortunately, that leads people to take dependable partners too much for granted," says Liebowitz. "They think, oh well, somebody else is very attractive, and my long-term relationship is not as exciting as that." Thirsting for the amphetamine high again, many will eventually abandon their partners for someone new.

32   Even here, in betrayal and divorce, evolutionary theorists such as Fisher see a form of natural logic. Research has shown, she notes, that the powerful attraction phase of love generally lasts from two to three years. And statistics suggest that divorce rates peak in and around the fourth year of marriage. In Fisher's view, the timing is significant. As it happens, women in traditional hunting and gathering societies—which resemble those in which humans first evolved—frequently nurse infants for as long as four years. During that period, they depend on their mates to supply some food and protection. But once a child is weaned and can be cared for by others, the mother may consider switching mates.

33   "I think four million years ago, there would have been advantages to primitive divorce," says Fisher. "If a male and a female raised a child through infancy and then broke up and formed new pair bonds, what they would actually be doing is creating genetic variety. And that's really critical to evolution."

34   But, as Fisher concedes, such biologically based codes of conduct may have served us far better in the grasslands of Africa than they do today in a world of divorce lawyers, property settlements, and child-custody battles. As she sets her empty glass on the table, the anthropologist shakes her head at the irony of it all. "Look at the incredible problem we're in. A drive to make a commitment, to love, to remain together. A drive to break up and pair again. And a drive to be adulterous on the side. No wonder we all struggle in every culture in the world." She pauses and smiles. "We are built to struggle."

Topics for Critical Thinking and Writing

1. Pringle's essay comments upon some anthropological studies that maintain that human mating behaviour is genetically programmed (think Darwin). After reading "The Way We Woo," are you convinced by the evolutionary scientists' theories, or do you believe that culture plays a part in mate selection?
2. Write a formal outline for Pringle's essay. (Review "Formal Outline" on pages 282–83.)
3. Explain Pringle's use of process analysis, comparison, analogy, example, expert evidence, and counter-argument.
4. Who fares better in this essay, men or women?
5. Conduct field research of your own, and then write a 750- to 1000-word essay applying or refuting the points and theories that Pringle illustrates in "The Way We Woo."

 ROBERT B. REICH

Robert B. Reich was born in Scranton, Pennsylvania, in 1946, and educated at Dartmouth College, Oxford University (he was a Rhodes Scholar), and Yale Law School. After working for the federal government he taught at Harvard University's John F. Kennedy School of Government until he was chosen by President Clinton to be secretary of labour. After leaving Washington, Reich accepted a post at Brandeis University and later at the University of California. He has written ten books, numerous articles, and a play, and he is the co-founding editor of The American Prospect *magazine. This essay, originally a memorandum circulated to undergraduate students in 1989, has been slightly revised for wider publication.*

The Future of Work

1   It's easy to predict what jobs you *shouldn't* prepare for. Thanks to the wonders of fluoride, America, in the future, will need fewer dentists. Nor is there much of a future in farming. The federal government probably won't provide long-term employment unless you aspire to work in the Pentagon or the Veterans Administration (the only two departments accounting for new federal jobs in the last decade). And think twice before plunging into higher education. The real wages of university professors have been declining for some time, the hours are bad, and all you get are complaints.

2   Moreover, as the American economy merges with the rest of the world's, anyone doing relatively unskilled work that could be done more cheaply elsewhere is unlikely to prosper for long. Imports and exports now constitute 26 percent of our gross national product (up from 9 percent in 1950), and barring a new round of protectionism, the portion will move steadily upward. Meanwhile, 10,000 people are added to the world's population every hour, most of whom, eventually, will happily work for a small fraction of today's average American wage.

3   This is good news for most of you, because it means that you'll be able to buy all sorts of things far more cheaply than you could if they were made here (provided, of course, that what your generation does instead produces even more value). The resulting benefits from trade will help offset the drain on your income resulting from paying the interest on the nation's foreign debt and financing the retirement of aging baby boomers like me. The bad news, at least for some of you, is that most of America's traditional, routinized manufacturing jobs will disappear. So will routinized service jobs that can be done from remote locations, like keypunching of data transmitted by satellite. Instead, you will be engaged in one of two broad categories of work: either complex services, some of which will be sold to the rest of the world to pay for whatever Americans want to buy from the rest of the world, or person-to-person services, which foreigners can't provide for us because (apart from new immigrants and illegal aliens) they aren't here to provide them.

4   Complex services involve the manipulation of data and abstract symbols. Included in this category are insurance, engineering, law, finance, computer programming, and advertising. Such activities now account for almost 25 percent of our GNP, up from 13 percent in 1950. They already have surpassed manufacturing (down to about 20 percent of GNP). Even *within* the manufacturing sector, executive, managerial, and engineering positions are increasing at a rate almost three times that of total manufacturing employment. Most of these jobs, too, involve manipulating symbols.

5   Such endeavors will constitute America's major contribution to the rest of the world in the decades ahead. You and your classmates will be exporting engineering designs, financial services, advertising and communications advice, statistical analyses, musical scores and film scripts, and other creative and problem-solving products. How many of you undertake these sorts of jobs, and how well you do at them, will determine what goods and services America can summon from the rest of the world in return, and thus—to some extent—your generation's standard of living.

6   You say you plan to become an investment banker? A lawyer? I grant you that these vocations have been among the fastest growing and most lucrative during the past decade. The securities industry in particular has burgeoned. The crash of October 1987 temporarily stemmed the growth, but by mid-1988 happy days were here again. Nor have securities workers had particular difficulty making ends met. (But relatively few security workers have enjoyed majestic compensation. The high average is due to a few thousand high-rolling partners in Wall Street investment banks.)

7   Work involving securities and corporate law has been claiming one-quarter of all new private sector jobs in New York City and more than a third of all the new office space in that industrious town. Other major cities are not too far behind. A simple extrapolation of the present trend suggests that by 2020 one out of every three American college graduates will be an investment banker or a lawyer. Of course, this is unlikely. Long before that milestone could be achieved, the nation's economy will have dried up like a raisin, as financiers and lawyers squeeze out every ounce of creative, productive juice. Thus my advice: Even if you could bear spending your life in such meaningless but lucrative work, at least consider the fate of the nation before deciding to do so.

8   Person-to-person services will claim everyone else. Many of these jobs will not require much skill, as is true of their forerunners today. Among the fastest growing in recent years: custodians and security guards, restaurant and retail workers, day-care providers. Secretaries and clerical workers will be as numerous as now, but they'll spend more of their time behind and around electronic machines (imported from Asia) and have fancier titles, such as "paratechnical assistant" and "executive paralegal operations manager."

9   Teachers will be needed (we'll be losing more than a third of our entire corps of elementary- and high-school teachers through attrition over the next seven years), but don't expect their real pay to rise very much. Years of public breast-beating about the quality of American education notwithstanding, the average teacher today earns $28,000—only 3.4 percent more, in constant dollars, than he or she earned fifteen years ago.

10   Count on many jobs catering to Americans at play—hotel workers, recreation directors, television and film technicians, aerobics instructors (or whatever their twenty-first-century equivalents will call themselves). But note that Americans will have less leisure time to enjoy these pursuits. The average American's free time has been shrinking for more than fifteen years, as women move into the work force (and so spend more of their free time doing household chores) and as all wage earners are forced to work harder just to maintain their standard of living. Expect the trend to continue.

11   The most interesting and important person-to-person jobs will be in what is now unpretentiously dubbed "sales." Decades from now most salespeople won't be just filling orders. Salespeople will be helping customers define their needs, then working with design and production engineers to customize products and services in order to address those needs. This is because standardized (you can have it in any color as long as it's black) products will be long gone. Flexible manufacturing and the new information technologies will allow a more tailored fit— whether it's a car, machine tool, insurance policy, or even a college education. Those of you who will be dealing directly with customers will thus play a pivotal role in the innovation process, and your wages and prestige will rise accordingly.

12   But the largest number of personal-service jobs will involve health care, which already consumes about 12 percent of our GNP, and that portion is rising. Because every new medical technology with the potential to extend life is infinitely valuable to those whose lives might be extended—even for a few months or weeks—society is paying huge sums to stave off death. By the second decade of the next century, when my generation of baby boomers will have begun to decay, the bill will be much higher. Millions of corroding bodies will need doctors, nurses, nursing-home operators, hospital administrators, technicians who operate and maintain all the fancy machines that will measure and temporarily halt the deterioration, hospice directors, home-care specialists, directors of outpatient clinics, and euthanasia specialists, among many others.

13   Most of these jobs won't pay very much because they don't require much skill. Right now the fastest growing job categories in the health sector are nurse's aides, orderlies, and attendants, which compose about 40 percent of the health-care work force. The majority are women; a large percentage are minorities. But even doctors' real earnings show signs of slipping. As malpractice insurance rates skyrocket, many doctors go on salary in investor-owned hospitals, and their duties are gradually taken over by physician "extenders" such as nurse-practitioners and midwives.

14   What's the best preparation for one of these careers?

15   Advice here is simple: You won't be embarking on a career, at least as we currently define the term, because few of the activities I've mentioned will proceed
along well-defined paths to progressively higher levels of responsibility. As the
economy evolves toward services tailored to the particular needs of clients and customers, hands-on experience will count for more than formal rank. As technologies
and markets rapidly evolve, moreover, the best preparation will be through cumulative learning on the job rather than formal training completed years before.

16   This means that academic degrees and professional credentials will count for
less; on-the-job training, for more. American students have it backwards. The
courses to which you now gravitate—finance, law, accounting, management, and
other practical arts—may be helpful to understand how a particular job is *now*
done (or, more accurately, how your instructors did it years ago when they held
such jobs or studied the people who held them), but irrelevant to how such a job
will be done. The intellectual equipment needed for the job of the future is an
ability to define problems, quickly assimilate relevant data, conceptualize and
reorganize the information, make deductive and inductive leaps with it, ask hard
questions about it, discuss findings with colleagues, work collaboratively to find
solutions, and then convince others. And *these* sorts of skills can't be learned in
career-training courses. To the extent they can be found in universities at all,
they're more likely to be found in subjects such as history, literature, philosophy,
and anthropology—in which students can witness how others have grappled for
centuries with the challenge of living good and productive lives. Tolstoy and
Thucydides are far more relevant to the management jobs of the future, for example, than are Hersey and Blanchard (*Management of Organizational Behavior*,
Prentice Hall, 5th Edition, 1988).

 Topics for Critical Thinking and Writing

1. Consider Reich's first three paragraphs. Has he taken account of his audience? What sort of personality does his voice reveal in these paragraphs?
2. In paragraph 7 Reich suggests that one should think twice before spending
   one's "life in . . . meaningless but lucrative work." What makes any sort of
   work "meaningless"? For instance is sorting or delivering mail meaningless
   work? Is working as a butcher in a supermarket? Being a criminal defence
   lawyer? Breeding or grooming dogs? Designing bathing suits? Explain.
3. Assuming that much of your career as a worker is in the future, how much
   of a role does prediction of the future play in your plans for a career?
4. In paragraph 11 Reich says that "Salespeople will be helping customers
   define their needs, then working with design and production engineers to
   customize products and services in order to address those needs." If you
   are old enough to have seen some jobs change in this direction, in five hundred words provide evidence that supports Reich's point. Or interview an
   older person, to gain information about what Reich is saying. (For advice
   on conducting interviews, see Chapter 15, "Interviewing.")
5. In his final paragraph Reich sets forth what he thinks is "the intellectual
   equipment needed for the job of the future." Read this paragraph carefully, and then ask yourself (1) if you think he is probably right about the

skills that will be needed; (2) if you think his suggestion about how those skills may be developed in university is probably right; and (3) if you plan in any way to act on his suggestions. Present your answers in an essay of about 500 words.

6. Changes have taken place in the job market since Reich wrote this memorandum. Rewrite Reich's advice for today's undergraduates.

 # DAVID W. SCHINDLER AND ADELE M. HURLEY

David Schindler is Killam Professor of Ecology at the University of Alberta, and Adele Hurley is Director of Program on Water Issues at the Munk Centre for International Studies, University of Toronto.

Rising Tensions: Canada/U.S. Cross-Border Water Issues in the 21st Century

1   Harmonious relations between the United States and Canada have long been a source of pride for both countries. The U.S. is Canada's largest trading partner, constituting 85% of our two-way trade with other countries. More than $400 billion in trade goods now flow across the border every year.

2   In the last decade, Canada has even become the largest supplier of energy to the U.S., surpassing the Middle East. Exports include uranium and hydroelectric power, as well as oil and natural gas (Grafstein 2004). As a result, the countries have created a number of mechanisms for dealing with cross-boundary environmental matters including air, water and migratory wildlife.

3   In particular, policies on water have enjoyed much cooperative environmental management. The International Joint Commission has provided a mechanism for joint management of the St. Lawrence Seaway, the Great Lakes, and other cross-border waters. Two binational agreements, The Great Lakes Water Quality Agreement and the Boundary Waters Treaty of 1909 have provided a framework for IJC undertakings.

4   But signs of disharmony in trade and environmental relations between the two countries have recently surfaced. Disagreements on softwood lumber exports from Canada to the U.S. have gone to arbitration under the North American Free Trade Agreement. Two rounds of resolution, generally favouring Canada, have been challenged by the Americans, and remain unresolved. The closure of U.S. borders to Canadian animals as a result of the BSE crisis has also had an unsettling effect on Canada/U.S. trade.

5   In September 2004, the U.S. announced that it would proceed with the Devils Lake diversion (described below) which is opposed by many Canadians as a threat to Canadian aquatic ecosystems. In short, the U.S. has become increasingly aggressive in its relations with Canada. Conflicts over water will likely increase in the years ahead.

A summary of current and potential areas of conflict over water

6   The Great Lakes and St. Lawrence River are the world's single largest source of freshwater. They supply drinking water to 45 million people, and sustain half of U.S.-Canada trade. Most of Canada's manufacturing and 25% of its agriculture occur

in the watershed of the Great Lakes. Ships transport $80 billion worth of goods annually through the lakes via the St. Lawrence Seaway. While the waters of the Great Lakes are vast, they are also heavily used. Urban and industrial growth on the Ontario side of the Great Lakes has resulted in increased water use and consumption. In particular, immigration from water poor regions of the world (Somalia, Sudan, China and India) is fuelling population growth in southern Ontario.

7   The Great Lakes Water Quality Agreement is scheduled for review and theoretically provides a unique opportunity for improving management of the Great Lakes. But given the emergence of the U.S. as the world's only superpower, and its aggressive behaviour on international matters, there will be pressure to skew the agreement in favour of the U.S. A case in point is a controversial draft agreement called Annex 2001. This Annex was initiated by the Council of Great Lakes Governors which represents the eight U.S. states in the Great Lakes basin. A 90-day period for public comment on the Annex began on July 19, 2004 and has just ended. This agreement would supplement the Great Lakes Charter and set a common standard for water diversion by both states and provinces. On the surface, the Annex appears to protect the Great Lakes. In fact, it is a means for permitting the export of Great Lakes water, as will be discussed below. In particular, there is no indication of how the Annex might affect water movement via the Chicago diversion, which already conducts Great Lakes water to the Mississippi drainage system.

Other areas of current and potential water conflict

8   Ongoing and potential conflict over water, or trade dependent on water has become a political reality in Canada. New hydroelectric developments in James Bay, designed to supply clients in the U.S. Northeast, are threatening another large piece of aboriginal territory in northern Canada. Large quantities of sulfur and nitrogen oxides still drift across the border from American industrial centers and acidify Canadian freshwaters and soils. While the emissions of pollutants have declined slowly over time, current emissions are still keeping many lakes acidic, and causing a small proportion to acidify even more. Soils are becoming leached of essential nutrients for forest growth, which in turn will decrease their ability to buffer waters from acidification.

9   Due to increasingly massive algal blooms scientists have raised concerns about the health of Lake Winnipeg. Much of the nutrient load that causes this problem originates in the Red River drainage basin which extends into the fertile farming country of the U.S. The cities of Fargo, Grand Forks, Moorhead and Winnipeg discharge sewage to the Red River, which drains to Lake Winnipeg. In North Dakota, the U.S. has recently decided to divert Devil's Lake into the Sheyenne River, a tributary to the Red River, in order to keep the lake from flooding surrounding lands. The U.S. Army Corps of Engineers has also proposed to connect Devil's Lake to the Missouri River, to stabilize and freshen the lake. This would connect the Mississippi-Missouri river system with the Nelson River, which drains Canadian waters from the Rockies to north-central Ontario. Alien species could invade and potentially disrupt natural food webs and the valuable fishery of Lake Winnipeg. The total annual value of the commercial and sport fisheries of Lake Winnipeg and the Red River is almost $50 million.

10   Complex agreements already exist for sharing the water of the Souris River, which flows from Saskatchewan to North Dakota and then to Manitoba. Since its original signing in 1958 the Souris River agreement has been renegotiated several times. Farther west still, in arid southern Alberta and northern Montana,

there is competition for the scarce waters of the Milk and St. Mary's rivers, a source for livestock and irrigation in both countries. A 1921 agreement apportioned the waters more or less equally between Alberta and Montana. However, Montana, one of the United States' least efficient irrigators, has recently asked the IJC to review the agreement, claiming that it should be entitled to more of the rivers' water. Following hearings in summer of 2003, the IJC must now decide whether Montana's complaint deserves further exploration.

11   In British Columbia, the Columbia River originates in Canada but eventually flows to the U.S. The 1964 Columbia River Treaty required Canada to build three dams on the upper Columbia to control flooding and maximize power production in the U.S. part of the watershed. Half the power generated was to have been Canada's. But the British Columbia government negotiated a lump payment of $254 million instead. This sum did not even pay for dam construction. In addition these dams have totally blocked anadromous salmon runs on the Canadian portion of the Columbia River. Nor did the treaty recognize considerable damage to Canadian agricultural lands, local communities and forests. The Columbia River Treaty will soon be renegotiated. It needs to be revisited with a view to equalizing benefits.

Increasing pressure on freshwater supplies in the future

12   Water scarcity has already affected many areas of the U.S., and a few parts of Canada. The reasons for these shortages include increasing populations and industry, climate warming, poor agricultural practices, poor prevention of water pollution, and watershed modification.

Climate warming

13   The effects of climate warming will likely cause governments to re-examine all existing transboundary water agreements, including inter-provincial agreements. Climate warming has already increased the pressure on water supplies in arid areas such as the Great Plains and populous areas such as the Great Lakes and the Greater Puget Sound area. The U.S. Global Change Research Program recently concluded in a regional paper "Rocky Mountain/Great Basin Region" (water resources) that, "There will be increasing competition for already limited water supplies and all water-using sectors."

14   The Great Plains of the western U.S. and Canada lie in the rain shadow of the Rocky Mountains and are semi-arid at the best of times. Annual average precipitation in this area ranges from less than 300mm to as much as 500mm. In general, average evaporation equals or exceeds precipitation, so there is little or no net water generated to flow from the area. Fortunately, some of the area receives flow from rivers or aquifers that originate high in the Rockies, where precipitation is higher. Economically important rivers that originate in the snowpacks and glaciers of the Rockies include the Colorado, the Missouri and the Platte rivers in the U.S. and the Saskatchewan, Athabasca and Peace rivers in Canada. In the 20th century, the Great Plains have come to rely on these mountain flows. Cities like Denver and Calgary and surrounding agriculture rely on these mountain "water towers."

15   But much of the Great Plains has already warmed from 1 to 3 degrees C. Evaporation has increased in proportion. Recent paleoecology studies show that intense droughts lasting for a decade or more were common in the Great Plains before the 20th century, which was unusually wet. Even the "dirty 30s," widely referenced as an example of the hardships of drought on the prairies, was a

minor drought compared to earlier centuries. Few humans of European descent ever witnessed the effects of these earlier droughts (see Palliser 1859). The relatively few aboriginal inhabitants of the Great Plains were nomadic and simply moved during times of drought. But even long-lasting droughts displaced or eradicated these well-adapted peoples.

16   These earlier droughts occurred under much cooler climatic conditions than occur today, or than are anticipated in decades to come (IPCC 2001). Given the large numbers of European settlers, huge populations of livestock, and vast areas of croplands the economies of the Great Plains are much more vulnerable to drought than ever before.

17   Warming temperatures have also affected mountain water supplies. Glaciers supply relatively small proportions of the total downstream flow in most rivers. But they release their water during the critical midsummer period when annual snowpacks have melted, evaporation is at its highest, and when fish and other organisms are stressed by high temperatures and oxygen deficits at lower elevations. The demand for water among irrigators is also greatest at this time.

18   Some glaciers have supplied increasing flows during the warming years of the late 20th century, compensating to some degree for drought and increasing evaporation downstream. But some glaciers have already receded so greatly that their contributions are dwindling. Many will have disappeared by 2100 or before. Once gone, they will not return, at least not until the next ice age.

19   The contributions of annual spring snowmelt in western Canada to river flows has also declined. An increasing proportion of winter precipitation in the mountains and foothills is falling as rain rather than snow, and periodic winter melts are increasingly allowing winter snowfalls to seep away gradually, so that they are not available to recharge rivers in the spring.

20   Altogether, climate warming will cause the already scarce waters of the Great Plains to dwindle.

21   Climate will have somewhat different effects on the St. Lawrence Great Lakes. Many naively consider the Great Lakes to be nearly inexhaustible sources of freshwater. But the apparent vast water supply of the Great Lakes is deceiving. The waters are not renewed very rapidly. The average water renewal time (the time it would take to refill the lakes if they were drained) is estimated at 100 years. In other words, an average of only one percent of the water is renewed each year. Lake Superior, the headwater for the system, is even longer with water renewal times estimated at 200–300 years. In short, only a small proportion of Great Lakes water can be used sustainably, and climate warming (generally already a degree or two at various places in the basin) will gradually reduce that available for sustainable use. Some climate models suggest that lake levels could drop by as much as a metre, and outflows could be reduced by 30% in the next half century.

22   Efforts to export Great Lakes water, divert it to arid areas, and otherwise squander it have been successfully defeated in the past for good reason. Even small reductions to lake levels and outflows can cause millions of lost dollars to shipping and hydroelectric production. Some engineers believe that dredging should be employed to deepen shallow shipping channels, an expensive and ecologically destructive activity. Dredging in the St. Clair and Detroit rivers has already lowered the levels of Lakes Michigan and Huron by more than 30 cm.

Vandalizing nature's plumbing

23   Between 50 to 70% of wetlands in the prairies and Great Lakes basin have been filled, drained or otherwise destroyed. Rivers have been channelled,

dammed and their riparian areas ruined. Lakes have been routinely dammed and their levels regulated for human convenience rather than for ecosystem health. In short, the natural systems that once kept water from snowmelt and large rainstorms on the landscape, and that once released waters slowly to recharge rivers and aquifers, are all but gone. This mismanagement of natural drainage areas amplifies flooding, land erosion, and many other problems. It will exacerbate the adverse effects of climate warming and the increasing human thirst for water.

Human demand

24   Human demand for water is increasing greatly in many areas on the continent, where water is in increasingly short supply. Both urban and suburban populations are growing rapidly in the northern U.S. and southern Canada. Intra-country migration has amplified water conflict in some areas. For example, a massive migration of people from the "rust belt" states of the Great Lakes, where heavy industry once employed many workers, to the still relatively pristine areas of the eastern slopes of the Rockies and the adjacent Great Plains has stressed existing water supplies. In Canada, a similar migration has occurred. People from job-scarce eastern provinces are moving to wealthy Alberta, where jobs in the oil industry and construction are plentiful. Calgary, already home to 1,000,000 people, is expanding in area at almost 5% per year. Canmore, at the very gateway to Banff National Park, is growing at a similar rate. If current growth rates continue over the next 50 years, Alberta's huge urban footprint will disrupt water flows, pave over water recharge areas, and challenge scarce water resources.

25   Population growth and industrial demands just outside the Great Lakes basin in Ohio, Michigan and Pennsylvania have also compromised the water supplies of the Great Lakes. Many out of basin communities have already exceeded sustainable water uses, or have polluted their surface and ground waters too much to use for drinking water. Demand in some areas has actually reversed the direction of flow of groundwater, so that water that used to flow to the Great Lakes now flows away from it (Nikiforuk 2004).

Water diversion schemes

26   In the past grand schemes to move water from the large rivers and lakes of the Canadian north to water-scarce regions of the US have made headlines. Today such schemes are given little credibility. Several studies have unmasked the dubious economics of such projects. Cities and communities now occupy many of the areas proposed to become reservoirs. Consequently any future attempts to divert or export Canadian water will be more surreptitious and less grandiose. Canadian business interests and politicians have heralded these lesser schemes. In 1999 a Conservative government in Ontario issued a five-year permit to tank water from Lake Superior to Asia. In recent years the government of Newfoundland has expressed repeated interest in selling water to the oil-rich yet water-poor Middle East. Throughout the 1990s the government of British Columbia entertained more than a dozen proposals to export water. The Canadian public loudly opposed and defeated these ventures yet the idea of turning water into a source of state revenue remains a temptation for many Canadian governments and their bureaucracies.

Annex 2001

27   As currently drafted, Annex 2001 could end up being the kind of "Trojan Horse" undertaking that would quietly move Canadian water to the U.S. The Annex pro-

poses to regulate the removal of water from the watershed of the Great Lakes with only seven conditions: The proponent must prove that there is no reasonable alternative, that there is no significant impact, guarantee a return flow (of unspecified proportions), prepare water conservation plans, meet all acceptable laws, request a reasonable quantity of water, and agree to "resource improvement," a vaguely defined notion at best. The decision process is somewhat vague, but it appears that a simple majority of states would be sufficient to allow a diversion to proceed, regardless of the opinion of Canadian provinces. There is no plan that would restrict the total amount of water allocated for removal, or tie removal to needs of the Great Lakes. In short, it puts water needs of humans outside the basin ahead of in-basin needs and the health of the Great Lakes ecosystem (Nikiforuk 2004).

28   Annex 2001 is a fundamentally flawed agreement. If passed in anything close to its present form, it could do great damage to Canadian environmental and economic interests.

Alien species

29   The biota of northern and southern watersheds is vastly different. Many species endemic to the Mississippi and Colorado systems have never reached the Saskatchewan-Nelson, the St. Lawrence, or the Athabasca-Peace-Slave-Mackenzie drainage basins. No one knows what the mixing of the continent's aquatic fauna and flora would do to the ecological integrity of a given drainage system. Recent experiences in other watersheds suggest that it is highly probable that at least a few alien invaders will harm the native species of any ecosystem. In recent years the invasion of the sea lamprey, zebra mussels, opossum shrimp, common carp, Eurasian milfoil, and tamarisk have created havoc in aquatic ecosystems around the world. Successive waves of alien invaders have made the understanding and management of freshwater systems increasingly difficult. Introduction of alien species has brought harm to the Great Lakes. Approximately 160 species have invaded the Great Lakes from other parts of the world, often via ballast water in ships (Mills et al. 1994). Zebra mussels and lampreys have caused costly and irreparable damage. They and other species have invaded ecosystems that are adjacent to the Great Lakes, often via bait buckets, contaminated boats and fishing equipment.

Cost

30   The costs of engineering projects have increased manifold in the past half-century. There is not enough water in southern Canada alone to satisfy U.S. demand. Northern rivers would have to be tapped. Huge diversion channels, many dams, and other infrastructure necessary to transfer huge volumes of water for thousands of kilometres would make the costs prohibitive unless heavily subsidized. Today, few would regard the benefits as worth the economic or ecological costs.

The North American Free Trade Agreement

31   Before the signing of the North American Free Trade Agreement, Canada came close to protecting its freshwater supplies. In 1988, the governing Conservative Party introduced the Canada Water Preservation Act to prevent large-scale diversions and exports of water. The legislation was not passed, thanks to an election call, and it was never reintroduced. Even so, it seemed reasonable to expect that a clause exempting water could have been inserted in the Free Trade Agreement when it was being drafted. This was not done, for reasons that have never been clearly explained. As a result of these ambiguities, there is

still considerable controversy over whether or not water exports are subject to NAFTA regulations (Boyd 2003).

32   As Boyd (2003) points out, many water uses that benefit the U.S. are already subject to regulation under NAFTA. One is the generation of hydroelectric power, much of which is sold to customers in the U.S. If we wished to reduce exports to the U.S. of electricity, NAFTA would require proportional cuts in our own power consumption.

33   Even prior to NAFTA, Canada struck deals that greatly favoured the U.S. The Columbia River was dammed to supply power largely to the lower portion of the basin in the U.S. But Canadians paid for much of the cost of construction of the necessary infrastructure. No compensation was ever negotiated for the huge runs of anadromous salmon that once entered Canada via the river. This renewable resource has been lost forever, as long as the dams on the system remain. Much of the hydroelectric power generated within Canada also goes to the U.S. The enormous damage to rivers, lakes and aboriginal society has been considered an "externality" in these arrangements to ship "virtual water."

34   To satisfy U.S. hunger for cheap hydropower, Canadians have already made more inter-basin transfers of water than any other nation. It seems somewhat hypocritical that the movement of water considered unacceptable between nations because of its great ecological liabilities (i.e. the Souris or Great Lakes) should be rendered acceptable simply by the fact that it occurs entirely within Canadian boundaries, especially when Americans are the primary beneficiaries.

35   Other possibilities seem to fit. How about the export of cattle or other agricultural commodities raised in Canada, on irrigation water? Such exports of "virtual water" have in many cases greatly harmed Canadian ecosystems. Over 60% of the energy from Alberta's oil sands is exported to the U.S. Again, cutting exports would require treating Canadian customers in proportion. Extracting oil from the oil sands currently uses three to six barrels of water for every barrel of oil produced. It is another "virtual water" export that degrades Canadian ecosystems.

Political Temptations—Profits to Canadians

36   In recent years Canadian water policy has become increasingly vague and ambiguous. Canadian governments of both dominant political parties have chosen to avoid legislation specifically preventing the export of freshwater. The Canadian economy is largely based on the export of raw materials. In that respect, it is almost unique among nations that enjoy a first-world lifestyle, equalled only by a few oil exporters from the Middle East. In fact, Canada has placed little emphasis on creating industries that could add value to the country's raw resources. Most of these industries are in other countries, where cheap Canadian raw materials make it possible to reap profits from secondary industries. But Canada's supply of conventional oil, gas, and forest products is declining. Climate and land availability limit agricultural exports. As we deplete or saturate these resources, the temptation among politicians to sell more hydropower, or even water, to wealthy U.S. customers will grow.

Water security

37   Recent actions by the U.S. indicate that it is willing to risk international scorn or condemnation to get its way. The invasion of Iraq without UN support is a dramatic example. Despite being described as an "illegal act" by United Nations Secretary General, Kofi Annan, the U.S. administration still defends its actions. It

is increasingly evident that the U.S. did not invade Iraq for "weapons of mass destruction," but to secure American oil supplies.

38   Recently, George W. Bush exhorted Canada to pipe its seemingly-plentiful water to the U.S. southwest. It seems likely that the U.S. will act aggressively to ensure its water security. Will Canada respond aggressively to protect its limited water supplies and watersheds?

39   In 1970, Canada passed the Canada Water Act, which is largely devoted to federal-provincial management and monitoring of water. At the same time, new programs in Environment Canada (including what would later become the Department of Fisheries and Oceans) placed Canada at the forefront of freshwater research. Water appeared to rise in priority for the next 20 years, culminating in the Inquiry on Federal Water Policy in 1984, which proposed a framework for federal water policies for the future. The final report of the Inquiry offered 55 recommendations for more coherent federal water policies and administration. The issues ranged from drinking water safety and water export, to research support and intergovernmental arrangements. In 1987, a Federal Water Policy was tabled in Parliament. It was never fully implemented, for reasons that remain obscure. Since that time, water policy initiatives have been de-emphasized in Canada under both Liberal and Conservative governments. Research has been severely cut in both the Department of Environment and the Department of Fisheries and Oceans. The Inland Waters Directorate of Environment Canada, which was to implement most of the new policy, was disbanded in the early 1990s. The government also cut funding for the former Canada Water Act to a few percent of expenditures in the 1970s and 1980s (Pearse and Quinn 1996). In view of the now-recognized problems with drinking water and the impending international problems outlined above, these actions appear to be high risk and short-sighted. In 2001, the Auditor General's office reported that Canada's water protection capabilities are adrift.

Canada's position on boundary waters needs to be strengthened

40   In recent years, the federal government appears to be abdicating many of its Canada-U.S. water responsibilities. The Annex 2001 process is a good example. The issue of diversions from boundary waters is clearly a federal responsibility. Yet in the Annex process, the federal government has chosen to let Ontario and Quebec bargain with eight U.S. states in an 8 to 2 negotiating situation. All diversions in the immediate future are likely to occur on the U.S. side of the basin. Passage of Annex 2001 would leave the provinces with no control over diversions in the U.S. It would also give the U.S. significant say over water-related developments in Canada. As such, it would weaken Canada's ability to protect Canadian interests under the Boundary Waters Treaty of 1909.

Short Term Solutions: A Role for the Office
of the Auditor General of Canada

41   The authors propose that the Office of the Auditor General make recommendations within one year's time concerning policy and funding requirements needed to protect Canada's water resources in keeping with the demands of the 21st Century.

References

Bocking, R. (1987). Canadian water: a commodity for export? Ch. 5 in M. Healey and R. Wallace. *Canadian Aquatic Resources.* Minister of Supply and Services, Ottawa.

Boyd, D. (2003). *Unnatural law: Rethinking Canadian environmental law and policy.* UBC Press, Vancouver.

Grafstein, Hon. J.S., Q.C. (2004). *The greening of the Great Lakes.* Speech to the 2004 International Association of Great Lakes and St. Lawrence Mayors' Conference, July 14-16, Chicago, Illinois.

Intergovernmental Panel on Climate Change. (2001). *Climate change 2001.* Synthesis Report of the IPCC Third Assessment Report. IPCC: Geneva, Switzerland.

Nikiforuk, A. (2004). *Political diversions: Annex 2001 and the future of the Great Lakes.* Munk Center for International Studies, University of Toronto.

Mills, E.L., Leach, J.H., Carlton, J.T., and Secor, C.L. (1994). Exotic species and the integrity of the Great Lakes. *BioScience*, 44: 666–676.

Palliser, J. (1859). *British North America: The northern branch of the River Saskatchewan and the frontier of the United States; and Between the Red River and the Rocky Mountains.* Her Majesty's Stationery Office, London.

Pearse, P.H. and F. Quinn. (1996). Recent developments in federal water policy: One step forward, two steps back. *Can. Water Resources Journal*, 21: 329–339.

Topics for Critical Thinking and Writing

1. Schindler and Hurley state that a fresh-water crisis is looming: how imminent do they think the problem is? What evidence do they provide? Do you think that a crisis is imminent? Why or why not?

2. What are the subject, purpose, audience, and methods of development used in "Rising Tensions"? Are they effective? Based upon this information, what kind of essay is it?

3. Schindler and Hurley make a proposal at the end of their essay: in your own words, what is that proposal?

4. Review "Outlining" in Chapter 13, and write a formal outline for "Rising Tensions: Canada/U.S. Cross-Border Water Issues in the 21st Century."

5. a. Write a 1000-word research paper on one of the fresh-water agreements or issues/potential conflicts that Schindler and Hurley discuss in their paper. *Or,*

   b. It has been said that water will be "the oil of the twenty-first century," a potential economic boon for water-rich nations and a cause for conflicts arising out of a shortage of water in other countries and regions. Write a researched persuasion essay on your views about a fresh-water issue of your choosing. You might want to start with a subject such as an issue of conservation, of cross-border conflict, of severe drought, of the impact of global population growth on water supplies, and so on. Remember to make sure that your topic is clearly focused.

BRENT STAPLES

Brent Staples, born in 1951, holds a Ph.D. from the University of Chicago. He is a member of the editorial board of The New York Times, *the author of a memoir,* Parallel Time: Growing Up in Black and White *(1994), which won the Anisfield Wolff Book Award, and contributor to several magazines such as* Harper's, The New York Times Magazine, *and* Ms., *where this essay appeared in 1986.*

Just Walk On By: A Black Man Ponders His Power to Alter Public Space

1   My first victim was a woman—white, well dressed, probably in her early twenties. I came upon her late one evening on a deserted street in Hyde Park, a relatively affluent neighborhood in an otherwise mean, impoverished section of Chicago. As I swung onto the avenue behind her, there seemed to be a discreet, uninflammatory distance between us. Not so. She cast back a worried glance. To her, the youngish black man—a broad six feet two inches with a beard and billowing hair, both hands shoved into the pockets of a bulky military jacket—seemed menacingly close. After a few more quick glimpses, she picked up her pace and was soon running in earnest. Within seconds she disappeared into a cross street.

2   That was more than a decade ago. I was 22 years old, a graduate student newly arrived at the University of Chicago. It was in the echo of that terrified woman's footfalls that I first began to know the unwieldy inheritance I'd come into—the ability to alter public space in ugly ways. It was clear that she thought herself the quarry of a mugger, a rapist, or worse. Suffering a bout of insomnia, however, I was stalking sleep, not defenseless wayfarers. As a softy who is scarcely able to take a knife to a raw chicken—let alone hold it to a person's throat—I was surprised, embarrassed, and dismayed all at once. Her flight made me feel like an accomplice in tyranny. It also made it clear that I was indistinguishable from the muggers who occasionally seeped into the area from the surrounding ghetto. That first encounter, and those that followed, signified that a vast, unnerving gulf lay between nighttime pedestrians—particularly women—and me. And I soon gathered that being perceived as dangerous is a hazard in itself. I only needed to turn a corner into a dicey situation, or crowd some frightened, armed person in a foyer somewhere, or make an errant move after being pulled over by a policeman. Where fear and weapons meet—and they often do in urban America—there is always the possibility of death.

3   In that first year, my first away from my hometown, I was to become thoroughly familiar with the language of fear. At dark, shadowy intersections in Chicago, I could cross in front of a car stopped at a traffic light and elicit the *thunk, thunk, thunk, thunk* of the driver—black, white, male, or female—hammering down the door locks. On less traveled streets after dark, I grew accustomed to but never comfortable with people who crossed to the other side of the street rather than pass me. Then there were the standard unpleasantries with police, doormen, bouncers, cab drivers, and others whose business it is to screen out troublesome individuals *before* there is any nastiness.

4   I moved to New York nearly two years ago and I have remained an avid night walker. In central Manhattan, the near-constant crowd cover minimizes tense one-on-one street encounters. Elsewhere—visiting friends in SoHo, where sidewalks are narrow and tightly spaced buildings shut out the sky—things can get very taut indeed.

5   Black men have a firm place in New York mugging literature. Norman Podhoretz in his famed (or infamous) 1963 essay, "My Negro Problem—And Ours," recalls growing up in terror of black males; they "were tougher than we were, more ruthless," he writes—and as an adult on the Upper West Side of Manhattan, he continues, he cannot constrain his nervousness when he meets black men on certain streets. Similarly, a decade later, the essayist and novelist Edward Hoagland extols a New York where once "Negro bitterness bore down

mainly on other Negroes." Where some see mere panhandlers, Hoagland sees "a mugger who is clearly screwing up his nerve to do more than just *ask* for money." But Hoagland has "the New Yorker's quick-hunch posture for broken-field maneuvering," and the bad guy swerves away.

6   I often witness that "hunch posture," from women after dark on the warren-like streets of Brooklyn where I live. They seem to set their faces on neutral and, with their purse straps strung across their chests bandolier style, they forge ahead as though bracing themselves against being tackled. I understand, of course, that the danger they perceive is not a hallucination. Women are particularly vulnerable to street violence, and young black males are drastically overrepresented among the perpetrators of that violence. Yet these truths are no solace against the kind of alienation that comes of being ever the suspect, against being set apart, a fearsome entity with whom pedestrians avoid making eye contact.

7   It is not altogether clear to me how I reached the ripe old age of 22 without being conscious of the lethality nighttime pedestrians attributed to me. Perhaps it was because in Chester, Pennsylvania, the small, angry industrial town where I came of age in the 1960s, I was scarcely noticeable against a backdrop of gang warfare, street knifings, and murders. I grew up one of the good boys, had perhaps a half-dozen fist fights. In retrospect, my shyness of combat has clear sources.

8   Many things go into the making of a young thug. One of those things is the consummation of the male romance with the power to intimidate. An infant discovers that random flailings send the baby bottle flying out of the crib and crashing to the floor. Delighted, the joyful babe repeats those motions again and again, seeking to duplicate the feat. Just so, I recall the points at which some of my boyhood friends were finally seduced by the perception of themselves as tough guys. When a mark cowered and surrendered his money without resistance, myth and reality merged—and paid off. It is, after all, only manly to embrace the power to frighten and intimidate. We, as men, are not supposed to give an inch of our lane on the highway; we are to seize the fighter's edge in work and in play and even in love; we are to be valiant in the face of hostile forces.

9   Unfortunately, poor and powerless young men seem to take all this nonsense literally. As a boy, I saw countless tough guys locked away; I have since buried several, too. They were babies, really—a teenage cousin, a brother of 22, a childhood friend in his mid-twenties—all gone down in episodes of bravado played out in the streets. I came to doubt the virtues of intimidation early on. I chose, perhaps even unconsciously, to remain a shadow—timid, but a survivor.

10   The fearsomeness mistakenly attributed to me in public places often has a perilous flavor. The most frightening of these confusions occurred in the late 1970s and early 1980s when I worked as a journalist in Chicago. One day, rushing into the office of a magazine I was writing for with a deadline story in hand, I was mistaken for a burglar. The office manager called security and, with an ad hoc posse, pursued me through the labyrinthine halls, nearly to my editor's door. I had no way of proving who I was. I could only move briskly toward the company of someone who knew me.

11   Another time I was on assignment for a local paper and killing time before an interview. I entered a jewelry store on the city's affluent Near North Side. The proprietor excused herself and returned with an enormous red Doberman pinscher straining at the end of a leash. She stood, the dog extended toward me, silent to my questions, her eyes bulging nearly out of her head. I took a cursory look around, nodded, and bade her good night. Relatively speaking, however, I never fared as

badly as another black male journalist. He went to nearby Waukegan, Illinois, a couple of summers ago to work on a story about a murderer who was born there. Mistaking the reporter for the killer, police hauled him from his car at gunpoint and but for his press credentials would probably have tried to book him. Such episodes are not uncommon. Black men trade tales like this all the time.

12   In "My Negro Problem—And Ours," Podhoretz writes that the hatred he feels for blacks makes itself known to him through a variety of avenues—one being his discomfort with that "special brand of paranoid touchiness" to which he says blacks are prone. No doubt he is speaking here of black men. In time, I learned to smother the rage I felt at so often being taken for a criminal. Not to do so would surely have led to madness—via that special "paranoid touchiness" that so annoyed Podhoretz at the time he wrote the essay.

13   I began to take precautions to make myself less threatening. I move about with care, particularly late in the evening. I give a wide berth to nervous people on subway platforms during the wee hours, particularly when I have exchanged business clothes for jeans. If I happen to be entering a building behind some people who appear skittish, I may walk by, letting them clear the lobby before I return, so as not to seem to be following them. I have been calm and extremely congenial on those rare occasions when I've been pulled over by the police.

14   And on late-evening constitutionals along streets less traveled by, I employ what has proved to be an excellent tension-reducing measure: I whistle melodies from Beethoven and Vivaldi and the more popular classical composers. Even steely New Yorkers hunching toward nighttime destinations seem to relax, and occasionally they even join in the tune. Virtually everybody seems to sense that a mugger wouldn't be warbling bright, sunny selections from Vivaldi's *Four Seasons*. It is my equivalent of the cowbell that hikers wear when they know they are in bear country.

 Topics for Critical Thinking and Writing

1. What did Staples learn, from the first experience that he narrates, about other people? What did he learn about himself?
2. In paragraph 3 Staples gives a second example (the response of people in cars) of the effect that he has on others. Why do you suppose he bothered to give a second example, since it illustrates a point already made by the first example?
3. In paragraph 12 Staples quotes Norman Podhoretz's remark about the "special brand of paranoid touchiness" that Podhoretz finds in many blacks. What would you say is Staples's view of Podhoretz's idea?
4. In paragraphs 13-14 Staples discusses the "precautions" he takes to make himself "less threatening." Are these precautions reasonable? Or do they reveal that he is, in Podhoretz's word, "paranoid"? Do you think he ought to be less concerned with taking precautions? Why, or why not?
5. Evaluate Staples's final paragraph as a way of ending the essay.
6. The success of a narrative as a piece of writing often depends on the reader's willingness to identify with the narrator. From an analysis of "Just Walk On By," what explanation can you give for your willingness (or unwillingness) to identify yourself with Staples?

JONATHAN SWIFT

Jonathan Swift (1667–1745) was born in Ireland of an English family. He was ordained in the Church of Ireland in 1694, and in 1714 he became dean of Saint Patrick's Cathedral, Dublin. He wrote abundantly on political and religious topics, often motivated (in his own words) by "savage indignation." It is ironic that Gulliver's Travels, the masterpiece by this master of irony, is widely thought of as a book for children.

From the middle of the sixteenth century the English regulated the Irish economy so that it would enrich England. Heavy taxes and other repressive legislation impoverished Ireland, and in 1728, the year before Swift wrote the satirical pamphlet "A Modest Proposal," Ireland was further weakened by a severe famine. Deeply moved by the injustice, the stupidity, and the suffering that he found in Ireland, Swift adopts the guise or persona of an economist and offers an ironic suggestion on how Irish families might improve their condition.

A Modest Proposal

For Preventing the Children of Poor People in Ireland from Being a Burden to Their Parents or Country, and for Making Them Beneficial to the Public

1   It is melancholy object to those who walk through this great town or travel in the country, when they see the streets, the roads, and cabin doors, crowded with beggars of the female sex, followed by three, four, or six children, all in rags and importuning every passenger for an alms. These mothers, instead of being able to work for their honest livelihood, are forced to employ all their time in strolling to beg sustenance for their helpless infants: who as they grow up either turn thieves for want of work, or leave their dear native country to fight for the pretender in Spain, or sell themselves to the Barbadoes.

2   I think it is agreed by all parties that this prodigious number of children in the arms, or on the backs, or at the heels of their mothers, and frequently of their fathers, is in the present deplorable state of the kingdom a very great additional grievance; and, therefore, whoever could find out a fair, cheap, and easy method of making these children sound, useful members of the commonwealth, would deserve so well of the public as to have his statue set up for a preserver of the nation.

3   But my intention is very far from being confined to provide only for the children of professed beggars; it is of a much greater extent, and shall take in the whole number of infants at a certain age who are born of parents in effect as little able to support them as those who demand our charity in the streets.

4   As to my own part, having turned my thoughts for many years upon this important subject, and maturely weighed the several schemes of our projectors, I have always found them grossly mistaken in their computation. It is true, a child just dropped from its dam may be supported by her milk for a solar year, with little other nourishment; at most not above the value of 2s.,[1] which the mother may certainly get, or the value in scraps, by her lawful occupation of begging; and it is exactly at one year old that I propose to provide for them in such a manner as instead of being a charge upon their parents or the parish, or want-

[1]Two shillings. Later in this article, "*l.*" is an abbreviation for pounds and "d" for pence.

ing food and raiment for the rest of their lives, they shall on the contrary contribute to the feeding, and partly to the clothing, of many thousands.

5   There is likewise another great advantage in my scheme, that it will prevent those voluntary abortions, and that horrid practice of women murdering their bastard children, alas! too frequent among us! sacrificing the poor innocent babes I doubt more to avoid the expense than the shame, which would move tears and pity in the most savage and inhuman breast.

6   The number of souls in this kingdom being usually reckoned one million and a half, of these I calculate there may be about 200,000 couples whose wives are breeders; from which number I subtract 30,000 couples who are able to maintain their own children (although I apprehend there cannot be so many, under the present distress of the kingdom); but this being granted, there will remain 170,000 breeders. I again subtract 50,000 for those women who miscarry, or whose children die by accident or disease within the year. There only remain 120,000 children of poor parents annually born. The question therefore is, how this number shall be reared and provided for? which, as I have already said, under the present situation of affairs, is utterly impossible by all the methods hitherto proposed. For we can neither employ them in handicraft or agriculture; we neither build houses (I mean in the country) nor cultivate land; they can very seldom pick up a livelihood by stealing, till they arrive at six years old, except where they are of towardly parts; although I confess they learn the rudiments much earlier; during which time they can, however, be properly looked upon only as probationers; as I have been informed by a principal gentleman in the county of Cavan, who protested to me that he never knew above one or two instances under the age of six, even in a part of the kingdom so renowned for the quickest proficiency in that art.

7   I am assured by our merchants, that a boy or a girl before twelve years old is no saleable commodity; and even when they come to this age they will not yield above 3*l*. or 3*l*.2s.6d. at most on the exchange; which cannot turn to account either to the parents or kingdom, the charge of nutriment and rags having been at least four times that value.

8   I shall now therefore humbly propose my own thoughts, which I hope will not be liable to the least objection.

9   I have been assured by a very knowing American of my acquaintance in London, that a young healthy child well nursed is at a year old a most delicious, nourishing, and wholesome food, whether stewed, roasted, baked, or broiled; and I make no doubt that it will equally serve in a fricassee or a ragout.

10   I do therefore humbly offer it to public consideration that of the 120,000 children already computed, 20,000 may be reserved for breed, whereof only one-fourth part to be males; which is more than we allow to sheep, black cattle, or swine; and my reason is, that these children are seldom the fruits of marriage, a circumstance not much regarded by our savages; therefore one male will be sufficient to serve four females. That the remaining 100,000 may, at a year old, be offered in sale to the persons of quality and fortune through the kingdom; always advising the mother to let them suck plentifully in the last month, so as to render them plump and fat for a good table. A child will make two dishes at an entertainment for friends; and when the family dines alone, the fore or hind quarter will make a reasonable dish, and seasoned with a little pepper or salt will be very good boiled on the fourth day, especially in winter.

11   I have reckoned upon a medium that a child just born will weigh 12 pounds, and in a solar year, if tolerably nursed, will increase to 28 pounds.

12   I grant this food will be somewhat dear, and therefore very proper for landlords, who, as they have already devoured most of the parents, seem to have the best title to the children.

13   Infant's flesh will be in season throughout the year, but more plentiful in March, and a little before and after: for we are told by a grave author, an eminent French physician, that fish being a prolific diet, there are more children born in Roman Catholic countries about nine months after Lent than at any other season; therefore, reckoning a year after Lent, the markets will be more glutted than usual, because the number of popish infants is at least three to one in this kingdom: and therefore it will have one other collateral advantage, by lessening the number of papists among us.

14   I have already computed the charge of nursing a beggar's child (in which list I reckon all cottagers, laborers, and four-fifths of the farmers) to be about 2s. per annum, rags included; and I believe no gentleman would repine to give 10s. for the carcass of a good fat child, which, as I have said, will make four dishes of excellent nutritive meat, when he has only some particular friend or his own family to dine with him. Thus the squire will learn to be a good landlord, and grow popular among the tenants; the mother will have 8s. net profit, and be fit for work till she produces another child.

15   Those who are more thrifty (as I must confess the times require) may flay the carcass; the skin of which artificially dressed will make admirable gloves for ladies, and summer boots for fine gentlemen.

16   As to our city of Dublin, shambles may be appointed for this purpose in the most convenient parts of it, and butchers we may be assured will not be wanting: although I rather recommend buying the children alive, and dressing them hot from the knife as we do roasting pigs.

17   A very worthy person, a true lover of his country, and whose virtues I highly esteem, was lately pleased in discoursing on this matter to offer a refinement upon my scheme. He said that many gentlemen of this kingdom, having of late destroyed their deer, he conceived that the want of venison might be well supplied by the bodies of young lads and maidens, not exceeding fourteen years of age nor under twelve; so great a number of both sexes in every country being now ready to starve for want of work and service; and these to be disposed of by their parents, if alive, or otherwise by their nearest relations. But with due deference to so excellent a friend and so deserving a patriot, I cannot be altogether in his sentiments; for as to the males, my American acquaintance assured me from frequent experience that their flesh was generally tough and lean, like that of our schoolboys by continual exercise, and their taste disagreeable; and to fatten them would not answer the charge. Then as to the females, it would, I think, with humble submission be a loss to the public, because they soon would become breeders themselves: and besides, it is not improbable that some scrupulous people might be apt to censure such a practice (although indeed very unjustly), as a little bordering upon cruelty; which, I confess, has always been with me the strongest objection against any project, how well soever intended.

18   But in order to justify my friend, he confessed that this expedient was put into his head by the famous Psalmanazar, a native of the island Formosa, who came from thence to London about twenty years ago: and in conversation told my

friend, that in his country when any young person happened to be put to death, the executioner sold the carcass to persons of quality as a prime dainty; and that in his time the body of a plump girl of fifteen, who was crucified for an attempt to poison the emperor, was sold to his imperial majesty's prime minister of state, and other great mandarins of the court, in joints from the gibbet, at 400 crowns. Neither indeed can I deny, that if the same use were made of several plump young girls in this town, who without one single groat to their fortunes cannot stir abroad without a chair, and appear at the playhouse and assemblies in foreign fineries which they never will pay for, the kingdom would not be the worse.

19   Some persons of a desponding spirit are in great concern about that vast number of poor people, who are aged, diseased, or maimed, and I have been desired to employ my thoughts what course may be taken to ease the nation of so grievous an encumbrance. But I am not in the least pain upon that matter, because it is very well known that they are every day dying and rotting by cold and famine, and filth and vermin, as fast as can be reasonably expected. And as to the young laborers, they are now in as hopeful a condition: they cannot get work, and consequently pine away for want of nourishment, to a degree that if at any time they are accidentally hired to common labor, they have not strength to perform it; and thus the country and themselves are happily delivered from the evils to come.

20   I have too long digressed, and therefore shall return to my subject. I think the advantages by the proposal which I have made are obvious and many, as well as of the highest importance.

21   For first, as I have already observed, it would greatly lessen the number of papists, with whom we are yearly overrun, being the principal breeders of the nation as well as our most dangerous enemies; and who stay at home on purpose to deliver the kingdom to the Pretender, hoping to take their advantage by the absence of so many good Protestants, who have chosen rather to leave their country than stay at home and pay tithes against their conscience to an Episcopal curate.

22   Secondly, The poor tenants will have something valuable of their own, which by law may be made liable to distress and help to pay their landlord's rent, their corn and cattle being already seized, and money a thing unknown.

23   Thirdly, Whereas the maintenance of 100,000 children from two years old and upward, cannot be computed at less than 10s. a-piece per annum, the nation's stock will be thereby increased £50,000 per annum, beside the profit of a new dish introduced to the tables of all gentlemen of fortune in the kingdom who have any refinement in taste. And the money will circulate among ourselves, the goods being entirely of our own growth and manufacture.

24   Fourthly, The constant breeders beside the gain of 8s. sterling per annum by the sale of their children, will be rid of the charge of maintaining them after the first year.

25   Fifthly, This food would likewise bring great custom to taverns, where the vintners will certainly be so prudent as to procure the best receipts for dressing it to perfection, and consequently have their houses frequented by all the fine gentlemen, who justly value themselves upon their knowledge in good eating; and a skilful cook who understands how to oblige his guests, will contrive to make it as expensive as they please.

26   Sixthly, This would be a great inducement to marriage, which all wise nations have either encouraged by rewards or enforced by laws and penalties. It would increase the care and tenderness of mothers toward their children, when

they were sure of a settlement for life to the poor babes, provided in some sort by the public, to their annual profit instead of expense. We should see an honest emulation among the married women, which of them would bring the fattest child to the market. Men would become as fond of their wives during the time of their pregnancy as they are now of their mares in foal, their cows in calf, their sows when they are ready to farrow; nor offer to beat or kick them (as is too frequent a practice) for fear of a miscarriage.

27   Many other advantages might be enumerated. For instance, the addition of some thousand carcasses in our exportation of barreled beef, the propagation of swine's flesh, and improvement in the art of making good bacon, so much wanted among us by the great destruction of pigs, too frequent at our table; which are no way comparable in taste or magnificence to a well-grown, fat, yearling child, which roasted whole will make a considerable figure at a lord mayor's feast or any other public entertainment. But this and many others I omit, being studious of brevity.

28   Supposing that 1,000 families in this city would be constant customers for infants' flesh, besides others who might have it at merry-meetings, particularly at weddings and christenings, I compute that Dublin would take off annually about 20,000 carcasses; and the rest of the kingdom (where probably they will be sold somewhat cheaper) the remaining 80,000.

29   I can think of no one objection that will possibly be raised against this proposal, unless it should be urged that the number of people will be thereby much lessened in the kingdom. This I freely own, and it was indeed one principal design in offering it to the world. I desire the reader will observe, that I calculate my remedy for this one individual kingdom of Ireland and for no other that ever was, is, or I think ever can be upon earth. Therefore let no man talk to me of other expedients: of taxing our absentees at 5s. a pound: of using neither clothes nor household furniture except what is of our own growth and manufacture: of utterly rejecting the materials and instruments that promote foreign luxury: of curing the expensiveness of pride, vanity, idleness, and gaming in our women: of introducing a vein of parsimony, prudence, and temperance: of learning to love our country, in the want of which we differ even from Laplanders and the inhabitants of Topinamboo: of quitting our animosities and factions, nor acting any longer like the Jews, who were murdering one another at the very moment their city was taken: of being a little cautious not to sell our country and conscience for nothing: of teaching landlords to have at least one degree of mercy toward their tenants: lastly, of putting a spirit of honesty, industry, and skill into our shopkeepers; who, if a resolution could now be taken to buy only our native goods, would immediately unite to cheat and exact upon us in the price, the measure, and the goodness, nor could ever yet be brought to make one fair proposal of just dealing, though often and earnestly invited to it.

30   Therefore, I repeat, let no man talk to me of these and the like expedients, till he has at least some glimpse of hope that there will be ever some hearty and sincere attempt to put them in practice.

31   But as to myself, having been wearied out for many years with offering vain, idle, visionary thoughts, and at length utterly despairing of success, I fortunately fell upon this proposal; which, as it is wholly new, so it has something solid and real, of no expense and little trouble, full in our own power, and whereby we can incur no danger in disobliging England. For this kind of commodity will not bear exportation, the flesh being of too tender a consistence to admit a long con-

tinuance in salt, although perhaps I could name a country which would be glad to eat up our whole nation without it.

32   After all, I am not so violently bent upon my own opinion as to reject any offer proposed by wise men, which shall be found equally innocent, cheap, easy, and effectual. But before something of that kind shall be advanced in contradiction to my scheme, and offering a better, I desire the author or authors will be pleased maturely to consider two points. First, as things now stand, how they will be able to find food and raiment for 100,000 useless mouths and backs. And secondly, there being a round million of creatures in human figure throughout this kingdom, whose subsistence put into a common stock would leave them in debt 200,000,000*l.* sterling, adding those who are beggars by profession to the bulk of farmers, cottagers, and laborers, with the wives and children who are beggars in effect; I desire those politicians who dislike my overture, and may perhaps be so bold as to attempt an answer, that they will first ask the parents of these mortals, whether they would not at this day think it a great happiness to have been sold for food at a year old in the manner I prescribe, and thereby have avoided such a perpetual scene of misfortunes as they have since gone through by the oppression of landlords, the impossibility of paying rent without money or trade, the want of common sustenance, with neither house nor clothes to cover them from the inclemencies of the weather, and the most inevitable prospect of entailing the like or greater miseries upon their breed for ever.

33   I profess, in the sincerity of my heart, that I have not the least personal interest in endeavoring to promote this necessary work, having no other motive than the public good of my country, by advancing our trade, providing for infants, relieving the poor, and giving some pleasure to the rich. I have no children by which I can propose to get a single penny; the youngest being nine years old, and my wife past child-bearing.

 Topics for Critical Thinking and Writing

1. Characterize the pamphleteer (not Swift but his persona) who offers his "modest proposal." What sort of man does he think he is? What sort of man do we regard him as? Support your assertions with evidence.
2. In the first paragraph the speaker says that the sight of mothers begging is "melancholy." In this paragraph what assumption does the speaker make about women that in part gives rise to this melancholy? Now that you are familiar with the entire essay, explain Swift's strategy in his first paragraph.
3. Explain the function of the "other expedients" (listed in paragraph 29).
4. How might you argue that although this satire is primarily ferocious, it also contains some playful touches? What specific passages might support your argument?
5. Although the conditions that the "Proposal" describes are not exaggerated, the solutions proposed are hyperbolic. How successful is Swift's (not the persona's) use of shock value in taking the absurd to its logical extremes?

VIRGINIA WOOLF

Virginia Woolf (1882–1941) was born in London into an upper-middle-class literary family. In 1912 she married writer Leonard Woolf, and together they founded an influential publishing company, The Hogarth Press. Woolf was a central member of the Bloomsbury Group and a prominent Modernist. She was a distinguished, innovative, and prolific writer of essays and novels, and is considered a foremost writer of the twentieth century. This essay was originally a talk delivered in 1931 to the Women's Service League.

Professions for Women

1 When your secretary invited me to come here, she told me that your Society is concerned with the employment of women and she suggested that I might tell you something about my own professional experiences. It is true I am a woman; it is true I am employed; but what professional experiences have I had? It is difficult to say. My profession is literature; and in that profession there are fewer experiences for women than in any other, with the exception of the stage—fewer, I mean, that are peculiar to women. For the road was cut many years ago—by Fanny Burney, by Aphra Behn, by Harriet Martineau, by Jane Austen, by George Eliot—many famous women, and many more unknown and forgotten, have been before me, making the path smooth, and regulating my steps. Thus, when I came to write, there were very few material obstacles in my way. Writing was a reputable and harmless occupation. The family peace was not broken by the scratching of a pen. No demand was made upon the family purse. For ten and sixpence one can buy paper enough to write all the plays of Shakespeare—if one has a mind that way. Pianos and models, Paris, Vienna and Berlin, masters and mistresses, are not needed by a writer. The cheapness of writing paper is, of course, the reason why women have succeeded as writers before they have succeeded in the other professions.

2 But to tell you my story—it is a simple one. You have only got to figure to yourselves a girl in a bedroom with a pen in her hand. She had only to move that pen from left to right—from ten o'clock to one. Then it occurred to her to do what is simple and cheap enough after all—to slip a few of those pages into an envelope, fix a penny stamp in the corner, and drop the envelope into the red box at the corner. It was thus that I became a journalist; and my effort was rewarded on the first day of the following month—a very glorious day it was for me—by a letter from an editor containing a check for one pound ten shillings and sixpence. But to show you how little I deserve to be called a professional woman, how little I know of the struggles and difficulties of such lives, I have to admit that instead of spending that sum upon bread and butter, rent, shoes and stockings, or butcher's bills, I went out and bought a cat—a beautiful cat, a Persian cat, which very soon involved me in bitter disputes with my neighbors.

3 What could be easier than to write articles and to buy Persian cats with the profits? But wait a moment. Articles have to be about something. Mine, I seem to remember, was about a novel by a famous man. And while I was writing this review, I discovered that if I were going to review books I should need to do bat-

tle with a certain phantom. And the phantom was a woman, and when I came to know her better I called her after the heroine of a famous poem, The Angel in the House. It was she who used to come between me and my paper when I was writing reviews. It was she who bothered me and wasted my time and so tormented me that at last I killed her. You who come of a younger and happier generation may not have heard of her—you may not know what I mean by the Angel in the House. I will describe her as shortly as I can. She was intensely sympathetic. She was immensely charming. She was utterly unselfish. She excelled in the difficult arts of family life. She sacrificed herself daily. If there was chicken, she took the leg; if there was a draught she sat in it—in short she was so constituted that she never had a mind or a wish of her own, but preferred to sympathize always with the minds and wishes of others. Above all—I need not say it— she was pure. Her purity was supposed to be her chief beauty—her blushes, her great grace. In those days—the last of Queen Victoria—every house had its Angel. And when I came to write I encountered her with the very first words. The shadow of her wings fell on my page; I heard the rustling of her skirts in the room. Directly, that is to say, I took my pen in hand to review that novel by a famous man, she slipped behind me and whispered: "My dear, you are a young woman. You are writing about a book that has been written by a man. Be sympathetic; be tender; flatter; deceive; use all the arts and wiles of our sex. Never let anybody guess that you have a mind of your own. Above all, be pure." And she made as if to guide my pen. I now record the one act for which I take some credit to myself, though the credit rightly belongs to some excellent ancestors of mine who left me a certain sum of money—shall we say five hundred pounds a year?—so that it was not necessary for me to depend solely on charm for my living. I turned upon her and caught her by the throat. I did my best to kill her. My excuse, if I were to be had up in a court of law, would be that I acted in self-defense. Had I not killed her she would have killed me. She would have plucked the heart out of my writing. For, as I found, directly I put pen to paper, you cannot review even a novel without having a mind of your own, without expressing what you think to be the truth about human relations, morality, sex. And all these questions, according to the Angel in the House, cannot be dealt with freely and openly by women; they must charm, they must conciliate, they must—to put it bluntly—tell lies if they are to succeed. Thus, whenever I felt the shadow of her wing or the radiance of her halo upon my page, I took up the inkpot and flung it at her. She died hard. Her fictitious nature was of great assistance to her. It is far harder to kill a phantom than a reality. She was always creeping back when I thought I had despatched her. Though I flatter myself that I killed her in the end, the struggle was severe; it took much time that had better have been spent upon learning Greek grammar; or in roaming the world in search of adventures. But it was a real experience; it was an experience that was bound to befall all women writers at the time. Killing the Angel in the House was part of the occupation of a woman writer.

4   But to continue my story. The Angel was dead; what then remained? You may say that what remained was a simple and common object—a young woman in a bedroom with an inkpot. In other words, now that she had rid herself of falsehood, that young woman had only to be herself. Ah, but what is "herself"? I mean, what is a woman? I assure you, I do not know. I do not believe that you know. I do not believe that anybody can know until she has expressed herself in all the arts and professions open to human skill. That indeed is one of the reasons

why I have come here—out of respect for you, who are in process of showing us by your experiments what a woman is, who are in process of providing us, by your failures and successes, with that extremely important piece of information.

5 But to continue the story of my professional experiences. I made one pound ten and six by my first review; and I bought a Persian cat with the proceeds. Then I grew ambitious. A Persian cat is all very well, I said; but a Persian cat is not enough. I must have a motor car. And it was thus that I became a novelist—for it is a very strange thing that people will give you a motor car if you will tell them a story. It is a still stranger thing that there is nothing so delightful in the world as telling stories. It is far pleasanter than writing reviews of famous novels. And yet, if I am to obey your secretary and tell you my professional experiences as a novelist, I must tell you about a very strange experience that befell me as a novelist. And to understand it you must try first to imagine a novelist's state of mind. I hope I am not giving away professional secrets if I say that a novelist's chief desire is to be as unconscious as possible. He has to induce in himself a state of perpetual lethargy. He wants life to proceed with the utmost quiet and regularity. He wants to see the same faces, to read the same books, to do the same things day after day, month after month, while he is writing, so that nothing may break the illusion in which he is living—so that nothing may disturb or disquiet the mysterious nosings about, feelings round, darts, dashes and sudden discoveries of that very shy and illusive spirit, the imagination. I suspect that this state is the same both for men and women. Be that as it may, I want you to imagine me writing a novel in a state of trance. I want you to figure to yourselves a girl sitting with a pen in her hand, which for minutes, and indeed for hours, she never dips into the inkpot. The image that comes to my mind when I think of this girl is the image of a fisherman lying sunk in dreams on the verge of a deep lake with a rod held out over the water. She was letting her imagination sweep unchecked round every rock and cranny of the world that lies submerged in the depths of our unconscious being. Now came the experience, the experience that I believe to be far commoner with women writers than with men. The line raced through the girl's fingers. Her imagination had rushed away. It had sought the pools, the depths, the dark places where the largest fish slumber. And then there was a smash. There was an explosion. There was foam and confusion. The imagination had dashed itself against something hard. The girl was roused from her dream. She was indeed in a state of the most acute and difficult distress. To speak without figure she had thought of something, something about the body, about the passions which it was unfitting for her as a woman to say. Men, her reason told her, would be shocked. The consciousness of what men will say of a woman who speaks the truth about her passions had roused her from her artist's state of unconsciousness. She could write no more. This I believe to be a very common experience with women writers—they are impeded by the extreme conventionality of the other sex. For though men sensibly allow themselves great freedom in these respects, I doubt that they realize or can control the extreme severity with which they condemn such freedom in women.

6 These then were two very genuine experiences of my own. These were two of the adventures of my professional life. The first—killing the Angel in the House—I think I solved. She died. But the second, telling the truth about my own experiences as a body, I do not think I solved. I doubt that any woman has solved it yet. The obstacles against her are still immensely powerful—and yet they are very difficult to define. Outwardly, what is simpler than to write books?

Outwardly, what obstacles are there for a woman rather than for a man? Inwardly, I think, the case is very different; she has still many ghosts to fight, many prejudices to overcome. Indeed it will be a long time still, I think, before a woman can sit down to write a book without finding a phantom to be slain, a rock to be dashed against. And if this is so in literature, the freest of all professions for women, how is it in the new professions which you are now for the first time entering?

7   Those are the questions that I should like, had I time, to ask you. And indeed, if I have laid stress upon these professional experiences of mine, it is because I believe that they are, though in different forms, yours also. Even when the path is nominally open—when there is nothing to prevent a woman from being a doctor, a lawyer, a civil servant—there are many phantoms and obstacles, as I believe, looming in her way. To discuss and define them is I think of great value and importance; for thus only can the labor be shared, the difficulties be solved. But besides this, it is necessary also to discuss the ends and the aims for which we are fighting, for which we are doing battle with these formidable obstacles. Those aims cannot be taken for granted; they must be perpetually questioned and examined. The whole position, as I see it—here in this hall surrounded by women practising for the first time in history I know not how many different professions—is one of extraordinary interest and importance. You have won rooms of your own in the house hitherto exclusively owned by men. You are able, though not without great labor and effort, to pay the rent. You are earning your five hundred pounds a year. But this freedom is only a beginning; the room is your own, but it is still bare. It has to be furnished; it has to be decorated; it has to be shared. How are you going to furnish it, how are you going to decorate it? With whom are you going to share it, and upon what terms? These, I think, are questions of the utmost importance and interest. For the first time in history you are able to ask them; for the first time you are able to decide for yourselves what the answers should be. Willingly would I stay and discuss those questions and answers—but not tonight. My time is up; and I must cease.

 ## Topics for Critical Thinking and Writing

1. The first two paragraphs seem to describe the ease with which women enter writing as a profession. What difficulties or obstacles for women do these paragraphs imply?
2. Try to characterize Woolf's tone, especially her attitude toward her subject and herself, in the first paragraph.
3. What do you think Woolf means when she says, near the end of paragraph 3, "It is far harder to kill a phantom than a reality"?
4. Woolf conjectures (in paragraph 6) that she has not solved the problem of "telling the truth about my own experiences as a body." Is there any reason to believe that today a woman has more difficulty than a man in telling the truth about the experiences of the body?
5. In her final paragraph, Woolf suggests that phantoms as well as obstacles impede women from becoming doctors and lawyers. What might some of these phantoms be?

6. This essay is highly metaphoric. What is the meaning of the metaphor of "rooms" in the final paragraph? What does Woolf mean when she says, "The room is your own, but it is still bare. . . . With whom are you going to share it, and upon what terms?"
7. Explain, to a reader who doesn't understand it, the analogy making use of fishing in paragraph 5.
8. Evaluate the last two sentences. Are they too abrupt and mechanical? Or do they provide a fitting conclusion to the speech?

LAST WORDS

A rich patron once gave money to the painter Chu Ta, asking him to paint a picture of a fish. Three years later, when he still had not received the painting, the patron went to Chu Ta's house to ask why the picture was not done. Chu Ta did not answer, but dipped a brush in ink and with a few strokes drew a splendid fish. "If it is so easy," asked the patron, "why didn't you give me the picture three years ago?" Again Chu Ta did not answer. Instead, he opened the door of a large cabinet. Thousands of pictures of fish tumbled out.

Literary Credits

Allende, Isabel. "If You Touched My Heart," pp. 81-91 from THE STORIES OF EVA LUNA, translated from the Spanish by Margaret Sayers Peden. Copyright © 1989 Isabel Allende. English translation copyright © 1992 Macmillan Publishing Company. Reprinted with the permission of Scribner, a division of Simon & Schuster.

Atwood, Margaret. "Happy Endings" from GOOD BONES AND SIMPLE MURDERS. Used by permission. McClelland & Stewart Ltd. *The Canadian Publishers.*

Atwood, Margaret. "Nine Beginnings" from THE WRITER ON HER WORK, II, edited by Janet Sternberg, pp. 150-156. Copyright © 1991 by Margaret Atwood. Reprinted by permission of the author.

Barnet, Sylvan. "Writing About Literature: An Overview" from LITERATURE FOR COMPOSITION: Essays, Fiction, Poetry, and Drama, Fourth Edition, pp. 430-452. Copyright © 1996. Reprinted by permission of Addison Wesley Educational Publishers, Inc.

Beckford, Sharon Morgan. "This Space Called Canada: Re-imagining the National Story" from STRANGERS IN THE MIRROR, TSAR publications. Reprinted by permission of the author.

Berton, Pierre. "Overview: The Worst of Times" from THE GREAT DEPRESSION, 1929-1939. Reprinted by permission of Elsa Franklin.

Bly, Robert. "Love Poem" in IRON JOHN: A BOOK OF MEN, p. 133. Copyright © 1990 by Robert Bly. Reprinted by permission of Perseus Books Publishers, a member of Perseus Books, L.L.C.

Bok, Sissela. "To Lie or Not to Lie?-The Doctor's Dilemma," The New York Times, 18 April 1978. Copyright © 1978 by The New York Times Company. Reprinted by permission.

Breda, Paola. "Caged: Ross's 'A Field of Wheat' and Munro's 'Thanks for the Ride'." Reprinted by permission of the author.

Campbell, Jim. "Riot Rocks Toronto" from PRISON NEWS SERVICE, September/October 1991 and reprinted in SEMIOTEXT(E) CANADAS.

Caragata, Warren. "Crime in Cybercity." MACLEAN'S, May 22, 1995. Reprinted by permission of *Maclean's* magazine/Rogers Publishing Limited.

Carpenter, David. "The Darker Implications of Comedy" from WRITING HOME. Copyright © 1994 by David Carpenter. Reprinted by permission of the author.

Choyce, Lesley. "Thin Edge of the Wedge." CANADIAN GEOGRAPHIC, March/April 1997. Reprinted by permission of the author and Pottersfield Press.

Cross, Amy Willard. "Life in the Stopwatch Lane." THE GLOBE AND MAIL, July 5, 1990. Reprinted by permission of the author.

Cuff, John Haslett. "Eat your Hearts Out Cinephiles, The Tube Is Where It's At." THE GLOBE AND MAIL, September 24, 1996. Reprinted by permission of *The Globe and Mail.*

Derman, Josh. "Deconstruction Pop: The Halo Benders" from *Harvard Crimson*, April 3, 1998. Reprinted by permission of the author.

Dey, Myrna. "A Present from the Past." CANADIAN LIVING, December 2000. Copyright © 2000 by Myrna Dey. Reprinted by permission of the author.

Dickerson, Debra. "Who Shot Johnny?" First appeared in The New Republic, 1977. Reprinted with permission of the author.

Didion, Joan. "Los Angeles Notebook" from SLOUCHING TOWARDS BETHLEHEM. Copyright © 1966, 1968 and copyright renewed © 1996 by Joan Didion. Reprinted by permission of Farrar, Straus and Giroux, Inc.

———. "On Keeping a Notebook" from SLOUCHING TOWARDS BETHLEHEM. Copyright © 1966, 1968 and copyright renewed © 1996 by Joan Didion. Reprinted by permission of Farrar, Straus and Giroux, Inc.

Doidge, Dr. Norman. Extracted from The Suit. Reprinted by permission of the author.

Doyle, Arthur Conan. "The Science of Deduction" from A STUDY IN SCARLET. Copyright © 1996 The Sir Arthur Conan Doyle Copyright Holders. Reprinted by kind permission of Jonathan Clowes Ltd., London, on behalf of Andrea Plunket, Administrator of the Sir Arthur Conan Doyle Copyrights.

Dubuc, Pierre. "Quebec Separation Was Not Laid to Rest in 1995." Reprinted by permission of the author.

Editorial. "The Myth of Canadian Diversity" from THE GLOBE AND MAIL, June 13, 1994. Reprinted by permission of *The Globe and Mail.*

Photo Credits

Index